Game Balance

Game Balance

Ian Schreiber and Brenda Romero

CRC Press
Taylor & Francis Group
Boca Raton London New York

CRC Press is an imprint of the
Taylor & Francis Group, an **informa** business

First edition published 2022
by CRC Press
6000 Broken Sound Parkway NW, Suite 300, Boca Raton, FL 33487-2742

and by CRC Press
2 Park Square, Milton Park, Abingdon, Oxon, OX14 4RN

© 2022 Taylor & Francis Group, LLC

CRC Press is an imprint of Taylor & Francis Group, LLC

ISBN: 978-1-032-03400-3 (hbk)
ISBN: 978-1-4987-9957-7 (pbk)
ISBN: 978-1-315-15642-2 (ebk)

Typeset in Garamond
by codeMantra

Writing a book together is a labor of love and a deathmatch. This is our third book together, and our spouses certainly must think we're about to kill each other as we debate endless topics into the ground, survey dozens of game designers we know, do more research, and ultimately arrive at a consensus. We love the process since it makes for a better book than either of us could individually create, and sure enough, we discuss "the next book" as soon as we're done with the current book. So, this book is for our spouses, both of them, Sharon Schreiber and John Romero, who have not only tolerated and encouraged us but participated in the discussions, making them richer and better.

Contents

Part I
Game Balance

8

9

15

Part II
The Mathematics of Balance

Part III
Spreadsheets

List of Case Studies

Acknowledgments

Very few game design books are written alone without consulting many friends and colleagues in the field. While many designers (knowingly or unknowingly) contributed to this work through sparking ideas in conversation, we wanted to call out the following: Daniel Cook, Joris Dormans, Andrew Friedman, Aki Jarvinen, Mario Izquierdo, Crystin Cox, Squirrel Eiserloh, Link Hughes, and Jenna Hoffstein for their assistance at Project Horseshoe for writing a report that became the basis for much of Chapter 11, and additionally Chelsea Howe for her excellent feedback on that chapter; Alex Jaffe for his insights that helped us to write Chapters 13 and 24; and Squirrel Eiserloh (again) for his work on random systems that gave us useful examples and content in Chapters 19 and 20.

Preface

Ian Schreiber has been fascinated with the topic of game balance for his entire professional life. When he first started making games professionally in 2000, there were not very many textbooks that covered *anything* about game design; the first widely read textbooks for game design classes would not be written until later that decade.

Even once the field developed to the point that there were a critical mass of how-to books on game design, there was still a dearth of information about game balance, specifically. Most books on game design didn't mention it, or if they did, they settled for some vague advice about how game balance is important, you should think about maybe doing it, and if you're not sure what to do with a number, then multiply or divide it by 2. While none of that was inherently wrong, it also wasn't reflective of the field; game designers use all kinds of techniques to balance games, but finding practical advice was challenging. Even at professional conferences, talks on game balance were few and far between, and they tended to be narrow and specific.

Ian had, meanwhile, developed plenty of techniques for balancing games on his own, through experience. But it left a question in his mind: what techniques did *other* designers use that they aren't talking about? He started asking this question in online spaces, in person at conferences, and among friends and colleagues. And what he found is that in general, yes, game designers do tend to use the same techniques that we have all apparently managed to discover independently of one another (aside from those lucky designers who got to learn by working alongside another more experienced designer, and could thus learn by direct observation). Ian found it fascinating that there are apparently universal, largely undocumented and unspoken, Natural Laws of game balance. And so, he began to document. (And then he recruited Brenda, with her own vast experience, to partner with him in their third book together, because he knew she would make everything she touched an order of magnitude better.)

This book is the culmination of several decades of documentation, conversations with designers, and teaching the subject in classrooms, workshops, and masterclasses. We hope that this becomes *the* definitive book on the subject and is able to stand on its own for many years to come.

How to Navigate This Book

There are many paths through this book. Sure, you start at page 1 and move forward in page order if you have the time, but there are many other possible paths on this journey. In particular, while the chapters are numbered sequentially, and the later chapters do tend to build on the material of earlier ones, the actual sequence of chapters looks more like this:

If there is a certain topic or chapter that is of particular interest to you, feel free to start there. However, certain concepts may be referenced from earlier in this book. For example, if you start on Chapter 8 (transitive mechanics and cost curves) but don't know anything about curves from Chapter 4, some of the topics might not immediately make sense. On the other hand, if you've already read Chapters 1–6, you could go sequentially to Chapter 7, or jump ahead to Chapter 8 or Chapter 9, and be just fine.

You may wonder why the chapters are in the order that they are if there are so many valid paths through this book. To start, we felt that the chapters should be in such an order that going through them sequentially would not violate any of the prerequisites in the "tech tree" diagram above. Within that constraint, chapters were grouped together thematically. For example, while Chapter 7 ("Trading Systems") could have been numbered anywhere from 6 to 15 by reordering the numbers, it is most closely linked to the material in Chapter 6 ("Economic Systems"), so those two chapters were placed together.

We also felt that the final ordering of chapters represents a reasonable flow through the broad topic of game balance. We start in Chapter 1 by defining what is meant by "game balance" and provide an overview of the process by which games are balanced. In Chapters 2 through 5, we introduce the basic tools of the trade, in terms of defining the numbers and "dials" that game designers can turn, twist, press, and change to improve the balance of a game. These chapters together set the foundation for the rest of this book.

Chapters 6 and 7 take a diversion into common topics in games, such as economics, negotiation, and trading mechanics, from the resource trading of the board game *Catan* to the auction house in *World of Warcraft* to the ways players can pay in *Clash of Clans*.

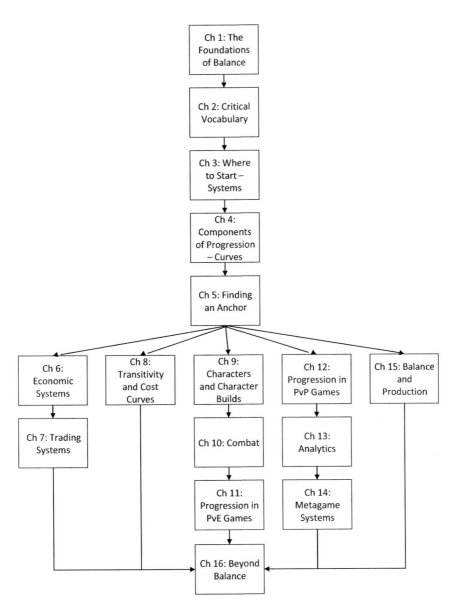

Chapter 8 examines transitive mechanics in depth: games where better things cost more, and how to relate the cost of an item to its benefits. While isolated in some ways, it is a key chapter that can be used on its own to balance trading card games, role-playing games, and other types of games. We then get up close and personal with character creation systems in Chapter 9 and combat systems in Chapter 10. While not all games have either or both of these, many do, so these are likewise key chapters that give direct advice on balancing a variety of games.

Chapters 11 and 12 then move into progression systems, which are the beating heart of most games. In Chapter 11, we look at these in the context of single-player and multiplayer cooperative games, where the player(s) struggle against the game's systems. In Chapter 12, we examine multiplayer competitive games, where the players struggle against one another.

Up to this point, this book looks at tools for game designers to balance games through manipulation of the numbers and systems of the game. But many games today are also balanced through playtesting and analytics, and we cover these topics in the following chapters. Chapter 13 shows how to use statistical tools to improve a game's balance through the powerful techniques of analytics. Chapter 14 takes a step back to look at ranking, rating, and tournament systems in competitive play, and how the design of those systems impacts the play experience. Chapter 15 gives direction on how to get good information to assist in balancing from running small-scale playtests, and also looks at how playtesting (and balance) fits with the bigger picture of a game's overarching project schedule.

In the final chapter of Part I, "Game Balance," we look at the limitations of game balance itself. Where do the techniques in this book fail, and at what point does a designer have to look outside of "balance" to fix a broken game? For a game designer interested in taking things even further than what's in this book, where do they go next? These questions are addressed in Chapter 16.

Part II of this book, "The Mathematics of Balance," covers the mathematical tools and techniques that are used in the various chapters of Part I. We felt that covering these topics here was important, because not all game designers are comfortable with heavy math skills, and looking these up in a typical math textbook is unwieldy: game designers use perhaps 5% of any given textbook on a single branch of mathematics, but we borrow from half a dozen different branches of mathematics. By putting the commonly useful parts all in one place, we provide designers with a handy reference guide for all of their mathematical needs.

Chapters 17 and 18 start the section with a survey of probability, useful when balancing systems of chance or randomness. Chapter 19 puts these in context, showing how to find a balance between luck and skill in a game, and how to alter that balance for a given audience. Chapters 20 and 21 show some limitations of probability: humans and computers, respectively, do not always obey the laws of probability in ways that one might expect, so here we cover design problems and solutions to dealing with the idiosyncrasies of human psychology and computer-generated "random" (actually *pseudorandom*) numbers.

Chapter 22 extends the discussion on probability to include some special kinds of probability problems that involve infinite series, and as such can't be solved in conventional ways. The techniques in this chapter are more technical and math-heavy than most other chapters in this book (save perhaps Chapter 25), and can be skipped for readers that are too intimidated, but it provides the answers to some very interesting problems for readers who make the trip.

Chapter 23 applies the previous chapters in this section back to Chapter 8 (transitivity and cost curves) in Part I, showing how to assign costs and values to random effects in a game using probability calculations.

Chapter 24 examines statistics (essentially, probability in reverse), providing tools that in particular are useful when looking at analytics (as covered in Chapter 13) or assessing the balance of rating and tournament systems (Chapter 14).

Chapter 25, as with 22, may be challenging for readers who are afraid of too much math. This chapter uses the branch of mathematics known as Game Theory in order to solve balance problems relating to intransitive mechanics (those that have a *Rock-Paper-Scissors*-type relationship, where some things are strong or weak against others). The kind of analysis done in this chapter is useful to a wide variety of games, but is also not in common use, and can be skipped by readers who find themselves having too much trouble getting through it.

Part III of this book, "Spreadsheets," covers another tool that is critical for game designers and especially for performing most kinds of balance: spreadsheets. Since spreadsheet programs are used so heavily for most of the topics in Part I, we felt it was important to include a how-to guide to give the reader familiarity with these tools of the trade. Even experienced designers may find a trick or two in here that they haven't seen before; spreadsheet programs have a truly monumental set of features, and even the most seasoned professional game designer doesn't know *every* hidden feature or spreadsheet technique. Even designers with decades of professional experience will sometimes see something they've never seen before in a spreadsheet. In this part, we assume no prior experience with spreadsheets and intend to take the reader from any experience level up to expert level. This could have just as easily been a separate book of its own—but we included it here since it is so relevant to the topic of balance.

This final part of this book starts with four chapters that cover the very basics of navigating a spreadsheet, meant for absolute beginners: how to enter data in cells (Chapter 26), how to format cells for readability (Chapter 27), how to write formulas to do computations and display graphs and charts (Chapter 28), and how to use absolute references inside of formulas (Chapter 29).

From there, we go deeper into more advanced formatting tools (Chapter 30) and then learn in more detail about functions with an emphasis on commonly used math functions so you don't have to calculate too much by hand (Chapter 31). We then use some of these functions and some new ones to learn some useful techniques for handling random elements, including how to actually shuffle a deck of cards inside a spreadsheet, as well as manipulating strings for display purposes (Chapter 32).

After that, we take a step back and look at practical ways to format and organize a spreadsheet for better viewing (Chapter 33), and some time and date functionality that can be helpful when putting together project schedules (Chapter 34).

The final three chapters look at more advanced topics and can be skipped if a reader is already feeling overwhelmed. We first look at some powerful techniques for implementing the passage of time or turns inside a spreadsheet (Chapter 35). We then look at more advanced techniques for using graphs as visualization tools, including how to embed certain types of graphs inside a single cell (Chapter 36). We finish up with how to perform the matrix operations from Chapters 22 and 25 inside of a spreadsheet (Chapter 37).

We welcome your feedback on this book, of course. On Twitter, Ian is @ianschreiber and Brenda is @br. Feel free to connect with us and let us know what you think.

Inside Each Chapter

The chapters in this book all follow a similar structure. After a brief survey of what the reader can expect to find in the chapter, as well as the chapter material itself, you will find at the end:

- **Additional Resources**: for those chapters that mention other outside sources such as other books, articles, websites, or online videos of conference talks, these are all mentioned and linked to at the end of the chapter.
- **Discussion Questions**: an assortment of basic reading comprehension questions to stimulate classroom discussion or for assigned homework. Part III of this book, "Spreadsheets," does not have discussion questions.
- **Sidequests**: more in-depth challenges that allow the reader to practice the tools and techniques addressed in that chapter. Chapters 1 and 16 do not have Sidequests, because they are more conceptual and do not introduce specific game balance techniques. Sidequests are for teachers

or group leaders who want to assign practical projects that allow participants to demonstrate competence or mastery of the chapter material, or readers who want to solidify the reading through diligent practice. A few Sidequests also lend themselves to contests or tournament play (these say so explicitly in their description). Some other Sidequests have variations:

- **Alternate challenge**: a variant that can be done in place of (or in addition to) the originally stated challenge in the Sidequest.
- **Greater challenge**: an additional challenge or constraint that makes the Sidequest harder, but gives the reader practical experience for doing so.
- **Ultimate challenge**: an even more intense version of a greater challenge, useful in classes as extra credit (or for more advanced students such as honors or graduate sections) or for readers who want to challenge their skills to the limit.
- **Main Quests**: there are three Main Quests in this book, multi-part long-term design projects broken up into individual milestones throughout the chapters. Chapter 1 introduces all three Main Quests (playfully named Rogue, Fighter, and Wizard) if the reader is in a position to choose the one that is the most interesting or relevant. Additional pieces of the Main Quests are added to chapters where the concepts required to complete them are introduced, so each milestone of a Main Quest provides as much practice as a Sidequest of that chapter, with the additional benefit of providing some extra continuity between chapters.

A Note about Terminology and Writing Style

This book uses a lot of jargon and terminology specific to the field of game design. When a term is used for the first time, it is **bolded** and then defined immediately in the text. Whenever possible, we use terminology that is standard and widely used and accepted in the video game industry. When we required a term that was not in common use or that had to be invented, we say so explicitly.

When referring to games such as *Chess* or *Minecraft*, we italicize and capitalize the names. This is done out of respect for the medium we work in, particularly for works that merit a specific mention because they provide a prime example or case study of an important concept in this book. We also use italics (without capitalization) to show emphasis on a word.

When talking from the point of view of a player in a game, we refer to "the player." When talking from the point of view of a game designer, we use "you" or "we." We do this to avoid confusion in situations when we are talking about both designers and players, and because we assume that the reader of this book is more of a game designer than a game player (else you would be playing a game, not reading about how to design them).

Authors

Ian Schreiber has been in the industry since 2000, first as a programmer and then as a game designer. He has worked on eight published game titles, training/simulation games for three Fortune 500 companies, and has advised countless student projects. He is the co-founder of Global Game Jam, the largest in-person game jam event in the world. Ian has taught game design and development courses at a variety of colleges and universities since 2006.

Brenda Romero is a BAFTA award-winning game director, entrepreneur, artist, and Fulbright award recipient and is presently game director and creator of the *Empire of Sin* franchise. As a game director, she has worked on 50 games and contributed to many seminal titles, including the *Wizardry* and *Jagged Alliance* series and titles in the *Ghost Recon, Dungeons & Dragons* and *Def Jam* franchises. Away from the machine, her analog series of six games, *The Mechanic is the Message*, has drawn national and international acclaim, particularly *Train* and *Siochán Leat*, a game about her family's history, which is presently housed in the National Museum of Play. In addition to a BAFTA and a Fulbright, Romero is the recipient of multiple lifetime achievement awards, a Grace Hopper Award, and a GDC Ambassador Award, and many of the games she has contributed to have won numerous awards. Romero is the CEO and co-founder of Romero Games based in Galway, Ireland.

Part I

Game Balance

This book is divided into three parts. This first part dives right in to the meat of the matter. We start by defining what "balance" is and what it looks like and defining some common terminology (Chapters 1–2), and then give general techniques for how to analyze and balance a game by relating the elements of the game to one another (Chapters 3–5). We then do a series of deep dives into specific kinds of common systems found in games: economic (Chapter 6), trading and auctions (Chapter 7), resources (Chapter 8), characters (Chapter 9), combat (Chapter 10), and progression (Chapters 11–12). We finish up this section by looking at practical approaches used in the industry: analytics (Chapter 13), ranking and rating system design (Chapter 14), and practical techniques for playtesting and fitting balance into a project schedule (Chapter 15). In the final chapter of this part of this book (Chapter 16), we look beyond the techniques of balance to see where "game balance" fits into the big picture of game design and game development.

The chapters in Part I assume the reader already has familiarity with mathematics (specifically algebra, probability, statistics, matrices), and the use of spreadsheets. For readers who are comfortable with these things already, Part I may be all you need. However, if chapters are referring to techniques that may be unfamiliar to some readers, they will note which chapters in Parts II and III of this book can be used as reference.

1

The Foundations of Game Balance

In This Chapter

- What is Game Balance?
- Kinds of Game Balance
- Balance as Fairness
- How Do We Know if a Game is Balanced?
- How Do You Balance a Game?
- A Note about Math

What Is Game Balance?

The success of a game depends, in part, on the game's balance, and as designers, we spend many hours trying to get that balance right. If a game isn't balanced properly for its audience and its design goals, the gameplay experience can be ruined—even if the mechanics are brilliant, the story is outstanding, and the execution is great everywhere else. Game balance is an important and critical part of game design, and is therefore worthy of study and investigation by itself.

Game balance is also hard to get right and easy to get wrong. You can't just "add more balance" to your game any more easily than you can "add more fun" to it. Balance is a property, not an ingredient. Because a game's systems are interconnected, even if you correctly identify and fix an imbalance, as often as not that change throws half a dozen other things off, and you then need to fix those as well. Balance is like swapping out a gear in the center of a bunch of other gears. You're not creating a single component in isolation; you're making a machine where all the gears work together.

If you ask 100 game designers what game balance is, you get 90 different answers. We know, we tried. Game balance is, first and foremost, a feeling, and you know it when you feel it:

- "That boss battle was way too easy."
- "This weapon is way overpowered."
- "The original *Starcraft* is the most well-balanced game I've ever played."
- "*Betrayal at House on the Hill* is a lot of fun. Totally unbalanced, but fun."
- "This character class was nerfed too much."
- "*Magic: the Gathering* was doing pretty well for awhile, but Tolarian Academy really destroyed the balance of the environment while it was out there."
- "*Bloodborne* is super challenging, and it's supposed to be."
- "I died 100 times an hour in *Super Hexagon*. I think I have the hang of it now."

Game balance is many things to many players. What follows are a few ways to think about balance.

Game balance is a gray area. What one designer or player considers balanced, another may not. That much is true of all game design: there are at least five ways to do or define anything correctly, and yet another ten ways to prove each of those five ways wrong. Throughout the course of this book, in fact, our definitions and explanations reflect this tension. Where we feel there is a generally agreed upon definition or process, we present it. If there are multiple schools of thought, they are presented as well. Multiple schools of thought are often necessary when one considers the balance of different types of genres. What's right for one is wrong for another.

Game balance is contextually sensitive. There is no one perfect answer to rule them all. Gamers and game designers use the term "balanced" in many different ways and contexts. Likewise, we have developed terms that suggest a lack of balance: unbalanced, overpowered, broken, nerfed, and so on. We might refer to individual cards in a card game, character classes in an MMO or Arena Shooter, units in an RTS, levels in an FPS, or the balance of an entire game overall. We might talk of the balance of single-player games, and also multiplayer competitive games and multiplayer cooperative games, even though the relationship between players and game and hence what is considered "balanced" is wildly different for each.

Game balance is a metaphor. When we think of a scale—a balanced scale—it seems obvious. One side is equal in weight to another and, in fact, that's precisely where the metaphor comes from. However, such a measurement isn't really applicable to games. You can't put monsters and their difficulty on one side of a scale and the experience points and loot they drop on the other to figure out if one is heavier than the other, nor can you weigh the current vs. desired challenge of a game that's too much for the average player. Interestingly enough, and to take this metaphor one step further, single-player and multiplayer cooperative games that are actually considered "balanced" are often slightly tipped in the player's favor and continue the slight tilt no matter how much weight (game mastery) the player puts on the scale (more detail on this can be found in Chapter 11).

Game balance is also a series of interdependencies. Let's change the metaphor from a scale to an engine. The gears in the engine are running perfectly. If you enlarge one gear and determine that it is at the right size, now the others are completely out of balance, if they're working at all. This process is a familiar one to many game designers who find themselves rebalancing previously balanced areas of play to accommodate a current change. For instance, if it is decided that the player characters are starting out too powerful, all other systems may need to be rebalanced to accommodate this lesser starting state. It is in this way that game balance is a dance of sorts with some give and take until at last the game as a whole seems to be balanced overall.

Kinds of Game Balance

The reality is that game balance means different things in different contexts. There is a pattern to its use, however, so we can at least offer a functional understanding of what people mean when they refer to a game's balance. In this book, we address seven different elements of game balance.

Mathematical Balance

In most contexts, when designers or players refer to a game's balance, they are referring to something mathematical, whether it be a level curve, the cost of items, hit points, or the rarity of an object (an object's "rarity" is often determined mathematically, too). It's for this reason that most designers spend an inordinate amount of time in spreadsheets. To properly understand game balance, one needs to understand numerical relationships, probability in several forms, cost curves, and statistics. Some of our readers may be quite comfortable with these concepts, while others could use a refresher or an introduction. Part II of this book is dedicated to balance math. We reference it as we go through this book.

Balanced Difficulty

The progression of difficulty over time is referred to as a **difficulty curve**. In general, difficulty scales over the course of the game experience to provide continuous challenge for the player as they grow in skill. In most cases, if a player is challenged at the level of their current ability, we call the game balanced. If the game is too hard or too easy for its intended audience, or if it has sudden difficulty spikes where it gets much harder or much easier in a short period of time, the game may not be balanced.

An understanding of both the designer's intent and the audience is critical here. In a masocore game, the appeal comes from a player being faced with insanely difficult challenges which they eventually overcome through diligent practice and persistence. The game is balanced toward a desired difficulty. So, we may call the game balanced if a player is destroyed again and again and makes progress only after many deaths. In a game meant for very young children, we may call the game balanced if it always skews in the child's favor making it nearly or completely impossible to lose.

In analyzing a game's difficulty curve, knowledge of its release date is also helpful. Early games such as *Defender, Robotron 2084, Gravitar,* and *Crazy Climber* were notoriously difficult, yet intended for an average audience. 1981s *Wizardry: Proving Grounds of the Mad Overlord* permanently erased characters from the disk if the player failed to resurrect them after two tries. While recent games have raced the difficulty curve as well, the average difficulty of games has gotten easier over time.

Difficulty curves are covered in Chapter 11.

Balanced Progression

Progression is defined as the rate at which the player passes through the power, difficulty, narrative, or gameplay ramp of the game. Progression is balanced when the player is neither stagnated nor rushed through play. Progression is covered in detail in Chapter 11.

Power progression refers to the increasing power of a player as they go through the game via stat improvements, level gains, and increased abilities or items. In games like *Chess* or some first-person shooters (FPSs), power progression is improved *only* through player mastery of the game. Power is what the player or their avatar brings to the game. Power progression shouldn't ramp smoothly. Rather, it has periodic spikes such as when players find an amazing weapon or unlock a new ability. Both may be overpowered for the player's current position in the game, but with that power, they will progress through the gameplay until it matches the level of difficulty. Power progression is a regular topic among game players who note that characters are overpowered and need to be nerfed, or underpowered and need to be buffed.

Difficulty progression refers to the increasing difficulty of a game which marches *mostly* in tandem with the increasing skill and power of the player. We say *mostly* because players expect and even need spikes in difficulty to keep things interesting and somewhat unpredictable, like a really challenging enemy that significantly tests their skill and ability. If a boss was just moderately more difficult than the creature before it, there would be yawns for miles. In fact, many developers create a smooth ramp in spreadsheets and manually add in these spikes. In general, players expect new challenges to match their increasing power and skill.

Difficulty progression is also related to a player's expectation that the more difficult something is, the more they should be rewarded for overcoming that challenge. A creature that requires ten damage to kill should give the player fewer XP than a creature that requires 100 damage to kill. Similarly, in most cases, the more time something takes to complete, the more players expect a big payoff. If a player *feels* like they are gaining in-game rewards (experience levels, loot, or other forms of power) that are worthwhile in relation to the time spent achieving them, they feel the game is balanced. If the player is showered with too many rewards for very little effort, or if the player must repeat the same core tasks again and again to move a small amount ahead, they feel it's unbalanced. Players use the term **grindy** to describe games like this. Players desire something of greater difficulty, thus having a greater reward, to prevent the game feeling too grindy.

Gameplay progression refers to the player's desire to try or see something new, whether it's a new gameplay mechanic, level, item, or enemy. Part of the reward for playing a game is seeing the vista of the game regularly changing while learning new things. If you've ever said, "this part has gone on long enough," you've experienced a failure of gameplay progression. If a player's interest is *mostly* sustained throughout play, we consider the progression of gameplay balanced. Since different players have different levels of interest, "mostly" is a good target.

Narrative progression refers to the progression of the game's story. Similar to gameplay progression, the progression of the game's story must mostly hold the player's attention or, metaphorically speaking, hold it enough so that they have a willingness to turn the next page. To do this, writers often follow the three-act structure or the 12-act hero's journey from Joseph Campbell's *Hero of a Thousand Faces*. Both of these structures are well covered in other books.

Balanced Initial Conditions

In multiplayer competitive (PvP) games, we call a game balanced if all players have a similar chance to win when the game starts, assuming equal player skill. Unbalanced games have an inherent bias that gives an unfair advantage to a player based on randomly determined turn order, starting position, the player's chosen character, class, faction, or some other initial condition that varies from player to player. In an effort to better balance initial conditions, many games employ matchmaking to ensure that players enjoy a game vs. someone near their relative skill level.

Balance between Multiple Strategies

In PvP games that are designed to support multiple strategies and paths to victory, the game is balanced if each strategy can be viable and competitive with other strategies, given equal player skill. In *Magic: the Gathering*, there are many deck-building strategies (such as aggro and control). If the game (or metagame) is biased such that aggro decks are too powerful and control decks aren't viable for competitive play, we call that an imbalance between those strategies.

This doesn't mean that every strategy or every particular implementation of a strategy must be equally good. Slapping 60 random cards together and calling it a "strategy" should not put a player in a position to have a 50/50 shot at winning against a well-tuned and focused deck that concentrates on one primary strategy and does it expertly.

It also doesn't mean that all games need to have multiple strategies or multiple paths to victory in the first place. In many games, there is just a single path to victory, and the game comes down to which player executes on the core strategy of the game better than the other players. But in a game that is designed to support multiple strategies, they should all be viable when played well.

Balance between Game Objects

Within a game, we may also describe individual **game objects** as balanced or unbalanced. For the purposes of this book, we define a game object as a single item in one of the game's systems: an individual card in a card game (Lightning Bolt in *Magic: the Gathering*), a specific weapon in a shooter (Chaingun in *DOOM*), a particular unit in a strategy game (Hydralisk in *StarCraft*), a specific piece of equipment in a role-playing game (Dragonbane in *Skyrim*), a single tech in a tech tree (Irrigation in *Sid Meier's Civilization*), a single character in a fighting game (Link in *Super Smash Bros.*), and so on.

An individual object is balanced with respect to other objects if everything about it in aggregate (its stats, cost, rarity, strengths, weaknesses, and so on) is comparable to other objects in aggregate, with reasonable tradeoffs between them—one sword might do more damage than another, but also be harder to find or cost more gold. Balance is experienced where each object has a reason why a player might use it, at least in some situations. If a particular piece of armor is so weak that the player never uses it, even at the start of the game—or if they receive a super-strong piece of armor in the first 5 minutes of a 100-hour game that is better than anything else and never gets upgraded or replaced—we call that item unbalanced.

Chapters 8 and 9 deal in detail with the balance of game objects.

Balance as Fairness

The common thread with each of these elements of balance is the concept of fairness. A balanced game is one that feels fair to the players. If players are assumed to have a level of skill within a certain range, a balanced game does not present challenges that are far outside of that range. If the game sets up an expectation of progressively increasing difficulty at a fairly constant rate, it is balanced if it doesn't deviate sharply from that difficulty curve without good reason. In a balanced PvP environment, each player feels like they have a reasonable chance to win, provided that their skills are equivalent and that their win or loss was not predetermined or otherwise outside of their control. If a game with an in-game economy is balanced, players expect that more expensive things are also more powerful and useful. If the player feels like the game isn't jerking them around, and the game seems to be playing by its own rules and conforming to the expectations that it sets up from the beginning, then it is balanced.

The use of the word "feel" here is not accidental. From the player's perspective, and as noted earlier, balance is something that arises from perception. As different players may have different perceptions of a game, players can disagree over whether a game is balanced in the same way that they might disagree over other subjective interpretations such as whether the game is fun. Somewhere out there, there is someone who hates *Half-Life 2*.

How Do We Know If a Game Is Balanced?

Pronouncing a game "balanced" is a lot like pronouncing a game "fun." Designers and players know it when they feel it. At the core of that feeling are really three metaphorical dials that are coming together to produce that feeling. It's not surprising that if these dials are tuned right, the game feels fair, provided they are in line with the game's target audience. The dials are the following:

- **Difficulty**: Is it too easy, too hard, or just right? This takes into account everything from winning a single encounter to beating a level to completing the entire game.
- **Quantity**: Is there too little, too much, or enough? This applies to all components of a game including all resources, players, creatures, etc.
- **Timing**: Is it too early, too late, or right on time? Timing is often a factor of difficulty or quantity (it was too easy, and they got through it too quickly), but it also often stands on its own in examples where the player isn't moving quickly enough or the conflict/pressure of a game is moving too fast.

The designer's intent is then tested through repeated, iterative play and tuning to get it "just right."

Along with these three dials are three modifiers to which these dials need to be tuned. These modifiers answer the question of what a game's core purpose is.

- **Target audience**: Who is this game being made for? Targeting for one demographic means you're ultimately making the level of conflict/play pressure in the game not suitable for another demographic. That doesn't mean it's unbalanced though. We'd say that is "as designed." Family games are designed to be approachable for a wide range of groups. Games designed for hardcore players like *Super Hexagon* or even the speed-tuned *Starcraft* one sees in Korea are nearly unapproachable for the non-hardcore.
- **Designer's intent**: Once the core demographic is decided, how hard does the designer want to make the game for her desired demographic? Masocore games are designed to be deliberately difficult for even skilled players. Meditative games are designed to produce a continuous series of activities where there's very little pressure at all.

- **Purpose**: Why is this game being made? Post-purchase/acquisition, is the designer balancing for fun or balancing for continued revenue? This is radically important question, obviously, which affects the core of a game's entire design. Games that are being designed to promote free-to-play friction-based monetization consistently balance the game to provide the player not enough resources, on average, for any given task. Designers often balance time against money (if you want it quicker, pay for it) and then craft external pressures to make sure that players feel the weight of that time either through game-applied pressure (you want to play more, but you are out of energy or still have quests or you are consistently just shy of one necessary resource) or through PvP-applied pressure (if you don't upgrade, you are going to get destroyed and lose what you have created). Games that are not designed to generate resource-based income post-sale must balance toward fun, knowing that players who are constantly struggling against "not enough" are unlikely to sign up for more of that with downloadable content (DLC), expansions, or sequels. This is not to suggest that free-to-play friction-based games which are designed toward income are not fun. What's fun to some is not fun to others no matter which game we pick. They are, however, balanced differently than other games and the metrics of the games are rigorously tracked to make sure they meet certain baseline thresholds.

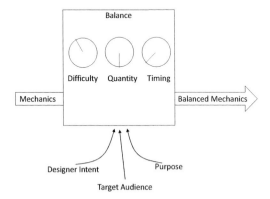

The last remaining factor that applies to game balance is progression. Slamming on the same creature throughout the course of play with the same weapon for the same rewards is ultimately very dull (unless one is going for a high score, in which case the game is actually about mastery and being able to do it better and be rewarded for that). There are certain tools we use that help us go in with basic baselines. For instance, in an RPG that is ten levels deep, one might say, "I want each level to be twice as hard as the previous level." That alone gives us some degree of progression. By the end of one level, we should have ramped the player for the next (or close to it, anyway).

When it comes down to releasing a game, the question of "is it balanced" is ultimately one of feel or what one feels the metrics should be.

Case Study: Is *Chess* Balanced?

On the one hand, it has been observed that there is a slight advantage to going first at the highest levels of tournament play, although as of this writing, it has not been conclusively determined why. Is there a mechanical reason, i.e., a bona fide tactical or strategic advantage to going first? Or is it merely psychological, where players assume there is a first-move advantage and thus mentally trick themselves into doing worse when they go second? Also interesting is that this advantage disappears at lower skill levels. Keep in mind that *Chess* has been played in some form for thousands of years, and we still don't know exactly how balanced it is, or how much the first-turn advantage is really worth!

Chess is also interesting in that a greater degree of player skill makes the game more unbalanced, not less. This actually happens in a lot of games; skilled players are more able to exploit the imbalances in the game. However, sometimes it works the other way around, where skilled players can correct an inherent imbalance through clever play. For example, in the board game *Catan* (originally *Settlers of Catan*), much of the gameplay involves trading resources with other players. If a player has a slight advantage (due to lucky die rolls, a favorable start position, and so on), other skilled players may simply agree to not trade with them, at least until such time as their relative positions have equalized. This might not happen in casual play, as novice *Catan* players are unable to recognize or act on a slight early-game advantage. At the tournament level, however, players are more likely to identify imbalances and act accordingly.

How Do You Balance a Game?

Now that we have established what balance is, how does a game designer go about improving the balance of their game? Is balance something that can be measured, evaluated, and modified? How is the work of balancing a game actually done in the field? The answers to these questions form the bulk of this book.

This book covers four general approaches to balance: designer experience, small-scale playtesting, analytics, and mathematics, each of which is covered in detail later on in this book. On any given game project, some combination of the four is used.

Designer Experience

The more experienced the designer, the more they have been exposed to in terms of different methods of balancing games. In truth, it's a bit of a black box. Odds are, you won't find the spreadsheets of your favorite game online. Talks on game balance are few and far between. Concrete knowledge is seldom shared and is guarded as a closely held corporate secret (really). Once a game is in circulation, the collective play of crowds is able to disseminate its play and reverse engineer it into spreadsheets and loot drop tables to show you what the designers arrived at, but not the route they took, or why they went there in the first place. With experience, especially experience that includes working with other experienced designers, laying the initial foundation for a game's balance becomes easier and the core starting point for many. One experienced designer we know prefers to start with 1.5 as her guiding number. By 1.5, she means that each area shall be 1.5 times harder than the previous area, and everything shall follow suit accordingly. She adjusts these numbers as she plays to give the game the proper feel she's looking for, but at its core, her experience saves her a good deal of trial and error. For designers working on sequels, the experience of the previous game literally feeds into the next: the same data is used and then tweaked to account for new play, items, locations, etc.

Early on in their careers, the best designers draw on their experience playing other games and their design instincts. As they design more and more games, they are able to draw on their past experience of knowing what does and doesn't work, based on similar elements of games that they've designed in the past. Experience has the benefit of being fast: you can sit down and make some changes, and the balance is modified in some way that you are ultimately able to predict with a high degree of accuracy.

Since experience cannot come from book learning (by definition), this book cannot teach you experience. However, the Main Quests and Sidequests at the end of each chapter should provide you with some useful practice that helps in building your experience, and simply making lots of games helps you as well.

Small-Scale Playtesting

Few, if any, designers have the ability to balance a game by hand and have it come out perfectly right away. While a designer must always start somewhere just to get a playable version of the game, it is critical to see what actually happens when the game is set in motion with real players. When observing a game in progress, balance issues can often be seen, clear as day. Furthermore, as designers become more and more expert in the systems they have created (this is referred to as "designer blindness"), they lose a feel for what a new player expects. Seeing someone play for the first time makes it apparent whether the game starts off too hard or just right.

There are many forms of playtesting. Early on in development, a designer may play the game on their own as a solo activity, simply to eliminate any obvious problems that waste anyone's time. Later, the designer may play with close friends, co-workers, or confidantes in order to get outside opinions. Eventually, these tests may be extended to a small set of friends-of-friends or even complete strangers who can play the game, while the designer observes or otherwise receives direct one-on-one feedback from the players. Playtesting is covered in Chapter 15.

Analytics

The collection and analysis of large amounts of play data are collectively referred to as analytics. Games that are designed to be living, dynamic ecosystems, such as MMOs, or those which are designed to bring in cash through either ad revenue or some form of free-to-play monetization test balance primarily through analytics. For games like this, the only way to test the success of the game's balance is by letting players in, letting them do what they do, and analyzing the data. Based on that data, both product managers and game designers work together to adjust the game toward certain pre-defined KPI (key performance indicators). Typically, certain performance criteria must be met before a publisher even launches a game like this.

Being able to collect data about how the game is being played on a large scale "in the wild," designers can have powerful tools to evaluate and tune the balance of the game. Analytics are covered in detail in Chapter 13 (with some useful tools for analytics covered in Chapter 24).

Mathematics

Every game has numbers, even if they aren't exposed to the player and even for games that don't seem overly "geeky." An FPS, for example, may have damage, range, and ammunition for each weapon; health remaining for each player; and current positions of all players, vehicles, and pickups on a coordinate grid, all of which are numbers.

What about the playground game *Tag*? It contains elements that could be measured numerically, such as each player's running speed and the amount of time that a player has been "it." While these numbers may not be tracked or studied on a typical playground, imagine if *Tag* were a professional sport; if it were, you had better believe there would be numbers and stats all over the televised broadcasts, sports websites, and trading cards of each player.

Some games are quite explicit about their use of numbers. RPGs (role-playing games), for example, often list numbers for hit points, damage, accuracy, and all kinds of other numbers used to determine whether a particular attack hits an opponent and if so, what effect it has on the target. Professional sports (and the video games based on them) provide all kinds of statistics on player and team performance over the course of a season or a lifetime.

Whether a game exposes or hides its numbers to the player, these numbers must be designed, and there are a wide variety of mathematical tools that can be used to understand a game's systems, analyze a game's balance, and identify and eliminate imbalances. How to find relationships between several game objects or systems is covered in Chapters 4 and 5, and analyzing randomness in systems is shown in Chapters 17, 18, 19, 22, and 23.

Balance between Types of Balance

While there are four different methods of balance (described above), that doesn't mean you can just pick your favorite method and do everything that way. All four methods have some place in a game development cycle, but they have varying degrees of emphasis depending on the game, genre, and project phase.

In some action games, there is less of a focus on numbers that fit neatly into spreadsheets. How do you compare the Gravity Gun to other weapons in *Half-Life 2* when it is such a unique game object? How do you mathematically compare the High Jump against the Varia Suit in *Metroid* when they do completely different things? In these genres, there tends to be more emphasis on playtesting and analytics where the designer can see exactly how players interact with the game.

In Multiplayer Online Battle Arena (MOBA) games like *League of Legends*, which tend to be highly stats and numbers based, numerical analysis with cost curves is useful to take an initial stab at getting the balance right. Playtesting is important but not as heavily emphasized in small scale, since these are games designed to have thousands or millions of players and that creates dynamics that you can't really get a clear picture of with just a few dozen playtesters (hence why so many of these games have an "open beta" period—yes, this is also good marketing for their game and a way to get players hooked early, but it's also useful for data collection for analytics). After launch, the game is still actively maintained in real time, so analytics based on player data is where designers get the most bang for their buck here.

In TCGs (trading card games), there tends to be a lot of math up front to get the costs and benefits of each card lined up along a cost curve, and then playtesting during development to smooth out the edges and improve the understanding of the supporting math. Analytics is much harder to use for tabletop TCGs because there's no way to have every game played in someone's dorm room get uploaded to your servers to collect the data in the first place; and even if you do find a gross imbalance in the game, it's harder to issue a "patch" to fix it.

With games that are meant more as Fine Art pieces, balance is done in service of the artistic statement of the game. In these cases, a game may be intentionally balanced or imbalanced based on what the designer wants the game to say. Many arthouse games aren't all that numbers-heavy to begin with, so the balance comes more from designer intuition than math, with playtesting in small scale to confirm that it's doing what the designer wants (these games typically don't have enough of a budget or a large enough player community to make large-scale analytics practical).

Other genres have their own mix of which types of balance are emphasized. The point here isn't to say that such-and-such a genre must have a specific percentage breakdown between the four types, just to point out that each type has its own strengths and weaknesses that make each one more or less appropriate to any given genre or any given game within that genre.

It's also worth adding that there is a fifth way to balance games: modeling the numbers after an existing game (referred to derisively as "cloning"). If a previous game is known to have good balance, then modeling the data and numbers from that game may be balanced in the new game, provided that game is systemically the same as the other game. However, designers should always understand why the elements of a particular game are or are not balanced, so that creating similar systems can be done with intent. Otherwise, a designer might copy something that works in the original game but not in the new game because of a slight mechanical difference that invalidates the original design. For this reason, cloning responsibly still requires the ability to analyze the balance of an existing game using mathematics or other methods, or else the designer runs the risk of breaking the balance of the new game without understanding why (or how to fix it).

A Note about Math

There is a cultural myth that every person is either "good at math" or "bad at math." Many people assume this is some kind of inborn trait, and everyone finds out which one they are around the time they learn fractions in elementary school. If you as a reader fear that you are not good at math, the thought of an entire book dedicated to the subject may be sending chills down your spine. Does a game designer need to be born with mathematical ability?

First, let's be clear that this is, in fact, a myth. Mathematics is a skill, and like any skill, it can be taught and it can be learned. Some people may say they're "bad at art," and yet, these same people can still learn to produce competent drawings by simply practicing a lot of drawing (perhaps while taking a figure drawing class or reading some books on drawing and anatomy). Some people who are "bad at learning language" can still learn to speak a foreign language through any number of successful programs, as long as they put in the time and effort. For people without inborn aptitude, it may seem to take slightly longer or be a little more frustrating, though mostly that is just coming from self-doubt… but it is still very possible for just about anyone to learn all of these skills.

For the purposes of this book, you are expected to know how to do basic arithmetic, and how to solve simple algebra equations, of the kind that you probably encountered in grade school as a teenager. That is it. This book will take you the rest of the way, on a strictly need-to-know, just-in-time basis. Most of the "math" is no more complicated than rolling dice or shuffling cards. If you've rolled some dice or played some card games before, you already have most of the math intuition you need as a game designer.

And if you do consider yourself "good at math" and are unafraid to move forward, you should be in for a wonderfully fun time. Let us begin, then, our journey into the arcane world of balancing games.

Discussion Questions

1. Select a game you know well that has particularly good balance in your opinion. What makes you think so?
2. Select a game you know well that is very poorly balanced in your opinion. What makes you think so?
3. Choose a well-known video game. What methods of balancing do you think are the most effective if the designers wanted to improve the game's balance further?

4. Examine a game of any type (board game, video game, etc.), and identify what features are assessed when considering how balanced that game is.
5. Do you consider yourself good at math, bad at math, or neither? What topics are you most looking forward to learning about as you progress through this book? What topics scare or intimidate you the most?

Rogue's Main Quest, Part 1: A Mini Expansion Set

At the end of each chapter in this book, there are some Sidequests, short exercises, and challenges to test your skills. In addition, some chapters have a Main Quest, a long-term project that involves a larger game balance task broken into multiple parts. There are three Main Quests to choose from, which we have named after common character classes.

The Rogue's Main Quest involves creating a small expansion set (as might be offered in a promotional pack) for an existing, commercially released game. You go through the process of analyzing what has already been released for the game and deriving a mathematical model to describe the relationship between the costs and benefits of the various game objects (in other words, how the costs of everything in the game are determined, based on how powerful they are and what they do for you). You then create an original mechanic of your own design that does not yet exist in the game, tentatively come up for what it costs based on the analysis you did and your intuition, and then create a small number (five to ten) of new game objects that showcase your new mechanic. You then balance those objects using the math you've established, then playtest the expansion, and make adjustments to both the objects and your underlying math based on the results of the tests.

To undertake this Main Quest, start now by choosing a game in one of the following genres: TCG, LCG (Living Card Game), deckbuilding game, miniatures game, or a tabletop RPG (role-playing game) that has combat resolution rules. Or, if you prefer video games, choose a TBS (turn-based strategy) or RTS (real-time strategy) computer game that has mod tools, such that you can modify the numbers and capabilities of various units.

Choose a game with relatively simple systems. You are doing some in-depth analysis of the game, so a game with dozens of stats and giant manuals full of charts (such as *Warhammer 40K* or *Advanced Squad Leader*), since it is time-prohibitive for you to do a full analysis.

Also choose a game with enough content to be able to do a reasonable analysis, but not so much that you are overwhelmed. Avoid *Magic: the Gathering* or *Dominion*, since those games have been around for so long that developing an entirely original mechanic is challenging, and both games have enough cards that it takes too long to sort through them all to develop any kind of mathematical model.

Choose a game. Then, if you haven't played it recently (or ever), go ahead and play it to familiarize yourself with it. Or, play several games, and then, pick your favorite.

Part 2 continued in Chapter 2

Fighter's Main Quest, Part 1: Analysis of an Epic Journey

The Fighter's Main Quest involves looking at the player experience and progression throughout a single-player (or multiplayer cooperative) game's campaign mode. You look at the numbers underlying the player's progression through the game and analyze play time through each section. In the process, you identify how the game's pacing changes throughout the campaign, and what areas are the most and least compelling in terms of challenge level and amount of time, effort, and skill required to progress.

To begin this quest, first choose an appropriate game. This should be a video game with some kind of campaign or story that has a clearly defined start and end point. Suitable candidates include most CRPGs (computer role-playing games), tactical RPGs, Action-RPGs, Roguelikes, FPSs or Third-Person Shooters, idle games, Metroidvanias, Survival Horror games, or Stealth games.

It is recommended that you choose a game that plays to completion in 20 hours or less, such as many older- or earlier-generation games in these genres. You will be poring over all kinds of charts, formulas, and level maps, and you want to keep the total content manageable.

At this point, simply choose a game. Do not play all the way through it unless you have the time, but you may want to play through the first few minutes to familiarize yourself with the core mechanics. Also find some sources for information on the game: physical strategy guides, online FAQs or Wikis, game reviews, developer interviews or conference talks, or Let's Play videos. You do not have to look through these thoroughly, but keep a record of what sources you have and where to find them (such as a list of URLs) and keep it handy for later.

Part 2 continued in Chapter 2

Wizard's Main Quest, Part 1: Creating a TCG

The Wizard's Main Quest involves starting with an existing core concept for a simple trading card game called Harmony and balancing the game, one step at a time. Normally, trading card games are not a good project to create from scratch for practice; they are large and complicated and take a long time to get right. This particular game was designed by the author specifically to have simple mechanics, be easy to learn, and easy to modify.

To get started, simply make a playable prototype of the game. You can either copy and cut out the cards on the following four pages or create them manually on 200 index cards if you don't have access to a scanner/printer or copier (or want cards that are larger and easier to handle). Separate the cards into four decks (A, B, C, and D) as marked on the bottom of the cards. In the next chapter, we learn to play the game and eventually modify the game to balance it, as its initial form starts out highly unbalanced.

Part 2 continued in Chapter 5

POWER +1 Bio (Deck A)	POWER +1 Bio (Deck A)	POWER +1 Bio (Deck A)	POWER +1 Bio (Deck A)	POWER +1 Bio (Deck A)	
POWER +1 Bio (Deck A)	POWER +1 Bio (Deck A)	POWER +1 Bio (Deck A)	POWER +1 Bio (Deck A)	POWER +1 Bio (Deck A)	
POWER +1 Magic (Deck A)	POWER +1 Magic (Deck A)	POWER +1 Magic (Deck A)	POWER +1 Magic (Deck A)	POWER +1 Magic (Deck A)	
POWER +1 Magic (Deck A)	POWER +1 Magic (Deck A)	POWER +1 Magic (Deck A)	POWER +1 Magic (Deck A)	POWER +1 Magic (Deck A)	
Awakening Cost: 1M Draw 1, Damage 2 (Deck A)	Awakening Cost: 1M Draw 1, Damage 2 (Deck A)	Inspiration Cost: 2X Draw 1, Damage 2 (Deck A)	Inspiration Cost: 2X Draw 1, Damage 2 (Deck A)	Medicine Cost: 2X Heal 3 (Deck A)	Medicine Cost: 2X Heal 3 (Deck A)
Depression Cost: 2X Discard 1 (Deck A)	Wall of spikes Cost: 2X Damage 2 (Deck A)	Natural heal Cost: 1B Heal 4 (Deck A)	Natural heal Cost: 1B Heal 4 (Deck A)	Regeneration Cost: 2B+2X Heal 6, Discard 1 (Deck A)	Spell scroll Cost: 2M+2X Draw 2, Damage 3 (Deck A)
Fairy glow Cost: 3M Draw 2, Damage 3 (Deck A)	Meditation Cost: 3B Heal 6, Discard 1 (Deck A)	Mindhack Cost: 6X Discard 2 (Deck A)	Oneness Cost: 6X Draw 2, Damage 3 (Deck A)	Thornwheel Cost: 6X Damage 4 (Deck A)	Warmth Cost: 6X Heal 6, Discard 1 (Deck A)
Light orb Cost: 6M Draw 3, Damage 4 (Deck A)	Cultivate Cost: 6B Heal 9, Discard 1 (Deck A)	Spellbook Cost: 4M+4X Draw 3, Damage 4 (Deck A)	Blossom Cost: 4B + 4X Heal 9, Discard 1 (Deck A)	Library Cost: 2M + 8X Draw 3, Damage 4 (Deck A)	Infuse Cost: 2B + 8X Heal 9, Discard 1 (Deck A)
Connectedness Cost: 8M + 4X Draw 4, Damage 5 (Deck A)	Treatment Cost: 8B + 4X Heal 12, Discard 2 (Deck A)	Brainstorm Cost: 6M + 8X Draw 4, Damage 5 (Deck A)	Rebirth Cost: 6B + 8X Heal 12, Discard 2 (Deck A)	Restoration Cost: 8B + 8M Heal 10, Draw 3, Discard 3, Damage.4 (Deck A)	Restoration Cost: 8B + 8M Heal 10, Draw 3, Discard 3, Damage.4 (Deck A)

POWER	POWER	POWER	POWER	POWER	
+1 Bio	+1 Bio	+1 Bio	+1 Bio	+1 Bio	
(Deck B)	(Deck B)	(Deck B)	(Deck B)	(Deck B)	
POWER	POWER	POWER	POWER	POWER	
+1 Bio	+1 Bio	+1 Bio	+1 Bio	+1 Bio	
(Deck B)	(Deck B)	(Deck B)	(Deck B)	(Deck B)	
POWER	POWER	POWER	POWER	POWER	
+1 Science	+1 Science	+1 Science	+1 Science	+1 Science	
(Deck B)	(Deck B)	(Deck B)	(Deck B)	(Deck B)	
POWER	POWER	POWER	POWER	POWER	
+1 Science	+1 Science	+1 Science	+1 Science	+1 Science	
(Deck B)	(Deck B)	(Deck B)	(Deck B)	(Deck B)	
Headache	Headache	Depression	Depression	Medicine	Medicine
Cost: 1S	Cost: 1S	Cost: 2X	Cost: 2X	Cost: 2X	Cost: 2X
Discard 1	Discard 1	Discard 1	Discard 1	Heal 3	Heal 3
(Deck B)	(Deck B)	(Deck B)	(Deck B)	(Deck B)	(Deck B)
Inspiration	Wall of spikes	Natural heal	Natural heal	Regeneration	Brain freeze
Cost: 2X	Cost: 2X	Cost: 1B	Cost: 1B	Cost: 2B+2X	Cost: 2S+2X
Draw 1,	Damage 2	Heal 4	Heal 4	Heal 6,	Discard 2
Damage 2				Discard 1	
(Deck B)	(Deck B)	(Deck B)	(Deck B)	(Deck B)	(Deck B)
Disassembly	Meditation	Mindhack	Oneness	Thornwheel	Warmth
Cost: 3S	Cost: 3B	Cost: 6X	Cost: 6X	Cost: 6X	Cost: 6X
Discard 2	Heal 6,	Discard 2	Draw 2,	Damage 4	Heal 6,
	Discard 1		Damage 3		Discard 1
(Deck B)	(Deck B)	(Deck B)	(Deck B)	(Deck B)	(Deck B)
Invasiveness	Cultivate	Neoplasm	Blossom	Surgery	Infuse
Cost: 6S	Cost: 6B	Cost: 4S+4X	Cost: 4B+4X	Cost: 2S+8X	Cost: 2B+8X
Discard 3	Heal 9,	Discard 3	Heal 9,	Discard 3	Heal 9,
	Discard 1		Discard 1		Discard 1
(Deck B)	(Deck B)	(Deck B)	(Deck B)	(Deck B)	(Deck B)
Fragmentation	Treatment	Segmentation	Rebirth	Transplant	Transplant
Cost: 8S+4X	Cost: 8B+4X	Cost: 10S	Cost: 6B+8X	Cost: 8B+8S	Cost: 8B+8S
Discard 4	Heal 12,	Discard 4	Heal 12,	Heal 10,	Heal 10,
	Discard 2		Discard 2	Discard 3	Discard 3
(Deck B)	(Deck B)	(Deck B)	(Deck B)	(Deck B)	(Deck B)

POWER	POWER	POWER	POWER	POWER	
+1 Gear	+1 Gear	+1 Gear	+1 Gear	+1 Gear	
(Deck C)	(Deck C)	(Deck C)	(Deck C)	(Deck C)	
POWER	POWER	POWER	POWER	POWER	
+1 Gear	+1 Gear	+1 Gear	+1 Gear	+1 Gear	
(Deck C)	(Deck C)	(Deck C)	(Deck C)	(Deck C)	
POWER	POWER	POWER	POWER	POWER	
+1 Magic	+1 Magic	+1 Magic	+1 Magic	+1 Magic	
(Deck C)	(Deck C)	(Deck C)	(Deck C)	(Deck C)	
POWER	POWER	POWER	POWER	POWER	
+1 Magic	+1 Magic	+1 Magic	+1 Magic	+1 Magic	
(Deck C)	(Deck C)	(Deck C)	(Deck C)	(Deck C)	
Awakening	Awakening	Inspiration	Inspiration	Wall of spikes	Wall of spikes
Cost: 1M	Cost: 1M	Cost: 2X	Cost: 2X	Cost: 2X	Cost: 2X
Draw 1,	Draw 1,	Draw 1,	Draw 1,	Damage 2	Damage 2
Damage 2	Damage 2	Damage 2	Damage 2		
(Deck C)	(Deck C)	(Deck C)	(Deck C)	(Deck C)	(Deck C)
Medicine	Depression	Ball of Spikes	Ball of Spikes	Machine Mask	Spell Scroll
Cost: 2X	Cost: 2X	Cost: 1G	Cost: 1G	Cost: 2G+2X	Cost: 2M+2X
Heal 3	Discard 1	Damage 2	Damage 2	Damage 4	Draw 2,
					Damage 3
(Deck C)	(Deck C)	(Deck C)	(Deck C)	(Deck C)	(Deck C)
Fairy Glow	Silver Grenade	Mindhack	Oneness	Thornwheel	Warmth
Cost: 3M	Cost: 3G	Cost: 6X	Cost: 6X	Cost: 6X	Cost: 6X
Draw 2,	Damage 4	Discard 2	Draw 2,	Damage 4	Heal 6,
Damage 3			Damage 3		Discard 1
(Deck C)	(Deck C)	(Deck C)	(Deck C)	(Deck C)	(Deck C)
Light Orb	Claw Hand	Spellbook	Warrior's Fury	Library	Infestation
Cost: 6M	Cost: 6G	Cost: 4M+4X	Cost: 4G+4X	Cost: 2M+8X	Cost: 2G+8X
Draw 3,	Damage 6	Draw 3,	Damage 6	Draw 3,	Damage 6
Damage 4		Damage 4		Damage 4	
(Deck C)	(Deck C)	(Deck C)	(Deck C)	(Deck C)	(Deck C)
Connectedness	Cruel Drill	Brainstorm	Shatter Body	Body Siphon	Body Siphon
Cost: 8M+4X	Cost: 8G+4X	Cost: 6M+8X	Cost: 10G	Cost: 8G+8M	Cost: 8G+8M
Draw 4,	Damage 8	Draw 4,	Damage 8	Draw 4,	Draw 4,
Damage 5		Damage 5		Damage 12	Damage 12
(Deck C)	(Deck C)	(Deck C)	(Deck C)	(Deck C)	(Deck C)

POWER +1 Gear (Deck D)	POWER +1 Gear (Deck D)	POWER +1 Gear (Deck D)	POWER +1 Gear (Deck D)	POWER +1 Gear (Deck D)	
POWER +1 Gear (Deck D)	POWER +1 Gear (Deck D)	POWER +1 Gear (Deck D)	POWER +1 Gear (Deck D)	POWER +1 Gear (Deck D)	
POWER +1 Science (Deck D)	POWER +1 Science (Deck D)	POWER +1 Science (Deck D)	POWER +1 Science (Deck D)	POWER +1 Science (Deck D)	
POWER +1 Science (Deck D)	POWER +1 Science (Deck D)	POWER +1 Science (Deck D)	POWER +1 Science (Deck D)	POWER +1 Science (Deck D)	
Headache Cost: 1S Discard 1 (Deck D)	Headache Cost: 1S Discard 1 (Deck D)	Depression Cost: 2X Discard 1 (Deck D)	Depression Cost: 2X Discard 1 (Deck D)	Wall of Spikes Cost: 2X Damage 2 (Deck D)	Wall of Spikes Cost: 2X Damage 2 (Deck D)
Inspiration Cost: 2X Draw 1, Damage 2 (Deck D)	Medicine Cost: 2X Heal 3 (Deck D)	Ball of Spikes Cost: 1G Damage 2 (Deck D)	Ball of Spikes Cost: 1G Damage 2 (Deck D)	Machine Mask Cost: 2G+2X Damage 4 (Deck D)	Brain Freeze Cost: 2S+2X Discard 2 (Deck D)
Disassembly Cost: 3S Discard 2 (Deck D)	Silver Grenade Cost: 3G Damage 4 (Deck D)	Mindhack Cost: 6X Discard 2 (Deck D)	Oneness Cost: 6X Draw 2, Damage 3 (Deck D)	Thornwheel Cost: 6X Damage 4 (Deck D)	Warmth Cost: 6X Heal 6, Discard 1 (Deck D)
Invasiveness Cost: 6S Discard 3 (Deck D)	Claw Hand Cost: 6G Damage 6 (Deck D)	Neoplasm Cost: 4S+4X Discard 3 (Deck D)	Warrior's Fury Cost: 4G+4X Damage 6 (Deck D)	Surgery Cost: 2S+8X Discard 3 (Deck D)	Infestation Cost: 2G+8X Damage 6 (Deck D)
Fragmentation Cost: 8S+4X Discard 4 (Deck D)	Cruel Drill Cost: 8G+4X Damage 8 (Deck D)	Segmentation Cost: 10S Discard 4 (Deck D)	Shatter Body Cost: 10G Damage 8 (Deck D)	Cataclysm Cost: 8G+8S Damage 10, Discard 4 (Deck D)	Cataclysm Cost: 8G+8S Damage 10, Discard 4 (Deck D)

2

Critical Vocabulary

In This Chapter

- (Please Don't Skip This Chapter, it's not as boring as it sounds)
- Understanding the Possibility Space
- Affecting the Possibility Space
- Curves
- Solvability
- The Metagame

Understanding the Possibility Space

Before getting into the nuts and bolts of *how* to balance a game, let's examine some key variables and tools (masquerading as concepts and terminology) that are used in game balance and in shaping the possibility space of a game.

What is a possibility space? To understand a possibility space, it is first necessary to define a game state.

- **Game state**: a game state is a collection of everything that describes the current position or value of a game-in-progress at a single point in time. If we take a break from *Chess* mid-game, what's left on the table is its game state.[1] The game state is everything that must be saved, including whose turn it is, in order to restore the game to the exact same point at a later time or in a different location.

- **Possibility space**: the possibility space of a game is the set of all potential game states. It is, in effect, all possible instances of that game that could ever be played. Most games are complex enough that it is not practical to actually list the entire possibility space, so it is more often just as a theoretical concept. The larger the possibility space of a game, the less predictable and more replayable it is.

The possibility space of a game varies widely from game to game. For instance, let's take the case of a typical coin toss. The possibility space for this game is incredibly narrow:

- Player A flips and wins/Player A flips and loses.
- Player B flips and wins/Player B flips and loses.

Contrast this game with *Minecraft*. In *Minecraft*, the game state contains the status of every block in that instance/seed of the world, everything the players have collected and built and all the tunnels they've created in the process. It also contains all the data associated with fixed monsters and **NPC** (Non-Player Character, that is, characters in the game that are controlled by AI rather than players) villages. Separately, the game state also includes the players and their individual inventory, although players are free to drop out of the game without affecting the world's game state. The possibility space of Minecraft is every game world that could ever be created. It is, in effect, infinite.

Within a single game, the possibility space can also vary depending on how we frame the word "game." Consider *Magic: the Gathering*. The entire possibility space of the game is vast—all games that could possibly be played with its many cards. Next, consider the much smaller possibility space of a game between two players who have already chosen their decks. Still smaller, consider that same game at the 15-minute mark. At that point, only so many different play paths are possible. For games of the non-infinite variety, the possibility space gets smaller and smaller until a winner is declared.

---

[1]For those readers familiar with *Chess*, technically its game state also includes whose turn it is, whether each king and rook has moved before (to determine whether the castling move is valid), and whether a pawn has recently moved two spaces forward (making it eligible for an *en passant* capture). These things would not always be apparent just by looking at the pieces on the board, but are still considered part of the game state.

Affecting the Possibility Space

Having created a possibility space for a game, designers have several tools at their disposal to constrain or broaden that possibility space. These tools are determinism, transitivity, information, and symmetry.

Determinism

Actions within games can be either deterministic or non-deterministic, and game designers balance these types of games differently from one another.

- **Deterministic games**: players start with a particular game state in the possibility space. If they take a particular action from that state, it *always* produces the same resulting new game state. While playing an early scene in the game *Inside*, if you trip over the branch in the water, the guards always come for you, and it's always game over.
- **Non-deterministic games**: players start with a particular game state in the possibility space. If they take a particular action allowed by that state, it does *not* always produce the same resulting new game state. While playing *PlayerUnknown's Battlegrounds*, jumping out of the plane at exactly the same time every game will most certainly not result in the same resulting new game state.

Analyzing game balance is done differently for deterministic and non-deterministic games, so identifying which elements of a game are one or the other is a necessary first step.

To increase the possibility space of a single game, a designer can make some of its deterministic events non-deterministic. For instance, if a sword always does 5 damage, the designer could make it non-deterministic so that it does between 1 and 7 damage. Now, instead of one outcome, we have seven possible outcomes. Conversely, designers can also add six more deterministic events to increase the possibility space: the sword does 1 damage on the first round of combat, 3 damage against slimes, 7 damage against dragons, 2 damage on alternate Thursdays, and so on. In general, adding randomness is easier than adding six new events.

Rock-Paper-Scissors is a purely deterministic game once players have chosen their throws: any particular pair of throws always gives the same result. In some games, particularly adventure games, all actions are deterministic, and therefore, we call the game itself a deterministic game. In *What Remains of*

Edith Finch, the narrative always progressions in the same way through the family tree. Likewise, *Chess, Go,* and *Checkers* are deterministic. If you start a game of *Chess* with e2-e4, the game state is exactly the same every time you start with that move, no matter what. Note that these games are non-deterministic from the frame of reference of a single player: when you choose a move, the end result may differ depending on what your opponent does, and you don't know what any given opponent is doing ahead of time.

World of Warcraft is largely non-deterministic. Hitting a monster with the exact same weapon is not always going to do the exact same damage or even successfully hit. Furthermore, killing that same monster is not always going to produce the same loot drop due to the random numbers involved in selecting the likelihood of that drop. The randomness inherent in the AI's behavior also affects the outcome. Similarly, *Candyland* and *Chutes&Ladders* are non-deterministic. Players move forward on their turn through a random mechanism (such as dice, cards, or a spinner, depending on the version). There is no guarantee that a player taking a turn from one game state receives the same random output each time. This means it is non-deterministic—you cannot determine the outcome. However, once the random element has happened, the rules for movement are deterministic (if you roll 1 in *Chutes&Ladders* when you are on the space marked 99, you always advance to space 100 and win the game).

Perhaps the clearest comparative example is two similar video games, *Pac-Man* and *Ms. Pac-Man*. Both games have similar mechanics: you guide your avatar around a maze, eating dots and avoiding the four ghosts that are chasing you. There are special dots in the corners that turn the tables, allowing you to eat ghosts for a short time. Twice per level, fruit appears in the maze for bonus points.

Pac-Man is deterministic. The ghosts follow an AI that is purely dependent on the current game state, specifically the positions of ghosts and Pac-Man in the maze. Because the ghost AI always does exactly the same thing in the same situation, a player can get the same results on separate playthroughs if they follow the same controller inputs. From this property of determinism, players are able to figure out patterns[2] to follow to beat the game. By making use of patterns, the game changes from chasing and being chased to a game of memorizing and executing patterns.

By contrast, the sequel *Ms. Pac-Man* is non-deterministic. The ghost AIs have random elements to them, and the fruit in the maze moves in a random path rather than showing up in a static location. As a result, *Ms. Pac-Man* has no patterns that work, and the focus shifts to quick thinking and reaction. A novice may not notice the difference between the two games, but an expert player plays the two games quite differently.

Calling a game deterministic or non-deterministic is not a value judgment. While *Ms. Pac-Man* has a larger possibility space and offers expert players more interesting choices, games like *Chess* and *Go* are entirely deterministic and have been played for thousands of years, a significant success given that most game designers today are happy if their game is still being played a mere ten or twenty years after it's published. In fact, the patterns in deterministic games give players a great degree of enjoyment as they seek to master them.

Transitivity and Intransitivity

Mechanics and properties within games can also be described as having transitive or intransitive relationships with one another:

- **Transitive relationships**: game objects or mechanics have transitive relationships with one another if "you get what you pay for." More powerful effects have greater costs, limitations or drawbacks. Said another way, if A is better than B, and B is better than C, then A is always better than C. Different power levels of spells are likewise transitive if more mana equals more power.
- **Intransitive relationships**: a game object or mechanic is intransitive if "better" or "more powerful" is a relative (and not absolute) concept. This happens frequently in games that have elemental strengths and weaknesses. Water might be strong against Fire, and Fire might be

---

[2] You can find many such patterns online. For example, http://nrchapman.com/pacman/.

strong against Ice, but Water isn't strong against Ice. Said another way, just because A is better than B and B is better than C does not necessarily mean that A is better than C.

From a literal perspective, and interestingly enough, transitivity has no effect on the actual possibility space of the game. However, intransitivity makes it more challenging to see through that possibility space since it is not entirely clear exactly what the right choice is. Therefore, the *perceived* possibility space seems greater because there are interesting vs. obvious choices. For instance, imagine ten swords each of which does one more damage than the last. While the possibility space contains ten swords, it's an obvious choice to select the sword with the most power. However, if we take these same swords and give them unique properties (the one that does 2 damage, say, also has a 50% chance of completely healing you), the choice becomes less obvious. This creates an intransitive relationship between the items and makes the choice less clear. The player must decide which item she values more. So, the realm of reasonable choice, thus the *perceived* possibility space, is generally larger in games with more intransitive properties.

To illustrate, RPGs have many transitive properties. For instance, the higher the level of the character, the better you expect that character to be. The more you pay for a spell in mana, the more powerful you expect that spell to be. Likewise, really good items tend to cost more or require a higher player level. Things are transitive when a Level 10 character is more powerful than a Level 5 character, which in turn is more powerful than a Level 1 character.

Player character choices, however, are often intransitive. For instance, consider characters in a typical street fighting game and their win rates one-versus-one against other characters. Suppose Character A beats Character B most times, and Character B regularly beats Character C. This doesn't necessarily mean that Character A has an advantage against Character C. Some are strong against one character and weak against another. Games in the *Civilization* series are likewise intransitive in terms of the civilizations represented and their powers vs. each other. However, they are transitive in terms of the cost and strength of their units.

Information

A game has **perfect information** or **complete information** if all players know all elements of the game state at all times. *Chess*, *Go*, and *Tic-Tac-Toe* are all games of perfect information. It follows that any deterministic game with perfect information is, at least, theoretically solvable.

Players make decisions in games based on the *perceived* possibility space before them. The more information they know, the better those decisions will be (provided their brain is with them that day). For example, if there are two otherwise identical enemies before a player, and they know that one enemy has low hit points, that's the one they attempt to take out first. If, however, they don't know the state of enemy health, their decision isn't as clear. The amount of information available to the player dramatically affects the size of the perceived possibility space.

Other games have various types of incomplete information, of which there are several varieties.

- **Privileged information**: information is considered privileged when it is a part of the game state that is known only to a single player or a subset of players and no one else, such as a player's hand in a card game or your health in an FPS.
- **Common information**: information is considered common or **shared** when it is known to all players, such as the health meters in a fighting game, the discard pile in most card games, or face-up cards in a collectable card game (CCG).
- **Hidden information**: information is considered hidden when it is a part of the game state but not known to *any* of the players, such as random enemy placement in a level or the next card on a draw pile. Similarly, the three hidden cards in the board game *Clue* are not only an example of hidden information, but also the objective of the game.

A single game may have many different types of information. Trading card games like *Magic: the Gathering* show just how many layers of information can exist in a single game. Each player has a hand of cards (privileged information), and there are cards in play (common information), as well as cards in each player's draw pile (hidden information). However, each player knows what cards are in their own deck (privileged information), even if they don't know the order of those cards (hidden information); the possibility space of each player's deck is thus privileged information (all possible decks that could be created from their specific set of cards). Beyond that, many CCGs have cards that give the player limited access to information: mechanics which let a player peek at some cards in one player's deck or hand, for example. Part of the challenge of deck construction in these games is deciding how important it is to gain access to information vs. how important it is to attack or defend directly.

Symmetry

Symmetry in games refers to the initial starting state of the players.

- **Symmetric**: A game is said to be symmetric if all players have the same beginning state, play by the same rules, and have the same goals. Cosmetic differences, such as pawn colors in chess, which do not affect game play are not a consideration. In level design, symmetric level design means the one part of the level is a mirror image of the other.
- **Asymmetric**: A game is asymmetric in design if there are multiple starting states, multiple paths within the game, or different rules for different players (or character choices). If anything is on Player 1's side that is not perfectly mirrored on Player 2's side, it is not symmetric. In level design, asymmetric level design means that most parts of the level are not mirrored by in other areas. The original *DOOM* games are an example of classic asymmetric level design.

A two-player map for a first-person shooter that has everything mirrored, including start positions and locations of objects in the level, is symmetric (assuming both players also have the same character capabilities and attributes). By comparison, asymmetric design means players start with *at least one* different component, be it weapons or different locations or a non-mirrored level. The more asymmetric a game is, the larger its possibility space. It may be more interesting to players specifically because there are a wider variety of potential interactions. This is also true of level design. In symmetric design, if players know half of a level, they therefore know the other half of the level and are able to make decisions based upon that. Asymmetric level design keeps players guessing.

Civilization: Revolution is an excellent example of asymmetric game design. The initial starting civilization abilities, when taken individually, seem impossible to beat. Each has such an obvious strong advantage. However, since each is overpowered in its own way, the game balances out. Furthermore, the maps are randomly generated as are the starting civilizations that the player plays against.

Mathematically speaking, symmetric games are by definition perfectly balanced: if all players have the same initial state and play by the same rules toward the same goals, obviously none can start with an unfair advantage. However, some resources or strategies in the game may still be unbalanced, at which point the game degenerates to who can reach the exploits first. Additionally, other elements of balance such as progression, pacing, and player vs. player skill may still be suboptimal from the perspective of player enjoyment. Sadly, "make the game symmetric" is not the ultimate solution (or even a lazy solution) to all game balance problems.

While symmetry narrows the possibility space of a game, its use is important. Symmetry allows players to make obvious comparisons and allows them to feel that the playing field is quite literally balanced. By contrast, asymmetric games, particularly those on the far end of the symmetric–asymmetric spectrum, can overwhelm the player with too many difficult decisions.

The use of the word "spectrum" in the previous sentence is not accidental. Very few games are purely symmetric or purely asymmetric. Rather, a designer would refer to a particular mechanic in a game as symmetric or asymmetric. In common use, a designer might refer to an entire game as symmetric if it is *primarily* symmetric in the case of most or all of its core mechanics, even if the game technically has some minor asymmetries (or vice versa).

For example, is *Chess* symmetric? Players have different colors (traditionally white and black), but that is a purely cosmetic asymmetry that does not affect gameplay. Likewise, the initial setup is mirrored (the king is to the right of the queen for white, and to the left for black), but none of the pieces have different movement rules when going right vs. left, so this does not affect play either. Both players have the same initial set of pieces and the pieces all play by the same rules, so that aspect is perfectly symmetric. The only asymmetry is that the game is taken in turns, and one player goes first. So, *Chess* is an asymmetric game (with many symmetries between the players)—to call an entire game "symmetric" implies it is symmetric in every respect.

Could you change the rules of *Chess* to make it symmetric? Absolutely! For example, suppose that instead of taking sequential turns, each player wrote down their next move at the same time and both moves were revealed and resolved simultaneously. In this case, the added symmetry requires added complexity: you need extra rules to handle cases where two pieces move into or through the same square, or when one piece enters a square on the same move that another piece vacates that square. There are, in fact, variants along these lines.[3]

Feedback Loops

Feedback loops are situations in a game where the result of some game action modifies that action in the future. There are two types of feedback loops: positive and negative.

- **Positive (amplifying) feedback loops**: A feedback loop is positive when systems amplify their own effect as they feed into themselves. In a multiplayer game, giving an advantage to a player who is already winning (or a disadvantage to a player who is losing) is a typical example.
- **Negative (dampening) feedback loops**: A feedback loop is negative when systems dampen their own effect and stabilize the game. In a multiplayer game, this gives an advantage to players who are losing, or a disadvantage to players who are winning.

Positive feedback loops are one of the most misused terms in games. In this case, positive means "additive" and not "good." This is particularly problematic because positive feedback loops are typically anything but positive. Positive feedback loops cause the rich to get richer and the poor to get poorer, and because of this, they tend to bring the game toward an irreversible conclusion or send the game into a state known as "the empire problem." *Monopoly* is a classic positive feedback loop with an irreversible conclusion. The more property you have, the more money you make. With that money, you make those properties even better and can easily withstand a periodic stay at another's hotel. Regrettably, the game often takes forever to drag itself toward an obvious and inevitable conclusion due to the house rules that people have added that counteract the positive feedback loop. What's happening in *Monopoly* is similar to the empire problem that happens in tycoon games. In these games, you're building a business in the game, whether it's a zoo or a pizza business. You improve your business, and it improves your income. Eventually, you're just rolling in cash, and there is no real challenge in the game anymore. This is known as the empire problem.

---

[3] As one example, see http://en.wikipedia.org/wiki/V._R._Parton#Synchronistic_Chess. (Last modified April 4, 2021.)

In video games, positive feedback loops are often ironed out before launch. For example, an issue once occurred in an RPG but was removed before launch. In that RPG, as in traditional RPGs, characters fight monsters, get experience, and get stronger. As they do, other things in the game progress as well, keeping a like mathematical relationship and level of difficulty between player and environment to produce a challenge. This is a progression curve, not a positive feedback loop. However, a special damage multiplier was added in which multiplied a wizard's spell damage by their level. This multiplier was not applied anywhere else, however. So, the result was that the wizard quickly progressed along the progression curve and became more and more powerful as they did so. In effect, this multiplier made it easier for them to increase their multiplier even further.

Used well, positive feedback loops can cause a game to end quickly once it reaches a certain point, so that players don't have to wait too long while going through the motions once a winner has emerged. Used poorly, positive feedback loops can be frustrating, throwing too much focus on the early game (as an early lead can snowball into an insurmountable advantage by mid-game) and giving the feeling of helplessness to anyone who is even slightly behind the leader (since it becomes harder and harder to catch up once you fall back).

Negative feedback loops bring all players together in standing, making sure that no one gets too far ahead or behind, and thus tends to extend the game by preventing anyone from winning too easily. Used well, negative feedback loops stop the game from ending too early, and keep all players feeling like they still have a chance (even if they made some early mistakes). Used poorly, negative feedback loops make players feel like they are being punished for doing well and rewarded for playing poorly, cause the game to drag on for too long since no one can get ahead too easily, and put too much focus on late-game actions since any advantages won early on are negated over time. In games, social dynamics are often the most obvious negative feedback loop. Once a potential winner has emerged, other players tend to work together to stave off that person's winning.

Some games may have both positive and negative feedback loops that counteract each other. For example, in many racing games, there is a positive feedback loop where once a player is in the lead, they have no opponents nearby and thus fewer obstacles to get in their way; however, there is often a negative feedback loop in the mechanics, where computer-controlled cars start driving faster when behind (termed "rubber-banding" because they act as if there's an invisible rubber band connecting them with the lead car).

Some feedback loops may be explicitly and intentionally written into the core rules of the game. Others may simply be a by-product of how the rules work when set in motion. And still others may occur from how the players choose to play. Consider the board game *Catan*. The game contains a positive feedback loop: as players build more settlements and cities, they generate more resources, which in turn let them build even more settlements and cities which lets them gain even more resources. While there are no explicit negative feedback loops to counteract this (no rules that reduce the resource gains for players in the lead or that grant additional resources to players who are behind, for example), the game contains mechanisms for players to help or hurt one another. Since players get a lot of resources through trading with each other, a player who is strongly in the lead has difficulty convincing anyone else to trade with them. Additionally, on each turn a player occasionally gets the chance to move the Robber, which reduces the production of players of their choice; a single player who is leading tends to be targeted by the Robber from all other players.

Curves

In game design, we use the term **curve** to describe a graph of numbers representing the relationship between two resources in a game that shows what happens to one game resource when the other increases. Despite the name, curves might simply be a straight line, or a gently sloping curve, or a series of jagged or smooth hills and valleys.[4] Curves plot **progression** through the game, whether it's experience level to experience level or the hit points of varying levels of creatures.

You have likely heard or used the terms learning curve and difficulty curve no matter how experienced you are in game design. If a game has a steep **learning curve**, it means that players are expected to learn rapidly as the game gets progressively more challenging. The term **difficulty curve** is sometimes used synonymously with learning curve, but can be referencing many other things (the monster's strength relative to the player, the change in competitive level between two PvP arenas, and so on). Last, the term **ramp** is sometimes used synonymously with curve because many curves in game design look like ramps one might drive over.

---

[4]A synonym for a game curve is a **function**. In mathematics, a function provides a mapping from one set of numbers to another (for example, if you give a particular function a character's level, it returns the number of experience points required to reach the next level). For this reason, game designers may more precisely refer to a curve by *two* names, those of the two numbers that are being mapped. In this case, one might call it the "level/XP curve" rather than the "level curve"; the only reason the latter is commonly used is that enough games have one of these that the "XP" part is implied and understood.

One of the most common curves in games is the level curve. **A level curve** shows how many experience points are needed to gain a level, based on a character's current level.

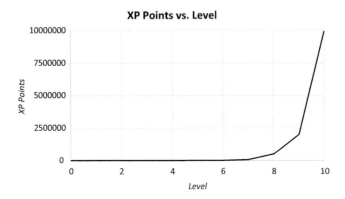

Experienced game designers recognize the shapes of curves and often design to a particular shape on purpose, either because it has worked in the past or because it does the job they need it to do. In free-to-play games, for instance, it is common to **ramp the player out**: increasing the difficulty of the game rapidly at a specific point so that only the monetizing (paying) players stick around. This quickly lets the product managers focus on the core, monetizing group.

There are a few types of curves used commonly in games that we discuss in this book: identity, linear, exponential, logarithmic, triangular, and designer-created curves. While each is discussed in depth in the various sections of this book, it is useful to define them briefly here:

- **Identity curve**: An identity curve is the simplest type of curve where two objects equal one another. You can trade 10 food for 10 gold.
- **Linear curve**: A linear curve is created when one object increases as a multiple of the other. You can trade 1 food for 5 gold, 2 food for 10 gold, 3 food for 15 gold, and so on. In this case, we have a 1:5 linear relationship between food and gold. For every 5 gold, you get an additional 1 food.
- **Exponential curve**: An exponential curve is created when one of the objects is multiplied repeatedly by a number to determine the progression (mathematicians call this number the "base"). Let's say our base is 4. To start, you can trade 1 food for 2 gold, 2 food for 8 gold, 3 food for

32 gold, 4 food for 128 gold, and so on. Each end result is multiplied
by 4 to get the next result.

- **Logarithmic curve**: A logarithmic curve is just the reverse of an exponential curve. In the above example, the food progression is logarithmic. For each new unit of food, it requires 4× the number of gold. Level
  curves are often logarithmic, while XP is often exponential, at least up
  until a certain point.

There are other types of curves that are used as progression in games as well
as curves created by designers, but this is a good start to get us going. Where
curves are common to a specific type of resource or problem, we explain their
use in depth.

Solvability

The possibility space coupled with those things that shape it—determinism, transitivity, information, and symmetry—ultimately come together
to determine the game's solvability. A game is **solvable** if it has a single
knowable "best" action to take when you encounter *everything* in the game.
So, for instance, some adventure games are solvable as are any games which
are deterministic and transitive. For any possible game state, there is a best
answer. This applies for the first time you play it right through to the fiftieth.

Solvability is important as a concept because a game's solvability (or lack
thereof) influences how we evaluate a game's balance.

Types of Solvability

There are three different types of solvability:

- **Trivial solvability**: A game is trivially solvable if it is possible for the
  human mind to completely solve the game, either in real-time during
  play or ahead of time by memorizing best-move lists.
- **Theoretical solvability**: A game is theoretically solvable if it is *possible*
  for the human mind to completely solve the game, but it's *not realistic* to
  do so due to either time constraints or the size of the possibility space.
  Players know all the information in the game state and could deduce
  the outcome, but it's just not realistically possible.
- **Computational solvability**: A game is computationally solvable if it is
  possible for a computer to solve the game, but not the average or even

better-than-average human mind. Computers are capable of running many simulations to determine quickly if there is an optimum play path.

Tic-Tac-Toe is a common example of a trivially solvable game for adults. For young children who haven't solved it yet, it is a challenging game of strategy. Once their minds grow to the point where they can figure out the entire possibility space, it no longer holds much interest. In video games, most tutorials are trivially solvable. They are fully deterministic, and the possibility space is incredibly narrow by design. Players follow a set path, press a few buttons or keys, take out a monster, and then are allowed into the game.

We can still talk about the balance of trivially solvable games. Is *Tic-Tac-Toe* balanced? You could say that it is, in that optimal play on both sides always leads to a draw. You could also say that it's not, in that the possibility space contains more ways for the first player to win than the second player, so there is a first-player advantage at the novice level. Or that if the only way to lose is to make a mistake, there's actually a second-player advantage because the first player has the first opportunity to make a mistake and thus lose the game. Or you could take statistics of a large number of games played by players of various skill levels to see how often each player wins, and note any first or second player advantages from actual play.

In contrast, *Chess* and *Go* are examples of theoretically solvable games that have such a large possibility space that the human mind can't realistically solve the entire game perfectly for all positions. These games may be solvable in theory, but they are still interesting because their complexity is beyond our capacity to solve them.

When assessing the balance of a theoretically solvable game, we can't grasp the complete solution, so we do not yet have the means to perform the same analysis we did above for *Tic-Tac-Toe*. We don't know if perfect play on both sides yields a win for one player or a draw. We don't know if there are a greater number of game states that are a win for one player over the other in the entire possibility space. The best we can do is make an educated guess. How do we guess? We may use our game designer intuition. We may look at the (sometimes conflicting) opinions of world-class, expert players. If the game is widely played and has a rich recorded history, we may look at documented tournament stats across a large number of championship-level games.

When computers get involved, we can again use brute-force simulation of the entire possibility space to do the same kind of analysis as with *Tic-Tac-Toe* in terms of assessing balance. As memory gets larger and cheaper and computers get faster, more and more games become computationally solvable, although these games may still be unsolvable by the unaided human mind. As of this writing, *Checkers* and *Connect Four* have been completely solved by computers, while *Chess* and *Go* have a large enough possibility space that we do not yet have a complete solution. For those games, AIs use a set of heuristics rather than a full brute-force lookup in order to play, so these games remain theoretically solvable at this point and we can only rely on second-order metrics to assess balance.

Solving Non-deterministic Games

Since non-deterministic games don't have predictable paths through them, can they be "solved" like *Tic-Tac-Toe* can be? It turns out they can, although the solution looks different from a solvable deterministic game. Remember, solvability just means that there is a single best action; it does not require that this action always succeeds. It means that it succeeds more often than any other action, and a complete solution might also state what that probability is.

The gambling game *Blackjack* is non-deterministic and solvable in several forms. If no card counting is allowed, and the next card could be anything in the deck that isn't showing on the table, one can find many tables and charts online that tell when to hit, stay, split, or double down, and some even tell you the house advantage. If the player counts cards, then the optimal play changes depending on whether there are more high cards or low cards remaining in the deck, and depending on the particular card counting algorithm you're following, the probability of winning any given hand may differ from the non-card-counting strategies. The card-counting player is still not guaranteed to win a given hand, or a set of hands, but the probabilities shift in their favor. Casinos disallow this strategy and include countermeasures to prevent it (watching player betting habits, dealing from a multi-deck shoe, and other methods).

Solving Intransitive Games

Perhaps the best known example of intransitivity is *Rock-Paper-Scissors*, and it provides a useful example in terms of solvability. Since the outcome depends on what you do and what your opponent does, there isn't an obvious optimal move, and therefore, the concept of "solvability" does not seem to apply here. But in fact, the game is solvable, although the solution looks very different from solutions discussed previously.

The solution is a ratio of 1 Rock to 1 Paper to 1 Scissors, meaning you should throw each type as often as the others. Why? Because if you favored one throw over the others in the long term (maybe out of every 100 throws, you always did 50 Rock, 23 Paper, and 27 Scissors), then an opponent could beat you by always playing whatever beats your dominant throw (a strategy of 0 Rock, 100 Paper, 0 Scissors beats 50/23/27 more often than it loses to it). This doesn't mean that you must always keep your throws exactly equal at all times, but just that this should be your general trend in the long term, to not favor one over the others.

The Metagame

The term **metagame** literally means "the game surrounding the game" and is how we describe the things that players do that affect their chances of winning a game, but that happen outside of actual play. In championship Poker, this may mean studying the playing habits of upcoming opponents. In trading card games like *Magic: the Gathering*, activities such as constructing a deck (especially if you consider other popular decks in the play environment) fall into this category. In professional sports, there are many metagame activities, including salary offers, drafting and trading players, how much players are trained, and what training methods are used.

The balance of the metagame can have a profound effect on the balance of the game itself. For example, consider a professional sport that simply lets teams hire who they want, at whatever price they can negotiate, and team revenue comes from ticket sales of their games. What happens? The teams that win a lot have a stronger fan base and more ticket sales, which gives them more money; they can use that money to hire better players, which then gives them an even better chance of winning—a positive feedback loop! In many popular sports, the metagame has rules to control this loop, such as

- **Drafting**: each season, teams choose among the players looking to join a new team, in some order. In this way, the worst teams still have the opportunity to grab some good players, and the best get spread out among several teams and not collect in a single team.
- **Salary caps**: there is some upper limit to how much an individual athlete can get paid by their team, and/or an upper limit to how much a team can spend on their athletes in total, so that a wealthy team can't just outbid everyone else for the best players.

- **Revenue sharing**: rather than ticket sales only benefiting the teams that were playing, some or all of the ticket revenue gets put in a pool that is evenly distributed to all teams. In this way, a team that wins a lot doesn't have drastically more money than everyone else.
- **Team size limits**: by placing strict limits on how many players can work for a team, a good team can't hire an infinite talent supply.

These kinds of metagame restrictions are not arbitrary or accidental. They were put there by people who understand game balance, and it's part of the reason why any given Sunday, the weakest team in the NFL might beat the strongest team.

Case Study 1: Gray Ogre vs. Granite Gargoyle

In the very first set of *Magic: the Gathering*, there were two cards: Granite Gargoyle and Gray Ogre. Gray Ogre cost 2R (two colorless and one Red mana) for a 2/2 creature with no special abilities. The Granite Gargoyle cost the same 2R for a 2/2 creature with two special abilities (Flying, and ability to gain +0/+1 by spending one Red mana). Even if you've never played the game, it is clear that the gargoyle is more powerful than the ogre even though it has the same cost, so this is clearly unbalanced. What's going on here?

The answer is that in this game (and most other trading card games (TCGs)), some cards are more common or rare than others. Granite Gargoyle was more rare than Gray Ogre. The original designers assumed at the time that players have some kind of reasonable limit to what they spend; thus, by making a rare card better, it is balanced by the fact that there are fewer of that card in circulation and that if a player wants to use a particular rare in their deck, they likely have to trade for it (probably with another rare from their collection), so they have to do with fewer rares of other types.

Unfortunately, this did not actually work as intended. The original designers did not realize at the time just how popular the game would be, or how different players would spend vastly different amounts of money on the game, or that a full set of many copies of every card was achievable (and highly unbalancing), and therefore that rarity as a balancing factor only served to give a gameplay advantage to players who spent more. Today, TCG designers are more aware of this issue, and players are less likely to put up with overly aggressive "pay-to-win" design.

Case Study 2: Anti Raigeki

Another issue that particularly plagues non-digital TCGs is that once a set of cards is released, it is difficult to fix any imbalances that are found post-release. While an online game might be able to release a patch to modify some numbers and fix imbalances that way, a non-digital designer's options to fix balance at this point are limited and harsh. Cards can be restricted or outright banned in tournament play, which of course angers any players who were (un)fortunate enough to have those unbalanced cards in their collection. The designers can issue errata that changes the effects of the cards in competitive and general play, but that relies on getting the word out to players; enforcement is difficult, and players can become very frustrated (and rightly so) if they find out in the middle of a paid tournament that their deck no longer works! These solutions may be necessary if a card is so drastically unbalanced that it ruins the environment, but for cards that are not quite that powerful (but still noticeably better than intended), the designers are stuck.

One solution occasionally tried by TCG designers is to balance a powerful card or strategy by issuing a new card in the next set that serves as a direct counter-strategy. Here is an example from the card game *Yu-Gi-Oh*: a card called Anti Raigeki. It's a Trap card with the following text: "When your opponent activates 'Raigeki', all of your opponent's monsters are destroyed in place of your own."

Even without playing the game, it is pretty clear that this card was created as a direct counter to a card called Raigeki. This card does absolutely nothing for a player unless the opponent plays one specific card. It can be inferred that Raigeki is probably a very powerful card that was heavily unbalancing the metagame, and this was created as a way to allow players to defend themselves against it. (If you're curious, it destroyed all of the opponent's monsters when activated.)

This is a metagame solution: if the competitive environment is full of people playing a single dominant card, deck, or strategy, players are given a new card that lets them fight against that strategy. It essentially turns the metagame into *Rock-Paper-Scissors*: the dominant deck beats most other decks, the counter-card beats the dominant deck, and other competent decks beat the counter-card (because the counter-card is an inefficient use of resources if the opponent isn't playing the thing it selectively counters). While a *Rock-Paper-Scissors* metagame is still preferable to a metagame with only one dominant strategy (a game of Rock-Rock-Rock), it is not much better because the focus of play is shifted to the metagame. If the dominant strategy and counter-strategy are sufficiently powerful, players may as well just tell their opponent what deck they're playing, and not bother going through the motions of actually playing. This is an extreme example.

Counter-cards might have other useful effects in their own right, or the game overall might be designed such that the outcome of the game is determined more from player choices during the game than from the contents of each player's deck.

Metagame Balance: Benefit or Bane?

Why is it that balancing the metagame in professional sports is a way to make the game more balanced, while attempting to balance the metagame in a TCG feels more like a kludge?

In the case of sports, the imbalance exists in the metagame to begin with, so a metagame fix is appropriate. In the two TCG case studies mentioned in this section, the underlying imbalance lies in the game mechanics or individual game objects; the metagame imbalances resulting from these are a symptom and not the root cause. A metagame fix for an imbalance in the game just fights this symptom while doing nothing to address the initial problem.

Thus, as a general principle, if a game balance problem exists in one part of your game, it can easily propagate to other areas, so the problems your players experience in playtesting are not always the exact things that need to be fixed. When identifying an imbalance, before "fixing" it, start by asking why it is happening and what is really causing the problem… and then fix the imbalance where the root cause exists and not in some other interconnected system.

Discussion Questions

1. Define the difference between game state and possibility space.
2. Select a game you know well, analyze its possibility space, and discuss the things which affect it.
3. Select a video game, and identify three deterministic properties and three non-deterministic properties.
4. Analyze three game properties, objects, systems, or mechanics as either transitive, intransitive, or a mix of both. Provide examples for the same.
5. Choose a well-known game (board game, video game, or even a sports game), and analyze the information in the game in terms of privileged, common, and hidden. Find at least one example of each.

6. Identify a game with an asymmetric starting state, and explain how it might change the play experience if it had a symmetric starting state instead.
7. Examine a video game and identify at least one positive or negative feedback loop within it, as well as the effects it has on play overall.
8. Select a game of your choice and compare it against another in terms of solvability.
9. Select any game and analyze some number progression in it. Determine which type of curve that number progression is.

Sidequests

This chapter was mainly about just building a critical vocabulary that lets us describe the balance of games, so there are not a whole lot of skills to practice. Instead, use the opportunity to build intuition.

Sidequest 2.1: Balance Intuition Log

Next time you play or watch a game, don't just do it for fun. Instead, observe the actions in the game, and decide whether you think the game is balanced or not (hint: no game is perfect, so there are imbalances somewhere even if they are slight). What are the imbalances? How severe are they? What are the root causes of these imbalances? If you were in charge of the game, how do you fix them? Write down your thoughts as you go.

Later on, you can return to your intuitive thoughts on the balance of this game and apply mathematical principles to either confirm or disprove your initial suspicions.

Rogue's Main Quest, Part 2: Find the Exemplars

Continuing from Part 1 in: Chapter 1

For the game you've chosen, identify game objects (cards in a TCG, Living Card Game (LCG), or deckbuilding game; units in a miniatures, turn-based strategy (TBS), or RTS (real-time strategy) game; or items, character classes, feats, etc. in a tabletop RPG) that are clearly overpowered, others that are clearly underpowered, and others that feel "just right" as ideal paragons of balance. You will be using these later to construct and test your own mathematical models, to make sure that your math identifies the most broken objects as such. For this reason, don't worry about objects that are only slightly off; concentrate on those things that lie at the extremes, or else that are on the cusp of balance perfection.

If you are very familiar with the game, you may do this using just your own experience and intuition. Otherwise, you may wish to supplement by looking online for strategy articles, player or developer forums, or similar sources to see what the player community has identified.

Part 3 continued in Chapter 4

Fighter's Main Quest, Part 2: Fast Parts, Slow Parts

Continuing from Part 1 in: Chapter 1

For the game you've chosen, first make a rough outline of the main storyline or narrative, divided into levels or sections that the player must traverse in order (feel free to use a FAQ, strategy guide, or similar if you don't remember). Then, for each section, mark it as one of the following:

1. **Slow grind**. Section is very difficult when first encountered, has multiple roadblocks, is overly large compared to other levels, or otherwise requires the player to do a lot to pass through. Feels frustratingly, artificially slow.
2. **Slight grind**. Feels a little slower than normal, but not enough to stand out as one of the most frustrating parts of the game.
3. **Average**. Difficulty is consistent with most of the game, or with what you think of as ideal.
4. **Slightly easy**. Feels a little more rapid than normal, but not enough to stand out as something the player blasts through instantly.
5. **Fast and easy**. By the time the player reaches here, they are overleveled, have built up an excess of skill, or are otherwise so prepared that it provides little challenge. The player then proceeds to pass through the section extremely quickly, facing little or no resistance.

Also mark each section that contains one of the most memorable points of the game, such as an important plot point or reversal in the story, or a particularly fun or interesting boss fight or puzzle.

Record all of this in a spreadsheet program, with the first column containing the name of each section, the second column a number from 1 to 5 (as above), and the third column an 'x' if that section contains one of the high points of the game.

In later parts of this meta challenge, you will analyze the numbers and balance of the game in order to explain why the difficulty of certain sections deviated from the mean, and where such deviations were beneficial or harmful to the overall play experience.

Part 3 continued in Chapter 3

3

Where to Start—Systems

In This Chapter

- Where to Start: Put It All on the Table
- Critical and Fuzzy Thinking about Systems
- Types of Resources

Where to Start: Put It All on the Table

> I was brought in to fix a game that wasn't meeting publisher expecta-
> tions. The developers told me about the game's story, showed me the
> game in action, showed off the game assets and discussed the concept.
> The game itself, however, felt lifeless and was no fun. I said, 'Show me
> your economy,' and they didn't have any idea what I was talking about.
> Ultimately, it was easier to cancel it than to fix the game.
>
> *A veteran system designer and producer with 30 years' experience*

To understand what's happening in a game, whether that game is just starting or in production, it's critical to understand what the various **systems** in
a game are and how they work together. The word "system" in game design
follows the standard dictionary definition: a set of interacting or interdepen-
dent parts that form a complex whole. More formally, a system in a game is
a designer-created collection of game mechanics and resources which can
be understood mostly in isolation from other systems and that controls a

significant group of related, nontrivial behaviors of gameplay toward a specific outcome.

We balance how objects and resources flow between these systems. We could reskin *Monopoly* with 100 different narratives, make it digital, or keep it analog, but it's the underlying systems of turns, currency, property, and improvements that make the game. We can't break the game by changing its narrative. We *can* break the game by changing its resource economy. If everyone just takes whatever cash they need when they need it, it's busted.

In order to approach balance, and as an early step in game design, we need to know what we're balancing and how these things work with one another. It is at this point that game designers generally list all the resources in their game as well as how these resources work with one another. In some cases, lists aren't used professionally, because the genre's balance patterns are so baked in that a list isn't deemed necessary (role-playing games (RPGs) almost always have experience points, levels, HP, and gold for instance, and it's well known how these work with one another).

If a game is already in production and unbalanced, this exercise in systems analysis is just as valuable. It stands to reason that something isn't right in the eyes of the player—it is too much or too little. Furthermore, rather than it being a singular resource that's too much or too little, it's probably a several things that are off kilter, one thing reacting to the other. We use the term "player" here to denote a player who is also privy to the system information and interaction. Oftentimes, our post-launch players are like patients in a doctor's office. They tell you what's wrong and how they think it should be fixed, but a doctor must listen to the systems, make a diagnosis, and tell the patient how she thinks it should be treated. Provided it's not completely obvious, the only way to ascertain what's going on is to take a step back and look at your game's systems from the macro-view.

In a sense, a quilt is an apt metaphor for knowing your economies: pre-production, you're figuring out the pattern, choosing the colors, cutting fabric apart, and seeing where the squares go. While in production, if it's not feeling right or looking good, you have to take a step back and assess your resources and how you connected those resources together.

Critical and Fuzzy Thinking about Systems

Before exploring the types of systems games have, it is necessary to note three important points.

First, a system is a rhetorical construction for analysis and discussion. For instance, if one wanted to speak of the combat system in a game and how it affects the player's health, one is referring to a player's health and all things that affect that health either positively or negatively. So, in this analysis, we could say that the player is taking too much damage or not getting enough health packs or isn't killing enemies fast enough or has weapons that are too weak or isn't gaining levels quickly enough. It could be any one or more of these things that's the issue. In this example, there are many ways to solve the symptom of the player taking too much damage. Thinking of things in terms of systems is useful and necessary for game analysis and balance.

Second, systems have blurry lines. A resource from one system might seem perfectly at home in another, and in fact, it is. So, be mindful not to think too rigidly when thinking of systems. For instance, if there is currency in your game, there is a question of where it comes from (a starting amount+loot drops, let's say) and where it goes (stores, NPCs, other players, paying to settle events). Game designers often visualize systems as a set of interconnected gears; think of the character system and the combat system. Resources might be considered the things that travel on those gears, moving system to system and keeping the whole game flowing. In this example, hit points are a critical shared resource between the character and combat systems. Hit points are in both systems. Anything considered to be a game resource is likely to find itself in the analysis of many different systems, and these resources are the means by which one system affects others.

Third, systems are fractal in nature. There are small subsystems that might be composed of just one resource and one mechanic, and then macro systems like the entire game economy that's an overview of how every resource in the game works together. Sometimes, designers analyze smaller parts of the game, while other balance issues involve examining the entire game as a whole.

Types of Resources

All games have some or all of the resources covered in this section. In this chapter, we use the term "resources" very broadly to mean any thing we can trade in exchange for another thing. There are five general classes of resources which we cover throughout this book. These tend to form an interwoven economy of tradeoffs.

While the designer can include any that she likes, it's strongly recommended you include only those things that are necessary for a game (and question that necessity regularly). Overcomplicating a game is like overcomplicating anything else. It usually ends poorly.

Time

Time is the most important resource of a game. If you have to make an important decision in an hour or in a split second, the weight of time as a resource is acutely felt. Furthermore, as designers, we literally have time to fill with gameplay. As a resource, designers consider time in the following ways:

- **Length of game (game macros)**: How long one expects the game to last determines the progression of everything in the game and is one of the most important decisions a designer has to make. In fact, it creates what are called the game's **macros**—a term game designers use to describe the high-level gameplay plans. To illustrate the importance of the length of game, consider an RPG that lasts, on average, 10 hours. Players have certain expectations which we as designers can loosely balance toward. For instance, let's say that by the end of a 10-hour game, a player could reasonably expect to be level 30. As gamers ourselves, we instinctively know level 5 is far too little, and level 70 seems far too much for that length of time. It's perhaps surprising how many expectations there are when your gamer brain thinks, "What feels right here?" Of course, as the game's designer, you can do whatever you like. However, for the sake of this example, we will go with level 30. Using that number, we can make predictions or decisions on all kinds of things. Note that the numbers below are our estimations or goals to develop toward and are used to illustrate the process. Your game might be different (and as with many things in game design, several different ways can be right):
  - **Number of level gains**: Players are actually gaining 29 levels, since games start at level 1.
  - **Levels per hour**: Players should gain approximately three levels per hour, probably 4 per hour in the early game and 1 or 2 per hour in the later game.
  - **Stages of content**: Players have approximately 15 "stages" to pass through if we have 29 level gains. A stage is defined as a more challenging level of content. We use 15 stages rather than 29 in this

example, because games often blend stages together so there is overlap between the current state and the upcoming stage thus giving us 29 effective stages of challenge. For example, if we have stage 10 enemies and stage 11 enemies, we gradually go from *all* stage 10 enemies to *mostly* stage 10 enemies to *mostly* stage 11 enemies to *all* stage 11 enemies (and maybe even some stage 12 enemies). Our stages are designed to meet the growth of the player. When a player gains a level, they typically get more HP, improved stats, and improved skills. These improved skills must be met with more challenging game content which demands more of their skills, and enemies which demand more and more of their HP. To be clear, stages are typically not triggered by the player gaining a level but rather by moving to a new zone and making forward progress in the game (it would seem weird if players gained a level and all the monsters suddenly changed).

- **Number of enemy configurations**: Players may expect to encounter a minimum of 45 enemy configurations, three enemies for each stage. This doesn't necessarily mean 45 distinct enemies. Rather, given our 15 stages, it is reasonable to expect that players encounter an introductory enemy, a mid-level enemy, and a tough enemy. These *can* be 45 distinct enemies, or they can use the same reskinned art assets such as Skeletons, Cursed Skeletons, and Cursed Skeletons of the Darkness. This means that the team can develop fewer core art assets, thus saving time and money. As the player becomes more powerful, the current stage's mid-level enemy might become the next stage's weak enemy. Games can stretch this out and create even more stages by carefully staggering the introduction of enemies—ranging from, say, a couple of weak enemies to four weak enemies with one strong enemy to four strong enemies and one boss enemy. Content stages and enemies aside, players expect you to be reasonable. Consider the variety of monsters you might want in a 10-hour RPG vs. one that lasts 100 hours.

- **Bonus stat points per level**: Designers set the starting player stats of a game (either precisely or approximately by letting players allocate their bonus stat points where they choose). Likewise, we determine the approximate ending stat points of a game. Our preference is for players to hit the end of a game being exceptional in one or two stats, high in a few, mid-level in the rest, and still low in one. So, if we know our starting number and can rough out an ending number, we likewise know the difference between the two. That difference divided by 29 equals the point gain per level. Most games offer a random number within a range (say 5 ± 2 points). Why not just let players max out their stats? Because, if players don't max out, the decisions they make are meaningful decisions. Players can choose to improve along one vector or another, but not all of them.

- **Bonus skill points per level**: There are many ways that bonus points work. In some games, players can directly assign them on level gain. Some games allow players to progress their skills through use, not just through bonus points upon level gain. Games also unlock one per level in a skill tree or have a set of skills accessible from the beginning of the game, each with its own value, where the values level up (either with use like in *Elder Scrolls*, or they just improve automatically on level up, or the player gets skill points to assign on each level up, etc.). Whatever method one uses, the designer must likewise take these gains into account.

- Notice how all of these resources—stats, skills, levels, enemies—all come directly from the total desired game length. While you might not normally think of enemy lists as something associated with time, in fact these are all related.

- **Turn-time**: Is the game real-time or turn-based? David Brevik, creator of the *Diablo* series of games, has discussed what he referred to as his "lightning moment" when he changed the original game from turn-based to real-time. It was then that he knew he was on to something big. In addition to turn-time (either real-time or turn-based), we might also ask how long is each turn supposed to take? For pencil and paper RPGs, there is often a direct relation between turns and time; while players may take as much real-world time as they wish to decide on an action, that action might take place within 6 seconds of time within the game's narrative. Some board games use sand timers to force players to move quickly or to limit the length of a turn. Sometimes, games are a blend of real-time and turn-based gameplay; *Mario Party* moves between turn-based game play and real-time minigames for instance.

- **Time to level in a genre or on a platform**: Players have expectations about how long it should take them before they gain a level. This is particularly true in casual games and **F2P** (free-to-play) games where showing players progress quickly is important. These games are often balanced toward ensuring that players level in a set amount of time. "Feels like the player should have gained a level by now," is a common refrain. While our RPG example above suggests the player reach level

30 within 10 hours, in a casual game or F2P game, the ramp is likely quite different.

- **Time of actions**: In some games, players have action points that they can use during a turn. Depending on the complexity of the action, it may cost a point, two points, or be entirely free. Some games don't incorporate time in this way at all.
- **Effect timer/cooldown time**: Some actions are powerful enough that you wouldn't want the character doing them constantly. To prevent that, designers incorporate a waiting period before the player can do the action again. Similarly, timers are also used for effects such as poison, sleep, invincibility, and the like that affect players for a limited amount of time. The amount of time these effects last is a variable, set by design.
- **Production/build time**: Similar to cool down time, production/build time is the amount of time a player has to wait before something is ready to use. This typically occurs when players are waiting for an upgrade to complete.
- **Movement speed**: The rate at which players move through the world is likewise a resource, both for game feel and for game play reasons. In any action game, the timing of player actions and how quickly and fluidly they move can make or break the experience.

While there are many more uses of time in games than these listed here, this list illustrates that it is a critical resource used in a wide variety of ways, all of which affect game play and some of which affect each other.

Currency

Currency is an all-purpose resource, which allows a player to trade some of its quantity in exchange for something else, be it other resources, information, or a savings of time. While some games have no currency or an economy in which players trade one item for another, there is typically an all-purpose resource which is used to purchase things in a game. That resource—be it gold, ducats, gems, or dollars—is the currency of the game. Beyond that, some games (particularly F2P games) also incorporate premium currency and real-world currency.

- **In-game currency**: currency earned by a player through their actions in a game is referred to as in-game currency. Some games allow players to purchase in-game currency with real-world money. In these instances, in-game currency is often obfuscated from real-world currency so that developers can have more granularity (spending €2 for 500 jewels for instance) or so that players have a harder time thinking of how much money has been spent (purchasing 20 jewels for €3, for instance).

- **Premium currency**: currency purchased with real-world cash which is not otherwise easily obtainable in the game is referred to as premium currency. Premium currency is often used in games for vanity items and for pay-to-win opportunities (rushing production of armies, for instance). Steambucks are an example of a premium currency which can be used to purchase in-game vanity items such as hats in *Team Fortress 2* or items on the Steam Marketplace.
- **Real-world currency**: plenty of games, most notably gambling games, allow players to use real-world currency in the game in exchange for a chance to win real-world currency or some other valuable. Other games like *Star Citizen* and *Shroud of the Avatar* sold in-game property for real-world currency. It is also common for game Kickstarters to offer in-game, exclusive rewards in exchange for real-world cash.

Note that if a player can pay real-world money in exchange for saving time, that is referred to as "pay to win." Pay to win has been incredibly lucrative for some game developers, particularly in competitive games such as *Clash of Clans*. If you want it done quicker? Pay money. The *Civilization* series allows you to rush things with in-game currency. Many free-to-play games allow you to do the same with real-world currency.

Game-Specific Objects

Game-specific resources are the things players collect, find, mine, win, or otherwise take possession of which can be used now or in the future to improve the player's game state. In *Minecraft*, for instance, there are many resources with which we are all familiar: wood, iron, gold, and diamonds, among them. Players can use six diamonds to create a diamond pickaxe. That diamond pickaxe, in turn, does more damage, mines faster, and lasts much longer than, say, the wood pickaxe. Minecraft's economy is one entirely composed of resources. Better resources help you live longer and mine faster. Board games like *Catan* are similar in terms of resource production and trade. The resources players collect by investing their time or by trading them with other players allow them to progress in the game itself. First-person shooter games like *Hitman* or *Call of Duty* use bullets as their primary resource and also lack any other form of currency.

It's worth noting that resources can appreciate or depreciate in value as the game goes on; we cover this fully in Chapter 6. When you first start to play *Minecraft*, for instance, your wood axe is amazing. It saves you another resource—time—over your bare fist. Iron saves you time over wood, thus depreciating wood, and diamond saves you time over iron, thus depreciating iron. If *Minecraft* were free-to-play, we could imagine that players would pay money for diamonds so that they could progress faster in the game. Trading money for time (making things go quicker) is the hook of most free-to-play games.

Hit Points/Lives

Although it's not often thought of as a resource *per se*, hit points, hearts, or whatever resource a game uses to track a player's health or lives is one of the most important resources of all. Hit points are present for both players and enemies. Game-specific objects like healing potions or health packs are consumed to restore hit points, and armor or powerups are used to slow or prevent any loss of hit points. On the other hand, weapons, magic spells, or other aggro actions cause loss of hit points. Players trade other resources in exchange for hit points, too: either money for healing potions or time to allow their characters to heal over time. In arcade or pinball games, players can spend real-world currency in exchange for another ball or additional lives.

The entire challenge of a game is largely connected to the player's ability to manage this resource effectively. While this may seem like the most obvious statement in the world, it's also one worth considering at length when one is balancing a game. The player's ability to manage this resource hinges on the designer's ability to pace the game appropriately—not presenting them with challenges before they are ready for them, and presenting them with opportunities to heal up when necessary. Statements such as "too easy," "impossible," "unfair," and "not fun" are words no designer wants to hear, and for many games these critiques are tied to how the designer handles this single resource. Allowing players to select from different difficulty levels as well as putting players into skill or platform brackets allows gives players meta-game options for managing this resource as well.

Experience and Levels

In games that measure character or player growth over time, there is an economy of experience. For roleplaying games, character progression is core to the form and that progression is often measured in terms of experience. The resource of experience typically includes the following components:

- **Experience points**: experience points are awarded to players for successfully completing game tasks. The amount of experience points awarded per game task is set by the game designers in the game data.
- **Experience levels**: experience levels are awarded when the player accumulates a set amount of experience points. Players usually require progressively more experience points per experience level.
- **Faction/relationship levels**: relationship levels in a game track how the player is perceived by others groups within the game.
- **Skill/performance levels**: the more a player uses a skill, generally, the higher the character skill becomes. Often, players can add points to skills during level gain.
- **Ranks**: the accumulation of experience levels is sometimes mirrored in profession or class ranks. For instance, a level 5 character might gain a rank from "beginner" to "novice" thief. This may be a purely narrative or cosmetic change, or the new rank might come with certain gameplay benefits.
- **Level cap**: level caps are often introduced in games that don't have definitive win states. For instance, games like *World of Warcraft* have had multiple level caps, beginning with level 60 and rising over time. As expansions release, the level cap increases with it. Level caps are a critical component of a game's experience economy and a means to ensure player enjoyment. To gain the next level, a character needs to **grind** (engage in repetitive play to generate enough of a resource such as experience to progress) for experience points. This is fine so long as the game's content is keeping pace with their ever-increasing experience point needs. At some point, however, if the content fails to grow with the player, the player must grind longer and longer to eke out those points. As an example, let's say you need to kill ten monsters worth 100 XP each to gain the next level. That's fine when you need 1000 points to gain a level. Let's imagine that there's no level cap beyond this though and that the XP needed for the next level keeps doubling. At some point, the player needs to dispatch thousands of enemies taking potentially weeks of time. To make matters worse, since players hit the *content cap*, encounters merely repeat the same enemies again and again. It's obviously not the best experience. As an added point, without a level cap, designers find themselves starting from an uncertain state

for downloadable content (DLC) or expansions. Early RPGs often had no level cap and allowed the player to continue playing even after they had killed the end boss of the game. When sequels were released following the game's success, designers lowered or flattened player experience levels, even if they transferred in high-level characters. Having a cap is infinitely preferable from a player perspective, compared to taking away levels which were earned. In games where players can compete with each other, lack of a level cap can effectively lock out new players from the top-tier leaderboards, unless they've been playing since early beta. For example, in many early Facebook games such as *Mafia Wars*, players would generally gain levels and power over time, unbounded; since players were progressing in the game at about the same rate over time, a player's standing in the global leaderboards had more to do with how much time they had been playing than anything else, and there was virtually no way to catch up to a player who was ahead of you as long as they stayed as active in the game as you did.

In games that have no experience points or a capped experience economy, player progression and growth is often reflected in items and equipment that they find, instead. Short-play RPGs in arcades award players with new items and more powers as they progress, such as permanent stat-gain potions that can be found occasionally in *Gauntlet*. In *World of Warcraft*, once players level cap, they receive an heirloom item which itself levels up. Other games reward the player with story, new character abilities, or some other vector for growth.

Establishing Relationships between Resources

As you undoubtedly noticed, there are relationships between different resource types and game objects. In fact, one could argue that if an economy of some sort stands alone in a game, it might not belong in the game at all. In the next chapter, we take a deeper look at the numerical relationships that exist between these resources.

Discussion Questions

1. In what ways is time integrated into the game as a resource?
2. Why might a game institute a level cap?

3. Compare games without level caps. What are the differences between those games and games that do have them?

4. Discuss how a currency-based economy is integrated into a game.

5. Can time be used as a form of currency?

6. Can currency be used as a form of time?

7. What kinds of resources might a free-to-play game allow a player to purchase for real-world money?

8. Of the resources in the previous question, which of those might be considered "pay to win," which would not, and which might or might not depending on how they were implemented?

9. What relationships might there be between health (hit points) and time?

10. Choose any physical sport. List the resources that individuals or teams manage within this sport.

Sidequests

Sidequest 3.1: Make a Resource Flow Diagram

Choose any game with multiple types of resources. Start by trying to list all of the resources in the game that you can.

Next, think about how these resources are related to each other or exchanged for each other during play. Draw a diagram where each resource is a box, then draw arrows between boxes to indicate relationships or exchange rates.

For example, consider *Ori and the Blind Forest*. In this Metroidvania game, the player explores a world while collecting several types of resources. There is health, of course (and some rare items that increase the main character's maximum health). The player also collects energy, which can be used for special attacks or to create impromptu save points (and items that increase maximum energy). The player also collects ability points (through both finding ability-point-granting items, and through defeating enemies in combat) which can be used to upgrade techniques along three separate tracks—one that makes it easier to find secrets (such as more health, energy, and ability points); one that improves the main character's combat abilities; and one that lets the character reach new places on the map by letting them jump or swim farther. For this game, you could produce the following resource flow diagram.

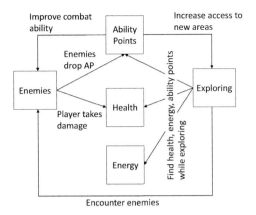

Fighter's Main Quest, Part 3: Grinding for Loot

Continuing from Part 2 in: Chapter 2

Analyze all ways that the player grows stronger in this game (e.g., new loot found in a specific chest or as a mandatory drop from a specific boss, new feats the player gets when they level up, or new abilities that the player finds as they explore the world) throughout the entire game. How often do they appear and when? Label this as a timeline broken into different sections, where each section represents a region, zone, quest line, or similar area in the game that the player must encounter. The amounts of time on the timeline need not be exact, but should be a reasonable example of what might be expected on a given playthrough of the game.

Identify any parts of the game that have either particularly large numbers of rewards or a small number of very strong rewards (such as a weapon found in a certain place that is far more powerful than anything before it, leading to a big jump in power). Also identify parts of the game that have relatively few noteworthy rewards.

For rewards that are random in nature, such as loot drops on wandering monsters that have a 0.1% chance of dropping a powerful artifact, create a model in a spreadsheet using RAND() or RANDBETWEEN() or similar pseudorandom number generators to give an example of what these rewards might look like on one or more playthroughs.

With reward schedule in hand, look back at your guesses from Part 2. Is there any correlation between the number/strength of player growth in a section with your label of how easy or grindy it was?

Part 4 continued in: Chapter 9

4

The Components of Progression—Curves

In This Chapter

- The Importance of Numerical Relationships
- Types of Numerical Relationships
- Types of Game Curves
- Everything in Moderation

The Importance of Numerical Relationships

In game economies, everything is relative to everything else. I remember watching a friend play WoW. He had a max level character, and I was just starting out. Every hit of his seemed like it did an obscene amount of damage, numbers higher than I had seen in any other game. However, those numbers were actually balanced considering the HP of the creatures he faced. The numbers worked with all the other numbers.

A narrative designer with two years' experience

Chapter 3 laid the foundation for game economies. In this chapter, we look at the relationship of numbers within those economies.

Let's say a player does 250 damage. In most games, that's a really nice hit. In the late stages of a game, however, that's a tragic fumble. Numbers (including zero) are only meaningful and useful in relation to other numbers. If you do 250 damage vs. a monster with 25,000 HP, it will probably kill you before you kill it. Likewise, if you do 250 damage, but the sword is capable of doing 2500 per hit, clearly you're on the lower end of the scale.

Numbers within game economies, like those covered in Chapter 3, are only meaningful when given context within the game economy as a whole. If we consider a standard level progression, experience point requirements for the next level often double level after level. In order for the game to remain fun, this level progression must work in concert with other components of the game including the amount of experience points the player is awarded from combat and quests. Further, gaining a level must reward the player in a way which feels meaningful in terms of their hit points and other tangible stats, skills, or spells.

What about games where characters gain no levels? Most first-person shooters work this way. In these games, the progression is on the player's skill instead of the character's. The game gets progressively harder in a variety of quantifiable ways (number of monsters, HP of monsters, challenge of the terrain, number of bullets, quantity of health packs) in order to compensate for the player's increasing skill. While the player might find new weapons that give them more tactical options to a point, in many FPSs an individual gun doesn't get any more powerful over time, and the focus is more on the player learning to use it effectively than in leveling it up. As another example, team-based esports games balance the teams against each other, so there are still numbers to relate to one another in a game like *Rocket League* or *Overwatch* even if players don't level up during a match.

As these examples (hopefully) reveal, the challenge and reward of gameplay are made in the relationship between numbers, and getting a feel for these relationships—many of which you already know from your experience playing and designing games—is critical to your success as a game designer.

Types of Numerical Relationships

There are two core types of numerical relationships in games we cover in this chapter:

- **Tradeoff relationships**: represent relationships where a game asks the player to give one thing in exchange for another.
- **Progression relationships**: represent relationships where the player is making progress, whether it be in experience levels, game narrative, or improved player skill.

Balance is determined not just mathematically, but by the player perception of these relationships. Does it feel like the player paid way too much for that sword in relation to the damage it does? Has it been forever since they gained a level? Is that monster incredibly overpowered compared to others in this area? Numbers in games are like that. They don't exist in a vacuum, but only in comparison with other numbers, in this case, the accumulated gameplay experience that builds expectations in a player's head. Balancing a game isn't just changing numbers or balancing a single economy, but understanding the relationships between them and changing them relative to each other.

In addition to these core relationships, in this chapter, we also show how these relationships tend to represent themselves in terms of a **curve**, the term game designers use to describe the shape of their progress or the cost of their tradeoffs as they increase or decrease (or sometimes both). We'll cover these types of curves: identity, linear, exponential, logarithmic, triangular, and custom crafted curves or functions. If this sounds complex or boring (it often seems to be one or the other), give it a chance. If you are a game player, you have already seen these curves in action, even if you don't have a specific name for them yet.

In this chapter, we'll take a look at the relationship of numbers to one another, explore different curves, and discuss how these relationships affect our balance decisions. Along with the material presented in the previous chapter, these concepts lay the groundwork for the material in later chapters.

Tradeoff Relationships

All games have at least one resource—the player's time. Most games have more than that, of course, such as some form of currency, items, hit points, and mana. These resources, including the player's time, have a cost in relationship to other resources. Whether we consider that cost acceptable or not depends on its relationship to other numbers. In fact, most interesting decisions within games involve some kind of tradeoff. How much gold is the player willing to spend for a particular item? How much mana does that spell cost? How much real-world currency must the player spend to rush the completion of a particular unit in a free-to-play game? How much time per day must a player invest to become truly competitive at a professional level?

For instance, consider a simple combat: a player's character vs. a monster. When the player attacks, they do 50 damage. To determine if this is balanced, there are many factors to consider:

- How does this amount of damage fit in with its place in the game according to the game's economic macros?
- How much damage does a monster take before it is defeated?
- What's the weapon's range of power?
- What armor or other protections does the monster have?
- What is the location of the monster in comparison with the player (a thrown projectile that just barely hits a creature before it falls to the ground won't do much damage).
- How long does the designer want the encounter to last (how many hits)?

The amount of damage the player does is only meaningful in relation to these other numbers.

Let's take another example: you want to buy a *Sword of Ultimate Awesomeness*, and it costs 250 gold. Is that a lot or a little? It depends: how often does the player find gold, how much of it is found at a time, and how difficult is it to earn? Now, let's say in this game you double the cost of the sword to 500 gold, but you also double all gold awards in the game; the sword appears more expensive, but in reality, it takes exactly the same amount of time and effort as it did before.

Progression Relationships

From beginning to end, games are about progression—progression from point A to point B, through a series of quests, from noob to legendary, and from level 1 to level 100. Players upgrade their swords and skills and improve upon their stats, too. They advance the plot, clear the stage of all enemies, or make moves that bring the game toward its conclusion. In essence, progression is a tradeoff between two resources where the player gives up something (such as their time) in exchange for progress in the game. As designers, we generally class progression in one of four ways:

- **Character progression**: the character in the game grows in some way through player action.
- **Player's skill progression**: the player's skills in the game grow through repeated practice.

- **Narrative progression**: the in-game story progresses through character action or time.
- **Mechanical progression**: the more the player plays, the more mechanics get added, making the game deeper, more complex, and more challenging.

A single game may have one or more of these (or none, depending on the game).

These relationships between two things (character/time, player/time, narrative/time, mechanics/time), while not always obvious to the player, nonetheless create a recognizable pattern whose timing players can feel ("it's been forever since I leveled!"), and furthermore, these expectations become deeply embedded affordances that dominate genres.

In the mind of the player, progression is often cause for celebration. For us designers, however, it's a design decision. How fast do players progress? When do they cap? The answer to each of these questions is actually a curve. Experience point (XP) curves, cost curves, and difficulty curves are common examples that you may have heard of. XP curves in RPGs, for instance, often start with exponential progressions which cap or level out over time. We'll cover common types of curves next.

Types of Game Curves

In game design, the term **curve** is used in the mathematical, not aesthetic, sense: a curve tracks what happens to one game resource when another increases. For example, an XP curve (sometimes called a level curve) shows how many experience points are needed to gain a level, based on a character's current level. Game designers sometimes use the term **ramp** as well.

Despite its name, a "curve" might simply be a straight line, or gently sloping curve, or a series of jagged or smooth hills and valleys. A curve is just a graph of numbers representing a relationship between two resources in a game.

Experienced game designers recognize the shapes of curves and often design to a particular shape on purpose, either because it has worked in the past or because it does the job they need it to do. In free-to-play games, for instance, it is common to "ramp the player out": increasing the difficulty of the game rapidly at a specific point so that only the monetizing (paying) players stick around, choosing to pay money to keep pace with the game's scaled progression. This very quickly lets the product managers focus on the core, monetizing group.

There are a few types of curves used commonly in games that we discuss here: identity, linear, exponential, logarithmic, triangular, and designer-created curves.

Identity Curve

An **identity curve** represents the simplest relationship between two numbers: they are equal. If one number increases by +5, the other number also increases by +5. The curve between two resources in an identity relationship looks like the graph $y = x$:

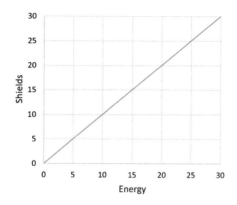

This curve, taken from certain versions of the classic game *Spacewar!*, represents a tradeoff between energy units and shield units. Each player starts with full energy (which decreases when they fire their weapons at the other ship) and full shields (which decrease when their ship is hit by enemy fire). A player wins by doing damage to the opponent's ship when they have no shields remaining. Either player can transfer any amount of energy for an equal amount of shields or vice versa, at any time. Part of the tactical nature of the game is in managing when to put more power to shields to protect against incoming hits, and when to transfer into energy to blast the opponent out of the sky.

Let's consider another example from a different genre: an RPG where party members must consume food on a regular basis to avoid starvation, and 1 unit of food costs 1 gold in town. Players can buy any quantity: 10 food for 10 gold, 100 food for 100 gold, and so on. As long as the party is standing right outside of the food store, food and gold are more or less equivalent with a 1-to-1 relationship—an identity.

You might wonder: if the two resources are completely equivalent, why bother having two resources at all? Why not just have a single resource?

In many cases, an identity relationship does suggest that you may as well just use a single resource type. In this case, there are a number of reasons why it might make sense to keep food and gold separate:

- If players can only buy food in towns and not while exploring in dungeons, food becomes a limited resource while adventuring, and only gains this identity relationship in specific situations. In a dungeon, a player might pay an NPC 30 gold for a single unit of food. If the resources could be converted easier—such as a magic spell that could freely convert food to gold and vice versa—then it might make more sense to just do away with one of them, use the other, and explain that the party is using food as currency because "alchemy."
- Thematically, it makes no sense to have your adventurers eating gold or using food as currency, unless the game world is strange.
- If you can only buy food but not sell it, gold is more versatile since you can use it to buy other things as well, and the player must then be careful to buy enough food to survive but not so much food that they have a gold shortage. Meanwhile, food is consumed on a regular basis, while gold is not. The two resources thus behave very differently and feel distinct, and each has their own separate reasons for inclusion in the game.
- In games with multiple uses for a single resource, that resource may have different curves for each resource. So while the food/gold has an identity curve, swords/gold may have something else entirely.

Linear Curve

A linear curve occurs when one number increases (or decreases) as an exact multiple of the other number. In RPGs, for instance, the relationship between hit points/health (HP) and magic points/mana (MP) is often linear. Suppose a healing spell costs 5 MP and heals 25 HP; this is a 1-to-5 linear relationship between MP and HP. In a simple game where this is the only healing spell and that is the only use of MP, you could simply add five times your MP to your current HP and know about how many effective HP you have, total, before you have to find other non-spell-based methods of healing or find a way to restore your MP.

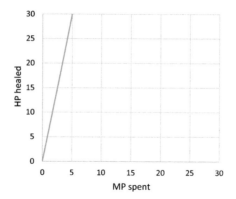

Another common example of a linear relationship in games is between damage and cost of an item. The more damage an object does the more it costs. For every 1 point of damage it does, you may have to pay 100 gold for its purchase price, for instance. Designers commonly assign values to item properties like "cost per point of damage," each of which has a linear relationship to its cost. Something that does double damage against giants might add 1000 to the cost of the item, for instance.

As a note, an identity relationship (a 1-to-1) is a linear relationship where the multiple is exactly 1. Linear relationships satisfy the equation $y = mx$, where m is a fixed number (the multiplier), y is a resource, and x is the other resource. So, HP = 10MP (10 magic points get you 1 hit point).

Exponential Curves

An exponential progression or tradeoff is used when designers want to get somewhere big quickly, and to get even *bigger* even *faster* as the player progresses. They do that by multiplying a **base** number, say 5, a certain number of times. That number of times is the **exponent**. Let's take 5 as the base and 10 as the exponent.

    5 = 5
    5 * 5 = 25
    5 * 5 * 5 = 125
    5 * 5 * 5 * 5 = 625
    5 * 5 * 5 * 5 * 5 = 3,125
    5 * 5 * 5 * 5 * 5 * 5 = 15,625
    5 * 5 * 5 * 5 * 5 * 5 * 5 = 78,125
    5 * 5 * 5 * 5 * 5 * 5 * 5 * 5 = 390,625
    5 * 5 * 5 * 5 * 55 * 5 * 5 * 5 = 1,953,125
    5 * 5 * 5 * 5 * 5 * 5 * 5 * 5 * 5 * 5 = 9,765,625

When writing exponents, we generally use what's known as exponential notation: the base is written first, then followed by the exponent as a superscript (a small number written above and to the right of the base). So, this progression would actually be written as $5^2 = 25$, $5^3 = 125$, $5^4 = 625$, and so on up to $5^{10} = 9,765,625$.

Exponential curves are often multiplied by a single constant; for example, an XP curve might have double the XP requirement at every level, but it would start with 100 XP to gain the first level, then doubling to 200, then 400, and so on (rather than starting at 1 and doubling to 2, then 4). Mathematically, this might be written as $100 * 2^{Level}$, where Level is the current player level.

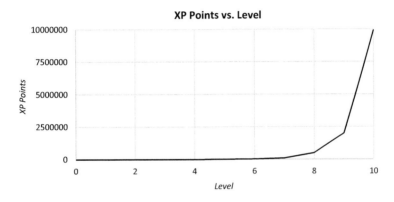

Exponential progression is most often used in early character leveling where the experience points required for a level double each time (a base 2 progression). Due to the nature of exponential progression, however, at some point, players give up progressing further due to the time it takes to get to that next level. In the example above, if these were game levels, you would need nearly 8 million XP to go from level 9 to level 10! Before this point, most games institute a level cap.

Exponents are also used to produce dynamic, incredible outcomes. Take the game *Hearthstone* for instance. Some creatures/cards double their damage whenever they are hit or targeted. At first, this may seem limited, particularly if the base damage is just 2. However, every time this creature is targeted or hit, the current value doubles. It becomes ridiculously powerful in a short amount of time, and often factors into the strategy of the player who may repeatedly target the card themselves to produce this effect.

Because exponential curves tend to start slow and then ramp to extreme levels over time, in many systems, an exponential effect can be highly unbalancing or, in the case of a level curve, cause the game to drag on, an imbalance of its own kind. In most strategy games and trading card games (TCGs), for example, an effect that doubles the strength of a card or unit is relatively rare, especially if that effect gets stronger over time or can stack with other multipliers. Those effects that do have exponential effects are often sharply limited in some way, such as having a short duration, having a negative effect to counterbalance the positive, or being expensive to bring into play. For example, in the very first edition of *Magic: the Gathering*, one card in the entire set had the word "double" on it (Berserk, which doubled a creature's attack power for the turn), and it was restricted in tournament play for a long time. In *Hearthstone*, there are quite a few cards that double some number or other on a card in play, and the only reason these do not unbalance the game is that cards in play are inherently fragile: most are vulnerable to many types of removal, and even a powerful card usually doesn't survive for more than a handful of turns which tends to limit just how big things can get even with multiple doublings.

If you look at games which have multipliers that grow or stack over time, there is typically a clear design intent behind it; for example, in *Civilization: Revolution*, various player abilities, city upgrades, and researched technologies can create incredible multipliers in the end game leading to what appears to be an unbalanced state. This was done intentionally to both speed the end game (where a winner has usually already emerged and players are just going through the motions anyway), and give the players a sense of epic victory when they win. Had the game been designed with these multipliers coming into play earlier on, it would have caused games to end prematurely and clear, early-game dominant strategies to emerge that would have unbalanced things. As it is, these only happen toward the end where they only serve to bring the game to a satisfying conclusion.

BOX 4.1

Rule of 2: Designers often use the **Rule of 2** (credited to game designer Sid Meier): if you need to change a number and don't know how much to change it by, double it or cut it in half. By doing this, you get a good sense of that value's effect on the game. It proves much more effective than cutting by 10% and then 10% again (and again). This may seem counterintuitive, since doubling or halving is drastic, and you won't think that your numbers are off by all that much. Give it a try, though. You may be surprised at how well it works.

Logarithmic Curves

A **logarithmic** relationship curve is the reverse of an exponential curve: a harsh law of *decreasing* returns. In games, we often see a logarithmic progression in character levels. For instance, to get from level 1 to level 2, you need 20 XP. To get from level 2 to level 3, you need 40 XP. This means that for every level you gain, you need *double* the experience points to get there.

Recalling the XP curve we discussed earlier, XP represents an exponential curve whereas levels are generally logarithmic. XP has a many to one relationship with levels whereas levels have a one to many relationship with XP.

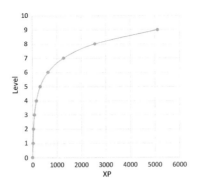

The equation is $y = \log_b x$ (or, $x = b^y$), where b is a fixed number. So, New Level = Current XP * 2. This is really the same as an exponential, just looked at with the resources reversed.

Triangular Curves

Triangular numbers are a series of numbers that are commonly used in game design, particularly in resource progression in board games. The series is called "triangular" because the sequence follows the pattern of a triangle shape made of dots, where you keep adding a row.

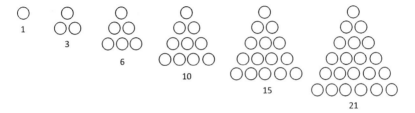

These numbers appear in many board games including *Hare and Tortoise*, *Ticket to Ride*, and many more and are probably the most commonly used increasing-returns formula in game design because they increase but not as fast as an exponential, and the sequence of costs is familiar. The cost pattern is also simple for players to understand. In *Baldur's Gate: Dark Alliance*, the XP curve was purely triangular. If you start looking for triangular progressions, you'll be surprised at how often you find them.

If you need a curve that is increasing at a rate somewhere between linear and exponential, try a triangular curve to start and then modify from there. Mathematically, triangular numbers can be expressed by the function $y = (x^2 - x)/2$.

Custom-Crafted Curves, Formulas, and Outcomes

Sometimes, the standard curves just don't cut it for designers, and they prefer a specific progression or tradeoff relationship that's not necessarily exponential or logarithmic but hand-crafted. It might be a unique formula for a spell (the first three levels cost 150 mana, but the fourth level costs 300), or it might be a set of numbers chosen by the hand of the designer that don't fit any discernible mathematical pattern at all (incredible damage on a weapon whose effective drop rate is never +0.01).

Sometimes, curves start logarithmic or exponential, but change to a custom-crafted curve over time. This is often the case with the amount of XP needed to reach the next level. It may start exponentially for the first few levels or so, but is custom-crafted after that to reduce the extreme level-to-level increases. As mentioned before, XP commonly follows an exponential curve, but the numbers are rounded down to end in zeros to make them easier for players to remember.

Take a look at the following chart, and notice the difference beginning at level 13. On the left, we have a pure, base 2 exponential progression. On the right, it changes to a base 1.5 progression at level 13. If you think from a player's perspective, you can imagine the time difference required to gain levels.

Total XP Required	XP Level		Total XP Required	XP Level
100	2		100	2
200	3		200	3
400	4		400	4
800	5		800	5
1,600	6		1,600	6

Total XP Required	XP Level		Total XP Required	XP Level
3,200	7		3,200	7
6,400	8		6,400	8
12,800	9		12,800	9
25,600	10		25,600	10
51,200	11		51,200	11
102,400	12		102,400	12
204,800	13		153,600	13
409,600	14		230,400	14
819,200	15		345,600	15
1,638,400	16		518,400	16
3,276,800	17		777,600	17
6,553,600	18		1,166,400	18
13,107,200	19		1,749,600	19
26,214,400	20		2,624,400	20

Example: Weapon Cost and Damage   As another example of custom curves, let's examine the following situation involving weapon cost and damage. Suppose you have a game where most enemies have 4 hit points. An attack doing 1 damage needs to hit four times in order to defeat one enemy. An attack doing 2 damage only needs to hit twice, making it twice as powerful as only 1 damage. But an attack doing 3 damage *still* needs to hit twice; it is no better than doing 2 damage! It may be slightly better, in that if you can do 3 damage, getting hit with a −1 damage penalty won't hurt you, and a +1 damage bonus helps a great deal, but it is certainly not *three* times as powerful as 1 damage. Meanwhile, 4 damage means you can defeat one enemy per attack, so by default, 4 damage is twice as powerful as 3 damage. Beyond that, 5 or more damage is not much better than 4 damage. We might therefore create the following relationship between damage and how powerful that damage actually is (or how much it should cost):

Damage	Cost
1	1
2	2
3	2.5
4	4
5	4.5
$5 + n$ (for every n additional after 5)	$4.5 + (n/2)$

In this case, the relationship is mostly linear, except with a sudden drop between 2 and 3, a sharp increase from 3 to 4, and a very slow increase thereafter.

Example: Roll through the Ages   One final example is found in the dice game *Roll Through the Ages*, players roll several dice. One of the possible results is a skull icon on each die. If your entire roll contains no skulls or only one skull, it doesn't affect you at all. With two skulls, the player loses 2 points, an unfortunate result. With three skulls, the player's *opponents* all lose 3 points, a very good result. With four skulls, the player loses 4 points, a very bad result. And with five or more skulls, the player loses some of their other resources, effectively loses their turn, may lose additional points and experiences one of the worst results possible. The relationship between skulls and points looks something like this:

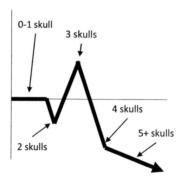

While this function isn't strictly increasing or decreasing and fits no obvious pattern, it works well within the context of the game. Since players can reroll their non-skull dice up to twice per turn, this can create dramatic tension during a turn. At just about any point, either players are hoping to not get any more skulls (if they already have one, three, or four) or they *are* hoping to get one more (at two skulls). This can lead to multiple reversals of fortune within a single turn, causing much anticipation and excitement, brought about through a custom function that was carefully hand-crafted and tuned by the designer.

Cost Obfuscation Curves

In free-to-play (F2P) games, it is common for companies to obfuscate the value of the in-game currency in relation to the real-world currency it takes to get it. So, the numerical relationship might start like this: $2 = 15 units of in-game currency. It scales from there, often in even more confusing ways. For starters, few players are going to remember or to calculate that 1 unit of in-game currency equals 13.3 cents. Even fewer are going to do the math to calculate how much 9 units equals and even fewer are going to examine the effect of bulk purchases or special, in-game savings events. Games could make this math easier (each unit of in-game currency is worth 10 cents, for instance), but keeping the math more complicated means fewer players question the actual cost of their purchases and may spend more money as a result.

In some games, bulk purchases actually cost *more* per unit than smaller purchases as you can see in the chart below (note the *per unit* price of 3500 units is more than the *per unit* price of 500 units). Such questionable methods take advantage of player's good faith, believing that if they buy more, they save more.

Units	Per Unit	Cost
15	0.133	2
30	0.133	4
50	0.133	7
100	0.12	12
250	0.12	30
500	0.12	60
1000	0.14	140
3500	0.16	560

This obfuscation between real-world currency and in-game currency sometimes goes a step further. Some mobile games use dual *grind* currencies, coins, and gold, for instance, to cloud the actual costs still further. Dual currencies are nothing new to games, of course; typically, the currencies are delineated by those you get in the grind (during gameplay) and a premium currency you generally purchase for cash. These F2P games treat dual currencies as both grind and premium currencies. So, you can purchase both and get both in the grind, though one is significantly more rare than the other. While on the surface it seems beneficial to reward the player with something he or she perceives as a premium currency, the average player is challenged when the cost of an item asks for both currencies as payment, simultaneously. If something costs 500 coins and 3 gold, what am I really spending? If I can both buy and earn coins and gold, how much have I earned compared to what I need to purchase to have enough in-game currency? Do I feel I have earned enough to justify the "top up" purchase? In this case, both currencies are available for cash and through the grind, so it makes the job of determining actual cost or worth more difficult. If players have the cash and want the item, they may be more likely to get it than to spend time figuring out the value (in either cash or time) that they are spending.

Curve Summary

While there is no hard and fast rule, in general, these are the curves that different economies tend to use:

- **Experience Points**: Exponential
- **Experience Levels**: Logarithmic
- **Item Values**: Linear in relation to damage caused or protected with custom-crafted values that take into account rarity and amount of utility to the player
- **Skill Trees and Stat Increases**: Identity (one bonus point is spent to gain one skill point)
- **HP Increases**: Linear with a randomized value within a certain range. Level 5 might mean +25 HP, give or take 10%.
- **Monster Strength**: Linear
- **Loot Drops**: Linear, tied to create strength, with a randomized value within a certain range.

In the case of monsters and items, smooth curves are the rare exception. It is common for designers to hand-edit spreadsheets to include peaks and valleys and adjust the rarity, if need be. Some of the best moments in games are when we get an amazing sword or meet an enemy that poses an unbelievable challenge.

Everything in Moderation

Taken to an extreme, every curve and every formula presents a problem for designers and players. For instance, as noted, exponential and logarithmic curves are often capped or forced into a designer-created curve instead. This illustrates a common issue with games balanced to a math formula: even if the math is good and generally balanced, it often breaks at the extremes. If your math works in most cases but not at these edge conditions, you might not need to fix the general formula. There are two common options:

- Create special-case math to handle the extremes
- Place hard caps to prevent a player from reaching the extremes.

Discussion Questions

1. Discuss what is meant by progression in a game. Select a game and note the types of progression present.
2. What is an identity relationship?
3. Why might a resource's identity relationship change to a linear relationship?
4. What is an exponential curve?
5. Why are exponential curves potentially problematic for game designers?
6. What are triangular numbers?
7. Give an example of two systems in the same game and identify shared resources between the two.
8. Give an example of a custom-crafted curve and why a designer might chose to use one.
9. Select a mobile game and analyze its monetization structure.
10. In creating curves, designers often create spikes (a super powerful weapon compared to where the player is at in the game) and valleys (a weak monster). Why do you think designers do this?

Sidequests

In this chapter, we learned how various numbers relate to each other.

Sidequest 4.1: Level Curve

Choose any computer game that has a mechanic where you gain experience points (XP) and, at certain thresholds, you gain a Level. Through a strategy guide, online FAQ, or walkthrough, find a chart that lists how many XP you need to achieve each Level. If you cannot find one, pick a different game.

If you graph Level on the *x*-axis and XP on the *y*-axis, what kind of shape is the curve? Is it an identity, linear, exponential, logarithmic, polynomial, or something else? Does it behave one way in the early game and then shift to something else later on? Try to describe the XP-Level relationship using the vocabulary we have developed in this chapter.

Sidequest 4.2: Level Curve Fitting

As with Sidequest 4.1, choose any computer game where you gain XP and ultimately Levels, and find a chart that lists how many XP you need to achieve each Level. In a spreadsheet program, put the Levels in one column and required XP in another, and graph it as a scatter plot. Then, use a trend-line to connect the points, and have it display the R-squared value. Try various types of trendlines: linear, polynomial ($n = 2$ and $n = 3$), and exponential, at least. Which one gives the best R-squared fit? If the curve looks like it has several segments that behave differently, try breaking up the plot into those sections and do a trendline for each.

Sidequest 4.3: Machinations

One of the useful game design tools that has come out of the academic world is *Machinations*, originally a Ph.D. project by Joris Dormans (currently found at http://machinations.io). *Machinations* is a visual diagramming language that can be used to model the flow of resources in a game. The tool supports saving and loading functionality so you can share your diagrams with others, and runs in a browser. It also has several functions for setting the diagram in motion, so that you can see what happens in real time.

Go to the Machinations website, sign up for free, and read through the documentation, tutorials, and examples to familiarize yourself with the language. Then, choose a game that is not mentioned in any of the examples and diagram the resource flow.

Note that Machinations can work at any level of abstraction. For example, the board game *Catan* could be modeled with each of the five individual resources, the Progress cards, and so on, down to the micro level of trading; you could theoretically make a fully working version of the game, although it would be a very large and complicated diagram. Alternately, you could simply model "resources" (a single resource that represents all five resource cards) and "resource generators" (settlements and cities) and some general concept that you spend resources to build resource generators. Choose whatever level of abstraction is most appropriate.

Also, you may find it helpful to add labels to your diagram. Make it clear what each item represents.

Sidequest 4.4: Optimizing Idle Game Play

Idle games, popularized by *Cookie Clicker*, are games where players gain both active income (typically from clicking on things) and passive income (from waiting). Players then spend their income to improve their rate of income. While there is typically no way to lose progress, there is still a good deal of strategy in terms of choosing which things to upgrade in what order. Do you take the cheapest upgrade that improves your income? Or do you hold off for a higher-cost upgrade that has a better cost-to-benefit ratio, but in the meantime, you're earning a lower level of income for longer?

Here is a very simple design for an idle game:

- At the start of the game, the player gains 1 gold per second.
- The player may purchase the following items to improve their income:
  - **Small Gold Mines**: increase income by 1 gold/s each. Base cost: 15 gold.
  - **Medium Gold Mines**: increase income by 5 gold/s each. Base cost: 100 gold.
  - **Large Gold Mines**: increase income by 20 gold/s each. Base cost: 300 gold.
  - **Huge Gold Mines**: increase income by 100 gold/s each. Base cost: 2000 gold.
  - **Massive Gold Mines**: increase income by 700 gold/s each. Base cost: 15,000 gold.
  - **Alchemical Gold Mines**: increase income by 10,000 gold/s each. Base cost: 250,000 gold.
- The cost of each mine is equal to the base cost multiplied by 1.1^N, where N is the number of that mine already owned (rounded up to the next highest integer). For example, the first Small Gold Mine costs 15 gold, the next one costs 15 * 1.1 = 16.5 rounded up to 17, the next costs 15 * 1.1^2 = 18.15 rounded up to 19, and so on.

In a spreadsheet, create a simulation of this game:

- In Column A, show the time elapsed in seconds. Start at zero in the first row and then add one for each row down.
- In Column B, show the player's current gold. For the first row, this starts at zero; each additional row is the previous row's gold, plus that row's income (one gold as the base plus income from all mines), minus the cost of any mine purchases.
- In Columns C through H, list the player's current number of mines of each of the six types. These all start at zero. In subsequent rows, these are equal to the number of that mine type in the previous row, plus any that were purchased in the previous row.
- In Column I, give the player's income at this point in time: one gold, plus income from the mines in Columns C through H (multiply the number of each mine type by that mine type's income).

- In Columns J through O, list the cost of purchasing one additional mine of each of the six types, calculated using the formula given above based on the number of each mine type owned in the current row (from Columns C through H).
- Columns P through U represent the number of mines of each type that are being purchased during this second. These are numbers that the user of this spreadsheet should enter manually in order to "play" the game. For our purposes, assume the player can purchase any number of mines of each type, all at the current listed price in Columns J through O.

After creating the first and second rows (plus a header row, if desired), take Row 2 and Fill Down to Row 900 (this represents the first 15 minutes of gameplay, if each row is one second). Enter in some sample values in Columns P through U in several rows to confirm the effect on gold and income.

Ultimate challenge: Instead of leaving Columns P through U blank or with test data, try to fill in the columns in such a way as to maximize income by the end of Row 900. You can try to do this either manually by hand or through a series of formulas (in these columns, and possibly additional columns off to the right that you create on your own). Although it may not look like it, this is actually an implementation of an AI for this game, using no code and only spreadsheet values and formulas!

If going through this book with several other people (as in a classroom setting), have an Idle Game Tournament: have each player turn in their own AI, and compare the incomes of each at the end of 15 simulated minutes. Compare algorithms and discuss the strengths and weaknesses of each.

Alternate challenge: do the same for an existing idle game. You want to find a game that has all of its cost and benefit formulas published somewhere. Also, as most idle games include some kind of active component (such as gaining income for every mouse-click), you may want to either ignore that entirely or make a simplifying assumption like five mouse-clicks per second. Keep in mind that even relatively simple idle games are significantly more complicated than the example in this Sidequest. The benefit, however, is that a "tournament" could involve playing the game for a certain amount of time and seeing who has progressed the farthest, without having to compare spreadsheets.

Sidequest 4.5: Detangling the Obfuscation of an F2P Game

In the mobile/tablet game *Gordon Ramsay Dash*, the player can purchase gold (the game's premium currency) at the following rates:

Amount of Gold	Cost (in US Dollars)
10	$0.99
35	$2.99
125 ("Most Popular!")	$9.99
300	$19.99
1000	$49.99
2500	$99.99

Among other things, you can then use gold to purchase supplies at the following rates:

Amount of Supplies	Cost (in Gold)
50	10 G
115	20 G
250	40 G

Suppose a player wanted to buy a total of 500 supplies—no more, no less, with no intention of buying anything else in the game in the future. They would first do this by using real-world cash to buy gold, then purchasing supplies with that gold. What is the cheapest that this player could pay for their 500 supplies?

Greater challenge: suppose that the developers have a special event, Supply Saturday Sale, where all supplies are 20% off *and* you get a bonus 20% of supplies for each purchase (e.g., you can get 60 supplies for only eight gold at the lowest purchase tier). *Now* what is the cheapest way to purchase exactly 500 supplies?

Ultimate challenge: Some F2P games obfuscate costs. If someone were to redesign the pricing tiers above to obfuscate the costs, how might they do so? Increase the cost of purchasing exactly 500 supplies (without a "sale"), without making this evident or obvious at a casual glance. Explain why you made the choices you did, and why you think they would work.

Rogue's Main Quest, Part 3: Identifying Key Resources

Continuing from Part 2 in: Chapter 2

In the game you chose, list all of the resources in the game state that you can think of. In a card game, this might involve the resources used to put cards into play (mana, gold, etc.), cards in hand (or in a draw deck or in a discard pile), life points or victory points. In a turn-based or real-time strategy game, this might include resource units (gold, oil, or whatever is used to bring more units into play), military or other units in play, structures and upgrades, advancement along a tech tree, and so on. For a tabletop miniatures game, these are usually not resource-heavy (you start with an army in play and simply manage those units throughout play), so in this case, you'd be thinking of your units, individual units' health, and combat stats (defense to improve survivability, attack to remove opponents' units from play). In a tabletop RPG, you might consider currency, experience points/levels, player stats, and health/hit points.

Also identify the relationships between resources. Can some resources be converted to others, either by the core mechanics of the game or by the special rules of a specific game object?

Express the resource flow of the game through a diagram. You might use a diagramming language like *Machinations* (see Sidequest 4.3) or just a manual diagram of boxes and arrows drawn by hand or in a computer program.

Part 4 continued in: Chapter 8

5

Finding an Anchor

In This Chapter

- Establishing an Anchor
- Finding an Anchor
- Scaling an Anchor with Curves
- Finding an Anchor in Skill-Based Games
- Finding a Comparative Anchor
- Interactions between Systems
- Granularity
- Completing a First Pass

Establishing an Anchor

> When I'm ready to begin balancing a game, I need to find an anchor - it's basically the alpha number of the game and all other numbers need to fall in line. It's often hit points or the game currency. And even in saying that, you can usually buy hit points with currency via a healing spell or health pack, so they are sometimes one and the same. Once I decide that number, though, I can determine everything else.
>
> *A lead designer with thirty years' experience*

Having explored economies in Chapter 3 and the relationship between individual game objects that leads to progression in Chapter 4, here in Chapter 5 we show how designers connect these things together to build the actual mathematical structure of a game. Of particular importance here is the scaffolding presented in Chapter 3 under "Length of game (game macros)." In effect, those macros are the outlines we fill here, and the progression relationships discussed in Chapter 4 are the means by which these macros grow. If you skipped over Chapter 3 for whatever reason, please do go back and have a read of that section.

Finding an Anchor

All of the relationships we've seen so far in Chapter 4 relate two resources to one another, such as experience points to experience levels. What about relationships between three or more resources? For example, let's consider any RPG with four stats: hit points (HP), magic points (MP), attack damage, and defense. Clearly, all of these relate to each other in some way. For instance, you can use MP to deliver damage, up your defense, and increase your HP, and that's just one of many possible ways to look at these four stats. In order to balance them, however, you need to figure out a means of understanding their relationship to one another. To do that, you find what game designers refer to as an **anchor**.

An anchor is a resource that can be related directly to every other resource. If you find an anchor, then you use that number as the number to "rule them all." Most games have an anchor, and it's usually the very stat that is the win or loss condition. HP is a common anchor in RPGs, for example, while victory points are a common anchor in board games. Once the anchor is found, designers set the value of the anchor manually and craft all other numbers in relation to that number, typically with a mix of procedural and custom-crafted numbers.

To find an anchor, let's explore the relationship between the various stats in this example.

- *Is there a relationship between Defense and HP?* Yes: Defense reduces the damage taken, which means the player's character can survive more hits. Raising Defense is analogous to raising HP. In both cases, the character is able to last longer in combat.
- *Is there a relationship between Attack and HP?* It turns out that raising Attack is *also* similar to raising HP: characters with higher Attack can defeat enemies faster, which means the enemies get fewer chances to attack, and they are therefore taking less damage from each enemy.

This lets them survive a greater number of combats, just as if they had the same Attack but higher HP. While HP, Attack, and Defense are not wholly equivalent, it is apparent that increasing any of them does the same thing: they all let a character survive a greater number of enemy encounters.

- *Is there a relationship between MP and HP?* In this game, we'll assume a small set of standard spells. The player can heal (converting MP to HP) or cast attack spells that cause damage (defeating enemies faster, which prevents further loss of HP from their attacks, so this is *also* a form of converting MP to extra HP). In addition, there are spells that temporarily improve the character's stats ("buffs") or decrease an enemy's stats ("debuffs"), both of which would also let the character survive a combat in better shape and essentially be converting MP to HP.

As you can see here, not only is HP the loss condition (if you run out of that resource, you die), but it is also related to everything else. So during balance, the worth of an item or action comes down to its net effect on HP. HP is clearly the anchor for this game. For example, to balance a healing spell against an attack spell, figure out how much extra damage the player takes if they don't use the attack spell in a typical situation where they'd need it, vs. how many HP they'd restore with the healing spell. Or, if you're trying to balance the gold cost of an item that increases Attack vs. one that increases Defense, figure out how many HP the extra Attack saves in typical combat by reducing the number of attacks the enemy gets in, vs. the HP that the extra Defense saves by reducing the damage taken from every hit.

It's worth noting here that anchors are not just a construct of games. They are a critical part of our day-to-day lives. When you go to a store, everything there has an anchor—the financial value of that item. This is why most real-world economies are based on a unit of currency rather than a barter system where one might trade milk for a loaf of bread. There are millions of consumer products that could be traded, which means trillions of potential exchange rates between every combination of two goods. Using an anchor—currency—each good or service can be assigned a single price, and then anything that could be bought or sold can be related through this one number—much simpler! Sometimes, that anchor is supplanted with another as in the oft heard phrase, "Time is money." At some point in life, provided basic needs are met, time becomes more important than money. You can make money, but you can't make time.

Scaling an Anchor with Curves

To illustrate how anchors work within a game, we provide three examples below which illustrate how game designers set item prices, ramp item prices, round item prices, and provide peaks within a range of items.

To begin, we set the value of our anchor. In this case, HP is our anchor, and we decide to give it a value of 10 gold per point of HP. Since we're dealing with weapons in this case, it's per point of HP *damage*. Furthermore, we establish an improvement rate of 25% which means that each item does 25% more damage than the item before it. We show this as 125% to allow for ease of multiplication in our generated tables. Our rate of improvement is purely a designer choice.

The following table illustrates the damage range as it grows over time. All gray-colored fields are *manually* entered numbers which we use to *generate* numbers in a spreadsheet. In addition to "Value per HP" and the "Improvement Rate," the designer also sets the starting values for item damage. Delineating manually entered fields by color allows the designer to quickly rebalance the game with a few minor changes. For instance, if players find that weapon growth is too slow, you can raise the improvement rate, the maximum damage, or both. Generating numbers also means fewer errors as a result of inputting bad data. As a note, you do not expressly *need* to set these numbers manually. You could generate everything off a single, starting number which was set randomly, but in our experience, that's often more fun for a designer that loves spreadsheets than the player.

Each item is 25% more powerful than the item before it. Costs are based on the maximum damage range, but could also be based off the average damage or lowest damage.

Value per HP	10		
Improvement Rate	125%		
Weapon	Damage Range		Cost
Sword	5	10	100
Sword +1	6	13	125
Sword +2	8	16	156
Sword +3	10	20	195
Sword +4	12	24	244
Sword +5	15	31	305
Sword +6	19	38	381
Sword +7	24	48	477
Sword +8	30	60	596

Games often round the cost of items to the nearest 5 to make the math easier for players to work out as shown here:

Value per HP	10		
Improvement rate	125%		
Weapon	Damage Range		Cost
Sword	5	10	100
Sword +1	6	13	125
Sword +2	8	16	160
Sword +3	10	20	195
Sword +4	12	24	245
Sword +5	15	31	305
Sword +6	19	38	385
Sword +7	24	48	480
Sword +8	30	60	600

Designers also *manually* add "peaks" which fall outside of the normal procedural bounds. The "Special Sword" below is one such item. While it fits in terms of cost per HP, its damage range falls outside of the established growth range of 25%. An item like this might be in the store, or it might be a rare loot drop available to players well before the Sword +8. Having a high cost would also improve its sell-back value, provided the game allowed that (sell value is typically half of its purchase value). Peaks surprise the player and provide for excitement and moments of power in gameplay.

Value per HP	10		
Improvement rate	125%		
Weapon	Damage Range		Cost
Sword	5	10	100
Sword +1	6	13	125
Sword +2	8	16	160
Sword +3	10	20	195
Special Sword	10	50	500
Sword +4	12	24	245
Sword +5	15	31	305
Sword +6	19	38	385
Sword +7	24	48	480
Sword +8	30	60	600

If we graph the curve, we see both its standard trajectory and its peak. Peaks are particularly important for the variety they provide. If weapons, characters, and enemies go up at the same trajectory, the challenge remains constant and that makes for a boring game. Having peaks in creatures and items is critical to prevent boredom.

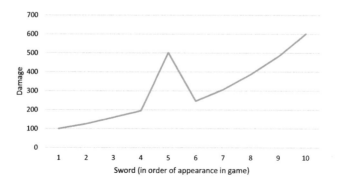

Finding an Anchor in Skill-Based Games

In games where the progression is based on the player's skill, anchors are still necessary, even if the items have no particular financial value in the game. Consider the classic 1993 first-person shooter *DOOM*. In that game, players have their choice of eight weapons, each of which allows for a different style of play: a fist, chainsaw, pistol, shotgun, chaingun, rocket launcher, plasma gun, and the BFG. The anchor of *DOOM* is clearly HP. The monster HP is set by the HP damage the weapons do. If the player runs out of HP, they die. In deathmatch, if a player runs out of HP, their opponent gets a frag. Weapons, of course, remove HP from monsters and opponents, fragging them before they can take damage from the player.

Looking at our previous examples in this chapter, the more damage a weapon did, the more it cost. In *DOOM*, however, there is no cost to weapons. So, since some weapons do more damage than others, how could something like this be balanced? The weapons' designer, John Romero, differentiates the weapons in a variety of ways. The double-barrel shotgun, for instance, does more damage than the pistol, but takes longer to reload and does its best damage in close range. The rocket launcher does amazing damage at a distance, but causes blast damage within a radius as it detonates. If the player fires it at close range, they might frag themselves as well. Ammo, proximity to player, time to reload, time to fire, placement within the level (will the player go for this weapon or the armor on the other side of the level?), and other factors allowed Romero to balance the properties of the weapons off each other so that no one weapon became obsolete once the player got another weapon, something that happens by design in virtually all games that are based on character progression.

Finding a Comparative Anchor

Depending on what part of a game we're designing at any one time, sometimes a **comparative anchor** is necessary. A comparative anchor is a number or collection of features which allows us to make one choice more or less equivalent to the other, all things considered. Such is often the case when creating different starting characters that players can choose from. Similarly, if players can select from a choice of starting races and professions as is the case in most fantasy RPGs, as designers, we need a means to differentiate between those different starting states so that no one character is overpowered vs. another. If you've played online games with these attributes, you know that this is often a challenging thing to get just right as developers regularly iterate upon stats even after a game is released.

To find a comparative anchor in these situations, we use a combination of methods presented in Chapter 3 and this chapter: establish a starting set of numbers based on player expectation, sum those numbers, and, using that sum as an anchor, design the other classes from there.

In the following table, we list common RPG stats for three different types of character progressions: fighter, wizard, and ninja. At the bottom of each column, there is a summary of the character stats which we would consider a comparative anchor. In this example, the Wizard and Ninja have equal stats totaling 350. The Fighter, however, is coming up low. We could address this deficiency by making the intrinsic value of one stat better than another (constitution, which is tied to the character's HP growth, is often considered better than the other stats), or we could give the fighter extra abilities or a lower XP curve to compensate. While lower XP curves were common in early RPGs, they are rarely used anymore. Easiest of all, we could adjust some of the Fighter's stats upward to make them roughly equivalent to the others.

	Fighter	*Wizard*	*Ninja*
Strength	80	40	60
Intelligence	30	80	60
Agility	50	40	80
Dexterity	60	50	70
Constitution	85	60	40
Charm	12	80	40
Stat Sums	317	350	350

Stats don't need to be perfectly equal. In fact, in the game Brenda is working on now, there are 13 different characters, and their stat sums are quite different from one another. They compensate by making up for it in other ways than their starting stats. In this, there is also a lesson. After the stat sums, that's where the comparative anchors as pure numbers end. At some point, it comes down to designer intuition about different play styles and what players might like. A great example of this is the asymmetric design of the different civilizations in *Civilization Revolution*. Each civ seems overpowered in its own way. Trying to imagine them reduced to numbers on a literal scale seems somehow impossible. This design is different than the design of the more symmetric PC-based *Civilization* games. However, it works.

Giving Value to Extras

Rarely are items a collection of plain damage stats. Rather, they are often a collection of extras such a double damage or critical hits against a certain type of enemy. Sometimes, they benefit the player by giving them protection from something like all damage or healing them slowly while an item is equipped. Each of these effects needs to be assigned a value, typically a percent increase on the original cost of the item or be offset in some other way, such as the rarity of the item, a cool-own time on its use. This is covered in detail in Chapter 23.

For instance, if the Sword of Destiny is valued at 50,000 gold, a Sword of Crit Destiny might be valued at 100,000 gold, or double its value due to its chance to crit. It is always useful to study the values of comparative games to see how designers handle the value add of extras. You may find that similar games all treat a certain type of extra the same way, in which case you know what's standard and can think about why that's such a common mathematical pattern. In other cases, every game treats it differently, and you can observe different approaches and their respective effects on the play experience.

Interactions between Systems

When designing a game, we often think of things in terms of systems. A single system comprises all gameplay elements, mechanics, and resources that work together as a cohesive and logical unit. Common systems in games include combat systems, physics systems, exploration/mapping systems, economic systems, dialogue systems, and narrative systems, though individual games may have their own unique, custom systems as well. It's understandable, then, that there is a resource exchange between systems.

For larger games, each system may be designed and balanced individually, at least early on. All seems well until the game reaches alpha, when all these systems come together, often for the first time. It's then that we clearly see the often surprising interaction between systems and how these interactions can affect game balance: a chain of resources affects another that affects yet another across multiple systems, such that linear, exponential, triangular, or other types of relationships combine to either intensify or cancel one another out. Progression can be dramatically altered, and designers must analyze the intersections to figure out precisely what is happening. Sometimes, these surprising interactions remain undiscovered until launch.

Example 1: Rocket Jumping and Bunny Hopping

Rocket jumping, now considered to be standard fare for the FPS genre, was actually the unintended result of two systems coming together. As *Quake*'s designer John Romero points out, "Rocket jumping is not something we planned. It effectively broke all the levels as they were intended to be played. Obviously, the game with or without rocket jumping worked, but the flow of levels with rocket jumping is quite different than it is without."

In *Quake*, when a rocket hits a surface, it does an area-of-effect damage roll, and physics pushes objects away from the area of impact. So, when players point the rocket at their feet, jump, and then fire the rocket below their feet, the physics pushes them farther into the jump. Players take damage from the area-of-effect of the rocket, but the benefits of rocket jumping far outweigh any damage it may do. Players rapidly traverse the level in ways it was not intended to be traversed.

Similarly, a phenomenon known as bunny hopping allows players to traverse a level at an ever-increasing speed. First, the player presses the key to move forward and then turns the mouse left and right while jumping. The angular velocity while jumping translates into faster forward movement. Timing the turning and jumping keep the velocity increasing far beyond the maximum movement speed normally attained by pressing the forward movement key alone. Normally, players traverse levels at 320 units of speed. However, by bunny hopping, players can traverse a level at three and four times that speed. Watching a competitive match between world-class players, bunny hopping and rocket jumping are regularly employed. Because both require a degree of mastery, particularly bunny hopping, a player's ability to effectively employ them adds to the competitive nature of the game. Bunny hopping is emergent behavior caused by a bug in *Quake*.

Example 2: How to Nuke Your Income

Sometimes, unintended interactions between systems can have real-world negative consequences. Prior to its 2010 release, coin drops in the web and mobile game *Ravenwood Fair* were deliberately very generous to facilitate the game's testing. With lots of coins, developers and external testers could easily purchase items and speed their way through game. Approximately two weeks after launch, the generosity ended, and drops were set to a more appropriate level. Surprisingly, the actual income of the game plummeted by more than 50%.

Designers immediately rolled back that change as they tried to figure out what had caused such a profound effect on monetization. The answer? With loads of coins to spend, players likewise purchased loads of buildings. However, these buildings required "balloon payments" to complete; otherwise, they sat there looking half-built, a timber framework of sorts. Balloon payments consisted of other resource drops in the world which were not nearly as easy to come by as coins. So, in order to clean up their world and make it more aesthetically appealing, players spent real-world currency to purchase their way through the balloon payments. However, with fewer coins in circulation, players purchased fewer timber framework buildings and were therefore not inclined to spend actual money to purchase their way through the balloon payments. An important lesson was learned that day. Coins were left at the generous level.

Granularity

When designers speak of the **granularity** of a number, what they are referring to is the proximity of one number in relation to another. When numbers are said to be too granular, they are too close together, like fine-grain sand. When they are not granular enough, they are too large to be meaningful to players, like giant boulders. When the granularity is right, it gives designers the room they need to balance the game. To illustrate, here are two different XP/leveling systems:

Level	XP	Level	XP
1	0	1	0
2	1	2	100
3	3	3	300
4	6	4	600
5	10	5	1000
6	15	6	1500

Really, these are the same system, except the one on the right has its XP amounts multiplied by 100. If all XP awards from the system on the left are multiplied by 100 as well, then proportionally the two systems are exactly the same. However, the system on the right has more granularity and that granularity is critical to game designers attempting to balance and grow games.

If granularity is too low—that is, there is not enough space or separation between numbers—this can cause problems in design. Simply, as designers, we won't have room for the game to grow except at the high end. For example, let's say that a game allows a range of damage from 1 to 10 and has 10 swords that do 1, 2, 3, 4, and so on up to 10 damage. We cannot add another sword in there without going into fractional damage (which, sure, we could do if we also had fractional HP, but who wants that?). However, if we have those same swords and stick a zero on the end of their damage, we suddenly have room to add in 90 other swords. If enemy HP increased by a factor of 10 as well, then proportionally it is the same, but the granularity allows us to have much more flexibility. By providing meaningful gaps between power levels to provide for future expansion, we have plenty of room to insert new things in between. Instead of making something 1 through 10, make it 10 through 100 or 100 through 1000.

Granularity that's too low can be a problem for any game, but particularly for games that are expandable by design, such as trading card games or online RPGs that get regular expansion packs or other updates. Low granularity constrains the design space.

Can granularity that's too high also be a problem? Yes, although it's not quite as bad as having too little. If a player has a million HP and damage is on the order of tens of thousands, you could divide everything by a hundred or a thousand and not lose anything. At some point, the numbers become so large as to lose their perceptual meaning. What's the difference between 100,000,000,000,000,000,000 and 100,000,000,000,000,000? A lot, it turns out, if you have time to catch it as it flashes by on your screen. Likewise, needlessly large numbers are difficult to manage, particularly in board games. In digital games, needlessly large numbers make numbers at the low end trivial and therefore essentially worthless.

The last consideration with granularity is purely aesthetic rather than functional. Numbers that are easy to manage, calculate, and compare are ideal. Fractions and decimals are much harder than whole numbers for most people, so if a game has fractional values, it's usually better to multiply everything to get it up to a whole number. Furthermore, it is way more exciting to get 100 gold than 10 gold, and it's even more exciting to get 1000 gold.

This "adding a zero" is often referred to as "pinball numbers." Throughout the history of pinball, in order to increase player excitement, makers added more zeros with each new generation of machines to make scores more exciting.

Completing a First Pass

At this point in this book, believe it or not, you have everything you need to complete a first pass balance on your game. Starting with Chapter 3, you can determine the skeletal structure of your game's macros. In Chapter 4, you can determine the progression styles of your game (depending on the game, you most certainly need a combination of styles—exponential for XP, logarithmic for levels, custom-created for items, and so on). In this chapter, you find an anchor and use that anchor, whether precise or comparative, to scale your game's breadth (such as character classes or weapons as in *DOOM*) or depth such as a wide variety of ever-increasing items, creatures, and effects.

We strongly recommend studying the weapons in the *Diablo* series as well as the character balance in games like *World of Warcraft* or *Overwatch*. As a company, Blizzard has the time, resources, and experience to hit close to the mark more often than not. Since their games are so popular, the various components and statistics of the same are also well documented online.

Discussion Questions

1. What is an anchor?
2. Select any game and attempt to find its anchor.
3. What is the anchor of an adventure game? Is there one?
4. Why are peaks useful for designers?
5. Too little granularity in a game may cause what issues?
6. What issues are introduced by too much granularity?
7. If *DOOM* were an RPG and had character progression as well as player progression, what changes do you think this might necessitate?
8. What is the anchor of chess?
9. Select a game. Provide an analysis of the various resources or stats and how those relate to one another.
10. Discuss an imbalance you remember in a game and analyze it. How did it relate to the game's anchor?

Sidequests

In this chapter, we learned about the need for anchors, how to find one, and how to build upon that anchor.

Sidequest 5.1: Arcade Analysis

Choose any classic arcade game that has multiple resources of some kind. First, list out each type of resource, as shown in the previous chapter. Next, draw arrows between the different resources to show all of the direct numeric relationships between pairs of resources. Finally, choose whichever one you think would make the most appropriate anchor.

As an example, consider the classic *Super Mario Bros.* In this game, the player manages the following:

- **Lives**: when the player is hit by an enemy or falls into a pit, they lose a life and start the current level over (with coins, enemies, and time reset). When they lose all their lives, the game ends.
- **Coins**: the player finds these scattered throughout each level. Each one is worth points, and if the player collects 100 coins, they earn an extra life.
- **Time**: the player is given a certain amount of time to finish each level. If they run out of time, they lose a life.
- **Enemies**: the player can avoid enemies by jumping over them, but defeating them through various means earns points.
- **Score**: when the player collects coins or defeats enemies, their score goes up. They also get a score bonus for time remaining when they finish a level.

Already we can see relationships between these five resources. Time earns points (100 points per unit of time remaining at the end of a level). Enemies earn points when defeated (between 100 and 1000 points, depending on the enemy—more dangerous enemies are worth more). Coins are also worth points (200 each). 100 coins also earns +1 life, while both enemies and running out of time can cost a life. When a life is lost, it resets the level, so the player is essentially exchanging a life for the opportunity to collect more coins and defeat more enemies, and it also resets the timer. You might, then, draw your diagram as shown below.

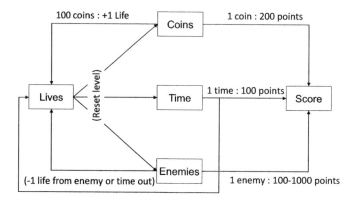

From here, it's easy to see that everything ultimately points to score, which would make that the natural choice for an anchor. If you were balancing the numbers in this game, you could now use this diagram and these numbers to determine, for example, how many coins are equivalent to a unit of time.

Now, choose your own arcade game (other than *Super Mario Bros.*) and perform this analysis to find an anchor and the numeric relationships between each resource.

Wizard's Main Quest, Part 2: Building Intuition

Continuing from Part 1 in: Chapter 1

You should have four pre-constructed decks of cards available from Part 1 of this quest in the previous chapter. Now we learn to actually play the game. Find a partner or get prepared to play against yourself.

Harmony is a game meant for two players. Each player starts with their own custom deck of 50 cards. To start the game, each player shuffles their deck and then draws ten cards into their hand. A player is randomly chosen to take the first turn. A player immediately loses the game if their hand or their draw deck is ever empty; the object of the game is to force the opponent to empty one or the other before they do the same to you.

There are two types of cards in Harmony: Power cards and Action cards. Power cards provide one of four types of power: Bio, Gear, Magic, or Science. Action cards all have some Power requirements; you must have at least that many Power in play in order to use that Action card. An Action card might require specific types of Power or "generic" Power that can be any type, or some combination of the two. For example, a card might require 2 Bio + 2 Generic, which could be satisfied by having 4 Bio in play, or 2 Bio and 2

Magic, or any other combination of at least four Power where at least two are Bio.

A player's turn is divided into three steps: Draw, Power, and Action. If they have not yet won the game, it then becomes the opponent's turn, and this continues until one player loses. The steps are as follows:

- **Draw phase**: the player draws two cards from their deck.
- **Power phase**: either the player can play one Power card from their hand into play, or if they can't or choose not to, then they must discard one card from their hand to their discard pile.
- **Action phase**: the player can either play one Action card for which they meet the Power requirement of all of their own Power cards in play, or else they must discard one card from their hand to their discard pile.

Action cards can perform some combination of the game's four core mechanics:

- **Damage**: for each point of damage done to the opponent, take the top card of their draw pile and move it to their discard pile.
- **Healing**: for each point of healing, take the top card of your discard pile and put it on the bottom of your draw pile. If there are fewer cards in your discard pile than the amount of healing, move all that you can and ignore the rest (for example, if your discard pile has seven cards and you Heal 9, move all seven cards to the bottom of your deck and the remaining 2 are ignored).
- **Draw**: for each point of draw, take the top card of your draw pile and put it in your hand.
- **Discard**: for each point of discard, the opponent must choose and discard one card in their hand to their discard pile.

For example, a card that says "Damage 5, Draw 4" means you draw four cards from your own deck, and the opponent takes the top five cards from their deck and put them in their discard pile.

That's it! Go ahead and play each deck against the others (this is at least six games total: Deck A vs. B, A vs. C, A vs. D, B vs. C, B vs. D, and C vs. D). By then, you should be comfortable with the rules and core mechanics and have a general sense of how powerful Damage, Healing, Draw, and Discard are relative to one another.

As it is, you'll find the game to be heavily unbalanced. Each of the four mechanics is costed similarly, even though they have drastically different value in play, as you'll see when you play. For now, just make a mental note of which of the decks and which of the mechanics seems the most and least powerful. You may want to take some written notes to this effect as well, so you can refer back to them in later parts.

Part 3 continued in: *Chapter 8*

6

Economic Systems

In This Chapter

- What Are Economic Systems?
- The Language of Economic Systems
- Common Economic Systems
- Mechanical Characteristics of Economic Systems
- Supply and Demand
- Market Price
- Inflation
- Open and Closed Economies

What Are Economic Systems?

> It's amazing what a difference a single percent, a half percent, even one-tenth of a percent can make. Over the course of a single game, you can be talking about thousands of added HP in the form of health drops from enemies.
>
> *an economic designer discussing how small percentages*
> *scale over time to dramatically affect a game*

Chapters 3–5 demonstrated the core building blocks of game balance. In reading them, you have a solid understanding of the *foundations* of game balance. As the word "foundation" makes clear, there is much more to game balance than its foundation. Chapter 6 builds upon this foundation by introducing economic systems.

The terms "economy," "game economy," and "economic system" are used frequently and interchangeably in games. What do we mean by these terms?

When game players refer to a game's **economy**, they often mean the types and amount of currency earned and spent in a game. Meanwhile, Merriam Webster defines an economy as "the process or system by which goods and services are produced, sold, and bought in a country or region." While a system in a game is a collection of elements that work together and may be thought of as one unit, an **economic system** in a game deals specifically with how resources are generated, how players can control them through production, acquisition, and trade of those resources, and how players use up their resources.

Creating an economic system can be challenging, because (like much of design) it is several steps removed from the player experience, and game designers do not directly design or control the player experience. Rather, we design the *possibility* for players to experience certain things through the rules and mechanics of the economic systems in the game. For instance, in *Monopoly*, a designer cannot make a player trade Park Place to their opponent. The economic systems, in turn, influence and incentivize certain player behaviors. Those behaviors, when acted out in the game, contribute to the player experience. For example, while both *Monopoly* and *Catan* have economic systems, *Monopoly*'s system pits players against each other with its limited resources and winner-take-all auctions, yet *Catan*'s system has players constantly trading and negotiating with each other for mutual gain. This is why, in part, the two games feel so different during play (*Monopoly* being so much more cutthroat, and *Catan* feeling more collaborative). In contrast to both *Monopoly* and *Catan*, free-to-play (F2P) games often pit players against one another and those who are willing to spend the most win. Earlier generations of F2P games played heavily on the collaborative "gifting" of friends to spur virality.

The Language of Economic Systems

Ahead of our discussion of common economic systems, it's useful to define a few terms since they come up often in discussions of game economies.

- **Resources**: anything a player receives in a game which may be used or traded in the acquisition of something else. For instance, magic points can be used to get HP, wood can be used to build, fire can be used to provide light, and gold can be used to purchase armor.

- **Consumables**: a type of resource that a player consumes in the acquisition of something else. Once used, consumables are gone. Health packs are common consumable.
- **Permanent Items or Objects**: a found, traded, or purchased object which exists in the world, which cannot be consumed or used in the acquisition of something else, and will theoretically exist after the player gets rid of it. For instance, if a player drops a sword, that sword exists on the ground. If the player sells that sword for gold, the sword theoretically exists in the store inventory. Swords cannot be consumed nor can they be used as resources to build something else.
- **Quest/Mission Objectives**: a specially designated item whose acquisition, trade, or delivery solves a quest. These objects are often similar to permanent items and even consumables, at least at face value. For instance, in *World of Warcraft*, an early quest requires the player to get many Red Bandanas. Once the player collects the requisite amount, the items will be removed from the player when they turn in the quest.

Common Economic Systems

There are four common types of economic systems seen in games, and companies often employ game designers, product managers, and game economists with specialization in one of these areas.

- **Fixed economic systems**: All resources in the game come from within the game itself. The prices are set by the game's designers prior to launch, and players cannot affect the prices. Likewise, players cannot inject real-world currency into the game economy or perform actions such as watching advertisements to earn in-game currency. In a fixed game economy, the game is the only seller, and if the game allows for players to sell their goods, the game (usually through NPCs) sets the price at which it buys them. In most single-player RPGs such as the *Final Fantasy* or *Dragon Quest* series, for example, the purchase price of any item in a shop is chosen by the designer. The player can't bargain with the shopkeeper; all they can do is go out and grind to earn more in-game currency.
- **Player-dynamic economic systems**: All resources in the game come from within the game itself, but players can affect the value of goods in the game. They generally do this through trade or auction houses which

use in-game currency. The former auction house in *World of Warcraft*, where the players set their own prices, is an example of this. Players trading resources among themselves to their mutual benefit in *Catan* is another example.

- **Free-to-play (F2P) economic systems**: Some resources in the game can be purchased for real-world currency or earned by performing "monetizing" actions such as watching ads or sharing the game with the player's friends. These purchases augment the player's game in some way, typically from a performance perspective, trading a player's money for a reduction in time, often called "pay to rush" or "pay to win." While many games are considered F2P, for the sake of a game economic system discussion, when we refer to F2P games, we are referring only to those games which create friction to incentivize the player to purchase. Players feel friction when the game's difficulty, typically quite easy in the beginning but getting harder as the game progresses, outpaces their ability to keep up. This is usually the point at which players are first encouraged to monetize to improve their performance. Adding friction to progression-based games is discussed in detail in Chapter 11.

- **Prestige economic systems**: Some resources in the game are paid for with real-world currency and have no effect on the actual gameplay, except as prestige items. Examples are virtual land holdings in MMOs, custom avatar apparel, hats in *Team Fortress 2*, custom vehicles, or unique items signifying the player's contribution. These goods are often limited edition and contribute significant income to the company.

- **Real currency economic systems**: Some resources in the game are real-world currency. Gambling games that require money to play or games that offer real-world currency as a reward are real-world game economies

While we have given these different economic system descriptive names for the sake of having a vocabulary to talk about these concepts, in the field, with the exception of F2P economic systems, the systems themselves tend not to be named. Rather, they are dictated by the mechanics, platform, and connectivity of the game.

While these five are the most common game economic systems, there are as many edge cases that don't fit neatly in one grouping or another. In some cases, games feature more than one type of game economy. Game designers often use phrasing such as "the economy of armor" or "the economy of combat" to isolate all game objects that touch that particular aspect of the game for the purposes of discussion. Furthermore, by using common mechanics of one and mixing it with another, entirely new patterns may still emerge. To be clear, the field of economics is huge, and any exploration of it here is limited and specific to games.

Mechanical Characteristics of Economic Systems

Most games that have economic systems contain several common mechanics that specify how resources are generated, populated, traded, and consumed.

- **Resource generation**: players receive or produce resources over the course of the game by purchasing them with in-game or real-world currencies, performing in-game "grind" actions like combat, or through accumulative growth over time such as mining resources in *Minecraft* or in *Starcraft* and similar RTS games. In most games, there are typically several ways to produce resources. This is often presented to players as a tradeoff between time and money (buy it instantly or work/wait for it).
- **Resource conversion**: players can convert resources of one type into something else, either another resource or a permanent item. Crafting is a common type of resource conversion. In *Minecraft*, converting two sticks and three iron into an iron axe is considered resource conversion. Purchasing from an in-game store is also a common resource conversion: the player is converting the resource of game currency into something else they can use. Resource conversion differs from resource consumption: you consume resources to change an existing thing. You convert resources when creating something new.
- **Resource trading**: players can trade resources with others, typically through some form of negotiation, haggling, or gifts. Trading gives players a powerful reason to interact with one another and is a key element in games that rely on a strong player community or inter-player social dynamics. We go into detail on trading mechanics in the next chapter.
- **Resource consumption**: players use resources to gain some kind of in-game benefit or remove an in-game barrier. While items in games may be considered permanent or consumable, resources in games are almost always considered to be consumable items. Designers can control the consumption of resources by controlling the demand for, quantity of, timing (i.e., once per day) and effect of the consumption of resources.

- **Resource limits**: the total sum of resources in the game is unlimited or else limited to some degree, and designers control just how much of a resource a player receives. To do so, designers may affect an item's rarity or make it wholly limited so that there are only a certain number available in any given game. **Zero-sum resources** are a special case of limited resources where players cannot generate or consume resources, but can only take them from other players. Zero-sum resources are covered in Chapter 12.

The more of these mechanics a game has, the more likely designers are to say it has an *economic system*. Consider the game *Super Mario Bros.* in which the player gains a life for every 100 coins they find. While this does involve converting coins to lives, most people would not think of this simplistic conversion as an economic system. The game *Monopoly*, by contrast, includes examples of all of these. Players generate money by passing Go. They can convert money into permanent goods, such as buying properties on the board or buying houses or hotels to place on their color groups. Players can trade money, undeveloped properties, and Get Out Of Jail Free cards with each other at any time, in any quantity that is mutually agreed to. Money is consumed by landing on Income Tax, Property Tax, paying to get out of jail, or drawing certain cards that require the player to pay to the bank. The properties, houses, and hotels are all limited: if all 12 hotels have been purchased and are on the board, for example, the rules state that no further hotels can be built until an existing one is sold. The exchange of rent money when a player lands on an opponent's property is zero sum: the amount of money that the property owner gains is exactly equal to what their opponent loses.

Supply and Demand

Central to the study of game economics (and economics in general, for that matter) is the concept of supply and demand. In the simplest sense, one could look at the effect of supply and demand upon price of a given item. If there is high demand and low supply, odds are, the price is high. Likewise, if there is low demand and high supply, prices are low. We can see this effect in games like *Magic: The Gathering* where powerful, rare cards can cost hundreds if not thousands of dollars on the open market. We also saw the effect of this in real-world markets when bitcoin miners purchased high-end graphics cards, traditionally aimed at gamers, for their mining operations. Demand dramatically increased, and so did the price. This simplified chart illustrates supply and demand's effect on price:

Condition	*Effect on market price*
Demand and supply do not change	Prices remain constant
Demand decreases and/or supply increases	Prices decrease
Demand increases and/or supply decreases	Prices rise
Demand and supply both increase or both decrease at the same time	Indeterminate: may cancel each other out or one may outweigh the other

The Supply Curve

Let's explore the implications within games by imagining an economy with only one resource: iron. Those selling iron want to make as much as possible. Those buying iron want to pay as little as possible.

Each seller has a minimum price at which they're willing to sell their iron. Some may have lower production costs, so they can afford to sell for less than their competitors, while others may just be greedy and demand a higher minimum price. We can also assume that sellers will accept more than their minimum price for iron; if a blacksmith is willing to sell iron for 20 gold and they're offered 25 gold for it, they're not going to refuse. If we knew the minimum sale price of each seller, we could construct a **supply curve** that relates the sale price to the number of sellers willing to sell at that price or above. A sample supply curve might look like this, where low prices mean few sellers are willing to part with iron, but as prices rise more become willing to sell.

The curve may or may not be a straight line, but we know that as the price increases, the number of sellers willing to sell iron at that price increases or stays the same.

Gameplay Effects of Scarcity

Scarcity is a term used to describe the prevalence of a given thing in a game, be it a resource, an item, or even other players. There are, of course, degrees of scarcity. How much of an item there is in any given instance of a game affects not only the supply of them available to the player, but the demand for them as well.

Scarcity can have a profound effect on the gameplay experience and player strategies. Consider a first-person shooter with limited (*DOOM*, *Half-Life*) vs. unlimited (*Overwatch*) resources. Where ammo is scarce, the player switches to use the weapon that has more ammo respawning or available in the level. When ammo is plentiful, by contrast, a player is more likely to fire at enemies liberally and use multiple weapons.

Similarly, imagine a strategy game with limited (*Fire Emblem*, *Final Fantasy Tactics*) vs. unlimited (*Advance Wars*, *Wargroove*) resources. In most tactical RPGs, the resources on the map are limited: players come to a location with only the characters in their party, and if the map contains any special items to be found, the player can only find so much before the level is entirely depleted. Anything that gets destroyed stays destroyed and does not get replaced, so the game focuses heavily on careful control of combat and who has the least casualties. The primary focus of the game becomes keeping one's own units alive, since there are so few of them, and they can't be replenished. Management of the game economy takes a back seat to fast-paced tactical action.

If the resource limits are infinite, however, players are not as concerned with keeping individual units alive because they can build even more resource-generated units. Mind you, they still care, but it's not at the same level of intensity as one might care if the 10 units they have are the only units they will have for the rest of the game. With infinite resources, income generation becomes a positive feedback loop: players build units or dedicate workers to generate resources, which then can be used to build even more. In tactical RPGs with resource generation such as the *Advance Wars* series, players generate resources from locations they control on the map, then use those resources to build military units to take over more locations, and keep going until they control the entire map or meet a given objective. 4X games such as the *Civilization* series take resource management even further. In *Civ*, resources on the map are marked by different icons. By locating a city near the resources or expanding the city's borders to encompass those resources, workers can mine them indefinitely. Once the player's income per unit of time is sufficiently high, they shift to building an offensive military and face off against opponents. More units are built continually throughout the game. If all players have similar economies and incomes, the game may take a very long time, as players pay to replace anything that was lost in battle. The only way a player is eliminated is if an opponent invades with an overwhelmingly large force that wipes them out… which would only happen if they are very far behind their opponents in terms of production capability. *Civilization* offers multiple paths to victory, insuring that the game doesn't always take this route. The focus in this game is on the efficiency of ramping up an economy and trying to outproduce the opponents; the death count of military units is much less important here since they are infinitely renewable.

Resource limits in strategy games act not only as a determinant of strategy but as a delimiter of time. Games sometimes mix both limited and unlimited resources, and maps are also designed to change the focus of the game. If the resources located nearby the players' start locations are very limited but other more distant resources are effectively unlimited, the early game focuses mainly on establishing defendable supply lines to mine the more distant resources while attacking the opponents' mining units.

The Demand Curve

The buyers work the same way, but in reverse. Buyers each have a *maximum* price that they are willing (or able) to pay for iron. We can draw a **demand curve** that shows how many buyers are willing to purchase a specific item at

any given price. A sample demand curve might look like the following; note
that when prices increase, there are fewer buyers willing to purchase:

As the price increases, the demand curve always decreases or stays the same,
but never increases. When there's a price increase, a few people who *were*
buying at the lower price might decide it's too expensive and refuse to buy
at the higher one. For instance, most players expect games on the App Store
to be free or cost less than $5. As with supply, the demand curve might be
straight or curved or wavy or just about any shape you can imagine, except
that unlike the supply curve it is always decreasing or staying constant as
the price increases. Auctions are great examples of demand curves in action.
As the auction progresses, fewer and fewer people are participating until at
last, one person is declared the winner. (Auctions are examined in detail in
Chapter 7.)

Marginal Supply and Demand

The amount a seller is willing to sell a resource for, or a buyer's maximum
amount to pay, is not always constant. In particular, it can depend on
how many resources that the buyer or seller already has. Economists use
the term **margin** to describe the *last* resource bought or sold, compared
to all the other ones. In short, a player's demand for an item *may* decrease
if the player has a lot of something, so that a single player's demand looks
like this.

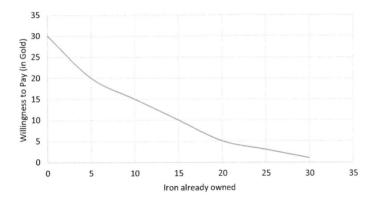

In the action-RPG *Diablo*, players have limited inventory space which can be used to hold their gold, equippable items, and consumable items. Consumables such as healing and mana potions can save a character's life, and players will generally want to take at least a few with them in order to escape an unexpectedly bad situation. However, taking too many of these clogs the player's inventory and doesn't allow for them to bring back much in the way of additional treasure, and on top of that, the player is unlikely to get into such a bad situation that they would need dozens upon dozens of potions. In this situation, a player's demand for their first consumables will be high and will get progressively lower as they carry more and more of them. In the game, the price for consumables is fixed, so the demand is not reflected in the game's prices. Players therefore buy as many consumables as their marginal demand—and their wallet—dictate. Similarly, in *Minecraft*, players may keep all the stone blocks they're mining through, paying little attention to their inventory until they realize it's full. Then, the stone blocks that had some worth as potential building blocks get cast off in favor of higher value items.

Can there be situations where demand *increases* with the amount of resources a player owns? In F2P games, the margin is quite important and, interestingly, sometimes works in this way: the more players have, the more they are willing to pay provided they are close to their goal. If players need 20 units of iron to complete an upgrade, they may be completely willing to work for those units for a while. The closer they get, however, the more likely they are to monetize the few remaining units. Players rationalize that they did most of the work, and in competitive games, urgency to complete the upgrade may be greater. Developers count on this margin pressure to monetize.

The same can be true for supply curves. In some cases, producing a lot of resources at once may be less expensive per unit (often referred to as "economies of scale"). For instance, in *Civilization*, some terrain generates double of a resource while not requiring any more time or units to do so. In other games, producing additional resources of the same type gets *more* expensive per unit, in order to encourage players to produce a broader range of resources or pursue other strategies. For example, in most idle games such as *Cookie Clicker*, each time the player buys a resource generator of any type, subsequent purchases of that same resource generator increase in cost.

Adding mechanics to your game that influence supply and demand based on the amounts of a resource already owned can change player strategies a great deal. Once players own a majority of a color group in *Monopoly*, their demand for the remaining property in that group goes up. Similarly, in other games, if each unit of a particular resource is more useful than the last, the game tends to quickly organize into players attempting to control each individual good, and once a player has the majority of a particular good, they want to acquire the rest of them. If designers don't want the game to go that way, they can change the awards, avoid such groupings, or give players other reasons to get rid of their resources (maybe they can cash them in for some necessary other resource and they need to do so regularly, or maybe the resources have a use-it-or-lose-it mechanic that limits how much players can hoard—*Catan* features both of these). Conversely, suppose instead each additional unit of a good is less useful to a buyer; then having a decreasing cost for producing the good might make a lot of sense if you want the price of that good to be more stable.

Supply and Demand with Multiple Resources

Economies get more interesting when there are multiple types of trade goods, because the demand curves can affect one another. This interaction leads to two specific types of interactions: imperfect substitutes and complements.

Imperfect substitutes are items that are nearly substitutes for one another. For example, suppose a game has two resources that give similar effects: a healing potion that heals 50 HP, and also a mana potion that restores 5 MP which can then be used to cast a healing spell that heals 50 HP. These may not be identical, but they're close enough that if one of them is very cheap, and the other is very expensive, players tend to buy the cheap one. The extent to which they do this tells you how efficient the substitution is. In the case of imperfect substitutes, increased price (for example, from a decreasing supply or greater demand) of one good can increase the demand (and number of units sold) of the other good. Likewise, if one good has a lower price (from increased supply or lower demand) compared to a substitute good, players buy more of the "sale price" good which then lowers demand for the substitute.

There are also cases where several goods are **complements**: demand for both tends to go up together or down together. The extent to which they do tells you how closely they complement each other. One example is a set of matching gear that gives a character an additional stat bonus if they are wearing multiple pieces of gear from the same set. In this case, if a single player has several pieces of the set, their personal demand for the remaining pieces goes up, and they are willing to pay more for the final piece that completes the set than they would for their first piece.

Market Price

In any economy with buyers and sellers, the **market price** is exactly the price where the supply and demand curves intersect. In the following chart, combining our earlier supply and demand curves, we see that the market price for iron is around 6 or 7 Gold, but if either the supply or demand curve changed, that would cause a shift in the market price.

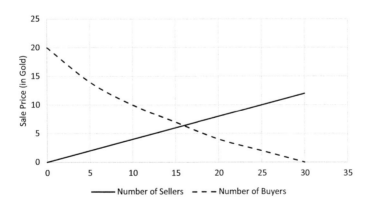

While this concept applies in economic theory and, for the most part, in real currency game economic systems, its application in other game economies is a little murkier. How does one set a "market price" in a game? It's not an easy or straightforward question to answer, because there are many design dials that affect market price depending on which type of economic system designers integrate (of the types covered earlier in this chapter).

Fixed Economies

In fixed economic systems, the game economist or designer sets the market price or cost for objects in the game. In general, the market price of items is often tied to both the game's anchor (like HP) and rarity. For example, the more HP damage an item does, the more it costs. These costs are augmented if the item has extra abilities, HP regen, for instance. In fact, it's common for designers to assign a per-unit value to everything in a game (10 gold per HP, for instance), and then take the sum of those values for the item's price. This book goes into more detail about the process for assigning prices based on an item's value in Chapter 8.

As players progress through the game, they are in need to better items and are reliant upon some combination of item and currency drops to make those new purchases. If players have an abundance of money and can buy everything whenever they want it, we would call the game unbalanced.

In essence, the goal of any economic system is to introduce scarcity so the player has to make tradeoff decisions: how should they spend their money?

These decisions make games interesting, fun, and strategic. At the same time, players may grow frustrated if they need to grind too long before having enough currency to keep up with the game's difficulty curve. In setting market prices, the designer may change the prices in the store or change the rate of currency drops to address the imbalance. Generally, these adjustments are completed during alpha- or beta-testing, but sometimes are altered in post-launch if an item is determined to be worth more or less than it was initially thought to be.

Player-Dynamic Economies

Player-dynamic game economies, often found in MMOs and board games, are similar to fixed game economies, except that players also give or trade items and in-game currency with one another or sell goods in an auction. As such, players establish the transactional price for the goods. The market price in these auctions, however, is established based on supply and demand. If something is priced too high in the auction house, it sits there. Likewise, if a player demands too much in trade as they might in *Catan*, *Monopoly*, or any trading card game (TCG), the trade may not be accepted.

In player-dynamic economies, the market price in the game guides the trading price for items in the auction. If players can sell their item to an NPC or store for a certain amount, they are not going to auction it for less.

Depending on the rarity of the item, however, they may indeed auction it for more.

Designers can directly affect the market and trading price of an item by

- **Controlling availability**: Items that are available in the game's stores are unlikely to sell above that market price in the auction. Items which are not available in the game's stores will follow the rules of supply and demand. If an abundance of people start crafting a particular type of armor and release it in the auction house, the price will likely go down in response to the oversupply.
- **Controlling the rarity of the loot drops**: The rarer the item, the higher its value is likely to be, other things being equal. If it's a rare yet worthless drop, its value may be limited.
- **Controlling the placement of stores**: If it can be sold or purchased nearby and that is an advantage to the player, he or she is unlikely to auction the item for less.
- **Controlling the properties of the items**: Some items may only be used by specific classes, thus limiting their potential market value.

Over time, the market price in player-dynamic markets fluctuates because supply and demand curves are changing. Every time a new item is put on the market, or someone buys an item from the market, that modifies the supply of that item. Also, the set of buyers logged in to the game is changing over time. In short, player-dynamic markets, like real-world markets, are not perfectly efficient, and the player base and resource pool is finite, so you see unequal amounts of each resource being produced and consumed over time, hence the fluctuations.

In player-dynamic economies, the fewer the number of players, the more prices tend to fluctuate, because each individual player controls a greater part of production or consumption. In a three-player game of *Catan*, the going rate for one clay varies widely from game to game, and even within a single game, because player demand is constantly shifting and each player controls a third of the game's resource supply. In comparison, the price of any given card in *Magic: The Gathering* is expected to remain more stable over time, simply because there are a lot more of that item and more players in the game, and massive shifts only happen when there are major changes to the game environment such as a new expansion. While the volatility of the market isn't something designers can control directly, we can at least predict it and design accordingly. In designing a board game for three to six players, one can expect larger price fluctuations with three players than with six; if a stable market is important to the functioning of the game, you may then need to add some extra rules with fewer players to account for the naturally higher volatility.

The Invisible Hand

In player-dynamic economies, it turns out that even absent knowledge of the true value of an item (the value in the store, for instance), players converge rapidly on the market value that is predicted from the supply and demand curves. Economists call this the **invisible hand**, meaning that the market prices are guided to the "correct" values, as if an invisible being was intentionally manipulating them. For example, if players are trading between two resources of equal gameplay value where one is rarer than the other, the rarer one usually trades for more... even if players have no hard statistics that *tell* them which is more rare or what the total number of either resource in circulation. It can even be a deliberate design choice to reveal or conceal economic market information from the players. Making this information fully available aids players in making good decisions, while concealing the information gives the player community more to learn about the game as a community. Think of all the game-based wikis that players use to analyze every last element of the game.

Free-To-Play (F2P) Economies

Markets in F2P game economies are some of the most interesting, complex, and dynamic game markets to study. The very lifeblood of the game depends upon its ability to get players to spend money after receiving the game for free. It's not an easy task.

In these economies, players spend money to purchase in-game currency or perform actions which are worth money to the game's publisher (such as watching ads or inviting friends on their social graph). Setting a market price in a F2P game economy is a combination of market data and competitive analysis, A/B testing the market, targeting a specific market, keeping prices flexible and player psychology.

Analyzing Historical Data

Market price in F2P game economies is initially set based on historical data. Companies analyze their own data as well as market prices in a range of competing products from significant publishers and significant trending games.

For instance, most F2P games offer bulk purchases of in-game currency. In developing a game, an analysis of the price points for various quantities of in-game currencies is undertaken to determine a baseline for what the market is presently bearing. It is not uncommon to find the same prices/amounts across a wide range of games, particularly from a single publisher. Furthermore, it's not uncommon for cloned games to copy game economies exactly, only bothering to rename and re-skin items. This analysis gives the team critical starting information for what works (or what may work), even if they don't have that information in their own metrics.

Testing the Market

Unlike fixed game economies, F2P game economies are initially tested in monetizing regions which are reflective of but still not the main demographic region for the game. For instance, games intended for release in the United States are often test marketed in the Philippines where there is low cost of acquisition, similar play patterns and high English competency. Developers iterate the games based on feedback and then test in Scandinavian countries and Canada for monetization before a US and worldwide launch. Different market price ranges may be experimented with to see tolerances toward pricing and to explore player retention and drop off points. Product managers have specific **key performance indicators** (KPIs) that they are looking for which include a specific level of average monetization and retention (players coming back to play the game again after x hours, x days, etc.) and average session play time. Through testing of the game this way (called a **soft launch**), product managers have more closely aligned their desired KPIs (which, of course, includes pricing). Games are then rolled out into the desired target regions, typically still in soft launch. This book goes into more detail on choosing KPIs in Chapter 13.

Targeting the Market

Targeting the market in F2P games is quite an interesting field. As you might expect, F2P games attempt to get as many players into what designers call "the funnel" as possible. Players are quickly "ramped out" by increasing game difficulty. If you've played these games, you know the moment—it seems easy at first, but then you start to feel pressured and that you can't keep up. At about this time, you are offered something in the game for premium currency which would make you more efficient and able to compete. Designers are interested in creating and tuning a game which is designed to elicit purchases from monetizing users who spend the most money. The quicker they ramp non-monetizing players out, the more they can optimize the game for players who do. This is known as targeting the **whales**—the small group of players who spend hundreds, thousands, or tens of thousands of dollars on a single game.

To illustrate, consider a recent F2P game: a new player has played the hell out of it, but they're at that point where the game is ramping more quickly than their skill. In the initial stages of the game (be they levels, or challenges, or however the game is structured), they were doing great. The game ranks performance on each level, and the player was consistently at the top. Shortly thereafter, typically on the second or third day of play, the game starts aggressively ramping in difficulty. Where the player was previously a "three out of three stars" performer, they're now a two- or one-star performer. They feel the pressure from the game as it suggests purchases to improve performance. However, they can't afford those purchases with the in-game currency they have available. They see some people on their friends list with seemingly impossibly high scores or highly sought-after resources, things they couldn't achieve even if they performed optimally, but which they *could* do by monetizing. This is a pivotal point for the game's success. The player either does or does not monetize, and it's the people that do monetize that game designers want to tailor the game toward. As sad as it sounds, in all but a rare few cases, players that do not monetize do not get the attention; if monetizing players request a feature or a fix, it has priority over requests of non-monetizing players. Players who don't pay are instead deliberately ramped out so that the desired target market can be best catered to. While the largest number of purchasers may seem to set a traditional market price, F2P games aim to cut off the lower end of that spectrum (non-purchasers and low-amount purchasers) to focus on the whales for whom higher market prices are a non-issue.

Developers want to optimize the game to best cater to the players who spend money, and the more money they spend, the more priority they get. Developers want to assess their metrics and pressure points. They want to know when the monetizing players are dropping out and improve upon those KPIs while still making sure legions of non-monetizing players funnel into the product, hopefully monetizing at some point.

As a note, since most F2P games also have ratings in the app store, games are careful to make sure that players have a great early ramp experience to ensure that the largest number of people is having fun, enjoying the experience and therefore likely to leave a positive review. The initial net is cast as wide as possible, and players are funneled and sieved to retain those who spend. As players become increasingly aware of F2P monetization practices, it's common to see them complaining about the precise moment the difficulty begins to ramp players out. Similarly, games often prompt players to review the game *before* the ramp takes effect.

Keeping Prices Flexible

In launching a F2P game, there's an old adage (well, as old as F2P is, anyway) that you can always lower prices, but you can't raise them. Players react negatively to rising prices, and as game communities develop over time, the public data on historical prices becomes more widely known among networked players. This seems to create a dilemma for F2P developers. What if you want to raise your prices to see if people are willing to spend more than you're currently charging? What if you initially set your prices too low?

Developers have a variety of ways to keep pricing flexible in order to continually optimize market pricing to best fit their target audience. The most common methods used are the following:

- **Offering percent-off sales**: Product managers set an initial high price and incentivize users with a variety of "percent off" sales to see what price gives the greatest return. This way, the high price remains constant, and players are not surprised when sales end or are changed. Sales are known to be events of a fixed duration. Furthermore, sales incentivize to purchase before the sale ends.
- **Adjusting the drop rate**: If developers want to make more money without raising prices, one way to do that is to give players less, thus forcing them to buy more. For instance, in most games, players are given rewards for completing certain tasks. These rewards are typically random, ranged drops (between 50 and 100 gold, for instance). Product managers can alter the global drop rate and have a dramatic impact on the game. Players who refuse to buy must now play longer, accept lesser performance, or be funneled out. In effect, they increase the friction upon players.
- **Changing quantities on in-game currency purchases**: Another method of raising prices without raising them is to change quantities on in-game currency purchases while maintaining the same pricing structure. For instance, if the player used to purchase 125 units for $10, they now purchase 120 units for $10. Another method used is to raise the amount of units purchased while also raising the price per unit. While this is a clear raising of prices, the message may be muddied with "Now more gold!" without mentioning that there is now also more cost involved.

- **Using Per-Player Cost**: In an effort to monetize more players, some F2P games offer different prices for different players playing the same game. Players who are not monetizing or not monetizing at a level the product managers desire receive lower prices or better specials than those that are already purchasing at a sufficient level. Pushing it one step further, some games have actually offered higher prices to those players who monetize knowing that they are likely to purchase regardless of cost. This is particularly true for new items for which there is no known historical data among players. The ethics of such practices are regularly questioned by both game designers and players.

Prestige Economies

Setting a market price for prestige items in a prestige game economy is a classic case of supply and demand. What will the market bear? If the item is priced too high, no one will buy it. If it's priced too low, everyone can get it, so it's not a prestige item at all. Prestige items almost always have one or both of these properties:

- **Visibility**: For items to truly be considered prestige items, they must be visible to other players in some way. For example, in 2010, *World of Warcraft* launched its first prestige-class mount. Priced at $25, before launch, many questioned the price of the item noting that its cost was nearly double the subscription cost. Within the first 4 hours of its release, however, Blizzard made $2 million.
- **Limited Quantity**: To incentivize the uniqueness of an item, prestige items are often limited either by time or by quantity available. Both incentivize those on the fence to rush their purchase.

Setting a market price for prestige items is an inexact science and continuously surprising. Virtual property and item purchases in games have snapped up $10K or more per item. In *Shroud of the Avatar*, for instance, a castle sold for $12,000). In setting the prices so high, Richard Garriott, the game's designer, told Eurogamer that he would regularly see virtual property sell for approximately $10,000 on eBay. In his first MMO, *Ultima Online*, there was no precedent for such a thing. So, the designers weren't prepared to handle it or shepherd it. *Star Citizen* made dozens of headlines with its prestige purchases. Today's developers have a marginally better idea of market tolerance, though such high prices continue to make news. It's hard to say where the top is.

Inflation

Inflation is defined as "a continual increase in the price of goods or services" according to the Merriam-Webster dictionary. What might cause inflation to happen in a game? Clearly, something has changed with either the supply or the demand curves to cause such a shift in market price.

Supply-Side Inflation

On the supply side, *World of Warcraft* offers an interesting case study. When it released, *World of Warcraft* was a fixed game economy. With the addition of its auction house, it became a player-dynamic economy before it reverted to a fixed game economy. **Gold farmers** quickly began to exploit the game to earn real-world cash. Gold farmers are players who grind the game to collect currency through a combination of bots and individuals employed expressly for that purpose. In at least one case, prisoners were forced to farm for gold. Representatives of the farmers would then approach players in game and offer to sell them gold in exchange for cash which was sent via a third-party app such as PayPal. Gold farming created significant problems in *World of Warcraft*'s economy and resulted in the banning of accounts associated with gold farming and the creation of developer tools designed to detect and deactivate bots. At its peak, the *New York Times* estimated that there were over 100,000 people employed as full-time gold farmers. The results of the labor of these farmers was a dramatic oversupply of gold in the game. It sent prices skyrocketing in the auction house, putting items out of reach of ordinary players. The only way to counteract the over-abundance of gold is to raise prices or create **money sinks**, a term designers use to describe things in the game deliberately designed to remove money from the economy (like an item that can only be purchased for 1M gold). Since all players hadn't availed themselves of farmer gold, however, such a measure couldn't be taken. The gold from farmers worked its way through the community, going from farmer to player to auction seller and so on. Companies with in-game currencies now employ several methods from in-game tokens to account monitoring to keep inflation and economic effects low.

Even without gold farming, most MMOs still experience inflation (albeit slower) since players kill monsters and gain loot which is then added to the economy. Over time, if the amount of money entering the game's economy through players collecting loot exceeds the amount of money leaving the economy through money sinks, players will on average become richer.

With more gold to spend, players are willing to spend more, which drives up prices for any items that have a limited supply provided the games allow for player-to-player purchases or support an auction house.

Demand-Side Inflation

Recall that a demand curve for most types of game economies shows how many players are willing to pay each possible price for some resource. Normally, we think of the demand curve as mostly fixed, perhaps fluctuating a bit in the case of different players being active or being in different short-term situations, but over time, we would expect it to balance out. However, there are a few situations that can permanently shift the demand curve in one direction or another.

Obviously, demand for a resource can increase or decrease when that resource's usefulness in the game changes. Examples of how this might happen:

- A game balance change modifies the game environment. Whenever cards are changed in an online CCG, the cards that are strengthened become more valuable in trade while those that were **nerfed** (weakened) are less valuable.
- New content is introduced that changes the metagame value of existing content. Expansion sets for CCGs and MMOs often include new content that is more powerful than the old which reduces the value of old stuff; or new things that combine particularly well with certain other old things, thus increasing their value.
- A new strategy or exploit is discovered in the player community. If a particular character in a MOBA suddenly starts doing well in competitive play because some players figured out how to use them particularly effectively, that character (and any skills and items that support this strategy) suddenly becomes more valuable to a lot of players.

Another more interesting case is where the game environment is the same, but each player's maximum willingness to pay for things increases. This mostly happens when players gain more purchasing power within the game. Consider a game with a **positive-sum** economy: that is, more resources enter the economy than leave the economy. A common example is in currency and loot drops in MMOs: a player defeats a monster, and the monster leaves resources behind; the player collects these resources; and the act of doing this does not take any resources away from any other player. Over time, with many players defeating many monsters, the overall amount of loot in the game's economy increases. With more total in-game currency in the economy (and especially, more currency *per player* on average), we see what is called **inflation**: the demand curve shifts to the right as more players have more in-game money and are thus able (and willing) to pay higher prices for the same goods. Developers may introduce new, higher priced goods, increase the market price of existing goods (a decision players wouldn't like), or decrease the drop rate to compensate.

Inflation in game economies has the potential to be a problem for all players. On the one hand, prices may be increasing, but that is because those very players are richer in-game and thus able to pay more for everything. Seemingly, this is not an issue. However, if inflation is due to gold farming or pay-to-win meaning people have to pay more to keep up, it unfairly tips the scales toward those who are willing to pay. For some games, this is highly problematic. For others, it is their business model. Inflation can be a major issue for new players, or inactive players that are away for a while and then come back, because these players enter the game to find that they can't earn enough to keep up. If players can earn 10 gold for every 5 hours of play, and anything worth having in the game costs several hundred gold, those items are going to seem unattainable. Even if a player is highly persistent and works hard to get enough gold to buy those items, by the time they've collected several hundred gold, inflation has pushed the cost of the goods even higher. How might a game designer fix this? There are a few ways: adding negative-sum elements to the economy, removing positive-sum elements from the economy and resetting the economy itself.

Adding Negative-Sum Elements to the Economy

A **negative-sum element** is a mechanic that removes resources from the economy. A **positive-sum element** is a mechanic that deposits money into the economy. If the economy is inherently positive-sum where resources are created without being destroyed elsewhere, some **negative-sum** mechanics can be added that allow resources to be removed from the economy without others being created (sometimes called **money sinks** or **gold sinks**). Resource sinks take many forms. Computer-controlled (NPC, short for "Non-Player Character") merchants and shopkeepers typically give players items in exchange for in-game currency, and the currency is removed from the economy. These purchases are a sink, particularly if the items sold are consumable or otherwise go away over time and they have to be purchased again. Another common sink in some types of games is in-game money paid for maintenance and upkeep; an example is paying gold to repair a weapon and armor periodically. Penalties for dying (such as losing some money or things that cost money to replace) can be a resource sink that triggers on death. When an in-game economy has gone too far out of control, developers sometimes offer limited quantities of very expensive items (often items that are purely cosmetic that serve more as status symbols than a gameplay advantage) which can remove large amounts of cash from the economy in a very short time when a few very wealthy players buy them. In other live games, expensive items have appeared as mandated quest items designed to forcefully drain gold from all players. Once the economy stabilizes, the price can be lowered over time to correlate with the economic changes taking place in the early game.

Ideally, a resource sink takes about as much out of the economy as the positive-sum elements (**money sources**) add in. In a persistent, online game, these things can be measured by determining the average gold per player and seeing if it's growing or shrinking over time. The sources and sinks can be adjusted accordingly.

Removing Positive-Sum Mechanics from the Economy

Instead of adding negative-sum mechanics to fight inflation, an alternative is to remove the positive-sum mechanics that are causing the inflation in the first place. This tends to be more difficult in games where players are used to killing monsters and getting loot drops. If the monsters are limited so that they don't respawn, the world becomes depopulated very quickly; if the monsters respawn but give no rewards, players won't bother killing them at all. In live games, designers gradually reduce the amount of gold in the drops over time so that less and less gold is entering the economy.

Economic Resets

Then, there's the nuclear option: occasionally reset the entire economy so that everyone loses everything and has to start over. In online games, this is referred to as a **server reset**. This doesn't solve inflation—a positive-sum economy is still positive-sum, and a player coming in at the end of a cycle has no chance of catching up. However, it does mean that if a new player waits for the next reset, they'll have as good a chance as anyone else immediately following the reset. Economic resets are incredibly rare, to be sure. Generally, they occur in live games when it transitions from alpha to beta or from soft launch to full launch.

Occasionally, a game can be designed with regular resets in mind that players can expect and anticipate; many TCGs do this in a mild way by having seasons of play, rotating old cards out of active play at the end of each season. A more interesting example was an older game played in a web browser called *Archmage* (now defunct). In this game, players generally gained power over time, but there was one late-game spell in particular that players could cast—Armageddon—that painted a giant target on them, allowing all other players in the game to attack them with impunity. However, if seven players cast this spell in succession, it would destroy everyone in the game, resetting everyone to a brand-new character just starting out, and those players who cast it would have their names permanently inscribed in the Hall of Immortality (the game's high-score list). This made a total server reset essentially a win condition of the game, unpredictable but ultimately inevitable, and a cause for excitement as enough players got powerful enough to make the attempt.

Interestingly, games themselves go through economic resets. As games transitioned from premium to subscription to F2P, the publishers have had to find new ways of making money. These changes often affect the actual game economy. For instance, *Diner Dash* was once a pay-to-play game and, at other times, a free game. However, when the game switched to F2P, the overall design of the in-game economy changed as well.

Case Study: *Catan*

In *Catan*, on each player's turn, they roll two dice to determine resource production. With one rare exception, dice rolls generate resources for some or all players but do not remove resources from the game economy. As players generate resources, they then spend these to build new settlements and cities on the board, which then further increase their resource production (the build cost of settlements and cities can be thought of as a resource sink, though an ineffective one long term since they are improving production and eventually pay for themselves). As the game goes on, players are producing more and more resources per turn (on average), so there is an inflation of resources (or at least resource production) over time. However, this doesn't affect the balance of the game, for a few reasons. All players start at a similar position from the beginning, so no one is disadvantaged by entering the game late. By the time players are in the late game and *willing* to trade large quantities of goods to get the one thing they need, they're also at the point where they are so close to winning that their opponents refuse to trade with them. In any case, the game ends with one player winning before the economic inflation gets hopelessly out of hand.

Case Study: *Monopoly*

The board game *Monopoly* provides an interesting example of a game economy. Money sources include passing Go, as well as some of the Chance and Community Chest cards. Money sinks include landing on Income Tax or Luxury Tax spaces, paying to get out of jail, and some other Chance and Community Chest cards. Purchasing property, houses, and hotels are also partial money sinks, though the player can get half of the value back by selling the improvements or mortgaging the property, and the player tends to get their money back eventually through others landing on their space and paying rent (if the player did not expect to make their money back, they wouldn't buy the property or improvement in the first place). Note that collecting rent itself is neither a money source nor a money sink; it is zero-sum, because money is simply transferred from one player to another.

If only examining the involuntary money sources and sinks, *Monopoly* is a strongly positive-sum economy: players earn $200 every time they pass Go, and only lose money sometimes when landing on one of two specific spaces. Of the voluntary money sinks, buying property and improvements is an investment that eventually pays for itself; and getting out of jail is only worth paying for if the loss of $50 is made up for by greater opportunities to buy good properties. Thus, over the course of the game, the game economy should be positive-sum, and we should see inflation in the long term. In other words, players get richer over time.

The object of the game is to bankrupt all other opponents. If players are getting richer over time, this becomes more and more difficult as the game goes on. This is, in part, a reason why games of *Monopoly* are notorious for taking a really long time to finish. Some people play with an additional house rule that money paid from spaces like Luxury Tax and Income Tax is put in the center of the board and awarded to the next player to land on Free Parking, which only serves to eliminate some money sinks, which makes this problem even worse!

Open and Closed Economies

When talking about any system (economic or otherwise), we say that a system is "open" if its internal parts can be directly influenced by things outside the system itself and "closed" if the system is entirely self-contained.

Most AAA and analog game economies are closed systems. There may be some kinds of resources or "money" within the game, but no way to influence that from outside the game. In fact, if a game is designed as a closed system, players typically get very uncomfortable if someone tries to change it to an open system. As an example, next time you play *Monopoly*, try this: at the start of the game, decide that people can purchase extra *Monopoly* money for real-world currency and see what happens. (What probably happens is that you won't be playing *that* game with the same people ever again, or everyone will declare that it's a dumb idea and go back to playing it in a normal way.)

Many competitive F2P games are open systems. In contrast to a closed system, players can influence the money and resources inside of the game from outside, whether it's purchasing additional in-game currency for real-world currency or rushing production of resources or units.

Closed systems are easier to design and balance, because designers have complete control over the resource production and consumption within the system. Open economies are more difficult since the designer no longer has control over the game economy.

How can a designer balance an open economy, where players can spend real-world money for in-game resources, and players might spend vastly different amounts? There are a few ways: limiting spending, limiting power, providing competitive gates, and survival of the richest.

- **Limiting Spending**: In tournament play of *Poker*, players typically start with the same amount of chips, and additional buy-ins are either strictly limited or disallowed entirely. This is obviously not practical for most games that rely on additional player purchases as their business model.
- **Limiting Power**: Design the game such that player spending gives more options but not more power. This is the typical model for collectible card games (CCGs). When a player buys a new pack of cards, it lets them build more decks with a greater variety of strategies, but as long as all cards are balanced with one another, players who own all the cards don't necessarily have the best decks. An alternative seen in some other CCGs is to make cards generally more powerful if they're rare, which *does* reward players for spending more.
- **Providing Competitive Gates**: If a game is balanced in such a way that players who spend more become more powerful, designers can balance the game so that players are competitively matched with other players at their skill level. This has the benefit of making the game

feel fun and competitive for all players, not just those at a high level. Using similar gates, designers can protect lower level players from higher-level players so that they don't become fodder for them. There are a variety of ways to do this, from providing no experience points or other value in doing so to providing safe starting areas for new players.

- **Survival of the Richest**: F2P games that rely on player spending for all of their revenue follow a strategy of making the most powerful items or equipment only achievable through spending money. In this case, players who spend more are generally more powerful than players who spend less (or nothing); such games are often referred to as **pay-to-win**. Some F2P games also allow players to pay-to-rush. These players are inherently more powerful than other players because they invest money over time.

In general, money tends to segregate players by how much they've spent; once a player has paid a lot of money, if they only get to play with others who have similar win/loss records or power level, they end up facing other players who have also paid a lot of money—and the gameplay advantage they paid for is no longer there. Interestingly enough, although it seems that the players might become frustrated and quit, the opposite is actually true. High monetizing players are actually more likely to spend even more to catch up. It is helpful to compare this to an auction. Someone is driving the bid. In a best-case scenario for F2P games, high-monetizing players are driving one another on. One common design for F2P games that's less drastic than the pay-to-win strategy is to allow players to exchange money for time. For example, suppose a player unlocks a new area to play in after 10 hours of gameplay, and the play is fun enough that this can be done without feeling like the game is forcing an arbitrary, meaningless grind. However, the game also offers the player the option of skipping ahead and unlocking it now by paying some small amount. In this way, money doesn't give a gameplay advantage, but merely speeds up progression on the same progression curve that a free player would experience.

Player Trades in Open Economies

One final consideration in games with open economies is whether and how players can trade (or give away) resources within the game. If players can buy things with real-world money and then trade them to someone else, it's a sure bet that the game develops a secondary economy where players exchange real-world money for in-game stuff among themselves. When designing these economies, there are a few additional practical considerations that can affect not only the play experience, but even the experience of the game developers when dealing with the player community.

One option that many early games tried was to expressly forbid the trading of items for cash saying it was against the game's Terms of Service. Any player found to have done so has their account terminated. This is not a very useful solution, mainly because it's a customer support challenge. Tracking and banning players who have done this takes a lot of time, and dealing with angry comments from players who were banned takes even more time and can lead to nontrivial social media issues. Ultimately, if designers don't want people trading in-game goods for cash, the trading system that as designed should not allow it. More often, developers declare that trading goods for cash is okay but unsupported by the game developer. If two players engineer a trade and one of them takes the other's virtual stuff and reneges on giving the cash, that's the player's problem and not the developer's. As an alternative to this, designers can formalize trading within the game, including the ability to accept cash payments and transfer that cash to other players.

A more balance-oriented trade issue is whether trades can themselves unbalance the game. For example, in an online game, having an experienced player trading a lot of in-game money and powerful equipment to a low-level player may make that character too strong. One common solution to this is to place additional restrictions on items; for example, a given suit of really cool armor might require that the player be at least Level 25 to wear it, so a Level 3 character might be in possession of it but still have to wait to make use of it.

Examples of Economic Systems

Any combination of production, trading, and consumption mechanics surrounding a particular type of game resource forms the groundwork for an economic system in the game. While this chapter discusses five kinds of common economic systems, this is by no means an exhaustive list. Prestige and F2P systems only recently became commonplace when we consider the history of games. Let's look at some existing examples:

- Single-player computer RPGs such as the *Final Fantasy* or *Dragon Quest* series. In these games, currency is a resource which is produced through grinding. Some permanent and consumable items are purchased in shops for currency, while others may be found through grinding.

Advancement and prestige items do not exist. As a single-player game, trading only exists between the player and NPC agents of the game, so this is a purely command economy. Most resources are theoretically unlimited, although some powerful permanent items may be scarce due to number (only one copy, found in a specific location in the game or featured as a one-time reward for a certain quest) or time (generated as a very rare item drop in a single zone of the game, so the player can find multiples, but it takes much grinding to do so).

- *Candy Crush Saga*. This F2P game has the player going through a series of single-player levels. There is a single premium currency that can be used to buy consumable items, which can assist in helping the player to pass a level. The player can pay cash for premium currency and is also awarded occasional consumable items through play. The levels are tuned to be challenging to win without the use of consumables, but much easier if they are used—when a player loses a level they are usually very close to finishing.

- *Second Life*. This now-defunct game had economic systems that were very different from other MMOs, in that players could design and create their own custom items and then sell them to other players. The game featured a single currency which players could get through the sale of items to other players or by buying it for cash. In this sense, the means of production was entirely player-controlled. As the game didn't feature progression mechanics (it was more of a virtual world than anything else), all items were essentially prestige items.

- *Poker* and other casino and gambling games. These games feature a single currency that can be exchanged for cash in either direction and that is its only means of production—the two-way exchange is, in effect, what differentiates gambling from non-gambling games in the first place. Resource exchange happens between players as a consequence of play.

Discussion Questions

1. What is a closed economic system?
2. What is an open economic system?
3. Select a game with a closed economic system, and imagine that game as an open economic system. How would it change the core gameplay experience, if at all?

4. Discuss ways that a designer might remove money from a game economy? Why might they want to do that?

5. How does inflation occur in a game economy?

6. What is a player-dynamic economic system?

7. Discuss the reasons that F2P designers might ramp players out? Why is it advantageous to do so? Stretch discussion on this point: are there ethical considerations for designers to consider here?

8. How do designers set prices of prestige items?

9. Blizzard removed the auction house from their games. What economic considerations led them to do that?

10. What is the difference between a positive-sum mechanic and a negative-sum mechanic?

Sidequests

In this chapter, we learned about how to apply some basic principles of economics to predict how players react to mechanics that deal with limited resources.

Sidequest 6.1: Fixing Monopoly

In this chapter, we examined the board game *Monopoly* as a case study and identified one game balance problem: the goal is to bankrupt one's opponents, but the game has a positive-sum economy that makes the goal get further away over time, making the game take a potentially very long time. Propose one or more rules changes to fix this imbalance in order to shorten game time.

Sidequest 6.2: Fixing TCG Expansion Sets

One concept discussed in this chapter was inflation and different solutions that could fix it. TCGs, by their nature, suffer from a similar issue: power inflation.

TCGs regularly release new cards, typically in the form of expansion sets. When a new card is added to the play environment, it's either more powerful than previous cards, or about as powerful, or less powerful. If it is less powerful, then it is mostly ignored in competitive play. Ideally, it should be about as powerful. But TCGs are hard to balance perfectly, so every now and then a new card gets released that's slightly more powerful than previous sets, even if this only happens by accident. In this way, over time, the power curve of the game—that is, the average usefulness of a card relative to its cost—increases (we discuss power curves and cost curves in Chapter 8).

As the power curve increases, future expansion sets need to be balanced on the new (increased) curve; if they are balanced on the older power curve, then most cards are too weak relative to the set of "most powerful" cards in all past sets. And the trend continues, with cards getting more powerful over time, forever.

Now, to be fair, this does have the benefit of incentivizing players to buy new cards each time an expansion is released. But the feeling that one has to continue buying just to keep up, that one's old decks are no longer viable at all after a while, can turn away veteran players.

Suppose you wanted to design a TCG where power inflation would not happen in the long term. Knowing what you know about *resource* inflation, how would you apply those lessons to reduce or eliminate *power* inflation?

7

Trading Systems

In This Chapter

- What are Trading Systems?
- What's a Trade?
- Mechanics of Direct Trades
- Mechanics of Gifting
- Mechanics of Auctions
- How Trading Affects Balance
- How Gifting Affects Balance

What Are Trading Systems?

If we go back to the earliest examples of trading that I can think of, whether it's card games, board games or trading items with other players in an online game, there is always the principle of reciprocity. We are trading for mutual benefit. This entire principle was taken to its zenith in the early days of social and casual games. The incredible growth of games like FarmVille and Clash of Clans is entirely dependent on your ability to trade or, in some cases, 'gift' your friends with resources. The concept of trade went from a convenience factor to a means of survival for online games, and the success of their trading systems was core.

a product manager with ten years' experience in mobile games

Chapter 6's introduction to economic systems paves the way for Chapter 7's discussion of trading systems and the mechanics associated with the same, something which has become increasingly important as games continue to go from single-player to multiplayer online persistent worlds.

Why do players trade? If there are multiple resources in a game, it stands to reason that some resources may be more valuable to some players than others. So, games allow players to trade with one another. For instance, in *Monopoly*, if a player has two yellow properties, the third yellow property is going to be way more valuable to them than to someone else.

To facilitate trade between players, games use trading, negotiation, and bartering mechanics within their game economy. Some online game marketplaces take trading to the meta-level. For instance, Steam allows players to trade items from one game for items in another.

A player's desire and need to trade is caused by design. In general, by giving each player an assortment of things and ensuring enough scarcity so that not all players have exactly what they need when they want it, players have a reason to trade with each other. Games can, of course, play up this need/want relationship to affect the amount of trade that happens in a game.

In competitive games, trading inherently acts as a negative feedback loop, especially within a closed economic system. Players are more willing to offer favorable trades to those who are behind, while expecting to get a better deal (or refusing to trade entirely) with those who are ahead of them.

What's a Trade?

What seems like the most superficial question in this book is actually a sincere one. A **trade**, by definition, is when one player trades something they possess to another player in exchange for something the other player possesses. In this definition, note three key things:

- There is prior ownership of a resource, meaning the player could, in theory, do something with this resource if they wanted to, such as selling it, using it, or disposing of it. This resource may be inside the game or outside of it, such as real currency.
- The trade transfers that ownership to someone else.
- Each party in the trade now has ownership of something new to them post-trade which they can likewise do something with.

In games, this definition of trade is typically all we need. However, what if a player gives something away and gets nothing in return? Furthermore, what if the thing they are "giving away" isn't something they own in the first place? In F2P games, that's often the case. In these games, **gifts** are far more common than trades are, and some games actually call them "trades," further confusing the issue. In F2P, when one player gifts something to another (such as ammo, a unit or a rare resource), these rules typically apply:

- There is not prior ownership of the resource being traded. Rather, the player is typically allocated a certain amount of something to give away to other players within a certain period of time (typically a day). If players do not give it away, they cannot use it themselves.
- Players get nothing in return for "gifting" another player. The game may suggest the other player reciprocate from their gift allocation, but it is not required.
- Players can request "gifts" from players not yet playing the game, thus potentially extending the reach of the game and its player base.

Trades and gifts obviously differ from one another. However, in the lexicon of game design discussions, they often co-mingle under the term "give": you give something and sometimes you get something in return. The distinction between trade and gift is important for balance reasons, however, and so, throughout this chapter, when we say "trade," we mean *trade*—you give up something you own to get something someone else owns and ownership is transferred as a result. Where appropriate, we also add analysis of how gifting can affect a game's economy.

Mechanics of Direct Trades

There are many ways to include trading in a game, but simply saying "players can trade" isn't really enough. Sure, it could be left open ended, but it also leaves the designer with far less control over the game. So, designers add mechanics, which turn simple resource trading into interesting and complex decisions. For instance, the card game *Bohnanza* only allows you to trade with the active character on her turn and only during a certain phase of it. These mechanics also give the designer a lot of control over the player experience. Of course, there is no "right" or "wrong" way to design trade in games. In fact, simple and straightforward trading is great in children's games or games which appeal to a mass audience.

What follows in this section is a menu of options for a designer, along with the considerations of how each choice impacts the play experience. The most common elements of direct trades involve limits, information, costs, and futures.

Establishing Limits

Some games allow players to trade but impose limits on that trade. In *Team Fortress 2*, players can trade any items in the game except for milestone achievement weapons or items crafted from the same and other items labeled "Not Usable in Trading." In many RPGs, players can trade items, but they cannot trade XP, levels, stats, or any other details core to the character. In *Minecraft*, players can trade any resources and items, at any time, with no restrictions whatsoever.

There are multiple reasons why limits are placed upon trades. Let's examine some of those reasons.

Prolonging Play

In the card game *Bohnanza* and board game *Catan*, there is a trading phase as part of each player's turn, and trades only happen during that phase. Players may only trade with the active player, which gives that player a trade advantage. By placing restrictions, even fairly light ones, these games maintain some level of tension by forcing players to strategize by planning ahead, prevent a single player from dominating all trade, and encourage players to remain engaged even if it's not their turn.

If games limit the number of potential trade partners, timing of the trade and/or the number of trades, as is the case in many board games (i.e. one trade per turn on your turn or trading only with members of your team), it takes players longer to gather the resources they need and also reduces the game's emphasis on trading and inter-player negotiation. As a result, adding trade restrictions tends to prolong play. We cover the length of play and why a designer would need to change it in Chapter 12.

Preventing Exploitation

As in the real world, where trading exists, so do people willing to take advantage of other people. Games have added mechanics to minimize the effects of scammers. In Steam trading, for instance, items may be placed on hold for up to 15 days, depending on a variety of factors including whether Steam Guard is enabled and whether the players are friends. The goal is to prevent unscrupulous players from taking advantage of other players within the community.

Where casual games are concerned, exploitation was also common, but came in a different form. Players sometimes create dozens of fake accounts within online games so that they can gift between the accounts, accessing loads of extra resources. Since these games are primarily F2P, this essentially cuts into the profits of the game publishers and developers who can't sell what people are gifting for free. Having multiple accounts is a grind of sorts that adds extra consumables to the player's economy at the expense of their time.

Preventing Kingmaking

To prevent unbalancing trades, some games may only allow players to trade a specific amount per day or may prevent them from trading entirely if they are knocked out of the game. This is particularly important in "kingmaking" situations, where one player who is hopelessly behind chooses to trade all of their stuff to another player to let them win (either in exchange for real-world favors, or just as a poor-sport way of ruining the game for everyone else). This book examines kingmaking in more detail in Chapter 12.

Reducing Complexity

Games don't just place restrictions on what can be traded, but also when. For example, in *Monopoly*, trades can take place at any point except when die rolling and movement are actively in progress, because this would otherwise leave open questions about how to handle the timing if property ownership changes hands just as another player is landing on that property. Rather than having extra rules to deal with this special case, simply preventing trades during that critical time keeps the rules simpler without unduly inconveniencing players.

Limited Information

Usually, trades are open: players know exactly what they're trading and also what they're getting in exchange. However, adding some uncertainty to the trades can greatly change how trades feel. In the card game *PIT*, for instance, players are dealt a hand of cards that each has a resource on them, and the goal is to collect all of one type of resource. Players trade matching sets of cards for the same quantity of card from another player. A player may hold out two cards of the same type and shout "TWO!"; another player may trade two matching cards of some other type. But players do not announce what they are trading, only how many cards. Since trades are made blind, players are encouraged to trade frequently. Since players are trying to collect all of a resource, they are also encouraged to trade with a variety of opponents and not just a single trading partner. As the round continues, players tend to consolidate around their preferred resource, and players see more single-card trades and fewer double- or triple-card trades. As trades get more frantic and also progressively more weighted toward only single cards, all players realize that everyone is getting closer to completing their full sets and that the end of the round is very close. This change in play patterns that emerges naturally from the mechanics gives each round a clear progression and gives experienced players a way to read their opponents.

In the board game *Advanced Civilization* (not to be confused with Sid Meier's video game series), players draw resource cards from a random deck every turn which they can exchange for points to purchase technology. Each resource is worth exponentially more points the more resources the player has of that type, so players are encouraged to trade with each other to collect resources of the same type. However, shuffled into the resource cards are a few Calamity cards which do bad things to a player still holding that resource at the end of the turn. Most Calamities can also be traded to opponents, but of course, no opponent is foolish enough to knowingly accept one of these in a trade. To get around this, players may only trade three or more cards at a time, and players are allowed to lie about one card. Thus, a player may claim that they are trading two Fur and one Salt, and really be trading two Fur and a Calamity. This leads to a tense dynamic where players are obligated to trade in order to get enough points to buy the technology they need (technology is part of the game's victory condition), while at the same time putting themselves at risk whenever initiating a trade.

The TV game show *Let's Make a Deal* (which we analyze further in Chapter 18) often asked contestants to make trade decisions blindly. For example, the host might give the player a box with unknown contents, and then offer to trade them for whatever's behind Door Number One. In this case, the player has no idea what is on either end of the trade; it is a game of pure psychology, with the contestant having to decide whether the game show host is offering a good trade or a bad one.

Costs

In some games, a trade actually has a cost associated with it. For instance, in *Warbook*, an early game played on social networks, players send their armies to other players, as either trades or gifts. However, only 90% of the armies sent would ultimately arrive. The cost, then, is the 10% that perished.

The concept of adding a cost to trade has several potential effects:

- It forces more strategic trading in that players are less likely to make trivial trades if they know there is a cost to doing so.
- It provides an economy sink where designers can regularly remove currency from the economy to prevent economy inflation.
- If the cost is a percentage of the total amount, this mechanic reduces the likelihood of large trades since the perceived cost is greater even if the actual costs are still just 10%.
- If the cost is a flat fee, this mechanic discourages small trades and incentivizes larger ones.
- If the cost is time-based, designers can limit the amount of times per day a player can trade to limit exploitation. For example, if players have a trading area where they can offer a trade of their choosing, the developer may choose to only allow players to post a certain number of trades at a time to prevent unscrupulous players from spamming the trade board with bad trades.

Adding costs to trades allows designers to control the flow of resources between players.

Futures

Trading a future favor or future resource for something in the present is known as trading futures. For instance, asking another player to trade you iron now in return for not attacking them the next five turns is an example of futures trading. While most instances of futures trading in games are implicit (not stated in the rules), making them explicit and stating so in the rules gives players additional options when negotiating with each other. They may buy "on credit," give each other loans, offer favorable deals in exchange for specified or unspecified future considerations, or form short-term or long-term pacts or alliances with other players. The ability to make future trades also may make the system more complicated during play if players must remember what they have promised.

The *Sid Meier's Civilization* series offers futures trading between the player and other civilizations within the game. Players or their in-game rivals offer non-aggression treaties hoping to gain access to a new tech, to stave off imminent destruction, or to maintain an uneasy (and sometime brief) peace between the two groups. Sometimes, the trade is an either/or scenario: give me this tech now or face certain destruction. The game remembers the trade and attempts to enforce it. For instance, if players receive a tech from the Spanish in exchange for five turns of peace, they are not allowed to attack them until those five turns have passed. Sometimes, however, players break their agreements. In some games in the Civilization series, if players agree to peace with another civilization without a goodwill trade, they may immediately break that truce on their turn. There is a penalty, however. All computer opponents (not just the one they lied to) reduce their willingness to be diplomatic with the offending player. A player who breaks a truce finds trades and future treaties harder to come by as a result.

If the rules of the game state that all future trades made between players must be carried out once agreed to, this makes players more likely to make future offers. As designers, of course, we must then implement a means to report and resolve disputes. Is there a simple way to record deals made, so that players who forget the exact details can find them? Is there a means to mark the deal as closed? For most games, these extra steps aren't necessary, as deals between players tend to be simple and implicit (remembered by the player and not by the game). However, if it comes up frequently because the nature of your game encourages players to make many complex ongoing deals, further in-game tools for players may be necessary. These kinds of implementation details are the primary reason why future trades are more common in tabletop than digital games.

If future trades are non-binding – that is, players can simply refuse to live up to their end of the deal – this obviously makes such trades more dangerous for players to accept. When a player does break their promise, that can be frustrating for the other player, and it can carry some very real-world negative feelings of mistrust and betrayal. One well-known example is the board game *Diplomacy*, where players first negotiate with one another about where they intend to move, in a completely non-binding way, and then write down and reveal their actual moves. The game is notorious for destroying friendships,[1] specifically because players are not only able to backstab one another, but the mechanics of the game virtually require that they do so. In some cases, the tension of having a threat of betrayal may be the point of the game and

---

[1] Regarding the "destroying friendships" comment, we mean this literally. This line was flagged as a potential exaggeration, but a post on Facebook asking game designers if they had, in fact, seen friendships destroyed revealed that the majority had. A friend of Brenda's specifically noted that he does not play *Diplomacy* with friends. Ian suggests that any designer interested in negotiation mechanics play this game to see it in action, but that they play it either with such dear friends that even a horrendous betrayal would not harm the relationship or with complete strangers, but not with relations between these extremes.

exactly the kind of dynamic that the designer wants. In other cases, the non-binding nature of future trades just means that players tend to not offer or accept them or that the social nature of the game causes players to naturally keep their promises (under threat of universal retaliation by all other players otherwise). Most online games advise players to trade with caution and at their own risk, and note that all in-game trades between players are final.

Mechanics of Gifting

Gifting is a term used in games to describe the transfer of an item that the players do not own to another player.[2] As mentioned earlier in this chapter, in many F2P games, players may give other players a resource that they don't actually have possession of themselves. For instance, in the mobile game *Merge Dragons*, each day a player may give up to five other players a random gift which they can collect the next time they play. If the player chooses not to give away these things, they don't get to use them for themselves or save them up for later. They just go to waste, effectively, since the next day brings five more resources for gifting. Because the players can't use the resources themselves, they are encouraged to give them away daily in hopes that others reciprocate in kind. In other similar games, players can sometimes request specific resources from their friends which don't come from their friend's pool of resources but are nonetheless given to the player if the friend agrees to the request.

In this way, gifting is designed not as a conduit for players to move things between one another but rather to promote virality and strengthen retention. As such, gifting in F2P games doesn't work the same way as trading or even giving a gift in other games or real life. Most of the differences come down to possession and intention. If you give a gift in real life, you have possession of the gift until you give it to the other person.

Strengthening Retention

The design of these gifting mechanics encourages players to come back on a regular schedule (usually once per day) to dole out their daily allotment of gifts. This is known as an **appointment mechanic** (players have an

---

[2]There are also situations in some games where players may use direct-trade mechanics and trade something for nothing, essentially giving away an item that they *do* own—whether for future considerations or just out of kindness. While this may also be called "gifting" when it happens, in this chapter we're specifically referring to "gifts" that are created out of nothing.

appointment to come back at a specific time). Typically, the more you give, the more you get. Games that allow gifting also make for easy reciprocation. "You received a box of ammo from Ian. Say thanks and send him a box of ammo back!" The timing of the gift resource is geared toward promoting day-to-day retention. Furthermore, designers know that the bigger your social network in a game, the more likely you are to continue playing it.

Promoting Virality

Typically, the resource that players can gift is rare enough that players communicate outside of the game in an effort to get real-world friends to sign up and play, thus strengthening their gifting network. So powerful is this mechanic that many online communities around these games have whole threads devoted to "add me." This virality is particularly important in mobile F2P games since the cost of acquisition of new players continues to spiral toward prohibitive levels. As of this writing, the cost of acquisition per paying player is upwards of $2.50 each. So, any new players which come in organically through such mechanics prove that those mechanics are quite valuable.

Mechanics of Auctions

An auction is a special kind of trade that is common in games. In an auction, one or more resources are offered to a group of players, with each player bidding their own resources in exchange for whatever is being auctioned. The players or the game itself may be offering the items for auction. When something comes from the game, by definition, it's not a "trade" in the formal sense, but rather enters the game economy as a form of "production."

Like other forms of trade, auctions work best when the resources in the game have different value to each player, particularly if the value is situational. A thief's blade is obviously worth more to a thief than to a mage. It's worth even more if the thief's old blade just broke.

As noted in the previous chapter on game economies, each person in an economic system has a maximum amount that they are willing to pay for any given resource. An auction is a pure form of determining each player's willingness to pay, because each player in the auction must decide what price they are willing to buy at and then bid for the item accordingly. There can also be meta-strategies for bidding: a player might not only think of how much they want the auctioned items for themselves, but also whether they'd like to buy it to avoid letting an opponent get it because it is too powerful in their hands, or even whether it's worth bidding up the price in the hopes that an opponent pays more for it than they would have otherwise.

Ideally, a seller would like an item in an auction to fetch the highest price possible, i.e., the maximum amount that any player is willing to pay. In most cases, however, an auction actually gets a lower price than that: commonly the second-highest price that any player is willing to pay or very slightly higher. This may seem counterintuitive, but it is explained below.

Suppose there are four bidders in an auction, Ayla, Brock, Celes, and Dalamar. They respectively have a willingness to pay a maximum of $1, $2, $5, and $20. Once the auction price gets as high as $5.01, Dalamar is the only bidder willing to buy it at that price, but not knowing what the others are going to bid, he says $8 and wins the auction at that price. If all bidders had perfect information about each other's willingness to pay, Dalamar would have walked away with the win for $5.01. With imperfect information, as in the case of this auction, the actual auction price is usually higher, but it would still likely be far below the $20 that Dalamar would accept.

When designing auctions, designers take into consideration whether they want to emphasize buying or selling, and what kinds of strategies they want players to employ: negotiation between players as they haggle with one another during the auction; bluffing as the players cajole, wheedle, and extort their opponents; or value calculation as each player tries to weigh the value of the item(s) up for auction to themselves and to their opponents to come up with their personal maximum bid. Some mechanics can even incentivize or disincentivize high bids, or even bidding at all, which then determines how often players engage with the game's auction mechanics. There are many other mechanics that can be added on or combined with other auctions to create a different result. Some of these mechanics are detailed below, to give you an idea of just how broad the design palette can be for auctions.

Setting Time Limits

An auction may involve a time limit to keep things moving and add additional time pressure to players. In an open auction with a time limit, the winner is the highest bid before time runs out. This makes it more difficult for players to do a perfect value calculation in their head and allows for extra tension as the timer elapses and last-minute bids get thrown.

Setting Reserve Prices

An item for an auction may have a **reserve price** which can be either made known to the bidders or hidden. If the highest bid is lower than the reserve, no one wins the auction. This can give players incentive to bid higher to start than they normally would, out of the fear of a wasted bid – particularly if there is a cost to bidding or if the number of bids is sharply limited.

Setting Buyout Prices

An item may also have a buyout price, where any bidder can immediately pay that price to end the auction and win the item. If no one pays the buyout price, the winner of the auction is determined normally instead. Depending on the timing rules for the auction, this can give every player a chance at winning it at any time, or it can allow early bidders to deny the item to later ones if they're willing to pay up, giving an extra layer of meta-strategy to the auction.

Setting Negative Effects

An item may have a detrimental rather than positive effect, and players may be bidding to avoid getting stuck with that effect (a **negative auction**). If auctioning multiple items as a group with some of them positive and some negative, players have to weigh the consequences of bidding at all.

For a series of auctions, if winning too many in a row is deemed unfairly powerful, the designer may add a negative feedback loop, such as giving a bonus on subsequent auctions to the players who didn't win or a penalty to the player who did. Usually, this isn't necessary, as the loss of resources paid upon winning an auction is sufficient. However, if the items being auctioned give the winners more resources with which to win future auctions, this can create a positive feedback loop that requires negative feedback to counteract its effects.

Limiting Information

The items themselves may or may not be known to the players. If some or all of the results of an auction are hidden information until the auction ends, bidding becomes more of a probability problem and less a problem of determining the actual value. If the contents up for auction are privileged information that is known to some players but not all, there can even be an element of bluffing, where the players who don't know the item may watch the ones that do to see if they are bidding high or low and then follow suit accordingly.

Enabling Sellers to Bid

There are some situations where the seller may be permitted to place a bid on their own item. In the card game *Modern Art*, players take turns each putting an item up for auction as the seller. Normally, the seller collects the money from the winning bidder; however, the seller may bid on their own work and pay the proceeds to the bank instead. This is usually a poor strategy (the seller is better off getting money from another player), but allows the seller a way to keep their item cheaply if other players are bidding significantly less than what the seller believes the item's true value is.

Auction Formats

Just as there are many kinds of trading, there are also many kinds of rules governing an auction including an open auction, fixed-price auction, circle auction, silent auction, and Dutch auction. Each offers different potential gameplay dynamics in both analog and digital games.

Open Auction   The best known type of auction is the **open auction**. It's the most common kind of auction on eBay, for instance. Any player may make a bid at any time, as long as it is higher than the previous bid. This all happens in real time with no one taking turns. Eventually no one is willing to raise the bid further, and the most recent high bid wins the auction. In an open auction, as soon as the bid exceeds the second-highest willingness to pay, it is sold to the top bidder. On eBay, there is a time limit, of course. The classic auctioneer call of "going once, going twice, sold!" is indicative of an open auction.

Circle Auction   A **circle auction** is turn-based and requires a turn order. In this auction, each player can either choose to make a bid (which must be higher than the previous bid, if any) or pass. Circle auctions are relatively common in analog games, but not so in digital ones. In one variant of a circle auction, the bid goes around the table only once, with the final player deciding whether to bid higher than the current highest bid, or letting the highest previous bidder win the auction; this gives an advantage to the last player, since it essentially becomes a fixed price auction for them (see next section). In another variant, the bid continues to go around until all players pass, which gives a slight advantage to earlier bidders (if the top two bidders have the exact same maximum willingness to pay, the first one to bid that amount gets the item). In this second variant, there is the additional consideration of whether players who passed previously can bid again on a subsequent round. Allowing this can increase the tension of an auction near the end, where it's possible that anyone could raise the bid even higher (and it essentially turns the auction into a slower-paced open auction), but it does make the auction take longer. An example of a game that allows bidding after passing is *Contract Bridge*, where bidding is not only an attempt to win an auction, but also a way for a player to give information about their hand to their partner.

Fixed-Price Auction   As you might guess, a **fixed-price auction** is where the seller sets a price and waits for a buyer to accept it. It is the most common type of auction in video games. The original auction house in *World of Warcraft* used fixed-price rules. Fixed-price auctions may be done in real time on a first-come-first-served approach (more like a sale than an auction, although you may see a "Buy It Now!" button on auction websites like eBay), or they may be done turn-based where each player in turn order is given the option to purchase or decline, and it goes around until someone accepts or everyone declines. In the turn-based version, this does give an advantage to the first player, who gets the option before anyone else. If it's offered at less than that player's maximum willingness to pay, they get to pay at less than they would have otherwise. This type of auction is interesting in that depending on how well the seller chooses the price, it can be either the most or least efficient of the bunch. In our earlier four-bidder example, if the seller chose a fixed price of $20, Dalamar would still buy it and they would get the maximum possible amount for the item; but if the seller chose a price of $1, even Ayla would buy it, and the seller would receive far less than they would in any other type of auction. As such, a fixed-price auction requires multiple layers of strategy for the seller, in trying to anticipate the highest price they can get away with given their knowledge of the other players' needs. This type of auction is a lot more interesting (and treacherous) as the seller than as the buyer—the reverse of most auction types.

Silent Auction   In a **silent auction** (or blind auction), all bidders choose a bid secretly and simultaneously. The bids are all revealed at once, with the highest bid winning. Silent auctions are very common in analog games and digital recreations of them. This type of auction has some interesting psychological qualities to it: players are not only thinking about their own maximum willingness to pay, but also that of the other bidders. In our four-bidder example, if Dalamar knows that the item is much more valuable to him than to the others, he may bid significantly less than $20 for the item because he expects other players' bids to be low, such that he can still bid low and expect to win (and Dalamar's opponents, anticipating this, might bid a nominal amount just to keep Dalamar honest). Note that silent auctions always need some mechanism for resolving ties, since it is possible for two or more bidders to choose the same highest bid. This may be as simple as a coin flip or using turn order or some other mechanism as a tiebreaker, or as psychout-inducing as ignoring ties and giving the auction to the highest unique bid (e.g. if there are bids of 8, 8, 6, 5, and 3, the person with the highest unique bid of six wins). The card game *Fist of Dragonstones* is essentially a series of silent auctions, where most auctions either give a player one or more stones or else allow a player to convert some of their stones into victory points, and resolves ties with a second silent auction among the tied players using a special tiebreaker-only currency (and if players tie again in the tiebreaker round, they lose their bids and no one gets the item).

Dutch Auction   A rare type of auction in games is a **Dutch auction**, which is lesser known because its classic form requires special equipment in the form of a countdown timer that's marked with currency amounts. In this auction, an item starts at a high fixed price (hopefully chosen to be higher than anyone's maximum willingness to pay), and then, a timer counts the price down at a fixed rate, e.g. dropping by $1 per second or per turn. At any time, any bidder can stop the counter and pay the current price. The advantage of this auction to the seller is that once the price hits the top willingness to pay of all bidders, they should accept and thus this auction is one of the most efficient. However, if bidders are able to look at each other in real time to figure out who is becoming interested and who isn't, there may be some bluffing involved as players try to wait as long as possible. The card game *Queen's Necklace* features cards with costs that start high and get reduced every time a player doesn't buy them, a turn-based form of a Dutch auction that avoids the need for special equipment. The classic videogame *M.U.L.E.* features a multiplayer trading system that is similar to a Dutch auction, with the added wrinkle that the seller doesn't merely drop the price over time, but can also increase the price or keep it the same at their discretion.

Quantity of Items Up for Auction

As you can see, there are many types of auction formats, with each one having its own general efficiency in terms of extracting maximum value from the bidders, and also each one having its own feel and progression of rising and falling tension. Even once you decide on a format for an auction, there are a number of ways to auction items when there's more than one item to auction. These include single item auctions, multiple item auctions, and item drafts.

Single Item   The most common method of auctioning is to put a single item up for auction at a time. The top bidder receives the item, and the other bidders get nothing. If multiple items are being auctioned, these are done in succession. Bidders may wait out high prices in an auction, hoping for an increased supply to lower demand and thus lower prices. Likewise, they may snipe items they perceive are exceptionally good deals. In digital games, bidders have no knowledge of how many other players are considering a particular item. In analog games, bidders with limited resources may delay or try to get others to spend more on auctions that do not matter as much to them, so that they have more money to spend on the auctions that help them the most. This type of sequential single-item auctions can also lead to different behaviors based on whether the players know what other items are coming up for auction in the future or are actively being auctioned simultaneously vs. whether the future items are unknown such as being drawn from a shuffled deck or put up for auction at an unspecified later date by players unknown. If known, that encourages players to plan ahead and only change their plans if they unexpectedly win or lose a particular item; if unknown, it encourages more calculated risk-taking, as players do not know if the upcoming items are more or less valuable than the one currently up for bid.

Multiple Items   Items can be auctioned in a group (sometimes called **auctioning in a lot**). The items are bid on as a group, all of which go to the top bidder. This increases the stakes, but can also draw interest from a wider variety of players if the auction includes some items that are useful to each player and others that are not. The board games *Ra* and *Medici* both involve auctioning multiple items at once, with added restrictions that players have some control over how many items to auction at once, so that the auctioneer might keep an individual lot small if it contains things that they (and only they) want or make it larger if they want to induce a bidding war between several opponents. Digital games that offer auctions in lots typically restrict the lot to being multiple items of the same type for ease of UI design.

Item Draft   Another method is an item draft, where there are a set of items and the winner of the auction has the right to choose one item for themselves; then, the second-highest bidder chooses a remaining item, then the third-highest bidder chooses another remaining item, and so on. If the number of items is equal to the number of players, this may mean that the lowest bidder gets the one item no one else wanted (this may give players incentive to bid zero, since they still get something for free). If the number of items is less than the number of players, so that one or more low bidders get nothing, that is a stronger encouragement for disinterested players to at least bid some nominal amount to avoid getting stuck with no item at all. If there are more items than the number of players, then bidding zero may be even more tempting, as the last player gets not just a single unwanted item, but a choice of several. Also if there are more items than the number of players, the items not chosen by anyone may be discarded; or they may stay around and go up for auction again next time; or they may be given to the high bidders as the draft goes around several times, and each of these offers different considerations that will change typical player behaviors.

While not an auction *per se*, in *Magic: The Gathering*, booster drafts are a popular form of play. In a booster draft, each player opens a pack, takes a card of their choice, and then passes the remains of that pack to the next player. The result is that each player gets first choice at least once. In raiding in MMOs, it's also common for players to employ a form of drafting for loot drops. Drafting on its own without auctions can also appear in games as its own mechanic, typically where either players draft simultaneously (each from their own selection) or players draft from a common pool in turn-based fashion (and in this case, typically, the ability to draft first for the next round is one of the things that can be chosen in the current round).

Payment in Auctions

As if there aren't already enough options for a game designer to consider when adding auction mechanics to a game, there is also the question of what happens to the resources that are bid during the course of the auction.

Winner Pays   For a single item auction, the most common method is that the top bidder pays their bid, and the other players spend nothing. This makes bidding relatively safe: a player only pays if they get something in return.

All Pay   Another possibility, common in item draft and occasionally seen in silent auctions, is where all players pay their bid, regardless of who won. If players can only win a single item, this makes players more hesitant to bid at all (because of the desire to not "waste" resources on a bid that doesn't win). For important auctions, players may tend to bid extremely high, even if everyone else bids zero. Conversely, occasionally players may make very small bids when hoping to get an item for cheap if everyone else bids zero.

Some Pay   There are variants where some, but not all, players pay their bid. Depending on who pays and who doesn't, this can deeply affect the dynamics and bidding strategy. For example, if the top two players pay their bid (where top bidder gets an item and second-highest bidder gets nothing), making low or medium non-zero bids becomes dangerous and puts a bid at risk of causing the player to lose resources for no gain. Here, the strategy is to do what other players do not: if a player thinks others plan to bid high, then they'll bid zero and avoid losing anything; if other players are anticipated to bid zero, then the player bids a small amount to win the auction cheaply; and if other players are bidding small amounts, the player bids high to win (or zero if they don't want the item). This kind of variant also has a very different feel depending on the auction format. In a silent auction, players are never sure of what the opponents are bidding, so the final reveal is a high-tension high-stakes moment. With an open auction, things can get out of hand quickly, as each of the top two bidders may be better off paying the marginal cost of outbidding their opponent than losing the current amount they have bid. Consider, for example, an auction where the top bid gets $1.00 and the second-highest bid gets nothing. If current high bidder Edward offers $0.99 and the next highest bidder Fiora offered $0.98, it is worth it for Fiora to offer $1.00 (even though winning at that price would simply break even, because it is better to break even than to lose $0.98). At that point, it is ironically better for Edward to bid $1.01, because losing one cent is better than losing 99 cents. And then, Fiora is better off bidding $1.02, and so on, up to infinity.

Other Variations Bidders don't necessarily have to pay their own bids. Another option is that the top bidder of an auction wins, but pays the second-highest bid. The field of game theory tells us, through some math that need not be repeated here, that in a silent auction where the top bidder pays the second-highest bid, the best strategy is for all bidders to bid their own maximum willingness to pay (and the seller then sells the item at the second-highest maximum willingness to pay, which as we have already seen is typical for most auction formats).

Another variant has all players paying the difference between their bid and the next highest bid below them (with the lowest bidder simply paying their bid, i.e., the difference between their bid and zero). Here, the seller still gets the amount of the highest bid, same as with a standard auction where the winner pays everything, but in this case, the price is distributed among all bidders, and the players paying the most may not be the one that got the item. To work around the perceived injustice of a high bidder paying next to nothing while the losers shoulder the major burden, there could also be the additional rule that top bidder pays their entire bid, and it is only those who don't win who pay extra.

Yet another possibility is to only have the top and bottom bidders pay their bid (where the top bidder wins the item, and the bottom bidder just loses their bid for no gain). If players can bid zero, this may make low bids feel safe (since there is always the possibility that another player bids and pays zero). If players must all bid something, there is a strong incentive to bid at least a moderate amount, to decrease the likelihood of losing even if the player doesn't expect to win.

Another option is that all players pay their bids except the lowest bidder (or the lowest several bidders). This gives players an incentive to bid either really high or really low, and it is the moderate bids that are risky. As you can see, the mechanics of who pays (and how much they pay) can be chosen to emphasize or de-emphasize certain types of bidding strategies to encourage the game dynamics you wish to see.

Where Does the Money Go?

In addition to considering who pays and who doesn't, there is also the question of where that money goes. It may be paid to the "bank," that is, the resources are removed from the economy which leads to deflation. It may be paid to some kind of holding area that collects auction proceeds, which can then be distributed to players at a later time. The proceeds may be paid to other players (typically but not always those who are auctioning the items), thus making the auction zero sum with respect to the game economy.

Underbidding

What happens to the item(s) up for auction if there are no bids? If the auction has a time limit, the item is removed from the auction and returned to the player's inventory. The player may choose to relist the item at the same price or a lower price hoping to attract a buyer.

As an alternative, an auction with no bids can have additional items or incentives added to the pool, and then repeated until at least one player finally decides it is worthwhile to open the bidding.

The item may also be given away if it draws no bids. It could be that one player gets the item for free or some minimal cost. If that player is known in advance to all bidders, it gives everyone else incentive to bid at least a nominal amount to prevent that player from getting a free item. If the player is unknown, such as the case where the item is given out to a random player if there are no bids, players may be more likely to not bid in the hopes of getting lucky.

If one of the players is the seller, they may be forced to buy it (or keep it). If they pay a penalty for doing so, this gives sellers incentive to offer items that other players perceive as valuable enough to bid on.

The unwanted item can also just be thrown out, with no one getting it, and the game proceeding forward from there as if the auction never happened.

How Trading Affects Balance

How can trading and the mechanics of the same affect game balance? Simply, trades open what is otherwise a closed game economy and introduce a degree of unpredictability into an economy and its balance. Players find exploits, buy time, and have that very behavior incentivized. This doesn't mean games should avoid trade, of course. It just means that as designers, we need to be mindful of the opportunities we introduce when we allow trading and gifting.

Players Buy Time

Games are often about the grind, and the grind requires time. If there is a means to shorten that time, players are often willing to pay for it. That's the whole basis of many free-to-play games. In games where "**pay to rush**" isn't allowed and where players can trade with one another, players may use the trade function to trade money for time. Purchasing in-game gold in *World of Warcraft* for cash which is exchanged outside the game system is just one example. This has the effect of incentivizing currency miners who then introduce much more gold into the economy than they, themselves, are spending. To address these issues, some games have simply removed auctions, while others have introduced a performance economy outside the main cash economy so that players are rewarded only for actions within the game and not merely by what they can afford.

Players Look for Exploits

If there is a means for a system to be exploited, eventually players find it, and once having found it, word spreads online like wildfire until the exploit is fixed or shut down. A simple search of "game exploit" turns up thousands of valid search results. Many exploits involve item duplication. Having doubles and triples of the same sword is not useful for players, particularly if items cannot be sold within the in-game economy. However, if the player is duplicating fire bombs or healing potions that can be used or traded to other players, it is valuable. Another method of exploitation opened up by trade is the creation of duplicate accounts. Players use the duplicate account as a farm of sorts, trading its items to the main account. This was a particular problem for games on Facebook during their heyday. Players would create alternate accounts and use their increased "friend network" for the purpose of gifting back and forth.

Players Are Encouraged to Trade

If trading is allowed in a game and even encouraged through scarcity, players become a conduit of item value rather than a hoarder or a garbage bin. Through trade, players are encouraged to participate in the game's economy and with one another. This is particularly important when players are able to incentivize participation of new players in a game by being incentivized themselves (the more friends they have, the larger their trading network is). From an economy perspective, more players in the game increase both the potential demand for particular game resources as well as the supply of them if players are allowed to mine or craft. When other players are allowed to affect the overall economy of their fellow players, the game has an added level of strategy, decision-making, and attachment.

Players Have a Mind of Their Own

Players are predictably unpredictable. When one of the authors of this book started *World of Warcraft* years ago, a high-level character suddenly gifted her with far more in-game currency than she could have collected in a week's worth of play at her given level. While this had zero effect on the currency economy of the game (the total currency in the game remained the same), it had tremendous effects on the play balancing of the game for her. Items that were out of reach were now affordable. This would have been even more interesting if *WoW*'s auction house were still available. How can a game designer mitigate the effects of such things? In *WoW*'s case, items have particular requirements for use. So, even if a player could afford a ridiculously impressive item, there's no guarantee that they can actually use the item. Designers can also gate items in other ways, so that a lower-level player would be able to purchase a whole lot of low-level items which, all in all, wouldn't do them a whole lot of good. Even taking such measures into account, opening your game to trade means that you have to be both watchful and mindful of the immense goodwill and interesting behaviors it welcomes.

How Gifting Affects Balance

In F2P games, gifting is a common mechanic to encourage players to create a community around them in which they can both give and receive an important resource in the game. It helps the game grow its player base and improve its day-to-day retention. Without limits, however, it could affect the game's overall monetization. For instance, let's say that iron bars are the most important limited resource in the game. You need them to do just about anything. If players can send unlimited amounts of iron bars to their friends, there is no need for them to purchase iron bars from game's premium store. Two friends can work together to send each other all they need every day. So, games typically place limits on the amount of gifts a player can give to another player in a single day. These daily limits encourage players to expand their network so that they can't rely on a single friend for their resource needs.

Discussion Topics

1. Select a game and identify the various types of trading available to players.
2. What are the pros and cons of introducing an auction into a game?
3. How does limited information affect trading? Give an example of its use or potential use in an existing game.
4. In what ways is trading different in an online game vs. an analog game?
5. Other than providing a mechanism which allows players to trade, how can designers encourage trade?
6. Other than removing the option to trade, how can players discourage trade within a game?
7. Why would designers want to encourage trade?
8. Why would designers want to discourage trade?
9. What are the differences between trading and gifting?
10. Choose any game that has some kind of trading or auction mechanic. Now choose a different kind of trading or auction, from the mechanics presented in this chapter. If you wanted to replace the existing mechanic with your new chosen one, how would you do it, and what effect do you think it would have on the game?

Sidequests

In this chapter, we saw many ways for resources to be transferred between players, through trading, negotiation, and auction. While these are common activities in games, you hopefully have an appreciation for just how many options there are for the designer to customize the play experience through the mechanics of trade.

Sidequest 7.1: Multiplayer Auction Chaos

Design the mechanics for an eight-player auction, where four players are buyers and four players are sellers. Assume each seller has one resource they are trying to get top dollar for, so they can each sell to only a single buyer. Assume that the resources are equivalent, so each seller has exactly the same item as the other three sellers. Assume that a single buyer may buy from multiple sellers, or none at all, but that buyers generally want to purchase for as low a price as possible.

In considering your options, think about whether you want buyers or sellers (or neither) to have an advantage. Also think about the play experience: what mechanics make for an interesting, boring, tense, or frustrating experience for some buyers or sellers?

Sidequest 7.2: The Trading Game

Take a handful of nearby objects of various types: paper clips, coins, colored glass stones, index cards, or whatever you happen to have on hand. Count out six each of five different objects. Using only these components, design a game for five players where the objects are distributed randomly and evenly at the start of the game, and the only mechanism for acquiring new objects is in trading with other players. You need to provide a goal, the mechanics that govern what kinds of trades are or aren't allowed, and what information is public or hidden. Make the game interesting, and design it in such a way that no player is likely to be advantaged or disadvantaged just from their own starting resource distribution (or, design this to be a very short experience and then play multiple rounds, so that the luck of a single distribution evens out over time).

Alternate challenge: Instead of six each of five different objects, use four, five, six, seven, and eight of each type of object, respectively. This makes some objects more rare than others and introduces some inherent inequality that you have to balance.

8

Transitivity and Cost Curves

In This Chapter

- Transitivity
- Costs and Benefits
- Cost Curves
- Peaks and Valleys
- Supporting Math
- Creating the Cost Curve for player vs. environment (PvE) Games
- Creating the Cost Curve for player vs. player (PvP) Games
- Creating the Supporting Math
- New Games
- Expanding Cost Curves For Existing Games
- Analyzing and Studying Existing Analog Games
- Analyzing and Studying Existing Digital Games
- Analyzing and Studying Free to Play Games
- Cost Curve Guidelines

Transitivity

> You get what you pay for.
>
> *Brenda's mother*

A key part of game balance is finding an anchor as discussed in Chapter 5. Anchors are a critical part of our balance foundation, of course, a starting point from which we build as we continue to develop the content necessary for the game. Transitive mechanics[1] are the means by which we do that.

"You get what you pay for" is the hallmark of transitivity. A transitive item list, for example, is one where some things are better than others, but they cost more. The same is true of many things in games including spells, DLC, armor, weapons and power ups. Similarly, the more difficult something is, the more we expect to be rewarded for it, with either a rare drop, higher experience points, or an achievement of some sort. Balancing transitive data in games means figuring out what each thing should cost, so that the costs have some kind of relation to the benefit it provides. In referring to "data," we mean all the numbers that come together to bring a game object like a monster to life: it has 2000 HP, does 60–80 damage per hit, may hit one or two times per turn, has 87 AC, and so on. These numbers pass through mechanics in a system and produce transitive outcomes.

Many types of games have transitive data. For example,

- In RPGs (*Final Fantasy, Dragon Quest*), costs of items bought in stores is usually transitive: the more powerful a sword, armor, or potion, the higher the cost. Leveling is also transitive: the higher a character's level, the more powerful that character tends to be and the more experience points it takes to reach the next level.
- In FPSs with progression mechanics where a player upgrades their weapons or abilities (*BioShock, Borderlands*), the more powerful upgrades typically cost more.
- In Sim games (*The Sims, Sim City*), the various objects available for purchase have costs, and generally, the more expensive, the more useful or powerful.
- In Tower Defense games (*Desktop Tower Defense, Kingdom Rush*), the upgrades for an individual tower are transitive: higher levels of upgrades cost more but make that tower better at what it does.
- In trading card games (*Magic: the Gathering, Hearthstone*), individual cards usually have some kind of cost to play, and the more resources it takes to put a card into play, the better the effect from playing it.

---

[1]We borrow the term **transitive** from the field of mathematics. Transitive relationships are those where, if two elements A and B have this relationship, and a third element C has the same relationship with A, C must also have that relationship with B. Equality is transitive: if $A = B$ and $B = C$, then $A = C$. Inequalities are also transitive: if $A < B$ and $B < C$, then $A < C$. The game *Rock-Paper-Scissors* is not transitive: Rock beats Scissors, Scissors beats Paper, but Rock does not beat Paper. While "transitive" and "intransitive" are not terms widely used among game designers, we use them in this book to make the distinction, since these types of mechanics are balanced differently.

- In retro arcade games (*Space Invaders*, *Asteroids*), the scoring rules are transitive. The more dangerous or difficult it is to defeat an enemy, the more points a player gets for doing so.
- In professional sports (*Football*, *Baseball*), better athletes demand higher salaries, and better teams tend to cost more money when they are sold to a new owner.
- For that matter, in real life, a higher price tag on some good or service often implies it is of higher quality in some way.

When balancing a game with transitive data, an ideal anchor is often the resource cost of each item, whether that resource is dollars, gold, mana, experience points, or something else. Recall from Chapter 5 that very different game elements can be compared directly by using an anchor that all others can be related to. There, we used the victory condition or loss condition of a game. For games with transitive data, the resources used to acquire stuff offers a third option. We use that anchor and scale all the other data along with it to develop a mathematical relationship between what the item costs and what it does for you, referred to as a **cost/power curve** (or sometimes just a **power curve** or **cost curve**—these terms are used interchangeably by designers, and in this book, we'll mostly refer to them as cost curves). If a lesser sword costs $300, we would expect a sword that does double that amount of damage to cost $600, all other things being equal. This chapter details how to create a cost curve for your game and how to use it to balance various objects in your game against one another.

Costs and Benefits

We can describe each element of an object's data as having a set of **costs** and a set of **benefits**. The costs include the resource cost to acquire the thing, but also more generally, any other negative aspects, such as drawbacks or limitations. The benefits, meanwhile, are anything good or useful or beneficial to the person or character acquiring the item. Benefits are the reason they want the thing in the first place.

Some attributes are a gray area that could be thought of as either a cost or a benefit. Suppose a sword does double damage against dragons. Is that a benefit (higher damage in vs. dragons) or a limitation (it gets only regular damage against all other enemies despite its increased cost)? What about gun that fires at a slow rate compared to other available weapons (an obvious drawback), but which does more damage (an obvious benefit)? This cost-benefit relationship is obvious when creating characters in RPGs—each archetype has its own strengths and weakness. There is a cost you pay for the benefit of those strengths—the weaknesses! As designers, our goal is to make sure there is a defined numeric relationship between costs and benefits; it doesn't matter exactly how we view something—a cost in some cases while a benefit in others—as long as the sum of everything balances out between other like objects. For example, in a game with multiple characters to choose from, players expect those characters to each be about as strong as the others, over-all, when you take into account all their strengths and weaknesses together; whether a particular limitation on a special ability is counted in the "costs" column of your spreadsheet or a reduction of the value in the "benefits" col-umn doesn't matter as long as it comes out to the desired result.

Cost Curves

While its relatively easy to grok the concept of balanced transitive data in a single item (if it's powerful, it better be worth more or have something to offset that power) or even among a small group of objects (the player's start-ing character choices have different strengths and weaknesses), it is the game designer's task to figure out how these relationships—all the data relation-ships across the whole game, sometimes thousands of data points—form a cohesive, balanced experience for the player. For example, how is it that in well-balanced games, you have the opportunity to get the right weapon at *just* the right time to meet the rising challenge the monsters? Furthermore, when you get the loot drop or experience points, as a player, it just feels right. Obviously, it's not a coincidence. This happens by design. Ask any game designer who's wrangled these numeric relationships from beginning to end, and they'll tell you the same thing: it is simultaneously exciting, fun, cool, and daunting.

How are these relationships—weapons, creatures, characters, loot drops, etc.—made meaningful to one another? We can see the relationship using cost curves and the intersections between them.

To do so, it is first necessary to state both the costs and benefits of any object in terms of numbers. Game designers typically start with a single object that they declare to be balanced. Now, in reality, it's only balanced because the designer says it is. However, if we shape all other things to it, in fact, we will have achieved a first pass at a balanced game, since these items are about equal in power level relative to each other.

There are four general approaches to creating a cost curve, depending on the type of game and nature of the relationship:

- In competitive games (referred to as **PvP**, short for "player vs. player") where the various game objects have costs, it's often simplest to use an identity curve (see Chapter 4) as the relationship between costs and benefits: one point of costs=one point of benefits, and an item is balanced if the total costs equal the total benefits. For games like TCGs and MOBAs where players accumulate in-game resources and spend them to purchase items to help them, this method keeps the math easy to do and to conceptualize.

- For PvP games where the game objects do *not* have costs, such as fighting/brawling games or MMOs where players control a single character and different characters have their own sets of strengths and weaknesses, you can still treat costs and benefits as equal-but-opposite (one point of costs counterbalances one point of benefits), but it may feel odd to try to get everything to add to zero, since you generally want characters to feel useful and powerful, with more strengths than weaknesses. In this case, you'd use the same method as above, except "balanced" might be a constant positive number instead of zero. Once you make a single character that you consider balanced, figure out what their benefits minus their cost is numerically—maybe it's 50 points—and then, balance every other character so that they too add up to 50 points.

- Other games are either single player or cooperative, guiding the player through a game experience where enemies or obstacles are controlled by the computer or the game system (these are referred to as **PvE**, short for "player vs. environment"). These games may still have objects with costs: weapons for sale in shops in a computer RPG, for example, where the player finds progressively more powerful weapons as they travel through the world. Some of these may be purchased in shops for in-game currency, while others may be found in treasure chests or as item drops from defeating monsters. In these games, designers assign a value to the various benefits of the object and negative value to its costs (or flaws). Adding these together (benefits minus costs) determines the overall worth or value of the item. This might be a financial value (in the case of a sword) or difficulty level (in the case of a wandering monster). A designer could then sort like objects by worth or difficulty and plot these along a curve in a spreadsheet. Rather than all objects being equal in value, there's a progression of value throughout the game in order to give the player a sense of long-term growth. If building these data from scratch, designers commonly add a progression value procedurally such that, for instance, every object is 5% greater than the one before it. In an actual game development studio that makes these kinds of games, you'd be unlikely to hear these referred to as a "cost curve"; you're more likely to hear terms like "item list" and "monster list," though the methods of their creation are as described here, and they are in fact cost curves.

Anything that gives a higher level of benefits than the curve suggests for a given cost is said to be **above the curve**, and anything that gives a lower level of benefits is **below the curve**. Colloquially, both game designers and gamers will sometimes refer to items above the curve as **overpowered** or **OP** for short (though in fact they are sometimes not too powerful, just too inexpensive). If an item is below the curve, it is likewise sometimes called **underpowered**, although this does not have an abbreviation like "UP" for some reason.

Remember, "cost" isn't just financial here. It can also be rarity or other limits imposed upon the item. A cost curve for a PvP game with resource costs, for example, might actually be plotted on a graph that looks something like the graph on the left, while a cost curve for a PvE game might look like the graph on the right:

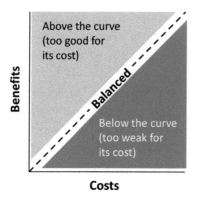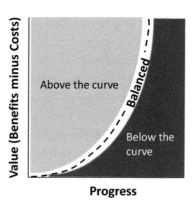

If you find something that is above the curve, you can either reduce the level of benefits or increase the cost or rarity, in order to get it back on the curve (rarity would be considered a cost in that players are unlikely to find it in an average playthrough). Likewise, if something is below the curve, you can add more benefit or decrease the cost to bring it in line with other game items.

Maybe that sword that costs 43,000 gold is deemed to be too powerful; you could raise the price, reduce its damage a bit, and make it rare or a combination of the three.

If something is off the curve, how do you know whether to adjust the costs or the benefits (or both)? It depends on the situation. In most cases, the game designer can do either or both; the easiest way to decide is to ask whether you'd rather keep the cost the same, or whether you'd rather keep the benefits the same, and then, choose the thing that you don't mind changing. For example, you might have a card with a really interesting effect that doesn't need to be modified, and it's clear it only needs a cost adjustment. Or, you might find an item that is just too weak, even at no cost at all, so it really needs to be more powerful and not just cheaper.

Otherwise, you risk having something overpowered in the game which can most certainly affect the game's balance and time to completion. An overpowered sword can allow players to slash their way ahead more quickly than you planned. This is typically not much of an issue, surprisingly, as the player is only able to race ahead until the content meets their ability.

Peaks and Valleys in the Cost Curve: Deliberately Unbalanced?

Before we needlessly throw ourselves at the mercy of these cost curves to make sure every item, creature or whatever gets right in line, let us make something perfectly clear: ***you should absolutely violate the cost curve whenever you want***. Cost curves should be your servant, not your master.

In PvE games, perfectly mathematical and regular progression rarely makes good gameplay. The challenge in such a game is constant and predictable, and the player becomes bored. Deviations from the curve allow you to surprise the player. Kickass items are okay, so long as not everything is kickass. Monsters that kick your ass are okay, too, since they remind you that you might be powerful, but you're still up against powerful enemies. You might not want to deviate *too* much—a sword that makes the player so powerful that it carries them through the entire game with no challenge, or an enemy so powerful that the player gets stuck in an area for an inordinate amount of time, would feel bad—but slight perturbations that give the player unexpected boosts or challenges can create memorable moments (something we cover in more detail in Chapter 12).

Likewise, in PvE games, if everything is exactly on the curve, then the game may be mathematically balanced, but it may also give players the sense that their choices don't matter. After all, if everything has the same value, then it doesn't matter what choices you make, one is as good as another. Player communities delight in arguing about the balance between respective characters or items, making tier lists and spending inordinate amounts of time analyzing a game to find any way to gain even the slightest edge over their opponents. By deliberately creating some items that are very slightly above or below the curve, you give players something to do—hunting through the game to find the hidden gems—while allowing players to sometimes surprise each other by using less popular or powerful stuff to win in unexpected ways.

Supporting Math

If the numeric relationship between costs and benefits is a cost curve, where do the individual numbers describing the costs and benefits—the **supporting math**—come from?

The answer is to find the numeric relation between everything using an anchor. As noted earlier, this can be the currency cost of the weapon, but it can also be the damage the weapon does. If you're balancing weapons in an RPG, the anchor might be the gold cost of a weapon or the amount of damage it inflicts per hit. Each additional point of attack can be put in terms of how much gold a point of attack is worth. Special effects like stat bonuses or healing can also be put in terms of gold as well. Limitations and drawbacks (such as only being equippable by certain character classes) can be thought of as a negative gold cost: They make the sword less valuable and therefore act as discounts. The goal is to have each individual stat, special ability, or mechanic put in terms of your anchor: +1 damage has a benefit of 5, elemental attacks are worth 40 each, regeneration is worth 100, "only usable by a specific character class" cuts 25% off the value, and adding an elemental vulnerability to the wielder is a drawback worth −20. Or whatever numbers you happen to come up with.

The wonderful thing about cost curves and supporting math is that if you have these in place, and they are correct, then balancing every item in the game is straightforward. If you want to invent a new item, you can figure out what it does and you can then calculate how much it should cost. If you want to evaluate an existing item to see if it's balanced, which could be the case if you are evaluating the work of someone else on your team or evaluating a previous version of the game in preparation for a new expansion, count up its numeric benefits and costs, and see if it falls on the cost curve. Having this math in place speeds up the design and balance of a game.

There is a down side to this technique: The initial creation of a cost curve and its supporting math is a lot of work, taking the form of trial and error and a good amount of playtesting and/or analytics. Every possible effect in the game, cost or benefit, must be identified and the numbers derived. So once you get this done, balance is straightforward, but actually getting to that point is hard. In short, a lot of the work to be done for game balance is paid up front, and then, you reap the benefits later.

Creating the Cost Curve for PvE Games

When a designer wants weapons that grow more powerful or monsters that grow more damaging over time, a designer builds a cost curve. We use the term "builds" because rather than comparing a new item to the curve of existing items, as with a PvP game's cost curve, we actually construct the data and the cost curve procedurally.

For example, perhaps you have a sword that does 36–50 damage per hit and has an attack rate of two hits per second. We determine its value to be as follows:

- For every point of damage a weapon does, the designer gives it a cost value of 200.
  - The average damage of this weapon is 43.
  - The value of the damage is 200 * 43 = 8600.
- For every hit per second a weapon does beyond the first hit, the designer gives it a *multiplier* of 5:
  - The rate of hits per second for this weapon is 2 per second (so, one additional hit above the baseline, for a single ×5 multiplier).
  - The value of this *multiplier* is 5 * 8600 = 43,000.

In this example, we have decided to make the "hits per second" a multiplier on the damage. It could also have been a value you add vs. a multiplier. *It actually doesn't matter so long as you are consistent.* Even though players may not see the pattern or work to determine the math behind it, they can *feel* the pattern, just as you do when you say, "this weapon sucks," "that boss is overpowered," or some other statement which translates to "this thing does not feel balanced to me."

Value per HP	10		
Improvement rate	25%		
Chance to Crit	5%		

Weapon	Damage Range		Crit Value	Cost
Sword	5	10		75
Sword +1	6	13		94
Sword +2	8	16		117
Sword +3	10	20		146
Sword +4	12	24		183
Crit Sword	15	31	5%	240
Ninja Hammer	18	100	5%	500
Crit Sword +1	19	38	5%	300
Crit Sword +2	24	48	5%	376
Crit Sword +3	30	60	5%	469

Let's take a look at another example where the worth of an object is built by the spreadsheet.

In this spreadsheet, there is a value assigned per HP of 10. Each weapon is 25% better damage-wise than the weapon before it. Furthermore, weapons that have a chance at a critical hit cost 5% more than those that don't. The cost of these items is calculated by averaging the damage range and adding on any benefits. In this case, there are no costs.

Making a curve of these data (plotting the "cost" column in order), we can see a clear outlier which is not fitting the expected curve.

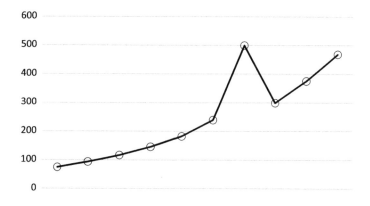

Looking at the original data, it's the Ninja Hammer that's causing this issue. In this case, the designer may believe that it is too powerful and needs a benefit decrease. That decrease could come in the form of its rarity, its limitation that only a ninja can use it, or we could lower the range of damage it's capable of to bring it in line.

Entire item lists are typically built this way in PvE games.

Creating the Cost Curve for PvP Games

As noted earlier, for PvP games where items have a resource cost, we usually want the sum of the costs to equal the sum of the benefits on a single object—our cost curve is the identity curve ($y = x$). This keeps the math easy to conceptualize. If you take the benefits and subtract the costs, a result of 0 means it's balanced; a negative result means it's below the curve, and a positive number means it's above the curve. The more positive or negative it is, the more unbalanced the item is.

What if the resource cost does not scale linearly with benefit level? In many RPGs, costs increase exponentially compared to stat bonuses because the player is earning progressively more gold per enemy encounter. In many collectible card games (CCGs), benefits increase much faster than resource costs, such that late-game cards tend to have extremely powerful game-finishing effects while early-game cards are relatively minor. In these cases, simply treat the resource cost as one of the "costs" in the game, and scale the resource cost accordingly. For example, here is the underlying math for a weapon in a simple MOBA:

- **Costs**:
  - Gold cost: 1 point for 1 gold; 2 points for 3 gold; 3 points for 6 gold; and so on triangularly.
- **Benefits**:
  - +1 Attack: 1 point

In this case, a sword that costs 1 gold gives +1 Attack; 3 gold gives +2 Attack; 6 gold gives +3 Attack, and so on. The gold cost increases triangularly with benefits. And yet, by putting gold cost in terms of "points," the cost curve itself can still be kept as the identity, with +1 point of costs granting +1 point of additional benefits. If you designed a weapon that gave +4 Attack and cost 6 gold, you'd know that 6 gold = a 3 point cost, 4 attack = a 4 point benefit, so this would be $(4-3) = 1$ point above the curve.

Yes, you could just as easily model the above with gold costs of 1 point per 1 gold, benefits of 1 point per +1 attack, and a triangular-shaped cost curve. But then it would not be so obvious whether something was above or below the curve just by looking; 6 points of costs (6 gold) for 4 points of benefits (4 Attack) is still above the curve (on a triangular curve, balanced would be 6 costs for 3 benefits), but at first glance, it looks like the reverse since there are more costs (6) than benefits (4).

Creating the Supporting Math

If the cost curve is trivial (just make it the identity, and you're done), the supporting math is a bit more involved, but there is a process.

- First, make a list of all costs and benefits in your game.
- Then, determine the value of resource costs which may be any kind of numeric relationship, depending on the game.
- From there, determine the value of the most common benefits, those that appear on just about everything you're trying to balance.
- Last, work your way up to more rare and complex things, progressively.

What are the less common costs and benefits worth? What about individual items that combine several benefits: Are they more than, equal to, or less than the sum of their parts? A single item with multiple bonuses might be more powerful than several separate items each with one of those bonuses, because the single item gives it all in one package; in an RPG where the player only has a certain number of equipment slots, or a TCG where merely having a card take up space in the player's hand is an opportunity cost, this might be the case. In other cases, a single item with multiple bonuses might be *less* powerful than having those on separate items, if the bonuses aren't always useful, are situational, or work against each other. It all depends on the nature of your particular game.

What about benefits or costs that are modified in some way? If a benefit only works 50% of the time on a coin flip, is that worth exactly half as much as if it was always "on"? That would be a good starting guess. However, if the game is such that having a known, consistent effect is important for strategic planning purposes, then having a benefit that might or might not happen becomes a serious drawback and that modified benefit would cost less than half of a 100% effect. On the other hand, in a game where players have lots of effects that let them modify or influence coin flips, this benefit might be worth more than half of a 100% effect.

What about a combined effect that is part benefit and part drawback, so that it could be considered either a benefit or a cost? As mentioned before, it doesn't actually matter: If the cost curve is the identity, then a negative benefit is the same as a cost, and a negative cost is the same as a benefit of the same value. You may find it easiest to simply treat it as a benefit if the net value, overall, is more benefit than cost (and vice versa). In that way, all values for costs and benefits can be consistently positive numbers, and you'll only need to add and not subtract to combine all costs and all benefits.

Cost Curves in New Games

Creating the cost curve and supporting math for a brand new game, one that doesn't exist yet, is harder than deriving a cost curve for an established game. Established games have established cost curves. Assigning costs to untried benefits, for instance, is at best an educated guess. The more original and innovative your design, the more challenging this is. As designers, we rely on a lot of playtesting as the project progresses once the mechanics have been solidified and expect that once playtesting begins, we can improve upon initial estimates in response to player feedback.

When creating your initial numbers for a game, it's important to generate numbers formulaically, typically referencing specific cost cells in a spreadsheet. Why? Suppose you come up with a complete set of supporting math… and then find out later that one of your formulas is off and needs adjustment. Everything that number touches needs to change and that may be many or all of the things in your game. Being off is a given, and correcting it becomes quite tedious when a single math change requires changing dozens or hundreds of affected items. However, if this is all calculated automatically in a spreadsheet, we just have to change a single formula, Fill Down, and all the other numbers are changed appropriately without us having to do a ton of manual labor.

If there is one last bit of advice we can impart to you as experienced designers, don't sweat the first iteration of your numbers. Just apply things consistently and formulaically (i.e. if something resurrects characters, it always adds 10% cost to the item or something). No matter what you do, your numbers will be off. So will ours. So will every designer you know, no matter how great. Game balance is a process. The more you do it, the closer you get to the bullseye on the first shot, but the odds of hitting a bullseye on that first shot? It's unlikely, particularly considering player desire changes regularly. *Bloodborne* and *Dark Souls* are both ridiculously challenging games clearly balanced toward a more masocore audience. A similar balance style was common in the early 1980s, but it's not always in vogue.

In any event, the best approach for original games is to take the best educated guess you can, get something in playable form as fast as possible, and allow for as much playtesting and revision as you possibly can. Write down and keep all the options that you didn't take in your initial guess, in case you find them useful to try out later on. Meanwhile, continue playtesting and let the game tell you what direction it needs to go in. It's also helpful to study other games, mapping out their cost curves to learn from them. Understand that games differ from one another, however, and it's not recommended to merely take another game's math for your own—it will probably be wrong (and even if they're right, lawsuits have been filed and won on this basis).

To give you an idea of how this works, let's consider *Micro TCG*, a two-player game created by one of the authors of this book specifically to illustrate this point. In this game, each card represents a character, and players choose characters to battle one another on their behalf. Cards have three numbers on them: their Cost, Strength, and Damage. Here are the rules:

- **Objective**: reduce the opponent's health to zero.
- **Setup**: each player brings their own deck of ten cards. After shuffling their deck, they draw an initial hand of three cards. Each player starts with 10 health.
- **Play**: the game is played in a series of rounds. Each round has five phases: Select, Reveal, Battle, Damage, and Cleanup. These phases are repeated until one or both players are reduced to zero health or below, at which point the game ends immediately.
  - **Select phase**: each player chooses one card in their hand and places it face-down in front of them. Proceed when both players have selected.
  - **Reveal phase**: both played cards are turned face-up. Each player loses an amount of health equal to the Cost of the card they played. (Yes, if a player plays a card with Cost greater than or equal to their remaining health, they would lose the game at this point.)
  - **Battle phase**: compare the Strength of the two cards. If one card's Strength is lower than the other, it is discarded from play and has

no further effect. If Strength is tied, both cards remain in play to the next phase.
- **Damage phase**: any card that is still in play does its listed Damage to the opponent's health.
- **Cleanup phase**: all cards in play are discarded, and players draw one card from their deck (if their deck is depleted, then they simply don't draw).
- **Resolution**: if a player's health is zero or less, their opponent wins. If both players' health is zero or less, the game is a tie. If one or both players are completely out of cards at the start of the Select phase—they have exhausted their deck and played out every card in their hand—then the player with the highest remaining health wins (if both players are tied in health, the game is a tie).

Let's take an example round of play. Two players, Aerith and Barrett, start with 10 health each. Aerith selects a card with Cost: 1, Strength: 3, Damage: 3. Barrett selects a card with Cost: 2, Strength: 5, Damage: 5. When they reveal these cards, Aerith pays her cost of 1 and now has 9 health. Barrett pays his cost of 2 and has 8 health. Next in the Battle phase, the cards' Strengths are compared; Aerith's card has the lower Strength and is discarded from play, and will not do anything further. Barrett's card remains in play and does its listed 5 damage to Aerith during the Damage phase, leaving Aerith with 4 health remaining and Barrett with 8. Barrett's card is now discarded, both players draw another card, and they continue with another round since they both still have health remaining.

Now that we know how *Micro TCG* works, suppose we're tasked with designing the actual cards. We come up with four cards to start and throw some numbers on them that feel about right:

	Cost	Strength	Damage
Thief	1	4	2
Cleric	1	3	3
Fighter	1	5	1
Hero	2	5	5

Are these cards balanced? How would we come up with a cost curve? In this case, we'd start by using some mathematical intuition and trying to derive as much as we can with logic and common sense.

Cost seems very straightforward here: each point of cost guarantees that the player loses a point of health when they play it. As this damage can't be prevented (at least, not with the rules and cards we have right now), one point of cost is exactly equal to losing a point of health. This suggests using health as our anchor.

How much health is a single point of Strength worth? Strength does two things: it makes it more likely that your card will stay in play so that your Damage will get through, and it also makes it more likely your opponent's card will be removed (which prevents the incoming Damage from their card). How likely, exactly, is Strength to have an effect? This depends on what cards exist for the game (is it just these four? What if we design a hundred more?) as well as what cards are popular in the metagame, but those can both change over time, and we must have some basis for defining the value of Strength in a way that it doesn't change. Here's what we'll choose: we'll say that Strength should generally vary from 1 to 5 with each number appearing equally often. If we produce a 50-card set, there would be ten cards with each Strength value from 1 to 5. As long as the cards are relatively balanced, we hope that the metagame won't favor specific Strength values, and we can design accordingly within this constraint.

If we know that the opponent's Strength is equally likely to be any number from 1 to 5, then a Strength of 1 will never eliminate the opponent's card, and only has a 1 in 5 (20%) chance of not being eliminated itself—only if the opponent's card is also Strength 1. A Strength of 2 has a 20% chance of eliminating the opponent's card (if their Strength is 1) and a 40% chance of remaining in play (opponent's Strength is 1 or 2). Each additional point of Strength increases both the chance of it eliminating the opponent's card and the chance of it not being eliminated itself by 20%.

Strength's value in terms of damage prevention, then, is equal to ((Strength-1)/5) * (opponent's Damage). What is the average of the opponent's Damage? Let's suppose we decide to make Damage, just like Strength, vary from 1 to 5 with an equal chance of each across every card set we produce. This makes the average Damage equal to 3. So, we can say the benefit of Strength is equal to ((Strength-1)/5)*3.

How do we find the value of Damage? Each point of Damage is equal to -1 health of the opponent… but only if the card has a high enough Strength to not get discarded during the Battle phase. The amount of damage our card does, on average, is (Strength/5)*Damage. To put this another way, if Strength is 5, then we are guaranteed that our Damage will get through since the opponent won't have a Strength that's higher. For every point of Strength below 5, there's a 20% chance that our Damage doesn't get through at all, so we reduce the expected value of our Damage by 20%.

Putting these together, we can write out a formula for the value of a card that adds up its benefits (Strength and Damage) and subtracts its cost:

((Strength-1)/5) * 3 + (Strength/5) * Damage – Cost

Creating this calculation in our spreadsheet, we see the following:

	Cost	Strength	Damage	TOTALS
Thief	1	4	2	**2.4**
Cleric	1	3	3	**2**
Fighter	1	5	1	**2.4**
Hero	2	5	5	**5.4**

Immediately, we see a problem: *all four cards* are listed as being significantly above the curve, which obviously shouldn't be the case. Thinking about it some more, the reason is that we're combining the entire outcome of a turn— our cost, our card's ability to prevent incoming damage, and our card's ability to deal damage to our opponent—but we left out the fact that there's still an average 3 damage incoming from the opponent's card if it isn't prevented. We could either leave it like this (and say that a total value of 3 is balanced) or amend our formula to the following so that a total of zero is balanced:

((Strength-1)/5) * 3 + (Strength/5) * Damage – (Cost+3)

That gives us the following totals:

	Cost	Strength	Damage	TOTALS
Thief	1	4	2	**-0.6**
Cleric	1	3	3	**-1**
Fighter	1	5	1	**-0.6**
Hero	2	5	5	**2.4**

Now we see another problem: the first three cards are a bit on the weak side while Hero is drastically OP relative to the others. With our formula, we could fiddle around a bit with the numbers manually to find something a bit closer to the curve:

	Cost	Strength	Damage	TOTALS
Thief	1	4	3	**0.2**
Cleric	0	3	3	**0**
Fighter	1	5	2	**0.4**
Hero	2	5	3	**0.4**

Once we created this cost curve and the supporting math for the three core stats of Cost, Strength, and Damage, we could then get more sophisticated, perhaps creating new cards that have special abilities such as healing, winning ties of Strength, and doing some damage to the opponent even if the card is eliminated. Each of those could be derived similarly. If you'd like to see an expanded version of this game that shows how to cost these abilities and more, you can download a slide presentation and spreadsheet from bit.ly/ AlgebraNotMagic that goes into greater detail.

Cost Curves in Existing Games

If you have a game that has already been released and is already being played, and it was developed by hand (or through much playtesting and/or analytics), but no one actually created a cost curve and supporting math for it, why would anyone need to figure this out if they didn't do it before?

In the case of a game that may release future expansion sets, knowing the cost curve and supporting math of the original game aid in creating new assets for the later games based on the same math. If the original cost curve or spreadsheets are unavailable (as sometimes happens with acquisitions relaunches of older IP), deriving the math after the fact can provide a valuable resource for future developers on that game, while also potentially identifying items that are above or below the curve in the original. Remember that some of these items may be classed as "peaks," and a well-balanced cost curve is *not* a perfect progression. Blizzard's games excel at revealing peaks, in part because they are so well documented online.

Designers are not the only ones who seek cost curve information. Competitive players may make their own mathematical models of the game balance in order to identify the items or strategies that are most above or below the curve to give them an edge over their opponents. At a recent first-person shooter (FPS) deathmatch tournament, Koopa (competitive *Quake* player Sam Singh from Ireland) brought his own cathode ray tube (CRT) monitor because it offered a split second timing difference that improved the reticle accuracy over an liquid-crystal display (LCD) monitor connected to the same computer, something he actually proved via side-by-side video at the event. As competitive gaming continues to grow, such seemingly trivial player-created proofs are the difference between winning and losing.

If you're studying an existing established game, as either a player or a designer on the project, it may be worth your time to look at what the player community has done already, in terms of publishing strategies, tier lists, or even their own math and cost curves that they derived after the fact. This can provide a starting point for your work, or at least, a point of comparison to see how close your analysis is to that of others.

Analyzing and Studying Existing Analog Games

To further understand cost curves and their application, studying existing analog games is quite useful. It helps us to better understand why things cost what they cost while viewing the game through the lens of a game designer vs. a player. What follows are extensive analyses that use *Magic: The Gathering* as their basis.

If you are sufficiently familiar with a game, you may have a basic idea of what things cost. This may or may not have any relation to how the game is actually balanced, and may be closer or further from a well-balanced state than the game as is.

Let us take *Magic: the Gathering* as an example. In this game, most everything has a mana cost, except for Land cards which are the resources that provide mana. Typically, a player can play up to one Land card per turn, each of which provides one mana per turn. This mana cannot be saved up over turns, so on turn N, a player has no more than N mana available. Also, a player starts the game with seven cards in their hand, and they draw one new card per turn (the first player to take a turn does not draw, to reduce the advantage of going first). While many cards can accelerate this mana curve or provide extra card drawing, we use it as a baseline.

Likewise, based on many tournament decks, we estimate of about 20 Land cards in a 60-card deck. While competitive decks can have a wide range of Land to non-Land cards (adjusted as appropriate based on how expensive the non-Land cards are), 20 would be a reasonable starting point to consider "average." Thus, we expect one out of every three cards to be Land.

By turn three, the player who went first has drawn nine cards (their starting seven, plus one on the second turn, and one on the third turn), and we would expect an average of three of those cards to be Land. Thus, this player should be able to play one Land per turn for the first three turns. What about their fourth Land? On average, the next three cards they draw contain one Land. It might be drawn on the fourth, fifth, or sixth turn—but the fifth turn would again be the average. Thus, we expect to see the fourth Land on turn five, not turn four. From there, the player draws about one Land every three turns: the fifth land enters play on turn eight, the sixth on turn eleven, and so on. Of course, a random shuffle (and cards that modify the mana curve) means we may see plenty of variation from this average in actual play. However, we balance the mana cost based on these expected values. See Chapters 17 and 18 for more about calculations like this.

Because of this, we might expect that the benefit from each point of mana is constant for the first three mana; the fourth mana would be worth more; and every mana after the fourth would be worth much more. Specifically, we might make the following cost table:

Mana	Value
1	1
2	2
3	3
4	5
5	8
6	11
$6+N$	$11+3N$

Additionally, *Magic: the Gathering* has a concept of colored and colorless mana. There are five colors: black (B), green (G), red (R), blue (U), and white (W). Most lands provide one color only. Cards with mana costs may require some of that mana in specific colors, while part of the cost may be "colorless" meaning it can be paid with any color. Thus, a card might cost RR3 (five mana total, two of which must be Red), or W1 (two mana, one of which must be White), or UUUUU (five Blue mana).

Should we make a distinction between colored and colorless mana for the purposes of modifying this cost table? It depends. If a deck consists of only cards that use a single color, then colored and colorless are identical. It doesn't matter, and we need make no distinction. However, *Magic: The Gathering* is designed so that each color has certain strengths and weaknesses, so a single-color deck has some clear deficiencies that the opponent can detect and possibly exploit; using only one color is thus a disadvantage because the player is severely limited in what cards are in their deck.

If a deck contains three colors, there is a separate type of disadvantage: with the expectation of having three Land by turn three, and six Land is only expected by very late game (turn eleven), the player can only rely on cards that cost a single-colored mana of a given type until late in the game. In this case, a card that costs, say, GG would not be expected to be playable before turn eight on average, even though it only requires two mana! With four or all five colors, this disadvantage becomes even worse.

For this reason, most competitive decks combine two colors, which provide a balance between being versatile and offering many options without effectively preventing most cards that require several colored mana from being playable. Thus, we use a two-color deck as a baseline.

In a deck that uses equal amounts of two mana types (thus, 40 non-Land cards, 10 land of one color, and 10 land of a second color), what is the relationship between colored and colorless mana? Simply, a player must draw an average of two land to find one of a specific color. Therefore, colored mana can be thought of as being twice as costly as colorless.

How does this affect our earlier cost table? That table simply looks at total mana, so it is equivalent to colorless costs. Colored mana should have a value twice that of colorless:

Colorless Mana	Value	Colored Mana	Value
1	1	1	2
2	2	2	5
3	3	3	11
4	5	$3+N$	$11+6N$
5	8		
6	11		
$6+N$	$11+3N$		

When studying cost curves using intuition-based math, our goal is to analyze a game and attempt to identify cards above and below the curve, so we might use this as a starting guess for the cost value of each point of mana on the cost curve. In this example, we use a known game for the purpose of analysis. The actual cost curves for *Magic: The Gathering* may differ expansion to expansion, and for the purposes of this example, it doesn't particularly matter. If it does not agree with the actual supporting math that the game is balanced on, the discrepancies become obvious very quickly; and then we could decide, through playtesting or through looking at winning decks from high-level tournaments, whether the discrepancies were later refined by the game's designers (it has happened with numerous cards) or whether they are a mistake in our tentative math above.

This method of analysis, then, may be used to study and identify patterns and outliers in the original cost curve and supporting math that the designers used to balance the game. It is also critical in helping us to understand why things have the value they do. Trying to figure out why is incredibly instructive and teaches more than looking at a completed spreadsheet. It is useful, then, to compare our analysis to the actual costs we find online.

Looking at Trends

If we wish to reverse-engineer the original math that the game was first balanced on, we may do this by looking at the actual costs and benefits of each card, and look for consistent patterns. We can think of each card as an equation that relates the set of costs to the set of benefits on that card. We can treat each individual cost and benefit as an unknown variable, and just need to solve for that variable.

The easiest way to do this is to look for "equations" that only have a single unknown. If you already know that a cost of W2 provides a value of 5, and a creature's base stats provide a value of 4, we could assume, then, that if it has a single special ability, that ability has a value of 1 on the cost curve. We can apply this value to other cards with that same ability and potentially derive anything else that's missing on those other cards.

Cost $W\,2$(3 mana, 1 white); Power 2; Toughness 2; Special ability

$$3m + 1w = 2p + 2t + 1s$$

$$3m = 3;\ w = 2;\ p = 1;\ t = 1;\ s = ?$$

$$5 = 2 + 2 + s$$

$$1 = s$$

"Solving for X," as it were, is great if you just have a single unknown. But when you're first starting out, every card in the game has at least two unknowns: its point cost on the cost curve, and at least one effect, stat, or something similar. For example, in *Magic: the Gathering*, all creatures have two stats, Power and Toughness, denoted as numbers with a slash between them (so a 3/4 creature has 3 Power and 4 Toughness), in addition to the mana cost of playing the card. Where do you start when there are no cards that have only a single unknown thing on them?

One method is to find several very basic creatures that have only the most basic parts to them—a cost and the core stats that every creature has (colloquially called "vanilla" creatures). If you have three unknowns (Cost, Power, and Toughness), then you only need three equations to solve for all unknowns, and a set of published cards in a TCG typically has plenty more than just three.

Another method is to find two cards that are nearly identical, except for one small difference. If you have two equations that are the same except one difference, you can combine them to find the value of the one missing thing. For example, suppose you have these two cards: B2 for a 3/2 creature, and B3 for a 4/2 creature. On the cost side, there is a difference of one colorless mana; on the benefit side, there is a difference of +1 Power. Thus, we might suspect that the value of 1 colorless mana is the same as the benefit of +1 Power... even if we don't know the rest.

$$\text{Cost} = \text{Power} + \text{Toughnesss}$$

$$4m + 1b = 4p + 2t$$

$$3m + 1b = 3p + 2t$$

(Subtract bottom equation from top equation)

$$1m = 1p$$

In the same way, there is a 2/1 creature that costs W, and a 2/2 that costs W1, suggesting that the value of one colorless mana is the same as the benefit of +1 Toughness (and therefore, Power and Toughness are themselves equivalent).

This method is useful for games that have enough "equations" to make it easy to find lots of pairs that are similar. If there are only a dozen or so game objects that are all completely different, of course, you must use other methods.

However, just as often you'll run into the opposite problem: there are many game objects that just do not agree with each other. If you have two equations and two unknowns, you can (usually) find a unique solution. If you have six equations and two unknowns, and some of the equations are not compatible with others. A unique solution may not be possible, and you'll have to start taking guesses.

Consider these creature costs and power/toughness ratings, assuming no other special abilities:

Mana Cost	Power / Toughness
W	2/1
W1	2/2
W4	3/5
U1	1/3
U4	2/5
B2	3/2
B3	4/2
R1	2/1
R3	3/3
G1	2/2
G4	5/4

We would like to find the relationship between mana cost, power, and toughness: three unknowns and eleven equations. Assuming each color is equivalent (one point of Black mana should be just as valuable as one Green or one Red), we immediately run into problems when comparing the creatures that cost 1 colored and 1 colorless. W1 and G1 both provide a 2/2 creature; U1 gives a 1/3; but R1 only gets a 2/1, making the red creature strictly inferior to the white and green ones at the same total cost. Comparing the W4, U4, and G4 creatures (3/5, 2/5, and 5/4, respectively) gives similar problems. There is just no logical math where 2/2=2/1, or where 3/5=2/5. How would we proceed from here?

There are a few possibilities to consider:

- Perhaps the designers intentionally designed some of these cards to be above or below the curve. If we see three cards that offer 2/2 or 1/3 (a total of four power and toughness) for two mana, and only one card that provides a 2/1 creature, we might suspect the 2/1 is under the curve and we could ignore it for the purposes of trying to identify the original ("correct") math.
- Or, our assumptions may be incorrect. Perhaps the five colors are not equivalent and that some colors are more efficient at creatures than others. For example, if you know *Magic: The Gathering*, Green tends to have lots of big creatures (but less versatility in other types of spells),

while Blue tends to have a very useful toolbox of spells and thus might
be expected to have weaker creatures.

- Or, there may be other metagame considerations. For example, maybe
there are several red spells that give bonuses to weak creatures, and
therefore, simply being a weak red creature is itself an inherent bonus
that isn't accounted for in our math. Or maybe some of these cards are
more rare than others, and the designers chose to make the rarer cards
slightly more powerful.

How do we know which of these is correct? Knowing the game might help us
make an educated guess. Otherwise, we could just keep going and see if we
can find other patterns or trends that explain it.

If we accept from before that one colorless mana is worth 1 Power or 1
Toughness, we can look at all eleven of these basic creatures in an attempt to
find the cost curve. If we put it in a spreadsheet and sort all rows by the total
mana cost (and if tied, sorting by Power + Toughness), we get this:

Cost	Total Mana Cost	Power / Toughness	Power + Toughness
W	1	2/1	3
R1	2	2/1	3
W1	2	2/2	4
U1	2	1/3	4
G1	2	2/2	4
B2	3	3/2	5
B3	4	4/2	6
R3	4	3/3	6
U4	5	2/5	7
W4	5	3/5	8
G4	5	5/4	9

Here, we bolded the columns for mana cost (which is the only cost of these
cards) and Power + Toughness (the combined benefits of these cards) to see
if we can find some relation between cost and benefit for these creatures.
Here, we see a definite pattern: Power + Toughness is usually equal to the
total mana cost plus two. It is the exceptions we must look at: the R1, W4,
and G4 creatures.

As noted before, the R1 creature appears to be below the curve. The
other red creature (costing R3) seems to be on the curve, so the possibility
that red creatures are intentionally disadvantaged across the board seems
unlikely.

The other area of note is the creatures that cost five total mana. Here, there seems to be three different cards each with a different result. What's going on here, and what do we do about it? Lacking further information at this point, we might take the average of the three and say that a cost of five mana is worth eight and that merely costing five mana is enough of a disadvantage to put the creature squarely in mid- to late-game territory and therefore it gets an extra point of benefits to compensate (and the variation is due to an existing imbalance in the game, whether intentional or not).

This limited set of data also leaves many open questions. All eleven creatures here have exactly one colored mana; how much is a second (or third, or fourth) colored mana worth, compared to colorless? The most expensive creature here costs five total mana; what does the player get for six, or seven, or more? To find out, we'll have to examine more cards. Let us extend our search to creatures that have one or more special abilities that are "keyworded"—a term game designers use to describe abilities that exist on so many cards that the designers saw fit to create a single word to describe the effect in shorthand.

Mana Cost	Power/Toughness	Special Abilities
G	0/3	Defender, Reach
W1	2/1	Flying
B1	2/1	Lifelink
GG	3/2	Trample
WW	2/2	First Strike, Protection from Black
BB	2/2	First Strike, Protection from White
W2	2/2	Flying
B2	2/2	Swampwalk
G3	2/4	Reach
R3	3/2	Haste
U3	2/4	Flying
W3	3/2	Flying
WW2	2/3	Flying, First Strike
GG3	3/5	Deathtouch
WW3	4/4	Flying, Vigilance
WW3	5/5	Flying, First Strike, Lifelink, Protection from Demons, Protection from Dragons
GG4	6/4	Trample
GG5	7/7	Trample

Here, we see a number of special abilities. Even if we don't know what they all mean, we can still take a pretty good guess as to what each of them is worth, just by isolating the ones that have a single "unknown."

We start with creatures that have similar cost to those with no abilities, where we have already established the beginnings of a cost curve. We know, for example, that a three-mana creature with one colored mana has a value of 5. Here, we see a W2 creature that is 2/2 and Flying, and a B2 creature that is 2/2 and Swampwalk, so both Flying and Swampwalk should have a value of 1 (both equivalent to +1 Power or +1 Toughness). We also know that a two-mana creature with one colored mana has a value of 4; here, we see a W1 creature that is 2/1 and Flying, and a B1 creature that is 2/1 and Lifelink, so Lifelink also appears to have a value of 1 (and Flying, at a value of 1 here, is consistent with our previous observation with the W2 creature). Notice that we can perform this analysis even if we have no idea what Flying, Swampwalk, and Lifelink actually do!

Lastly, we know that a four-mana creature with one colored mana has a value of 6; here, we see a G3 with 2/4 and Reach, an R3 with 3/2 and Haste, a U3 with 2/4 and Flying, and a W3 with 3/2 and Flying. From these, we can guess that Haste also has a value of 1, and the W3 confirms yet again that Flying has a value of 1, but we run into problems with both the G3 and U3: both of these would appear to be on the curve without any special abilities. What do we do here?

The U3, at least, is very likely above the curve. We have three other cards that all list Flying as having a value of 1, and four other cards that cost one colored and three colorless mana that have a value of 6 for that cost.

What about the G3? It uses a keyword we have not analyzed before. Without knowing what Reach does, we might consider the possibility that it is worth zero: perhaps it has both benefits and drawbacks that cancel each other out. It's also possible that the card is above the curve. And as before, it's possible there are other metagame considerations we haven't taken into account here. Let us dig deeper.

Knowing the game helps here. In *Magic: the Gathering*, creatures can attack, and when they attack an opponent that player can assign their own creatures to block the attackers. Flying is a special ability that makes a creature unblockable, except for enemy creatures that also have Flying. In this way, Flying is both offensive (makes a creature harder to block) and defensive (can be used to block the opponent's Flying creatures). Reach is a special ability that lets a creature block Flying creatures, but does not give it any other powers when attacking; it is, effectively, the defensive half of the Flying ability. If Flying has a value of 1, then we might guess Reach has a value of one-half. But this game does not allow mana costs that are fractional, so a creature with Reach as its only ability is destined to be either slightly above or slightly below the curve. Here, the game designers apparently chose to make it slightly above.

Knowing the value of Reach lets us analyze the G 0/3 with Defender and Reach. This has a base cost of 3 (for the mana cost of G), and a benefit of 3 from its Toughness, plus 1 for Reach, which gives Defender a value of −1 (that's negative 1) as a benefit. This is another case where knowing the game can help; after all, Defender sounds like some kind of special ability, so having a negative value sounds like we've done some math wrong. However, in this game, Defender is a restriction: it means the creature cannot attack. Knowing this, it makes sense that Defender is actually a cost, equivalent to an extra cost of one mana.

Our chart now looks like this, with our suspected benefits and costs given in brackets for those that have already been derived:

Mana Cost	Power / Toughness	Special Abilities	Benefits + Costs
G [−3]	0/3 [3]	Defender [−1], Reach [1]	0
W1 [−4]	2/1 [3]	Flying [1]	0
B1 [−4]	2/1 [3]	Lifelink [1]	0
GG	3/2 [5]	Trample	
WW	2/2 [4]	First Strike, Protection from Black	
BB	2/2 [4]	First Strike, Protection from White	
W2 [−5]	2/2 [4]	Flying [1]	0
B2 [−5]	2/2 [4]	Swampwalk [1]	0
G3 [−6]	2/4 [6]	Reach [1]	+1
R3 [−6]	3/2 [5]	Haste [1]	0
U3 [−6]	2/4 [6]	Flying [1]	+1
W3 [−6]	3/2 [5]	Flying [1]	0
WW2	2/3 [5]	Flying [1], First Strike	
GG3	3/5 [8]	Deathtouch	
WW3	4/4 [8]	Flying [1], Vigilance	
WW3	5/5 [10]	Flying [1], First Strike, Lifelink [1], Protection from Demons, Protection from Dragons	
GG4	6/4 [10]	Trample	
GG5	7/7 [14]	Trample	

We have added another column on the right, simply adding the benefits and subtracting the costs. If the benefits and costs are equivalent to one another, they sum to zero, which lets us know the card is on the curve. A positive number means the benefits are larger than the costs, showing a card that is suspected to be above the curve. A negative number would mean costs outweigh benefits, with a card below the curve.

At this point, we would appear to be stuck. There are no creatures for which there is exactly one unknown; in particular, we don't know what happens with a second colored mana, nor do we know what happens to the cost curve at six mana and above. However, there are still a few things we can do.

First, we can look for two cards that are highly similar, except for two differences. With two "equations" and two "unknowns," we can find the value of the differences. In particular, the two creatures at GG4 and GG5 have a difference of just a single colorless mana, the same special ability and a difference in power and toughness of +4. We can then guess that going from six to seven mana gives an extra 4 benefits.

We also have two creatures costing WW3, both of which have Flying. One of them is 4/4 with Vigilance, and the other is 5/5 with First Strike, Lifelink, and Protection from Demons and Dragons. This tells us that Vigilance is either an extremely powerful ability or that one of these cards is above the curve relative to the other. There is no way to know which one just from the information given here. Such is the danger of trying to derive the cost curve of a game from cards that are not all exactly on the curve (which, as noted earlier in this chapter, is normal and even at times desirable).

The last thing we can do is start making educated guesses, realizing these may be wrong and need to be corrected later. For example, there is a creature that costs GG for 3/2 Trample. We know that the Power and Toughness benefits are 5. Since most keyworded special abilities seem to provide a benefit of 1, we might guess that Trample has a benefit of 1 also, bringing the total benefits to 6. We know that the mana cost is 1 to start, +2 for the first G, which means the second G would cost +3.

We could then compare this to other cards with a cost of two colored mana to see if it is consistent. There are several relevant white creatures. We already know that W1 gets us a plain 2/2 creature; WW gets us a 2/2 with First Strike and Protection from Black. If First Strike and Protection from Black are each worth a benefit of 1, and the second W mana is a cost of 3, then this is consistent. So we can now revise our math: one colorless mana has a cost of 1, the first colored mana has a cost of 2, and the second colored mana has a cost of 3.[2]

We can look further. There is a WW2 creature with 2/3 Flying and First Strike. The cost is a base of 1, +2 (colorless)+2 (first W)+3 (second W)=8. Benefit of power and toughness is 5, +1 for Flying, and +1 for First Strike, for a total of 7. Oops! Maybe this should have been a 2/4 or 3/3 creature. Maybe that second W mana isn't so expensive after all. Let's suppose for now that

---

[2] If we ran into a creature with three colored mana, we might initially guess that the third colored mana has a cost of 4, but we would have to see.

it actually is under the curve by 1. Going up to the WW3 creature with 4/4 Flying and Vigilance, we can calculate the cost (base of 1, +3 colorless, +2 for first W and +3 for second W, and an additional +1 for crossing the threshold to five mana for a total cost of 10); if Flying and Vigilance each provide a benefit of 1, that card is balanced according to our system. (This means the other WW3 is probably a bit too cheap and might have been more properly costed at WW4 or WWW2.)

Returning to Trample: if we accept that a second colored mana has an extra +1 cost (we've seen further evidence that this is the norm), then the GG creature with 3/2 Trample shows a cost of 6, confirming that Trample does indeed provide a benefit of 1. From here, we can examine the most expensive green creatures to see what happens when we go up to six or seven total mana. The GG4 creature with 6/4 Trample gives a total benefit of 11 (6 power+4 toughness+1 for Trample). We know the cost is a base of 1, +4 for colorless, +2 for the first G, and +3 for the second G, and +1 for being above the threshold of five mana, for a total cost of 11. This seems balanced as is, which means that there is no additional cost for having a mana cost of 6... either that, or this card is under the curve.

Let's compare to the GG5 creature with 7/7 Trample. This creature has a total benefit of 15 (7 power+7 toughness+1 for Trample). We know the cost is a base of 1, +5 for colorless, +2 for the first G, +3 for the second G, and +1 for being at or above five mana, for a total known cost of 12, implying that the jump from five mana to seven mana has an extra cost of +3. Either all of this cost is in the jump from six to seven mana if there is some major difference between the two, or more likely, there should have been an extra cost of +1 to go from five to six mana, and an extra cost of +2 to rise from six to seven mana—thus, the GG4 should have been 7/4 or 6/5 Trample to be on the curve.

This leaves one more ability we haven't addressed: a GG3 creature with 3/5 Deathtouch. The GG3 cost is a base of 1, +3 for colorless, +2 for the first G, +3 for the second G, and +1 since it's five mana, for a total cost of 10. The benefit is 8 from power and toughness, suggesting Deathtouch has a benefit of 2. Since most other abilities are 1, this might initially suggest that this creature is below the curve. However, if you know the game and what Deathtouch does (it kills all opposing creatures in combat automatically), it is a pretty powerful ability and is probably worth the high benefit level that it appears here.

We can then, finally, fill in our entire chart of costs and benefits:

Mana Cost	Power / Toughness	Special Abilities	Benefits + Costs
G [–3]	0/3 [3]	Defender [–1], Reach [1]	0
W1 [–4]	2/1 [3]	Flying [1]	0
B1 [–4]	2/1 [3]	Lifelink [1]	0
GG [–6]	3/2 [5]	Trample [1]	0
WW [–6]	2/2 [4]	First Strike [1], Protection from Black [1]	0
BB [–6]	2/2 [4]	First Strike [1], Protection from White [1]	0
W2 [–5]	2/2 [4]	Flying [1]	0
B2 [–5]	2/2 [4]	Swampwalk [1]	0
G3 [–6]	2/4 [6]	Reach [1]	+1
R3 [–6]	3/2 [5]	Haste [1]	0
U3 [–6]	2/4 [6]	Flying [1]	+1
W3 [–6]	3/2 [5]	Flying [1]	0
WW2 [–8]	2/3 [5]	Flying [1], First Strike [1]	–1
GG3 [–10]	3/5 [8]	Deathtouch [2]	0
WW3 [–10]	4/4 [8]	Flying [1], Vigilance [1]	0
WW3 [–10]	5/5 [10]	Flying [1], First Strike [1], Lifelink [1], Protection from Demons [X], Protection from Dragons [Y]	+3+X+Y
GG4 [–12]	6/4 [10]	Trample [1]	–1
GG5 [–15]	7/7 [14]	Trample [1]	0

We can also list out all of the tentative supporting math that we have derived:

Costs	Benefits
1 for just existing (baseline)	1 per point of Power or Toughness
1 for each colorless mana	1 for most keyword abilities (Flying, First Strike, etc.)
2 for first colored mana	1 for Protection from a color
3 for second colored mana	2 for Deathtouch ability
1 for total mana cost ≥ 5	Either 1 or ½ for Reach ability
1 for total mana cost ≥ 6	
2 for total mana cost ≥ 7	
1 for Defender keyword	

From here, if we were inclined, we could examine the majority of other creatures in the set, as most of them are a combination of cost, power, toughness, some of these basic keyword abilities, and one other custom special ability that is specific to that creature. This custom special then becomes our one unknown. It would be simple enough to then find out the benefit or cost of most of these unique specials (or at least, what the game designer decided to cost them at). Even though many creature abilities are unique, as designers we can at least get a feel for what kinds of abilities are marginally useful vs. those that are extremely powerful, we can put numbers to them, and we can compare them with each other to see if they feel right.

We could go even further. Since this is an established game with a vibrant and active player community, there are plenty of player-run strategy websites, as well as publicly available deck lists of tournament-winning decks. If our analysis shows a particular set of cards to be vastly above or below the curve, we could see if actual real-world play bears this out. For example, in this analysis, the WW3 with five special abilities seems to be ridiculously powerful. Does it consistently show up in the top ranks of card-ranking tier lists that players have put together? Does it appear in deck lists of the contestants in high-profile tournaments? On the open market, does this card fetch a high price relative to others of its rarity? Likewise, our GG4 card seems to be a bit below the curve; is it virtually absent from competitive play, and does it find itself in the lower tiers on strategy sites' tier lists? If real-world data seems to generally agree with our cost curve and supporting math, that can give us extra confidence that our model is reasonably accurate. If there are particular cards that show a big difference—our math shows them as top-tier cards, while the community rates them as mediocre or vice versa—then we may have found an exploit in the game that the community hasn't discovered yet, or more likely, something in our math is wrong. We can then examine the specific cards that seem "off" in our mathematical model, looking for commonalities. If, for example, we have four cards that we show as above the curve that do not seem to be treated that way by players, and all four of those cards have the same special ability, it could be that our supporting math rates that ability too highly. Or, if we have a set of cards that we rated as below the curve, but they are all consistently seen in the most popular and winning decks, and all of them have multiple special abilities, it could be that our model takes each special ability as its own thing and adds them together, but these cards have abilities that synergize and work really well in combination, making them stronger than the sum of the parts.

Analyzing and Studying Existing Digital Games

Similar to analog games, digital games can likewise be studied to analyze how the game's designers valued object attributes along a cost curve. You can use the same process as used above, of course. Because digital games tend to have larger data sets (computers are not as limited as game boxes), the process of working backward from the data tends to be more complex. It is highly recommended that any aspiring designer search for item lists online and apply similar methodology to that used above to see if they can determine the cost curve the designers applied. For large games with thousands of game objects, using formulas in spreadsheets becomes a necessity in order to do the analysis in any reasonable period of time.

Analyzing and Studying Free-to-Play Games

Cost curves in F2P games are a different beast than traditional games. In a F2P game, in the first few days of play, players generally have what they need to do what they want to do. If we graphed a cost curve for this, we'd see that things were neither above nor below the curve. They are balanced.

As the demand rose for specific things, the player had enough of that specific thing to do what the game demanded of them. For example, in a restaurant game, as customers come in, you are able to meet their rising demand with your current skills and items. The goal of those first few days is retention, with Day 1 retention and length of play session being an important key performance indicator (KPI). Their goal, of course, is to get you to come back tomorrow. The following day's play is much the same. They've given you some premium currency and required you to purchase a restaurant improvement that will help you meet rising customer demand.

On Day 3, something happens to change the pace of the game. As your character and, in this example, your restaurant improves, you are no longer able to meet the rising demand, at least not as well as you could. What may have been a three-star performance on the first day is now a one-star performance. You're working much harder to excel, yet you're trying because you've invested time into this game. The items available in the general in-game currency store are "costed," neither under or over the curve, but the game pressure itself *is* above the curve, pushing you harder than before without giving you the resources to meet the increased pressure. F2P designers might call this the beginning of the ramp, the point at which players make a decision to stay and monetize, to grind it out with skill, or to leave. In these games, things are neither below or above the curve. They are costed according to what will monetize.

On average, the player has just too little of what they need and to succeed, they must spend money. The items in the cost curve are balanced relative to their benefits and costs, it's just that those benefits, and costs won't meet the rising challenge of the game itself.

Cost Curve Guidelines

Whether you're making your own original game or deriving the cost curve to an existing game, there are a few things you can count on.

First, a limited benefit is never negative. Even if the benefit is so limited in its use (a sword that does extra damage against dragons when you forgot to put dragons in the game), on its own the ability can't be worth less than zero.

Second, giving the player a choice between two effects (one or the other but not both) is never less than the most expensive of the two individual effects, because even if players always exclusively choose the better of the two effects, it is worth as much as that choice. Having an extra option, even one you never use, is never so bad that it's worse than not having the option at all. At worst, the extra option is completely worthless and thus has a benefit of zero (and the choice of "something worthless or something with a benefit of 5" has a benefit of 5). That said, if you are giving players a choice of two things, you usually want the two to be relatively similar in benefit levels so that the choice is an interesting one.

Third, if you are creating a game with several abilities where you don't know their costs, attempt to figure them out separately. Like a scientist, control for one unknown variable at a time. For example, if you don't know how much the Flying ability is worth, and you also don't know how much of a benefit First Strike provides, figure those out separately; don't start off with a creature that has both of them and try to figure out the individual costs. For one thing, trying to figure out the benefit of two unknowns together is hard. But even if you do manage to figure it out properly, you still won't necessarily know how much of that combined benefit comes from Flying, how much comes from First Strike, and how much of a bonus or penalty there is for combining the two. Even if you do figure out the benefit of Flying+First Strike, it doesn't give you any additional information about the cost curve or supporting math of the rest of the game.

Fourth, if you are uncertain how cost something in a game, err on the side of making the thing too weak rather than too strong. An object that's severely below the curve doesn't get used much, but it also doesn't affect the balance of everything else in the game. A single object that's severely above the curve always gets used, effectively preventing everything else on the curve from being used because the objects that are actually "balanced" are too weak by comparison. A too-strong object destroys the balance of the entire game, not just the balance of itself!

Fifth, test, iterate, and test again.

Finally, there is a long-term issue for persistent games that offer expansion sets or add-ons, where new content is added over time. The cost/power curve over time is not constant; it is increasing. Why? In order to make the new content viable, the designer must create a new cost curve that's balanced with respect to the best objects and strategies in previous iterations of the game, so that players find the new stuff useful and desirable. Since some of the new content is slightly above the new (higher) curve, the cycle repeats indefinitely. Over time, the power level of the game increases. It might increase quickly or slowly depending on how well balanced each set of content is, but there's always some non-zero level of "power inflation" or "power creep" over time.

While a designer's goal may be to get everything as close to the curve as possible in the initial and subsequent sets, in reality, a few things are a little better than they're supposed to be (even if the difference amounts to just a tiny rounding error). Over time, with a sufficiently large and skilled player base, anything that gives a player a competitive edge (no matter how tiny) rises to the top and becomes more common in use. Players adapt to an environment where the best-of-the-best is what is seen in competitive play, and players become accustomed to that as the "real" cost curve.

This is not necessarily a bad thing, in that it does force players to keep buying new stuff to stay current. Eventually, old strategies and objects that used to be dominant fall behind the power curve, and players need to get the newer stuff to stay competitive. By the same token, things that were above the power curve and disallowed from competitive play sometimes return. If players perceive that the designers are purposefully increasing the power level of the game in order to force new purchases, that gives players the opportunity to exit that game and find something else to do with their time.

Discussion Questions

1. Identify and discuss an overpowered item, character, or object in a game. How did it affect the balance, not just in the immediate sense, but long term?
2. Under what circumstances would a designer lower an item's price vs. lower its power?
3. What is item inflation?
4. Why might a designer create a cost curve?
5. What is transitivity?
6. How do cost curves apply to F2P games?

7. What is meant by "peaks and valleys," and why might a designer want them?

8. What is your favorite item from a game of your choice? From a balance perspective, why is that so?

9. Think of an item that felt underpowered to the point of frustration. How might you change that item?

10. If a boss were accidentally shipped with double the HP that had been intended, how might you address this in a subsequent update if you could not change that HP?

Sidequests

In this chapter, we learned how to use simple algebra to figure out how much items in a game should cost. There are many ways to practice this skill, from creating your own game to analyzing existing games. Note that most games that are complex enough to require cost curves takes far too long to analyze in the fullest, for the purposes of a short assignment for a game design course, so the sidequests presented here are intentionally abridged from the "real thing."

Sidequest 8.1: Using the Supporting Math

Using the cost curve and supporting math for *Magic: the Gathering* in this chapter, provide the following:

- A creature costs W4 for a 2/3 creature with the special ability that its owner gains 3 life when it enters play. How much is this special ability worth, assuming the card is on the curve?
- A blue creature is 2/2, with a strong special ability that is worth a benefit of 2. How much should it cost? (There may be several valid answers for this.)
- A black creature has a mana cost of B4 and has a drawback worth an additional cost of 1. If it has a power of 4, what should its toughness be?

Sidequest 8.2: Weaponization

Assume that in a particular game, a weapon should have a gold cost that is related in some way to the average damage per second (taking into account the accuracy of the weapon, i.e. the percentage of attacks that don't miss).

Thus, the Dagger does 1 damage per attack and attacks twice per second, and has an accuracy of 100%, so its expected DPS is $1 * 0.5 * 100\% = 2$. Assume the first three rows of this chart are balanced along the curve. Find a formula that fits, and then use that formula to fill in the rest of the numbers in this chart so that all weapons fit along the same curve (you may find it easier to enter these numbers into a spreadsheet to check your calculations). Note that there may be several valid answers.

Weapon	Cost (Gold)	Damage Per Attack	Seconds Per Attack	Accuracy
Dull Sword	10	1	0.8	80%
Dagger	40	1	0.5	100%
Battle Axe	160	10	1.25	50%
Mace	?	4	1	75%
Magic Sword	?	5	0.9	90%
Halberd	40	?	2	50%
Great Sword	?	6	1.4	?

Rogue's Main Quest, Part 4:
Finding the Cost Curve

Continuing from Part 3 in: Chapter 3

For this part of your quest, you first want to identify some subset of the game's mechanics and game objects that are meaningful within a relatively self-contained system. For a CCG or similar card game, this might be a particular class of cards; in a turn-based or real-time strategy game or tabletop miniatures game, consider the combat units of the game; for a tabletop RPG, you might look at item and equipment lists, or a list of spells or feats or other capabilities. There should be enough material to be able to find similarities and patterns, but not so much material to sort through that it becomes unwieldy—usually, this is somewhere between 30 and 60 game objects, once you remove any that are so unique that they can't be reasonably compared with anything else.

Derive the cost curve and supporting math for these objects, as best you can. List any assumptions you are making. When running into situations where several objects seem to conflict (one is clearly better than another so that they're not balanced along the same curve), use your own knowledge of the game, or else strategy articles online, to form a guess for which of the objects is above or below the curve.

In addition to the cost curve and supporting math, create a spreadsheet with formulas to calculate the balance, to show how far above or below the curve any given card is.

Next, apply a common-sense test. Identify the objects that you analyzed that are the most above or below the curve, given your work so far. Do the things at the extreme ends of your list make sense? Are your top five objects all things that are currently dominating the metagame? Are your bottom five objects all things that get used seldom if at all in competitive play? For the objects you previously thought of as being perfectly balanced—those that should be exactly on the curve—are they at least close?

If the answer to any of those questions is "no," then go back and look at your math. Why are certain objects being incorrectly classified by your math? Once you identify a problem, fix it in your formulas, then go back and repeat the process, until your set of objects seems like it's a reasonable representation of reality.

Part 5 continued in: *Chapter 10*

Wizard's Main Quest, Part 3: Updating the Costs for Harmony

Continuing from Part 2 in: *Chapter 5*

From playing Harmony, you should have a general sense of which of the four mechanics (Heal, Damage, Draw, and Discard) is most or least powerful, and whether there is a law of increasing or diminishing returns with each (e.g. is "Discard 3" three times as good as "Discard 1"... or more or less than that?). You should also have an idea of what the cost curve looks like: does something that costs 4 Power give twice as powerful an effect as something that costs 2 Power? Does increasing Power requirement scale linearly with the benefit, or is it a polynomial or triangular increase, a logarithmic increase, or some other type of curve (or a custom curve that behaves differently at various points and doesn't fit a single equation)? What is the relationship between Power of specific types (Bio, Gear, Magic, or Science) and Generic Power— how many Generic are worth one specific?

Make an attempt to develop a cost curve and supporting math for these four mechanics, based on your sense of their general power levels. Create a spreadsheet with columns for each of the four specific Power types and a fifth for Generic Power, and then four columns for Heal, Damage, Draw, and Discard. Finally, add a column that adds the benefits and subtracts the costs using some formula that you develop on your own, such that 0 is on the curve, negative is below the curve, and positive is above the curve.

Finally, put each card into the spreadsheet with its benefits and its original costs, and adjust the costs only to get each card to be as close to the curve as possible. Do not change type of Power, only quantity (notice, for example, some cards that have the same effect but one has only specific Power, one has only generic, and one has a mix of both). Your spreadsheet will look something like this, but with a formula in the rightmost column, and the costs modified appropriately:

Bio Cards			*Costs*				*Benefits*			
Name	*Bio*	*Gear*	*Magic*	*Science*	*Generic*	*Heal*	*Damage*	*Draw*	*Discard*	*Balance*
Natural Heal	1					4				
Regeneration	2				2	6			1	
Meditation	3					6			1	
Blossom	4				4	9			1	
Rebirth	6				8	12			2	
Cultivate	6					9			1	
Full Treatment	8				4	12			2	

Gear Cards			*Costs*				*Benefits*			
Name	*Bio*	*Gear*	*Magic*	*Science*	*Generic*	*Heal*	*Damage*	*Draw*	*Discard*	*Balance*
Ball of Spikes		1					2			
Machine Mask		2			2		4			
Infestation		2			8		6			
Silver Grenade		3					4			
Warrior's Fury		4			4		6			
Claw Hand		6					6			
Cruel Drill		8			4		8			
Shatter Body		10					8			

Magic Cards			*Costs*				*Benefits*			
Name	*Bio*	*Gear*	*Magic*	*Science*	*Generic*	*Heal*	*Damage*	*Draw*	*Discard*	*Balance*
Awakening			1				2	1		
Spell Scroll			2		2		3	2		
Library			2		8	9			1	
Fairy Glow			3				3	2		
Spellbook			4		4		4	3		
Brainstorm			6		8		5	4		
Light Orb			6				4	3		
Connectedness			8		4		5	4		

Science Cards			Costs				Benefits			
Name	Bio	Gear	Magic	Science	Generic	Heal	Damage	Draw	Discard	Balance
Headache				1					1	
Brain Freeze				2	2				2	
Surgery				2	8				3	
Disassembly				3					2	
Neoplasm				4	4				3	
Invasiveness				6					3	
Fragmentation				8	4				4	
Segmentation				10					4	

Misc. Cards			Costs				Benefits			
Name	Bio	Gear	Magic	Science	Generic	Heal	Damage	Draw	Discard	Balance
Inspiration					2		2	1		
Medicine					2	3				
Depression					2				1	
Wall of Spikes					2					
Mindhack					6				2	
Oneness					6		3	2		
Thornwheel					6		4			
Warmth					6	6			1	
Restoration	8		8			10	4	3	3	
Transplant	8			8		10			3	
Body Siphon		8	8				12	4		
Cataclysm		8		8			10		4	

Part 4 continued in: Chapter 12

9

Characters and Character Builds

In This Chapter

- Character Creation Systems
- Levels of Viability
- Balancing for Character Progression
- God Stats, Dump Stats, and Meaningful Decisions
- Balance and Player Perception

Character Creation Systems

> I have a Level 85 dwarven paladin, an 82 shadow priest, and I'm currently leveling a warrior through Northrend, although I spend most of my time tanking instances in the Dungeon Finder. I've held off on getting Mists of Pandaria because I got burned out on endgame progression after Wrath of the Lich King and the Cataclysm content is still new to me. Plus monks seem redundant in an era of dual specialization and viable hybrid DPS, and while I know they're well-established in the lore, Pandaren don't appeal to me. So I'm wrapping up a Taunka questline in the Borean Tundra, trying to determine if I should go to Dragonblight or Grizzly Hills, and now you know how I feel when you won't shut up about sports.
>
> *Comedian Nathan Anderson, @NathanTheSnake*

In the earliest days of video games, the concept of customizing the player's avatar was rare. The player is in control of a spaceship, or a paddle, or a Pac-Man, but there were no meaningful tradeoffs of choosing different stats or builds, no heated discussions over whether to take a faster but smaller paddle in *Pong*.

The ability to make a custom character was first popularized in tabletop role-playing games, notably *Dungeons & Dragons*, and many of the ideas from that game were later adopted by video game designers. These days, it's common for games across many genres to give the player some form of choice when selecting or creating a character, and further choices to develop that character over the course of play. These character-based mechanics can give players meaningful and interesting choices, support multiple play styles, and improve replay value of a game.

There are a few common methods for providing choices to players in this context, detailed here. Some games use all of these together, while others only allow customization in one category and keep everything else fixed.

Character Selection

The simplest way to give a player choice is to have a set of distinct pre-generated characters, and the player chooses one. This is common in games that have a relatively short play time (MOBAs, Fighting/Brawling games, racing games, and co-op board games). Each character is designed to support a particular role or play style within the game, and may have wildly different abilities. In these types of games, players will pay close attention to the balance between characters.

Character selection is also sometimes an option for longer-form games like RPGs, even those with more robust character creation systems, as a quick-start option for players who want to just get into the game without mucking about in attribute screens for half a day.

Attributes (or "Stats")

For games where the player character is central to the play and where the player is expected to use their character in many different ways to influence the game world, the character needs to be defined in terms of exactly what they can do. In the original *Dungeons & Dragons*, characters had six attributes (Strength, Dexterity, Constitution, Intelligence, Wisdom, and Charisma) and even today some games take strong inspiration from those.

Some early games had attributes assigned randomly, and the player would have to do the best they had with what they rolled. Today, it's much more common to see a **point-buy** system where players are given a certain number of attribute points which they spend to increase their attributes beyond some base level. Some games make a distinction between **primary attributes** (which the players can buy) and **secondary attributes** (which are determined by some combination of primary attributes, but the player cannot purchase them in a point-buy system directly). For example, in some games, Dexterity might be a primary attribute that the player can buy with attribute points and that has a number of effects on play, while Evasion might be a secondary attribute that is determined by the player's Dexterity plus any bonuses from skills or equipment. With an attribute system, it is the balance between the attributes themselves that players pay attention to: is it better to max out one or two attributes or to spread them around? Is one attribute just more powerful than the others for all characters or for a particular character type?

Skills

Characters can have a wide range of special abilities that designers refer to as **skills** (or sometimes "feats" or "techniques/techs"). Skills either enable a player to take a new action in the game that they couldn't without the skill (**active skills**) or provide the player an additional bonus that is in play all the time or that happens automatically in the right situations (**passive skills**). The distinction between a skill and an attribute is that player characters may not have a particular skill at all, but *all* characters share the same set of attributes and have some attribute score in each.

During character creation, a player may select certain starting skills, and often, they choose to add new skills (or in some games, level up existing skills to make them more powerful) as their character levels up. In some games, all skills are available at the start of the game, which gives the player the greatest number of customization options but can also be overwhelming for new players. In other games, they are introduced in linear fashion (you learn your first Healing spell at level 7, and an advanced Healing at level 25, always) which gives the designer the most control over character growth and makes the game easier to balance, but removes a lot of the feeling of ownership of the character from the player. In still other games, the player navigates a **skill tree** (also sometimes called a **tech tree**—the two terms are used interchangeably[1]) which splits the difference between the extremes: the player starts with a small selection of skills, and taking one skill can unlock more skills later on.

---

[1] If you're wondering why these are called trees, the term is borrowed from Computer Science since they tend to behave similarly to data structures of that name. Technically, skill trees as commonly implemented are not actually "trees" but "directed acyclic graphs"—but the name "tree" stuck early on, probably first used by the programmers that implemented them, and people have called them "trees" ever since.

This gives the player a reasonable number of options at any given time, while still giving the designer the ability to create some powerful skills that are only unlocked later, and offer the player interesting short-/long-term tradeoffs like "have a pretty good skill now that's a dead-end in the tech tree, or a mediocre skill that will let you get a *really* good skill a few levels from now."

In any case, games with skills can be analyzed in terms of the balance of these skills. Does a skill learned later make an earlier skill obsolete, or are even the early-game skills still useful in the late stages? If the player has a choice of several branches of the skill tree, is one clearly more powerful, or are they equally good and just support different play styles? Sometimes, there are strong links between skills and attributes: if the "fireball" skill does damage equal to twice your Magic attribute, then characters who learn this skill will have a reason to increase that attribute above the others.

Equipment

Characters might have a variety of gear that they can equip. In an RPG, this might involve various weapons, armors, and magic items. In an FPS, it might involve a main weapon, sidearm, and one or two slots for gear or grenades. In some games, skills are treated this way, where a player might have a large selection of skills for a character but they can only equip a small number of them at a time.

Usually, games like this provide each character with a set of **equipment slots** that each can only hold a certain type of equipment. You might have one slot for a helmet, one for body armor, one for a weapon, two slots for magic rings, and four slots for consumable potions. You can't equip a weapon in your helmet slot, as much as you might want to. In some games, all characters have the same equipment slots; in others, characters (or character classes) are differentiated from one another by how many and what type of slots they have available. Players refer to a specific equipment set for a character build as a **loadout**.

Character Classes

In some games, your character is the sum of your attributes and/or skills, and that's it. Want to play a character that's like a healer? Take a bunch of healing skills and the attributes to support those skills. Want to play a character like a fighter? Max out your combat-related attributes and take a bunch of skills that do damage or buff your ability to take hits when you wade into a sea of enemies. But all skills are available to all characters, and so official designations like "healer" or "fighter" are not given by the game itself, and a player could choose to mix and match with impunity.

In other games, characters are organized by their **class**. Classes may come with attribute bonuses or penalties, but what really differentiates them is class-specific skills. If your character is a thief, they can backstab; if your character is a fighter, they can't, no matter how much you want them to. A class tends to push a character in one or more specific directions, certain kinds of roles that the character can play and strategies they can pursue. A rogue will usually be good at sneaking around and will usually be bad at going toe-to-toe with fifty ogres in open ground in a combat arena.

Where classes exist, the first consideration is balance between the classes. If your Druid class acts basically just like your Cleric class except with a skill tree that isn't as good, players will complain that Druids are underpowered. The other consideration is variety within a class: is there only one role or play style for the class that it locks you into, or does it support multiple play styles?

Levels of Viability

We have a term for all of the choices that a player makes when creating a character—their class, equipment loadout, skills, attributes, and any other areas of customization that affect gameplay: a **build**. Sometimes, it isn't a specific character class or a specific piece of equipment that's overpowered in and of itself, it's a build that is overpowered, but the reason for the imbalance comes down to several elements of the build that work particularly well in combination.

When the player makes choices in the creation of their character build, we can speak of four broad categories that a particular build might fit into, in terms of balance:

- **Optimal (or "min-maxed")**: these characters contain the best performance that one can mathematically squeeze out of the game's systems. A player who has created an optimal character has probably spent a fair amount of time reverse-engineering the game's systems, comparing numbers, finding ways to stack bonuses or identify broken skill combos… or they've found an online guide from someone else who has.
- **Viable**: these characters may not be mathematically perfect, but they provide a playable experience throughout the game. A typical player should be able to beat the game at the default difficulty level without major problems, if they're playing a viable character.

- **Marginally viable**: these characters are suboptimal, but can still potentially be used to conquer the game's content in the hands of a skilled player. Such a build would be nonviable for most players, but expert players might create such a build on purpose as a personal challenge.
- **Nonviable**: a nonviable character is completely hopeless and could not be salvaged, even in the hands of an expert.

These terms are not industry-standard (the industry doesn't have standard terminology for this concept), but we use the terms in this chapter because differentiating between these categories is important. In particular, your best players will make optimal characters, while the majority of your players will end up making viable characters, and the difference in power level between "viable" and "optimal" (and how you balance your game content within that range) has strong implications for the play experience.

This concept is important for another reason: if a player creates a nonviable character, they will, at some point, have to abandon their game and restart from scratch. Sometimes, nonviability is immediately apparent: a player's first-level wizard with low Intelligence dies when a nearby rat sneezes on him, they realize their mistake and try a new build. Sometimes, though, it doesn't happen until much later: a build that's viable for the first 30 hours of play of an RPG, but then is literally unable to defeat the final boss because you built a fire mage and the boss happens to be immune to fire, and now the player has to abandon and replay the entire game if they want to progress. More likely, they'll stop playing entirely, and they won't recommend *that* game to their friends any time soon.

Balancing for Character Progression

For games where characters improve their skills and/or attributes over time (usually when leveling up), the game's challenge should increase to compensate. Players will find new zones with more powerful enemies, and the cycle repeats. For these games, a common design problem during development involves the difference between viable and optimal builds.

At the start of character creation, there will be *some* power difference between viable and optimal builds, of course. As characters level up, this gulf becomes wider, as the min-max players are going to optimize every little decision in character progression, improving their character even more than your typical viable build on every level gain.

How, then, do you balance the game's difficulty within this range? If you balance the content to be challenging but reasonable for a viable character build, your content will be absolutely trivial to conquer with an optimal build, and expert players will complain that your game is too easy. On the other hand, if you balance to provide a challenge to an optimal build, the game will be way too hard for the majority of players. And because the difference between viable and optimal increases over time, this problem of balance becomes the most notable with your end-game content. This is where a balance mistake leads to a final boss that goes down in one hit and feels anticlimactic, or conversely, a final boss that's impossible to beat and that stops a player cold. Neither of these is what a game designer would consider a good play experience.

There are a few potential solutions to this, depending on the game. If your game is very clearly made and marketed for a more casual, less experienced audience (or conversely, if you're catering to the hardcore powergamer crowd), you can balance toward one extreme or the other. More commonly, to support all player skill levels, games ship with multiple difficulty levels: an easy mode that's tuned to provide very little resistance for players who want to focus on the story, a normal mode that's tuned for most typical builds, a hard mode that's challenging for a typical build, and a hardest mode tuned to be a challenge even to optimal builds, for example.

Another method that can help is to reduce the power differential between viable and optimal builds, by making most of the character's power come from things the player doesn't choose (such as the base damage of weapons that they find in the game) with their attributes and skills providing minor bonuses. If a player in a particular zone is given a weapon that does 80–100 damage and their attribute scores and passive skills can potentially raise that up to the 100–130 range, that is still a noticeable improvement that min-maxers will appreciate, but not such a huge difference that it will invalidate any balance choices you made about how powerful enemies are. If, on the other hand, the player does a base damage of 80–100, a typical player will be at 85–110, and a min-max player can pump it to 300–600, there will be some people complaining about the balance of your game.

God Stats, Dump Stats, and Meaningful Decisions

Let's return to the idea raised at the start of this chapter: that character creation is about providing the player meaningful decisions.

What does "meaningful" mean in this context? It means a decision that has some impact on the game and that offers a choice between several viable alternatives.

Here are some examples of decisions that are *not* meaningful:

- A choice between two weapons, a sword that does 50 damage and a sword that does 75 damage, where the two are identical in every other way. The solution here is obvious—take the better one—so players are presented with a "choice" where there is a clear best answer, which isn't really a choice.
- A blind choice between two unknowns, where the player has no way of evaluating the choice, such as taking the prize behind Door Number 1 or the prize behind Door Number 2. Here, the player must simply guess (and then reload from save and guess again, or look up a walk-through online) because they aren't given the tools to own the decision themselves.
- A choice between two things that end up giving the same result, so that the player's decision did not matter. Sometimes, these choices can have emotional value (choosing the hair style for your avatar even when it has no gameplay effect), but if you have the player deliberating for hours over which attribute to give +1 to and none of the attributes actually do *anything*, that is a meaningless choice that players do not appreciate.

When the player is making decisions about their character build, they are choosing to assign points among their attributes, or choosing new skills on their skill tree, or choosing an equipment loadout. As designers, we want these decisions to be meaningful. Before we do that, let's look at ways to provide decisions that are *not*.

In player (and game designer) speak, a **god stat** is a stat that is overpowered or, at the very least, necessary for an optimal build. If you're trying to make a damage-heavy archer and bow damage is based entirely on your Dexterity, then Dexterity is a god stat for you: you'll want to put as many spare points into Dexterity as you can get away with.

The opposite of this is a **dump stat**—something that a player can safely ignore, because it simply isn't required at all. If the Intelligence stat in your game does nothing other than increase the number of spells the character can cast, characters that are not spell users gain no benefit from Intelligence, and if the game allows it, they'll do best to *remove* points from that stat during character creation in order to assign those points elsewhere.

The presence of anything in your game that's "god" or "dump" suggests, by definition, a decision that is not meaningful. If a player fails to maximize a god stat or puts otherwise perfectly good attribute points into a dump stat, all they've managed to do is weaken their character. There may be a perfectly good reason why they want to do this (such as creating an elaborate backstory for their character, and choosing the attributes and skills that match), but from the perspective of the game's systems, the character will end up being less powerful than it could have been. To avoid this situation, a designer attempts to make all elements of a character build at least marginally useful to *all* characters, and if you notice that there's a particular attribute or skill that all of your playtesters seem to take (or avoid), that suggests an imbalance to be addressed. For example, a stereotypical magic user class isn't particularly strong so a player might assume Strength is a dump stat... but if Strength also affects carrying capacity (how much loot you can carry back from the dungeon on each run) and ability to push obstacles like heavy doors (allowing you access to treasure rooms that you wouldn't be able to enter otherwise), then even magic-using characters will get some use out of Strength and it won't be such a no-brainer to use it as a dump stat.

As an extension of this, the presence of *completely* nonviable characters can be seen as a signal of imbalance, since that means the player has been presented with a choice where some of the options are simply not okay to choose.

For equipment loadouts and skill trees, things work a little different than stats. Each stat is, by definition, present in all characters, so the design focus should be making each stat meaningful. With equipment and skills, characters choose a subset of these from a larger pool of available ones, so a particular piece of equipment or a specific skill does not have to be useful for *every* character build, so long as it is useful for at least *some* builds. Think of each item as having a purpose that it serves—a particular role or play style that it supports—and since builds are based around optimizing for a play style, this means there should be at least one viable (or optimal) build where each item is useful.

A particular scenario to watch out for is characters in playtesting that seem viable early game and become nonviable later on, or else testers that are intentionally trying to make good characters that make nonviable ones anyway. This suggests that the player is making a blind choice without having the information to understand what their character build will do or what challenges they'll face. To avoid this, either modify the game's content so that these characters become playable, modify the character attribute/skill system so that the characters are viable, or find ways to prevent a player from making a nonviable build (such as making certain essential skills "standard" and automatically chosen or required for a given character class).

On the flip side, if you're finding that just about every character is viable but they all play exactly the same, the same general strategies work regardless of build, and the choices made during character creation don't seem to matter because the player ends up in the same place anyway... then first check your code, because the programmers might have forgotten to implement the effects of one or more of the attributes (yes, this has embarrassingly happened with more than one shipped title). But if you confirm the code is working properly, then consider increasing the effects of these decisions, which will widen the gap between "viable" and "optimal" but will also increase the impact of the decisions made when building a character.

Balance and Player Perception

If you notice in playtesting that something seems unbalanced, such as a particular attribute being overvalued by just about every player, or a skill that no one ever chooses, there are two possibilities. One is that there is a legitimate, mathematical imbalance and you need to **buff** or **nerf** something (these terms are used as shorthand for strengthening or weakening something to improve the balance of the game, by both designers and gamers).

Another possibility is that the game systems are fine, but the game has not communicated the value to players, so they make decisions based on misinterpreted information about the game's systems. When this happens, it usually comes down to the game failing to communicate effectively and transparently to the player. Here are a few ways players can fail to understand the power of something in the game:

- Assumptions based on prior game experience, if your game violates expectations. For example, many players will assume that Wisdom is a dump stat for rogue-class characters because that's how it is in a lot of games, and if Wisdom is important to rogues in your game, then you'll have to take extra steps to make sure the player realizes this.
- Lack of feedback from the game interface. For example, if the player is currently leveling up and can add +1 to an attribute of their choice, how are the effects of this choice made visible to the player? You might have it so that when an attribute is selected, it shows how much secondary attributes go up, highlights any skills that are affected, and so on, so the player can immediately see at a glance what they get. If the player has no information and only sees the effects after they irreversibly make their choice, they might choose differently than they should.

- Confusing or overwhelming feedback from the game interface. On the other end of the scale, if the game gives complete information but it's difficult for a player to parse, they may simply ignore it. An example of this might be a skill with a text description that's so long and intricate that most players don't bother reading it. Another example might be a math operation that's hard to conceptualize, like a "+13%" modifier to damage when your damage range is 65–78, something that players probably won't do in their heads.
- The way the data is presented can influence player decisions. Consider the difference between these two systems where the player's Strength stat is in the range of 1–9: in the first system, the player has a base attack damage of 1 and gains +1 attack damage for every point of their Strength stat (so their damage will range from 2 to 10); in the second system, the player has a base attack damage of 6 for a default/average Strength of 5, +1 attack damage for each point above 5, and −1 attack damage for each point below 5. These are exactly the same mathematically, of course, but in the latter case, players will tend to have a stronger aversion to an Attack below 5 since that is presented to them as a penalty.

Additional Resources

- Josh Sawyer, *Gods and Dumps: Attribute Tuning in Pillars of Eternity* (GDC 2016), https://www.gdcvault.com/play/1023481/Gods-and-Dumps-Attribute-Tuning
- Richard Bartle, *Clubs, Diamonds, Hearts, Spades: Players Who Suit MUDs*, https://mud.co.uk/richard/hcds.htm

Discussion Questions

1. What is a character build?
2. Choose any game with some kind of character creation or character build system. What are some of the most popular character builds? (If you're unfamiliar with the game, you might look this up in online forums or strategy guides.)
3. For the same game as in the previous question, what are the different play styles that the game supports? (Looking at the different character builds may give you some clues here—each popular build probably fits neatly into one particular play style.)

4. If a particular character build is found to be overpowered, what are some possible root causes that a designer should look for?

5. Think of a game that allows a great deal of character customization. Is it possible to make a completely nonviable build in this game, and if so, give an example.

6. In games with a point-buy stat system, why is the presence of a 'god stat' or 'dump stat' a potential sign of imbalance?

7. What is your favorite character build, in any game? Why?

8. Think of any skill or any single piece of equipment in a game you're familiar with. What kinds of play styles or character builds is this item optimal for, and which ones would it never be used with?

9. Which would be worse: shipping a PvP game with ten character classes where one of them is entirely nonviable, or where one of them is extremely overpowered?

10. Choose a single-player game that involves some kind of progression, where the player makes choices about how to level their character (either through point-buy stat gains on leveling up, finding new equipment in their loadout, unlocking new skills in a skill tree, or similar choices). How forgiving is this system to suboptimal choices—that is, how much does a player have to optimize in order to beat the game, or how suboptimal can a character build be while still having the game be theoretically beatable?

Sidequests

In this chapter, we talked conceptually about character build systems. As with some other chapters, most of the games that have elaborate character builds are too large in scope to just create one yourself for practice unless you seriously constrain yourself, so the sidequests here are a bit less mathematical and a bit more hypothetical than most in this book.

Sidequest 9.1: Three Attributes, Three Builds

Let's suppose you're designing a multiplayer RPG (this could be either a tabletop game, an MMO, or a couch-coop experience, or any other situation you might imagine). You're designing such that each player controls a single character, and the players work together in a small group to overcome the game's challenges.

You want there to be three general roles: a "DPS" role whose primary function is to do large amounts of damage to enemies; a "Tank" role who draws enemy attacks away from the DPS character so they don't die; and a "Support" role whose job is to keep the Tanks alive and/or buff the damage output of the DPS characters in order to increase the overall effectiveness of the team.

Design an attribute system for this game where all characters have exactly three attributes. You may name these attributes whatever you want. Design the attributes such that all three attributes have at least *some* value to all three roles. You do not have to go into great detail describing exactly how each attribute should work; rather, give a general description of what kind of effect the attributes have.

As an example of the level of complexity to go for here, you might design an attribute called Compassion which you describe as a stat that increases all buff and debuff effects that the character creates. (This would be a terrible design for an attribute since it would be a god stat for Support characters and a dump stat for both DPS and Tanks.)

Sidequest 9.2: Classes for Players

Game designer Richard Bartle wrote a widely read essay on four types of players that commonly play MUDs (games that were the precursors to today's MMOs). A link to the original article is given at the end of this chapter. If you haven't encountered this article before, in summary:

- **"Achievers"**: players who want to "win" the game (even though there isn't technically a win state). These are the players who want to create optimal builds, collect all of the rarest loot, get to the top of the rankings in PvP arenas, and generally just create the most overpowered character possible.
- **"Explorers"**: players who want to see everything the game has to show them. These are the players who would gleefully draw maps of the world if there were no auto-mapping feature and who would experiment with the physics, mechanics, and other elements of the game just to see how they work.
- **"Socializers"**: players who are there for the company of other human players. These people prefer to spend more time talking and interacting with their fellow players, sometimes casually, sometimes role-playing in character, and might be more concerned with how their character looks than what kinds of stats they have.

- **"Killers"**: more commonly called "griefers" today, these are the players who find fun in ruining the experience of other players. This may take the form of attacking other players and looting their bodies, and/or verbally abusing them in chat.

Choose any MMO, past or present, that has the concept of distinct character classes. If you are not familiar with the game, look up a strategy guide or wiki online that lists the classes available. Choose any three character classes in the game (try to go for a variety), and read about the general role that class plays in the game, general play style, and what strategies players can do to optimize their builds. Once you've done this research, for each of the classes you chose, write a single paragraph noting whether you think that class was created specifically to appeal to one or more of Bartle's four player types listed above. If so, mention why: what is it about the strategy or play style that would appeal to which types? If not, what kind of player (not listed above) *do* you think it would appeal to, if any?

Fighter's Main Quest, Part 4: Analyze a Combat

Continuing from Part 3 in: Chapter 3

For the game you've chosen, do a design analysis of the combat system (or closest reasonable equivalent). How would you model a typical combat, such as a random encounter, mathematically?

Choose any specific combat at any point in the game, with player characters that are at an appropriate power level for the situation they're in. Determine all of the player characters' combat stats and inventory, which you can make up so long as it is reasonable for that point in the game that you've chosen.

Then, look up the monsters' combat stats, as well as all relevant formulas to determine whether an opponent is hit, how much damage attacks do, and so on. The exact formulas are usually not given in the game's tutorials or manual (though there are occasional exceptions), so you may have to find this in an online FAQ/walkthrough/wiki or a published strategy guide. Online MMOs such as *World of Warcraft* tend to have well-documented stats published online by the community.

Create a spreadsheet that uses the game's formulas and the stats you've compiled in order to simulate the outcome of a combat. In particular, look at several situations:

- What is the worst-case scenario? If all random rolls go against the player, are they going to die, or are they merely going to lose a few more hit points than they would otherwise? How likely is this to happen?
- What is the best-case scenario? Does the player's adventuring party walk away unharmed, or are they just taking slightly less damage than they would normally? How likely is this, compared with the worst-case outcome?
- What is the average or expected outcome? You might compute this using probability calculations, or a Monte Carlo simulation… or ideally, both, to confirm that they are the same (and if you get two different answers, then re-check your calculations to find the problem).

Finally, state the implications of your findings. How many combats like this would a party be expected to survive before they're wiped out (and how does this compare with the number of combats between towns or other places where the party can fully heal)? Based on the rewards for winning the fight, how many of these fights does a player have to beat before the characters level up significantly, and/or before they find enough gold to purchase better equipment? How much of a threat is losing entirely (and having to restart the game), and how much of that depends on a player's choices vs. being determined by good or bad die-roll results?

Part 5 continued in: Chapter 10

10

Combat

In This Chapter

- What Combat Is
- The Feel of Combat
- Feel vs. Solution
- The Pillars of Combat
- The Constraints of Combat
- The Variety of Combat
- Time Outside of Encounters
- Genre Specialization and Player Pressure

What is Combat?

> Ever tried. Ever failed. No matter. Try again. Fail again. Fail better.
>
> *Samuel Beckett in Worstward Ho*
>
> *Samuel Beckett was not a game designer, although he
> was obsessed with Chess. Never has a quote so perfectly
> summed up how one balances combat in a game*

Combat is first and foremost a drama, and it's a drama choreographed with math, and the game designers who understand this stand out from those who don't. It's why this chapter begins with a discussion on the design of this drama and not spreadsheets to model or algorithms to implement. If you ask a group of gamers, or game designers for that matter, to describe the best combat they remember, notice the words they use. The collection below comes from a conversation held with six graduate students:

Unforgettable	Hope	Shock	Panic	Closure
Movements	Theatrical	Celebration	Lost	Win
Tension	Funny	Chaos	Anticipation	Memorable
Struggle	Prayer/ritual ("Hail Mary" moves)		Unexpected	Drama
Closeness of shared experience (in a multiplayer game)			Realization of mastery/learning	

The notion of *combat as drama* is as true in games as it is in movies or books. It's what the players are here for, and it's our job to give it to them, not by accident, but by design. We want to give players moments where they feel like a badass. So, as a combat designer, your job is to determine what you want your players to feel, to see, to hear. Then, you can determine the means by which this drama is going to unfold. Last, you direct that drama with math.

The *Feel* of Combat

Good combat is something you *feel*. Look at any reviews for any combat-centric game like a first-person shooter (FPS).

> Combat just feels good.
> The gunplay feels incredible.

What exactly are people referring to here? It's a combination of many different things which, when taken in together, result in something that is deeply satisfying for players. Combat should make the player feel like they are **empowered**, capable of making winning decisions. To make players feel empowered, it's necessary for the game to have one or more counters for every action an enemy can take. If the player fails in combat, they blame themselves for not using a counter properly or not having it yet vs. blaming the game for being unfair or unbalanced.

Combat should, at certain points, make players feel **heroically badass**. If they don't feel this way, *even if combat is perfectly mathematically balanced just as you intend it*, players may struggle to like your game. This doesn't mean you need to script the plans for one linear move after another or script the entire game end to end. It means you need to nail the **combat loop**: a short repeatable section of play.

Former Bungie designer Jaime Griesemar, echoing some of the *Halo* team ethos, referred to it as 30 seconds of fun, suggesting that if you could nail that and repeat it again and again, you could stretch it out into an entire game. While that phrase is often repeated, what's missing is the deeper context of Griesemar's quote: you need to *vary* it. If you take that 30 seconds and put it into different environments, with different weapons and enemies, this combat loop becomes incredibly effective.

In an interview with Engadet, Griesemar expanded upon his initial quote, recalling a conversation he had with then *Halo* AI programmer Chris Butcher. "The premise was that he was the AI programmer, and I was the designer working on characters and we were going to explain where we overlapped on *Halo*. To do that, we talked about how the AI handles all the decisions on the 30-second timescale; where to stand, when to shoot, when to dive away from a grenade. And the mission designers handle what happens on the 3-minute timescale; when to send reinforcements, when to retreat, encounter tactics. But in between, design and programming had to work together to come up with behaviors and a combat loop that would serve as the bridge between the 30-second AI and the 3-minute mission script. So that's where the idea of a short, repeated segment of gameplay first showed up." (A link to the full interview is given at the end of this chapter.)

We examine these key elements below.

The Camera

Where is the camera looking? How is it moving? Is the player able to get the information he or she needs and able to do what needs to be done? This takes into account not just the camera movement, but the critical things that the player must see like the reticle or the enemy he or she is tracking.

Of course, the look depends on the perspective of the game itself. For third-person games, programmer Ian Pilipski cites *Legend of Zelda* for its ability to lock onto your enemy in a way that feels natural. "A game that gives you this ability either directly or indirectly automatically gives you a natural way to express an ability you would do in the real life. Without it, you have to take conscious effort and control to simply keep your target tracked, and that doesn't feel natural." In first-person games, Pilipski notes that more emphasis is needed on the environment. After all, the player is tracking their own view. "Lens effects, blur, shaking, movement bob, crosshairs, visual cues, all become much more important when your perspective is limited."

Gears of War level designer Lee Perry notes that, "If the camera is shaking, you have to work out specifically how so. Ideally, you want the crosshair position being meticulously managed by game logic, but the subtle camera roll works well, minor FOV bumps as well as moving/bumping the camera position but leaving the aiming point specifically where you want it."

Programmer Tom Plunket noted that a game's camera is nearly invisible when it's done well. "I've done a lot of camera work in the past and considered my job done when nobody says anything about how the camera moves since it's at that point when it's not noticed that it's correct."

The Sound

Audio fills all the space between the code, the art, and the player's imagination and sets the mood. Great weapon sounds are like that, as are great impact and enemy reaction sounds. Try turning the audio off in any game, both soundtrack and effects, and notice how much less satisfying it is. A crisp, punchy, distinct sound is critical for the player's different weapons, even down to the microseconds when at first that weapon's sound plays. Think about the rocket launcher sound in *DOOM*. It's iconic and everyone knows it. Likewise, the sound of the plasma rifle in *XCOM Enemy Unknown* is incredibly satisfying.

In his talk *Gods and Dumps* on character attribute tuning (see additional resources in the previous chapter), game designer Josh Sawyer relayed a story where a systems designer was running a playtest and the players felt one particular gun in the game was severely underpowered. In the next patch, the developers changed the audio sound that played when the gun fired, but didn't change any of the stats on the gun, and the players felt like the problem was fixed and the gun was good now. Good audio counts more than we often give it credit for when it comes to the player perception of value.

The Look and Feel of the Weapons

The feel of the weapons is determined by the visual feedback in player character and the weapon motion (and physically, in the case of vibration on the console controllers). Players often want to see that they are carrying heavy guns which make them feel badass. Animation in gun carry is deliberately oversold. Artist Josh Jay notes that "the weapon has to feel impactful via recoil animation effects, have a satisfying sense of weight and crisp audio." Jay cites the *Fallout 3* Gauss Rifle as an excellent example. "There was a really great metallic ring to firing (and reloading) and the induction slugs and the rifle conveyed a sense of heft, like you were lugging The Pain with you everywhere you went."

The Look of the Impact

When a weapon fires upon or hits an enemy, the obvious and palpable response in the enemy to the impact of these weapons is key to making combat feel good and, in response, making the player feel good.

First, players want to see where their shot went. Games use tracers to help players follow the action. In multiplayer games, these tracers are also useful in giving away the player's position. Next, players want to see that their attack had an effect appropriate to their expectations. If it exceeds those expectations, so much the better. For instance, you can already imagine the effect of a rocket launcher, and so that's what players expect you to deliver.

Lee Perry, citing his work and the work of colleague Cliff Bleszinski on the *Gears of War* series, offered specific insight into the importance of good hit impact visuals. First, Perry suggested using "small detail particles as well as larger subtle volumes that linger." Likewise, Perry highlighted "*fast* impact effects, too. Whatever most people do, double or triple the playback rate so it's visceral and immediate instead of a particle guy's demo reel in slow motion." Bleszinski has been quoted saying that shooting is "touching the world," so it needs to feel and look great.

Think about how oversold impact visuals are in movies or in professional wrestling. It works. Admittedly, there is a nuance to this design that is difficult to encompass in words. Describing good combat feel, *Monday Night Combat* designer John Comes says, "It's when no one notices it. When the weapon feels so good that it's just natural. Building *Monday Night Combat*, we literally spent two weeks on this. Getting the spread right, the recoil, the trace, the client-side prediction, and more. We studied our favorite games like *Call of Duty*, *Modern Warfare 2* and *Team Fortress*." It's important to understand that your game balance fits into and relies upon this nuance. In the words of *Empire of Sin* combat designer Ian O'Neill, "You need to sell it!"

The Celebration

Once the combat is over, there needs to be a focus on celebration which adds a significant amount to how the player feels independent of how good the action combat loop is. Celebration from a *feel* perspective involves audio, of course. It also typically involves some kind of animation (from a gun flourish to a full-on dance). Showing players that their player character *feels* how they should feel goes a surprisingly long way.

Clarity

What appears on the screen gives the player the necessary information to act upon and accurately displays what has just happened. The units themselves telegraph the gameplay they are capable of and have clear and distinct visual signatures. The information about all units, including the player, clearly displays their key attributes such a health/max health. If the player needs the information to make a decision, it's either already visible or within obvious reach (a hover over or focus button).

Game designer Will Kerslake notes, "The constant struggle is removing chaos, particularly in co-op situations where the number of combatants increases. It's hard enough to get players to understand cause & effect under pressure when their focus narrows. But in multiplayer, there are additional actors creating new causes, often offscreen, compounding the problem. Typically, the best solve is a combo of clear presentation of new enemies, and simplifying individual enemy behavior so that each is very easy to understand."

"Finding the right balance between over-communicating and letting players figure out how to best put bodies on the ground, well, it often leads to over-communicating because players in a focus test will be more vocal about 'I didn't understand that; it sucked' vs. 'Wow, that was great! I struggled just enough with that and it felt great to figure it out.'" says designer Jonathan Hamel. "Designers solve problems, so when someone brings us a problem, we feel compelled to solve it. It takes a great deal of restraint, careful observation, and a publisher relationship built on trust, to put down the pencil and let players struggle a little. Which is fun, at least for players who crave challenge."

Struggle and challenge is good. If the player is struggling to understand what's happening because it's either inconsistent or not clear, however, that will be their focus, not the action itself. In a worst-case scenario, players may feel like they randomly die without any indication as to why this might have happened, even if there are very good reasons for it happening.

Underneath the hood, it feels like it's making sense and following patterns. Things act as the players expect they will act and as they are advertised to act. Players are able to learn from what they see based on feedback which tells them they did it right or still have room to improve.

The Timing

Timing and pacing in games is critical, and nowhere else is it more critical than combat. If things are happening too quickly and the players don't have time to consider what's happening, they will not be able to formulate a response. They grow frustrated, hopeless, and quit. In PvP games, this can happen if players are mismatched, or there is no matchmaking. In both single- and multiplayer games, it can happen if the AI overwhelms players and doesn't give them enough time to think through their options. It can also happen if the AI doesn't give them enough to recoup. Conversely, if the pacing is too slow, players become bored. They've made their decisions and wonder what's taking so long. The timing of *Starcraft* provides excellent examples of all these principles. In South Korea, the game is optimized to account for the extreme speed of the players. If left to the Western version, South Korean players become bored. Conversely, Western players find the pacing of the South Korean versions simply overwhelming.

Feel vs. Solution

In considering combat as drama and something to choreograph, and in understanding our intuitive or research-led answers, what we are doing is directing. We're writing the script of how we hope the encounters play out, and with that, we engineer our way there through code, art, audio, and design. It's not the other way around. It certainly *can be* the other way, but it will take a lot less time to know what you want and work your way there than to assign some numbers hoping it works out for you. In looking for these answers, it's sometimes surprising to find that the answer is already there or that we at least have opinions about what is *not right* at a given point in time. By having an idea of what combat looks like 5 minutes, 1 hour, or 5 hours into play, you create the target of for the combat space you're trying to balance toward.

This discussion on combat may seem counterintuitive to those of you who don't see it as a drama to be choreographed with math, but rather a math problem to be documented and overcome. You might see it as something to be solved vs. the fuzzy, uncertain space it is when you factor in players, weapons, enemies, and the wide possibility space that exists in between. To those of you in the "solve" camp, many examples abound. The mathematical wiring of nearly every game you can imagine is now online.

The Pillars of Combat

The pillars of combat are the core decisions you, as the game's combat designer, must make. Like design pillars, combat pillars are words that people might use to describe combat in your game. The pillars of combat are

- Genre
- Time
- Pacing
- Feel
- Participants
- Progression
- Volume

It is necessary to know these things first, both as a guide for making decisions about how combat will unfold and for making decisions later on when it comes time to cut or to add elements to your game. These topics must be addressed in a non-linear fashion where one informs the other. Sometimes, in these discussions, the answer to, "What is combat like?" is a canonical game which has been universally praised by both players and designers alike. *XCOM*, *Final Fantasy Tactics*, and *DOOM* are regularly mentioned in discussions of combat. In saying, "Combat is going to be like *XCOM*," one must understand the questions the designers of those canonical games asked of themselves.

These seven core pillars, when evaluated and decided upon, result in the definition of your combat. For instance, in Brenda's game *Empire of Sin*, the combat could be described as

- **Genre**: Strategy/Empire Building
- **Time**: turn-based
- **Pacing**: methodical and calculated
- **Feel**: visceral, gritty, tactical
- **Participants**: single-player, squad-based
- **Progression type**: player and character progression
- **Volume**: one-third, with empire and crew management being the other two-thirds.

Let's look a little more closely at each.

Genre

It's safe to assume that decision of genre is already made by the time you reach the combat discussion. Otherwise, it's like ordering a main course in a restaurant without previously having made the decision to go to a restaurant. We add genre here as a key checkpoint for readers. In some genres, like fighting and FPS, combat is the entire game. In others, it's a component of the game.

When working solidly within the space of an existing, well-defined genre, players have certain expectations based on their prior experience with other games in that genre. As game designers, we don't want to just recreate a previous game in the genre, so we must find ways to differentiate our game from the others in a way that attracts players.

The lesson here is to understand the genre you're working in: what are the mechanics that must be there and are non-negotiable, what mechanics are commonly used and you will change them (understanding that this will emphasize different parts of the play experience, which will then be the focus of how your game differentiates itself), and what other common things in the genre will then have to change to support your key changes.

Time

Is combat real-time or turn-based? Real-time combat unfolds as it happens. This is true of all first-person shooters, many strategy games, and some RPGs. On the other hand, turn-based combat unfolds according to character or player initiative and in rounds. Everyone takes a turn according to initiative (usually based on the character's speed or agility stat). When everyone has taken their turn, a round passes, and we begin again. There are minor variations on these standards which are employed to heighten the drama. For instance, at a specific moment, combat might go into "bullet time" which slows the combat down dramatically so that players can attempt to avoid a bullet in real time on their turn-based turn. Turn-based combat can have a time limit or timers that advance if the player does nothing, as in the "Active Time Battle" system found in many *Final Fantasy* games. In the classic card game *Slap Jack*, players take turns flipping a card face up into a pile. If a player flips a jack, then the game enters real-time where the first player to slap their hand on the jack wins the entire pile. The variations here are endless, but all employed to heighten the drama.

In the initial development of *Diablo*, designer and programmer David Brevik was asked to change the time of combat from turn-based to real-time. As he tells the story, he initially balked at the suggestion, but decided to give it a go anyway. He describes it as a "lightning bolt" moment in which transformed the game.

Pacing

Think of two or three words to describe the pacing of your game. How do you want *players* to describe it? You need to know these things before you begin your own combat design and balance. Is combat intense or methodical and calculated? Is it pre-planned and tactical? Is it a mix of both? Consider *DOOM* vs. *Hitman*. In the former, combat is intense. There are rarely breathers to collect your bearings. In *Hitman*, combat is methodical and calculated. Even initiating a hit must be well timed, with many different circumstances taken into account. These questions are important regardless of whether it's real-time or turn-based. A turn-based game can have a time limit on its turns, making it feel as visceral and intense as a real-time game. Likewise, a team-based esports match is heavily pre-planned and tactical even if the game itself is real time. Sure, many decisions happen on the fly, but odds are those decisions are based on pre-planning.

Feel

Think of one word each to describe how you want people to feel as they approach and then enter combat. Are they scared, tense, and fearful? Are they coordinated, organized, and hopeful? Are they examining the odds of success before deciding to proceed with combat or back out? Are they walking through a real or metaphorical escape room taking terrified steps forward (equal parts anticipation and dread)? Consider the team's mood pre-raid in *World of Warcraft* and compare that to a player planning a battle in *XCOM* or a player contemplating but then backing out of a battle in *Mutant Year Zero*. Consider the actual, physical side-to-side movement of FPS players as they react to their opponents. Each of these feelings was a deliberate creation of game designers. If you want a player to feel scared, for instance, you need time and space to build that scare. If you want players to feel like they are planning, you need to give them stuff to build a plan about and sometimes a place to do that planning. People plan a raid. People choose their load outs. They plan all kinds of scenarios for professional sports matches. These intentions are critical for the drama of combat.

Most importantly, ask yourself, "How do I want them to feel?" and then follow that with, "What am I doing to make them feel that way?" Moods (like tense or scared, especially) take time to percolate. When looking at combat through this lens, it's apparent it is so much more than a mathematical construct.

Participants

Is it player vs. player (PvP) or player vs. environment (PvE)? Is this single player or multiplayer? Is it team play or solo? Are AI combatants involved or is it humans only? Is it squad-based or solo character? The number and type of participants on the stage determines who the game designer needs to direct and, as with everything here, affects the decision you might make in regard to time, pacing, and volume.

Progression Type

Consider how players get better in your game. There are two primary progression paths for this: player progression and character progression. With player progression, the player's skill gets better over time, even though the game itself remains unchanged. This is true of most FPS games as well as games like Chess or Poker. With character progression, the character the player controls gets better over time, generally by gaining experience points in the game. These experience points are then converted into levels which are then converted into increased skills, abilities, and performance improvements. Sometimes, you might have a mix of the two. See Chapters 11 and 12 for more about various kinds of progression.

With player progression, if you have attended any deathmatch events in which professional players are involved, the mastery of the players is most certainly on display. In games like *Quake*, even bugs are exploited to give professional players an edge (bunny hopping and rocket jumping being the result of bugs within the original *Quake* code). If the game is about players finishing or "beating" mastery of the gameplay only, at some point, the player masters it and either they require new gameplay (such as new weapons, monsters, or levels) or they become bored. Who's still trying to get better at an adventure game? If the gameplay includes PvP play, which is almost always the case in cases where player mastery of play is key, the player requires progressively better players to match their level of play. In this case, the volume of "enemies" is virtually endless so long as players can find new opponents. The possibility space of the game is vast.

With character progression, the possibility space of the game is more narrow. Players encounter only what's in the game, and the designers need to account for the appropriate level of variety and challenge in the game itself to keep players entertained and engaged from beginning to end. At its most narrow are the types of RPGs that feature a linear narrative arc through which the characters pass while engaging in combat along the way in pursuit of the story's goals. A purely narrative game would be even narrower, but those traditionally do not involve character progression in need of balancing in the way we have defined it here. In such an RPG, designers need to consider ingame variety to keep it fresh. See "Variety of Combat" later in this chapter an expanded discussion on this.

Volume

Where does combat fit within the game itself? Is it the game or is it only one aspect of the game? Combat is the game in *Fortnite,* and even the building aspects of *Fortnite* are there to support the combat. Combat is a part of the game in *Red Dead Redemption* where exploration and story share the stage. Combat is likewise a part of *Civilization* where building and expanding one's civ are equally important.

The Constraints of Combat

The constraints of combat form the boundaries of dramatic combat encounters and work in concert with your pillars of combat in terms of making decisions about what combat should be. Sometimes, they are design set (enemies always show up in groups of two or more), and sometimes, they are code set (you can't have more than 15 units on the screen for memory reasons). Building upon the pillars of combat, the constraints determine timing and quantity, and not surprisingly, these numbers have less to do with balance, *per se,* than they do with drama, player expectations and technical constraints. In fact, it's these things we balance toward. The constraints of combat revolve around three key things: length of game, length of combat, and number of hits.

Length of Game

How long is your game predicted to be? For the sake of this discussion, however, let's assume that your game is 10 hours long. Furthermore, let's assume that combat is one of three game pillars (with exploration and story being the other two). How many enemies do you need there to be to give you this 10 hours of gameplay? What at first seems like a difficult-to-answer question actually isn't. For instance, consider this scenario: at least once in every college class, there's a student with a list of 100 weapons and 200 monsters for a game he or she expects to be approximately 10 hours long. Is this excessive? It means you need to get to know and master 20 creatures per hour and 10 weapons per hour of gameplay. Consider the overlap between the weapons and monsters (what weapons are best for which monsters), and you can see that the potential game space with that many weapons and monsters is much too large for the time allotted. From a production viewpoint, the cost of creating and animating the monsters is nontrivial, and from a code point of view, crafting unique AI for these different enemies or even a subset of these different enemies is a lot of work. While someone could absolutely design a game with these constraints (10 hours, 200 monsters, and 100 weapons), it's more than is needed to provide a good gameplay experience.

So what is the answer to this question? We look more closely at that in the next section, "The Variety of Combat." For now, it's important to know the length of the game. When we refer to "game," we mean the entire game and not just a gameplay session. At the time of this writing, the campaign of most games that involve combat is roughly 10+ hours long. Of course, this doesn't take into consideration rogue-likes or deathmatch which extends the combat procedurally or with the aid of AI opponents. Your game might be shorter or longer, obviously. Some RPGs still clock in at the 30+ hour mark, whereas old-school RPGs routinely hit the 50+ hour mark for gameplay. Many designers survey existing games in their genre to see what the average play length is. Sites like HowLongToBeat. com have plenty of data.

Length of Combat and Number of Combatants

How long do you believe it should take to kill an average enemy? Furthermore, how long would you expect the average combat to be? While playing a game, you have undoubtedly exclaimed, "This combat has gone on forever," or "That was quick," based on both your expectations for the game you're playing as well as similar games in the genre. Consider these questions and attempt to form answers for your own game. Your answers may differ dramatically depending on whether your game is real-time or turn-based and further be dictated by genre.

In a turn-based game like *Civilization*, an average combat may be 3 minutes with more intense combats gusting upwards of 20 minutes, particularly if other units need to travel in. Simple combats with Barbarians can be under a minute. Conversely, one could argue that an FPS game is all combat, and therefore, length is immaterial, but even in those games, combat tends to come in waves, in areas, or in segments. The player has periods where they are not in combat after clearing an area. Choose a game you've played recently and ask yourself how long a single period of combat lasts, when the player is in the action; just take a guess. Now, go and play that game and actually time the combat with a stopwatch. How close was your guess? Does the combat feel longer or shorter than it actually was?

Thinking about the number of combatants as well as the time-to-kill for an average combatant helps us shape a desired length of combat or the number of combatants or both. For more difficult, longer combats, we may choose to scale the type of enemy or the quantity of enemies. These numbers can become our goals, metrics to measure against.

When you have an idea for the average amount of time such an encounter takes, how often do you expect these combats to happen? Do they change in frequency and intensity as the game goes on?

Frequency of Combat

How often do you expect combat to happen? In the beginning of the game, combat may be less frequent. As the game progresses, combat may happen more often, either player led or AI led. Conversely, one could argue that an FPS game is all combat, and therefore, "how often" is immaterial, but even in those games, length can be a player-set metric, be it number of frags or most frags in a given amount of time in a multiplayer or AI game or the size of the map. Many strategy games also allow you to choose the number of enemies and the hostility of the same, and even then, the game designer may still offer some default values based on what they figure would make for a good first-time play experience. In considering the frequency of combat, consider also whether they change in frequency and intensity as the game goes on? They often do in both real-time and turn-based games.

Number of Combatants

In addition to the frequency of combat, the number of combatants is a critical balance question. Does the number grow over time? What are the limitations in terms of game performance, maximum cognitive load on the player, project hours/budget available for the design team to create content, etc.?

If you want only a few enemies, but want combat to last 10 minutes or more, other factors will have to fill that time, or everyone had better have a lot of hit points or stages, as bosses tend to have.

Number of Hits

How many times do you need to hit a creature in order for it to die? This question, not the math, comes first. While this may seem simplistic, players have built up expectations in terms of the amount of time it should take. You see the complaints online—it took too long to beat or was too easy to beat. A good metric *to start* is this: for an average monster, average character, and an average weapon, how many times would you expect to hit it before it died? Of course, you likely have different answers for a boss monster.

For instance, in *DOOM*, John Romero felt like players should have to hit the Cyberdemon two or three times for it to die. Math-wise, the numbers here really don't matter. The Cyberdemon could have had 3 hit points or 30 or 300. What mattered is that you had to hit it two or three times in order for it to die. The Baron of Hell, on the other hand, required many more hits. Boss monsters, particularly those in console games or in MMO-style raids, also frequently involve different stages which are choreographed in expectation of a particular play style. A single monster here may require 20–30 minutes of time before it has passed through all its stages and the players are victorious.

The metric of "average number of hits before a creature dies" allows us a median point from which to start from as we adjust both weapon and creature numbers. We discuss that further in the next section.

The Variety of Combat

The questions in the previous sections help designers to create the size, scope, and pacing of encounters. This section focuses on keeping the interest of players and providing them agency through variety. Even the greatest Bruce Lee fight is only going to be so interesting if you're forced to watch it 100 times, and then, only the super hardcore fans will stick around (okay, it's Bruce Lee, so maybe most of us would stick around, but you get the point). *DOOM* designer John Romero notes that in the creation of the original game, they didn't so much design combat itself, but rather, they spent their time creating an interesting variety of monsters coupled with an interesting variety of player weapons which would then hopefully react to one another in a variety of interesting ways. They also allowed creatures within the game to fight with other creatures, deepening not only the possibility space of combat, but the strategy of combat as well. When coupled with Romero, McGee, and Petersen's level design, the result was combat that stands the test of time.

Variety is important in a number of different ways. It's not just about having ten different enemies. It's *what's* different about those enemies that forces a player to react, to plan, and to play differently. In the first seconds of any first encounter with an enemy, players are absorbing information, making decisions based on their assumptions about that information, and preparing to react via a literal fight or flight response.

Veteran game designer Greg Costikyan thinks in terms of what he calls "axes of differentiation" when designing combat systems. "I think in terms of axes of differentiation. Not just 'rock-paper-scissors,' which is one legitimate approach, but in terms of 'How can I create orthogonally different combat dilemmas which require different strategies to deal with?' Zerg rushes work, but can be defeated by grenades. Lasers are effective, unless your opponents have reflec armor, so you better have a backup weapon. Cover defends, but reloads are necessary, so you can maybe time when you break cover to get off a shot. Flamethrowers are great, but have limited range and god forbid someone get off a shot that blows up your fuel tank, etc. It shouldn't be about DPS. It should be about different situations requiring different strategies."

In discussing variety, among other things, we're considering the enemy's visuals (seen vs. invisible), size, speed, mode of movement (flying vs. walking), cover-seeking ability, weapon abilities (ranged vs. close up), HP, and AI behaviors (do they hang back or rush the player, for instance).

Variety of Visuals

A player's first response to a creature is always going to be how it looks or, in the case of an analog game, how they perceive how it looks. Referring again to *DOOM*, the Cyberdemon is roughly two times the size of any other enemy, and his sheer scale tells players that he is not to be messed with. In *Shadow of the Colossus,* the enemies are grand in scale, unlike any in a game before it. While they are effectively levels, their size tells the player quite clearly that this is an encounter that's not going to end in a minute or two. Raid bosses in *World of Warcraft* have a similar effect on players.

Visuals also telegraph what an enemy is capable of. For instance, if you saw an enemy was on fire, what might you also assume about its abilities?

If an enemy was huge, you might guess that it's lumbering or certainly slower than, say, a creature capable of flying. Variety of visuals keeps players interested, sure, but it also provides an important insight into the prospective behaviors of the enemy.

Designers also often use visuals to telegraph increasing levels of difficulty. For instance, compare a soldier in a basic soldier's outfit vs. that same soldier something extra added to its outfit. That extra, whatever it is, tells the player that this enemy is both known and unknown. Players need to discover what's new about this creature—more HP, an additional ability, or something.

Variety of Numbers and Numbers within Levels/Areas

In the math of combat, these numbers are both simple and key:

- Your HP
- The enemy's HP
- The number of enemies
- The amount of damage you do
- The amount of damage they do.

A player's HP, of course, is usually fixed, but grows over time as he or she gains experience. The others, however, must vary. Why? Imagine if your weapon always did five damage, and the enemy always had 20 HP. Four shots, and it's dead, every time. Approaching a group of three enemies, the player could perfectly calculate the outcome, and if the game also stood rigid on initiative, it would be even worse. The combat would become more a box-ticking exercise than an uncertain encounter. Uncertainty keeps the player on their toes, keeps things interesting and gives a chance for highs and lows. Therefore, designers often vary damage and enemy HP within a range. Similarly, they sometimes set a range for the number of enemies that spawn at a particular location. The latter is not true of every game, of course. Some games are precise about the number of enemies that appear. When balancing combat, designers need to keep this range in account—what if the game spawned the max number of enemies consistently? Is this something a player could withstand?

Designers also include variance within the game, creating necessary peaks and valleys which surprise players and break the illusion of a well-balanced ramp. A perfectly balanced game with a perfect ramp is predictable, and we, as humans, are bored by predictability. Within a level, area, or range, designers also include variance. Just as there is variance within an enemy (it might have between 75–90 HP), designers also like to provide enemies that are seemingly above in either the amount of HP they have or the amount of damage they can do. Players can *feel* patterns. If your game is always progressing at the same rate—everything is getting just a little bit harder in unison—it's as good as asleep as far as the player is concerned.

That said, there also has to be *some* consistency, or else the game is entirely unpredictable and just feels like noise to the player, which destroys the feeling of mastery over the content. The designer must find a balance. This is true in the arts as well: a concept from music composition and from visual design is "repetition with variation": give the audience enough repeated themes and riffs that they can sense a pattern, with enough surprises and modifications to keep them interested in seeing what happens next.

In addition to the numbers above, designers also vary:

- **Strength**: Enemies have a range of damage they can sustain, even within specific areas or levels.
- **Speed**: Enemies might be fast or slow or have varied speeds depending on terrain. In *DOOM*, while both Cacodemons and Lost Souls are flying creatures, Cacodemons tend to be pretty slow, while Lost Souls rush the players. In multiplayer games, player vs. player speed is critical as are player expectations and desires about speed. We discuss this further when we discuss variety of players.
- **Damage range**: Does the enemy's base hit do a ton of damage or just a little? Does it depend on the player's armor?

Variety of Behaviors

An interesting thing about combat balance is that, in many cases, it is not about math. Accusations of "it's unbalanced" sometimes arise because the game doesn't have the features or player options which allow the player a means to control, counter, or predict the situation.

If you think of a sizeable encounter you recently had in any game, what thoughts ran through your head? "I'm going to take out these guys first, before they can summon more enemies. Then, I'll deal with these guys, because they don't do much damage." It's exactly this situation that designers *want* you to be in. To do this, designers vary the behavior of enemies.

The base behavior of an average enemy is to give and to take damage in some form or another. How that happens is up to the designer.

In a well-designed game, designers attempt to strike a balance between enemy behaviors so players must learn a variety of counters to outsmart or eliminate the threat. Furthermore, they tend to take the combat stage itself into account so that the stage/area itself determines how enemies act. If it was all just getting hit with swords in a field, with enemies who all behaved exactly the same way, a game wouldn't be that interesting after all. The player would just learn one tactic that works and repeat it until they got bored.

Designers vary:

- **Attacks based on range**: As an example, in *DOOM*, the Baron has two primary attacks: one for distance and one at close range.
- **Range preference**: Enemies may prefer to hang back, while others operate as tanks, heading straight for the player.
- **Abilities**: Enemies typically have different abilities which they will use in response to their situation (i.e., low health might provoke them to heal), the environment or the stage of combat. In RPGs, their different abilities might mirror those of player classes. In *Minecraft*, Creepers blow up. Skeletons shoot arrows at range. Witches cast spells on the player. In *Magic: The Gathering*, enemies might have Trample, Plainswalk, or Flying abilities, each allowing different types of actions.
- **Vulnerabilities**: In keeping with their abilities, enemies often have vulnerabilities. Wizards can be silenced, magical beings can be dispelled, and slow moving creatures can be outrun. These vulnerabilities form part of the possibility space that players need to master and consider as they enter combat.
- **Solo vs. Squad behavior**: In conjunction with their own individual behaviors, enemies tend to have crowd behaviors. Do they show up alone or in squads? Do they have different or additional squad behaviors? For instance, on their own, Demons in *DOOM* aren't much of a threat. However, in groups, they tend to outflank the player which can quickly become a problem.
- **Enemy stages**: Some enemies, particularly boss enemies, have different stages of combat which players must master to defeat them. Each stage is the very definition of a choreographed combat with enemies performing specific attacks and sometimes revealing necessary vulnerabilities.
- **Location**: Players appreciate variety of location. This often means varying the size, shape, and cover offered in a location. Sometimes, however, it might be the difference between light and dark or enemies on different angles. Obviously, you can only do what your engine allows you to do.

From a balance perspective and a player mastery perspective, the list of variables above is near endless. However, it's often best to go with a light touch, giving individual enemies between 1 and 5 things each, with those on the higher end of the scale reserved for more important enemies, enemies which are typically scarce. For instance, consider the Imp in *DOOM*. It has ranged and close up attack, and that's it. The Baron of Hell also has ranged and close up attack, but in addition to those abilities, it can take a whole lot of damage, meaning it likewise can deliver a lot more before you take it out. The Demon is quick, does average damage, and can be dangerous when in a group. The Spectre one-ups the Demon because of its invisibility. Taken as they are, none of this becomes particularly complex to remember. However, if weapons are added which have unique effects depending on the creature, and we further complicate it by terrain, the possibility space of combat grows. You might see how this could quickly grow beyond the player's ability to keep pace.

One of the most important things you need to balance in a combat in a game is the player's ability to remember the possibility space you have created. It's that which results in mastery, and that's the reason they keep coming back. If they feel they can't remember the space you've created, examining all the different options they have, your game may not enjoy the success it otherwise would have. It's worth noting that it's fine to complicate things provided that complication comes in waves and layers. You don't need to memorize every card from *Magic: The Gathering* to play it. However, you do need to grok the basics so that when something new presents itself, you know how it fits in.

Variety of Counters

When players accuse combat of being unbalanced, what they sometimes mean is that they simply have no way to counter or protect themselves from an enemy attack. Without options, certainly, it seems unbalanced and unfair. Of course, means of countering enemies, whether it is weapons, cover, or evasive actions, is quite game-specific. Comparing *Super Meat Boy* to *Minecraft* to *DOOM* to *Dark Souls* illustrates the problem perfectly. There's no one-size-fits all recommendation for combat counters. However, there are some general guidelines to follow.

For games where movement takes place on a grid or a map with discrete spaces (such as *XCOM* or *Into the Breach*):

- **Items**: Does the player have a range of weapons that they can choose in response to different enemies or even player preference?

- **Cover**: Does the player have a means to block damage, seek cover from damage, or back out of the encounter if they desire?
- **Movement**: Does the player have the ability to move to cover in a way that is efficient and doesn't feel as if it's lagging?
- **Enemy review**: Is there a way for players to counter or to protect themselves from what an enemy is dishing up? It's fine if the enemy can destroy the player in a single hit provided that the player has a means to evade that hit behind cover. Then, it becomes a test of the player's agility and timing. Does the play space support that?
- **Targeting range**: Does the player have options at a variety of ranges? Do they have an attack that works well close up as well as far away? This isn't strictly necessary, but if you have a creature which has a ranged attack, it's useful if the player does, too.
- **Predictability**: Games are full of patterns, and players rely on these patterns to decide what to do next. Is your enemy predictable in a way that allows player to plan? The ability to plan serves as a means to counter the enemy. If it's just random and players can't plan at all, then the outcome feels like either an unfair loss or a lucky win, neither of which are appreciated by players.

For continuous movement games (side-scrolling platformers, bullet hell games),

- **Hindsight**: Will the player realize what they could have done better to make it successfully through the level/area next time? Did they learn something from their defeat? This is particularly important—the player feels they learned something, they could do it better next time, and they will be inclined to keep playing.
- **Predictability**: Similar to non-continuous movement games, is the game telegraphing expected behavior with enough lead time for the player to respond to it or is it just completely random?
- **Evasion**: In continuous moment games, "blocking" is often about evading things, jumping over them, timing movement from A to B, and so on. In these games, the ability for players to evade things is critical as is the ability to predict their timing.

Fortunately, it's often in this cross section of weapons, counters, and enemies that some of the most interesting play occurs. One weapon and five different enemies give you a possibility space of five different combat scenarios (provided we keep it one on one). Two weapons and five different enemies doubles the possibility space. Since weapons, enemies, and cover are particular to their own world, the key here is to make sure that players have both aggressive and defensive (or evasive) options in combat. If they don't, combat becomes unfair in the eyes of the player. They say it's unbalanced because they expect to be able to counter what's coming at them. The other option (which isn't really much of an option) is to give the player no counters other than a ton of HP. This leaves no room for mastery and isn't considered fun by many players. Players have even given names to these type of "counter" characters—bullet sponges.

Some designers take a more constrained and controlled approach to the possibility space of combat and approach it in a "rock / paper / scissors" style where different unit affordances affect other units in ways that players can immediately recognize and understand. It means that units have an orthogonal relationship to the other units in ways that make them both powerful and weak. RTS games often use this approach for both player and enemy units. We go into more detail on how to analyze these kinds of mechanics in Chapter 25.

Variety of Players, Player Characters, and AI Characters

Considering the types of variety we have discussed to this point—weapons, counters, terrain, behaviors, and visuals—we have created an interesting combat space for the player and noted reasons that players might say a game is unbalanced or unbalanced. That said, the biggest provider of variety and balance issues in multiplayer games (or single player games with multiple characters) are the players or, by extension, the player characters themselves. Let's take a look at a few examples:

- **Halo 2 multiplayer server**: When *Halo 2* opened their online servers to both console and PC players and allowed them to play vs. one another, the result was a graveyard of controllers. PC players were faster and more precise than their console playing counterparts. The game was considered unbalanced because players didn't have the same potential. Limitations on the console controller prevent players from moving as quickly as PC players.
- **Starcraft**: Over the years, South Korean players have developed incredible skill in the game, and as a result, the speed of the gameplay itself has been altered to accommodate both their skill and their player preference.

- ***Quake***: Originally released in 1996 and still played competitively, both *Quake Arena* and *Quake Champions* have received criticism from new players who struggle to compete with veteran players.
- ***Ultima Online***: One of the earliest massively multiplayer online games, *Ultima Online* provided game developers critical insight into the behavior of other players and, in turn, how that behavior can affect other players. When new players created characters, they started in town where combat was not permitted. Eventually, those new players would wander out of town in search of adventure. What they found, however, were what became known as "PKers" or "player killers," existing players who waited just outside the safe zone to mow down the newbies before they could even rightly defend themselves.

In addition to the examples noted above, games have also developed lingo to describe character-to-character balance issues. We talk of a character being "OP" or overpowered. To correct for this, developers "nerf" the characters. It is an incredibly challenging balancing act which requires a degree of experience and intuition, but also requires a great deal of playtesting. Additionally, for multiplayer PvP games, it's often a matter of introducing lobbies or ranks where players of similar skill can play against each other.

In single-player games, fundamentally, the same questions apply, but they apply in the context of each character type: how many times would I expect a fighter to hit an average creature before it dies? How about a wizard? You might immediately think, "But a wizard wouldn't hit an enemy. It would attack it with a spell from a distance away." Players also have these affordances. (In editing this book, one reader noted that she often looks up "how many times should I have to hit this enemy before it dies" online if it seems excessive.)

When designing for player characters, there are two schools of thought:

- **Symmetric design**: Players all have the same abilities and opportunities. Players may be able to choose different paths (you can select from x1 or x2 as an ability), but the same paths are available to all players in the game. You and I may start as Charlemagne, but by the end of the game, we are two different possibilities of what Charlemagne could be.
- **Asymmetric design**: Players have different starting states, often wildly so. These starting states might give them a huge advantage in one area or another or give them access to abilities and weapons completely closed off to others. Although asymmetric, the various abilities of the

characters have are of similar value in the context of the game as a whole. And excellent example of this is *Civilization Revolution* where each starting civilization has something which is seemingly imbalancing—the Mongols, for instance, get a new city for every Barbarian they conquer. The Indians have access to every resource from the beginning of the game. When taken individually, each civilization is in a "how could they not win?" position. However, when everyone's in that position, no one is. So, rather than an imbalancing aspect of the play, it adds variety and fun. Because all civilizations are equally overpowered, it ultimately comes down to player skill.

In addition to different player characters, players themselves have different play styles. Providing multiple avenues for players who have different skill levels and supporting players who employ different tactics in getting through encounters not only makes for a better game, but expands your player base. Lee Perry notes that "with *Gears [of War]* it was cover based players who wanted to play tactically, and point blank shotgun players who wanted to dive and roll around a map like crazed combat chickens relying on reflexes. Similarly, it is part of the popularity of *Fortnite*. The construction system has evolved into not being about base building at all, but rather like summoning magic cover, and the great players use that to a skill level that's just insane."

Game designer Jonathan Hamel of *What Remains of Edith Finch* as well as the *Tomb Raider* series discusses the challenges of identifying an audience for a game. "Different audiences have very different preferences when it comes to 'well-balanced combat.' I struggle with this most on projects that are not sequels. Players who love the challenge of execution very often feel accessibility is eliminating their desire to challenge and express themselves, and players who prefer feeling powerful will find that challenging execution is too hard and not accessible enough. Finding the right design goals among these and other combat dualities is often the biggest challenge even when you have an experienced and talented team, especially if they have different backgrounds and preferences. Even more so if the developers you are leading and the audience you are aiming for have different tastes. That's not an ideal situation, but that's often the reality. You not only have to design for the right audience, you have to signal through all aspects of your game's design and marketing that this game is for them and not for another audience with very different preferences and strong opinions."

When it comes to AI, however, there are very different considerations:

- **Less than perfect**: The goal of AI in a game is to challenge the player and provide a compelling game experience. Since this compelling experience usually means making the player feel clever and skillful, this principle has been stated as "the AI's job is to put up a good fight and then lose." However, the AI in a game knows everything about the game state, except what's presently in your head (though it can learn from you and anticipate this). Therefore, the AI in any game needs to be dumbed down otherwise, it will destroy the player or other AI agents in the game. Often, you'll find that teaching an AI to play poorly is a lot of work; controlling a paddle in *Pong* or finding the perfect shot in *Pocket Billiards* is easy, but intentionally missing in a way that makes the player think they won from their own superior skill (and not because the AI suddenly had a fainting spell) takes a bit more work—especially if the AI tries to do something like intentionally set the human player up to make a great shot. Games are often referred to as unbalanced if the AI doesn't do this and instead outpaces the player to the extent that it puts the player regularly in a suboptimal state. Sometimes, however, AI bots are slightly better than the player and are used by players to become better at the game.
- **Believable**: While it's unrealistic to expect that most players would confuse an AI for a human opponent in most games (getting "human-like" behavior is a very hard problem), the AI should at least not do things so wildly inappropriate or stupid that it breaks the player's immersion. Usually, this is a matter of iteration: start with a fairly simple AI, see what things stand out in playtesting that make it easily beatable or that otherwise stand out in a bad way, then add additional code and rules to prevent those situations, and try again until no one complains. Helpfully, in many cases players can be extremely forgiving when they don't know how the AI works: a simple *American Football* AI that simply picks a random play on each down might be seen as acting "intelligently" if it picks a play that the player would have expected, and might be seen as "clever" if it picks something that the player wouldn't have anticipated. The most difficult part is usually getting the AI to *lose* in a believable way, so that the player doesn't think that the AI decided to throw the game (even if that's legitimately what's happening).
- **Mutual opportunity**: If the AI can do it, the player should be able to do it, too. And the same is true of the player actions for the AI. If the AI is allowed to do something that the players can't do, players will perceive the game as unbalanced or call the game unfair. If the AI is

unable to do something players can do, particularly in hardcore strategy or action games, the players may perceive that they were thrown a win. This is one of the reasons many players dislike so-called "rubber-banding" AI in racing games: if the player is racing well and one of the AI cars puts on an unrealistic burst of speed to catch up, that feels unfair to the player because *they* have no such ability... and this is in auto racing, where *in real life*, one of the expectations is that everyone has the same (or similar) cars in order to emphasize the skill of the driver. If an AI wins the race because they essentially cheated, players don't like it.

- **Conforms to player expectations**: Ultimately, all of these come down to the idea that players are going to have a mental model of how they expect an AI to behave, and if the AI violates these expectations, players will complain. This may seem unfair to a game designer: are we supposed to read our players' minds now? But in reality, we often find out what typical players expect by simply observing early playtests and seeing what they complain about. We also have the ability to shape these expectations, somewhat. For example, if we name our difficulty levels "Ridiculously Easy / Normal / Hard / Unfair," then if the AI cheats in the player's favor on the easiest mode and cheats in its own favor on the hardest, the player has already been primed to expect that, and so they may not complain about the lack of mutual opportunity.

Time Outside of Encounters

Time in an encounter is as important as the time *outside* of the encounter in two separate ways, all of which, if implemented improperly, can cause players to accuse a game of being unbalanced. The two purposes of out-of-combat time are **anticipation** (building up to the next combat) and **recovery** (release after the previous combat).

In a discussion of time and space, designers are often focused on filling and then leaving empty both time and space. This empty space is the key to building anticipation for a player. No game does this better than *Resident Evil*, and outside of games, no genre does this better than horror. Empty space—where something *could* happen—gives the player the necessary time to build up tension for the delivery.

After a combat, players or player characters may need time to heal. Putting one well-orchestrated combat right after another doesn't give players this time and will result in cries of "too much combat." The reality is that there may just be the right amount of combat, but not enough space in between said combats or, alternatively, not enough differentiation in the combats such that a big encounter relative to player strength is followed by a small encounter. In an FPS, this recovery time is more down to placement of items that allow the player to rejuvenate their health. In fighting games, obviously, "recovery" time isn't applicable in the same way. In this case, the games are often broken down into rounds with time between rounds designed to allow players to rest.

Recovery doesn't just involve mechanics (for games without health, there is no recovery of HP). The post-combat period also provides a mental space for the player to get their bearings. If the player just made it through an intense combat by the skin of their teeth, that powerful post-combat feeling of "woah, I can't believe I barely made it" goes away if the player is immediately thrown into yet another fight. The player needs some time to process what just happened and to feel powerful, or scared, or triumphant, or whatever it is that the designer wanted them to feel. You can observe this in other media, too: in an action movie, there is almost always a quiet period right after a chase scene or fight scene. If a character barely makes a near-impossible jump over a deadly drop, they'll take the time to peer back over the edge, to contemplate the consequences of the failure they almost experienced.

Anticipation and recovery can happen simultaneously. In the original *BioShock*, for example, many levels were designed with empty spaces in between important or difficult fights. After a boss fight, the player might then have to backtrack a small distance through empty corridors to get back to the main path; or after a challenging fight against a swarm of enemies in a small room, the player might have to traverse a long, featureless corridor. There is already some anticipation in both of these cases, as the player might not know if the game will drop a surprise on them as they're walking, and the longer they walk, the more uneasy they might get about when the next combat is coming. Additionally, the player would find audio tapes scattered throughout the levels and was given the opportunity to play them immediately (and these were generally in locations where there wouldn't be any combats before the tape was done playing, so the backstory that the player was listening to wouldn't be interrupted by enemies). These voice recordings also built anticipation for future fights, for example, by introducing characters that you would encounter as bosses later, or hinting at the dangers just behind the next door. All of this was happening at the same time, as the player was recovering from the previous combat and looking toward the next.

Genre Specialization and Player Pressure

Video games have been around a long time, 61 years as of this writing. During that time, players have gone back and forth in terms of the difficulty level they prefer. In the 1970s and 1980s, games tended to be more difficult, assuming that players were becoming better at games and therefore needed more challenging games to play. To an extent, this was true. Players were no longer focused on learning the machine, but rather the game inside the machine. So, designers began to fill out the game space, making games more difficult and extending the length of the play session. Back then, players were often penalized and their characters killed for seemingly trivial things.

By the mid-1990s, games regularly included difficulty levels to account for the variety of player ability and taste. In addition, games that specifically billed themselves as expert-level games came into vogue, and playing them became either a badge of honor or a huge frustration, depending on the player's opinion of the game in question. If they liked it, they fancied themselves great players. If they didn't, they figured the designers couldn't balance a game to save their lives. After all, they bought the game thinking themselves good players. If they weren't, they were hardly going to blame themselves for the waste of money.

In the late 1990s into the 2000s, games began to get easier, adding auto-saves, catch-up mechanics, and other player-friendly features. Players were no longer willing to tolerate being whacked for going the wrong way, and in an effort to expand the player base beyond those who had been playing for years on end, some games became more accessible, peaking in 2010s with casual games. Yet, and perhaps as a response to those games and their ease, maso-core games began to rise. Games such as *Super Meat Boy*, *Super Hexagon*, and *Getting Over It with Bennett Foddy* presented players with an incredible level of masterable challenge. One of the oldest game genres, shoot-em-ups (or **shmups** for short), even morphed into a subgenre commonly known as **bullet hell** where the screen is routinely filled with bullets that the player must dodge by flitting between the few places on the screen that will *not* kill them instantly. In the mid-2000s, news of players creating their own gameplay modes such as **permadeath** became common. Players restart a game from scratch if they die, regardless of where the game itself respawns them.

Designers continue to iterate on finding a balance between difficulty and accessibility. In the 2010s, game designers tried combining the two, with interesting results. In *Bastion* and *Transistor*, the player can enable a number of added challenges (such as higher enemy health or the player taking more damage from hits) but also giving additional XP/loot for each one, thus allowing the player to fine-tune the game's difficulty while also giving the player a reward incentive to seek the highest level of difficulty they are able to handle. In *Celeste*, the core game is an extremely difficult masocore platformer, full of precision jumping, dashing, and climbing that must be executed flawlessly to proceed, but it also includes a wide range of options for players to reduce the difficulty (for example, by giving immunity to spikes or allowing the player to hold onto a wall and climb infinitely), thus adding accessibility options to allow just about anyone of any skill level to enjoy a masocore experience.

This level of tuning, whether player- or designer-led, is in direct response to desired player pressure. As designers, it's a decision we need to be conscious of, either designing for it directly by making the game more difficult than the average market game or by giving players the tools to adjust the difficulty themselves. What passes for "average market game" is, of course, subjective. To gauge this, game designers play a lot of games or engage with user research (UR) firms to get an idea of the player's response to the game's difficulty. It's also dependent on the style or events of the decade. If it's F2P, the average market game is going to pressure the player to monetize, underdelivering on at least one key resource (often the player's time or ability to keep up with the speed of the game without purchasing an in-game improvement). If it's an arcade game of old, it was designer-led to last about 3 minutes.

Calculating Player Power vs. Enemy Power

Let's imagine a typical game where the levels, areas, neighborhoods, or what have you, are populated with enemies for the player to beat. How do we figure out the player power and hence the enemy power from that point?

In games with player character progression where the player improves over time, we know the player's relative power—how much damage the player can deliver, on average, as well as how much damage the player can take. We can calculate this based on the XP awarded by all enemies placed to this point in the game and determine the level of the character in turn based on our level curve. If there are other sources of XP, those would also be factored into account. Once that is known, we return to the questions which choreograph encounters. How many times do we expect the player to hit this enemy before it dies? What is the power of the weapon you have given it? How long would it take, on average, for the player to expire? The answers to how strong the player is and how strong the enemies should be are densely woven, so that one is incredibly dependent on the other, hence the term "balance." As mentioned in earlier chapters, the concept of an anchor is critical here. What thing comes first so that you can use it to balance all other things?

In games with skill-based progression, player power is often assessed one of two ways. If it's a PvP game, players often work their way up through ranks based on wins or on another match-making metric established by the designers. If is a skill-based game with solo play, designers generally rely on you having made it through the last level do decide that you're ready for the next one.

Dr. Cat, a veteran game designer, discusses the challenge of adapting the AI to fit the player's growing power. "In a team, my biggest concern is team members who think the primary goal for opponent AI is either 'more realism' or 'a smarter, tougher, better opponent.' The ending of that latter path is a game people almost never win, which isn't fun. People should win at games more often than they win at 'real life', so people will want to play them. While you do want the AI to be 'tough enough to have some challenge rather than being a cakewalk', what you have to teach people on your team if they don't already know it is, enemy AI design is about forming the ideal shape of the 'negative space' that they imply. Every kind of tactics, movement algorithms, etc. that you put into a computer controlled monster or enemy implies one or more highly effective player behaviors that would beat that opponent." What you *want* to design is opponent behaviors that cause those ideal player responses to meet as many as possible of these criteria:

1. The stuff the players would do to beat them should be interesting and fun to do.
2. If there are multiple effective counter-strategies, that's more fun than just one. But you can also get this by having many enemy types, each of which has one "unique but very cool" counter-strategy. This can be better in some ways because see point 3.
3. The visible aspects of the monster's behavior should give the players sufficient clues to work out what their best counterplay against the monster might be.
4. Beating the opponents by taking advantage of their tendencies or quirks should feel significantly better than just slogging it out against them without thinking about it much, so the player feels rewarded for being clever. Opponent goes down faster, player takes less return-attack damage for using the good strategies, gets to see a different cool death animation, or other rewards.

Play is Required (and Required (and Required))

At its most basic, designing combat requires a player, a weapon or two, a space, and an enemy. Designing a good combat requires a designer who plays the game again and again, tweaking things here and there, to make sure that the game feels just right. The importance of *feel* cannot be understated. To go back to *DOOM*, when you play a level of that game, you're not playing a level as much as you are playing the result of literally thousands of playthroughs by its designer. Each playthrough tests a change and assesses how it feels within the scope of everything else. As a rule of thumb, a game designer plays the game every day. There is always something to be polished. Balance passes on games are typically left until after alpha when systems are in and then the real work begins after beta when all the content is in. It's hard to perfect a recipe when you don't yet have all the ingredients.

Throughout these many playthroughs, designers and testers often become experts at their own game before its release. If the game's difficulty level is not adjusted for players, complaints of "it's too hard" abound. In the creation of levels for *SIGIL*, John Romero's default setting was "ultra violent" from a pistol start. If he couldn't beat a level that way, he deemed it too difficult. Playing through on Nightmare was, appropriately enough, a nightmare. Conversely, sometimes designers must design their games knowing that players will ultimately become *much* better than they are. This can become noticeable in a game's consistency where one set of levels, say, designed by a good player are then followed by a set of levels designed by an expert-level player. There is a noticeable ramp in difficulty which affects balance, pacing, and player enjoyment.

In his work on *Dungeon Siege 2*, John Cutter talked about a challenge in designing boss battles. "One of the toughest challenges I faced was how to make these fights fair and entertaining when I only had a rough idea of the player's level, gear, spells, and skill at that point in the game."

Difficulty Levels

Games often have different difficulty levels to suit different levels of player desire and skill. Games that dynamically adjust their difficulty during play based on how the player is doing are considered to have **dynamic difficulty adjustment** (DDA). The original game masters or dungeon masters were likely the originators of DDA, having spared a player's life on many more than one occasion to keep the adventure going. In digital games, DDA either makes the game more difficult or makes it easier depending on the player's skill or on the nature of the game's pay model.

Response to Player

In some AAA games, the AI is designed to recognize different styles of play and hit the player with an appropriate opposition to challenge their play. Games in the *Halo* series, for instance, adjust but let the player set the place. In "Half-Minute Halo," Jaime Griesemer discusses how it works. "Most games have a single difficulty, or you know, maybe they have multiple difficulty levels, but at any one time you are only playing on one difficulty. And the AI does a set amount of damage and each encounter has a certain challenge, and you either are good enough to beat it or not, and if not maybe you learn or get lucky the next time and get through it. *Halo* is fundamentally different in that it lets the player set the pace."

"It doesn't do any magical dynamic difficulty; it doesn't make itself easier if you suck. But just naturally, how it is tuned, it waits to see what you will do, how hard you will push, and then it pushes back at just the right resistance. If you play carefully and pick guys off, you can work your way through a big encounter without too much risk, but if you charge in, guns blazing, it will push back really hard and probably kill you. But then if your shields go down and you run for cover, it backs off and lets you catch your breath. In most games, if you hide behind cover, the AI comes around the corner and roots you out, but the enemies in *Halo* won't usually do that."

More games have been adopting this model in response to players' desires not to run and gun through games. Most notably games in the *Assassin's Creed* and *Dishonored* series allow players to complete the game without even getting into combat.

Pay-To-Win

Mobile game developers also allow players to adjust the difficulty of their game by buying their way to easier gameplay. For instance, players can often purchase extra units to prop up what they have built up through play. For pay-to-win games, this is the entire business model and therefore developers create a situation that is ultimately unbalancing for other players but also quite profitable for the publisher.

Melee vs. Ranged Combat

One of the most challenging combat issues comes in games which feature both melee and ranged combat. Depending on how the design is tuned, one or the other might be considered "out of balance." Close and ranged combat have their own set of mechanics, tactics and strategies, and some of the strategies that make one great can actually work against the other to make it feel unbalanced or weak. Jonathan Hamel who worked on the *Tomb Raider* series notes that "in a primarily ranged game, solving for 'not backing up' is hard… I and others have spoken publicly about the challenge of balancing axe melee in *Tomb Raider* with the core of ranged. It's tricky for one not to overwhelm the other and create degenerate strategies that are just not as fun as the complicated, interesting, and varied combat you have designed the enemies and tools around. In a melee game, as mentioned above, it's the reverse: it's hard to balance ranged tools so that they feel rewarding but not, again, a degenerate strategy that takes all the fun out of the rich melee combat system."

There is not really an off-the-shelf solution to this challenge. Making each satisfying is critical, obviously, as if they were the only option in the game. When paired, the challenges arise. How do you keep the player from using the same mode of combat again and again? Is it environment? Yes. Is it enemy behavior? Yes. For both questions, the answer is also no. Keeping the player in close quarters forces a melee, but has the risk of making the player feel constrained. Having enemies rush players forces melee or provokes them to back up. As with so many game design problems that have no textbook solution, a designer deals with this issue through repeated playtesting, iteration, and analyzing what successful similar games (same genre, same difficulty, same camera view, etc.) have done.

Managing for Degenerate Strategies

The primary goal of players in combat is to put bodies on the ground. Sometimes, they will find a loophole and exploit that, using a single action or strategy that is effective in every situation against everything. Designers refer to such a thing as a **degenerate strategy**. Players always go for the optimal solution over the fun solution. "Since players are looking for the best corpse-to-risk ratio, they always optimize, even if it isn't fun, rather than explore the system," says designer Jonathan Hamel. "They're not looking for fun when facing with an enemy. They're looking to put ragdoll bodies on the ground quickly." Degenerate strategies typically reveal themselves in testing. No amount of pretty flourish will fix it. Degenerate strategies need to be removed, or players find them and use them. While a novice designer might want to complain that they've created a system that's extremely fun if players engage in it the way it was intended, if players are not playing the game the way the designer wanted, that is still the responsibility of the designer to create additional restrictions and affordances to pushing the player in the direction of playing the game in a way that is actually fun. Needless to say, if following a degenerate strategy ends up being even more fun than the originally intended gameplay, the designer can instead refocus the game with that strategy as the core and give the player the means to execute that strategy with enough variations on the theme to keep it interesting. Rocket jumping is one of the best-known degenerate strategies that is now standard in FPS games.

The Illusion of Winnability—Chris Crawford

In his seminal text *The Art of Computer Game Design*, Chris Crawford discusses the need to make sure that players believe in the illusion of winnability which applies as much in combat as it does everywhere else.

THE ILLUSION OF WINNABILITY

Another important trait of any game is the illusion of winnability. If a game is to provide a continuing challenge to the player, it must also provide a continuing motivation to play. It must appear to be winnable to all players, the beginner and the expert. Yet, it must never be truly winnable or it will lose its appeal. This illusion is very difficult to maintain. Some games maintain it for the expert but never achieve it for the beginner; these games intimidate all but the most determined players. TEMPEST, for example, intimidates many players because it appears to be unwinnable. The most successful game in this respect is PAC-MAN, which appears winnable to most players, yet is never quite winnable.

The most important factor in the creation of the illusion of winnability is the cleanliness of the game. A dirty game intimidates its beginners with an excess of details. The beginner never overcomes the inhibiting suspicion that somewhere in the game lurks a "gotcha." By contrast, a clean game encourages all players to experiment with the game as it appears.

Another key factor in maintaining the illusion of winnability arises from a careful analysis of the source of player failure. In every game the player is expected to fail often. What trips up the player? If the player believes that his failure arises from some flaw in the game or its controls, he becomes frustrated and angry with what he rightly judges to be an unfair and unwinnable situation. If the player believes that his failure arises from his own limitations, but judges that the game expects or requires superhuman performance, the player again rejects the game as unfair and unwinnable. But if the player believes failures to be attributable to correctable errors on his own part, he believes the game to be winnable and plays on in an effort to master the game. When the player falls, he should slap himself gently and say, "That was a silly mistake!"

Additional Resources

- Ludwig Kietzmann, *Half Minute Halo: An Interview with Jaime Griesemer,* https://www.engadget.com/2011-07-14-half-minute-halo-an-interview-with-jaime-griesemer.html
- Harvey Smith, *Orthogonal Unit Differentiation,* http://slideplayer.com/slide/4321830
- Chris Crawford, *The Art of Computer Game Design,* https://www.digitpress.com/library/books/book_art_of_computer_game_design.pdf
- Jan Willem Nijman, *The Art of Screenshake,* https://www.youtube.com/watch?v=AJdEqssNZ-U

Discussion Questions

1. What is the role of math and numbers in combat design?
2. Look up a gameplay video of any first-person shooter where a player is firing one of the guns (any of the guns). Describe the gun aesthetically: what does it look like and what does it sound like?
3. For the gun in the previous question, describe its purpose in the game (what situations is the weapon the best at?). Does its look and sound match its gameplay?
4. Find a game where combat is part (but not all) of the experience—most RPGs, 4X games, and Metroidvanias would qualify, for example. Now, suppose you wanted to create a similar game except with much more emphasis on combat—nearly all of the game is now combat, and the other elements are virtually nonexistent. What would you imagine that game to play like, and what changes would you have to make to the combat systems to compensate and make it work?

5. For the same game in the previous question, now imagine removing the combat entirely so that the game focuses on its other elements. How would that change the game, and what other changes would you have to make to the other systems to make up for the loss of combat?

6. Choose a game that has a memorable AI in some way (particularly good or particularly bad). What about the AI stood out in the game, and why?

7. Find any game with combat. By either looking it up online or from your own experience, about how long does it take to play through the game beginning to end, and how many total enemies are there in the game? Now divide to get the average time it takes for the player to encounter a new enemy in the game.

8. Repeat the previous question with several similar games and compare them. Which games have the most new enemy content and the least? Which games were seen as better (either through sales or critics' ratings)?

9. Take any game with combat and describe its pillars (genre, time, pacing, feel, participants, progression type, volume).

10. Repeat the previous question for a second game in the same genre as the first, and compare the two. How are they alike, how are they different, and how do the differences in combat pillars manifest in a different play experience?

Sidequests

Sidequest 10.1: Roll-and-Move Combat

Choose any board game of the "roll-and-move" genre that has no combat system (examples include *Monopoly*, *Chutes & Ladders*, *The Game of Life*, *Clue*, *Candyland*, or *Trivial Pursuit*). Design a set of "house rules" that add a PvP combat system to the game. Things you'll need to specify include

- What kind of "feel" do you want the combat to have? Give two or three words to describe the combat and/or the feelings you want the player to have from engaging in combat.
- When does combat initiate—every turn, when landing on or passing over another player, when landing on a specific board space, or something else?

- What are the actual mechanics of combat? How do these mechanics support or enhance the core gameplay?
- What happens after combat? That is, how is resolution determined, and what happens to each player who was involved?

Your goal is to write these rules in a way that is clear for the reader, feels integrated with the core game, and is a natural extension of it, and that the combat has the right kind of drama and choreography to provide the feelings and goals that you were designing for.

Sidequest 10.2: RPG Asset Budget

Congratulations, your team has just successfully pitched a 60-hour epic RPG where the player spends about a third of that time is in combat (the rest is split between exploration, narrative, and optimizing their party in equipment subscreens). You expect a single typical combat to last about 2 minutes (with boss fights being a bit longer).

How many distinct enemies should your team expect to design for this game? Justify your answer through math, making any additional assumptions that you need to for other numbers that aren't provided here.

Rogue's Main Quest, Part 5: Create a New Mechanic

Continuing from Part 4 in: Chapter 8

As you examine the spreadsheet for the cost curve and supporting math that you developed in the previous part of this quest line, each column in the sheet that isn't just a core stat (such as resource cost, or health) can be thought of as a mechanic. For TCGs or similar card games, those might be common abilities or keywords. For a turn-based or real-time PC strategy game, it might be a general capability or class of unit. For tabletop miniatures games, you might see some common unit special abilities. For tabletop RPGs, you might have some general types of abilities, feats, or similar.

Create one new mechanic along these same lines, essentially adding one more column to your spreadsheet that's blank or zero for all of your existing rows. Based on your current knowledge of the game, tentatively add the supporting math for your new mechanic to the spreadsheet. Describe the mechanic clearly in the sheet (such as in a cell comment), along with your justification for why you costed it the way you did.

Part 6 continued in: Chapter 12

Fighter's Main Quest, Part 5: Combat Simulator

Continuing from Part 4 in: Chapter 9

Extend your spreadsheet from Part 4 to be a generic combat simulator, where you have some "input fields" (color or otherwise format these to make clear they are meant to be changed by the user) for the player character and monster stats, and "output fields" that display the combat outcome.

Use your combat simulator to compare relative outcomes at various points in the game, particularly those that you suggested were either very fast or very slow back in Part 2. Did your intuition match up with your simulation?

Part 6 continued in: Chapter 11

11

Progression in PvE Games

In This Chapter

- Balance in PvE
- Resistance to Progression
- The Four Elements of Perceived Difficulty
- Progression Arcs and Loops
- Types of Progression
- Reward Schedules
- Common Problems in PvE

Balance in PvE

> If you don't know where you are going, you might wind up someplace else.
>
> *Yogi Berra*

This chapter is about advancement, progression, and difficulty in the context of PvE games. This includes single-player games, tabletop RPGs, and multiplayer co-op video games. In multiplayer PvE, players progress as a group the same way that a single player would progress, so the overall forms of progression are similar no matter how many players are involved.

Progression mechanics also have to be balanced in terms of how quickly or slowly players gain power and whether this happens continually or in short bursts at specific places.

It is worth reminding ourselves what "balance" means in this context. Back in Chapter 1, we said that in terms of progression there are three things to consider:

1. Does the difficulty increase over time at a good rate, or does it get harder too quickly or too slowly, leading to frustration or boredom (the **difficulty curve**)?
2. Does the player's power in the game increase at a good rate relative to the increase in enemy power—or, does the player gain power too quickly, making the rest of the game trivial after finding some all-powerful weapon… or does the player gain power too slowly, requiring a lot of tedious grinding to compensate (the **power curve**)?
3. Is the *overall* difficulty level appropriate for the audience (is the game too hard or too easy)

Resistance to Progression

By its nature, progression requires that the player overcome some form of resistance, often referred to by game designers as **friction**. Without friction, the player would reach their goal and reap the rewards immediately, without having to engage with any kind of progression system. Friction may come in many forms, generally requiring some combination of player skill, luck, and time investment in the game to overcome it.

Friction can be visualized over time on a graph. In effect, this is a way of viewing the difficulty curve of a game. An individual unit of resistance—a single challenge or puzzle that forms an atomic piece of content in a progression system—goes through a rising and falling curve that can be divided roughly into four phases. The length and intensity of the friction (essentially "difficulty") varies in each phase, based on the type and complexity of the challenge, the game state, and also on the relative player skill and power. These stages are:

1. **Discovery**: the player discovers the existence, nature, and scope of this particular problem. The player transitions from ignorance to awareness.
2. **Learning**: the player invests time and effort in the now-defined problem, interacts with it, pushes at its boundaries, and thinks about it.
3. **Mastery**: the player's understanding of the problem finally reaches critical mass, and the pieces start falling into place. The process accelerates as the player unravels more of the problem, until it is finally resolved.

4. **Fluency**: after successfully navigating the challenge, the player internalizes the lessons learned from it and starts generalizing and abstracting from there. The player ultimately adds the new skill to their skill set, and can now use the skill on other similar problems encountered later.

As an example, here is what a simple lock-and-key puzzle might look like:

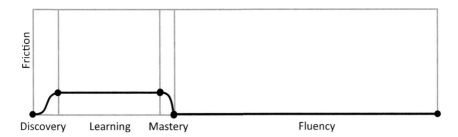

The friction in this case is never particularly high, because the process of finding a locked door and searching for the corresponding key isn't typically a great challenge. The Discovery phase is short: it doesn't take long for a player encountering a lock to realize they must search for the key. The Mastery phase is also short: once the player has the key, all that remains is to return to the lock and use the key on it. The Learning phase is longer and consists mostly of exploring the area and searching for the key. Note also that the Fluency phase has no friction; once the player owns that key, they can typically bypass all matching locks without taking any further effort.

By contrast, consider the resistance to mastering an entirely new skill, such as learning to use a specialized unit in an RTS game:

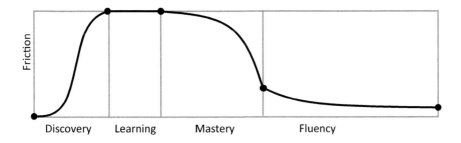

Here, the Discovery phase—simply learning the nature of the problem—is an extended task. The possibility space of the unit is not clear up front, and the player must do some experimentation just to learn about the unit: how to best direct it, what are its abilities, strengths, and vulnerabilities, and in what situations is it the most useful. The Mastery phase is likewise extended compared to the lock-and-key graph, as it takes some practice and trial-and-error to execute the strategies and tactics of the unit. Even in the Fluency phase, there is still some small amount of resistance, as the unit always requires some small amount of player skill to use, even when fully understood.

While not shown in this graph, there are many potential moments of joy that are scattered throughout the solving of a challenge. During Discovery, the understanding of a new challenge invokes the player's curiosity and generates interest; if the reward for overcoming an obstacle is known or hinted at, some anticipation of that reward may also be created and sustained throughout. During the Learning portion, the player may experience alternating frustration and excitement as they try new things, fail at some of them, and learn more of the boundaries and edge conditions. In the first part of the Mastery phase, the player gets the "aha" moment where everything finally comes together, and during the latter part of this phase, the player is savoring their new skills as they push toward an inevitable victory. In the Fluency phase, the player can call on their new skills or knowledge on demand, occasionally reminding them of how far they have come in the game.

Actual vs. Perceived Progression

While the game designer may be aware of what the friction of a particular puzzle looks like based on playtest observations, it turns out that players in the middle of the puzzle are unlikely to perceive the future parts. Instead, players tend to perceive the difficulty of a task relative to their current trajectory, assuming that their progress is linear even when it is actually a sharper downward-facing curve in the Mastery phase most of the time. This means that while still in the Learning phase and the early part of Mastery, the player is experiencing near-constant friction, making it feel like it never decreases and leading to player frustration (even if the actual rate of progress is quite high and the player masters the challenge relatively soon after). Midway through the Mastery phase, the player notices the downward trajectory of resistance so the end is in sight, although even then completion is closer than it appears.[1]

---

[1] If you have studied calculus, you can think of the player's projected perception of how long it takes to complete the Mastery phase as the first derivative of the curve at the point where they currently are, and the point of inflection on the curve is where the player shifts from spending most of their time figuring out *how* to proceed, to concentrating primarily on implementing the known solution. (If that means nothing to you, it isn't necessary for your understanding of this concept.)

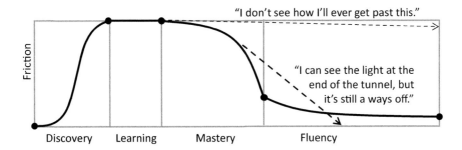

Designers should be aware that many players perceive difficulty as being much greater than it actually is and the ultimate point of mastery being much further away than it is. By putting more of the challenge in the Discovery and Mastery phases and shortening the Learning phase, this effect can be reduced somewhat. For challenges that allow it, visually showing the player an accurate indicator (such as a progress bar) can also help.

The Four Elements of Perceived Difficulty

When progressing through a series of challenges in a game, how does one track the level of challenge (or friction) that the player is feeling, so you can tell if it's increasing too quickly or too slowly, or whether the level of challenge is just right? This is actually tricky to answer, because the player's perceived difficulty is not a single item; rather, it is the combination of *four* things. The player experiences it only as a single "am I being challenged?" feeling, but there are four design knobs that can affect this. These four elements that affect perceived difficulty are[2] as follows:

- **Player skill**: the level of the player's actual **skill** at the game (the player's ability to make optimal decisions). The more skilled the player is at the game, the easier the challenges seem, other things being equal.
- **Virtual skill**: the player's power level in the game (sometimes referred to as **virtual skill**). Even if the player isn't very skilled at the game, doubling their health or the amount of damage that they do on a successful attack improves their ability to win.

---

[2]Note that while some friction can be in the form of time investment (requiring the player to "grind," using known and mastered skills repetitively in order to progress), this does not increase perceived difficulty. A tedious task is not difficult, merely time-consuming. For that reason, there is not a one-to-one mapping between friction and difficulty.

- **Virtual challenge**: there is the virtual difficulty of the game, based purely on power level of enemies or challenges in the game: increasing the health or attack or speed of enemies in the game (or just adding *more* enemies in an area), without making the enemies any more skilled, still increases the challenge of the game, because the player must execute their strategy for a longer period or at a higher rate of precision.
- **Skill challenge**: lastly, there is the level of skill-based friction that the game subjects the player to, where the player is not only executing the same tactics and strategies better, but where the player must develop new and novel ways to play in order to succeed. Examples of this type of resistance might be enemies that have more sophisticated AI that make them more challenging to defeat, introducing new types of challenges, or deep puzzles that require multiple skills used together.

The sum of player power + skill, minus the power-based and skill-based challenges, can be thought of as the perceived challenge as experienced by the player, and tracking this throughout a complete playthrough of the game can be thought of as the difficulty curve. If numbers could be assigned to each of these, they could be graphed. An example is shown below.

This graph would represent a game that requires a constant (and low) level of skill throughout, but increases its power over time, such as a simple idle game. The player may increase slowly in skill (for example, getting better at clicking the mouse quickly in *Cookie Clicker*), but mostly the player is gaining power through raw stat increases, and the game's difficulty curve also involves a linear increase in stat-based challenges.

If the level of challenge remains constant (not getting harder or easier), and the player's power is also constant (player does not gain or lose power over time), the perceived challenge still decreases over time, simply because the player is improving in their ability:

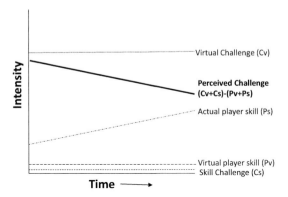

Thus, to keep the player feeling challenged once they get better, the game must get harder in some way.

Progression Arcs and Loops

If a single puzzle or other challenge has a difficulty curve, what does it look like when these are chained together? If an individual "unit of friction" is the microlevel of what is happening in a game's progression mechanics, then what does the macrolevel look like? Usually, an individual unit of friction does not exist in isolation, but is part of a larger progression system. That system may form a **progression arc** (one-time progression from one point to another) or a **progression loop** (repeating cycle of progression).

When the player recognizes a challenge as part of a repeating loop or ongoing arc of related challenges, the player may be looking ahead in a number of ways. Here are some things that the player may be aware of at any given time:

- **The current iteration in the current loop**: what the player is doing *right now.*
- **Foresight in the current loop**: the player's understanding of the future outcome of progressing in or mastering the current loop.
- **Near-future loops**: the progression loop(s) that become available once the player progresses in or masters the current loop. This may be clear or fuzzy, depending on the game.

- **Far-future loops**: a series of additional steps the player must do, where they don't have foresight into what they are or how they will do them… yet.
- **Anchoring goals**: the ultimate long-term goals that the player is aware of and desires. This forms the player's base motivation to go through all of these individual iterations through the loops in the first place (in addition to added motivations to advance or complete any particular loop for its own sake).
- **Exits**: ways for the players to leave the current loop, stopping their current behavior in the game, to do something else. One reason to exit would be to pursue other progression systems (or entirely different non-progression-based systems) in the game. Leaving the game entirely out of frustration, boredom, or futility is always another option, however.

The player's view of the present and future interaction loops in some game might be summarized as (1) Do Something; (2)???; (3) Profit! The first step here is the current loop. The second (unknown) step represents the future (as yet unknown) loops. The third step is the anchoring long-term goal.

Keep in mind that engaging with a progression loop has a cost. This includes direct costs to the player (cognitive load and time spent), sometimes resource costs (spending in-game resources to progress through the loop), and opportunity costs (choosing not to interact with other loops—or other activities outside of the game). These costs become an investment in the system over time. In a player's brain at a faster-than-conscious-thought speed, there is an economic calculation being evaluated constantly that considers and compares the perceived future payout of the current progression loop, the sunk cost of previous interactions with the loop, and alternate actions that may yield more than continued investment in the current loop. Many interesting game designs have this kind of choice (continue along current path or switch to alternate strategy?) as a core dynamic.

In Metroidvania and Adventure games, the player is motivated by a desire to gain access to new areas and new skills and abilities, which leads to a desire to master the most recently acquired skill or explore the most recently discovered area. This loop is repeated with each successive skill and area throughout the game. The player may not immediately know where *all* future areas are, but they may see some places they can't get to right away (giving them some idea of where to return to later), or some objects in the game that they can't interact with yet (but they know that there will be some future skill or ability that allows them to).

In a game with progressive resource management mechanics (this would include idle games like *AdVenture Capitalist*, deck-building tabletop games like *Dominion*, and even real-time strategy games like *StarCraft*), the player has a motivation to acquire more options for resource acquisition, which grants the ability to create an efficient economic engine—in essence, the core game loop in these games is about modifying the core game loop, and player satisfaction comes from meta-progress. In the case of competitive (PvP) games with a clear end condition, this continues until one player's engine ultimately allows them to dominate the game and triumph over their opponents for the win. For games with no defined endpoint and only a transition to some sort of elder game, this resource loop continues until the player chooses to exit the loop, either out of boredom with the mechanics or frustration with sufficiently diminishing returns for their effort.

In narrative-driven games (such as *Her Story* or *Life Is Strange*), the player is motivated by seeing the story develop and resolve. On successive iterations of the narrative progression loop, the player gains a greater understanding of the plot and world and backstory, and relatedness to the characters.

Note from the above examples that even games that are vastly different at their core still share similar progression models, in the abstract. If you are working on a game now, putting your game's progression design in terms of this model may help to refine the design, spot potential issues, or pinpoint the source of known issues. Keep in mind that each individual interaction loop may have several motivators.

Velocity and Acceleration

A player's rate of progression is affected by the level of resistance and can in fact be thought of as the inverse of resistance: the higher the resistance, the slower the player's progress. Each progression arc or loop in a game can be further described by how fast the player progresses through the system, and in what numeric relationship.

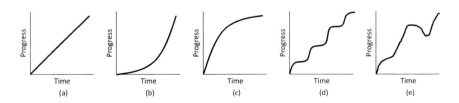

The player may progress linearly (at a constant rate), as in *Minesweeper* with an expert player that is constantly clicking to clear away squares, shown in (a) above. Progress may be exponential, starting slow and then speeding up over time, as in *Catan* where players generate a few resources over time and then (through a positive feedback loop) use those resources to increase their resource generation, shown in (b). Players may initially progress quickly, then see their rate of progression slowing over time, as often happens in RPGs or idle games, where the progression curve is designed to give players some early victories and level them up quickly in the early game to give the player a sense of power, and then slow the rewards to stretch out the content later on once the player has become hooked on the game, shown in (c). Or, progress may follow a common pattern of increasing and decreasing velocity and acceleration, giving an overall sense of increasing difficulty over time with breaks, following a repeated tension-and-release model, shown in (d). Progress may also follow no single formula, but speed up and slow down over time at multiple points, either intentionally to give the player some variety or unintentionally due to poor balance, as in (e).

We could speak of two elements here. First is the player's **velocity** of progression: what is the change in a player's power level over time? A fast velocity would imply a player is progressing quickly through the game's content or levels, a slow velocity means a player is only making slow, incremental gains, and a negative velocity would happen if a player is losing progress (for example, by dying and having to restart at a previous save point).

Another element to consider is the player's progression **acceleration**, or the rate of change in velocity. Even if a player is progressing slowly, if they detect that their rate of progress is increasing so that they move forward faster if they just keep going a little longer, that can be enough to make them not feel so demoralized at their perceived lack of forward movement. By contrast, if a player was progressing quickly but starts to notice that their rate of progression is slowing down, they would get mentally prepared to make a choice as to whether it's worth it to continue progressing in that loop or to abandon it in exchange for some other loop (or some other game) with a faster progression model.

There is no single "correct" velocity or acceleration rate that is appropriate for all progression systems. The designer must decide what pattern of progression is the most appropriate for each point in their game and then design the content accordingly.

Regression and Loss

As noted in the previous section, progression isn't always forward; a player can lose progress through failure or error. The fear of losing hard-earned progress—**loss aversion**—can be extremely emotionally impactful and is also related to the concept of overall perceived difficulty of a game. Loss can be a powerful motivator for a player to proceed with caution or flee out of fear—and also a motivator for the player to rage-quit your game if pushed too far.

In early editions of *Dungeons & Dragons*, some monsters (particularly higher-level undead) had an attack that could literally drain experience levels from a player's character. Many early GMs (Game Masters) noticed that players were even more cautions around an undead like a Wight than a more powerful creature like an Ancient Dragon. After all, if your character dies in combat from loss of hit points, there were resurrection spells, and failing that you could always roll up a new character and rejoin the adventure later. But if your character loses several experience levels, you may have just lost several weeks to months of progress that you'll generally have to earn back the hard way. While many players absolutely hated the level-drain mechanic for obvious reasons, it was highly effective at giving players the same healthy fear of the undead that their characters should have.

A player's fear of loss, then, is governed by two factors: the extent of the potential loss and the probability of loss. In *Super Meat Boy* and most other masocore games, the difficulty level is extreme and the player is expected to die a lot before they succeed on any given level... but levels are very short, so even the worst-case scenario of a player dying right before reaching the goal only sets them back about 30 seconds or so of progress. In such a game, the player can play recklessly and carelessly, not worrying too much if they die because they can just try again.

By contrast, consider a game with permadeath (the player's character is literally and permanently destroyed and the save file erased if they lose) but with a relatively easy difficulty overall. In such a game, dying could be a massive setback costing the player dozens of hours of progress, and the threat of losing everything is always there in the background like a weight. On the other hand, it probably won't happen as long as the player is sufficiently careful, so the player can feel all that much more powerful when they beat the game and cheat death. The total time to beat the game might be about the same as a masocore game—a small number of high-stakes restarts vs. a large number of expendable short-term lives lost—but it feels very different from the player's perspective.

Now compare both of these to a classic roguelike such as *Nethack*, where the difficulty is high (the game has many unexpected ways to kill the player) and the penalty for failure is also high (permadeath). To beat the game, a player must play flawlessly for perhaps 50 hours on a single character, and that's not counting the time they've sunk into characters who died along the way. This is why the number of people who have legitimately beaten *Nethack* (without using cheats or mods) is remarkably small.

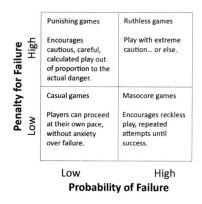

	Punishing games	Ruthless games
High	Encourages cautious, careful, calculated play out of proportion to the actual danger.	Play with extreme caution… or else.
Low	Casual games	Masocore games
	Players can proceed at their own pace, without anxiety over failure.	Encourages reckless play, repeated attempts until success.

Penalty for Failure

Low   High

Probability of Failure

Juiciness

Designers may speak of the **juiciness** of a system: the type and intensity of sensory feedback used to inform the player of their progress. This may include a dramatic change in music or a sound effect or fanfare, particle effects or similar graphical flourishes, screen shake, glow or flash or blink effects, or other audio or visual effects that happen during progression.

Juiciness is not easily quantifiable. It can't be solved for numerically. Getting the right amount of juiciness isn't a matter of fiddling with numbers in your spreadsheet until they work out right. And yet, it makes a huge impact in how your players experience the game's progression systems. Adding juiciness to a game at the moment of progression (such as the player leveling up, finding a treasure chest, or entering a new zone) can increase the player's perception of how much they just gained, especially in relation to the juiciness of other lesser gains.

As such, an extremely juicy bit of the game happening during a rare but significant point of progress (such as solving a major puzzle or clearing the game's most difficult area) can make that moment stand out in a player's mind, while a distinct lack of juiciness can make a moment feel particularly anticlimactic. Even though juiciness isn't directly related to the balance of a game (by definition, it has no impact on the game's systems at all), it still influences player perception... and as we've learned, balance is about the player's perception as much as it is about reality.

Types of Progression

How is a progression system designed—what are the necessary component parts? Typically, they begin with a **motivator** that gives the player the incentive to enter a progression arc or loop. When completed, the progression arc or loop provides a **reward** that satisfies the original motivator.

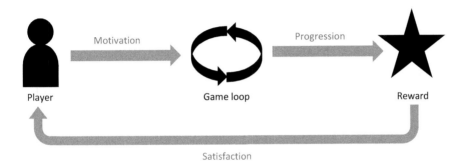

We can subdivide further. Some forms of progression are individual in nature, affecting the player and/or their character only, in relation to the game environment. Other forms of progression are social, affecting the player's relationship with other players.

Individual progression arcs include the following:

- **Accomplishment**: progress toward the completion of tasks or quests that can be finished
- **Discovery**: progression through exploring the game's virtual spaces, narrative, and dialogue.

Individual progression loops include the following:

- **Difficulty**: increasing the challenge level over time
- **Complexity**: enabling new game mechanics or features that give players new strategies and tactics

- **Power**: increased attributes or stats of the character
- **Cosmetic content**: collecting cosmetic or status items that don't have in-game effects and exist mainly for bragging rights or character customization.

Social progression may involve the following:

- **Influence**: increasing the number of other players that the player is interacting with or getting "shares" or "likes" from many friends
- **Ranking**: increased standing in leaderboards, ladders, or other ranking or rating schemes
- **Guilds**: joining player-created groups and then within that group gaining rank, responsibilities, privileges, and prestige.

Motivations for Progression

There are many reasons a player may wish to enter or advance a progression arc or loop. Motivations can be either **intrinsic** (motivated by the player's own internal drives and desires) or **extrinsic** (motivated by player's desire to be given an external reward, or to avoid an external punishment). According to self-determination theory from the field of psychology, intrinsic motivation is far more powerful of a driver for behavior, and yet it can paradoxically be displaced by the presence of weaker external motivators. In particular, if a player is performing an activity due to an intrinsic motivation to do so, and then an extrinsic motivator is added and then later removed, the intrinsic motivation is extinguished and the original behavior stops. Designers should therefore be cautious about rewarding players for "good" behavior or punishing them for "bad" behavior; this works well to motivate players to do rote tasks that they wouldn't have done otherwise, but in the long term handing out an achievement, trophy, or the like is actually antimotivational for nontrivial tasks or goals. Because of this, intrinsic motivators are more desirable to examine as a hook for progression arcs and loops. Design progression systems to focus on the actions that players are driven to do naturally: actions that are engaging and enjoyable in their own right and that become their own rewards.

Here are some examples of intrinsic motivators and some types of progression and rewards that naturally follow:

- **Agency**: control over one's environment and one's own fate. Motivates player to seek improved character stats or abilities, which give increased virtual skill as the reward.

- **Mastery**: greater understanding over how to manipulate a system. Motivates player to increase the difficulty or complexity of the game, which results in increased player skill at the game as a natural reward.
- **Curiosity**: finding out what happens next. Motivates player to enter a discovery arc, which when completed grants additional knowledge of the game to the player.
- **Closure**: finishing what one started. Motivates player to enter an accomplishment arc, which ultimately satisfies the player's completion-ist desires when the arc finishes.
- **Expression**: a show of one's individuality and uniqueness. Motivates player to collect cosmetic content or make character-defining choices in the game, which allows the player to use the game as a form of self-expression. Depending on the context, the player might be putting themselves in the game or else creating a fictional character of their own devising.
- **Connection**: relatedness to and fellowship with other humans. Motivates a player to enter guilds, which provide the player with a feeling of social inclusion.
- **Superiority**: showing domination of one's peers. Motivates a player to climb leaderboards and other ranking systems, which rewards the player with the thrill and recognition of competing and winning.
- **Community**: showing value to one's fellow players, be they opponents, allies, or guildmates. Motivates a player to enter an influence loop, performing behaviors that win friends and provide recognition of the player's value.

In addition, there are some people who are motivated by negative behaviors, either from the thrill of breaking social taboos within the magic circle of a game, or from the rush of power that comes from causing pain to others (often referred to in games as **trolling** or **griefing**). Designers rarely create systems specifically to support griefing. Rather, this behavior arises from systems that (unintentionally) allow or enable it, among those players who feel this as a strong intrinsic motivator.

We examine each of these motivation-progression-reward links in turn.

Desire for Agency → Stat-Gain Loop → Virtual Skill

Increased player power can involve stat boosts, new weapons or capabilities, and so on. These are generally straightforward and can be balanced using techniques found elsewhere in this book. A special case of these is a new item that actually increases the player's strategic, tactical, or exploration options (examples might be the ability to jump high or fly, which not only lets the player reach new areas, but also move around in combat in new ways; or a special weapon that lets the player fling enemies into each other, which opens up new ways to approach a room with lots of monsters). If these new "toys" are particularly fun to use, it can be valid design to give those to the player early in the game so that they can enjoy using them for most of the game (think of how early the player is given the gravity gun in *Half-Life 2* or how early they get the portal gun in *Portal*). However, in the case where the player receives all their powers relatively early in the game and goes the rest of the game without further progression in this area, there is a risk that the player starts feeling like their power is stagnant and they are not progressing. In that case, you'll need to make sure the player has plenty of ways to use everything in combination so that the rest of the game doesn't feel repetitive, and you'll need to rely on other kinds of rewards (other than progression via new toys) to keep the player engaged through the longer final parts of the game. Or, make the game shorter.

Player power and power-based challenges are much easier to balance mathematically than those relating to skill: compare the player's power curve with the game's opposition power curve. The game designer has complete control over both of these: when the player gains power, and also when the enemies rise in power to counter the player's increases. What do these curves tend to look like? Part of this depends on what you expect the skill curve to be, since power can be used to compensate for greater or lesser skill in either direction. As a general guideline, though, one common pattern looks like this on the micro-level:

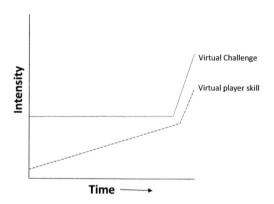

Here, within a single area (an individual dungeon, level, or play session), the player sees a sudden jump in difficulty, since they are entering a new space after mastering the previous one. As the player spends time in the current area, the player's power increases (through item purchases, level-ups, item drops, and similar), while the area itself generally keeps showing the same types (and difficulty) of challenges within its region. At the end of an area, there may be another sudden, brief difficulty spike in the form of a boss or other final challenge, and then following that a bump in player power when they get new loot from the boss or reach a new area that lets them immediately upgrade their character further.

Some levels may be split into several parts, with an easier part at the beginning, then a mid-boss, then a harder part, and then a final boss. This can just be thought of as the same pattern repeated several times within a level, without a corresponding change in graphical scenery. If many such patterns are strung together, that is what the power curve of the game might look like:

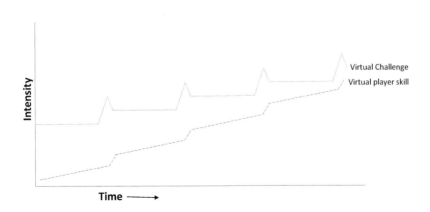

Computer/console RPGs often have this pattern of progression, where the player mostly increases their power level (moreso than their skill level). Older CRPGs tended to be even *more* based on stats and less on skill than more recent games, requiring a lot of level/xp/gold grinding and little in the way of skillful play. Most games made today give the player more abilities as they level up, giving more options and increasing the tactical and strategic skill required to win difficult fights. Winning more fights lets the player level up, which in turn makes it easier to win *even more* combats (a positive feedback loop, which is examined later this chapter), counteracted by the fact that the enemies also get stronger as the player progresses, and slowed by the property that players typically need more and more victories to level up again in the same area. As such, the actual rate of gain in player power is closer to linear.

Desire for Mastery → *Difficulty/Complexity Loop* → *Player Skill*

You might assume that the player skill curve is not under the game designer's control. After all, players come to the game with different levels of skill at the start, and players learn and improve at different rates. However, designers do have *some* control over this, based on the game's mechanics.

If we design deep mechanics that interact in many ways with multiple layers of strategy, so that mastering the core mechanics just opens up new ways to look at the game at a more abstract meta-level, the player's skill should increase for a long time, probably with some well-defined jumps when the player finally masters some new way of thinking (such as when a *Chess* player first learns book openings).

If the game is more shallow or has a significant luck component, we expect to instead see a short increase in skill as the player masters the game's basic systems, and then, player skill quickly plateaus. This may be a valid design decision, for example, in gambling games which must be taught quickly, or educational games where the player is expected to learn new skills from the game and then stop playing so they can go and learn other things.

The game designer can also influence how quickly the player learns, based on the number and quality of tutorials and practice areas provided. One common model is a three-stage approach: first, give the player a new capability in a safe area where they can just play around with it; then introduce them immediately to a relatively easy area where they are given a series of simple challenges that let them use their new toy and learn about all the cool things it can do; then, give the player a harder challenge where they must integrate the new thing into their existing play style and combine it with other previously acquired concepts. By designing the levels of the game to teach the player specific skills in certain areas in a given order, you can ramp the player more quickly so they can increase their skill faster, if that is your desire.

If you want to slow down player skill progression instead, you can use **skill gating**. Instead of teaching the player how to play your game or holding their hand through it, simply offer a set of progressively harder challenges. In this way, you are at least guaranteed that if a player completes one challenge, they are ready for the next. Each challenge is essentially a sign that says "you must be at least *this skilled* to pass," but the player's progress is slow, as they must learn each skill on their own the hard way.

Player skill is hard to mathematically measure on its own, since it's combined with player power and a player's performance includes both (so it is hard to separate out the individual elements). The best clues come from playtesting and analytics: how often players die or are otherwise set back, where these failures happen, how long it takes players to get through a level the first time they encounter it, and so on. We examine this more in Chapter 13.

If the skill challenges and player skill were plotted on this same graph as the power curves, their shape would tell a lot about the depth of the mechanics. If both skill curves increase at a regular rate, it means the game starts off simple but is layering additional complexities and considerations on a regular basis, making the game more and more challenging over time. More often, the progression curve in a CRPG looks more like this:

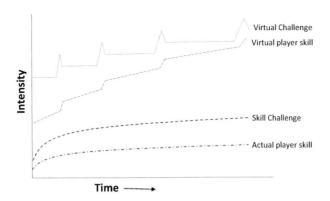

Here, there is some depth to the mechanics, but it plateaus maybe a third of the way in or so, once the player is out of the "tutorial" section and all of the core combat mechanics have been introduced. From that point on the player is playing by the same rules, and while they are learning new capabilities and getting new weapons from time to time, these usually don't cause massive shifts in the player's core strategies (which generally amount to "do damage to enemies, heal self when damaged, and default to using unlimited actions before using limited but renewable actions, which in turn should be exhausted before resorting to limited, consumable actions").

MMOs like *World of Warcraft* follow a similar skill and power curve, except that beyond a certain point, they transition to the elder game (when players reach the level cap), at which point the concept of "progression" loses a lot of meaning. But during the progression phase of the game, the two types of games look similar. We discuss the elder game later in this chapter.

That said, this is not the *only* pattern of power and skill curves, and may not even necessarily be the best for any particular game. These curves vary based on the genre and the intended audience. For example, here's another set of curves, this time for a retro-style arcade game, such as *Space Invaders*.

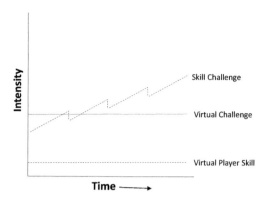

In the classic arcade game, the game presents a single skill-based challenge to the player. Wave after wave, a formation of aliens march back and forth across the screen, descending when it reaches the edge and meanwhile firing at the player's ship. The player has no way to gain power over the course of the game. They start with three lives and cannot gain extra lives in any way. There are no temporary or permanent powerups. On the other hand, the player doesn't really lose power either: whether the player has all three lives remaining or just one, offensive and defensive capabilities are the same.

The player's goal in *Space Invaders* is not to win (the game predates the concept of "beating" an arcade game) but rather to survive as long as possible before the increasing challenge curve overwhelms them. Interestingly, this challenge curve *does* change over the course of a wave. Early in any level, the aliens are numerous and move slowly, so it's easy to hit a target (in spite of their greater numbers, only one enemy shot can be on the screen at a time, so there is no safety in numbers for the aliens). As the player progresses in eliminating aliens, the survivors start moving faster (and there are less of them), meaning that it becomes much harder to hit a target with any single shot. With just one alien remaining, it travels quite fast—and if the aliens ever manage to make it to the bottom of the screen, it's an automatic game over no matter how many lives the player has remaining. If the final alien in a wave is killed, a new wave appears. The new wave is harder than the previous one, but the difficulty is still decreased initially when the aliens move slowly and there are so many of them again.

Note that player skill is not shown on this graph; its height could be anywhere, but would vary based on the skill of the player. Over the course of a single game, however, it would remain relatively constant most of the time (though it might be expected to increase slowly over repeated play). The point at which the combined challenge level exceeds the combined player skill+power is when the player would finally lose.

This provides a pattern of rising and then falling tension in the mechanics, which incidentally was also mirrored in the sound effects (the aliens make a brief sound every time they move, and the tempo speeds up as the aliens move faster during a level).

Another interesting case is the genre of games known as Roguelikes (such as the classic PC games *Rogue*, *Angband*, and *Nethack*). These games have the leveling and stat-based progression of a CRPG, but traditionally have the mercilessness of a retro arcade game. A single successful playthrough of *Nethack* looks similar in progression curve to a CRPG:

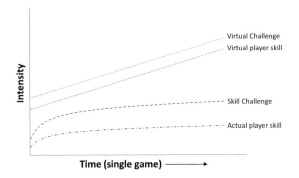

However, looking at a player's progression over multiple plays tells a more interesting story. A core property of many of these games is that they are designed to kill the player character if the slightest mistake is made. In this case, "dead" does not merely mean "reload from previous save," but rather, the game literally deletes the save file (permadeath). The player must then start over from scratch with a brand new character. While a single *winning* game may take dozens of hours, the player likely has died many, *many* times in order to gain the skill it takes to reach that point without dying. Over time, then, the power curve may look something like this.

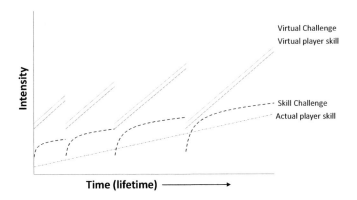

Across a series of playthroughs, the player is gaining power through the game then must reset, but in doing so, their skill increases as they reflect on what killed them and how to avoid dying in exactly that way in the future. This allows the player to get a little bit further, at which point, something new kills them, and the cycle repeats… but with each time, the player gets a little bit more skilled and is likely to survive a little bit longer. The sheer amount of time a player must dedicate to winning even one of these games is an intimidating barrier to entry for new players, but a source of endless fascination to devotees of the form.

By contrast, many early-generation social games (like *FarmVille*) have a very different progression curve:

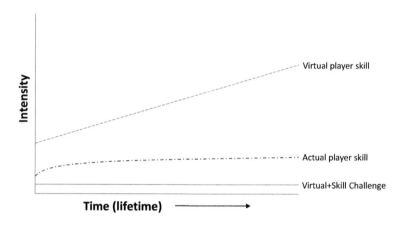

In stark contrast to Roguelikes, these are games where the player can essentially click the mouse to progress. It is virtually impossible in these games to lose any progress at all, and the player is constantly gaining power. If the player's skill is higher, it merely allows progression at a faster rate. Unlike MMOs, these games tend to not have a hard level cap; the player can continue happily gaining experience and resources and increasing their rate of resource gain. However, after a certain point, the rewards decrease in frequency and eventually stop entirely. When the player has earned all the ribbons and trophies the game has to offer, their ability to increase their rate of further progression has slowed to a crawl, and there are no apparent rewards for continuing on… and at that point, the player either stops playing or starts playing in a different way (to the extent to which these games support alternate forms of play, such as decorating one's farm in *FarmVille*).

Idle games (such as *Clicker Heroes*) take the constant low-risk progression model of *FarmVille* and add the ability to reset the game state (referred to in those games as **prestige** mechanics[3]), reducing the player's virtual skill and the game's power and skill challenges, but typically with a permanent stackable bonus that speeds player progression. In this respect, idle games look like a hybrid between the Roguelike and *FarmVille* models.

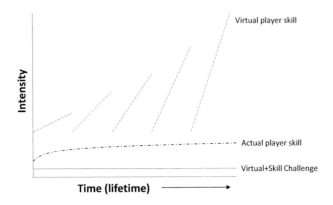

In this case, while there may be a low skill ceiling, and the constant forward progression supplies little resistance other than the time it takes for resources to accumulate, the player's virtual skill is increasing over time and then reset to the baseline after each reset. However, with each reset comes additional multipliers that further improve the player's rate of progression. As such, we could examine not only the progression curve of a player's virtual skill in a single playthrough (which could be linear as depicted here, but in these games is more often logarithmic so that the slowing progression eventually incentivizes a player to reset), but also the progression curve of a player's *maximum* virtual skill before each reset (which might be exponential as shown here or any other relationship).

In many F2P games, particularly those that appear to have a strong skill component (such as the F2P puzzle games *Puzzle & Dragons* and *Candy Crush Saga*), the required skill to pass levels with the highest rating starts out small and then ramps up considerably once the player has played a bit, learned the mechanics, and become invested in the gameplay. While the player might be able to easily beat the first few levels with the maximum three-star rating, after that the same amount of skill will only get them two stars, then one, and then being on that borderline between barely passing or just missing. The games then provide a means to boost the player's performance (for example, consumable items that give an advantage on the

[3] Not to be confused with high-status prestige items in a game economy

current level) that reduce the difficulty to manageable levels once more… but after burning through the first few of those items that were given for free, the player will have to pay real-world money to acquire more. Here, increasing friction is used as a means of forcing players to a decision to monetize or go away.

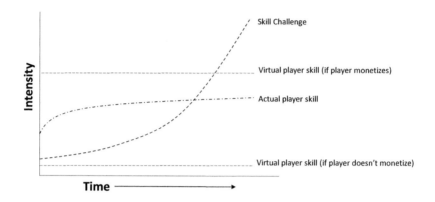

Curiosity → Discovery Arc → Player Knowledge

There are two main types of discovery arcs: exploration of virtual spaces and advancing the narrative.

Progression through level transitions (that is, when the player enters a new level or area) is a special kind of reward, because it shows at a visceral level that the player is moving ahead. The speed at which players move to new spaces should be chosen carefully. Too many transitions in a short period of time is disorienting, but too few makes the whole game feel like one giant series of identical levels with no progression. A common model (not the only one) is to have relatively short levels at the start of the game and have each successive level take slightly longer to traverse than the previous one, on average (with some variation to keep things from getting too predictable). This lets the player feel like interesting things are happening at the start of the game when they aren't yet emotionally invested in the outcome; a player can tolerate longer stretches near the end of the game, especially when leading up to a major plot event. Interestingly, level transitions can rely as much on environment artists as level designers. For example, if players are traversing a large dungeon, visual elements can be added to make each region of the dungeon feel different, such as having the color or texture of the walls change as the player gets further inside. Even something as simple as a color change can signify progress to the player.

Story progression has its own nuances that game designers have to be aware of, because in many cases, there is a separation between story and gameplay. For example, knowing the characters' motivations or feelings toward each other or their respective backstories usually has no meaning at all when dealing with combat mechanics or the xp/level curve. And yet, in many games, story progression is one of the rewards built into the game.

Additionally, the story itself has a "difficulty" or "friction" of sorts (story writers would call it **dramatic tension**), so an important consideration is whether the dramatic tension of the story overlaps with the perceived difficulty curves of the game. Many games do not: the story climax is often near the end of the game, but the hardest part of many games is in the middle somewhere, before the player finds a powerful weapon or levels up or masters the core mechanics to the point where the rest of the game can be played by rote. For example, here is Freytag's Triangle, a visual representation of the five-act structure, next to the difficulty curve for some poorly balanced RPG.

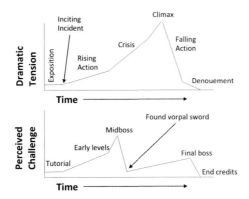

In this case, there is a mismatch between the most dramatic elements of the story and the most challenging parts of the game. A boss that appears just before a major crisis ends up being one of the hardest battles of the game; by the time the crisis of the story reaches its climax, the player has already gained so much power that the actual resolution of the crisis in gameplay is relatively trivial, making the final boss fight anticlimactic. Instead, it would be ideal for rising tension in the story to happen while the difficulty curve is increasing, with dramatic climaxes at the hardest parts, and so on. This would help the story feel more integrated with the game mechanics… all accomplished, oddly enough, through game balance and math![4]

---

[4]An alternative would be to keep the difficulty curve of the game the same, and instead force the story writers to adjust the dramatic moments of the story to match the existing difficulty curve, but in practice, it's generally easier to change a few numbers than to rewrite whole sections of story.

Desire for Closure → Accomplishment Arc → Completion

One thing you may have noticed is that the model of progression loops presented here can operate at any level of abstraction. Short-term tasks (navigate this hallway, beat this random encounter combat, solve this puzzle) can chain together to larger tasks (navigate this level, beat the boss of this dungeon, solve this series of puzzles), which in turn chain together for even larger tasks (navigate this world, beat the final boss of the game, solve a large meta-puzzle that requires solving several puzzle series). At the highest level, the player's long-term goal is to finish or complete or master the game and its mechanics.

There is a difference between **finishing** a game and **completing** it (though these terms are often used interchangeably in common speech and even among game designers—we only make the distinction here in this book to make a point). Here, the term complete is used in the sense of the term completionism (a player is called a "completionist" if they want to finish *all* of the tasks set out in the game, not merely the single stated long-term goal). For example, a player can typically finish a computer RPG by fighting and defeating the final boss, which results in being shown the ending sequence; but the player may have received a number of optional sidequests that they did not complete, and they may have passed by some optional locations that they did not explore (which may have contained even more quests, if they had). If the player manages to take 100% of all of the game's progression mechanics to their final state, then the player has completed the game.

What drives some players to completionism? The field of psychology describes the **Zeigarnik effect**,[5] which states that it is easier for people to remember incomplete tasks than completed ones. In the context of games, this means players are automatically, intrinsically motivated to complete known unfinished tasks. Players feel a sense of persistent cognitive load as long as they leave a task unfinished, and they experience a sense of relief when completing a long-standing goal.

Sid Meier's Civilization is a game that is notorious for being particularly compelling. Players may sit down for just a few minutes, intending to take one or two turns… only to find an entire evening has passed because they kept taking "just one more turn" repeatedly. In the context of progression loops and the Zeigarnik effect, we can gain insight into how and why this happens, and why this game series in particular is so good at trapping players into a seemingly never-ending cycle of play.

---

[5] Named after Russian psychologist Bluma Zeigarnik

In *Sid Meier's Civilization*, many progression loops are active at any point in the game. A player's current research is in the process of completing; a stack of military units might be approaching enemy territory; a building or Wonder in one or more cities might be about to finish; and so on. Some loops in the game are short term (a new unit that takes three turns to build) and others are long term (research that takes twenty turns to complete), but the experience of the game is such that all of the progression loops share two key qualities:

- The active progression loops are constantly open and ongoing. Any loop that a player is currently advancing is not yet complete, but as soon as it is completed, it immediately opens up the next iteration of that same loop. In this way, each of the progression systems in the game (technology, exploration, military, economic, and so on) remains open indefinitely.
- The progression loops overlap. Because the game has so many distinct progression loops active at once, and they are staggered, the player is never more than a turn or two away from completing one or more goals.

Because the player not only has a number of open goals, but is also very close to completing one of them at any given time, the player is psychologically compelled to take one more turn to complete the next goal, so that they can close a loop to save themselves the cognitive load of having an almost-but-not-quite-completed task. This is a trap, however, because as soon as the player does close that loop, it just opens another one, and next turn, there's some other almost-complete goal to complete on that turn. This cycle continues throughout the game, until either one of the loops finally closes (at the very end of the game—and games may take 10 or 20 hours or more to complete in some games in the series) or the player is forced to walk away against their cognitive desires.

In contrast to a game like *Sid Meier's Civilization*, some games are designed to feature total completion, where all open loops close down at the same time. There are some benefits to designing a game that provides one or more natural points in the play that work like this. The ongoing cost of maintaining active skills and working knowledge of the game drops off dramatically, allowing players to let the game go for a time, freeing their mental resources and reducing their cognitive load. This provides a wonderful feeling of satisfied completion on the part of the player. It provides a natural breakpoint where the player can step away to deal with life tasks outside the game. If these moments are spaced regularly and sufficiently close together, the player won't feel that the game is "holding them hostage."

Total completion can be tricky to design in a game that has multiple progression loops active at a time or a series of open loops that lead into other loops on completion. The solution is to synchronize the various loops in the game (rather than staggering them as in *Sid Meier's Civilization*) so that all of the loops come to a climactic conclusion at about the same time. One might speak not just of *completion* (when a progression loop finishes, giving the player the sense of moving forward) but also of **closure** (coming to a satisfying conclusion, giving the player the ability to leave things behind). For completion to lead to closure, the player must have the opportunity to look back and reflect on the play experience thus far. Closure is easier with longer-term progression loops and closing off the ability to revisit earlier parts or phases of the game. This inability to go back might happen through loss (the player grieves over a lost party member) or through relief (the player realizes they have grown to the point where they don't need a certain thing anymore). An ideal but hard-to-design case is providing players with a sense of closure (i.e. an interesting play session or episode) even if the player fails to accomplish their goals.

One can also design in the opposite direction, holding up completion or closure as a goal that is in fact virtually unattainable. F2P games, in particular, are notorious for making use of **gacha mechanics** (this is where the player acquires a new game object chosen from a long list of collectable objects, with some being more rare than others). Prior to the rise of F2P games, these were also seen with TCGs, as well as non-game collectables such as sports trading cards, or cereal boxes where you get one of several toys inside a box and are encouraged by a television commercial to "collect all six!" While players, seeing a list of characters in a game to recruit, will naturally want to collect them all, getting all of them can involve many random rolls in a gacha system. For example, suppose in one game there are merely ten rare, ten uncommon, and ten common characters, and when the player purchases a new character in game, it has a 10% chance of being rare, 30% chance of uncommon, and 60% chance of common. If the player can't purchase or trade for specific characters directly other than buying a random character and hoping for the best, on average a player would have to purchase 293 characters to get a full set. If there were instead a hundred characters of each rarity, you'd have to buy over 5000 characters to get them all! You can hopefully see where tying a monetization hook to this process (charging a player, say, a dollar per random character) could cause a player to spend a *lot* of money without realizing how difficult it is to collect a full set... and why some governments have looked at implementing legal restrictions on the use of gacha mechanics.

Social Progression

> Desire for Expression → Cosmetic Content → Self-Expression
> Connection → Guilds → Fellowship and Social Inclusion
> Superiority → Leaderboards → Competition and Recognition of Skill
> Desire to have Value to the Community → Influence → Recognition of Value
> Sociopathy → Griefing → Negative Attention

These social progression loops all have one thing in common: they all require interaction with other players to have meaning. They may or may not be supported by the systems and mechanics of the game; if they aren't, players sometimes take it upon themselves to build the scaffolding for these interactions on their own (for example, early-generation online multiplayer games that didn't formally recognize "guilds" still had players forming their own unofficial groups). To the extent that these *are* supported in the game, however, progression through these loops can be explicitly designed, and integrated with other progression arcs and loops.

False Progression

Some random systems can be tuned to give the impression that the player is progressing, even when they aren't. This is best illustrated with slot machines. Slots are mathematically balanced to trigger a false sense of progression in players. As an example, when a player has a "near miss" where it appears they are just one reel away from a jackpot, this can make the player feel as if they're getting closer to hitting a true jackpot... even though each spin is independently random and the player isn't actually progressing toward anything except more randomness.

This was also seen in the video game *Destiny*. On initial release, most loot drops did not give players anything better than what they already had, so new loot didn't actually bring these players closer to their goal in any way. And yet, it gave a perception of progress. Some players feel that in a random system, there is an unknown number of loot drops that the player must find before getting the next useful one, so even a "failed" drop takes them one more step closer to their goal.

However, this sense of progression is not guaranteed. Hope is a necessary component if the outcome is partly random. If the player perceives the chance of success as too low, they may feel a sense of futility instead.

In multiplayer games, there are other workarounds for "failed" random drops. In many MMOs, there is a sense of fairness in social groups, where players who have not received useful loot in a while may be able to get one from their guild (this is manifest in entering a loot queue where players can request a specific type of loot the next time one is found, or a "Need vs. Greed" system where players can request a specific item that was just found).

Another multiplayer workaround is the ability to trade between players. For example, if all items can be bought or sold at an auction house, and every item is bought or sold in gold, rare items may cost a lot of gold, but it can feel attainable to all players (they just have to grind for sufficiently large amounts of gold). However, there is little perceived movement toward a goal in this case, because there is no granularity. A player has enough to either buy the item they want now or they don't. There isn't a compelling resistance curve.

A third option is to allow players to use their useless items in some way. The simplest way is to allow players to sell them to an NPC shopkeeper or otherwise convert them into in-game resources, which can later be used to purchase more useful items (either from the same shopkeeper or from other players). In some games, useless items can also be fused together to become a stronger and more useful version of the item, or else they can be sacrificed to power up one of the player's currently equipped items. In this way, even a "useless" item can still be used in one or more ways. Even if it isn't what the player wanted, they can convert a sufficiently large number of unwanted items into one thing that they do want. One important design consideration for these types of mechanics is the exchange rate: how many unwanted items (or proportionally, how much play time spent grinding to get those items) does it take to get one item that the player *does* want?

All of this leads to an interesting paradox: both randomness and control can satisfy a player's desire for certainty when dealing with the intermittent progress from a random system. A player with more control can improve their skill at the game and don equipment that gives them a better kill rate or drop rate, so that they have a better probability of finding valuable loot. A player who submits to the randomness can be content to grind and wait for the RNG to give them sufficiently good loot eventually, either due to luck of the dice *eventually* giving them what they want, or due to item fusion or exchange mechanics that get the player there eventually with enough unsuccessful drops.

Reward Schedules

Progression is strongly related to what is sometimes referred to as the **reward schedule** or **risk/reward cycle**. You don't just want the player to progress automatically. Rather, you want the player to feel like they *earned* their progression and that they are being *rewarded* for playing well. In a sense, progression can be considered a reward in itself: as the player continues in the game and demonstrates mastery, the ability to progress through the game shows the player they are doing well and reinforces that they're a good player (an example in shorter games is the concept of a **speedrun** where players attempt to beat the game as quickly as possible, and repeated play serves to improve their time). A corollary here is that the player needs to notice that they are being rewarded (this is usually not much of a problem, but additional flourishes that call attention to the progression can be nice).

Another corollary is that the timing is important when handing out rewards. Giving too few rewards, or spacing them out so that the player goes for lengthy stretches without feeling any sense of progression, is generally to be avoided in games that focus on progression mechanics. The player can become demoralized and feel like they're playing the game wrong if they aren't making progress… even if in reality they're doing just fine.

Ironically, giving too many rewards, and/or rewards of too great an intensity within a short span of time, can also be counterproductive. One thing we've learned from research on happiness is that experiencing some kind of gain or improvement produces a short-term gain in happiness, but it does not increase linearly with the amount of the gain; it follows decreasing returns. As a result, many small gains earned gradually over a long time generally make a person happier than many small gains (or one large gain) granted in a short space of time… even if they add up to the same thing in total. Giving too many rewards too quickly diminishes their impact.[6]

Another thing we know from psychology is that a random or intermittent reward schedule has more impact than a fixed schedule. Note this does *not* mean that the rewards themselves should be arbitrary. They should still be linked to the player's progress throughout the game and should happen as a direct result of positive actions taken by the player. It's far more powerful to reward the player because of their deliberate action in a game, than to

---

[6] For this reason, the reader should never hope to get rich quick by making a wildly successful game. Rather, get rich *slowly* by making many *mildly* successful games over the span of an entire career, to maximize enjoyment.

reward them for something they didn't know about and weren't even trying for. Some examples of this done poorly are as follows:

- In some casual and free-to-play (F2P) games, the game starts immediately with some kind of trophy or achievement or bonus just for logging in the first time. This reward is arbitrary and actually waters down the player's hard-earned achievements later. It gives the immediate impression that the game is easy and that the player can win without taking any effort at all. In some games, you may *want* the game to give this impression of being easy, depending on the audience, of course... but there is a danger in reducing the *fiero* of genuine accomplishment that the player would get later on.

- "Hidden achievements" exist in some games, where the player may know that there is some kind of goal to be unlocked, but the game won't say what it is until after it is completed (unless the player looks up a hint guide or FAQ). If an achievement is supposed to be a reward for skill, the player can't demonstrate that skill if the goal is unknown.

- Some games feature "achievements" that are not under direct player control. One example might be an achievement for winning a luck-based gambling game five times in a row (yes, this rewards the player for gambling many times, but the player can't do anything to improve their odds other than playing a lot and hoping... and being frustrated when they randomly lose after three or four wins in a row and they have to start over again). Another example might be "do exactly 123 damage in a single attack" where damage is dealt through a formula with a large random component to it. When designing these kinds of goals, ask yourself what the player is going to feel rewarded for, exactly.

Here are some examples of spaced-out rewards done well:

- Random loot drops in typical RPG or action games. While these are random, and occasionally the player gets an uncharacteristically good item, this is still tied to the deliberate player action of defeating enemies, so the player is rewarded for their skill (but on a random schedule, tuned so that the expected value of the big rewards is not too far apart or close together). In many games, the probability of receiving really good loot is in proportion to the difficulty of the enemy, so that the player *might* get an epic drop from a weak creature, but they're more likely to see an epic drop from a powerful foe.

- The player is treated to a cut scene once they reach a certain point in a game, particularly if it is triggered by the player doing something significant (like defeating a challenging boss). While this isn't technically random—it is scripted to happen at exactly the same point in the game, every time—a player on their first playthrough won't *know* where these moments are embedded, so from the player's perspective, these can't be predicted, so they are random from the player's frame of reference.

- Looking back at *Sid Meier's Civilization* (examined earlier in this chapter), we can see another reason why the game is so compelling to so many players. This game has many progression loops running concurrently, and they are each staggered so that there is a lot of overlap, with small rewards from completing one iteration of a loop happening every few turns. While the timing of the rewards isn't "random" *per se* (the number of turns it takes to complete any given task is a deterministic calculation, and the player is made aware of it), there are so many different progression systems that the schedule for when the player receives *some* kind of reward behaves a bit erratically.

Note that while various types of rewards are different in their nature and the design considerations surrounding them, they still have similar effects on the player, in terms of making them feel *rewarded* for playing. Therefore, a designer doesn't just have to consider spacing out the rewards of each category individually, but also how they look when interleaved. Avoid too many overlaps, where (for example) a transition to a new level, plot advancement, and power level increase all happen at once: those should be reserved for major dramatic moments where a large reward feels appropriate. Since level transitions are fixed and tend to be the simplest to design ahead of time, power-based rewards can be sprinkled throughout the levels as rewards that happen in the stretches between transitions. While it might be nice to also intersperse story progression in any gaps, that can be tricky: if placed in an area that's otherwise uninteresting, the danger is the player getting a story-based reward arbitrarily when they feel like they weren't doing anything except walking around and exploring, which then fails to feel like any player behavior is being rewarded. One rarely used but effective technique is to have some small backstory elements given randomly after combats (as party members converse with each other to learn more about one another) or in small snippets during exploration (so that finding an audio tape, bit of writing, or similar item that feels like a reward for exploring the level thoroughly if they are sufficiently hidden).

One thing a designer can do is to actually attempt to put all of the rewards on a progression chart, showing approximately where in the game each reward is found. While these can't usually be exact (the game designer can't control *exactly* how long a given level takes any player, or what order a player encounters various challenges in a non-linear level), they can at least give a general approximation of where things happen in order to spot any gaps:

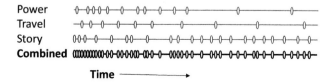

The diagram could be made even stronger by the addition of intensity data, so that the greatest gains in power, the most marked differences in level transitions or permanent changes to the game world, and the big climaxes and reversals in the story are drawn larger, and then, the combined intensity of everything is drawn as a graph over time to show generally what progress feels like in the game.

One of the most challenging aspects of designing progression systems is to design them in such a way that failure is also interesting, and doesn't just feel like rewards withheld. One common design pattern is to let the player keep their progression after failure: for example, a player defeated in an RPG might restart from the last save point with all experience, levels, and loot they had accumulated up to their death. This greatly lessens the sting of failure since the player no longer perceives death as wasted time or a setback. On the other hand, there is a danger that overcoming a challenge now feels meaningless: if the player can just keep bashing their character into a metaphorical brick wall and eventually pound their way through out of sheer stubbornness, progression feels like a function of time investment more than player skill. Another design (seen in some more modern Roguelikes such as *FTL*, *Desktop Dungeons*, and *Dungeon of the Endless*) is to unlock new gameplay elements when the player wins or dies. Even if the player loses all progress in a game with permadeath, it still gives a sense of overall progress if the player immediately learns on death that they just unlocked a new character, new starting options for the next playthrough, a new dungeon, and so on. This method is particularly well suited to games with lots of randomness or a harsh difficulty curve, where progress would otherwise feel slow and futile.

Common Problems in PvE

In PvE games, there are a few things designers should consider...

Increasing Player Skill

If you have studied game design before reading this text, you have probably encountered the concept of **flow**, as described by psychologist Mihaly Csikszentmihalyi. In brief, if a task is far too challenging compared to the player's current level of skill, the player feels great anxiety and frustration. If a task is too easy compared to the player's advanced skill, the player feels bored. But if a task is in the middle, challenging to the player and requiring the player to act near the upper boundary of their own skill without being overwhelming, the player becomes engaged and (we hope) finds the game more fun.

This suggests an obvious problem: as a player progresses through the game, they gain proficiency and get naturally better at making decisions in the game. Even if the game's challenge level remains constant, it gets easier *for the player*, changing their flow state into boredom as they get strong enough. This is often seen in longer PvE games, where the player has enough time and experience in the game to genuinely get better throughout a single playthrough. The solution is to have the game compensate by increasing its difficulty through play to make the game seem more challenging. This is the essence of what game designers mean when they talk about a game's difficulty curve: making sure that challenge level increases in line with player skill so that the player stays in the flow for the duration of the play experience.

Differing Player Skill Levels

Another problem with designing the game to provide an optimal level of challenge to put players in a flow state: not every player comes to the game with the same pre-existing skill level. What's too easy for some players is too hard for others.

The typical solution is to implement a series of difficulty levels, with higher levels granting the AI power-based bonuses or giving the player a power disadvantage, because that is relatively cheap and easy to design and implement. However, there are some caveats with this. If you continue using the same playtesters throughout development, those testers quickly become experts at the game and thus be unable to accurately judge the true difficulty of the easiest mods of play. Easy should mean *really easy*, and it's better to err on the side of making the easiest mode *too* easy, than making it so challenging that some players are unable to play at all. Bring in new playtesters on a regular basis in order to accurately judge the novice reaction. Another suggestion is to set and manage player expectations up front, especially about higher difficulties and *especially* if the game actually cheats. If the game pretends on the surface to be a fair opponent that just gets harder because it is more skilled at higher levels, and then players find out it's actually manipulating the numbers to give itself an unfair advantage, this can be frustrating. If the game is clear that the AI is cheating and the player chooses a high difficulty level anyway, there are less hurt feelings: the player *expects* an unfair fight, and the whole *point* is to overcome the unfair challenge through their extreme skill. This can be as simple as choosing a creative name for the game's highest difficulty level, like "Insane."

There are other ways to deal with differing skill levels. High difficulty levels can increase the skill challenge of the game (as opposed to just increasing power-based challenges). For example, the AI can actually be designed to play with a greater or lesser overall level of skill; this is expensive but can make the game feel like an entirely different experience once the player gets better and goes up to the next difficulty. In some games, the design can also be modified on higher difficulty levels to simply block off the easiest paths to victory, forcing the player to go through a harder path to get to the same end location.

Another method used in some games is **dynamic difficulty adjustment** (DDA), a special type of negative feedback loop where the game tries to figure out how the player is doing and then adjusts the difficulty level during play based on how the player is doing. This must be done carefully. As with other negative feedback loops, DDA punishes the player for doing well, and some players don't appreciate that if it isn't set up as an expectation ahead of time. Worse, in some games it's possible for players to understand and predict the DDA system in such a way that they intentionally play poorly for most of the game and then use the benefits of being behind to rush to victory in the end game—probably not what the designer had in mind!

Another method is to split the difference: try to figure out how well or poorly the player is doing (as with DDA), but then give the player the option of changing the difficulty level (or not) themselves. Some examples of how this might be done are given as follows:

- In *flOw*, the player can go to the next (more challenging) level or the previous (easier) level at just about any time. A confident player who wants to be challenged can dive deep quickly. A timid player who wants a more relaxed experience can spend extra time on each level, power-ing up a bit to make subsequent levels easier. If the player gets in over their head, the game knocks them back a level (*that* part is more like traditional DDA) but otherwise the difficulty is under player control.

- In *God of War*, if the player dies enough times on a level, the game offers the player the chance to change the difficulty level when on the game over/reload screen. Some players might find this patronizing, but on the other hand, it also gives the player no excuses if they try and then die again.

- In *Sid Meier's Pirates!* the game actually gives the player the opportu-nity to increase the difficulty level when they come into port after a successful plundering mission. It also gives the player an incentive to do so: they keep a higher percentage of the booty on future missions if they continue to succeed.

- In many games, there are alternate, optional paths through the game that increase the difficulty for the player if taken. Many of the race-tracks in the *Mario Kart* series contain shortcuts that are hazardous, but allow for faster lap times if the player finds and masters them. *Cave Story* and *Braid* both have secret objectives that open up a final, very difficult level and a new ending if the player is tenacious and clever enough to find it.

- In both *Bastian* and *Transistor*, difficulty isn't a game option, but rather a game mechanic. In both games, the player is given the opportunity to increase the difficulty in specific ways (such as taking more damage from enemies, or making enemies tougher, or having enemies explode or come back from the dead when killed), and each individual chal-lenge can be turned on or off in between levels. The game also rewards the player with extra money and experience points the more of these are turned on, so players are strongly incentivized to seek their highest acceptable level of difficulty.

The Commander Problem

One problem specific to certain types of multiplayer PvE games is when one player can dominate the entire game, telling other players what to do and generally turning the experience into a solitaire game where they are making all of the decisions and directing the other players to follow their orders by rote. This problem is common in many earlier tabletop cooperative games, such as *Pandemic* and *Flash Point: Fire Rescue*. It is referred to by many names, among them the **commander problem** or **alpha player**.

For this to be an issue, information about the game state known to any player must be known to all players. Otherwise, no player would have the privileged information to make optimal decisions on another player's behalf. Also, it usually only becomes a problem when there is a major difference in the skill level of players (such as one expert player teaching the game to several beginners).

The extent to which this is a true problem depends on the interpersonal dynamics and personalities of the players involved. Some expert players care more about winning than about everyone having a good time, and they try to take over even to the detriment of other players' enjoyment. Some expert players would actually *like* to just take their own turn and let everyone else deal with their own decisions, and feel uncomfortable being thrust into a role of *de facto* leadership. On the flip side, some players are timid by nature and would actually rather defer to a trusted authority if they are uncertain of how to proceed, and some players are comfortable offering advice to their companions when asked, without overstepping their bounds and dominating the conversation.

There are many ways to address this issue, but it is something that the designer of any multiplayer cooperative (PvE) game must consider. Here are some established solutions, which may be implemented individually or in combination; this is not a complete list, and there are surely many other solutions that have yet to be discovered:

- **Real-time mechanics**: if players only have 30 seconds to perform their actions for a turn, even if an expert player would *like* to take everyone else's turn for them, there just isn't time to do much more than take their own turn and hope that everyone else did a reasonable job. This is why the commander problem is rarely seen in video games: without growing an extra set of arms, a player who controls their own character with keyboard and mouse in *Left 4 Dead* makes them unable to control anyone else's actions, and some tabletop games like *Wok Star* and *Space Alert* also use this method.
- **Privileged information**: players can't make optimal decisions on another's behalf if they are lacking information. The restriction of information passing must be done carefully, however. In the board games *Lord of the Rings* and *Shadows over Camelot*, the rules prohibit players from speaking about specific cards in their hand, but do allow players to make generalizations. However, in both games the dividing line between what is okay and what is not is ambiguous, and left to the players to decide, making it feel like a kludge rather than a core mechanic.

In the card game *Hanabi*, this is done in a more central and interesting way: all players hold their hand of cards in reverse, so that they can see everyone else's cards except their own (and they must play cards from their hand blindly). Giving other players information about their hand is an action that can be taken in the game, and such information is treated as a sharply limited resource, making the choice of what to share with whom (and when) the critical decision that players are making.

- **Restricted communication**: if players must work together but *can't* directly tell each other what to do, then they must each make their own decisions. This can be challenging in practice (if the point of the game is about players working effectively in a team, shutting down lines of communication makes it harder for players to feel like they're together), but it can be done, particularly in combination with other mechanics. For example, in *Magic Maze*, each player has specific moves they (and only they) can perform on the board, and players are playing in real time to perform certain actions against the clock. It's often the case that a particular move must be made in order to progress, with only one player able to perform it. However, players are not allowed to tell each other what to do; the only means of communication are to stare intently at another player to get their attention or to place a large pawn (the game actually calls it the "Do Something pawn" in the rules) in front of them in order to indicate that they're supposed to do something. All of the information is out in the open; it's just a matter of how quickly players see it.

- **One against many**: is one or more of the players is the enemy, working to undermine the efforts of the rest of the group, sharing information between players carries the cost of revealing that information to the opposition. This can be seen in the dynamics of board games such as *Scotland Yard* and *Descent: Journeys in the Dark*. In some games, not only are there players who are working to get the team to fail, but their status as enemies is hidden. Board games such as *Battlestar Galactica* and *Dead of Winter* have the potential for one or more players to be **traitors**, and deciding who is and isn't a traitor is one of the key goals for the team. Since other players may or may not be on their side, games with traitor mechanics tend to feature a general feeling of paranoia, and information sharing is naturally limited because players do not want to give too much information. These games also may limit information sharing, which just increases suspicions when something goes wrong: did something bad just happen because of bad luck or a bad draw, or was it sabotage? The online game *Among Us* combines the traitor mechanic with restricted communication; most players are cooperating to complete tasks on a ship, but one "impostor" is attempting to sabotage the ship and kill the rest of the crew. Players can only talk during specific times and usually that involves establishing an alibi or making an accusation. During most of the play, players are on their own and can't really help one another.

- **Play to cultural expectations**: In the card game *Sentinels of the Multiverse*, each player is given their own deck of cards to represent their superhero character. In most games with cards, players keep the cards in a closed hand by default. Merely by habit, players are not going to share information or show cards, because that isn't normal behavior for a card game. Each card has small text on it, making it difficult to read from a distance, which further discourages playing with an open hand. Additionally, the theme of the game helps discourage unwanted kibitzing: since when does a superhero turn to their comrades and say "well, gosh, I'm not sure what my next move should be... anyone want to tell me what to do?" Superheroes are, well, *superheroes*, and they are expected to make their own decisions, for better or worse.

- **Don't play with jerks**: one final "solution" worth mentioning is to accept that some players destroy the fun of the game by dominating discussions and that this is more of a problem with the player than the game. You can suggest to your players to not play with those kinds of people, if they are finding it a problem that gets in the way of their enjoyment, much the same way as a tabletop RPG group might oust a disruptive player rather than trying to find a system that doesn't allow for disruptions.

The Elder Game

Normally when we think of "progression," we think of games that have a defined end, where progress is being made toward that end. The goal of many video games is to finish the game, for example, by beating the final boss, being rewarded with the final ending sequence, and (hopefully) a satisfying sense of closure.

For some PvE games, however, there is no such thing as an "end" (MMOs, Sims, tabletop RPG campaigns, idle games, and others). In this case, progression is used as a reward and incentive structure (particularly in the early game when the player is being taught the game's mechanics) rather than as a way for the player to finish the game entirely. This has an obvious problem that is seen in just about all such games: at some point, additional progression just isn't meaningful. The player has seen all of the content in the game that they need to. They've reached the level cap, unlocked every special ability in their skill tree, maxed their stats, or generally completed whatever other forms of progression the game offers. When the player reaches this point, the player has to find something else to do, and there is an (often abrupt) transition into the **elder game**, where the objective changes from progression to something else. For players who are used to progression as a goal (this is what the game has been training them for up to that point, after all), that transition can be jarring. The players who enjoy early-game progression may not enjoy the elder game activities as much since there is such a different focus (and likewise, some players who would *love* the elder game never reach it, because they don't have the patience to go through the progression grind). What kinds of elder game activities are there?

- In Sim games (like *The Sims*) or social games (like *FarmVille*), the elder game is artistic expression: making one's farm or house pretty or interesting for one's friends to look at, or setting up one's own custom narratives.
- In MMOs (like *World of Warcraft*), the elder game consists of a number of activities. There are high-level raids that require careful coordination between a large group, and PvP arenas where players are fighting their maxed-out characters against other maxed-out characters (either one-on-one or in teams). Other aspects of the game's social elements can be explored, like taking on a coordination or leadership role within a Guild. The developers also add new content on a regular basis, including live events, tournaments, and expansions.
- In tabletop RPGs (like *Dungeons & Dragons*), the elder game is usually finding an elegant way to retire the characters and end the story in a way that's sufficiently satisfying. This is an interesting case, because the elder game can really be thought of as a quest to end the game!

Progression as Artificial Gating

In most games, one important goal of a designer is to create a strong and enjoyable **core loop** (the main activity that the player repeats continually throughout play). The moment-to-moment gameplay should be enjoyable and meaningful, or otherwise meet the design goals. In this context, forcing the player to grind an area before being allowed to progress can be accepted by players. After all, if the play of the game is engaging, then doing more of it is hardly a punishment.

However, some games attempt to use progression systems as a way to fix broken gameplay. If the core interactions with the game do not meet their goals, artificial in-game progression-based rewards (or even threats of loss of progress) don't increase player enjoyment. Such tactics that hold the player hostage to the game. They may be effective at increasing or sustaining length of play in the short term, but if a player is forced to do something that they don't particularly want to do—especially if the reward they get doesn't seem worth it relative to the time they spend achieving it—they become resentful. When these players leave the game, they do not do so with the intent of eagerly awaiting the sequel; they leave bitter, feeling like the game has wasted their time through cheap psychological tricks.

As you design your games, think about what your design goals are, and what the purpose is of your progression systems in the first place. Do they enhance the player's engagement with the game, or do they act as a barrier to engaging with the game's most compelling systems?

Difficulty Appropriateness for Audience

How challenging should a game be? What percentage of the time should a game end in failure, or how many times should a player or group have to play a game before they succeed? In PvP, we think of balance as giving each player an equal chance to win (assuming similar player skill levels); does that carry over to PvE, where a player has an equal chance of winning or losing?

This depends greatly on who the intended audience of a game is, what their expectations are, and what the design goals of the game are. For a masocore game, the genre is rooted in heavy difficulty, where the player must master the intricacies of the game at a very high level in order to proceed; it is expected that a player fails early and often and succeeds only rarely. For a casual game, losing may not even be possible, and the game is just about how quickly or slowly a player progresses. For many multiplayer co-op games, the game's job is to make the players feel awesome and skilled and powerful, and it should therefore be weighted to give the illusion of putting up a strong fight and then losing. In this way, "balanced" may actually be weighted slightly (or greatly) in favor of the player.

Additional Resource

- Many of the topics in this chapter are adapted from *Progression Systems*, Project Horseshoe 2015, accessible at http://www.projecthorseshoe. com/reports/ph14/ph14r3.htm.

Discussion Questions

1. What is friction in a game?
2. What are some ways a game designer can modify their game to change the difficulty as perceived by the player?
3. What is the difference between a gameplay arc and a gameplay loop?
4. Choose any game that features permadeath as a mechanic. Suppose you changed the game so that when the player died, they simply respawned in a safe place a few feet away with no further penalty. How do you think this would change the play experience—would players play the game differently, would it appeal to a different kind of player, and how would the "feel" of the game change overall?
5. Of the motivations listed in this chapter (agency, mastery, curiosity, closure, expression, connection, superiority, community), which of these most motivates you when you play?
6. What are some ways to keep the player feeling challenged in a game as their skill increases?
7. Choose any co-op game that you're familiar with. What, if anything, does the game do about the Commander Problem? Is it effective?
8. Choose any game that keeps going after a player reaches the end, into an elder game state. What does the game do, if anything, to maintain player interest in the elder game?
9. What is a core loop? Why is it important?
10. Choose any game that has a reputation for its difficulty level (either very high or very low). Search for the marketing materials for this game, such as trailer videos or advertisements. Based on this marketing, who do you think the target audience was intended to be? Does the difficulty make sense based on that audience?

Sidequests

In this chapter, we have looked at forms of progression in PvE games. Players progress through the content of the game while being kept on a somewhat random but still regular stream of in-game rewards. These rewards can be a combination of power gains within the game, the ability to enter new areas or levels, and the advancement of the storyline and plot. The rewards tend to happen frequently at the start of the game, then slow over time as the player has built more of an emotional investment in the game, although it should not slow so much that players feel frustrated and quit due to a lack of perceived progress. Ideally, the reward schedule is timed so that the story, gameplay, and player power within the game all come to a satisfying conclusion by the end of the game.

Sidequest 11.1: Removal of Level Caps

Choose any game that has a "level cap" or some other hard limitation on one or more forms of player progression, leading into an elder game.

Think for a moment about why that cap exists at all.

Suppose for a moment that the cap was removed, and players could continue progressing indefinitely. How would this affect the game? What problems or issues with the existing game would be fixed? What new problems or issues would be created?

Sidequest 11.2: Reward Schedules

Choose any game that has one or more progression arcs or loops in it, preferably a game you have played a lot and are very familiar with. Looking at the game's mechanics and content, reverse-engineer the reward schedule for the game. Analyze it as follows:

- What are the different kinds of progression in the game and the rewards for each type?
- For each kind of progression, how often do rewards happen? Is it on a fixed or random schedule (or does it *seem* random on the first playthrough, but it's actually fixed if the player is already familiar with the game)? Does the schedule follow an obvious pattern, or is it irregular?
- Do certain types of progression (or rewards) get emphasized over others, either at certain times in the game or overall?
- Consider the combined reward schedule of all progression loops overall. Specifically:
  - How often does the player receive a reward? What's the approximate mean time between rewards?
  - Are there any points in the game where the player receives a larger number of rewards at once, where all or most of the progression loops finish an iteration at the same time? How does the game feel at that point—is there a strong sense of closure? How often do these points occur?
  - Are there any long stretches in the game where the player receives few or no rewards? How do those sections of the game feel when playing, relative to other sections of the game? Do they stand out in some way?

Sidequest 11.3: Modeling Rewards

Choose any game with a progression or loot system or similar (such as a computer RPG). Model that system over the course of the game, either in a spreadsheet or in a visualization tool like *Machinations* (as seen in Chapter 4, Sidequest 4.3).

Fighter's Main Quest, Part 6: Reward Schedules, Revisited

Continuing from Part 5 in: Chapter 10

In Part 3, you examined power rewards that increase a player's capabilities in the game. Now, take that reward schedule and add other types of rewards (location-based and story-based progression).

Comment on the following:

- Are there any areas that have either a surplus or dearth of rewards, across all types? Are any of those areas particularly memorable (in a good or bad way) in a way that can be traced back to these rewards?
- Do any of the *types* of rewards get emphasized over others, either overall or in particular points in the game? Is this what you would expect, considering the genre of the game?

Part 7 continued in: Chapter 13

12

Progression in PvP Games

In This Chapter

- Why Progression in player vs. player (PvP)?
- Positive, Negative, and Zero Sum
- Feedback Loops
- Power Curves
- Game Length
- Revisiting Flow
- Common Problems in PvP

Why Progression in PvP?

> The essence of games is competition, and I think that's a remnant of our past as animals, and the competition of the survival of the fittest.
>
> *Gunpei Yokoi*

Normally when using terms like "advancement" and "progression" and "difficulty curve" as with the previous chapter, we think of single-player (or multiplayer co-op) games, i.e., player vs. environment (PvE), and the rate at which the player advances through a defined gameplay and/or narrative arc. However, PvP games also have players progressing and getting more powerful during play, and providing greater or lesser challenges to one another over time. For example,

- In *Magic: the Gathering* and many other CCGs, players have access to more resources and more powerful attacks as the game progresses.
- In *Catan*, players start out generating very few resources per turn, but as they build they gain access to a greater variety and quantity of resources.
- In *StarCraft*, players field more powerful units (or large swarms of small units) in the late game than they're capable of producing at the beginning.
- In *World of Warcraft*, progression of player characters is built into the core mechanics of the game (through the XP/leveling system), even on PvP servers.

In PvP games, we are not only concerned with the rate at which players gain (or lose) power in absolute terms, but also the relative rate of change compared to the other players. In PvP games, balance (the subjective feeling of fairness) in progression means that players feel like the game's progression is not arbitrary but instead comes about as a direct result of their choices during play, and that all players feel like they have the opportunity to win, given sufficiently skillful (or lucky) play.

It's worth stepping back and asking: what is the purpose behind progression mechanics in PvP games to begin with? One would expect that if we're devoting an entire chapter to this topic, it should be a useful design tool. What is it useful *for*?

In many cases, the purpose of progression is to bring the game to an end. For shorter games especially, the purpose is to make sure the game ends in a reasonable time frame and doesn't drag on for too long. Whether you're making a game meant to last 3 minutes (a retro-style arcade game), 30–90 minutes (a family board game), 6 hours (a strategic tabletop wargame), or 100 hours (a console roleplaying game or CRPG), any game you're designing may have a desired game length, and if you know what that length is, progression mechanics can keep it moving along to guarantee that the game actually ends within the desired length of time (or at least within a reasonable range). We address optimal game length later in this chapter.

This leads to a problem: if players are gaining power throughout the game and this serves as a reward to the player, the game is going to end right around the time when the players are reaching the peak of their power. This can feel anticlimactic: just around the time when the player feels like they are all-powerful, the game ends without them being able to enjoy feeling like they're o' top of the world.

Conversely, there are some games where the player is *losing* power throughout the game (like *Chess*). In that case, at the end the player may feel like they've been ground into the dirt for the entire experience. This isn't much better.

If PvE games are all about rewards for progression along a defined linear arc, then PvP games are about gains and losses relative to the opponents. Either directly or indirectly, the goal is to gain enough power[1] to win the game, and there is a kind of tug-of-war between the players as each is trying to reach the goal first. Sometimes, the victory condition of the game is to reach a certain level of power directly (e.g., eliminate all other players from the game). In other games, victory is indirection, where the goal is to gain something abstract like victory points, and the player's power in the game merely enables them to score those VPs. In some cases, of course, players *don't* gain power, they lose it, and the object of the game is to get the opponents to run out of power first (as with *Chess*). In any of these cases, though, gaining power *relative to the opponents* (whether that means gaining power or the opponents losing it) is usually an important player goal.

Tracking player power over time can follow many different (and perfectly valid, from a design perspective) patterns. In PvE, you usually see an increase in absolute player power over time (even if the player power relative to the challenges around them increases), but in PvP, there are more options, since everything is relative to the opponents and not compared with some absolute "you must be at least THIS POWERFUL to win the game" virtual yardstick.

Positive, Negative, and Zero Sum

When talking about player power in a PvP game, one question is what happens to the *sum* of power among all players over time. Borrowing terms from the field of game theory, we say that a game is **positive sum** if total player power increases over time, **negative sum** if it decreases, or **zero sum** if it is constant and merely redistributed between players over the course of play.

Catan is an example of a positive sum game. With each roll of the dice, resources are generated for all players, and all players can gain power in the game simultaneously without any opponent losing power. This game does

---

[1] "Power" in this context of progression means the sum of all aspects of a player's position in the game, including having more pieces or cards in play, more resources, better board position, taking more turns or more actions, gaining better stats or equipment, or really *anything* that affects a player's standing.

have some zero-sum elements, however. Space on the game board is constant, so if one player builds on a certain location, other players can no longer build there. Also, there are two bonuses (Largest Army and Longest Road) that can only belong to one player at a time, and if another player surpasses them they simply take the bonus.

Monopoly is also a positive sum game, because every trip around the board gives the player $200 (and that money comes from the bank, not from other players). There are a few spaces on the board that take money out of the economy and are negative sum (Income Tax, Luxury Tax, and a few of the Chance and Community Chest cards, and sometimes Jail) but on any given trip around the board, the expected value of the negative elements is less than $200, so on average more wealth is created than destroyed over time. Some players use house rules that give additional payouts from the bank on Free Parking or landing exactly on Go, which serve to make the game even *more* positive sum. Note that players paying rent to another is zero sum: whatever one player pays in rent goes directly to another player, a redistribution (but not creation or destruction) of wealth. This helps to explain why so many people have memories of childhood *Monopoly* games taking forever: it's a positive sum game (so the average wealth of players is increasing over time), and yet the goal of the game is to bankrupt all opponents… which can only be achieved through zero-sum methods!

Poker is an example of a zero-sum game. Players can only gain power (money) by taking it from other players, and whatever one player wins in a pot is exactly as much as the other players collectively lost. When played in a casino or online where the House takes a **rake** (a percentage of the money bet in each hand), *Poker* actually becomes a negative sum game for the players, because the sum of money at the table decreases with every hand.

In PvP games, changes in player power are the primary motivators and rewards: the player's goal is to win, and they feel rewarded when they have gained power relative to their opponents, because they then feel like they have a better chance of winning after making a particularly good move. This is true whether the game is positive, negative, or zero sum.

Feedback Loops

A **positive feedback loop** is a reinforcing relationship in a game (a "snowball effect" that grows over time), where the output of one system amplifies the input of the same system. In a system with positive feedback, receiving a power-based reward makes it more likely that player receives *even more* power rewards. Positive feedback loops reward a player for doing well and punish them for doing poorly. Positive feedback loops can be beneficial when they draw the game to a close; if a player is already clearly winning a game, it's better to just end the game quickly rather than go through another hour of play where everyone is just going through the motions to reach an outcome that feels predetermined. Positive feedback loops can be detrimental to the game experience when they give players the perception that the player in the lead is untouchable, or the player who is trailing early can never catch up; it can give a sense of futility to the play, unless counteracted by negative feedback loops. Since positive feedback loops amplify over time, early-game positive feedback has a much more pronounced effect than if it only kicks in late-game.

Monopoly has a positive feedback loop, which is what prevents it from never ending, in spite of its positive sum nature: when one player gets ahead in cash, they can use it to buy houses and hotels, which then make it more likely they'll get *more* cash when someone lands on those, which lets them build *even more* houses and hotels, which gets them *yet even more* cash, and so on.

Chess, as noted before, is mostly negative sum… except for one element, that of pawn promotion, which is positive sum. However, pawn promotion usually happens near the end of the game and serves the important purpose of adding a positive feedback loop that brings the game to a close: once one player has an extra queen in the end game, they are very likely to be able to get even further ahead or turn that into a win directly.

A **negative feedback loop** is the opposite. It is a damping relationship that reduces its own intensity over time, where the output of one system reduces the input of that system. In a negative feedback loop, being in the lead carries additional liabilities, while being in a lesser position gives the player extra help to compensate. Negative feedback can improve play by keeping the outcome uncertain up to the end, or it can detract from the experience by giving players the sense that they are rewarded for playing poorly and punished for showing skill. Since negative feedback counteracts players being far apart in relative power, negative feedback has a larger effect in late game when players have had time to establish a large power differential.

Computer racing games are notorious for their strong negative feedback loops. When racing against computer opponents, if the player is racing very well, the AIs tend to drive unnaturally fast in order to catch up; if the player is driving poorly, the AIs slow down to let the player catch up. In the *Mario Kart* series of racing games, players can pick up randomized weapons by driving over certain sections of the track; the weapons tend to be less powerful for the player in first place, and more powerful for players in last place. The design purpose of these negative feedback loops is to keep the game interesting: racing games are more exciting when the player is in the middle of a pack of cars and needs to consider not only how to race on the track, but also how to maneuver around opponents. In order to keep the player in the middle of the pack, the opposing cars speed up or slow down with the player.

Catan has a positive feedback loop in its resource production: as a player gets more resources, they can build cities and settlements that get them even more resources. To counteract this, there is a natural negative feedback loop that emerges in the multiplayer dynamics: since players generally cannot produce all of the resources that they need, they must trade with the bank (which is highly inefficient) or with other players. If one player is clearly in the lead, the other players may refuse to trade with them.

One property of feedback loops is how they affect the players' power curves. With negative feedback, the power curve of one player depends on their opponents' power: they increase more when behind and decrease more when ahead, so a single player's curve can look very different depending on how they are doing relative to their opponents. With positive feedback, a curve tends to increase (or decrease) more sharply over time, with larger swings in the end game. Power curves with positive feedback don't always take the opponent's standings into account; they can reward a player's own absolute (not relative) power. Now, this is not *always* the case—it is possible to design a negative feedback loop that depends on a player's own absolute power (this forces all players to slow down around the time they reach the end game), or a positive feedback loop that depends on relative power between players. However, if we understand the game design purpose served by feedback loops, we can see why positive feedback is usually independent of opponents, but negative feedback is usually dependent.

Feedback loops are not specific to PvP games; they can exist in PvE as well. However, in a PvE game, the loops manifest in the difficulty curve or the player's power curve. For example, a positive feedback loop in player power in PvE makes the game suddenly feel much easier, allowing the player to rush through the last part of the game. The player experiences this as a shorter duration of play through later sections of the game, and this might be modified by changing the feedback loop or by extending the amount of content that the player must progress through in the later stages. In PvP games, however, feedback loops are concerning because they can drastically alter the balance of power between players, to the point that they define and dominate the multiplayer dynamics.

Power Curves

What do power curves actually look like in a PvP game? It depends on whether the game is positive, negative, or zero sum in nature, and also whether there are positive or negative feedback loops that dominate the power curve.

Positive Sum, Positive Feedback

Here is what a power curve for a two-player positive sum game with positive feedback might look like.

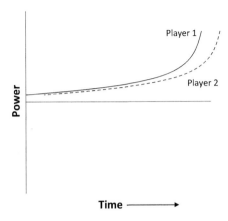

Here, the players are both gaining power over time, and the more power they gain, the more they have, so each player has an increasing curve. But since it is the difference in power (not absolute power) that is of primary importance in PvP games, we should also graph the difference between the two players.

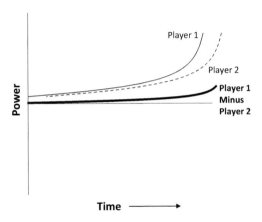

What should naturally happen in a positive sum positive feedback game is that one player gets a slight early lead and then keeps extending that lead and riding it to victory throughout the game (unless they make a serious mistake along the way). Notice how in this graph, the power curves for both players are drawn in exactly the same shape, just shifted over very slightly (as if Player 2 got a later start, perhaps losing one turn in the early game but otherwise keeping pace). Early in the game, the power difference is tiny, but it grows over time, and is quite significant by the time the game ends. This is a common power curve in the 4X genre (like *Sid Meier's Civilization*) where all players start building up their forces in the early game, and by the time anyone finds their opponents on the map through exploration, often one of those players is way ahead of the other on the tech tree, and one player ends up attacking with tanks against the defender's spearmen and archers.

This brings up an important point with this type of game: since one player is usually in the lead for most of the game with very little back-and-forth, which is normally quite frustrating for any player who is not in the lead. 4X games avoid the feeling of futility by hiding player standings from one another: no player has any idea what kind of forces other players have or how well others are developing their position, until players get strong enough to explore and find their opponents. At that point, if it isn't a close race, the weaker player often gets eliminated in short order, putting them out of their misery. As such, players are under the illusion that they are doing well for the bulk of the game, and if they are trailing, their defeat is swift. Other types of games may similarly hide player standings from one another in some fashion, to let all players feel they may have a chance to win.

Positive Sum, Negative Feedback

In a positive sum game with negative feedback, the players are still on an increasing absolute curve, but their trajectory is altered by their position relative to the other players. This reduces the gains for the leader and increases the rate of power gain for players who are trailing behind. The curve looks like a tangled braid.

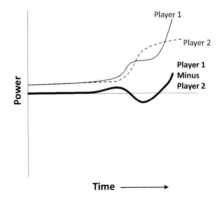

The combined curve—the difference between the players' power curves—swings back and forth between the two players (this is true of *any* negative feedback loop). In this case, since players are climbing the power curve, the end game can involve big gains with each player overtaking the other with ever larger plays. The end game can be exciting and dynamic.

One example of a positive sum game with negative feedback is *Catan*. In this game, players can never lose anything that they built on the board, and can only ever lose resources in a few special cases that mostly involve the player taking a known risk (or being ahead in the game already), yet players can receive new resources on any turn. This makes the game positive sum. This game also contains a pretty powerful *positive* feedback loop, as well: players receive resources from the settlements and cities they have in play, and those resources allow them to build more settlements and cities which then give them even more resources (and building these things is not only a way to get resources, but also the primary victory condition). At first, one might think that this leads to a situation where the player with the best initial placement of settlements or who gets better resource generation early in the game should dominate... and that would be the case if players couldn't trade with each other. But in the game, players can rarely generate *all* the resources that they need in order to continue building, which means they must trade. Trading with the "bank" is possible but has a terrible exchange rate, so players are strongly incentivized to trade with their opponents instead. This allows the players themselves to exert an even more powerful negative feedback loop to counteract the game's inherent positive feedback: if a player is well in the lead, other players can refuse to trade with them (or only trade at exorbitant rates), which slows the lead player down and lets the other players catch up fairly quickly.

Another example is a car or kart racing video game. Because the victory condition is to travel a certain distance, and players are almost always making forward progress toward that goal, this is a positive sum game as well. Many video games in these genres include a strong negative feedback loop that keeps all players feeling like they still have a chance through most of the race (and also tend to put human players near the AI-controlled opponents, where there's a lot more action), using what is sometimes called "rubber-banding" (opposing cars speed up or slow down to keep pace with the human players). Kart-racing games add an additional negative feedback mechanic in the form of random weapon pickups that are weighted to be more likely to be power-ful if the player is trailing. This provides an interesting tension: players in the lead know they just have to keep the lead for a little bit longer, while players who are behind are racing against the clock to close the gap quickly before the race ends. On the other hand, these methods feel artificial to a lot of players, because the player standings in the race are being modified by factors outside their control.

In fact, real-life stock car racing *also* has a negative feedback loop, because the driver in the lead is running into a lot of air resistance, so they are burning extra fuel to maintain their high speed. This means they need more pit stops to refuel, which cost precious seconds and allow others to overtake them a great deal. Meanwhile, the drivers who are drafting behind the leader are much more fuel-efficient and can take over the lead later. This negative feedback isn't arbitrary, like the weapon pickups in a kart-racing video game; it's a law of physics that affects all drivers equally, and it's up to each driver how much of a risk they want to take by breaking away from the rest of the pack.

Notice that while all three of these examples have the same pattern of progression, they all feel very different to players (or spectators). In *Catan*, the negative feedback is under player control through trading. In video game racing, the negative feedback comes from factors that are outside of player control entirely (computer-controlled opponents and weighted random die rolls). In real-life racing, the negative feedback comes from known factors that affect all players; while the players can't control air resistance, they can have some control over how much it affects them (with a tradeoff between fuel efficiency and overtaking opponents). Some of these situations feel more fair (and balanced) than others. So it is not merely the pattern of progression, but also the means by which the play progresses, that leads to a general feeling of fairness (or not).

Zero-Sum, Positive Feedback

In a zero-sum game, players take power from each other, so it is *only* the separate player power curves that have any real meaning here. The sum of player power in the game is constant, as a player can only take it from their opponent or lose it to their opponent.

With a positive feedback-driven game, the game may end very quickly as one player takes an early lead and presses it to gain even more of an advantage.

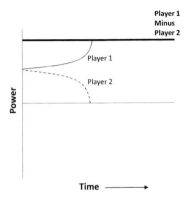

This can be appropriate for games that are designed to have very short play times, where it doesn't last long enough for the losing player to get demoralized. Most arm wrestling matches look like this, for example, since the stronger player is likely to start with an early lead, then the weaker player has to work against gravity to come back. Longer matches with multiple reversals are exciting in arm wrestling, partly because they are so rare in casual play.

Zero-Sum, Negative Feedback

With a negative feedback loop in a zero-sum game, we see swings of power that pull the leader back to the center. This keeps players close in power to each other and can lead to many exciting reversals of fortune before one player wins:

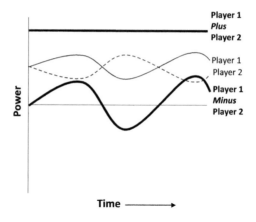

However, if the negative feedback loop is too strong, this also makes it hard for any player to actually win! The game can easily end in a stalemate where neither player can ever amass enough power to claim a decisive victory, since the further they are in the lead, the more pressure the game puts on them to relinquish that lead. A game like this might have an end condition based on time or number of turns, and whoever happens to be in the lead at a certain point of time is declared the winner. Such a game can have multiple layers of strategy. On the one hand, each player is constantly jockeying for position to be out in front, particularly if the game is coming to an end soon. On the other hand, knowing that the game can swing back and forth, players may try to intentionally take the lead at the right moment (or not), trying to plan ahead by anticipating when the big swings in power happen so that they aren't on a strong down-swing just as a victor is declared.

Zero-Sum, Positive, and Negative Feedback

Since zero-sum games with positive feedback can end too early, and zero-sum games with negative feedback can fail to end at all, another common structure for zero-sum games is to have a combination of positive and negative feedback loops. Early in the game, the negative feedback dominates, making it difficult for any player to get solidly in the lead and end the game too quickly. Later in the game, the negative feedback system plays less of a role, and the positive feedback dominates.

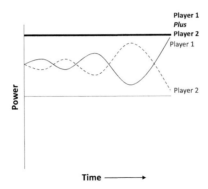

This can lead to an exciting game that starts off with a lot of back-and-forth reversals where each player spends at least *some* time in the lead, before one final, spectacular, irreversible triumph that brings the game to a close.

In limit *Poker*, players are limited in how much they can bet on a single hand (a player cannot risk all of their chips right away, no matter how good their first hand is), and the limit is typically raised at certain time intervals or after some number of hands are played. *Poker* does give an advantage to a player with more chips; they can afford to take more risks, and so they can grind down a player who has fewer chips by betting aggressively on so-so hands. Adding a limit prevents a player who takes a lucky early lead from dominating the table; but as the limit increases, eventually players can start making those big bets, often leading to one or two decisive hands where multiple players go "all in" against each other.

Negative Sum, Positive Feedback

Negative sum games look similar to positive sum games, except the power goes in the opposite direction. Here is what a negative sum game with a positive feedback loop might look like.

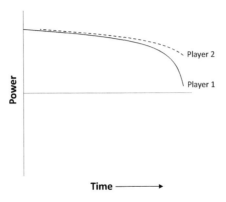

Here, the player who is in a losing position continues losing even faster in an increasing downward spiral. The more power a player has, the slower they tend to lose it... but once they start that slide into oblivion, losses happen more and more rapidly. As with positive sum games, losing for the entire game can be frustrating, so steps could be taken to hide player standings from one another, or combine with other systems that reduce the impact of the positive feedback.

Interestingly, one might expect *Chess* to follow this curve. Both players start with a set of forces and do not receive any reinforcements, nor are there any mechanics about resource trading, production, supply, or logistics that might be seen in more detailed army-level wargames. Players can generally not gain forces, but can lose them easily through capture. That makes *Chess* a negative sum game. It also has a mild positive feedback loop built in: if a player gets ahead in pieces, equal trades tend to be beneficial. Once the end game is reached, certain positions effectively let a player take an automatic win if they are far enough ahead. This can be demoralizing for the player who is losing, especially if the two players have unequal skill at the game, because the weaker player tends to start losing early and continues losing to an ever greater degree as the game goes on.

At first glance, this would seem to be a game that's not particularly compelling and poorly balanced. The game's saving grace is that against two equally skilled players, there does tend to be a bit of back-and-forth as players trade off piece advantage for board control or tempo, so that a player who appears to be losing in pieces has a number of opportunities to make up the deficit before long. Against well-matched opponents, we see instead a variable rate of decrease as the players trade pieces, based on how well they are playing. In such a case, the actual power curve looks more even, with players showing sudden but alternating drops in power, as if there were a negative feedback loop instead (see next section): There is not such a negative feedback loop, of course—it's simply that the game provides opportunities for player to make either short-term tradeoffs or gains that may be reversed later.

Negative Sum, Negative Feedback

With a negative feedback loop dominating a negative sum game, players are in a race to the bottom.

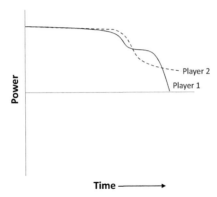

Players with more power are at a disadvantage and tend to lose it faster, relative to those who have already lost some power. Again, as with the positive sum version of this power curve, we see a "braid" shape where the players chase each other downward.

Game Length

"How long should I design my game to be?" is one of the most common questions asked in online game design groups. The short answer is, it depends on your game. The long answer follows.

All of the power curve graphs in the previous section lack numbers, because they are meant to just be general shapes to demonstrate what each situation tends to look like. However, it is possible to actually graph the power curves for a real game using playtest data, using real-time units or number of turns (as appropriate) on the Time axis, and using some kind of numeric formula for generally how well each player is doing in the game at any given time (this is easier to do with some games than others) on the Power axis.

If you do this for your game, one important thing to notice is the amount of time it takes to reach certain key points, because part of balancing the game is making the power curves scale so that the game ends within a certain time range.

The most obvious way to make sure the game ends at a desired point is by hard-limiting the turns or time. If you say that a turn-based strategy game automatically ends after ten turns or that a first-person deathmatch ends in 5 minutes, game length is fixed. Sometimes, this is necessary.

Sometimes, it's compelling and the best way to scale game length. Sometimes, it's a lazy design solution that implies the designer didn't playtest enough to know how long the game would take when played to a satisfying conclusion.

An alternative is to balance the progression mechanics that cause the game to end within a desired range. If the game ends on a certain condition that players eventually reach when they gain a certain amount of power, you can control game length by modifying how positive or negative sum the game is (that is, the base rate of power gain or loss), or by adding, removing, strengthening, or weakening the game's feedback loops. If you have the numbers to measure player power over time, this can be relatively straightforward, adjusting the numbers that control game length with some trial-and-error to get it just right.

Some PvP games have well-defined transitions between different game phases. The most common pattern is a three-phase structure with a distinct early game, mid-game, and end game (in *Chess*, not only are these phases well known and understood, but there are many entire books dedicated to just a single phase). As a designer, if you become aware of these transitions in your game (or if you design them into the game explicitly), you won't just be paying attention to the player power curve throughout the game, but also how it changes in each phase, and the length of each phase relative to other phases.

For example, if you find in playtesting that the end game isn't very interesting and mostly feels like players are just going through the motions to reach the conclusion that was arrived at during the mid-game, you could add new mechanics that come into play only in the end game to make it more interesting. Or, you could find ways to extend the mid-game and shorten the end game by adjusting feedback loops or the positive, negative, or zero-sum nature of the game during the various phases.

Another common problem in games: a game that starts off very slowly in the early game, giving players very little influence and interaction while they simply build up their own power, and then it becomes much more interesting and dynamic once it reaches mid-game. One way to fix this is to add a temporary positive sum mechanic to the early game in order to get the players gaining power and into the mid-game quickly. Another option is to start the players at a higher power level so that they effectively begin in mid-game (or close to it) from the start. A third possibility is to provide more interesting choices in the early game to make it distinct from the other phases but still compelling in its own right.

Some games have sharp, clear distinctions between the various phases of the game. In the board game *Shear Panic*, the game board is divided into four regions, and each region has its own scoring mechanics, giving an extremely different feel depending on where in the game the players are. Game shows often have abrupt transitions, too: in *Jeopardy!* the first round, second round, and final round each has their own feel.

Other games have phases that are not explicitly designed, may not be obvious to new or casual players, and have more gradual transitions. *Chess* is an example of this; nothing in the mechanics explicitly changes between the early and mid-game, but expert players recognize when it's time to stop developing their initial position and start attacking. Another example is *Netrunner*, an asymmetric CCG where one player (the Corporation) puts cards called Agendas into play, uses other cards to defend its Agendas, and ultimately attempts to use its resources to score its Agendas as victory points. The opposing player (the Runner) is meanwhile attempting to break through the Corporation's defenses to score points by stealing incomplete Agendas. After the game had been released and played for a while, players realized that most games follow three distinct phases: the early game when the Runner is relatively safe from harm and can attack before the Corporation has significant defense; the mid-game when the Corporation sets up a solid defense and makes it prohibitively expensive for the Runner to break through at the time; and then the late game when the Runner again gets enough resources to break through the Corporation's strongest defenses on a regular basis. Analyzed in this way, the Runner's goal is to score as many points as possible in the early game, use the mid-game to back off on attacking and instead concentrate on resource generation to transition from mid- to late game as quickly as possible. The Corporation's goal is to get a reasonable defense set up as fast as possible in order to minimize the length of the early game and then extend the mid-game for as long as possible while attempting to score enough points to win before the game extends too far into the late game where the Runner dominates. The dynamics between the players each trying to manipulate the length of each game phase provides much of the strategy of the game. So, placing the transitions between phases under partial player control is another way to add interest to the game.

All of this, of course, assumes that you know how long the game should take in the first place. How do you know? Part of this depends on the audience. Very young kids don't have the attention span to sit still for a very long game. Some busy, working adults prefer a game that can be played in short increments. Part of optimal game length also depends on the level and depth of skill. Games that are more casual and luck-based tend to be shorter. Deep, heavily strategic games can be longer. Another consideration is at what point a player is far enough ahead that they have essentially won already; you want this point to happen about the time that the game *actually* ends, so that the final part of the game doesn't feel like it's dragging on with no ability of any player to change the outcome.

For games that never end (such as tabletop RPGs, MMOs, and some free-to-play games), think of the elder game as a final never-ending "phase" of the game. In this case, the length of the progression portion of the game (pre-elder game) so that the transition to elder game happens about the time you want it to. How long should it take to reach the elder game? That depends on how much emphasis you want to place on the progression mechanics vs. the elder game experience. For example, suppose you are working on a game where players pay for subscriptions every month (so that it's to your advantage to keep players playing as long as possible), and you're seeing a lot of **churn** (lots of players leaving the game) when players hit the elder game, you might want to make several changes to the design: work on softening the transition to the elder game so you lose fewer people to a sudden shift in play; find ways of extending the early game (such as issuing expansion sets that raise the level cap, letting players create multiple characters with different builds so they can play through the progression game multiple times); or find ways to make the elder game more compelling to those players who find the progression mechanics fun.

Another interesting case where many games struggle is in story-heavy games such as RPGs, where the story often outlasts the mechanics of the game. It's fine to say "100 hours of gameplay!" on the box, making it sound like the game is delivering more value, but in reality, if the player is just repeating the same mechanics and going through a mindless grind for 75 of those hours, the game is really not delivering as much value and is mostly just wasting the player's time. Ideally, a designer wants the player to feel like they're progressing through the mechanics *and* the story at the same time; you don't want the gameplay to stagnate any more than you want the game to have tons of meaningless filler plot that extends the story without making it any more interesting. These games are challenging design because the length of the game must be tuned to match both story *and* gameplay, which either means lengthening the story or adding more game mechanics, and both of those tend to be expensive in development. The designer can also shorten the story or remove depth from the gameplay, but if you have a brilliant plot and inspired mechanics, it can be hard to rip those out of the game just in the name of saving some cash. Also, with RPGs in particular there is often a consumer expectation that games are long enough to give that "epic" feel, so the tendency in development is to add (not take away) from one side or the other.

Revisiting Flow

For PvP games, in most cases we *want* the more skilled player to win, so balancing the game to keep all players in a flow state (such that they are all challenged at the peak of their ability) is not a consideration. If an expert is playing against a novice, we would expect the expert to be bored and the novice to be frustrated; that is the nature of skill-based games. However, for games where we want less-skilled players to still feel like they have a chance while highly skilled players can still feel challenged, we can implement negative feedback loops and random mechanics to give an extra edge to the player who is behind.

In PvE games, we use multiple difficulty levels to keep players challenged regardless of their skill. The equivalent of "difficulty" in PvP is a handicapping system, where one player can either start in an advantaged position or else have an ongoing advantage over the course of the game, to compensate for their lower level of skill. In most cases, this is voluntary, because players entering a PvP contest typically expect the game to be fair by default, and they'll only add a handicap if they prefer an even match (each player has an equal chance of winning) over a fair game (most skilled play wins).

In PvP games with a large player environment, difficulty can also be scaled through use of a rating system and matchmaking, such that a player is generally matched with someone else of similar skill, thus eliminating the need for handicapping (we examine rating systems in detail in Chapter 14). When two players are of similar skill level, *that* is where both players tend to feel challenged at the peak of their ability, and these tend to be the most exciting matches since the outcome is generally uncertain (both players are capable of winning). When possible, finding ways to match players with those of similar skill tends to make for the best gameplay and is the preferred way to keep players in the flow in a PvP game.

Common Problems in PvP

In PvP games, especially those where there can be only one winner, there are some problems that come up frequently. These can be considered a balancing factor or an imbalance depending on the game, but they are things that are usually not much fun, so designers should be aware of them.

Turtling

One problem, especially in games where players are meant to attack each other directly, is that a player initiating hostilities toward an opponent takes a risk, as the opponent is now incentivized to defend themselves by attacking back, possibly damaging or eliminating the instigator. In some games, *even if a player is successful* with their attack, they still lose resources and power (as does the player they attacked) relative to other players who weren't involved. If attacking puts players at a disadvantage relative to other players who are standing by and minding their own business, the optimal strategy is to try to not get into any fights at all. Instead, players should build up their defenses to make themselves the least tempting target to anyone else. This intentional lack of interaction is called **turtling** (in reference to a turtle hiding in its shell). Then, when *other* players get into fights with each other, the one who was turtling suddenly swoops in and mops up the pieces while everyone else is in a weakened state. The root of the problem is that the game dynamics reward players for *not interacting with each other*, and if interaction is supposed to be the fun and interesting part of the game, you can hopefully see where this would be a concern.

Since the game balance problem is that attacking (i.e., playing the game) is not the optimal strategy, the most direct solution is to reward or incentivize aggression. A simple example of this is seen in the classic board game *Risk*. In that game, attackers and defenders both lose armies in combat so normally players would not want to attack. To overcome this, the game gives multiple bonuses and incentives for attacking. Controlling more territories gives a player more armies on the next turn, if they can hold their borders; the same is true for controlling entire continents. Players also receive a random card at the end of their turn if they capture at least one territory, and cards can be exchanged in sets for even more bonus armies... but those bonuses can only be achieved if the player attacks at least once per turn. Finally, a player who eliminates an opponent from the board entirely gets their cards, which can become yet more armies. These layered incentives are enough to force players to choose to attack on their turns, and while some turtling may still take place (a common strategy is to hide in Australia or South America where one's borders can be easily defended), eventually players must expand their borders or else they suffer a power disadvantage to those other players who have done so.

Another solution is to force the issue, by making it essentially impossible to *not* attack. For example, the card games *Plague and Pestilence, Family Business,* and *Nuclear War* are all light games where players mostly draw a card on their turn and then play a card. Some cards are defensive in nature, but most cards are designed to hurt the opponents. Since each player is obligated to play a card each turn (they cannot "pass"), before too long any given player is forced to attack *at least* one other player. It's simply not possible to avoid making enemies, at least not for long.

Killing the Leader and Sandbagging

In games where players can attack each other directly *and* it's clear who is in the lead, a common problem is that everyone by default gangs up on whoever's currently winning. This can be a good thing, as it serves as a clear negative feedback loop to the game, preventing any player from getting too far ahead. On the other hand, players tend to overshoot (the leader isn't merely kept in check, they're totally destroyed), and it ends up feeling like a punishment for doing too well.

As a response to this problem, a new dynamic emerges: that of **sandbagging**. If it's dangerous to be the leader, the optimal strategy is instead to play suboptimally to remain in second place intentionally. When the leader is heavily attacked and left a burning wreck, the second-place player can then zoom to victory before the rest of the table can target them, if timed properly. As with turtling, the problem here is that the players aren't really playing the game as the designer intended; they're working around the mechanics instead.

In order for this to even be a problem, three necessary conditions must be present:

1. Players must recognize a clear leader among themselves.
2. Players must see their best chance to win as eliminating the current leader.
3. Players must be able to coordinate to attack and take down the leader.

The good news is that this chain of events can be broken in any number of places in order to stop sandbagging from being a viable strategy.

If players can't figure out who the leader is, then even if they can coordinate, they won't know who to gang up on. If the game has hidden scoring, players may have a general sense of who is in the lead, but they may not be certain enough to commit to a coordinated takedown.[2] Likewise, if there are multiple victory conditions or the end goal can be reached by many different ways so that it's unclear which player is furthest along their current victory path.

Even if relative player standings are clear, players must see an attack against the leader as their best chance of winning. If the game has built-in opportunities for trailing players to catch up (such as negative feedback loops), a player's best bet may not necessarily be to go head-to-head with the most powerful opponent at the table, but rather to do their best to exploit the catch-up mechanics to overtake the leader by other means. In tabletop Eurogames like *Manhattan* and *Age of Discovery*, there are a small number of distinct scoring rounds in the middle of the game and at the end, and these are the only times when players can score points. Each successive scoring opportunity is worth more points than the last, so in the middle of a round it's not always clear who is in the best position to take the lead. Players also know that even if someone got the most points in the first scoring round that only gives them a minor advantage going into later higher-valued scoring rounds.

Even if players can identify the leader and players see attacking the leader as a viable strategy, the game can offer other viable strategies. For example, in the board game *Risk* it is certainly arguable that having everyone attack the leader is a good strategy in some ways; if one player controls a high-value continent, it's better for everyone to prevent them from holding onto it for too many turns. However, the game also gives players an incentive to attack weaker players, because anyone who eliminates an opponent gets their cards, and weaker players are also easier to take territory from which lets any player earn a card at the end of their turn.

Even if players can identify the leader and see their best chance to win as eliminating the leader, players must need some kind of mechanism to coordinate and "gang up" on them. If you make it difficult or impossible for players to form coalitions or coordinate strategies, attacking the leader is impossible. In a foot race, players can't "attack" each other at all, so kill-the-leader strategies aren't seen in marathons. In first-person shooter (FPS) free-for-all deathmatch games, players *can* attack each other, but the action is moving so fast that it's hard for players to form teams to work together

---

[2] An interesting case study here is to compare the two board games, *Vinci* and *Small World*. The two games have a different theme but are virtually identical in mechanics, with one key change. In *Vinci*, players score points at the end of their turn along a publicly visible scoring track, so every player always knows the exact standings. In *Small World*, players instead collect Victory Point tokens at the end of their turn when they score, and keep these in a face-down pile. This creates enough uncertainty that players in *Small World* may disagree on who is actually winning, making coordinated strikes against a leader much less frequent than in *Vinci*.

(in fact, it's difficult to do much of anything other than shooting whoever's nearby). Even *Monopoly*, for all its other issues, doesn't have this problem: if one player has multiple dangerous properties and no one else does, it's difficult for the other players to say "hey everyone, let's work together to take down that person"—the game just doesn't have a mechanism for direct interaction or attacks.

Even if all of these conditions are in place so that kill-the-leader strategies are theoretically possible, keep in mind that this simply manifests as a negative feedback loop in the game, so one final option is to keep it as is but add a positive feedback loop to compensate that helps the leader defend against attacks. This wouldn't eliminate kill-the-leader scenarios; instead, it would make it the focus of the game, where it may start off as an equal free-for-all and eventually transitions to one-against-many. As an example, the card game *Hacker* involved players rolling dice to attempt to hack in and establish accounts on various servers. The player who was in the lead (had the most accounts) got a +1 bonus when rolling. This gave players an incentive to become the leader, and also helped the leader to maintain and extend their advantage, even if other players were doing everything they could to slow the leader's progress.

Kingmaking

A similar but distinct problem is the situation where one player is too far behind to win at the end of the game, *but* they are in a position where their final action decides which of two *other* people wins. Sometimes, this happens directly, as in a game with trading and negotiation, where a player who's behind may choose to make favorable trades with one of the leading players to hand them the game. Sometimes, it's less obvious, where the player who's behind must make one of two moves as part of the game, and it becomes clear that one of the moves leads to a particular other player winning, and the other move hands the game to someone else. The losing player in this is situations is a **kingmaker**, ultimate decider of who wins without being able to choose themselves.

This is usually undesirable because it's anticlimactic. The winner didn't win because of superior skill, but instead because one of the *losing* players liked them better. In a game with heavy diplomatic elements (such as the classic board game *Diplomacy*), this might be tolerable or even expected. In that case, the game is all about players convincing one another to do what they want them to, after all. But in most games, a kingmaking situation makes winners feel like the win wasn't really deserved, so the designer may wish to avoid this situation.

As with kill-the-leader situations, there are three conditions that must exist for kingmaking to exist in a game at all, and the chain of events can be disrupted at any point. The conditions are

1. One player must recognize they cannot win.
2. The losing player must recognize that they can give support to any leading player.
3. The losing player must choose a leading player to win.

If every player believes they have a chance to win, either because the nature of the game allows it or because of hidden standings, there's no reason for a player to give the game away to an opponent. Likewise, if a player suspects they are losing but can't tell who else is winning, they would not know who to support and would have no incentive to help out a specific opponent. Or, if players just have no way to help each other so that kingmaking is impossible, that obviously solves the issue as well.

Player Elimination

Many two-player games are about eliminating the opponent's forces, so it makes sense that many multiplayer games follow this pattern as well. However, if one player is eliminated from the game and everyone else is still playing, the losing player has to sit around and wait for the game to end. Sitting around and not playing the game is usually not fun.

With games of very short length, this is not a problem. If the entire game lasts 2 minutes and players start getting eliminated 1 minute in, who cares? Sit and wait for the next game to start. Likewise, if elimination doesn't happen until very late in the game, it's less of a problem. If players in a 2-hour game start dropping out at 1:55, relatively speaking it won't seem like a long time to wait until the game ends and the next one begins. The loser can just go to the bathroom or grab a snack or drink. It becomes more problematic when players are eliminated early and then have to wait forever. There are a few mechanics that can deal with this:

- Disincentivize player elimination. Make the reward structure such that players only try to eliminate an opponent at the point where they feel strong enough to eliminate everyone else and win the game, too.
- Change the victory condition. If the goal of the game is to earn 10 victory points, players are more concerned with collecting VP than eliminating their opponents.

- Change the game end condition. Instead of ending when all players but one are eliminated, end the game when the first player is eliminated. Instead of victory going to last player standing, give the victory to the player in *best* standing (by some criteria) once the first player drops out. If players can help each other, this creates tense alliances as one player nears elimination: the player in the lead wants to win so they are trying to finish off the opponent, while the remaining players are trying to keep the weakened opponent in play until they can get in the lead. A softer alternative is to trigger the end game on elimination of the first player, but allow all remaining players to take some number of turns or give some short amount of time before the game formally ends.
- Make elimination fun. If eliminated players have something interesting to do after they're killed, it doesn't feel like as much of a penalty. Perhaps eliminated players can take the role of NPCs or monsters in the game, using them to harass the remaining players or retaliate against the player who eliminated them. In hidden-role/social-deduction games (such as *Mafia/Werewolf*), give eliminated players full access to information so that they can watch the drama unfold as the remaining players stumble around in ignorance; *Among Us* goes further, giving the "eliminated" players things to do (they can continue working on tasks and can chat to each other even if none of the living players can hear them).

Balancing Asymmetry

Symmetric PvP games tend to be easier to balance than asymmetric ones. For every element of symmetry, it may not be *automatically* balanced (there may be some exploits or strategies or game objects that are too strong or weak with respect to others, causing those things to dominate play), but at least, you don't have to worry about one player having an unfair advantage over the others simply because of unequal starting positions. When each player has a different game state at the start, or has different resources they can use, or are playing with entirely different sets of rules, it's much harder to ensure each player has the same opportunity to win.

First, the designer should start by simply being aware of what parts of the game are symmetric or asymmetric. Nearly every game has at least *some* asymmetries; *Chess* is symmetric except that one player goes first, and the first-player advantage is actually a major factor at the highest levels of tournament play. There are other types of asymmetry: different starting positions, different resources under a player's control, different goals or objectives, or even different core mechanics and game rules. Since there are different types of asymmetry, it's important to understand the nature of the game and what kinds of asymmetry are encountered.

Next, the designer should do their best to balance asymmetric elements of the game along the same cost curve and supporting math. For example, *StarCraft* has three extremely different factions (asymmetry in capabilities and, on most maps, starting position), but they all have the same core stats like health and damage, and they all have the same objective of eliminating the opponents from the map. This suggests the possibility of doing some mathematical analysis of units to balance the different factions with one another, or to identify the balances or imbalances in the data. In a game where players are *so* asymmetric that numeric comparisons aren't possible, of course, the designer should rely on other methods.

If players have radically different situations, it can be useful to include at least some intransitive elements in the game, so that each player can counter some strategies or moves of their opponents. This at least prevents a single dominant strategy with no counter (we examine intransitive mechanics in detail in Chapter 25).

As a general principle, the more asymmetric the game is and the harder it is to use mathematical analysis to compare the different sides, the more you need to rely on playtesting before release, and/or analytics after release. Make sure there is plenty of room for both in your project schedule.

Discussion Questions

1. Choose any game with a game economy that is, overall, positive sum. Suggest one or more fundamental changes to the rules to change the economy to negative sum instead.
2. Choose any game with a game economy that is, overall, negative sum. Without modifying the rules that make it negative sum, add one or more new rules or systems that counteract the negative sum elements, making the game zero or positive sum.
3. For either of the previous two questions, take a guess what the game will play like with the new rules. How will it feel relative to the original?
4. Take a PvP game that you know well, ideally one that is very short (less than 5 minutes). Draw an approximation of what you think the power curve would look like for a typical play of this game.
5. For the game in the previous question, actually play it if it is short, and track how close players are to the win condition over time. (If the game

is played in real time, have someone not involved in the game taking notes, or record yourself playing and go back and track it while watching the recording.) What does the actual curve look like, compared to your guess?

6. Choose a tabletop game (such as a board game or card game) that you know well. From memory, what is the approximate game length?

7. For the game in the previous question, look up the actual length of play. If it is a published game, you can usually find this on the bottom or back of the box (you can search the internet, such as the site boardgamegeek.com, to find an image of the box that shows stated play time). For a folk game, search for the rules and play time on a few sites and see if anyone lists an approximate play time. How does the listed time compare to your perception?

8. For the game in the previous question, do you think it is the optimal game length, or would it be better if it were longer or shorter? What makes you say this?

9. For the game in the previous question, if you wanted to make the game longer, suggest some rules changes that would preserve the core gameplay but lengthen the total game length.

10. For the game in the previous question, if you wanted to make the game shorter, suggest some rules changes that would preserve the core gameplay but shorten the total game length.

Additional Resource

- Designer Lewis Pulsipher wrote an article that goes into more detail on the common problems in PvP outlined in this chapter, in *Design Problems to Watch for in Multi-player Games*, accessible at http://pulsiphergamedesign.blogspot.com/2007/11/design-problems-to-watch-for-in-multi.html

Sidequests

In this chapter, we have looked at forms of progression in PvP games. The designer must choose an appropriate length for the game based on the audience and the depth of mechanics, and then tune the game's progression mechanics so that players move toward the game end condition at a good rate. If a full game can be thought of in terms of several phases, the designer also should make sure those phases are the right length within the context of the full game. Lastly, for most of the game, all players should feel like it's possible for anyone to win. If the outcome is certain, players may as well concede and not waste time playing it out; design solutions for this problem include adding catch-up mechanics (negative feedback), hidden information so that players don't know for sure if they are winning or losing, or just setting the end condition for the game so it happens earlier.

We conclude this chapter with a reminder that there are *many* things in games that are pleasurable and meaningful to players that are not related to progression at all. While this chapter and the previous one constituted a deep dive into PvE and PvP progression systems, keep in mind that progression is just one tiny element of game design, which may or may not be appropriate to use as a core or auxiliary system within any given game.

Sidequest 12.1: Player Power in Monopoly

Consider the board game *Monopoly*. Write a Monte Carlo simulation to play many games. This can either be done in a spreadsheet or in a programming language of your choice. Make any simplifying assumptions you like (for example, it cuts your time and complexity considerably if you ignore the Chance and Community Chest cards, and just treat those as blank spaces; you may also want to write a very simple algorithm for players, like "always buy a property you land on if possible" so that there are no choices to be made).

Treat each player's "power" as the amount of cash they have on hand, plus any other assets of value that you may be tracking. Graph average player power over time, after generating data for a few thousand simulated games. Also take a few randomly selected individual games and plot each player's power from those, to give an idea of what a single play might look like (as opposed to play in aggregate).

After doing this, answer the following:

- Does the game appear to be positive, negative, or zero sum?
- Does the game appear to have any feedback loops? If so, what kind (positive or negative), and do they exert a strong or weak effect?
- Does the game end slowly or suddenly? Do there appear to be distinct phases to the game, where the power progression behaves differently, and if so how long are those phases relative to each other?

- Do the progression model and game length seem appropriate given the audience and depth of the game? If not, what would you propose changing in order to fix these?

Alternate challenge: Do the same for a different board game of your choice.

Sidequest 12.2: World War III

Consider the following simple game:

- **Players**: any number
- **Setup**: each player starts with 2 forces.
- **Play**: on each player's turn, they can either gain 1 force or attack another player with any number of forces they wish. They lose all of those forces, and the opponent also loses an equal number of forces. If the player attacked with more forces than the opponent had, the opponent is also eliminated from the game.
- **End**: when only one player is left in the game, they win.

This game is horrendously broken. Players have no incentive to ever attack, so played optimally, the game never ends. With more than two players, several players might band together to selectively eliminate one of the competition, but once the game was reduced to two players, the game would stalemate.

Make this game more playable and compelling, to the point where attacking or defending is an interesting, non-obvious decision and where the game can reasonably be played to a satisfying conclusion given optimal play. Do this by adding, removing, or changing one rule at a time, testing the result, and repeating. Try to get there with the smallest number of rules modifications possible.

Rogue's Main Quest, Part 6: Create a Mini-Expansion

Continuing from Part 5 in: Chapter 10

Take the new mechanic you defined and costed in your cost curve and supporting math in Part 5, and create a handful of new game objects to showcase your mechanic. This doesn't mean every new object has to have the mechanic; some of them might just interact with it in interesting ways, such as working well in combination or providing a soft counter (works well against, while still being useful in its own right) to the mechanic.

In a collectible card game (CCG), this might mean five to ten new cards that each use or interact with your mechanic. In a turn-based or real-time strategy game, create five to ten new units (spread across multiple factions if the game has such a thing). In a tabletop miniatures game, create new units for a single faction, or an entire new mini-faction (or offshoot of an existing one). In a tabletop RPG, create a set of new abilities or feats *or* a new character class.

Then, balance all of your new creations along your existing cost curve and supporting math, so that your math (at least) claims that everything is exactly on the curve (or as close as reasonably possible).

Part 7 continued in: Chapter 13

Wizard's Main Quest, Part 4: Card Balance

Continuing from Part 3 in: Chapter 8

Here, you have a choice of two paths: balance the starter decks against each other, or balance the cards in a constructed-deck environment.

If balancing the starter decks: consider the four supplied starter decks (A, B, C, and D) as four single units. Your goal is to make the decks as balanced as possible against each other. That is, assuming equal player skill, either player should be able to play any two decks against one another and each player/deck should have as close to a 50% chance of winning as possible.

If balancing the starters, you can only make the following modifications to the starter decks, and no other changes:

- Modify the cost of an Action card (keeping the same Power types in the cost and only modifying how much Power is required to play it, as you did in Part 3). Note that most cards appear in several decks, so modifying the cost of a card in one deck means you have to change the cost of that card in all other decks that it appears in.
- Modify the number of each type of Power card in the deck. Each deck has two Power types, so you can swap one for the other directly, or you can add extra Power cards of either type by removing an equal number of Action cards, or you can remove Power cards and add extra copies of any Action card that is already in the game (whether it was formerly part of that deck or not).

Note that this means you cannot change the effects of any Action cards, create new Action cards with your own effects, or change the total number of cards in a deck (all decks must remain the same size).

Hint: Note that you are balancing decks, not individual cards. While you can certainly attempt to make every individual card balanced against every other card, you can also have some cards that are clearly above the curve, if the rest of the deck is weaker than average otherwise, for example.

If balancing the cards: assume a constructed-deck environment, where players can make their own decks using whatever cards they want from the list of cards supplied in the four starters (assume all decks must be exactly 50 cards, with a maximum of three copies of any Action card, but otherwise no restrictions). In such a format, each individual card must be balanced against the other cards on the same cost curve.

Make an attempt to balance the cards against one another, using the spreadsheets and any other tools you have developed for this game so far. As before, you can modify the power costs of Action cards but cannot alter the power type(s), nor the effects of playing the cards, nor the core rules of the game.

You do not have to playtest your attempt yet—that is coming in the next part—but just make a good-faith first-run attempt on paper for now, updating your prototype accordingly.

Part 5 continued in: Chapter 14

13

Analytics

In This Chapter

- What Is Analytics?
- Metrics
- The Process of Balance through Analytics
- Finding the Key Questions
- Strength of a Claim
- Case Studies
- Data Visualization

What Is Analytics?

> We look at all kinds of numbers in our daily lives to help us optimize. Some people track their monthly income and expenses to help improve their personal finances. Others watch their weight and exercise numbers to boost their health. Still others monitor their sleep schedule to keep themselves in peak mental performance. If you have the numbers available to help you improve your game, why wouldn't you use them?
>
> *A game designer with twenty years' experience.*

As you may recall from Chapter 1, there are four general methods to game balance: experience, mathematical models, playtesting, and analytics. So far, this book has concentrated mostly on mathematical modeling as an approach to balancing, because such an approach lends itself best to being taught in book form. Experience is important, but is best built through practice and not study. Playtesting is a skill that improves through a deep understanding of how games are put together and where the boundary conditions are—in other words, becoming a better designer also makes you a better playtester we'll also cover playtesting in more detail in Chapter 15). That leaves analytics, which is the subject of this chapter.

Analytics can be thought of, in some respects, as the intersection of playtesting and math. Instead of building hypothetical models of what we expect player behavior to be like, we use actual data from real games. Analytics takes the soft, fuzzy, non-mathy parts of game design that involve human psychology and human behavior (i.e., those elements that don't lend themselves well to mathematical models) and allow us to analyze these things quantitatively. This is made possible, mostly, when operating at a large scale. As we well see in Chapter 24, when dealing with statistical analysis, the more data you have the better. This means that while playtesting is more useful on a small scale (on your own, with friends and confidantes, and eventually with a small number of strangers), analytics becomes more useful as the size of the player base increases. As playtests become large enough to get unwieldy, analytics can take over as the preferred game way for designers to assess the balance of the game. This does mean that analytics is typically done late in the development cycle—you have to have a playable game and a large number of players already—but once your game reaches that point, analytics shines.

Metrics

Often, the terms "metrics" and "analytics" are used interchangeably, but they are actually distinct terms that are subtly different.

Metrics are measurements. In the case of games, many of the metrics we take are referred to as **KPIs** (an acronym for key performance indicators, i.e., numbers that say something important about how you're your game is doing). Here are some common metrics you may have heard of[1]

- **DAU**: Daily Active Users. How many unique people played your game today (or any given day)?
- **MAU**: Monthly Active Users. How many unique people played your game at least once this month?

---

[1]You may notice that many of these acronyms refer to "users" instead of "players." The term "user" comes from the broader field of software development. Culturally, game developers tend to refer to their users as "players," but the game companies that popularized the use of metrics were mostly headed by software moguls who initially came from outside of the game industry.

- **MAU/DAU**: By dividing MAU by the mean average of the month's DAUs, this provides a measure of how frequently the average player logs in. The lowest MAU/DAU can theoretically be is 1, meaning that every player logs in daily. The highest MAU/DAU should be is somewhere between 28 and 31, depending on the month (meaning that each player that logged in this month, logged in exactly once).
- **ARPU**: Average Revenue per User. Divide the total number of unique players of the game by the total amount of money spent by players, to get the average (mean) amount spent per player.
- **ARPPU**: Average Revenue per Paying User. The problem with ARPU is that in many F2P games, the majority of players pay nothing, and a small minority of players (unfortunately termed **whales** in the industry) spend large amounts of money. In short, the median and mode *are both zero* for many F2P games, making ARPU a bit misleading. ARPPU gives a better indication, in that it only divides by players who have spent more than zero. This tells you that *if* a free player can be converted to a paying player, on average they spend the ARPPU (which is typically much higher than ARPU).
- **ARPDAU**: Average Revenue Per Daily Active User. Gives a sense of how much players spend daily.
- **Churn**: There is a difference between having 100,000 MAU where all of those players are the same from month to month, and having 100,000 MAU where players come to the game, play for a month, then leave (but are replaced with new players). Churn is a percentage of players that leave and are replaced, per unit time (for example, if 10,000 players leave each month, but 10,000 new players find the game for the first time, this game would have a 10% monthly churn). Sometimes, this is stated instead as retention, which is calculated as 100% minus Churn.
- **ROI**: Return On Investment. Let R be the total revenue (money earned) for a game, and C be the total cost (including development costs, maintenance costs, marketing spend, and so on). ROI is calculated as $(R-C)/C$, expressed as a percentage. If the game exactly broke even ($R=C$), then the ROI is 0%. If the game cost \$100,000 to make and it pulled in \$200,000, the ROI is 100%. With big-budget ("AAA") games, publishers typically want the ROI to be either very high or negative. Games that lose money are tax writeoffs; big "hits" pay for the rest. But a game that makes a small amount of money isn't worth it—it keeps a bunch of money tied up in development. This is what people mean when they say that games are a "hit-driven"

industry: it's better for a game to succeed or fail spectacularly than to be a modest success.

- **Ratings**: In many digital app/game stores, players are allowed to leave a rating (typically 1–5 stars), and the ratings are shown in aggregate on the store itself to inform future prospective players. Another kind of rating, considered more AAA games, are those ratings given by professional game reviewers, and by averages of those reviewers on aggregation sites like Metacritic. Related metrics would be total downloads and app store ranking (out of all apps in a virtual store, how did this game do in terms of total number of paid or free downloads, or total revenue).

These metrics do tell something about a game. However, keep in mind that these are *second-order* effects: making change to the game leads to a change in player behavior, which in turn causes a change in the metrics. This means that while correlations can be found (change the color of main character's hat to pink, and see revenue increase 30% over the next week), the question of *why* cannot be answered. This makes **metrics-driven game design** (modify something in the game, see its effect on revenue or other metrics, undo it if the metrics get worse or leave it in if the metrics get better, then repeat) challenging to use effectively, for a few reasons. It does nothing to help the designer understand their game, which makes each change a stab in the dark (and given the vast possibility space of most game designs, there are a *lot* of potential stabs—so the designer is then left to their own personal intuition to prioritize which ones are most likely to succeed). Also, it relies on incremental changes, which do allow the designer to find a local maximum, an area in the design space that would actually be even better but requires a fundamental change or giant leap in the mechanics. And lastly, many of these metrics concentrate on money but say nothing about the human factor (do players enjoy the game? Is it enriching or destroying their lives? Would they play a similar game again, or are they suffering burnout?).

Analytics is not merely looking at numbers and making assumptions about causal effects. It is taking metrics a step further, using ways to use numbers to gain insight into how the game is actually working, so that the designer can be more informed about their choices. Analytics is meant to answer questions like: what are the players and systems doing, what happens when they do it, and how effective is it? More importantly, analytics helps to identify and prevent absolute disasters, the things that completely wreck the balance or play experience of a game: game objects or strategies that are never used (or always used, or used but only suboptimally), players who aren't learning or aren't winning often enough, and so on. Here, not only can analytics tell you what is happening, but—if you ask the right questions—also *why* (and thus, how to fix it).

A Question of Ethics

In some circles, metrics-based design has received a bad rep for its tendency to be used to maximize profit. Consider a case where, as the designer, you realize that your game is specifically exploiting a certain type of low-income player, causing them to spend more money than they can afford. Your game may very well be driving these players deeper into poverty, but in the meantime, your game is extracting the highest amount of money possible from them. Is this acceptable, since it is ultimately their decision to spend, and you are obligated as a developer to watch your own bottom line? Or is it ethically indefensible, because you're in the business of entertainment and yet you are measurably making your players' real lives worse?

Even if players can afford to play your game, if they are paying more than they normally would because your game is using psychological manipulation, is that acceptable practice as long as it's shown to bring in more money, or does the developer have obligations to their players and not just to their own health as a business?

Is there a certain amount of "strip-mining" going on in these cases, where players may pay money but later on regret it, and leave with a bad taste in their mouths, making it much less likely that they choose to play a similar game in the future? If so, does the developer have an obligation, if not to the player, then to the long-term health of the industry? After all, if you don't take care of your players and they permanently leave, every subsequent game you make now has that many fewer players as you drove out with the last game. Sure, if your only goal as a business is to swoop in, take a lot of money from people, and then exit, this is a valid business move. But there are other game studios who desire to be in this space for the long term, and if your company poisons the well, you might not just put your own company out of business, but take other companies down with you. The human cost to your fellow developers may be high. But then, business is business, so is this even your responsibility?

As with the other times in this book where ethical questions are raised, there is not necessarily a "right" or "wrong" answer. However, you should think, personally, about where you stand and where you would draw the line. If you don't, then someone else will make that call for you, and if you're uncomfortable with their decision, then it's your own job on the line, and you may not be in a position to make your own independent choice at that point.

The Process of Balance through Analytics

As with game design (and even game balance), analytics requires a mix of creative and technical abilities. But there is a series of steps to go through in order to get more informed about the balance of the game. In brief, the steps are

1. A game designer decides on some key questions that need to be answered.
2. An analyst (who may or may not be the same person as the game designer) looks at the question and decides what metrics need to be tracked to answer it.
3. A gameplay programmer (who is usually *not* the game designer, except on very small or highly specialized teams) adds analytics hooks in the code in order to track those particular features.
4. A database programmer (may or may not be the same gameplay programmer) decides how to store the data so that it's easily accessible.
5. These updates in code are pushed to the game players, and data are collected over a period of time.
6. The database programmer then "cleans" the data. The data collection software may have bugs. The data itself may be corrupt in some way. There may be outliers, missing values, or other anomalies in the data. These need to be identified, explained, and corrected or eliminated (and then the programmers may fix any bugs found in the code so that the data need not be scrubbed in the same way every time).
7. The analyst, with data in hand, now formalizes the key questions by putting them in quantitative terms that can be asked and answered by the data.
8. The database programmer creates queries into the database based on the analyst's requests from the previous step and runs those queries. This returns a new set of data that is scaled down from the full data set, including only the parts that are relevant to the particular questions being asked.
9. The analyst looks critically at the data to decide if there is a statistically meaningful pattern, or if it's just noise. In short, can the original questions be answered with this data? If not, then the team may need to return to previous steps to fix any problems identified, perhaps even going back to the beginning to rephrase the key questions.
10. Once meaningful data have been obtained, the game designer then interprets the data. This is where the game designer must ask the

question "why?" a lot. Why are the data behaving this way? What are the possible explanations? The goal in this step is to form hypotheses about all potential root causes. How does the team figure out which root cause is the correct one? By going back and asking even more detailed questions of the data, and continuing this process iteratively until the core answers are found.

11. The data leading to the answers are then presented, through visualization (such as graphs and charts), narrative (text explanation of what's going on), and metrics (individual numbers of key stats). This should explain succinctly what is happening in the game. Even if the game is being made by a single developer who is doing all of these things by themselves, it can be useful to have a record of the thought process so that it can be returned to in the future.

12. Lastly, the designer acts on the data by making actual changes to the game to address any deficiencies (or, if none are found, the designer chooses to deliberately *not* make changes).

Each of these steps could have an entire book written about it alone. Many steps are programming-related and therefore outside the scope of this book, but included in this list to show the overall process.

Finding the Key Questions

Analytics-based investigations can take several forms:

- **Improving the designer's intuition for systems and players**. This involves looking for correlations in the data that were previously unknown. An MMO designer might want to know what factors in the game influence the pace of leveling, so they know what design knobs they can tweak to make more coarse or fine adjustments. A fighting or brawling game designer might ask what factors influence character selection, so they know what to change in order to modify who the most popular characters in the metagame are. An FPS level designer might want to know what elements of a level most influence the length of time before map objectives are completed in team-based multiplayer maps, so they can optimize their designs to be exciting and dynamic but not too short.
- **Looking for general problems in the game**. The designer may have a general idea of how they'd like the game to behave, and they can

look for previously unknown situations where the game is deviating too much from the ideal. A roleplaying game (RPG) designer may wish to know if there are places in the XP/level progression where players tend to get stuck and have to grind a lot. A trading card game (TCG) designer could ask whether any cards or strategies are dominating the metagame. A designer of an action-platformer might wonder if any levels or bosses are too easy or too hard, relative to those immediately before or after them.

- **Finding answers to specific questions**. The designer may have a particular issue they have identified within the game, where they know something is broken but need to find out why. Or there may be a particular aspect of the game that the player community is complaining about, and the designer needs to evaluate whether it is truly out of balance, or if it's just a situation of a vocal minority making a big deal of nothing. A real-time strategy (RTS) designer might suspect that a certain unit is too powerful for its cost and dominating play, but wants to know for sure. A tabletop game designer may think that a particular action in their game is underutilized and wants to know if it is too weak or if players just have a hard time seeing its value (is it a balance problem or a perception problem?). The designer of a survival-horror game might feel that a particular enemy is too weak and therefore not enough of a threat to be scary to the player, and wishes to know if players tend to default to attacking the enemy or running from it.

- **Monitoring changes to the game on a continuing basis**. If the designer has made changes to fix balance problems in the past, they should follow up by looking at the key metrics used to make the changes in the first place, and seeing if they are changing as expected. An idle game designer might have changed the cost curve for a certain type of upgrade in the game to fix a point of progression that was too slow, and now wants to know if that change fixed the problem or if the progression is still too slow (or if the changes overshot and now it's too fast). An Action-RPG designer who changed the attack power of the final boss to make it harder should see if it is indeed more challenging. A stealth game designer who was having problems with players completing a certain section of a level may have removed some enemies and then should check how level completion rates and times are affected.

Always remember that at the highest level, the goal of analytics is to make sure the game meets its design goals (normally, that means that it's fun to play). Questions might include the following: how many people are playing?

How long are they playing for in a single session, and how often do they return to play some more? Are players improving? Are they progressing or winning, and is the game paced well? Across the player base, is play diverse or unpredictable? Is the game challenging?

For games with multiple game objects, strategies, or paths to victory, we may have a particular interest to make sure those are balanced against each other. How many players are playing a particular strategy? Are they getting better at that strategy over time, and how does the win rate compared to other strategies? Within a particular strategy, is the play diverse or unpredictable, and is the game challenging?

The designer may feel that they know the answers to many of these questions already. Opinionated players certainly claim to know the answers and post about it incessantly on player forums. But it is one thing to have a hunch, and another to be able to back that up with data. And there are more detailed questions that no one knows the answer to without using analytics.

Strength of a Claim

When forming a question, another consideration is the comprehensiveness and generalizability of the answer. As we will learn in Chapter 24, statistical analysis is never 100% reliable (some observed trends may be due to random variation and not an actual causal effect). The kinds of claims that can be made using analytics vary in strength. In order from the weakest to the strongest claims:

- **Observation**. You can tell that something is happening, but that's it. Often, that's enough. If you know that a particular thing happens, that is information that can sometimes be acted upon.
- **Correlation**. You can tell that when one thing happens, so does another. Often, we care less about a single game element in isolation, and more about a relationship between two or more elements. Finding correlations is harder than simply observing one variable, and is part statistics and part intuition (to make sure that the observed correlation makes some kind of logical sense).
- **Plausible causality**. As noted in Chapter 24, correlation and causality are distinct concepts, and distinguishing between them is one of the most important things an analytics designer does. Most of the time, designers need to understand the system causally: if you change X in the game, this causes a change of Y in player experience. Sometimes,

having a plausible explanation for why an observed correlation would have a particular cause (by understanding the game's systems, any potential confounding factors, etc.) may be enough to make changes and then see the effect of those changes. Other times, however, more certainty is required.

- **Verified causality**. When a possible causal link is found, the next logical step is to confirm it by changing the suspected root cause and observing the effect on the correlate. There are two ways to do this: prospectively (make a change then look for effects) or retrospectively (look at times in the past where a certain thing happened, and see if the expected correlates followed).

  - One common form of prospective study is the **A/B Test**, where players are separated randomly into two groups, making a change for only one of the groups, and then looking at the differences in the metrics of both groups (for example, on a game with multiple servers where players are randomly assigned to a server, the development team might make an update to one server but not others and then compare the metrics between different servers).

  - One useful type of retrospective studies is a **natural experiment**, where the conditions to divide players into two groups (as with an A/B test) happened on its own, by happenstance.[2] For example, many games have some natural randomness in the game, and this can be used to split players according to how the randomness affected them. When studying the effect of a certain card on winning in a CCG, if players receive cards randomly in booster packs, then some players naturally get more copies of that card than other players do.

- **Statistical models**. The most powerful claim is to go beyond a known causal link, to a statistical model. This goes beyond knowing *what* is happening, and is able to answer the fundamental question of *why*, as expressed mathematically. This allows the designer to predict certain events, infer generalizable "rules" about the game that may even apply to other games, and know where to look to find other interesting correlations. Of course, this is hard to do correctly.

It's important to consider not only the type of claim you're making, but also its reliability. If only two players do something and you have a

---

[2] It's arguable that if you can't frame a retrospective question as a hypothetical A/B test, then the concept of causality isn't meaningful in the first place.

player base of millions, then the "average" of those two players isn't very meaningful—it's a rare enough event that it has to be taken as an outlier and not treated as a trend. If a change to the game increases a particular strategy's win rate by 0.002%, that's also not meaningful—there's probably more noise than that in the system. Certainty is increased if you see a sustained trend over a longer period of time, if you have a larger data set, and if the observed effect has a larger magnitude… but you may only have limited control over these.

Using a Z test (as described in Chapter 24) is a great start to determining statistical significance, but it is not the only answer, nor always the most appropriate. Other tests also exist for various purposes (two commonly used ones are chi-squared and ANOVA), and the interested reader is encouraged to look them up and understand their appropriate uses and limitations; there are entire books dedicated just to statistical tests. Conversely, sometimes a designer can go simple and just put error bars on a graph that show standard error, and know that if the bars don't overlap between two groups, then they are probably distinct.

Essential Case Studies

FIGHTING/BRAWLING GAMES

Head-to-head action games like the *Street Fighter* or *Super Smash Bros.* series are a wonderful example of how analytics can be used to aid in balance, because these game genres are so focused. Each player chooses one character for a match (out of a roster of dozens of characters). Each character has its own attacks and move sets, and there are all kinds of numbers that vary between characters: reach and speed and damage of each attack, priority of each attack (if two moves are executed at the same time, which one hits), overall speed of movement and maneuverability, jump speed and height, ability to combo or stun opponents (where landing one or more attacks means a guaranteed opening to land further hits), and so on.

This is challenging to balance by hand. A player typically does not have the ability to create a custom move set; they just choose a character and that character comes as a package deal. A character with one particularly strong move may still be balanced with other characters, if their other moves are proportionally weaker (or if all other characters have one or more standout moves of their own). This means that even if a particular character is too good, there are so many potential things that a designer can do to weaken them, that it can be difficult to know where to begin.

Mathematical models are likewise challenging to put together for these kinds of games. Each individual character can be thought of as having a single power level (either the character is powerful or not) and yet this power level is a function of dozens of variables (all of the characters moves, abilities, etc.). Even one variable being misunderstood can throw off all of the calculations, and because of the complexity of inputs and simplicity of outputs of the system, this process would be error-prone and also hard to diagnose problems.

In this context, analytics becomes a powerful tool to help the designer not only balance the game, but also understand the key variables and zero in on problems. There are two general types of questions that are the most relevant:

- How is overall character balance? We expect there to be three broad categories (top, mid-, and low tier) and that can be fine, so long as each tier has plenty of options, and no single character is either entirely useless or else so powerful that it unbalances the rest of the environment. We might look at this at several intervals: during internal playtesting, private beta, open beta, and post-release.
- Is a particular thing a problem? During development or after release, some point of concern might be raised by the developers, playtesters, or player community. We would want to evaluate claims of a potential imbalance, and decide what (if anything) to do about it. This type of question should be asked on an on-demand basis, continually throughout development.

Let us consider how we might approach balance such a game, concentrating primarily on overall balance.

Win Rate

In a PvP game, win rate is effectively the strength of a character (or in other games, the strength of a strategy, a particular game object, etc.). This would seem at first glance to be the one and only metric you'd need: if a character wins more, then it is more powerful. But as we're about to see, there is much more to the story.

In a fighting game, matchups are typically one-on-one, so whether one character beats another is fairly straightforward; any character with a win rate of greater than 50% is stronger than average, and less than 50% is weaker than average. In a brawling game, matches are typically four-player free-for-all; in that context, what does "win rate" mean? A simple way of doing this would be the probability that each character wins a match against three opponents... but then the average win rate would be 25%. There are other dynamics in play: win rate is not entirely independent (some characters are strong or weak against others, giving a natural advantage or disadvantage in certain matchups), although we may need to make the (false) simplifying assumption that it behaves independently, at least to start out. For a four-player game, we may also prefer to instead treat a "win" as the probability of scoring higher than a particular opponent—so if, for example, players are playing a 3-minute match where their final score is some function of number of times they finish off an opponent minus the number of times they are killed, we can compare final scores and count a "win" for the top two players (since they did better than average), or some other scheme that puts the average win rate back to 50%.

Suppose in some fictional fighting game, we had twelve playable characters, with win rates displayed as follows.

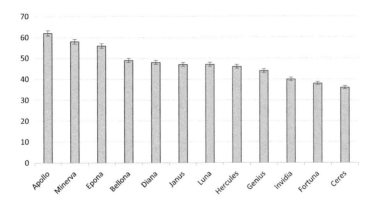

The bars in this graph show the win rate, and the whiskers are $\pm$ Standard Error (remember that Standard Error gets smaller the more data we have). This lets us visually confirm that the differences are probably real and not just random variation.

Another curious thing to notice is that only three characters have win rates above 50%, and the other nine have win rates below 50%… and that if you take the average of all twelve characters' win rates, you get below 50%. How is that possible? The key here is that the characters are not played with equal frequency; some are played more often than others, and usually the strongest characters are also the most popular. This suggests we should look not just at win rate, but also popularity.

POPULARITY

Popularity is often correlated with win rate, as might be expected, but this is not always the case for each character. Those characters who show marked differences between their popularity and their win rate can tell us interesting stories.

How do we measure popularity of a character? It is simply the number of times that character was chosen in a game. This leads to the additional question: if a character is chosen twice in a game (a "mirror match"), should we count that as one or two times? The answer is that we would count twice in that case, because we want the total number of times a player chooses each character.

Suppose in our game, the popularity of characters looks like this.

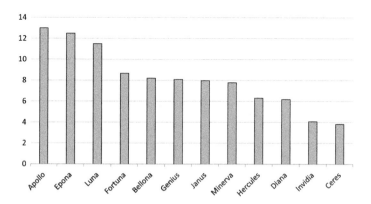

There are some marked differences between the popularity of each character and its win rate. Apollo and Epona are both clearly strong, being among the top spots for both win rate and popularity, so finding ways to make them weaker would be a reasonable balance change. Ceres and Invidia are both near the bottom of both charts, and probably deserve some kind of boost. But Luna is near the top in popularity, yet in the middle of the pack with win rate; does she need to be adjusted downward, or not? In short, which is more important for balance purposes: win rate or popularity?

What we actually care about is the *combination* of win rate and popularity. Specifically, the real psychological cost of an imbalance in the environment isn't just *playing* a particular character a lot, but *losing* to that character a lot. Competitive players won't mind so much if they keep playing against the same character, as long as it's one that they can always win against. Players also don't care if they always lose to a character who never gets played. What really hurts is when a player keeps going up against the same character and consistently losing to them. *That* is what causes a player to become frustrated and complain that such-and-such a character is too good. This also suggests that in a game where there is no correlation between popularity and win rate, the characters who are complained about the most by the player community are usually the popular ones (since that is what they see—and thus lose to—the most) rather than the ones who win all their games but are never seen in play.

Increasing the Granularity

We know that some characters are unbalanced in some way, and we have another couple of characters who are suspect (Diana, who is unpopular despite being near the top of the charts in win rate; and Luna, who is very popular but not particularly strong). But the data we have so far do not show us *why*. We can investigate further.

Win rate is a coarse metric. A lot of things happen in a match—players give hundreds of controller inputs in just a few minutes of game time—and yet win rate is but a single win/lose/draw result. More is going on, but we need to track metrics that are more granular in nature. Win rate is also difficult to change in any clear capacity; any change to a character (whether it makes them stronger or weaker) must be enough to push them across the threshold of winning a match, and many changes might cause the character to win or lose by a narrower margin without actually flipping the victory. Win rate may change, but it is usually subtle and not drastic.

One thing we can look at in a fighting game is how much damage is done in a game. In a brawling game where players can die and respawn multiple times in a single match, we can look at the kills, deaths, and kill/death ratio (or, if a player's score is some function of kills and deaths, we can look at the final score). You need to keep in mind known anomalies; for example, if one character has a highly aggressive play style such that it has an average kill/death ratio but lots of kills *and* lots of deaths, this makes the character stand out if you're just looking at metrics like number of kills or amount of damage done. You'll also want to acknowledge the implicit assumption here: that damage or kills is correlated with win rate (you'd expect it to be, but *always* check to make sure).

You can go even further, subdividing by each individual move of a character. You can look at frequency (how many times per match, on average, is that particular move used by the character?), accuracy (some moves are easier to avoid than others; of the times a move is used, how often does it hit?), and contribution to winning (how much damage, total, is done by a move over the course of the match—multiply frequency by accuracy by damage done when it connects). Here is Luna's totally made up move set.

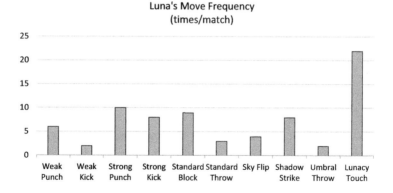

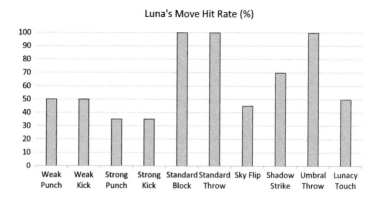

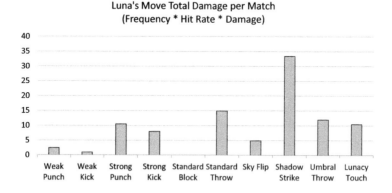

These charts tell a lot—some of it easy to understand, some of it downright misleading.

We first look for anomalies. Immediately, we see that block and both throws have a 100% hit rate, which seems much better than other moves—but this is probably because by design, a throw is unblockable if they player is up close and can land it, while a block can always stop a frontal attack that isn't a throw. While a player going in close for a throw attempt might be thwarted with a close-range attack, that might not register as such. This would have to be confirmed with the programmer who coded these metrics collection routines, but is likely not pointing to an imbalance there.

The next anomaly is that the bulk of damage done in a match—over a third, and more than twice any other move—is Shadow Strike. The move also has among the highest hit rate of any of the attacking moves. This would seem to imply that Shadow Strike is a potential culprit. Notice that this graph of Move Total Damage is essentially a combination of popularity and effectiveness—the same as we were examining with characters overall.

But wait. If Shadow Strike is so powerful, why is it used relatively few times in the match, compared to Lunacy Touch? In our example, suppose that Lunacy Touch is a low-damage move that stuns the opponent, opening them up to land a high-damage move, and then Shadow Strike is the most common follow-up? This would explain everything. Luna mostly tries to just stun the opponent by spamming Lunacy Touch attacks, and then, when she hits with one, she combos with Shadow Strike. Luna's relatively low win rate suggests that she is a bit of a one-trick pony, but one with a powerful trick. Players who know how to avoid Lunacy Touch can win handily, but those who don't are going to spend most of the match stunned and helpless. This suggests Luna indeed needs changes made, not necessarily because she's too powerful, but because she isn't fun to play (her strategy consists primarily of repeatedly attempting to connect with one move) and she isn't fun to play against (her opponent spends a lot of time stunned).

Given sufficient metrics, we could then look at the data even further to see if this is the case. We could, for example, ask what percentage of Shadow Strike hits are made against a stunned opponent, average number of times each character is stunned when playing against each other character, or how often any move is made as the initial strike versus immediately following the same or some other move as part of a combo.

If we confirm through further investigation that the issue is the Lunacy Touch/Shadow Strike combination, what is the appropriate response? In this case, it would probably be to limit the stun or lower the accuracy of Lunacy Touch. This may seem strange. After all, Shadow Strike is the move that is dealing damage so you might consider that as a better option. You might also consider doing nothing, as Luna has only a so-so win rate and is therefore not unbalanced in actual play. This is a case where considerations go beyond balance and encompass the broader field of game design. As a general design principle, players like to *play the game*, and anything that prevents players from actually playing is going to be perceived as not very fun. This includes being stunned in a fighting game, having to discard your hand in a card game, or having certain actions prevented due to an opponent's special ability in just about any game. Even if Luna wins less than half of her matches, the times she *does* win are frustratingly memorable to the opponent—and given how popular she is in the metagame, that is a *lot* of players who absolutely detest playing against her, mainly because of the helpless feeling when stunned. By making her stun move harder to land or adding some other limitation to reduce the amount of time that the opponent spends stunned, this can be mitigated.

Another option, interestingly enough, would be to *increase* the power of some of Luna's other moves. By giving her alternate strategies that are as good as her stun move, it could improve the diversity of her move set, making Luna more interesting and varied to play, and making her opponents less bored at having to defend against just one move all the time. This could be done in conjunction with fixing Lunacy Touch, to keep Luna in the mid-tier range of fighters.

Examining Player Ratings

We can go further. In a highly competitive PvP game, player skill counts for a lot, and the play styles and metagame of expert players may differ drastically from that of beginners. This is important; as a designer you want the game to provide an interesting and varied experience at *all* skill levels. If the game is finely balanced and tuned for the expert game but just isn't engaging at the beginner level, then few players bother sticking around to become experts. If the game is great for novices but a single dominant strategy is quickly discovered for higher levels of play, players will leave once they reach a certain level of skill.

Suppose that our game not only tracks data on games played, but also has player accounts and a matchmaking system with ratings. Then, we can subdivide all of our earlier analytics by rating. For example, let's examine win rate for each character as it relates to rating:

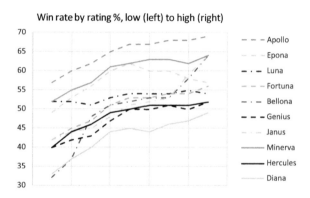

Win rate by rating %, low (left) to high (right)

We could then proceed to dig even deeper, looking for example at the popularity and effectiveness of a particular character's move set subdivided by rating. For example, Luna has a high win rate among low-skill players relative to other characters, but drops to the middle of the pack once you reach a reasonable skill level (because good players know how to counter her moves). Still, she dominates beginner-level play, in both popularity and win rate, so the solution here would be to reduce the power level of those particular moves that are used most often in beginner matches and less in expert games. This would shift the win rate down at the low end of the graph, but not the high end. Meanwhile, Bellona is the opposite, starting near the bottom of the pack for beginners but rising near the top for experts, suggesting that she is difficult to play but can be extremely capable in the right hands.

We could then proceed from here to find data on individual moves, broken down by player skill. If it's determined that a Lunacy Touch is the move that is dominating beginner-level play, weakening that move or just making it harder to connect with may reduce Luna's power level in low-skill games while preserving her power in higher-skill games, for example.

In short, as we drill down to get more granular information, the design solutions present themselves with less guesswork on the part of the designer. Everything has a context, and the more you know about the context, the more you can respond to it. Designers should care more about the specifics than the "average" or "typical" case, because games with large player bases don't have a single "typical" player, but many different player types that interact with the game in very different ways.

MOBAs

Multiplayer Online Battle Arena games (such as *Defense of the Ancients 2*, *League of Legends*, and *Heroes of the Storm*) involve teams of players, with each player controlling a single hero and working to level that hero up through a combination of fighting monsters, fighting enemy heroes, and spending gold to buy equipment. Like brawling games, MOBAs involve the relative balance of many characters, but there are additional considerations because of the more complex and layered systems.

PROGRESSION WITHIN A MATCH

Within a single match, you can look at the curve of gold, experience level, or character stats look like over time? Look for sudden spikes or flat areas overall to make sure progression feels good, and then, do the same by character to see if certain characters progress too rapidly or slowly at certain points in the game. Subdivide by skill level to see if certain characters work better for novices or experts. Since this is a team game, it can also be worth looking at not just individual character progression, but also in the context of team composition: do a character's progression curves correlate with the presence or absence of certain other characters on their team?

You can also look at the correlation between the game's ultimate outcome and a character's progression curves. Aside from just knowing the win rate of a given character, it's useful to know whether a character who falls behind early has no chance of catching up and winning later—or conversely, whether a character who gets an early lead ends up being just as likely to win as not, so that their superior early-game play ends up being irrelevant.

For a given character, it's also worth looking at variety. For games where that character is on the winning team, are there certain item sets that are always purchased, or are there several viable builds? A character may be "balanced" in the sense of having a reasonable win rate and progression curve, but still be boring to play because their strategy is fixed.

In general, an analysis should focus on identifying the worst possible case of system dynamics within the game, and then confirming that it isn't happening.

Progression between Matches

MOBAs also typically have long-term progression between matches, where players earn in-game currency and experience and use that to purchase new abilities, or characters, or other things. Interestingly, this inter-game progression acts similarly to in-game progression, just on a larger scale—and that is very much by design (you often see these nested loops of interactions in games where there's a connection between micro- and macro decisions).

Look at the curve of player progression (whether currency, experience, or however that is expressed in the game) over time. Does it spike or flatten at certain points, or for players of certain characters or character types?

Also examine how linked this macro progression is with game results. Do players who have lots of in-game currency win more, or is currency irrelevant? Conversely, do players with a high win rate progress faster, and if so, how much? What is the tradeoff between time spent in game, player skill (win rate), and money spent (currency)?

Are there multiple purchase strategies between matches, or do most players have the same purchases in the same order over the lifetime of their player account? What about when you subdivide by player skill—are there multiple *viable* purchase strategies, or do most *successful* (high-ranked) players have the same set of purchases?

TEAM MECHANICS

MOBAs are team-based games at their heart, and this is one of the key differentiators between MOBAs and brawling/fighting games. You can therefore use analytics to ask questions about the team elements of a MOBA. Going back to looking within a single game, in general, does teamwork matter?

You can examine what kinds of things players do when their teammates are in need of help. Do they get ignored, or do they get assisted? At the other extreme, do players feel that helping their team is a choice, or are some or all players (or characters) apparently forced to help others with no freedom, if they want to win?

It's also possible to look at team composition, and whether those choices are interesting, meaningful, and varied. Do successful teams all look the same, or is there variation (not just in characters, but also general classes of characters)? Are there certain pairs of characters that tend to succeed more when used together? Look for win rate of one character, only in games when another character is present, for any given pair—you could do this for triples as well, but beyond a point you either reduce the search space to be small enough that it's not statistically significant, or you're just looking at so many different possibilities that it's computationally too slow to give useful results. As with most things, you are looking to make sure team composition doesn't fall to either extreme: it's boring if the total number of team choices is small and each player feels constrained to a small possibility space, but it's equally undesirable to have a situation where teams don't matter at all.

Another area to consider is what the outcome of a game should be with teams consisting of uneven skill: how great is each player's individual contribution, and is it the strongest or weakest player that determines the performance of a team. Look in the data for teams where there is an outlier in skill, a single player that is significantly higher or lower rated than the rest of their team, and correlate that with win rate compared to a team of comparable rating but without the outlier. Can a single high-skill player carry their entire team to victory singlehandedly? Can a single low-skill player drag the rest of their team down to defeat? Or looking at the other extreme, can a high-skill player get dragged down such that they have no impact on a game if the rest of their team is mediocre? Can a low-skill player be a "free rider" who gets a win by hooking up with a good team, in spite of making only minimal contributions? In summary, what is the relationship between the personal ratings or win rates of the characters, the players, and the overall team, and which of the three tends to dominate?

Additionally, there may be players who are good at technical, individual play of a given character but who are just not fun to play with. If the game gives players surveys that allow them to rate the friendliness of their teammates and whether they would want to play with the same people again, how does that correlate with win rate, if other things are equal? Do teams that "get along" have higher win rates? Note that if players are surveyed about their team and they know about the survey ahead of time, this in and of itself can change player behavior (because players know that others are going to be rating them as well).

Teamwork is a system in itself, and one to not be neglected in games that feature it as a central element of gameplay.

MONEY

While most players would prefer not to think of business as something that drives game design, the reality is that game developers need to make a living wage if they are to continue making games, so any game studio needs to earn enough income to pay its people so the game can continue. Thus, many free-to-play style metrics (as discussed early on in this chapter) should also be considered. If a change is made that players love but that costs the studio money (everyone's favorite characters are now free forever!), and the studio has to shut its doors as a result, that isn't a positive outcome for anyone.

One of the key variables to look at is acquisition: the rate of players joining the game. If new players suddenly drop off, that's a problem that requires further examination of what has changed. It could be as simple as the download page being down, or a recent change to that page that turns people away. You can also look at the effects of various marketing strategies and how much is being spent versus what the game is making, to ensure that any advertising money is being spent wisely. If the game is mentioned in the press or by other sources and that drives a sudden rush of downloads, knowing where all of those new players came from can be useful in catering new content to them.

Another important question is that of conversion: how many players cross that barrier from playing for free to spending money, no matter how small the amount? Does the game's income come from lots of players spending small amounts, or from a small number of players who spend big (most free-to-play games are the latter)? You can also look at whether the game is too punishing to those who don't spend, by looking at win rates correlated with amount spent in the game.

A third common metric is retention: how long do players play in a single session, how often do they return, and how long do player accounts exist before players leave and never come back? When players do exit, what is that correlated with? You can look for connections with player win/loss records (do players leave if they have suffered some number of losses in a row?), specific dates (did a special in-game event like the end of a season or major tournament give players incentive to exit?), team composition (do players get bored if they see the same ten characters for a long string of games at a time, even though your game has over a hundred to choose from?), teammates (do players get frustrated if they are consistently put on teams of players who are weaker than they are, or players who are known to be abrasive based on reports by other players?), after reaching a certain rank or level (does the game become rote once a player masters the basics, or does the elder game feel too monotonous after the player has completed the main progression arc?), or lifetime of the account (does the game itself just seem to only hold interest for a limited time, after which players feel it lacks further depth and they leave to discover something new elsewhere?).

OTHER CONSIDERATIONS

Are there other interactions between players, like trading or other economic systems? Those are worth checking as well.

Does the game involve periodic updates, such as adding new characters or modifying old ones, or offering new maps or making core mechanics changes through patches? Everything mentioned up to this point can also be examined, not just as a single average, but also as a change over time by tracking over dates and marking the significant patch dates on the graph. If looking at data across multiple patches, keep in mind that the numbers are weighted toward the time period that had the greatest number of players.

The numbers may show trends over time even without game patches or updates. For example, if one character has slowly increasing popularity and win rate over time with no sign of stopping, that might suggest that someone discovered a strong strategy and it is spreading through the player community as more people play against it then attempt to copy it. If some metric that you're tracking has a sudden spike or drop and then returns to normal, you can then look at the single slice of time that's the most extreme to figure out what happened and what's so special.

Data Visualization

The importance of good visualization should not be underestimated; a good visual doesn't just present data, but often suggests the exact nature and root cause of the problem and thus the ideal balance solution. Even if only working on your own project without a team, visuals can be useful as a way to communicate with your future self, so that later on you can look back and remember why you made a particular choice.

In general, values in data sets come in two forms: **discrete** (must be exactly one of several distinct values) and **continuous** (can be any number within a range). Which character is played in a fighting game is discrete; there are a limited set of characters, and you are only playing one at a time (not half of one and half of another). Time of day is continuous; a timestamp can be at any time, down to the millisecond on most computers, and the difference between 12:31:04.003 and 12:31:04.004 isn't meaningful for most applications. However, time as measured in months is discrete again, because if you are dividing events by the month, then September is distinct from October, and you can't have data that is "between" months or some combination of several months.

Books have been written just on how to present the answers you find with analytics in a way that makes them easy to read and understand. Without going into too much detail, here are some quick rules of thumb:

- If you have a single value, whether discrete or continuous, you don't need a graph. Just give the number. Total number of active player accounts as of today: 3,024,710. But most interesting analysis comes from comparing two (or more) values.
- If comparing two values and one or both are discrete, use a **bar graph** or **pie chart** (bar graph if it's more important to compare the values side by side, pie chart if it's more important to highlight the largest or smallest values). For example, here's a graph of the favorite genre (discrete) of students in a class, where the number of students who listed that genre (discrete) is shown for each.

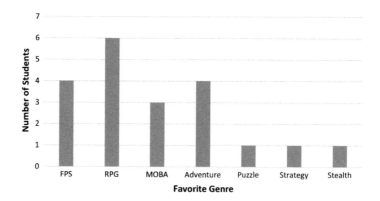

- If comparing two values that are both continuous, use a **line graph**. You can also use a line graph for discrete values that fall along a continuum with a clear progression. For example, here is a graph of console sales in number of units (technically discrete since they are integer values, but at this scale it's continuous because a difference of 1 in either direction is negligible) by month (discrete, but in time order).

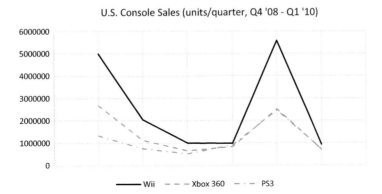

Note that in the preceding graph there is actually a third discrete value: the console itself (Wii, 360, or PS3). Comparing several discrete values on the same line graph (with one line representing each) can be useful for showing differences or similarities between the various lines.

- If you want to compare many values to one another, we run into a problem of a natural upper limit of how dense the data can be. The previous graph shows three values. We might theoretically be able to add a fourth value by color-coding each line so that the color corresponds with a continuous value, or even a fifth value by making the graph 3d, but it gets unwieldy very quickly. The solution here is the same solution to relating resources to one another that we addressed way back in Chapter 5: relate everything to one central anchor. You can then make a **dashboard** display that shows a series of line graphs, each one relating a different value to the same central one. For example, here is a dashboard that relates player activity to time.

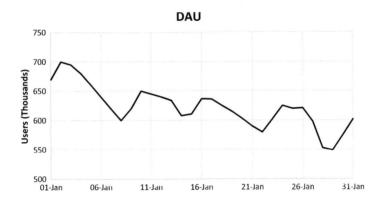

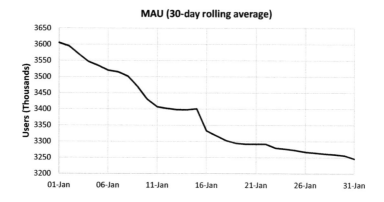

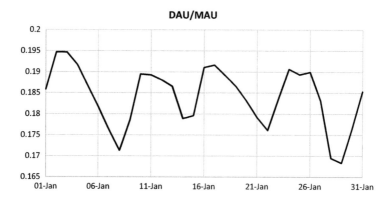

You might imagine displaying additional things over the same time period, such as 1-day, 7-day, and 30-day retention, the win rate of each primary strategy in the game, and so on.

- For spatial data, such as what happens in particular parts of a level map, use a **heat map** to show values by color intensity. In *Team Fortress 2*, player data are collected by Valve on the map coordinates where a player died. These visualizations show where deaths tend to happen on any given map, with brighter colors meaning more deaths (and thus showing the most dangerous parts of the map). You can view these by map at http://heatmaps.tf.

There are many other types of visualizations, including scatter plots, area charts, radar charts, and many others. Most can be done in a spreadsheet, although some (notably heat maps) benefit from having a custom software tool that interfaces with your game engine.

Additional Resource

- Alex Jaffe, *Metagame Balance*, GDC 2015. Viewable at https://www.gdcvault.com/play/1022155/Metagame

Discussion Questions

1. What is the difference between metrics and analytics?
2. What are the different development team roles (other than game designers) who would be involved in analytics?
3. Pick any F2P game that gets updated regularly. If you were in charge of making sure that game was profitable, what KPIs would you want to see first?
4. "Correlation is not causation," the refrain goes. What would you need to see in addition to a correlation in order to be satisfied it was a causal effect?
5. If you notice two variables are correlated, what are four different explanations for the potential root cause of this observation?
6. In a PvP game with online ranked play, when assessing the balance of different characters, play styles, or strategies, what are the most important metrics to pay attention to?
7. Why might metrics look different if you subdivide the data by player rating (or some other measure of skill or ability), compared to leaving it all combined?
8. What metrics would you look at to measure the churn rate of your game?
9. If your game's acquisition and retention rates are fine but conversion is lower than expected, what kinds of things might you do to the game to increase conversion?
10. Why is data visualization important when dealing with analytics?

Sidequests

Games, even (or *especially*) those that you design, are hard to understand at a fundamental level. You can gain some intuition through a lot of playtesting by yourself, and observing playtests with others. You can build mathematical models, but those that are developed without information may not reflect reality. Large amounts of data are a great way to inform design, when used properly.

Unfortunately, data can lie to you. It can show you numbers that suggest one thing, until you drill down and realize it's actually something else. Always be critical of any conclusions drawn from analytics, and use multiple views of the data and multiple calculations to confirm your suspicions. You may hear the saying "the numbers don't lie"—and while that is true strictly speaking, the way the numbers present themselves to you may very well lie, or at least mislead.

Sidequest 13.1: Analytics Plan

For this challenge, first choose your favorite genre of games that you like to play. Go ahead, pick a genre now.

Next, choose a notable game within that genre. It might be the first ever game that launched the genre, or a later game that popularized the genre, or else your personal favorite game within the genre, but pick one game. (This is easiest if you choose a game that lends itself well to use of analytics. This is most types of games.)

Imagine that you and your development team have procured the rights to do a remake (not a sequel) of that game. The expectation is that most of the core mechanics remain the same in the remake, but you *do* have permission to make some minor changes for the purposes of improving the game balance to fix the worst design errors of the original. Think of it as a "version 2.0"—remastered audio, updated graphics, new platform, and a few game balance updates.

First, define the questions. No game is perfect, so there surely must be *some* game balance issues with the game you chose, no matter how minor (if you honestly think the game's balance is perfect, then look harder, or pick a different game). You might suspect some imbalances from your experience with the game… but how would you prove it? List at least three game balance questions that you would want answers to—anything that could be answered by analytics.

Next, define the metrics. For each of your game balance questions, list the metrics you would need to collect in order to answer those questions. For each metric, specify how it would be collected (direct observation of playtesters in a lab, voluntary player surveys, database queries to server logs, etc.). For this challenge, you can assume you have access to a large supply of playtesters, and/or play usage data from the original game along with a full team of gameplay and database programmers, so that lack of data should not be a problem or a consideration here.

Then, set up your analysis. If you received the data you're asking for, how would you analyze that data to answer the original questions? What kinds of calculations would you perform? What kinds of graphs or other data visualizations would you make? And—most importantly—what kinds of things would you be looking for that would suggest one conclusion over another?

Rogue's Main Quest, Part 7: Playtest, Iterate, and Finish

Continuing from Part 6 in: Chapter 12

Develop an analytics plan (Sidequest 13.1) for your game, in preparation for playtesting. Since you will likely be testing with a small group or on your own, you won't have enough data for statistical significance, so focus on identifying key questions to ask and what the answers are expected to look like, so that you can be aware of them during playtesting.

Then, carry out your playtest.

When you find problems in your playtest, make a note of them, and modify your game objects (and/or fix your cost curve and supporting math) as appropriate. Then, repeat the playtest, fix more problems, and keep doing that as many times as you're able to in the time you have. Your goal should be to get your new mini-expansion as close to perfectly balanced in this way as you can get it.

This is the final part of the Rogue's Main Quest.

Fighter's Main Quest, Part 7: Analytics Plan for Remake

Continuing from Part 6 in: Chapter 11

Do Sidequest 13.1 for the game you have chosen.

This is the final part of the Fighter's Main Quest.

14

Metagame Systems

In This Chapter

- Rankings and Ratings
- Rating Systems
- Common Problems with Rating Systems
- Ratings as Outcome Prediction
- Ranking Systems
- Tournament and League Play
- Metagame Reward Systems

Rankings and Ratings

> Sure, Magic: the Gathering is a strategy game… but on the other hand, Garry Kasparov never lost a Chess game just because he went the first ten turns without drawing a Pawn card.
>
> *a game designer with 10 years' industry experience.*

The words "ranking" and "rating" are often used interchangeably in common use, but these actually mean subtly different things.

A player's **rank** is an ordinal number that shows their standing relative to other players; rank 1 means the player is better than all other players, rank 2 is better than all except the player in rank 1, and so on. A **ranking system** is a way of determining and updating the rank of each player. The absolute difference in skill or standing is not represented in a player's rank. A player of rank

N might be just slightly better than the player of rank $N+1$, or they might be a great deal better; all that you know is that there are no other players who fall between the two. Leaderboards and ladders are common examples of ranking systems.

A player's **rating**, by contrast, is a number that represents some kind of absolute attribute of the player (in most games with ratings, it is thought of as some kind of approximation of a player's skill at the game). Unlike rank, the numerical difference between two players' ratings tells how far apart they are in meaningful terms. As you might guess, a **rating system** is a method to assign and update player ratings. Elo is the most well-known rating system, and we start this chapter by examining and analyzing Elo and several variants in detail.

Rating Systems

Elo was not the first rating system ever developed, but it is the most widely used among games with ratings. It was originally developed as a rating system for *Chess*, as a replacement for the previous Harkness system.

Harkness

Harkness (named after its creator) was designed as a way to maintain player ratings in tournaments. Each player would enter a tournament with their former rating (new players who did not have a prior rating would be assigned a provisional rating instead, i.e., a starting number). In that tournament, the average rating of each player's opponents is computed (let's call this number R). If the player's win/loss record is exactly average (as many wins as losses), then their new rating after the tournament becomes R, regardless of what it started as. If they do better, their new rating is $R+(10 * P)$, where P is the percentage above 50/50. If they do worse, their rating is $R-(10 * P)$, where P is the percentage below 50/50.

For example, suppose a person enters a tournament with a prior rating of 1800, and they play against opponents of ratings 1500, 1700, 1750, 1900, and 1950, and they win 3, lose 1, and draw 1 game (in Harkness, it doesn't matter who a player wins or loses against, just their aggregate ratings and the player's final record against them). The average of the opponent ratings is 1760, so had the player won 2, lost 2, and drew 1, their rating would be 1760. In this case, they won 3, lost 1 and drew 1; if we treat a win as 1 point, a loss as 0, and a draw as 0.5, this player got 3.5 points out of a maximum of 5 or a 3.5/5 = 70%

win percentage. This is 20 percentage points above 50%, so $P=20$. Their new rating is then $1760+(10 * 20)=1960$. Note that the player would have this new rating regardless of what rating they had before the event.

It does not take much analysis to realize that the Harkness system leads to inaccuracies in a number of cases. Notably, a player's new rating after a tournament is purely a function of their performance and opponents' ratings in that tournament; their own prior rating is not a consideration, except for how it affects their opponents' new ratings. As such, player ratings can swing wildly if they do not perform consistently. Additionally, because rating is calculated as ±10 per percentage point above or below 50, a player's rating must be within 500 points of the average of their opponents. In theory, a novice player who managed to sneak into a grandmaster-level tournament would walk out of the event with a very high rating, even if they lost all of their games!

Elo

To deal with the deficiencies of Harkness, the Elo system (also named after its inventor) was created. In Elo, a player's prior rating is used as a baseline, and then, it is increased for each win and decreased for each loss. The amount of the changes depends on the opponent's rating relative to the player's. A player receives more points for beating an opponent at a higher rating, while receiving relatively few points for trouncing a weaker opponent. Likewise, a player loses few points when losing to a much more skilled opponent, but they lose more points if their opponent's rating was below their own.

The actual formula to determine a change in Elo rating is a two-step process. First, the expected number of wins for a player is calculated as follows:

$$E = \frac{1}{1+10^{(R_{opp}-R_{player})/400}}$$

In this equation, R_{opp} is the opponent's rating, and R_{player} is the player's rating before the game starts. E is the expected number of wins, based on the difference in the player ratings (a win is counted as 1 point, a loss as 0). For a single game, E is the probability of a win, which ranges from 0 if a player is infinitely worse than the opponent up to 1 if a player is infinitely better.[1]

---

[1] If you have trouble immediately seeing why, look at what happens if R_{opp} is much higher than R_{player}: then 10 raised to the power of a very big number is itself very large, which makes the denominator very large, and 1 divided by a large number is very small. The larger R_{opp} is relative to R_{player}, the smaller E becomes, approaching but never quite reaching 0. If instead R_{player} is much larger than R_{opp}, 10 raised to a highly negative power becomes very small, and if that term is close to zero, then 1 divided by (1 + almost zero) is very close to 1.

The number 400 seems strange. Why 400, and not some other number? It turns out that number could be anything, really, and is mostly an aesthetic choice, to offer a certain amount of granularity. When developing the system, Elo wished for a ratings difference of 200 to mean that the stronger player had an expected win rate (E) of about 0.75. In the actual formula, E is actually 0.7597469, which is fairly close to what Elo desired.

Another interesting property of this formula is that for any two players, their respective E values should add to 1 and that does turn out to be the case. This is not obvious from the formula itself, but is easier to see if you define two quantities, $Q_{player} = 10^{R_{player}/400}$ and $Q_{opp} = 10^{R_{opp}/400}$, and then reduce the formula to $E = Q_{player}/(Q_{player} + Q_{opp})$. Likewise, the opponent's $E = Q_{opp}/(Q_{opp} + Q_{player})$. Adding those two quantities together yields 1.

Once E is calculated for a particular player and their opponent, and the game is played, the result can be used to determine a change in rating. That formula is

$$R_{new} = R_{old} + K(A - E)$$

In this equation, R_{new} is the player's updated rating, R_{old} is their prior rating (the same number as R_{player} when calculating E), and A is the actual score (0 for loss, 1 for win). K is a constant that gives the maximum possible gain or loss from a single game, and is thus a measure of uncertainty: we accept that we do not know a player's actual skill at the game, the rating is an approximation, and we adjust the rating up or down after a game based on how far our prior estimate deviated from the actual result ($A - E$) and how uncertain we were to begin with (K). In *Chess*, K is typically higher for new (provisional) players since their skill is largely unknown, and very high-level tournaments might use a lower K.[2]

A useful property of Elo is that it can be calculated for a single game (as might happen at a *Chess* club where members play one or two "official" rated games in addition to other practice games that are unrated) or for an entire event such as a tournament. To calculate the ratings change for several games at once, calculate E for each game and add them up; A is the total score

---

[2] One common scheme is to use $K = 32$ for provisional players, reducing it to $K = 16$ once a certain number of rated games have been reached. The larger K at first allows new players to rise or fall to the general ballpark of their skill level fairly quickly. Some implementations also have K fall further for players above a certain rating, on the theory that highly skilled players are not going to change their skill level rapidly, and too high of a K value leads to too much volatility. In short, a balance must be struck so that K is not so low that the system doesn't respond quickly to an actual change in player performance, but not so high that a player's rating is dominated by only the most recent events. There is no universally accepted K value, and each implementation may vary from the others.

for the event. For example, if a player played against one very challenging opponent ($E = 0.2$), one equally rated opponent ($E = 0.5$), and one slightly easy opponent ($E = 0.6$), and they actually won two out of three games ($A = 2$), then the change in their ratings would be $K(2.0 - 1.3) = 0.7K$. For a typical K of 16, this player would thus gain 11.2 rating points (in some implementations that only allow integer ratings, this would be rounded down to 11).

Because Elo ratings go up or down in relation to the ratings of the opponents, there are practical upper and lower bounds. If, for example, players start off at a provisional rating of 1000, it is unlikely that you would ever see a player rated at 5000, so if you are doing some spreadsheet calculations to estimate the spread of player ratings and see someone rated 7724, there's probably an error in your simulation somewhere!

One final note here is that in *Chess*, draw games are possible, and the Elo system does not explicitly handle draws. Because two equally rated players both have E of 0.5, a draw is counted as half of a win. This means that a weaker player who manages to draw with their opponent actually sees their rating increase, and a stronger player who draws rather than wins sees their rating drop slightly.

While Elo is the gold standard for *Chess* and is used in many other games besides, it too has some drawbacks that make it impractical for certain types of games. In particular, it assumes that games are skill-based and that as one player gets infinitely more skilled than another, the probability of the favorite winning approaches 100% (not true in games with mechanics of chance that can allow a less skilled player a lucky win). Elo's treatment of draws is appropriate if a draw is indeed worth half of a win, but in a game where it is easier for a less skilled player to play for a draw (for example), that may not be valid. And, of course, Elo is limited to two-player games and requires additional modifications if one were to use it in any game that involves three or more players.

Glicko

There are many systems that are, essentially, minor modifications of Elo. Glicko (named after its creator, Mark Glickman) is one such modification.[3]

In Glicko, the K parameter in Elo's ratings change formula is not a constant. Rather, it changes over time. Each player has their own measure of

---

[3] The actual formulas for Glicko ratings calculations are quite complicated and not analyzed here. Some of its terms are similar to Elo, however, so conceptually it can be thought of as "Elo with a K that varies between players." For complete details, see http://www.glicko.net/glicko.html.

uncertainty, termed *RD* (for Ratings Deviation) that stays with them and updates after each game. In general, *RD* goes down after each game, but goes up slowly over time. The implication is that as a player plays more games, we get more certain of their rating, but if a player does not play for some time, they may be out of practice and their rating may have changed, so the system should adjust to allow larger deviations.

Since each player has both a rating and an *RD*, a Glicko rating can be shown not as a single number, but as a range of $R \pm 2RD$, with the expectation that 95% of players are somewhere within that range.

Glicko is an interesting illustration of how mathematics can clash with player psychology. From a practical perspective, having a decreasing *RD* with frequent play allows one to find a player's true rating within a small margin fairly quickly, which would be useful and efficient if that is the goal. However, a very low *RD* means that a player's rating doesn't change very much one way or the other with repeated play, leading to a sense that game outcomes don't matter and that it's impossible to raise one's rating unless they intentionally do not play for a while to get their *RD* back up. From that perspective, Glicko is a system that can disincentivize certain players from playing often, which can be a negative. For this reason, its creator even suggests having a minimum *RD* (such as 30) in practical implementations, to allow players to still have some amount of ratings gain or loss per game.

TrueSkill™

The TrueSkill™ system, developed at Microsoft™, is similar to Glicko in that each player has both a rating (here called μ, pronounced "mew") and an uncertainty (σ, pronounced "sigma"). A player's skill is characterized as a probability on a bell curve (also called a normal distribution) where μ is the mean and σ is the standard deviation. μ always increases for a win and decreases for a loss. The amount of the change depends on the ratio of players' σ (a player with a very high σ has a very uncertain rating, and if they play against an opponent of low σ with high certainty, the uncertain player's rating can change a lot because they have received very good information on where they stand relative to this opponent…and meanwhile, the opponent was already very certain of their rating and gains little information from a game against an unknown opponent, so their rating changes very little). The amount that μ changes also depends on the difference in μ between the players, as with Elo (an upset leads to more of a change than if the favorite wins).

One major innovation with TrueSkill™ is that unlike most other rating systems that came before, it has ways to explicitly handle multiplayer matches.

In free-for-all games, players are first ranked within a game according to their final standings (such as an FPS deathmatch game where each player is ranked according to their final score, or an auto race where players are ranked based on who finishes first). If the game has N players, then it is treated as $N-1$ one-on-one games played for each individual; the player is considered to have won against every player that they ranked better than, and each player they are ranked worse than is treated as if they had lost against them. If two players' final results are sufficiently close, that can be treated as a draw. The threshold for "sufficiently close" is chosen separately for each game, and some games may not even allow for such a thing (racing games, for example, may always have a strict ordering of finish with no draws allowed).

TrueSkill™ also includes a mechanism for team games. Each team is treated as an individual player with μ and σ equal to the respective sums of those values for all players on the team. It then calculates the ratings change for each team, and within each team, it then assigns those point gains or losses based on the individual players' σ values (the players with higher uncertainty have their rating change more).

Game developers are also allowed some leeway in their game-specific implementation of TrueSkill™. For example, some games might also keep track of how much an individual contributed to their team's result (a player in an FPS that hides in a corner all match is not contributing as much as one who is moving around and engaging opponents constantly) and then use individuals' contribution scores as an additional weight when assigning points to the team.

Online Rating Systems

For Multiplayer Online Battle Arena (MOBA) games such as *League of Legends*, as well as some other competitive online-only games like *Hearthstone* and *Dota Auto Chess*, there are some additional considerations and innovations over former systems, based on what is known of player behaviors.

It is generally accepted that the most exciting games are those between players of similar skill level. If a novice and an expert play together, the expert is almost certainly going to win, which is neither surprising nor particularly engaging for either player. If the novice does manage to win, it's probably from luck rather than skill, which is not something the novice can feel proud of, and surely frustrates the expert. As such, one goal of online games is to put players into matchups that are as even as possible.

To do this, most games have an MMR (Match Making Rating) for each player, which is generally updated similarly to Elo or TrueSkill™. When a player tells the system they would like to play a game, they are placed in a queue which attempts to match them against a player of similar MMR, but also attempts to match them quickly. If a suitable opponent cannot be found quickly, the acceptable difference in MMR increases, until eventually a match is found (even if that opponent is much better or worse than the player). MMR may or may not be displayed to players; often, it is purely internal, so as not to discourage players with low ratings. After all, if a player is winning about half of their games, they still feel like they are playing well, even if the reason is that they are bad at the game but matched against other weak opponents.

For team-based games, an ideal matchup involves teams where *every* player's MMR is similar, but that is often not possible or practical. In particular, if players can choose to form a "party" with their real-life friends, skill disparity is probably going to be larger than if an automated system simply looked for the nearest matches. In this situation, some kind of average is taken of all MMRs on a team, and teammates or opponents are sought who have a similar MMR to that average.[4] The game may even keep a separate MMR for each player when they enter into the game solo vs. when they group together with friends; players who play together regularly may be better at communicating and working together as a team, and therefore, a player's MMR on a known team may be different from when that same player is grouped with complete strangers.

Masterpoints

One other rating system bears mention here, used in the card game *Bridge*, the physical sport *Tennis*, and the collectible card game *Magic: the Gathering*, among others. In these systems, players gain points (termed **Masterpoints**) for each organized event they play in, based on their performance. A player might, for example, get 3 points for a win, 1 for a draw, and 0 for a loss for each tournament game played. A player's rating is simply the sum of all points they have accumulated over their lifetime.

Individual implementations have their own variations on this theme. For example, in *Bridge*, points are color-coded based on the prestige of the event; to be eligible to participate in an invitational event might require not just a

---

[4] This might be an actual mean average, or some kind of weighted average, depending on the game. There are many ways to approximate the skill of a combined team from the individual MMRs. For example, in a game where the strongest player on a team dominates play and everyone else is just along for the ride, the "average" might simply be the maximum (i.e., weighting the highest-rated player on each team at 100% and all other players at 0%).

certain number of points, but also a minimum of some number of points of a particular color or above (as a way to differentiate someone who plays a lot of club games from someone who has done well in national or international events). In *Magic: the Gathering*, players are given some points for merely participating in an event, in addition to the points gained from winning games. This is done to incentivize players to participate in many events.

In any case, a Masterpoint system is defined by a player gaining but never losing points, unlike other rating systems. An obvious down side is that there is no way to tell the difference between a player who has mediocre performance but plays a lot of rated games from another player who plays infrequently but wins most of their games. Most Masterpoint systems also don't take the skill of individual opponents into account, so a player is awarded the same number of points per win against a novice or an expert opponent. This gives something of an advantage to players who are consistently matched against opponents weaker than they are.

Common Problems with Rating Systems

To date, no rating system has been developed that is absolutely perfect. Each has its own strengths and weaknesses. But there are a few pitfalls that are common, and it's worth examining these issues, along with their potential solutions.

Encouraging Activity

For players who have achieved a high rating in Elo-like systems, they may feel compelled to not play in order to protect their rating, particularly if the player feels they are overrated and likely to lose points in the long run, or if the player is one of the best in the world and is afraid of losing their top spot.

There are other ways a rating system can disincentivize play. For example, the Glicko system has the concept of *RD*, which determines how many points can be gained or lost in a single game. *RD* goes down with frequent activity, and in a "pure" implementation of the system as originally proposed, the *RD* would approach zero with enough play. Effectively, that means an extremely frequent player could get locked in to their current rating, unable to move up much even if they win many games. The only way for *RD* to increase is if the player does not play for a length of time, so players are pushed to go through cycles of play activity to change their rating, then inactivity to increase their *RD*. Glickman even pointed this out as a flaw and suggested a minimum value of 30 for *RD* so that players could still have some marginal ratings gains.

Clearly, we would like our players to play our game, and a system that discourages play is not ideal.

One solution is to remove players from the global ratings if they do not show a certain level of activity per unit time. This is only a partial solution, as players who are otherwise incentivized to avoid play will just play the bare minimum they need to maintain their position. If the threshold is set too high, meanwhile, some casual players who can't play all that frequently might feel cheated if they play whenever they can and still can't have a rating or ranking.

Masterpoint systems explicitly encourage play, as player ratings can only go up and not down. On the other hand, these conflate experience with skill, making them poor tools for matchmaking, comparing player skill, or predicting the outcome of a game.

Other systems can be put into place to encourage play. For example, players could be given daily or weekly "quests" which involve playing or winning a certain number of games, and receiving free in-game currency for doing so. If players get paid to play (essentially), they may choose more in-game stuff over protecting a rating.

Hiding player ratings and using them solely for matchmaking can also help, particularly if there are other measures a player can look at, like ranking systems (as we see later in this chapter). If a player has no known rating to protect, they don't refuse to play—at least, not for that reason.

Luck and Skill

In the Elo system, the expected probability of winning varies in the range of 0–1. This means that an infinitely skilled player beats an infinitely unskilled player 100% of the time. In a skill-based game like *Chess*, this makes perfect sense. In a game where luck plays a role, like *Magic: the Gathering* or *Poker*, it does not.

In some games, an unskilled player can beat a highly skilled player occasionally, due to a lucky draw, good die rolls, or lucky guesswork. In those cases, the expected probability of a game result should never be 0 or 1, but should instead depend on the amount of luck in the game.

Suppose that in some card game, you are able to determine (somehow) that the game outcome is 95% skill and 5% luck. In other words, 1 in 20 games are determined by luck, and the rest are determined by skillful play.

In the case of an extreme skill mismatch, that means 19 out of 20 games are won by the highly skilled player, and the last game has a 50% chance of being won by either player (since it is luck-based and therefore favors neither player). As such, in this case, you would expect the rating system to have expected win probabilities in the range of 0.025–0.975 (instead of 0–1). More generally, if the amount of luck is N%, then win probabilities should max out at $N/200$ to $1-(N/200)$.

What happens if luck is not taken into account? The underdog wins slightly more games than a pure-skill system would predict. This creates something of a negative feedback loop, where highly skilled players tend to lose more points than they gain whenever they play someone of lower skill and vice versa.

How might you modify a skill-based system like Elo in order to take luck into account? If you compute the expected win rate $E=$ (something) which assumes pure skill, and your luck factor (the probability of a game being decided by luck rather than skill) is L, then

$$E = (1 - L)(\text{something}) + 0.5L$$

Where does that formula come from? It is simply an expected value calculation from probability: we multiply the probability of a result by the result itself and add all of those up. The first term shows that the probability of a game being decided by skill is $(1-L)$ and the probability of a win in that case is the original skill-based formula. The second term shows that the probability of a game being decided by luck is L (by definition), and in that case, the probability of a win is 0.5.

Matchmaking

A player wants to play a rated game. How are opponents chosen for them? The method is a game's **matchmaking system**.

In the early days of online games, a common method was to have a lobby. Players would select an opponent, challenge them, and begin a game. This system had several advantages. It was simple and required no automated process. It allowed people to choose their opponents, so it was easy to play with friends.

However, it also creates some problems when players can select their opponents. One issue is that any system whose expected win rate is different from the actual win rate is going to favor one player or the other when there is a large skill mismatch. A common example is a game that has some luck component that affects the outcome, yet it uses Elo or a similar skill-based system.

In that case, a low-rated player has some small chance of beating a much more skillful player due to luck, making their win rate higher than Elo predicts. In such a system, players are incentivized to challenge opponents who are much better than they are, and avoid challenges from players who are worse.

The reverse happens in a Masterpoint system, if players get the same number of points for beating a skilled or unskilled opponent. In that situation, players get more points for more wins, so the system encourages them to beat on players who are much weaker than they are.

In either situation, if all players optimized their challenges, no one would ever play. In any proposed match, one of the players is disadvantaged and more likely to lose rating points, and it is in that player's best interest to decline the challenge. The best compromise might be two equally-rated players to play, but in that case, both players are unhappy that they did not find someone better to challenge who would favor them. After all, a player who wants to gain rating quickly could wait until they actually increase their skill at the game, but they can do it faster by finding opponents where they are likely to gain more points than they lose.

Even if the rating system's expected win rates are exactly in line with actual win rates, players can still find exploits. At any given time, some players may have ratings that are a bit above or below where they should be, due to random variation. A player might choose to play against opponents who they believe are overrated, while avoiding those who are underrated, if they can tell the difference. For example, relatively new players often enter play at some kind of median rating and are therefore likely to be of lower skill than their rating suggests while they are first learning the game. At the highest levels of play, meanwhile, the top players likely know and follow each other and pay attention to tournament results, which might suggest to them which of their opponents is likely to be overrated.

The typical solution to this problem is to implement an automated match-making system. Players might be able to challenge their friends in unrated games for fun, but for rated games, players simply state their intent to enter a game. The system then looks at all other players waiting for a game and pairs them off. There are two considerations here. First, there is generally an attempt to match players with ratings as close together as possible; this makes for the most exciting and dynamic games and ensures that player ratings only increase if they are genuinely improving. Second, players do not want to sit around waiting for a match to be found for excessive periods of time, so there is a desire to pair up players quickly. There is a tradeoff here, as a perfect match can surely be found if players can wait for infinite time, but if a player must be paired immediately, then an unbalanced matchup is likely all that is available. A typical solution is a compromise, where the matchmaking system first looks for players of nearly identical rating and then increases the allowable rating difference for every second the player spends waiting.[5]

Rating Inflation and Deflation

Masterpoint systems are positive sum. Players gain points by playing, but never lose points, so the sum of all Masterpoints among all players in the system is only going to ever increase. But Elo, and most systems derived from it, are zero sum in nature: the number of rating points one player gains is the same as what their opponent loses.

There is a reason for this. All rating systems need some kind of starting point, a rating assigned to a new player with zero games. Perhaps in one system, new players all start with 1000 points. What does that mean? Really, it has no intrinsic meaning; the number is only meaningful in relation to other players' ratings. If the median player's rating is 1500, then a beginner is expected to be significantly below the median. If the median player's rating is 1000, then beginners are assumed to be at the median by default, and their first few games determine where they fall.

We might expect the median and mean player ratings, across the entire player base, to be relatively stable. But what if they aren't? If the average player rating tends to increase over time, we refer to that as **rating inflation**. If the average rating decreases over time, that is **rating deflation**.

Both inflation and deflation can be long-term problems, particularly where ratings are permanent, persistent, and exposed to players. Both suggest that a player's rating tends to drift in one direction or the other over time. That means a player's rating is no longer purely a measure of the expected outcome of a game, but also of how long they have been playing, which reduces the usefulness of rating as a metric for matchmaking. Inflation punishes new players (they must work harder just to catch up), while deflation punishes experienced players (they must win games just to break even).

Rating inflation and deflation can come from a variety of sources. One common method of rating inflation is if some kind of **rating floor** is implemented, a minimum rating beyond which a player is not allowed to drop.

---

[5] While it is generally preferable to give players even matchups most of the time, there may be design reasons to choose a different algorithm. For example, if a player is on an extended losing streak, they may be in danger of getting frustrated and leaving the game; in that case, giving the player an occasional match with a player of far lower rating—or even an AI that is programmed to simulate a weak human player and that is meant to lose—could end the losing streak and keep the player engaged. While no developer is likely to publicly admit to doing anything like this behind the scenes, it would probably increase player retention!

In such a situation, a player at the floor who loses a rated game doesn't lose any points, but their opponent still gains points, a positive sum event that leads to inflation.

On the flip side, a common method of rating inflation is players who leave the system. A player who exits the game permanently and never plays again essentially removes all of their rating points from the system. If their rating was lower than average, this leads to inflation; if it was above average, it would lead to deflation. However, while players of any rating might leave for a variety of reasons, players are more likely to quit if they are not doing well at the game and feel like they are poorly skilled and frustrated at their low performance. Such low-skill players may blame themselves, decide they are not good at the game, and leave out of shame or frustration; or they may blame the game itself, and leave because they perceive their own win rate to be lower than it should be, and thus that the game is unfair. This is, of course, far more likely to happen in an environment where player ratings are

In general, when designing and implementing a mostly zero-sum system, look at all conditions where the system might become positive or negative sum, and be aware of the potential for inflation or deflation. Average rating among active players is a useful metric to track over time, in order to identify how ratings are changing for real. If true inflation or deflation is identified, the designer can then seek the source of the change over time, and eliminate or counteract it. This is also much less of a problem with ratings that are reset regularly (as with season play), because player ratings don't survive to the point where inflation or deflation would be noticeable in the long term.

Handling Draws

In some games, draws are impossible. For example, in tournament *Go*, the second player is given some number of points to compensate for the minor disadvantage of going second, and this number includes a fraction. Since points in *Go* are otherwise integer, one player always wins.

In other games, draws can happen, but require skill. In *Chess*, draws are quite common at the highest levels of play, but a novice would not be likely to draw with a grandmaster.

One might imagine a game where a lesser player can force a draw if they focus more on not losing than on winning. In such a case, treating a draw as half a win (as most rating systems do) might be unfair: a low-skill player could virtually guarantee a rating gain by simply challenging high-rated players and playing to draw. The game designer might make an effort to change the rules of the game to prevent this situation, but if there is a valid reason for it, then the rating system would need to be restructured to place less emphasis on draws. Instead of treating a draw as 0.5 wins, for example, a draw might simply be ignored, with no rating gain or loss by either player, regardless of their relative ratings prior to starting. Or, if the higher skill player can still win sometimes even if the lesser player is trying to force a draw, the rating system could consider draws as a separate calculation from a win/loss situation, and the points gained or lost from a draw would depend on the expected number of draws compared to wins for a give ratings difference.

Multiplayer Games

Elo assumes a head-to-head game between exactly two players. In games that support more than two players, new tricks have to be devised, as with TrueSkill™. While there are many different relationships between players in multiplayer games, the sort of competition that lends itself to a rating system usually falls into one of two categories: free-for-all and teams.

In a **free-for-all** game, multiple players are all playing against each other at once. Each player is fighting on their own behalf, with no teamwork or alliances. A "deathmatch" mode in an FPS or a car racing game would be examples. In these games, the designer must determine what the best predictors of player performance are, and this varies from one game to another. The expected outcome might just depend on the average ratings of the opponents, or it might be dominated by the strongest opponent, or the weakest, or some other weighting of opponents.

In a **team** game, two or more players are grouped together with shared goals and a shared victory or loss. Two or more teams compete with one another, mimicking a head-to-head or free-for-all environment where each "player" is actually a team of players. The question here is what determines the overall strength and expected performance of a team. Each player on a team contributes, of course, but can a single strong player dominate the gameplay and carry an otherwise weak team to victory? Or in the opposite situation, can a single weak player manage to torpedo their own team, even if every other player is highly skilled? The team's overall rating might simply be the mean of the ratings of the individual players, or it might be weighted in one direction or the other. An additional consideration for team games is familiarity; a set of teammates that has played together many times and that works well together might be able to outperform a team of strangers who have never coordinated together before, but who individually are more skilled at the game than the opposition.

Disconnection

In online games in particular, an additional question is how to handle situations where one player loses their connection to the game in the middle of play. This might happen unintentionally if a player's internet connection chooses a bad time to go down, or it might happen temporarily through a random internet hiccough, or it might be intentional if a player is losing and decides to pull the plug out of frustration or spite. What happens to a player's rating if they or their opponent loses their connection to the game and fails to reconnect? How should this be handled in a two-player head-to-head game, or a free-for-all game, or a team game? What feels the most fair to players, given that it's difficult to tell the difference between an accidental disconnection and an intentional one?

Here are some options for a two-player game:

- Do not count the game as a rated game at all. Players who are about to lose have incentive to disconnect on purpose to avoid a loss, frustrating their opponent.
- Count the game as a loss for the player who disconnects and a win for the player who is still connected. Players with unstable connections become frustrated at losing when they lose a game they should have won simply because of a lost connection, and some players may try to find ways to use denial-of-service attacks to knock their opponents out of the game to claim an easy win. (Notably, this also adds an additional luck factor to the game, since there is a non-zero chance that either player might lose their connection and thus lose the game. The rating system might take this into account, although it does not impact all players equally, since some players have more stable connections than others.)
- Have an AI bot take over for the player who lost their connection, and have the game result stand. Less abusable than the above, but requires the developers to implement a reasonably competent AI, which may be very difficult (or they implement a terrible AI, such that a disconnect is essentially a loss in all but the most extreme situations, in which case it's the same as the previous option except with a lot more development work).
- Create some kind of algorithm to evaluate who is winning and by how much given any particular game state. When a player disconnects, use this algorithm to determine a partial winner. Players could then proceed to play with strategies designed to take an early lead and then disconnect on purpose before the opponent can come back.

With team games, the dynamics get even more complicated. If one player on a team loses their connection but the game continues, the rest of their team gets unfairly penalized. If the game simply ends when one player loses their connection, too many ten-player games may not play to completion.

Some of this can be mitigated in the automated matchmaking system, by not only matching people based on player rating, but also historical disconnect rate, or other metrics of general connection stability. Players can be matched with others who are of similar stability. In a large game that has multiple servers set up around the world, players can also be matched with others of similar ping times, which makes it less likely that one player has an unfair advantage in an action game due only to a faster connection, and less likely that any player loses connection if there are fewer machines to go through between players and the game server. It can also be minimized by finding ways to give players a reasonable amount of time to reconnect (so that a single dropped packet doesn't spell doom for an individual).

Speaking of servers, there are additional considerations depending on whether players connect directly to each other during a match or if they connect through a server. When players play through servers owned by the game's owner, it's easier to at least know which player lost their connection, and the game can also hide players' IP addresses from one another (to avoid a malicious player directly destroying their opponent's connection through a denial-of-service attack). If players connect directly to one another, and the players lose connection to each other, it's more difficult to even know who dropped and who didn't. Players can attempt to reconnect to the game server to upload their results, on the theory that if one player is no longer online, then they can't reach your server, which tells you who lost their connection and who didn't. But what if the problem was simply the connection between the two players, and *both* reconnect to the server without problems? Or, what if one player intentionally drops their network connection to avoid a loss and then re-establishes their connection just as it's time to reach your server (yes, there are players who are not above doing this sort of thing)?

Still, the question of what happens in case of a completely lost connection is something that must be answered by the designer. There may not be any perfect solutions, but at least you can pick your poison.

Cheating

In general, if it is at all possible to cheat the system, some players will make the attempt. It is therefore up to the designer to anticipate as many ways of abusing the rating system as possible, and add countermeasures to prevent it.

Cheating is a big deal in any game, but particularly in games that are competitive by nature, that have online communities, and especially in games where there are perks or prestige to doing well (such as invite-only tournaments to top-rated players with cash prizes). If it is discovered that a major tournament winner was cheating, that destroys player credibility in your tournament system, and players may leave the game if they feel like they can't compete fairly when there is rampant cheating among their opponents. Expect your team to spend a lot of time dealing with cheating in one form or another.

Simply leaving it to Community Management to catch cheaters and ban them from the game is not an ideal solution. It creates a heavy support burden and puts the onus of punishing players on the shoulders of the very people who are meant to provide customer service and support.

If players can choose their opponents, they might collaborate with friends to throw games. Each player might own several game accounts, one primary account to play competitively, and other throwaway accounts to provide cheap wins for their friends. Players could trade off, intentionally losing with their alternate account against their friend's main account and then vice versa. Players might also bribe other opponents to take a dive in exchange for in-game or real-world money (whether they follow through on their promise or not). Automated matchmaking and keeping players relatively anonymous makes this much harder.

If the rating system has any elements that are positive sum, such as a rating floor or "bonus points" for playing certain types of games, expect players to gravitate toward those elements and exploit them. Keeping the rating system zero sum prevents such exploits from existing. Of course, that is assuming that rating is what players are trying to maximize. In a game where MMR is hidden and the player's rank is what is shown, players seek cheats and exploits to maximize their rank (for example, if it's possible to have a high rank regardless of rating, a player might intentionally play in such a way as to *lower* their rating as much as possible, so they can get easier games from the matchmaking system).

Ratings as Outcome Prediction

In all zero-sum rating systems, it would be expected that a player at a certain skill level would have a rating that stayed more or less constant, unless they got demonstrably better or worse at the game. For the two-player case, if a player would gain X points for a win and lose Y points for a loss against a particular opponent, then the rating system is predicting that the probability of a win is

$$P(\text{win}) = \frac{Y}{X + Y}$$

Note that for the opponent, the probability would be $X/(X+Y)$, and the two probabilities would sum to 1 as expected. Also note the extremes. If $Y=0$, this means that the player would lose no points for a loss, suggesting that they are expected to lose and would thus not be penalized for losing; $P(\text{win})$ then becomes 0, regardless of the value of X. If instead $X=0$, this means the player would gain no points for a win, because they are expected to win every time; $P(\text{win})$ becomes Y/Y, which is 1, no matter what the value of Y is.[6]

Additional Predictors of Outcome

In reality, there are many factors that may contribute to a game's outcome, other than just player ratings. If these are not taken into account in the rating system, the ratings become inaccurate to some degree. Luck is one of these factors, which has already been discussed in this chapter, but there are others.

For games that allow a player to choose some game objects to start the game with—a constructed deck in a CCG, a character build in an MMO, a hero in a MOBA, or a character chosen in a fighting or brawling game— these create a mismatch to some degree from the beginning. A weak player who plays with a tournament-winning deck in a CCG may very well be able to outplay a strong player who uses a poorly constructed deck, for example. An online game may already have analytics hooks to collect data used to inform balance decisions made by game designers, such as the correlation between each game object, character, or strategy, and win rate. While most rating systems do not take this into account, it would theoretically be possible to factor these data into its expected outcome calculations when determining rating gain or loss.

For team games, the outcome may not just come down to individual players and their chosen game objects, but also how well those work together. In a MOBA, certain characters may have good synergy with each other, and a team with several characters that support each other well may be stronger than just the sum of its parts. As above, this information should be collected

---

[6] Technically, if X and Y are both zero, then $P(\text{win}) = 0/0$ which is undefined. However, there should not be a situation where the player is expected to both win *and* lose.

for analysis anyway, and factoring that into the rating could lead to a more accurate measure of outcome.

Another factor in team games is how well players on a team know each other. An established team of friends who play together a lot, know how to coordinate, and are used to reading each other's signals and responding fluidly to one another, may be able to take on a stronger team of strangers who do not have that level of teamwork. For games that allow players to choose their team, the game could keep track of how many games each player has played with each of their teammates, with higher numbers being counted as an effectively higher rating.

For games that end in more than just a binary win/loss state, final standings could speak to the relative skill of players. In a game of *Magic: the Gathering*, each player starts with 20 life; a player who still has all 20 life at the end of the game could be thought of as winning more solidly than a player who won the game with just 1 life remaining. In this way, rating systems might not only be used to predict the winner of a game, but also the point spread, and the difference in final scores could be used to further inform the ratings.

Similarly, player performance over time could be tracked in a game. Some highly skilled players, being good sports, are loathe to aggressively stomp their opponents into the ground, as they would not want an opponent to get frustrated and quit the game. Instead, they may play suboptimally in order to give their opponent the perception of a close game. In such a game, one player would be seen to pull ahead early on in the game and maintain a narrow lead throughout the entire experience. Such a pattern, if detected, would suggest a great deal of skill by the winning player, as they are able not only to win but to also control their opponent's experience.

Proving the System

Suppose you design a custom rating system for a game you are working on. How do you know if it is working properly? Once the game is released, how do you know if the ratings are accurate? We would like to know if our systems are any better than a random shot in the dark, after all.

You might be tempted to run a mathematical simulation on the rating system. For example, a programmer could code a simulation with a few thousand players that are each assigned a "true" rating that reflects their actual skill, and then that pairs players off into matches with opponents based on the matchmaking system. The simulation would then calculate an expected win rate based on the difference in true rating, generate a pseudorandom number to choose a result, and then use the rating system to update each player's system rating. By taking the difference between the system rating and the true rating, you can measure the error in the system. You could then track, for example, the **root-mean-square error** across all players (take each individual player's error, square it, take the mean average of all of these errors by adding them up then dividing by the number of players, then take the square root of that sum) and graph that in an initial state, and then after one game played by each player, then two games, then three games, and so on. This would give you a general idea of how many games each player would have to play before their rating was considered relatively accurate, and would also give a general sense of how much error is inherent in the system once it reaches steady state (there's always be some error, as a player who is currently at their "true" rating gains or lose points the next time they play a game, increasing their error).

While those numbers are useful, particularly when comparing two proposed systems to see which is more accurate or which one allows players to converge on their true rating faster, this method cannot be used to mathematically prove that the rating system is an accurate model that correctly predicts win rate. That is because the simulation must, by necessity, use the same model as the rating system itself. If the model you're using is not the same as what actually happens, you can't diagnose that with a simulation.

Using analytics is better for gauging the accuracy of your system, but doing so is not trivial. Unlike a simulation, you do not actually know the "true" ratings of your players, so there is no way to compute error in the system directly. However, what you *can* do is compare the expected win rate from the rating system to the actual win rate across all players, to see where your system is overestimating or underestimating the true win rate, and by how much.

If error is found that alone doesn't tell you the source, but by looking at subsets of match results, you can derive some useful information about the game. For games with some luck, you can look at extreme mismatches in skill and see how often an upset occurs; double that percentage to get the luck factor (since half of the time, luck favors the player who is expected to win anyway). In games with teams, you can look at only games where one team is all strangers and the other team is entirely players who have played together many times, to measure the amount that team experience plays a role in the outcome. For free-for-all games, you can look at the relationship between final standings and player rating in order to determine how often a player ranks differently in the game outcome than would be expected. If there are additional factors such as whether skilled players win by a greater margin, those are questions that can be asked of match results data.

Ideally, the programming team can add in analytics hooks for these things during beta, and this data can be collected and analyzed before the game is released (and before the rating system is even implemented). The data can then be used to design a fair system that can predict game outcomes as accurately as possible, and that can then be used for matchmaking to give players the most exciting and challenging games possible.

Ranking Systems

If the rating is displayed to players, and particularly if there are leaderboards or other status symbols that are based entirely off of rating, this matters a great deal to players. Since the vast majority of players are *not* in the Top Ten, and since (by definition) half of players are below the median rating, a great many players become demoralized if the game tells them so.[7]

For this reason, many online games use ratings purely as an internal metric for use in automated matchmaking, and do not display ratings to anyone. By hiding this information, players who are not particularly good at the game have less of a sense of where they stand. If they keep getting matches with other players at their skill level, they still win about half of their games and thus still feel competent (and engaged).

If ratings are hidden, then rankings can be an alternative way to give players some token of status or standing. Ranking systems are incredibly versatile, and there are many options, depending on the design goals and purpose they are meant to serve. In this section, we examine some of the design knobs available with rank.

Granularity

Rank can operate at either a high granularity or a low granularity. A high-granularity rank would be to give the player the exact number of their rank within the player base ("You are ranked #3,487 out of 65,234 players"). A low-granularity rank would simply give players a large range, and they would know they are somewhere in that range (Bronze/Silver/Gold/Diamond/Platinum).

Having a high granularity can help to clarify ratings by letting a player know exactly where they stand. This can be particularly useful for the few

---

[7]In fact, Valve has said that player opinions of the MMR system in *DOTA 2* are highly correlated with their recent win rates; see http://blog.dota2.com/2013/12/matchmaking/.

players at the very top (say, the best 5%), the players who would be eligible to join invitational tournaments, for example. Only showing high granularity at the very top has some additional benefits: merely becoming ranked via ordinal number is a significant milestone for top-tier players; and if players are only given their rank without further information, it need not betray the exact number of players of your game (some companies wish to keep exact player counts secret for various reasons).

Having a low granularity serves to mystify ratings by only giving a player a general sense of where they are. This can be useful for players who are *not* in the top tier, but who enjoy playing the game anyway. For these players, having a very general rank lets them feel like there is something they can work toward, without feeling like they are bad players. Designers can even make it so that only a very small percentage of players are in the lowest ranks, so that even weak players can feel like they aren't at the very bottom.

Community

Rank can be displayed to players as a global attribute (compared to all other players of the game worldwide), or some subset of players to have a more local feel. Players might, for example, be able to view the 30 players immediately above and below them in the global ranks, to see those who are closest to them. Players might see the relative rankings of those in their Guild, or those players who are in their Friends list, or those who play on the same server, or even those who are in the same physical city as they are. A game might display only one of these or several. The benefit of multiple ranking lists is that the player can be closer to the top on some of them, even if there can only be one #1 ranked player worldwide; the drawback is that multiple lists can be confusing if players aren't sure which is the "real" or "official" one that they should pay the most attention to.

How rank is displayed can also make a difference in the player's perception of their own ability, which affects such things as player retention and monetization. For example, if a game selectively shows a player near the bottom of their friends list in friend rankings, that might give the player an incentive to spend money to gain an advantage in the game so they can beat their friends. If the player is participating in a time-limited event like a tournament where their tournament rank is displayed to them, showing them increasing their rank early on in response to their play can make them feel like they're a good player, and if they appear to get outpaced by some other players (and thus fall in rank) later on, that could also drive sales of items they could use to regain their lost spots and place better in the tournament. On the other hand, showing a player that they are at or near the bottom of global rankings with no apparent change over time could lead to them simply quitting the game in frustration—which might be intentional if they haven't monetized and are just taking up the game company's bandwidth, or undesirable if their presence has other positive effects on the game. In theory, a game might even display ranks to a player that are inaccurate, and designed solely to influence their perception, though no game developers thus far have admitted publicly to doing so.

Permanence

Rank might be a lifetime attribute that stays with a player forever, as rating typically is. If rank is based purely on rating, this is usually the case. But rank can also be a separate system and thus be subject to occasional resets that put everyone back on the same playing field.

There are several benefits to regular rank resets. It gives players the perception that with every new **season** of play (a fixed period of time where ranked play is contained within that time), they have as good a chance as anyone else of rising to the top. It gives players a sense of progression, rather than the stagnation of a lifetime rating that stays relatively stable over time. Since players have to play again after a reset to regain their former rank, resets give players incentive to play the game on a regular basis; for players who felt like they had reached their peak before, a reset gives them a reason to come back and try again. For these reasons, seasonal play is quite common, particularly in online PvP games.

Subjectivity

In online games, most ranking systems are completely objective, based on player rating, game results, or other measures of performance. It is worth noting that in some professional sports, rankings of individuals or teams are subjective, assigned by a panel of expert judges who each may have their own systems, personal opinions, or whims. Fans of the sport may disagree with these experts, making the rankings a subject of much debate—particularly if the rankings are put to practical use, such as for initial tournament seeding.

Progression

There are many ways for players to go up or down in ranking, and the method chosen is at the core of how the ranking system operates. The simplest and most obvious is to tie rank to rating: simply order all players from the highest rating to the lowest and that is their high-granularity rank. For a low-granularity rank, either group people into specific numerical ranges for rating or divide into percentiles. The limitation with this is that it makes it more difficult to reset rank, without resetting the rating and thus reducing the usefulness of automated matchmaking to generate close matches.

Another well-known ranking system is a ladder system, where players gain rank by challenging and beating players with a rank above their own. There are many ways to handle this. Here are but a few examples:

- In a local *Chess* club, players might be paired in a ladder game, where each player is either matched with the player immediately above or immediately below them. If the lower-ranked player wins, they move up and the two players swap ranks; otherwise, the ranks remain unchanged. Games alternate so that a player in the same rank challenges up in one game and down in the next.
- In an online game with automated matchmaking, two players attempt to be matched with the closest rankings possible. If the lower-ranked person wins, they immediately move up to the higher-ranked player's position, and everyone else between the two players moves down 1. If the higher-ranked player wins, then both players stay where they are.
- In an online game where players can challenge one another, any player can issue a challenge to any other player. The winner moves up one rank, swapping places with the player immediately above them; the loser stays where they are.

The primary benefit of ladder systems is that the name alone suggests climbing a ladder, giving players an expectation and sense of progression. Additionally, at least half of the games played are usually free of risk; players challenging a higher position on the ladder typically either move up or stay where they are, but they do not lose standing if they fail. This provides a perception of safety.

The down side of ladders is that there can only be one player at the very top, which means everyone else feels disappointed. It can be demoralizing for players to feel like they're on a treadmill where they must play games not only to advance, but in some cases merely to maintain their current position. Climbing the ladder from the bottom is easy, but climbing further after reaching the halfway point is challenging for a majority of players.

Hearthstone has an interesting ranking system worthy of analysis as a case study. In this system, players start at rank 25. Each rank has a number of stars (the first ranks have two stars, progressively increasing to five stars per rank as a player improves), and winning a game grants a star. When all stars in the current rank are filled and a player gains another star, they increase to the next rank (24, then 23, and so on up to rank 1).

For ranks 25 through 20, players cannot lose stars, so a player who plays enough games eventually wins enough to get out of the bottom ranks. Since the system attempts to match players of equal rank and similar rating, players would be expected to win about half of their games at any point, so it would only be a matter of time before they progressed to rank 20. This gives just about all active players a sense of progression and of competence. By the time players get to the point where they can lose stars from losing games, they are already several ranks up from the bottom.

Up to rank 5, players gain a star for winning and lose a star for losing, but they also gain an additional bonus star if they won their last two games (i.e., if their current win streak is at least three games long, including the current game). The bonus stars for win streaks serve several purposes. One is that top-tier players can reach the top ranks much more quickly after a ranking reset, so players do not feel so bad about having to climb up again if they can make rapid progress initially. Another is that even a player who wins half of their games eventually makes slow progress up the ranks: assuming each game is an independent coin flip, occasional win streaks and loss streaks are expected, and every time that happens, the player has a net gain of stars. For example, if a player wins three in a row and then loses three in a row, they gain three stars for the wins and an additional bonus star for the last game of the win streak, and lose three stars for the losses, for a net gain of one star. Note that players gain extra stars for win streaks, but they do *not* lose extra stars for losing streaks—players only lose a maximum of one star per game, period.

On a monthly basis, ranks are reset. Upon logging in after the reset, players are immediately rewarded for the rank they achieved in the previous month, giving an incentive to log in and also to play to the highest rank they can manage in the following month. Players are also given bonus stars and ranks based on their prior standing, so that they do not start at the very bottom if they performed well. As with win streaks, starting higher saves time for the highly skilled players so that they do not have to play through the bottom ranks again. This type of reset makes players feel rewarded rather than punished (even if their rank is being lowered as a result) and also gives a constant sense of progression as players are regularly climbing the ranks, then getting knocked down after a reset and climbing again.

As you can see from this example, ranking systems can serve several purposes: as a progression system (particularly if they are perpetually being reset), a reward system (either a one-time reward if rankings are permanent or an ongoing reward if they are reset), a dominance system (players can strive to be better than their friends or to be Number One within their circle of friends or even worldwide), and also to clarify ratings *or* mystify them, depending on which of the two is more meaningful and enjoyable.

Tournament and League Play

Some games lend themselves to organized competitive events. As these events often have in-game or even real-world prizes associated with them, as well as high-level events being watched by many fans of the world's best players, it is important that players feel the event format is fair and does not give an inherent advantage to any of the players. There are many formats, each with their own quirks. We examine a few of the more popular ones presently.

Round Robin

The simplest and most fair format for tournaments is **round robin**, where every player plays against every other player. Players are ranked by win/loss record. For players with identical records, there may be a tiebreaking method,[8] a playoff game among the tied players, or they may share their standing and be considered equivalent. The main down side of a round robin is time; for an N-player tournament, there would have to be $N-1$ games played, making this impractical for more than a handful of players.

Single Elimination

A much shorter format is **single elimination**, where players are paired off against one another and the loser of a game is eliminated from the tournament while the winner continues on. For a two-player game, a single elimination tournament requires only $\log_2 N$ rounds for N players (that is, a four-player tournament takes two rounds; an eight-player tournament takes three rounds; a 16-player tournament takes four rounds; and so on).

Single elimination format requires deciding three things: pairings, draw games, and byes.

---

[8]One example of a fair tiebreaker is to take two players who were tied with one another and look at the record of games between those players. If players A and B tied in their overall record, and A won against B, then rank A higher. However, if the players drew against each other or if three or more players have identical records against each other, there would have to be an additional method to fall back on, such as performance against the top-ranked player (and then second-top ranked, and so on down the list). An alternative would be to use player ratings as a tiebreaker, but that gives high-rated players an inherent advantage going into the tournament that comes from outside their tournament performance, and might be considered unfair.

Pairings for a single elimination tournament are typically made ahead of time in a **bracket**, such that each pair of players plays their game, and then, the winner is written in the next round. For example, here is a sample tournament bracket for a 16-player single elimination tournament.

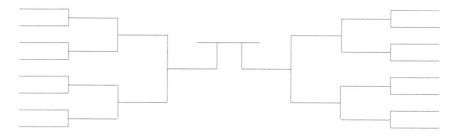

Players can be written in the outer leaves on the left and right sides. A completed bracket might look like this.

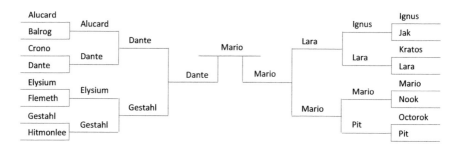

The initial pairings of players (referred to as the **seeding**, though the term is unrelated to pseudorandom number seeds) have a strong effect on the expected outcome of the tournament. For example, suppose if you ranked the players by actual skill, that each player has a 1% advantage per rank above their opponent; thus, the best player wins 65% and loses 35% of their games against the worst in a 16-person tournament. Here are two possible tournament seedings, where the number is the player's rank.

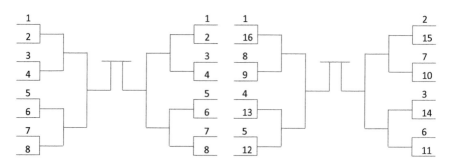

In the seeding on the left, the rank 1 player (the most skilled) does have the greatest chance of winning, but the rank 8 player has a far lower chance of winning the tournament than the rank 9 player (because 8 has to go through three matchups against better opponents, while 9 has three matches against worse opponents, just to make it to the final round). The seeding on the right does not have this problem; each player's probability of winning is higher than those ranked below them and lower than those ranked above them.

Knowing the relative player skill ahead of time for a fair seeding is, of course, not trivial. In a game with a global rating or ranking system, players can be seeded based on their ratings or rankings at time of tournament entry. If no such information is available, players might play a few preliminary rounds for the purpose of establishing a seeding, or players might be assigned randomly.

Once a fair seeding is established, the tournament organizer must still decide how to handle draws, in games where a draw is possible. Since elimination tournaments expect one player in each pair to drop out each round, what happens if both (or neither) are eliminated? The players could continue playing games until a definite winner is determined, but that may be impractical if a single match can delay everyone else indefinitely. Depending on the game, players might be able to start a new game in some kind of "sudden death" mode that plays quickly and does not allow for draws, or certain metrics in the game might be used to break a tie and determine a winner (such as the player with the greatest number of resources in play).

A final challenge is how to handle a tournament bracket where the total number of players is not a power of 2. In this case, the typical solution is to give the highest-ranked players a **bye** in the first round, meaning they do not play a match and automatically advance to the second round. Since the highest-ranked players would normally be paired against the lowest-ranked anyway, giving them byes causes the lowest chance of skewing the tournament results. (If players are paired randomly, then byes may also be assigned randomly; since this is a luck-based advantage, those players may be given some minor disadvantage to compensate in later rounds, such as automatically losing tiebreakers.)

Double Elimination

One disadvantage of single elimination is that in games with some amount of chance, a good player may be eliminated through bad luck in spite of strong play. As such, it may be desired to give players the ability to lose one game before being eliminated. The way to do this is with a **double elimination** format: there is one main bracket as with single elimination, but then there is also a loser's bracket that starts empty and is seeded from the losses in the main bracket each round. Eventually, the main bracket has one player remaining, and the loser's bracket also has one player who reaches the top. The top players in each bracket then play each other, with the main bracket player having to lose two games to be eliminated, and the loser's bracket player only having to lose one.

One could also envision additional loser brackets to have a triple elimination, quadruple elimination, or other similar formats; however, the bookkeeping becomes unwieldy, so higher-order elimination tournaments are rare. There are other formats that have similar characteristics, as we'll see shortly.

Swiss

Another disadvantage of single elimination is that half of the players get eliminated each round, so many players who might want to play a lot of games walk away having played only one or two. Double elimination doesn't do much to fix this problem; it just adds one extra game for everyone. For an all-day event, a compromise might be sought where players can play a lot of games but fewer than would be required for round robin. One such solution is a **Swiss** tournament (named after its country of origin).

In a Swiss tournament, all players are paired in a series of rounds, such that all players play the same total number of games. In the first round, players might be paired randomly, or seeded by player ratings or a similar metric.[9] After each subsequent round, players are ranked by their win/loss record (typically with a series of tiebreakers for players with identical records).[10] For each

---

[9] In the McMahon system (named after its creator), used in some *Go* tournaments, players are initially seeded with some points based on their rating, as if they came into the tournament having won some games already. While this may seem to give an unfair advantage to those who are already skilled, the practical benefit is that it pairs the more skilled players against one another in the early rounds, rather than having a few hapless players be paired against the best of the best early on and start off with one foot in the grave already. In such a case, the number of rounds would need to be high enough that a player starting with zero points due to rating would still conceivably be able to win the tournament if they win all of their games.

[10] While win/loss record is the most common method, technically Swiss players can be ranked according to any kind of cumulative score during the tournament. Often, "score" simply means 1 point for a win, 0.5 points for a draw, and 0 points for a loss; but in a game where players receive a final score (such as *Go* or *Scrabble* or *Bridge*), a tournament organizer could conceivably use game scores or some other metric to determine tournament score, allowing a player with strong performance in a match to reap further benefits than merely +1 point for a win.

round, players are paired with an opponent ranked close to them.[11] The process is repeated for however many rounds were chosen for the tournament, and the ranks after the last round are the final standings—best rank wins.

Since Swiss has no player elimination and no brackets, it can easily handle a number of players that is not a power of 2. At most, in any given round there is a single bye, if there are an odd number of players (although the tournament organizer needs to find a fair way to assign the bye, and also to decide how to count a bye since players are ranked on cumulative win/loss record). On the other hand, if there is an odd number of players, there is a bye in every round, as opposed to elimination where there are multiple byes on the first round and then never again.

The primary disadvantage of Swiss formats is complexity in determining pairings. Players must be scored, ranked, and reordered in real time after every round, typically using multiple tiebreakers and other exceptions to determine who plays who. The game designer has a great deal of control over how these algorithms are put together, and a number of established formats already exist, each with their own benefits and drawbacks relative to the others.

Hybrid

Note that for the purposes of determining a single winner, an N-player Swiss tournament with $\log_2 N$ rounds is the same length and gives the same result as a single elimination tournament. A Swiss tournament with $N-1$ rounds is a round-robin tournament. At fewer or greater than $\log_2 N$ rounds, it is nearly guaranteed that there are multiple players tied for top score, leading to the anticlimactic result of a winner being determined by tiebreaker algorithm. Swiss tournaments also often lack the exciting climax of the top two players facing off in the final round that an elimination format features.

For this reason, some Swiss tournaments start by playing for a certain number of rounds and then take the top four, or eight, or sixteen players into

---

[11] There are several potential methods of pairing players in Swiss. In the Dutch system, players are paired off against others of the same cumulative score, and within a single matching score, the player in the top half of the rankings with that score is paired against the corresponding player in the bottom half. For example, if there are six players that have a record of 2-1-0 (two wins, one loss, zero draws), the top ranked and fourth ranked of those six would play together, as would the second and fifth rank, and the third and sixth. In the Monrad system, top rank plays against second, third against fourth, fifth against sixth, and so on. There are plenty of other systems for pairing, as well. In each case, pairings may be further modified to prevent anyone from playing the same opponent twice, and to prevent any player from receiving more than one bye.

a final elimination tournament (seeded by Swiss rank). This gives, in some ways, the best of both worlds: a lengthy Swiss tournament without elimination that allows everyone to play plenty of games, while providing useful performance data that can be used to seed an elimination bracket. The final winners then must earn their victory through defeating the opposition, rather than simply being crowned by tiebreaker.

Other tournament formats might likewise be combined.

League and Season Play

While a tournament typically takes place over a single day or other short time period, **leagues** are organized as a group of players who play on a regular basis over an extended period of time (typically one or more months, up to a year). A league can be thought of as a tournament with many rounds and thus can follow any of the same formats, though typically not elimination since players are meant to play a lot of games. At the conclusion of the time period for the league, players are ranked and a winner determined based on overall performance throughout the league.

Leagues offer something partly between a tournament system and a rating system. In fact, a league could be run using a rating system rather than a tournament system, giving each player the same provisional rating at the start of the league and then treating the highest-rated player the winner at the end of the league.

As mentioned earlier, some games offer seasons. A season is like a league, except that when one season ends, another one begins, so that there is always a season in progress. The term is borrowed from professional sports, although in that case, there is usually one season per year with off-season play the rest of the year. With online games, there would generally not be months at a time between seasons, however; designers want their players to be playing regularly, without having long stretches of time where they might leave and not come back. Each season is typically treated independently, although the winners of one season might receive some slight starting bonus in the next season.

Handling Dropouts

In just about any tournament of sufficient size, at least one player is likely to leave early, whether due to life obligations, frustration at several early losses, or any number of other reasons. A tournament organizer must decide how their format should handle players that sign up, play a few games, and then leave before the conclusion of the event.

In round robin tournaments, players who exit can simply be removed, and any prior games played against them nullified. Alternately, players who won or lost against them before they left could have that information used (among other possible factors) to break ties at the end.

In elimination tournaments, a player leaving creates a gap in the bracket. The most obvious way to deal with this is to treat that player's next opponent as getting a bye, although in theory, the entire bracket could be restructured to give the bye to the top-seeded player who has not yet received a bye. Note that as more players are eliminated and only the strongest performers remain, late-round byes are more valuable than first-round byes, as they allow a player to bypass what was likely a strong opponent.

In Swiss tournaments, a player who leaves can be removed from the rankings, and pairings of future rounds would simply leave them out. Since players are already ranked according to win/loss record and then paired according to rank, a player leaving should have no effect on future pairings. If a single player leaves, they may affect whether byes are being given each round. Also, if one of the tiebreakers involves looking at the performance of each player's opponents, this would have to be defined for opponents who walked out early.

Metagame Reward Systems

In most free-to-play games, there is some form of in-game currency system (sometimes two currencies, one that is regular and one that can only be received easily through cash purchase or rarely through play). In the context of competitive games, a typical pattern is to unlock or add content available to the player through spending in-game currency. It's worth examining the design purpose behind this.

Part of the point of asking players to pay is, obviously, to make money. Game developers have to eat, after all. But many players have little tolerance for games where they essentially just pay to win, and those systems tend to be unsatisfying: players who pay to gain an advantage win some games initially, but then if they start consistently gaining rating, they eventually just rise to a level with all of the other paid players. At that point they no longer have an advantage over their peers; they have paid just to play games with other people who have paid.

Because the perception of "pay-to-win" is a negative one, players typically expect that they can eventually have the same capabilities whether they pay or not. If that is the case, the question for the game designer becomes: what do players earn in-game currency for doing? In general, the answer is anything that you want players to have incentive to do (which, in turn, means things that add value to your game in lieu of money). Three general categories you may want to reward include

- Playing against other human opponents. Players who actually play the game are essentially serving your game as a crowdsourced AI. They are providing entertainment and challenge to their opponents, whether or not said opponents are players who paid.
- Logging in on a regular basis. By making the game a regular and habitual part of a player's normal activities, other positive things tend to happen from that. Players typically do not log in, collect a bonus, and then leave immediately, even if the login bonus is all they initially came to do; there are usually other things they can do as long as they are there, and spending time in your game means adding value to the community. Players who come back frequently may also eventually be enticed to spend money.
- Performing other activities that pay the developer directly. The most obvious example is watching ads in the game, where the developer gets paid for each advertisement that is watched in its entirety.

Having an in-game currency system means that the game designer is free to use that as a reward for just about anything, however. For example, if the game has a ranking system that focuses on progression (with monthly resets), giving in-game currency for increasing rank can be one way to reward players for playing the game, without simply giving players money per game played. This makes players feel like they have earned their gold rather than simply chasing an incentive, since increasing their rank is probably something they wanted to do anyway. Similarly, players can be rewarded for playing in and winning tournaments (the dynamics can get interestingly complex if players also have to pay to enter those tournaments).

Giving players daily "quests" to win games or otherwise engage in certain in-game behaviors can benefit the game in multiple ways. Obviously, these give players an incentive to log in regularly to check and complete their quests. If the quests involve playing games, then it is also an incentive to play. And if it isn't just "win three games" but has some other requirement (such as playing with a particular character or strategy, with different ones being featured over time), that gives players incentive to explore the game's systems and appreciate some elements they may not have noticed otherwise.

Discussion Questions

1. What's the difference between a ranking system and a rating system?
2. What are the advantages and disadvantages of ranking systems vs. rating systems?
3. Choose any PvP game that doesn't have an official rating or matchmaking system. If you were going to design one, what considerations would you have to tailor a system to this particular game?
4. If you looked at an esport's match results and found that upsets happened more frequently than predicted by the rating system, what might that suggest about the game and the rating system?
5. Why might a game company choose to show or hide the MMR from players?
6. What are some possible causes of rating inflation?
7. What are the advantages and disadvantages of single elimination, round robin, and Swiss tournaments, compared to each other?
8. How might a rating system be changed to incentivize play?
9. How might a rating system be changed to deincentivize play?
10. How does a tournament's method of matchmaking (e.g. initial seeding in an elimination tournament) affect the outcome?

Sidequests

Sidequest 14.1: Elimination

Assume an eight-player single elimination tournament, where the players coming in have varying skill levels. In particular, the best player entering the tournament has a 55% probability of beating the next best player, a 60% probability of beating the third best, and so on in 5% increments up to an 85% probability of beating the worst. Likewise, each other player has a 55% probability of beating the next best player to them, 60% probability of beating the player two positions down, and so on.

Consider the following two starting brackets, with the best player seeded to the #1 position, second best seeded to #2, etc.; calculate the probability of each player winning the tournament. Which bracket is more fair?

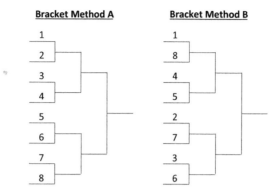

Sidequest 14.2: The Alpha Rating System

A developer has a two-player head-to-head game where players can choose who they challenge. They want to make a rating system, which they term Alpha, that gives players incentive to choose matches against others who are rated close to them.

Here is the system: let D be the difference in rating between the two players. If $D < 20$, the winner of the game gets 10 points and the loser loses 10 points. If $20 \leq D < 40$, the winner gets 9 points and the loser loses 9. For every additional 20 points of difference, the game is worth 1 fewer points, down to a minimum of 1 point per game. In short, each game puts $\max(1, 10 - \text{floor}(D/20))$ points at risk.

Does this system do what it was designed to do, making players seek out others of similar rating? If not, why not?

Hint: look at the expected value of rating gain or loss when playing against an opponent with higher, lower, or identical rating.

Sidequest 14.3: Elo with Luck

Take the Elo rating system and modify the rating change formula to be appropriate for a game where the outcome is determined 90% by skill and 10% by luck.

Sidequest 14.4: Swiss Deathmatch

Suppose you have a multiplayer deathmatch (free-for-all) game where four players battle at once. Throughout the game, players score 2 points when an opponent is killed and lose 1 point for being killed (players who are killed respawn quickly). Players start at 0 points and cannot go below 0. When any player reaches or exceeds 20 points, the game ends, with players ranked by score.

Design a Swiss tournament system for running a 16-person tournament for this game. Include how tournament scores are calculated and how players are grouped into matches, and how ties in scores are broken. Assume that you don't have to worry about odd numbers of players, nor players exiting the tournament early. Justify through any means you wish why you think your system is fair, or why players would perceive it as fair.

Greater challenge: additionally, create rules for byes if only 13–15 people show up for a tournament, and how to handle situations where one or more players drop in mid-tournament.

Wizard's Main Quest, Part 5: *Harmony* Ratings

Continuing from Part 4 in: Chapter 12

Design a complete ranking and/or rating system for *Harmony*. Justify your decisions in the design. If you're missing information (such as knowing exactly how much luck plays a role in the outcome), express that information as a variable in your rating formula, take an initial guess for what you think that variable might be, and mention how you might use analytics (see Chapter 13) to discover the value of that variable.

Part 6 continued in: Chapter 15.

15

Production and Playtesting

In This Chapter

- Balance Throughout Development
- Early Development
- The First Version
- Pre-Alpha
- Alpha
- Beta
- Post-Launch
- Playtesting for Balance

Balance throughout Development

> The first 90 percent of the code accounts for the first 90 percent of the development time. The remaining 10 percent of the code accounts for the other 90 percent of the development time.
>
> *The Ninety-Nine Rule, Tom Cargill, Bell Labs*

One of the most frequent questions that novice designers ask about balance: at what point in a game's development cycle do you start to balance the game?

It's a good question. If the core mechanics of the game change, that throws off the balance of the game entirely, and any balance work you did up to that point is largely thrown out and wasted, so it's possible to start too early.

If you wait until the very end of the development cycle, you won't have the time to balance things properly, so it's also possible to start too late.

The different methods of balance also become easier or harder over time. Early on when the game is just a rough prototype, observing a few playtesters is invaluable. Much later in development when you're nearing launch, finding enough playtesters to stick in observation chambers becomes impractical, especially if your company is doing a wider beta. Meanwhile, the use of analytics follows the opposite path: early in development, you just won't have enough analytics data to be statistically significant, but if you've got a few hundred thousand plays from a pre-release beta, that can be far more useful of a guide than just watching a few people play your game in front of you.

This chapter takes us through a full production cycle of a game from conception to post-release and talks about the kinds of tasks a game designer should be concerned with in terms of the balance of the game at each step.

Early Development

In the earliest stages of a game project, before the game is even barely playable, the mechanics are shifting wildly and constantly. The main concern here isn't having a balanced game but having a fun game or a game that otherwise meets its design goals. You want to get the "core" of the game—the moment-to-moment gameplay that's repeated throughout—to be solid. At this point, the game is changing too much for balance to be a meaningful activity. Make the game fun first, worry about balance later.

The one exception here is in the case where the game is *so* far out of balance that it's preventing meaningful playtesting. If I can't play your strategy game the way it was intended because I found a degenerate strategy exploit that lets me just win while bypassing most of the mechanics I'm supposed to engage with, then you'll need to fix that, because balance is now a blocker for your ability to meaningfully test and iterate on the game. In that case, yes, spend enough time balancing to fix the obvious killer problems. On the bright side, this is usually pretty easy: with a game *that* unbalanced, the issues are pretty obvious, and you can use some pretty blunt instruments to nerf the exploits enough to just get the game testable again (at this point, you don't have to have the game perfectly balanced, just enough that it isn't a showstopping block to your design process).

However, for the first iteration of the game you'll still need some numbers to attach to things, and you don't have any mathematical models, playtest results, or analytics data to draw from. Where do these numbers come from, when you have no basis other than your intuition?

One of the first and most important decisions you'll need to make in your game is this: either *everything* feels overpowered (but if it's all "overpowered" to the same degree, then it can still be balanced) or *nothing* is overpowered. Both can be perfectly valid approaches, depending on the game. In terms of how you want the game to *feel*, though, this question will drive your approach when it comes to choosing numbers. If you want the game to feel like an epic clash of powerful beings, the numbers you choose will tend to be on the ridiculous end. Armor that absorbs millions of hit points' worth of damage. Stackable damage bonuses that let you do so much damage in a single hit that you'll need scientific notation to display it on screen. Movement so fast that it seems instantaneous. In such a case, you'll want big numbers, big contrasts between different things in your game, and generally forcing your numbers toward the extremes (and only pulling back when absolutely necessary). For a game with a more realistic flavor, the numbers tend to be more muted, mostly tending toward a narrow range of average values, with large deviations from the range being notable exceptions that draw immediate player attention (and extra design scrutiny when you balance the game later). What you don't usually want is a game where most things are mundane and a few things are totally OP—then you end up with a game where only a small number of things matter, and everything else that you designed is seen as junk to be ignored or discarded.

After you know the extent to which you want to go wild with numeric spread, think about the purpose or role that each item plays in your game. What are the properties that define it? If you're designing a character class, what is it that they do—do they do piles of damage, do they protect the rest of the party, do they increase the amount of loot you find, or something else? If you're designing a weapon in a shooting game, is it best at long range in open terrain, close-quarters fighting in cramped tunnels, taking down large but slow-moving vehicles? If you're designing a piece of armor in an RPG, does it give protection against physical attacks or magical attacks, or does it give less protection but higher evasion to prevent getting hit at all, or giving stat bonuses to improve damage output without offering any protection at all? If you're designing a tower type for a tower-defense game, does it work best against clustered groups of enemies, single powerful boss-type enemies, armored enemies, fast-moving enemies, or does it do something else like buff nearby towers or debuff nearby enemies to make them more vulnerable to other tower types? If you're designing an enemy, is the purpose of this enemy to make the player feel strong, or clever, or afraid, or what? Think about the overall strengths and characteristics that define the thing you're designing.

Once you know what this thing is supposed to do, figure out what numbers will get it there. If you want a character class that's a "glass cannon" (does lots of damage to enemies, but can't take very much damage themselves before they fall apart), then maximize the stats that determine their damage output, minimize that stats that give them any kind of ability to soak incoming damage, and now you have the initial basis for that class. These won't be the final numbers by any means, but again, your purpose in the early stages isn't "balance" but rather, to set the tone of the game.

Since your goal is to get to a playable version of the game quickly (so that you *can* start playtesting and evaluating if it's any fun), you won't be creating all of the content for this game right now up front. If you're making a MOBA that will ultimately have 100+ playable characters, you shouldn't be designing that many in the earliest stages of development. Rather, find a small number of characters that are representative of the strategies you want to support. If, for example, you're designing the game so that most characters will fall into the three traditional roles of DPS, Tank, and Support, all you need up front is three characters to give you a general feel for the play of the game. If you can make a single "vanilla" character that is representative of every character in the game, then just make that one character as a baseline to show the general power level and set of skills that you want to balance against. Basically, create the bare minimum amount of content you can in order to have a game that can be playtested *and* that will showcase the main mechanics, strategies, and play styles that you intend to support.

Lastly, for each game object that you design at this point, you'll find it helpful to document their purpose. Write down a sentence to a paragraph about the purpose or role this particular thing has in the game, and where your "design knobs" are: what numbers can be changed, what numbers *can't* be changed, and any other design constraints that you can't violate without going against the spirit of why this object is in the game in the first place. Keep this documentation somewhere where you can find it later; when you do start balancing the game in earnest, you will almost always find that the balance is way off, and these notes will help guide you so you aren't making changes that will ultimately have to be undone later.

Remember, don't worry too much if your balance isn't perfect at this point. Your goal here is to get the game playable, get it fun, and start building your intuition for what feels good and what effects certain numbers have on play. While your initial guesses may be wildly wrong, the more you make these kinds of guesses, the better your design sense and intuition will get over time; even a "wrong" set of numbers still helps you grow as a systems designer.

First Playable

At some point (hopefully early on), you'll have the first version of the game that can actually be played in some form. The game may be broken, it may have many bugs (if it's coded on a computer), it's missing most of the content and several key systems, but you can actually sit down and play it and have some kind of experience. In the game industry we call this, intuitively enough, the **first playable** version of a game. This is where you'll start with playtesting.

Mostly, at this stage, you'll be testing with a small pool of people. For a commercial video game, the project may not have even been announced yet, so playtesting is limited to the development team only (or perhaps *very* trusted friends who have signed non-disclosure agreements). For a board game, the designer will probably be playing with their own family, friends, or (if they're lucky enough to have one) a local playtest group with a handful of players.

You still aren't testing specifically for balance, yet. You're mostly testing to see if the game is engaging, if the core mechanics work, if the vision of the game in your head is anywhere near the actual gameplay experience. (The answer to all of these questions is probably "nope, not even close"—which is why we playtest. That's fine, make changes, fix problems, repeat until it's working at a fundamental level.)

The one balance-related thing you *will* want to pay attention to here is at the macrolevel between broad strategies, character builds, or play styles, as appropriate to your game. If you have five "vanilla" character roles that are each supposed to represent a different play style, are they generally balanced against each other, or is one of these roles just inherently too strong or too weak—not from the numbers, but from how the core mechanics favor one form of play over another? If you find that, say, ranged attacks are too powerful relative to melee attacks in your game, that isn't a massive Priority One thing that must be fixed Now Now Now, but it is something you'll want to pay attention to for later and possibly adjust some of the mechanics to prevent it from getting out of hand.

As you get feedback from testers throughout development, remember that it is not the playtester's job to fix the game—it's the designer's job. The goal of a playtester should be to find problems, not solutions. Most testers, if they are not game designers, will not have the experience to be able to correctly diagnose a problem and identify the optimal solution. (Even experienced game designers aren't always great with this, if they don't already understand the big-picture vision of your overall game.) In other words,

- If a playtester says, "I don't like this particular thing about the game," that's useful information; they've alerted you to a problem. Your next step is to figure out why they don't like it, and then, what's causing this thing they don't like and addressing it at the source.
- If a playtester says, "I don't like this thing about the game, and here's why I don't like it" that's even more useful, since they've done half the work for you. All you have to do is find the root cause and take care of it.
- If a playtester says, "I think you should change this part of the game to this other thing," that is less useful, and you have twice as much work to do. First, you have to probe to figure out what element of the game the tester isn't having fun with, based on the suggestion they're making (what real or imagined problem are they trying to solve, given their suggestion?). Once you've uncovered that, *then* you can figure out why that part of the game isn't engaging them, what the cause of that is, and how to change the game to address it—and your change will usually not be the thing they suggested.

Usually, player criticisms of your game come down to this: the ideal game they're envisioning in their head is different from the one they're playing. Your goal, as the designer, is to first uncover what game they're thinking about, then deciding whether that is in fact the game you're trying to build and then changing either your game's presentation (to make it clear what kind of game you're *actually* making) or the game itself.

Pre-Alpha

Once your core mechanics are more or less solidified, here's the point where you can start creating mathematical models. You've probably done enough playtesting just to get the game fun, that you also have some general sense of what things are worth and what kind of shape you want the curves of the game to be. Balance still isn't a huge priority right now, but if you start setting up some spreadsheets with formulas to show the relationships between various mechanics in order to use it as a handy balancing tool later, you can front-load that work once you know that the mechanics aren't going to change out from under you.

Your initial spreadsheets will be wrong, of course. Just as the first numbers that come to your head are usually not perfectly balanced, the initial formulas you create to try to describe the relationships between the numbers in your game are also usually not an accurate reflection of reality. But you have to start somewhere, and the earlier you start, the more time you have to say "no, wait, this model is wrong, it's showing Poison as the most powerful spell in the game and Fireball as the weakest, that's not right at all… OH, I see, I had it treating damage over time as equivalent to immediate burst damage, here, let me discount future damage… ah, now that looks better."

Another thing you'll want to think about at this stage, if you plan on using metrics and analytics to assist with game balance later on, is to design your analytics hooks in the game. What kinds of data does the game need to collect and store, so that you can use that data later to inform your balance decisions? There are all kinds of tradeoffs to consider here: programmer time to build those analytics hooks (as opposed to spending that time actually making the game), as well as bandwidth and storage considerations (if you try to record literally *everything* and doing so drops the framerate considerably, that's a problem in a high-action game), so you may need to pick your battles on this and decide which things are the most important to record, and work that out with the programming team.

The emphasis still isn't on actively balancing the game, unless it's something that people deeply complain about during playtesting that's otherwise blocking your progress; it's on creating the tools you'll need to balance the game effectively, later on.

Alpha

There is no industry-standard definition of what, exactly, an "alpha" milestone is (it varies by company and by publishing contract), but in general, it's what we call **feature complete**, meaning that all of the mechanics are in the game, the basic engine is functional, and you can pretty much play with all the systems. The game is still missing much of its content (this is when the development content grind really goes into full swing) and the software has more bugs than an entomology lab, but at this point, the core design of the game is more or less locked down. (Changes can still be made and new features added, but after you reach alpha, those are much harder to get through, and there's often a formal Change Request process where any such additions need some serious justification since they can put the schedule of the entire game behind.)

This is where designers do much of the content grind, filling out all of the monster and item tables, character roster, dialogue trees, level layouts, and everything else that goes in the game. If you created one or more "vanilla" assets in earlier phases to test the core mechanics with, this is where you'll balance things *against* those baselines. For example, consider a fighting/brawling game like *Super Smash Bros.* which may feature over a hundred different playable characters. With a hundred characters and four players, even if two players can't choose the same character, that's still almost 4 million different matchups—far too many to individually playtest for balance. However, if there are a handful of character archetypes that have already been balanced against each other, all you have to do is balance each character against its archetype, so you only have to balance 100 matchups—much more manageable. Your initial baseline characters might not even make it into the final game; their purpose was not to be final characters, but instead to be measuring sticks to compare everything else against.

If you get every other character balanced against one of your "vanilla" archetype characters, will that make everything in the game automatically balanced against each other? Probably not, since individual character matchups may involve some natural advantages or disadvantages specific to that matchup. It is therefore possible that you'll have one character that is "balanced" in power level in theory, but that happens to have favorable matchups against a majority of other characters, and is thus unbalanced in the metagame, so you can't rest easy and assume your work is done. Still, the method of starting with a single set of baseline archetypes, then balancing everything else against the closest-match archetype, will get you in the general ballpark with the least amount of time and effort, particularly in genres like fighting games, Multiplayer Online Battle Arenas (MOBAs), and trading card games (TCGs) where you have to balance a large set of game objects against each other and won't have enough time to exhaustively test every single combination.

This phase of development is also where the mathematical balance work really starts to pick up. As you start churning out content, those spreadsheet models you created earlier will help you to produce reasonably balanced content for most things with a minimum of effort (you may have seen this firsthand back in Chapter 8, if you did any of the sidequests involving taking an existing cost curve with supporting math and using it to derive the proper costs and stats of individual items). As you create and change the numbers around, if you don't already have a good sense for how everything fits together, start by going to the extremes: if a number can be between

0 and 100, try it at 0 and 100 and then 50 to give yourself a general intuition for what it feels like, and then tune from there. When you change a number, make large changes—double or cut in half if you don't know where it needs to be, no less than 10% if you're more confident (anything less will probably not be noticeable anyway). You can use the experience you get from fiddling with numbers to build your spreadsheet models. If you don't have those mathematical models available, you'll still need to assign numbers to new things as you create them, but those numbers will probably need to be redone and you'll need to spend more time in playtesting later on.

Speaking of playtesting, that is still likely to be limited at this phase to the dev team and maybe close family and friends, but you might start asking people to test for balance specifically, trying to find exploits or otherwise break the game's systems in some way. Some people are much better at this than others. As before, your main goal here is to find the major exploits that prevent playtesting of anything else, but for the first time, you can also really start observing whether your models are accurate. If you think certain parts of the campaign mode of your game will be harder, or that certain weapons are more powerful, or whatever... see if your players agree. If your playtesters tend to gravitate toward certain strategies that seem effective but also out of line with what your models predict, this is a great time to go back and revise your models, now that you have more nuanced playtest data and an (ongoing) better understanding of your game.

As you test more, you'll also find that different testers have different strengths, and you'll learn different things from each of them. Pay attention not just to the feedback you get from a tester, but also who it's coming from. Game designer Jaime Griesemer, in a classic GDC talk (linked to at the end of this chapter), identified six particular types of testers:

- The tester who plays to win. Some testers find optimal solutions quickly and are great at breaking the balance of your game and finding overpowered exploits in your systems. If this kind of tester is using a particular character, item, strategy, etc. exclusively, that thing is probably overpowered.
- The angry tester. Some testers have a low threshold of tolerance for imbalances and will be the first to get frustrated, complain when they're losing, and (either metaphorically or literally) flip the table and ragequit if things aren't going their way. If this tester starts raging at your game, it means something is disturbing the flow of their experience; this kind of tester may feel unpleasant to be around, but is great at alerting a designer to rough spots since they're hyper-sensitive to them.

- The tester who always plays the same way. Some testers have a single preferred strategy that they always gravitate toward because it's their favorite, and whenever left to their own, they'll always try the same approach. You'll ideally want to find several of these, at least one for each play style that your game supports. For example, if you're making a first-person shooter, some players love sniping and will go out of their way to find the longest-range, highest-damage gun you have available and use it in every possible situation. Watch these testers to see if a particular strategy that you *want* to be viable actually isn't, since they might be the only testers even trying to get it to work (and they'll be experienced enough at this strategy to make a reasonable attempt at it).
- The tester who sucks at playing your game. Some testers are new to video games in general or haven't played many games in the genre of yours in particular. Testers that are naive or low skill are invaluable during development, since they give you insight into how newbies will experience your game, and what kinds of things will trip up players who are coming to your game for the first time.
- The tester who loves griefing other players. The reality is that for any multiplayer game, some players will have the most fun when they ruin someone else's fun. While you might not appreciate this kind of person yourself, and you don't necessarily want this kind of player actively advocating for changes to the game, you *do* want them playtesting your game. When you see this kind of tester laughing, it means one of the other testers is crying. Knowing what players can do to ruin one another's experience is helpful so you can set appropriate boundaries in your game.
- The tester who is a pro-gamer. While there is some overlap here with the "plays to win" kind of tester, the mindset here is a little bit different. Pro-level players rely on their inherent skill at a game (rather than specializing in finding unfair exploits), and while they want to win, what they *really* hate is losing to a less skilled player because of randomness or luck. Now, a certain amount of random element can be good for gameplay, even if a "pro"-type tester hates it; but these types of players are great for finding the *most* random elements of the game. If a pro-level tester wants to cut a particular mechanic from your game entirely, that means they perceive that mechanic to be too random; you might not remove the mechanic, but you can dial back the randomness a bit.

Beta

There's an old joke that "alpha" is Ancient Greek for "software is broken" and "beta" is Ancient Greek for "software is still broken."

As with alpha, there's no single industry-accepted metric for when a game goes to beta, but generally at beta, we are what we call **content complete** as well as feature complete. That is, the entire game can be played end-to-end in its entirety.

At this point, the game is "done" other than finding and fixing as many bugs as possible before release. It's a stressful time when team leads are regularly meeting to go over all known bugs and prioritize which ones need fixing immediately because they're blocking additional testing, which need to be fixed before release, and which can wait (a process referred to as **triage**, borrowed from the similar process that happens in the medical profession when you go to the ER and they prioritize the people who are about to die imminently over those who just need to be seen eventually). Here's where a lot of the final balancing of the game happens; while the programming team generally has its hands full just fixing bugs, the design team is mostly "done" in that the mechanics have been designed, the story written, the content finished, so all that is left is to answer "is this working as intended?" types of questions from programming and QA, and to fiddle with the numbers to get the balance right while the programming department is on fire.

As the game nears completion, this is also the time when the game may be sent out into the wild, either as an early release, or a **closed** or **open beta** ("closed" meaning it's by invite only, "open" meaning anyone can sign up from anywhere). For larger game projects with a large beta, this is where you can get some sufficiently large data sets to make analytics-based balancing worthwhile. If the company sets expectations with the player community that things will be changing regularly for balance reasons, this can even be a source of excitement among players (what will those wacky devs do next week?)—there was a great conference talk from the designer of *Slay the Spire* on how they did this very thing (linked to at the end of this chapter).

This is the final phase before release, so this is where you want to spend a lot of time thinking about the balance of the game, particularly the part that involves tuning individual numbers (since those are much easier and cheaper to change at this point than entire mechanics).

At this point, you should be guided by the principle that balance is about player perception as much as actual fairness. There's never enough time to fix *everything* so focus on the parts of the game that have the most impact and are the most visible. Balance the things that players see and perceive directly. For example, players have a hard time perceiving a random range, since the result varies over time. If you have a weapon that does some amount of base damage plus some random variance, changing the random range from "+0 to +10" to "−3 to +15" is not going to be nearly as noticeable as modifying the base damage, because players can't "sense" the range of a random roll, only the results… so it will take quite a few results for them to even notice that something has changed (unless you are explicitly displaying the range and showing dice rolling a number). As another example, if you have a choice between changing the physics of a platformer and changing the underlying math in a damage formula, the physics is much more immediate, perceivable, and visceral to the player than a bunch of hidden math formulas that are calculated in the background, so changes to the physics will have a more obvious effect on the play experience.

Post-Launch

For games that have continued development after release, such as MMOs, online TCGs, or free-to-play mobile games, regular development of new content and even full expansion sets will be ongoing. At this phase, you (hopefully) already have a pretty good idea of how the game is balanced, what "balance" looks like in the context of your game, and the general relationships between all the different numbers and how it all fits together.

Sometimes, a new piece of content or new expansion set will contain entirely new mechanics. Those may be in development for some time and will follow a process similar to the development of the original game in terms of the phases involved, just usually on a shorter timeline (but this time you start with more information about the nature of the game you're balancing). Here, you can concentrate your balance efforts on the new mechanics you're adding and how those relate to the old stuff.

You'll also have the benefit of live, post-launch player data (in large quantities, if your game is successful) that give you a better idea of what is and isn't balanced in your core game, allowing you to update your mathematical models to more accurately reflect the reality of how the game is played, which in turn should make it easier for you to balance your new content. Sometimes, you can even issue "balance patches" to fix some of the more egregious old stuff, buffing things that were worthless so that they have newfound value, and nerfing things that were powerful enough to be causing problems in the metagame.

Playtesting for Balance

At the stages of development where you are specifically playtesting for balance, it's one thing to say "go ahead and playtest the game for balance, it's important and you should really do that" but we feel that we should give a little more detail. Yes, some of your testers will be particularly good at testing for balance, but sometimes, it's the designer who playtests their own game (or a colleague's game), and the designer should be giving some direction to other testers about what to test for (simply telling most playtest groups "test this for balance" will be met with blank stares).

For small-scale playtesting, as you might do with a board game or paper prototype in a small group, all the typical general advice for playtesting applies:

- Respect people's time; you're asking for them to give up their time in exchange for helping you to make our game better, so stop the test early as soon as you've answered the core questions you came to ask. If further play won't help you, then don't waste everyone's time; just call it early, unless they specifically *ask* to keep playing. (Note that this is counterintuitive, since ending a game early when playing for pleasure is considered quite rude. But in a playtest, where the play is for another purpose, this shows respect.)
- Playtest with a purpose. Know what that purpose is (to answer a question) and then set up the test to answer that question. That question might be "is it fun?" or "is it balanced?" or any number of other things, but you should know what you're looking for.
- Unless secrecy is important to get a valid test result, instruct the playtesters of the purpose of the test and how they should approach the test.

If you're playtesting for the balance of a specific thing, make sure that thing happens. For example, if your question is "is this particular card overpowered if it's drawn early in the game?" then stack the deck and put that card on top. For video games, you may need to ask the programmers to put in a number of "cheats" in the game to aid testing. (Usually, these cheats are left in the final released version, since players like them too; if you look at the cheats available in any given video game, figure that those were probably the things that were the most important for streamlining playtests and bug testing.)

If you're playtesting for more general balance (finding if there are any strategies or game objects or whatever that are too good or too weak), then instruct your testers to play to win. This is a particular mindset that not all testers (or game designers) are great at, but if you playtest a lot you will eventually find some testers who are unnaturally good at this. Treat them well; they are like gold to you. In general, the kinds of things players can try:

- Try **degenerate strategies**. This is where the player latches onto one overpowered thing and just does that thing over and over whenever they have the option. If this is a TCG and there are no deck construction limits, take one overpowered card and put 100 copies of it in your deck. If it's a fighting game, spam one move over and over. If it's a tower defense game, build one kind of tower and ignore the others. Playing this way tends to be boring for the player and (if the strategy works) intensely frustrating for their opponents, so this is the kind of situation you want to avoid, where players are optimizing the fun out of the game.
- Be a total jerk. Stab other players in the back. Make moves that are totally unfair. Refuse to collaborate with anyone, unless doing so gives you a sufficient material advantage. Do everything you can short of cheating to gain even a small advantage, no matter how much fun it sucks out of the room. Ignore all normal rules of decency, and see if you can use this to your advantage. If a player can be rewarded in the game for being mean, they will, so you want to test for this to make sure that players are not incentivized to treat others poorly.
- If you'd like additional strategies on how to play ruthlessly, there's a wonderful book by designer David Sirlin on the subject that you can read online for free, called Playing to Win (see the "Additional Resources" section). It is, essentially, a retelling of Sun Tzu's *Art of War* in the context of competitive games/esports, and shows in depth the competitive mindset.

Additional Resources

- Jaime Griesemer, *Changing the Time Between Shots for the Sniper Rifle from 0.5 to 0.7 Seconds for Halo 3*, GDC 2010, viewable at https://www.youtube.com/watch?v=8YJ53skc-k4.
- Anthony Giovannetti, *Slay the Spire: Metrics Driven Design and Balance*, GDC 2019, viewable at https://www.gdcvault.com/browse/gdc-19/play/1025731.
- David Sirlin, *Playing to Win*, available at http://www.sirlin.net/ptw.

Discussion Questions

1. What happens if you start balancing the game too early in development?
2. What happens if you wait too long and start balancing the game too late in development?
3. When in development should you start with small-scale playtesting with tests observed by the designer directly?
4. What is the danger of creating a mathematical model of your game in a spreadsheet at the very beginning, as you're first designing the mechanics and before the game is playable?
5. What is the difference between "feature complete" and "content complete"?
6. What is the difference between how a game designer might observe the results of playtests in a closed-beta environment and an open-beta environment?
7. At what point in development would you be designing the analytics that a game will be collecting? At what point will you be making the most use of the analytics data collected?
8. Of the six kinds of playtesters listed at the end of the Alpha section of this chapter, which of those are you most like when *you* playtest? Which of those personas would be *hardest* for you to emulate, if you were asked to?
9. Suppose you're running a playtest of a Metroidvania game where the main character starts with a short-range gun as their primary attack, and a tester tells you that they think you should increase the range. How do you respond?
10. What are some reasons you might playtest a game *other* than testing for balance?

Sidequests

Sidequest 15.1: Cheat Codes

Choose any video game that has some kind of secret cheat code system (typically, the player enters some kind of special inputs through a keyboard or game pad that unlocks functionality such as invincibility, infinite lives, level select, infinite money, or any number of other things).

For the game you selected, research all of the available cheats (you can usually find lists of these by searching online for the name of the game+"FAQ" or "Walkthrough" or "Cheats") and put them in a list.

For each cheat, state how you think it might have been used by the development team during testing.

Sidequest 15.2: BattleBattle

This is a game designed by Eric Zimmerman specifically to teach game balance through playtesting. Download the game from: http://www.stonetronix.com/gdc-2013/battlebattle.pdf.

In the document, the rules are listed on the last page. This is a two-player game that requires 6d6 (or 2d6 and some other stackable tokens such as small coins or beads to keep track of health and special ability uses remaining).

First, familiarize yourself with the game mechanics. Near the end is a page with four copies of one card, called "Vanilla." This card starts with 5 health and 3 tokens which can each be used to add 1 to your battle die. This is the card that forms the baseline power level that all other cards should be balanced to. Start by playing a game of Vanilla against Vanilla, either on your own or (if playing as part of a class or study group) in pairs, until everyone is familiar with the rules.

Once you're comfortable playing the basic rules of *BattleBattle*, it's time to introduce the 28 characters that were designed as part of this game on the first seven pages. If playing on your own, choose a character at random; if playing in a group, distribute characters to each pair of players, one character per pair. Most of these characters are *not* balanced. Your ultimate goal is to balance them against each other, but rather than deal with the 756 possible pairings, you'll test them against Vanilla instead. Play the character selected for you against Vanilla, for long enough to determine if the character is too weak, too strong, or just about right. You may then make one or two changes to the character—modify their health or number of tokens, one of their special abilities, or one of the rolls of a battle die. This game has many "design knobs" to influence the power of a character. After making the change, put that character back in the rotation, choose a different character to play against Vanilla, and continue.

If doing this sidequest alone: choose four characters out of the 28, play all four of them against Vanilla (one at a time), making changes to each. Then, start playing these characters against each other; try to get all four of them balanced within their group, so that each character is about as powerful as Vanilla and *also* about as powerful as the other three characters in your set.

If doing this sidequest in a group: once each pair of players has made modifications to the one character they have, that character is handed back to the central pool of characters.

If doing this in a large group, you can continue playing and redistributing characters until each character has already had a balance pass. At this point, remove the Vanilla characters and have each group take two of the modified characters (at random) and play them against each other, modifying either or both of them to make them balanced against each other, then returning them, and getting two more characters. This can continue for a few minutes up to an hour or two, depending on what you have time for. Afterwards, discuss as a group what that process felt like, and whether any characters felt particularly overpowered or underpowered in their final modified forms.

Ultimate Challenge: if doing this in a group (as in a classroom setting), after balancing the characters in the document, give everyone a blank character. Each individual can now design one of their own characters. Consider the following when creating a custom character:

- Is the character fun to play? Does it allow for player agency and interesting choices?
  - Negative example: **Dalek** in the original set of characters has no choices at all; there's nothing to do when playing it. Even if the character were perfectly balanced against Vanilla, it isn't particularly interesting.
- Is the character balanced against Vanilla? Is it unlikely that many other characters will have strong (or weak) matchups against this one?
  - Negative example: **Cat** in the original set of characters works very differently from most others, in that it uses its tokens to avoid damage instead of its health. This means that any opponent who does extra damage or who interferes with opponents' tokens or token use in some way would tend to be either very strong or very weak against Cat. Cat might be balanced against Vanilla, but it's likely to be highly unbalanced in matchups against a number of other characters.
- Do the character's mechanics match its theme? Does the name of the card suggest what it does in a way that feels natural and seamless?
  - Negative example: **Sniper** in the original set has no special abilities that make it feel particularly sniper-like. In shooting games, snipers tend to be able to hit accurately (and with high damage) from a long range, but are fragile up close. None of that feeling is captured in the character as originally designed.

Everyone can then bring in their designed characters and have a tournament! Give each character out randomly (so that people won't be playing *their* character, but someone else's) and pair people up randomly to play with others. Have each individual record their own personal win-loss record, as well as the win–loss record (and final life totals) of the character they were playing. After a pair finishes their game, they can get matched up with different opponents and playing with different characters.

In this context, a way to measure "balance" objectively is through how close each match is. A game that ends in a blowout suggests one character was much stronger than the other. A game where one of the characters won but with only 1 health remaining suggests a close game between two almost-evenly-matched opponents. At the end of the tournament, winners can be determined by individual win–loss record (so that everyone is playing to win, even without playing their own character) as well as character records (characters with the lowest average health remaining at the end of their game, whether theirs or their opponents', can be considered the most balanced).

Wizard's Main Quest, Part 6: Playtest Your Cards

Continuing from Part 5 in: Chapter 14

Take the cards you modified back in Part 4, and find at least one other player willing to play with you. If you chose to balance the four starter decks, supply these decks to your tester(s). If you chose to balance the individual cards, provide the cards, along with instructions to your tester(s) that they can build their own custom deck of exactly 50 cards, with no more than three copies of any individual Action card.

In either case, the goal of each player (including you) should be to break the game. If balancing the starters, players should try to find one starter that they think is stronger than the others and use it to win consistently; or if they think they've found a starter that's weaker than they others, they can force their opponent to play it instead. If balancing the cards in a constructed-deck environment, everyone should try to build a deck that is so powerful that it dominates the play format, where everyone else would have to play a similar deck or else build a deck specifically made to counter it in order to stand a chance of winning.

If you find individual cards, card combinations, or decks in general that are too powerful through playtesting, make changes by hand to their costs as appropriate. You may also want to revisit your cost curve and supporting math to try to figure out where something went wrong; if you do, you may find other cards that should be changed that you might not have considered.

This is the final part of the Wizard's Main Quest.

16

Beyond Balance

In This Chapter

- Wrapping Up
- Perfect Imbalance
- Balance and Fun
- Numbers Aren't Always Balance
- What's Next?

Wrapping Up

> It doesn't matter if your game is fun, as long as it's balanced.
>
> *No game designer, ever*

Now, we come to the end of our journey through the sub-field of game design known as game balance. Throughout this book, we have learned many techniques to identify and fix imbalances in the game, mostly by looking at, understanding, and manipulating the numbers and mathematical formulas that underlie the game. In this chapter, we look at balance in the broader context of game design.

Perfect Imbalance

Game designer James Portnow coined the term **perfect imbalance** to describe how many games are, paradoxically, made better by adding minor imbalances to the system (see the "Additional Resources" section at the end of this chapter). This is not to say that a game designer should simply not care about the balance of their game, nor that they should put horrendously broken or ridiculously underpowered strategies in their game intentionally. But some minor deviations from the cost curve can, under some conditions, make for a more compelling game.

In particular, with games that have multiple strategies and multiple paths to victory, having some of them being very slightly off the cost curve (maybe 10% to 15% deviation) gives players the game-within-a-game of trying to figure out what the exploits are and how to best take advantage of them. If the game were perfectly balanced, any strategy would be as good as any other, so there would be no point in searching. Furthermore, with a perfectly balanced game, the optimal strategies would become known and rote after some time, meaning that rank beginners would find the game interesting with a vast possibility space, and world-class top-tier experts would know the game well enough to be developing new innovative strategies… but anyone in between the extremes is mostly going to have to spend their time studying the established knowledge of the game. Developing new strategies for a game is fun. Studying book openings, less so.

Portnow laid out the following conditions for a game that allow for intentional slight perturbations to the balance of the game:

- No matter how skilled a player is, they can't do *everything* well with their character/deck/army/etc.
- The balance curve of the game must be clearly understood, intuitively and mathematically, so that changes to the balance can be made intentionally and with purpose. This is not about making random changes, but deliberate ones.
- Players must have a wide enough pool of options in the game's possibility space, that a counter-strategy to just about anything can be found (without resorting to hard counters that specifically counteract a single game object and do nothing else). This prevents any single slightly unbalanced thing from dominating the metagame and in fact makes the metagame more dynamic as players go through cycles of identifying overpowered strategies, then countering them, and then countering the counters.

Counters All the Way Down

That last point about making sure that counters exist may bring up a question: how many layers of counters, and counters to the counters, and counters to the counters to the counters, have to exist?

In David Sirlin's book *Playing to Win* (see the "Additional Resources" section of Chapter 15), he identifies that games need exactly three layers of counter-strategies (he calls these **Yomi Layers**) for any given dominant strategy.

1. A player starts by identifying a dominant card, or move, or other in-game action, something above the curve that can be exploited to win games if it isn't stopped. If no counters exist, the dominant strategy ends up completely dominating the metagame and ruining the game's balance.
2. A counter-action is found, which is effective against the dominant action. Now, someone playing the counter can win all of the time.
3. The player who wishes to use the dominant action must now develop a counter-counter-action. This gives them the option to counter the counter or (if the counter isn't used) to revert to the dominant action.
4. The player who developed the original counter is now stuck. They can counter the dominant action, but not the counter-counter. So they must develop a counter-counter-counter-action. Now they have two choices as well: one to use when they suspect the dominant move (counter!) and one when they suspect the counter-counter (counter-counter-counter!).

No further layers of countering are necessary. If the original player suspects a counter-counter-counter, they can just use the original dominant action (which then goes uncountered). Since that action was overpowered to begin with, this would be preferred over trying to find an additional layer of counter-action.

Note that this is at the micro level, where players are taking many actions over the course of a game and can adjust strategies during play. At the metagame level, where players may be committing to an overall strategy at the start of the game and are unable to alter it for that game (such as bringing their custom deck to a TCG tournament), the number of counter-layers decreases by one:

1. A dominant core strategy is identified. As above, this is more powerful than most other strategies and starts to get popular enough in the metagame to become an issue that all players must consider when forming their own strategies.

2. A counter-strategy is developed, which is effective against the dominant strategy. If the dominant strategy is sufficiently strong in the metagame, the counter-strategy is successful and wins more often than it loses.

3. A counter-counter-strategy is developed, which works against the counter-strategy. This may, in fact, be an entire class of strategies that are reasonably powerful, are *not* weak against the counter-strategy, and therefore can beat it because the counter-strategy is inefficient when not countering the dominant strategy (it is putting resources toward countering something that is not present for the counter-counters).

You may recognize this as the same core mechanic from *Rock-Paper-Scissors*. In this case, we do not need a fourth layer of countering. To win against the counter-counter-strategies, simply use the dominant strategy.

For action-heavy games that don't give the player time to do much more than react to a situation, three Yomi layers may also be the limit; any more than two or three layers and players wouldn't be able to process what's happening in time to make a meaningful decision anyway. If you're playing a first-person shooter and see someone carrying a sniper rifle, you don't need to be thinking about what counters the thing that counters the thing that counters a sniper rifle; you just need to shoot them.

The significance of knowing how many layers of countering are required is that a designer doesn't need to implement too many soft counters in the game in order to still make sure that nothing in the game is uncounterable. It means that as designers, we can attempt Portnow's goal of perfect imbalance without requiring unlimited complexity.

Balance and Fun

The ultimate design goals vary from game to game—some games, particularly those made as Fine Art rather than as entertainment, may not prioritize "fun" as a goal at all—but in the majority of cases, an important goal of the game designer is to create a fun experience for the players. Many novice game designers, after understanding the basics of game balance and seeing some horrendously unbalanced games, may get the general feeling that a balanced game is fun, and a fun game is balanced, and therefore that the primary, overriding goal of a game designer is to get the balance of their game as perfect as possible. Or at least, to avoid having it be *too* unbalanced.

This is a common idea. In some cases, it is wrong. Let's take a look at some notable exceptions.

Imbalance in We Didn't Playtest This At All

Yes, there is a card game called *We Didn't Playtest This At All*. The game usually plays to completion in a couple of minutes or so. In the game, players each have a hand of cards, and they draw a card and play a card on their turn. Some cards score points toward a victory condition. Some cards allow players to make a simple choice (sometimes a blind choice, sometimes known). Many cards cause one or more players to be eliminated from the game. Usually, the winner is the last player to not be eliminated.

The game is horrendously unbalanced. It is quite common for a player to get eliminated before they even take their first turn, with no way to defend against it. Yet, the game is a commercial success and forms a key part of many players' game collections. Some people use it as a short filler game while waiting for the rest of their friends to show up. Some people use it as a simple way to determine who goes first for a longer game. Some people play it because they're drunk or tired and can't handle the cognitive load of anything more complicated, and the cards are hilarious. If fun is supposedly linked to game balance, why is such an unbalanced game so popular?

The primary reason is that the unfairness inherent in the game is obvious. The very title of the game implies that the players are about to experience an entirely untested, and therefore probably highly unbalanced, game.[1] If instead the game were called "A Perfectly Balanced Two-Minute Card Game," it would likely have been met with scathing reviews and would have been quickly forgotten. But the title instead serves to manage player expectations. The title is ridiculous, suggesting that the gameplay is likewise not to be taken too seriously, while simultaneously setting player expectations on the inherent imbalance of the game. If players choose to play at all, they have already decided that they are willing to explore an unbalanced system. Games tend to run into more trouble if players expect a fair fight and then find out only during play that it's not; *that* is where imbalances can cause a game to be less fun.

---

[1] According to the designer Chris Cieslik,

> We did test out earlier versions of it a bit, and I did a lot of spreadsheeting and math to make sure the appropriate number of cards ended the game vs. not ending the game. The final game was never playtested, and about 1/3 of the cards never saw paper until they were printed at the factory.
>
> Email to Ian Schreiber, September 1, 2015.

Imbalance in The Great Dalmuti

Richard Garfield's card game *The Great Dalmuti* (heavily influenced by a traditional card game known by various names, among them *Landlord* and *President* and some other names that cannot be printed here) is deliberately out of balance. In the game, each player sits in a different position around the table, with the seating order forming a definite progression from "best" to "worst." Players in the highest positions give their worst cards to the players in the lowest positions at the start of the round, and the lowest players must give up their highest cards to the players at the top. During the round, players play cards in turn from their hand and must play higher than the previous player or else pass; in this way, players with good cards can play more often, while players with a lousy hand must pass most of the time. Players are competing to play all of the cards out of their hand; the player who gets rid of their cards first takes top seat in the next hand, then the next player to finish takes the second best seat, and so on.

Obviously, the odds favor the players who start in the best seats. This forms a natural positive feedback loop: the players at the top have so many advantages that they're likely to stay at the top, and the people at the bottom have so many disadvantages that it's hard for them to climb the ranks. In some versions of the game, there is no scoring and no end; players simply play a hand, change seats, and then play another hand, continuing the cycle until everyone gets tired of it. Some groups can end up playing this game for hours at a time. It can be great fun, in spite of being obviously unbalanced. What's going on?

One reason is that the unfairness inherent in the game is obvious. It is, in fact, the whole *point* of the game, what differentiates it from other card games. As with *We Didn't Playtest This At All*, players enter the game expecting an unfair fight as soon as the rules are explained.

Another reason why *The Great Dalmuti* and similar games don't fail is the social dynamics. Players in different seats have different levels of power, and they often act accordingly; while this isn't a role-playing game, players do often act out their roles. Players at the top can have fun because it's good to be King. Players at the bottom can have fun because there's that thrill of fighting against the odds, being the underdog, striking a blow against The Man in the name of justice and The Little Guy... and every now and then, one of the players at the bottom does really well and overcomes the inherent unfairness to succeed, or one of the players at the top stumbles and is deposed, and these offer exciting, gratifying moments of play. The game is fun because everyone loves an underdog story.

It can also be exciting to play the game cautiously, by starting out from the bottom, and slowly and patiently, over many hands, holding your position... and then moving up when a particular hand offers that opportunity, and eventually reaching the top. This might act as a metaphor for upward social mobility brought about through a combination of opportunity, skillful play, and patience. Since the game replicates a system that we recognize in everyday life—the income inequality between the "haves" and "have-nots"—being able to play in and explore this system from the magic circle of a game has appeal.

There is a drinking-game variant where anyone can force anyone below them in the hierarchy to take a drink. (In the interests of personal health, you could instead play a variant where those at the top may freely take snacks and drinks at the table, but those below them can only do so with permission.) This layers on further social dynamics. How do your friends act when they're on top: are they nice to those below them, or are they merciless? If someone has been stuck at the bottom for a while and then suddenly has a string of good luck that catapults them to the top, are they gracious winners, or do they take revenge on the people who were formerly mistreating them? This game, through its unbalance, can become a wonderful social experiment that brings out the best and worst in people, and can let friends know each other's true nature in a deeper way that just about any other experience... all with nothing beyond a deck of cards, and an unbalanced game to go with it.

Imbalance in Betrayal at House on the Hill

The board game with the grammatically challenged title, *Betrayal at House on the Hill*, is not unbalanced intentionally, but it is unbalanced nonetheless.[2] In the game, players explore a haunted house room by room, drawing cards that represent events as they explore. At one point, one of the players (unknown to all at the start of the game) turns traitor; at that point, the traitor has one victory condition, and the remaining players band together to stop them through some alternate victory condition. The first edition of the game includes 50 different scenarios, and the particular scenario is chosen based on what room and what card triggered the activation of the traitor mechanic.

---

[2] The first edition of the game also had multiple printing errors, including, amusingly enough, an Underground Lake tile that could only be placed in the Attic. More than half of the scenarios required extra rules or errata, and many of them were literally unplayable as printed, as one side or the other was lacking the information about their victory condition! This suggests that the game was not unbalanced intentionally, but rather due to a lack of extensive playtesting for balance and printing errors—probably because the playtesters were having such a good time that they forgot to mention the flaws!

With so many scenarios, they tend to vary widely in terms of how easy it is for either side to fulfill the victory conditions. Some of them strongly favor certain players or teams over others. Some of them are much easier or harder if certain rooms have been revealed. Most do not scale well with the number of players (a scenario that is well balanced in a three-player game may be heavily unbalanced with six). The game has multiple layered random elements (random tiles drawn while exploring the house, some of which trigger a random card draw, and some card draws then trigger a random die roll) that make it likely for one or more players to randomly get a very strong advantage or disadvantage from a particularly lucky or unlucky encounter. In most scenarios, it's possible to have players eliminated early (on the turn right after the traitor is revealed), even if the rest of the game continues for another hour.

In spite of these issues, the game itself can be quite fun, especially if played in the right group. Why? Because no matter what happens, in nearly every game, *some* kind of crazy thing happens that's fun to talk about afterwards. Between the flavor text on the cards and in the scenarios, and the way they are designed to string together to form a narrative, the game almost always crafts a story of the experience of the characters in the game, and the stories are interesting. In addition to the crafted narrative bits in the game, the mechanics support the story: because of all of the random elements, it's likely that *somewhere* during play, players see something that feels highly unlikely and thus memorable: a player finds five items all at once because they draw items and events that let them draw other items; a player rolls eight dice and rolls all zeros; a player draws just the right card they need at just the right time; a player finds out the hard way that a new mysterious token on the board actually kills them. So, players are willing to overlook the flaws, because the core gameplay is about working together as a team to explore an unfamiliar and dangerous place, then having one of the team betray the others which shifts the game from purely cooperative to a one-against-many situation. As a general game structure, that ends up being unique enough to be interesting, and the camp-horror setting meshes really well with the core mechanics.

In *Betrayal at House on the Hill*, player expectations are actually *not* managed that well. Neither the theme, nor the box, nor the rules say anything about the imbalances inherent in the game. If a player who had never played before was just told "oh, this is a fun game," they might not have as good a time when they encounter all of the problems with it. If a new player is introduced to the game by saying "this game isn't balanced, but it is fun," then that usually helps them to enjoy the experience more. And incidentally, the game probably would be better if it were more balanced—but note that it is possible for a game to succeed in spite of a weakness in that area.

Balance in Story-Heavy Games

Is *Heavy Rain* balanced? What about *The Walking Dead*? *To The Moon*? *The Path*?

In some games, balance is less important than others. In particular, consider games that are heavy in narrative and light in mechanics—particularly those that are not meant or designed to provide much challenge or resistance to the player. Some games are designed more as an interactive story, and the entire core of the game and focus of the experience is on creating a compelling narrative. In these games, there are fewer mechanics, and balancing the mechanics isn't nearly as important as crafting a strong narrative experience. Again, this is because of design intent and audience expectations; players who pick up a game expecting an interactive story are going to be less concerned with balance, and a game that has a narrative-based core experience should concentrate on that part first, with all other elements of the game existing in service to the core.

Balance, Fairness, and Expectations

Ultimately, the purpose of game balance is to make the game feel fair to players.

In games where players expect a fair fight, balance is very important. One of the reasons that so many players hate the "rubber-banding" negative feedback mechanic in racing games, where an AI-controlled car suddenly gets an impossible burst of speed when it's too far behind the player, is that it feels unfair because real-life racing doesn't work that way. On the other hand, *The Great Dalmuti* is patently unfair, but players are expecting it to be that way so they accept the imbalance easily.

This is also why completely unbalanced, overpowered cards in a CCG are seen as a bad thing, since they dominate the metagame and destroy the balance of the rest of the game (and this is made even worse if the card is extremely rare, giving players the perception that the game is "pay-to-win"). However, in a single-player card battle version of a CCG, using the same mechanics against AI opponents can be a lot of fun and is less of an issue. With a head-to-head tabletop card game, players expect the game to provide a fair match, so they want the cards to be balanced. In the case of the single-player game, the core of the game is about character growth and progression, so getting more powerful cards as the game progresses is part of the expectation.

Just like everything in game design, balance is all about understanding the design goals of the game. What do you want the player to experience? If you want the player to experience a fair game, which is true in most (but not all) games, *that* is the function of balance.

Numbers Aren't Always Balance

In this book, we have often altered the balance of games by modifying the numbers in the game. This might suggest that "balance equals numbers": you balance a game with numbers, and the sole purpose of the numbers is to give the designer something to balance.

In fact, these two concepts do have a lot of overlap, but they are not identical. For example, in the very first chapter, we noted that sometimes balance is done through a game designer's personal experience where they just pick numbers that feel right, instead of with math.

While it hasn't been mentioned in this book (this is a book about game balance, after all), there are reasons to change numbers that don't involve balance. One important reason is to change the emphasis of play.

Bejeweled, one of the games that popularized the "Match-3" genre of puzzle games, provides a wonderful case study. It is a simple game; there is an 8x8 grid, and each location in the grid contains one of seven different colors of gems. A player must swap two adjacent gems in such a way that at least one orthogonal three-in-a-row or longer is created. All such matching gems disappear from the board, giving the player a score. This creates a void in the board, which is filled by having the gems above it fall down, with new randomly created gems appearing from the top of the board. If, in the process of falling, a new three-in-a-row is created, that disappears as well in a chain reaction, scoring more points. If the player makes a four-in-a-row instead, in addition to anything else, a gem is created that has the Flame property; when that gem is matched, it explodes, destroying all orthogonally and diagonally adjacent gems for extra points (and a likelier chance of combos). Matching five gems in a "T" or "L" shape (three horizontal and three vertical, all of the same color) creates a gem with the Star property; when that gem is matched, it destroys all other gems in the same row and column. Matching five gems in a straight line creates a Hypercube on the board. The Hypercube is a special gem that can be swapped with any color gem, and when this happens, all gems of the swapped color on the entire board are destroyed. The player also receives a score bonus if they match two different sets of gems at the same time (say, swapping a red and green gem to create a line of three reds *and* a line of three greens in a single move).

The board size and the number of distinct types of gems are core numbers that do in fact have a great deal of influence on the game's balance. Modifying either of those even slightly changes the game dramatically. The scoring system, on the other hand, has no impact on the balance of the game itself (a player's ability to survive by making matches is not impacted by their current score). This is the scoring system in the original *Bejeweled*:

- **Matching three gems**: 50 points
- **Matching four gems**: 100 points + Flame Gem
  - **Flame Gem explosion**: 50 points + 20 per gem destroyed = 230 points total
- **Matching five gems (T or L shape)**: 150 points + Star Gem
  - **Star Gem explosion**: 50 points + 50 per gem destroyed = 800 points total
- **Matching five gems (line shape)**: 500 points + Hypercube
  - **Hypercube explosion**: 50 points + 50 per gem destroyed = variable, usually about 500 points total
- **Chain reactions (cascades)**: +50 bonus each, cumulative
- All points are multiplied by the current level. Level increases by matching gems and is generally a measure of how many moves the player has made without losing.

As game designers, there are many questions embedded in such a simple game with such a straightforward scoring system. Why is matching five gems in a line worth *ten times as much* as a basic three-in-a-row, and more than three times as much as matching five gems in a "T" or "L" configuration? Does it balance out that the points gained from a Star Gem are usually more than a Hypercube? Why is making two matches at once a relatively tiny bonus compared to a multiple cascade? And what's up with that level multiplier?

If these numbers in the scoring system were changed, it would not make the game "wrong" or even imbalanced. The scoring system cannot claim to be "perfect" or balanced. Like we saw in Chapter 13 with the kill/death ratio in scoring, however, the scoring system here does tell us what is being emphasized.

The level multiplier means that long-term survival is heavily emphasized over short-term big combos. Survival requires the skill of being able to think several moves ahead, and make sure all available matches on the board aren't used up. Big plays can be set up by skill, but more often they happen by luck when the right pieces just happen to fall into place. The purpose of the level multiplier, then, is to make the scoring more a measure of skill than luck. Cascades are a linear bonus and not a multiplier, as they are in some other games, probably for the same reason.

The Flame, Star, and Hypercube gems are interesting cases, because they give an immediate score bonus on creation and then another score bonus on destruction. The Hypercube is harder to create in practice than the Star Gem, in spite of both of them granting about the same number of points total (after factoring in the bonus when the created gem is destroyed). But the Hypercube is much easier to use since it can match with anything at any time, while it is possible for the game to end with an unmatched Star Gem still on the board. Additionally, a Hypercube destroys gems that are scattered throughout the board, not on a single row and column, which means that in practice, there's a much greater chance of multiple cascades, for extra points and also opening up the board and giving the player more options.

If the scoring system for *Bejeweled* were changed, it wouldn't necessarily change the balance of the game… but it would change the kinds of moves and gameplay that were emphasized.

What's Next?

Another takeaway from the brief *Bejeweled* case study: even the simplest games still have many design decisions where changing the numbers can have an effect on gameplay. Looking at numbers when you play games is a great way to build your intuition for analyzing game balance. In fact, looking up online Wikis and FAQs or even buying printed strategy guides can be wonderful resources for a game designer, because they tend to give all of the underlying numbers and math of the game in nice, neat charts. Doing the analysis of *why* the designer(s) chose the numbers they did is an exercise left to the reader. If you want to improve your game balance skills, one of the best things you can do is pay attention while playing games and try to understand the design decisions and their implications on the play of the game.

The other way to improve your balance skills, of course, is to make games and balance them. There are three extended exercises ("Main Quests") in this book, if you aren't actively making your own original game (or modding someone else's with balance in mind).

Or, you can take the skills you've gained from this book, call it "good enough," and then go work on other types of game design skills like game writing, interface design, technical documentation, systems design, gameplay scripting and technical design, or whatever else interests you.

Either way, it is our hope that you've enjoyed taking this journey with us through the fascinating field of game balance and that you are able to use these skills to go out there and make great games. Good luck, and have fun!

- Ian Schreiber & Brenda Romero

Additional Resource

- James Portnow, *Perfect Imbalance – Why Unbalanced Design Creates Balanced Play*, Extra Credits (season 4 episode 22), viewable at https://www.youtube.com/watch?v=e31OSVZF77w.

Part II

The Mathematics of Balance

In this next section of this book, we examine the fundamental mathematical tools that designers will find useful when analyzing their games. We start with the branch of mathematics known as Probability, in order to better understand games that use random elements such as cards and dice (this is one of the most common types of math that come into play with balance, and one of the broadest, so we have split this up over Chapters 17–23). We then examine the field of Statistics in Chapter 24 (useful in particular for Analytics) and then touch the field of Game Theory in Chapter 25 (useful for analyzing intransitive mechanics such as *Rock-Paper-Scissors*).

Some readers may already be familiar with these kinds of math, and comfortable with skimming these topics (or skipping them entirely), which is why we put these in their own section rather than interspersed with the chapters in Part I of this book. However, for readers who are a bit shaky or rusty on their mathematical theory, we hope these chapters provide an easy-to-understand introduction that can be used as a reference guide to various chapters in Part I as needed. We would also encourage readers to at least skim the topics of Chapters 17–25 just in case there are some small tidbits in here that you aren't familiar with, particularly in Chapters 19–23 that cover the direct application of probability to game design in ways that may be new even to an experienced mathematician.

17

Independent Randomness

In This Chapter

- Non-deterministic Mechanics
- Die Rolls and Independence
- Probability, Odds, and Chance
- Computing Independent Probability
- Case Studies

Non-deterministic Mechanics

> In 1654, a French nobleman who liked to gamble a little too much started losing a dice game that he thought he should be winning. He asked about this to a friend of his, mathematician Blaise Pascal. Pascal then wrote a series of letters with another mathematician, Pierre de Fermat, and between the two of them managed to invent the field of study known as Probability. So the next time you think that math was just invented by a bunch of stuffy wig-wearing old guys, remember that an entire branch of mathematics was created, essentially, because some rich guy wasn't having enough fun playing a game.

Until this point, nearly every topic in this book has dealt with deterministic mechanics. Deterministic mechanics are those where there are no random elements—give it the same inputs and you get the same outputs. *Pac-Man* is deterministic which is why people could play the game perfectly by memorizing patterns. But many games have non-deterministic aspects to them. Take the same actions, and it may work out differently. *Ms. Pac-Man* added some random elements to the ghost movement so that patterns no longer worked the same every time, and you actually had to engage with new patterns that couldn't necessarily be memorized. Understanding the nature of randomness is important for game designers. After all, we create entire systems from both deterministic and non-deterministic mechanics in order to craft the player experience, and we need to know how these mechanics work.

Unfortunately, many aspects of randomness are counterintuitive (we go into detail on this in Chapter 20). It's very easy to think you have the right answer to a probability problem, while coming to an entirely wrong conclusion. There are a few ways to check your numbers to prevent the worst errors (which we examine later in this chapter) but for now, let us start with the basics.

Die Rolls and Independence

The simplest form of randomness is the die roll. In common use, it is assumed that a single die has six sides,[1] but there are many kinds of dice: dice with four faces, eight, ten, twelve, or twenty are commonly used in many tabletop games. Thirty-sided, hundred-sided, and other types of dice can also be found without too much effort.

In games and game development, dice are commonly called "d" followed by the number of faces on the die. Thus, a standard (six-sided) die is a d6; a twenty-sided die is a d20. In the common situation where one rolls several dice and then takes the total of all of them, the number of dice is shown before the "d": in *Monopoly* and *Backgammon*, players roll 2d6 for movement (two six-sided dice), for example. Sometimes, a constant number is added to the roll: d6+1 produces an equally likely result between 2 and 7, for instance. This die-rolling notation was popularized by *Dungeons & Dragons*, which then passed to general use in the game industry.

There are many other forms of random number generation that look different from a die but are equivalent and produce the same probabilities. You may have played a board game that has a spinner, where the player flicks a

---

[1]Note that six-sided dice are highly overused by novice designers due to familiarity. Most humans do not have six fingers on either hand. We don't count in Base 6. Six does not divide evenly into 100 to get nice, round numbers for percentiles. The only reason d6 is so popular is that it's a cube, so it is the cheapest and easiest type of die to manufacture. This may be a consideration for board game designers, but is mostly irrelevant for video game designers, who can roll any number or type of virtual dice as they want!

small plastic arrow with their finger, and it rotates around and comes to rest on a number from 1 to 6 (this is equivalent to a d6). You might write the numbers 1 through 6 on the sides of a standard #2 pencil and roll it along a desk to also simulate rolling a d6. A coin, when flipped, is essentially a d2. A dreidel (a four-sided top that is spun with a handle and eventually comes to rest on one of its sides) is equivalent to 1d4; a similar device (called a tee-totum) can be made with any number of sides, for that matter. A Roulette wheel with spaces marked from 0 to 36 is essentially a d37 (or d38 if it has an extra 00 space), though the design could of course be modified to make it a d50 or d78 or any other number. And of course, a computer can generate a simulated "dn" for just about any number n that you wish (more on this in Chapter 21). While these may look different, they are equivalent from the perspective of game balance: they have an equal chance of choosing a number from 1 to n. For this reason, when we talk about "dice" in the remainder of this book, we include all of these other things as well; a "die" is simply a shorthand for a random number generator that has an equal probability of giving any integer number from 1 to some other higher number.

Dice have some properties that are worth knowing. The first is that, assuming a fair die and not a rigged one, each side is equally likely to be rolled. If you want to know the mean (average) value of a roll of a particular die, which is technically referred to as the **expected value** of the roll, add up all of the sides then divide by the total number of sides. For a standard d6, this would be $(1+2+3+4+5+6)/6=3.5$.

This technique can come in handy when using custom dice. For example, suppose we have a special d6 where three of the sides are labeled 1, two sides are labeled 2, and one side is labeled 3 (so it behaves like a weird sort of d3 which is more likely to get a 1 than 2 and more likely to get 1 or 2 than 3). The average roll for this special die is $(1+1+1+2+2+3)/6=5/3$ (about 1.66). If a player rolls three of these custom dice and adds the results, you know they roll an average of 5 each time and can balance the game on that assumption.

Another important property of dice—in fact, one of the defining characteristics of them—is that each individual die roll is **independent**, meaning that it is not influenced by any past or future events. For a standard d6, the probability of rolling the number 4 is 1/6. If a single die is rolled enough times, it is very likely that streaks of numbers occur (several 4s in a row, perhaps), but if three 4s in a row occur on 1d6, then the probability of the next roll also being a 4 is still the same 1/6. It is not higher because there's a "4 streak and 4s are 'hot' right now," and it is not lower because "there were already several 4s, so it's time for something else.[2]" Dice do not have brains, and they aren't "thinking" anything. They are influenced only by chance—or physics, if you prefer.

Probability, Odds, and Chance

Before getting into the math, it's worth getting some terminology straight. The words "chance," "odds" and "probability" are often used interchangeably in common speech, but in mathematics (and game design), they have distinct meanings.

Probability is a number from 0 to 1 (this can be given as a decimal, fraction, or percentage) that tells how likely an event is to occur. A probability of 0 means it never happens, and 1 means it always happens. The probability of rolling the number 1 on a d4 can be expressed as 0.25, or 1/4, or 25%. Note that the probability, no matter how we express it, is always a number between 0 and 1. If you ever mathematically compute a probability and get a number that's negative or greater than 1, you have made a math error somewhere.

The term **probability** is sometimes used interchangeably with "odds," though the two have different meanings. The **odds** of an event happening are given as a ratio of two numbers, where the first number is how many times the event happens and the second number is how many times it doesn't, out of the total of the two numbers. The odds of rolling the number 1 on a d4 can be expressed as "1:3" (meaning, one time it happens for every three times it does not) or "3:1 against" (the same but in reverse). Sometimes, it is expressed in text instead of a colon: "1 to 3."

Because the numbers in the odds aren't as intuitive, they are usually not used when discussing randomness. Probability numbers are easier to conceptualize. Odds are most frequently seen in gambling games as a payout: that is, how much money a player gains off their bet if they win. For example, in *Blackjack*, winning a hand normally pays 1:1, meaning that if a player wagers any amount and wins, they get to keep the wager and get an equal amount from the casino. Winning with a blackjack pays 3:2, so wagering $2 means keeping the wager and also getting an additional $3 (and now, perhaps, you see why it is not as intuitive to those who are not familiar with it).

---

[2]On the other hand, if twenty 4s in a row are observed, the probability of rolling 4 the twenty-first time is actually quite high. A streak that is twenty long is astronomically unlikely under most conditions, so in that case, it means the die is probably rigged. In probability problems, however, unless stated otherwise we assume a fair die for this reason.

Casinos tend to use odds *because* they are less intuitive, in order to make them appear more fair to gamblers than they actually are.[3]

The word **chance** is a qualitative description, not a quantitative expression; we don't use math or numbers when using this word. Chance is relative; an event may have a high chance or low chance of happening, for example. If describing a general sense of how likely something is without giving numbers, "chance" is an appropriate word. If giving an exact measure of how likely, use "probability" (or "odds").

Computing-Independent Probability

As mentioned before, if rolling a fair die, each result is equally likely. If there are n faces on the die, the probability of each individual face being rolled is $1/n$. This is intuitive enough. But for more complex problems, how do you approach them? Generally, the way you do this is by counting.

First, count the number of possible results that satisfy your desired condition. Then, count the total number of possible results (including those that satisfy the condition and those that do not). Divide the first number by the second and that is the probability that the condition happens on any roll. So, assume there are three successful exits from a maze and 20 dead ends, and a player chooses one at random. That means the probability of finding a successful exit is 3 out of 23, or approximately 13%.

As we add constraints to die rolls, however, we also add complexity. Some examples follow.

Rolling One Die

What is the probability of rolling 3 or less on a d8? There are three ways to do this (roll 1, 2, or 3). There are eight possible rolls on a d8. So the probability is 3/8 (or 0.375, or 37.5%).

Rolling Two Dice

Here is a slightly more complicated example. What is the probability of rolling an even number on 2d6? There are 36 total results—6 results for each die,

---

[3]To make things even more confusing for gamblers, the payout for a casino game is never the actual odds of winning; it is lower, and the difference between the true odds and the payout is the casino's average (expected) profit. If you ever do express a probability in terms of the odds for any reason, be careful to specify whether you are talking about the true odds or the payout.

and since the dice are independent of each other, multiply 6 results by 6 other results to get 36 total combinations of the 2 dice. Now, we have to count the number of results that are even and divide that by 36 (the number of total results). However, this can be tricky, because it's easy to accidentally double-count a single result or neglect to count several similar results. For example, in this problem, there are actually three distinct rolls that produce the result of 4 (which is even): rolling 2 on both dice, rolling 1 on the first die and 3 on the second die, and rolling 3 on the first die and 1 on the second die. For the sake of probability calculations, those last two results are distinct (imagine that one of the dice rolled is red and the other is blue, if you desire). By writing out all possible way to roll an even number, we can count them manually:

		First die					
		1	2	3	4	5	6
	1	2	3	4	5	6	7
	2	3	4	5	6	7	8
Second die	3	4	5	6	7	8	9
	4	5	6	7	8	9	10
	5	6	7	8	9	10	11
	6	7	8	9	10	11	12

As you can see from this table, there are 18 different ways to roll an even number on 2d6 (out of 36 possible die rolls), so the probability of rolling an even number is $18/36=1/2=0.5=50\%$. The probability of rolling an odd number is the remaining 50%. This answer is not so obvious to many.

Rolling Far Too Many Dice

What if there are too many possibilities to count manually just by listing them? For example, suppose you want to know the probability of getting a total of 15 or greater on 8d6. There are a lot of distinct results in the possibility space for a single 8d6 roll, so counting one by one would take far too long.[4] Even if we found some tricks to group similar sets of rolls together, it would still take a very long time.

There are two ways to approach this. One is to write code. Inside a loop, evaluate and count the total number of distinct rolls, keep a running total of

---

[4]Specifically, each die has six possibilities, and each of the dice are independent, so there are 6 * 6 * 6 * 6 * 6 * 6 * 6 * 6 = 6^8 = 1,679,616 distinct results. If you were able to tabulate one result per second and continued to do this without sleeping, you would die of sleep deprivation before you'd finish counting. So don't do that.

results that sum to 15 or greater, and have it spit out the totals at the end. This does require some programming knowledge, however.

The second way to do this is in a spreadsheet. If you need a ballpark answer, you can use a random function to generate a bunch of d6 rolls (either =FLOOR(RAND()*6,1)+1 or =RANDBETWEEN(1,6) works), add eight of them together on each row, Fill Down to do this a few thousand times, and count the number of results that are 15 or greater. This doesn't yield an exact answer, but it's usually pretty close. If you don't know the answer and just try it a lot and hope you get a result that's close to the average, there is a name for that: a **Monte Carlo simulation** (named after a well-known gambling establishment). We encounter many uses for Monte Carlo techniques later in this book.

Rolling Dice in Sequence

The previous example, rolling 15 or great on 8d6, is an example of a dependent die roll. Since the dice are being added together and you care about the total, the result of one die affects the total needed on the others in order to succeed. If you roll high on one of those rolls, it takes the pressure of the subsequent roll and affects its chance of success. The previous problem is not something that can be split up into eight independent rolls, for instance.

What if you have several repeated but independent die rolls, so that the result of one roll doesn't affect the others? As an example of this situation, consider a dice game where the player rolls 1d6 up to five times in succession. On the first roll, they must get 2 or higher to stay in the game. On the second roll, they must roll 3 or higher. On the next roll, they need 4 or higher. On the roll after that, 5 or higher. On the final roll, they must get 6. In this series of five rolls, what is the probability that the player succeeds in all of them? In situations like this, there is an extra trick we can use to make things easier.

In this case, the rolls are independent. It's true that if the player fails one roll, then it affects the outcome of the entire dice game, but each individual roll's success is not influenced by whether the other rolls go well. If they roll very high on the second roll, that doesn't make them any more or less likely to succeed on later rolls. In fact, the rolls could be done in any order and the result would be the same. So, we can consider the probability of each of the five rolls independent of each other.

When you have separate, independent probabilities and want to know what the probability is that all of them happen, take each of the individual probabilities and multiply them together. In this case, the probability of making the first roll (2+ on 1d6) is 5/6. The probability of making the second roll is 4/6, the third roll is 3/6, the fourth roll is 2/6, and the final roll is 1/6. Multiplying these together gives 120/7776 or about 1.54%. It is very unlikely that a player makes all five rolls together.

Negation: the Probability of Failing

Interestingly, when it is a challenge to compute a probability of success directly, the probability of failure is sometimes much easier to compute.

Here's an example. What is the probability that a roll of 4d4 produces at least one die showing a 4?

There is a lot to compute here. There might be a single 4 (and the other three dice are all showing 1 through 3), and there are four different dice that could be the lone roll of 4. There might be two 4s, or three, or all 4s, and each of those is a separate computation. The complexity of computing this by hand can get unwieldy very quickly.

But there's another way to look at this problem: the player loses the game if none of the dice are showing 4. Here, we have four independent die rolls, each of which has a probability of 3/4 (the die can show anything except 4 for that roll to fail). The probability that all four dice fail is 3/4 * 3/4 * 3/4 * 3/4 (again, for multiple independent die rolls where they all must happen, multiply their individual probabilities together) to get 81/256, or about 31.6%—so there's a little less than a 1/3 probability of losing.

If you want to know the probability that an event doesn't happen, subtract that probability from 1. In this case, if we're not losing then we're winning, so the remaining 175/256 (or about 68.3%) of the time, there must be at least one 4 that was rolled.

Combining Results

A common mistake when dealing with independent probabilities is to add them together rather than multiplying. To see why this doesn't work, imagine flipping two coins and asking for the probability that both coins show heads. The probability of a single coin being heads is 1/2 (50%), but the probability of both being heads is not 100%, obviously. Instead, multiply 1/2 * 1/2 = 1/4 (25%).

Likewise, if asking for the probability that either coin shows heads, the probability is still not 100%. In this case, you could use negation, finding the probability that neither coin shows heads (both show tails) as 25%—for the same reason that the probability of both showing heads is 25%—and therefore, the probability of any other result (there is at least one heads coin) is 100−25=75%.

Is there ever a time when you can add probabilities together? Yes, but only in one specific situation: when you are trying to find the probability of any of several independent events happening in a single trial, where they do not overlap. For example, the probability of rolling 2 or 3 on a d4 is equal to the probability of rolling 2 plus the probability of rolling 3. The rolls of 2 and 3 do not overlap (it's impossible to roll both 2 and 3 on a single roll), so the probability of rolling either one is the sum of the two probabilities. However, be careful with this; the probability of rolling 1 through 5 and/or an odd number on a d10 (probabilities of 50% and 50%, respectively) is not 100%, because in some cases you can do both, and you don't want to double-count. In this case, you could add both probabilities together, but because you are counting the overlapping area twice (an odd number and a number 1–5), you must go a step further. Find the probability of rolling both 1 through 5 and odd (30%), and subtract that from the sum of the two so that you're only counting it once. That would give the correct result of a 70% probability of one or the other.

If you add up all possible distinct (non-overlapping) outcomes for an event, the sum should always be exactly 1 (or 100%), because there should always be some result every time. If you add up all probabilities and get something other than 1, your math is wrong.

Expected Values

So far, we've assumed that every single side of a die comes up equally often. That's how dice are supposed to work, after all. Occasionally, however, you may have a situation where each outcome has a different chance of coming up. This is common in board games with spinners, for example, where some segments of the spinner are larger (and thus more likely) than others. Another example would be the custom d6 mentioned earlier in this chapter, with sides of 1, 1, 1, 2, 2, and 3, that acts like a weighted d3. How do we handle these probabilities?

Recall that for a standard d6, to find the average roll, we summed all six sides and then divided by the number of sides. However, we could look at this a different way. What we are really doing here is multiplying each individual result by its own probability and then adding each of those together:

- The probability of rolling 1 is 1/6. $1 \times 1/6 = 1/6$
- The probability of rolling 2 is 1/6. $2 \times 1/6 = 2/6$
- The probability of rolling 3 is 1/6. $3 \times 1/6 = 3/6$
- The probability of rolling 4 is 1/6. $4 \times 1/6 = 4/6$

- The probability of rolling 5 is 1/6. 5 ×1/6=5/6
- The probability of rolling 6 is 1/6. 6 ×1/6=6/6
- Adding these together: 1/6+2/6+3/6+4/6+5/6+6/6=21/6=3.5

When multiplying a numerical result by its probability like this, that is properly referred to as the expected value. Thus, the expected value of a standard d6 is 3.5. This may seem like a needlessly overcomplicated way to determine the average roll of a d6, and it is. Painfully so. There are cases, however, where such a method is not only useful but necessary.

For instance, examine the following spinner.

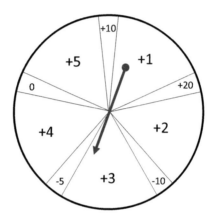

What is the expected value of a single spin? If you take out a protractor and measure, you'll see that each of the five large segments is 60°, or 1/6, of the total of a 360° circle. The probability hitting one of the larger segments is 1/6. The five small segments are each 12°, and the probability of each of those is 12/360=1/30. (For simplicity, we ignore spins that land so close to a line that they're ambiguous leading to a respin.)

In this case, we multiply each result by its own probability, then sum together:

- 1/6 probability of spinning +1=1/6
- 1/6 probability of spinning +2=2/6
- 1/6 probability of spinning +3=3/6
- 1/6 probability of spinning +4=4/6
- 1/6 probability of spinning +5=5/6
- 1/30 probability of spinning 0=0
- 1/30 probability of spinning −5=−1/6
- 1/30 probability of spinning −10=−2/6

- 1/30 probability of spinning +10 = 2/6
- 1/30 probability of spinning +20 = 4/6
- Adding these together: 1/6 + 2/6 + 3/6 + 4/6 + 5/6 + 0 – 1/6 – 2/6 + 2/6 + 4/6 = 18/6 = 3

Thus, over many spins, the expected value of a spin is exactly 3.

This technique also works if the results are equally probable, but the outcomes are weighted differently, such as "jackpots" where a player wins more than usual in certain circumstances. As an example, in the board game *Lords of Vegas*, one of the player options in the game is to make a wager (typically, this is used if a player is very close to affording a major purchase but can't quite make it, and it's worth it to them to wager a small amount in the hopes of getting enough). The way this wager works is simple: the player rolls 2d6. On a roll of 5–8 inclusive, they lose their wager. On most other rolls, they win at a 1:1 (keeping the original bet plus gaining an equal amount in winnings) payout. However, on the least common rolls of 2 and 12, they win at a 2:1 payout (keeping the original bet plus twice the wager). This raises two questions. First, how likely is a player to win anything if they make this wager? Second, what is the expected value of a single play of this game? Both of these factor into the question of whether a player should be willing to play this game or not.

2	1 1								DOUBLE WINNER!		
3	1 2	2 1							WINNER		
4	1 3	2 2	3 1								
5	1 4	2 3	3 2	4 1					LOSER		
6	1 5	2 4	3 3	4 2	5 1						
7	1 6	2 5	3 4	4 3	5 2	6 1					
8	2 6	3 5	4 4	5 3	6 2						
9	3 6	4 5	5 4	6 3					WINNER		
10	4 6	5 5	6 4								
11	5 6	6 5									
12	6 6								DOUBLE WINNER!		

Again, we count the probability of each result, then multiply by the outcome. There is one way to roll 2 on 2d6, two ways to roll 3, and three ways to roll 4.

On the high end, there is one way to roll 12, two ways to roll 11, three ways to roll 10, and four ways to roll 9. Adding it up, there are 16 rolls that result in a win (out of a total of 36 possible rolls). So, the probability of winning is 16/36 (slightly less than half), suggesting that the player is at a disadvantage.

That said, two of these rolls let the player win twice as much. If someone plays this game 36 times wagering $1 each time and gets each roll exactly once, they have $18 in winnings at the end ($16 for each of the winning rolls, plus an extra $1 for the roll of 2 and an extra $1 for the roll of 12). If they play 36 times and are expected to win $18, then that means this is even odds, right?

Not so fast. How many times do they lose? The probability of a loss is 20/36 (count up the ways to roll 5–8, or subtract the known probability of a win, 16/36, from 1). That means out of 36 plays at $1 each, the player is expected to lose 20 times, losing $20 in the process. This puts them very slightly behind, with an expected gain of $18 and loss of $20, or a net loss of $2, out of 36 rolls. The player would thus be expected to lose $1/18 (a little more than 5 cents) per dollar wagered on a single roll.

Another way of computing this: there are three different outcomes of a $1 bet.

- The player can lose their wager (−$1) with a probability of 20/36.
- The player can win their wager (+$1) with a probability of 14/36.
- The player can win double their wager (+$2) with a probability of 2/36.
- Just to check, 20/36 + 14/36 + 2/36 does indeed equal 36/36 = 1, so we can be confident that these are the only possible non-overlapping outcomes.
- Multiply each outcome by its probability, then add them all together: (−1 * 20/36) + (1 * 14/36) + (2 * 2/36) = −2/36 or −1/18.

Players should therefore not wager regularly, but only in cases where the potential gain outweighs the risk of a loss.

As you can see, calculating probabilities feels straightforward, but is easy to get wrong if you're not very careful. If you aren't sure of your result, it can help to run a Monte Carlo simulation in addition to an exact probability calculation, to make sure the two of them are roughly equal. If your math and your simulation give roughly the same answer, you can be a bit more confident you did your calculations correctly. If not… well, there may be an error in your math *or* an error in your simulation, so check both carefully.

Permutations

So far, all of our die rolls assume that order doesn't matter. If you're looking at the probability of rolling a combined 6 on 2d6, it doesn't matter whether the roll is 1 and 5, or 2 and 4, or 4 and 2. We can easily count the number of ways to have a combined 6. But in some cases, manually counting all of the different permutations to get a result is unwieldy, and it would be nice to have a math formula to calculate it for us.

Here is an example from the dice game *Farkle*. In this game, a player starts their turn by rolling 6d6. If they're lucky enough to roll one of each result (1-2-3-4-5-6), they get a huge score bonus. What is the probability this happens on the initial roll? As with all probability problems, we answer this by computing the number of ways we can roll one of each result and then divide by the total number of rolls. But there are a lot of ways to roll one of each number; how do we count them?

Here is one way to look at this:

- One (and only one) of the dice must be showing 1. How many ways are there to do that? Six, because there are six dice, and any of them can be showing the 1.
- One of the remaining five dice must be showing 2. There are five ways to do this.
- Continuing in this way, one of the remaining four dice must show 3, and there are four ways to do that.
- There are three ways on the remaining dice for one die to show 4
- There are two ways for the two remaining dice to show 5
- There is only one die remaining, so it must show 6

How many possible results are there from a roll of 6d6, regardless of what they roll? Each die can show six sides, so we multiply: 6 * 6 * 6 * 6 * 6 * 6 = 46,656, a pretty large number of possible rolls. How many ways can we roll 1-2-3-4-5-6 on 6d6? In the same way, we multiply, but our numbers are different since we're restricted in which dice can roll what numbers: 6 * 5 * 4 * 3 * 2 * 1 = 720. Divide the number of successes by the size of the possibility space to get our probability: 720/46,656, or about 1.5%.

This is interesting for a few reasons, but one important thing to notice is just how infrequently we actually roll exactly along the **uniform distribution** (that is, each roll is just as likely as the others) in the short term! Sure, if we rolled 6000d6, we would see approximately as many of each of the numbers

1–6 as any other. But by rolling just six dice, we almost never roll exactly one of each! This is why the score bonus for rolling 1-2-3-4-5-6 in *Farkle* is so large: it doesn't happen very often.

The Law of Large Numbers

As mentioned earlier in this chapter, the nature of independence is that "dice have no memory"; previous rolls do not affect future ones. As we just saw, die rolls along a uniform distribution are usually not split evenly in the short term. In a small series of die rolls (or coin flips, or what have you) we expect there to be some unevenness, and some "lucky" or "unlucky" streaks.

However, when we roll the dice a large number of times—thousands, or millions, of trials—we see the collective average be pretty close to the expected value. But wait, didn't we just say that dice have no memory? And now we're saying that rolling a lot of them causes them to tend toward average? What's going on here?

Suppose a player with far too much spare time on their hands rolls 1d12 ten thousand times, and a few thousand rolls in, they get a string of five 2s in a row. That string doesn't somehow "force" the die to roll the other eleven results more often from that point on to bring it back to average. It's just that a small streak like that has little influence on the collective results when rolling thousands of more times. Yes, there might get a bunch of 2s now, and it's just as likely that the player rolls a string of some other number before or after. This isn't because the die is being influenced by previous rolls; it's because in large sets of rolls, small streaks tend to get drowned out in the large ocean of data.

In fact, it turns out that small unlikely seeming streaks are actually very likely to happen somewhere within a large set of random rolls. Having some number on 1d12 getting rolled five times in a row is actually quite likely to happen at some point when rolling tens of thousands of times. This can cause all sorts of headaches for game designers.

For example, any programmer or game designer who has ever worked on an online game with some kind of random-number generator has surely heard this: a player posts on the game's forums to tell the developer that their random number generator is clearly broken and not random, and they know this because they just killed four monsters in a row and got the exact same loot drop all four times, and the player knows from a fan wiki of the game that those drops only happen 10% of the time, so this should almost never happen. Since it happened to them, clearly the loot drop tables are broken.

You do the math. There is indeed a 1/10 probability of that particular drop, so having that happen four times in a row should have a probability of 1/10 * 1/10 * 1/10 * 1/10 = 1/10,000, which is pretty infrequent (as the player is pointing out). Is there a problem, then?

It depends. How many players play the game? Suppose the online game in question is reasonably popular, and you have a hundred thousand players that play every day. How many of those players kill four monsters in a row? Maybe all of them, multiple times per day, but let's say that half of the players are just there to trade stuff at the auction house or chat and role-play in town, so only half of the players go out monster-hunting. With 50,000 attempts, you would expect that a four-loot-drop streak would happen five times a day, on average![5]

Essential Case Studies

RANDOMNESS VS. CERTAINTY

In his GenCon 2012 lecture *Volatility in Game Design*, game designer James Ernest constructed a simple game, *Kill the Elf* (see the "Additional Resources" section at the end of this chapter), to show some principles of probability. In the game, two players are competing to be the first to deal six damage to the titular third-party Elf, though it could just as easily be damaging each other, or even being the first to win a foot race. The warrior is steady and true, doing 1 damage per turn on every turn. The wizard is powerful but chaotic, rolling 1d6, doing no damage on 1–5, but six damage on a roll of 6. Who should win?

The expected value of both characters is the same: 1 damage per turn. One would expect this to mean that both characters have an equal chance to win, but in fact, they do not, because of what we have been discussing about the differences between short- and long-term rolls. Think of it this way: to win, the wizard must roll at least one 6 in its first five rolls and can tie by rolling a 6 on its sixth roll even if the first five rolls fail. We can easily compute the chance of failing to roll 6 in the first five turns (about 40.1%), meaning that the wizard wins almost 60% of the time. Of the times when the wizard does

---

[5] This is also why it seems like every few weeks, someone wins the lottery, even though that someone never seems to be you or anyone you know. The probability of winning is incredibly tiny, but if enough tickets are purchased, the probability of at least one obnoxiously lucky person somewhere in the mix is fairly high. At the same time, the probability of you winning, personally, is so low that it's never in your best interest to play, if going purely by an expected-value calculation.

not just win outright, there is still a probability of 1/6 that the game is a draw, so the warrior only wins slightly more than a third of all games. Even though the expected value of damage is the same between the warrior and the wizard, the game is unbalanced in favor of the wizard.

How do you balance this to make it more fair? One way is to make it a race to do 4 damage instead of 6. Then, the wizard only gets three rolls to win and then one opportunity to tie. The game is even closer to fair if players are racing to 10 damage and extremely close to a 50/50 probability of winning if players are trying to reach 1,000,000 damage. The greater the amount of damage required, the more that the wizard tends toward its expected value.

A HORSE RACE

Suppose we have a simple luck-based game: two players each roll 50d6, one die at a time, and sum their results. The highest total wins.

Let us suppose that on the very first roll, one player is lucky and rolls 6, while the other player is unlucky and rolls 1 (essentially, the players are now rolling 49d6+6 against 49d6+1, as the "lucky" player has a five-point lead). What is the probability of each player winning at this point?

Calculating all possibilities for 98d6 is time-consuming and best done with a computer, but you may be surprised to find that the player who rolled the 1 first now has only about a 25% probability of winning. What's going on? The answer is, once again, the law of large numbers. Over the course of 49 rolls each, the players are likely to roll very close to one another, as any short-term gains they have tend to average out with their losses over time. In that context, a five-point lead is significant enough to turn the tide in a fair number of cases.

The design lesson here is that a little luck at the beginning of a heavily luck-based game can actually dominate the play. If designing such a game, consider adding some negative feedback into the system if you don't want a situation where the player with the lucky first turn is just ahead for the entire game.

PIG

Pig is a traditional children's dice game with a central push-your-luck mechanic. Here are the rules:

- **Players**: any number, but at least 2
- **Objective**: be the first player to reach 100 points (or some other predetermined total).

- **Setup**: all players start with 0 points. Choose a player to go first and a turn order.
- The game is played in turns, with each player taking a turn in sequence. On a player's turn, they roll 1d6. If the die roll shows 1, then player's turn is over and they score no points for their turn. The die then passes to the next player in sequence. If the die shows 2 to 6 instead, the player can choose to stop, scoring the cumulative total of their die rolls that turn, and then pass the die to the next player in sequence. They can instead choose to roll again. Players can continue rolling as much as they would like until they either roll a 1 (losing all of their progress for the turn) or stop and take their current winnings.

What is the best strategy for this game? If the goal is to maximize one's probability of winning, when should a player keep rolling, and when should they choose to stop?

There are six outcomes on any roll. On 2 through 6, add that amount to the cumulative total for the turn. On a 1, a player not only scores zero, but also loses their previous gains (if any) that turn. You can thus think of each roll as having a 1 in 6 probability of scoring any of 2, 3, 4, 5, or 6 points or losing X points (where X is the current cumulative score in previous rolls this round). For example, with rolls of 6, then 4, then 1, the 1 can be thought of as being worth −10 points, canceling the gains from the earlier 6 and 4.

Now we can simply compute the expected value of a single roll by multiplying the probability of each outcome (1/6) with the result: $(2+3+4+5+6-X)/6=(20-X)/6$. So, if a player currently has 10 points from prior rolls in the current turn, rolling again has an expected value of $(20-10)/6=$ about 1.66. This is a positive expected value, so on average, they would improve their score by rolling again. If instead they have 25 points from prior rolls, the expected value of the next roll would be $(20-25)/6=-5/6$, so they would lose almost a full point on average by rolling and would do well to stop at that point. From the formula, it's easy enough to see that a player maximizes their long-term score by rolling on any current-turn total of 19 or less, and stopping on 21 or more. If they have exactly 20 points, then the expected value of the next roll is zero (any small potential gains are exactly counteracted by the small chance of a large loss), so it doesn't matter whether they roll one more time or not; their long-term score is the same either way.

That said, the strategy of the game is slightly more nuanced than simply rolling until reaching 20. That is fine for the very first player on the very first turn, but it is clearly not the optimal strategy in some circumstances. For example, suppose one player ends their turn at 98 points, and their opponent starts the current turn at 78 points. They roll 3, 5, 3, 2, 2, and 6, for a running total of 21. If they stop now, their score is 99, and the opponent with a standing score of 98 has a probability of 5/6 of winning on their first roll on their next turn. If the current player instead rolls one more time, however, they have a probability of 5/6 of winning right away. So in that situation, the player should roll again. (In general, a player who is behind should take more risks in order to catch up, because merely keeping steady with an opponent in the lead causes leads to a loss most of the time, as with the 50d6 horse race in the previous case study. When ahead, take less risk, preferring a steady and certain gain to close in on the win and not give the opponent the opportunity to have a run of good luck.)

RARITIES IN TCGS

One particular online collectible card game had a main set that contained 37 distinct cards with their rarity designated as Common, 90 cards that were Uncommon, 62 that were Rare, and 7 that were Very Rare. A booster pack contained 15 cards, of which 11 were Common, 3 Uncommon, and 1 Rare with a 25% chance of a Very Rare instead of a Rare. Within each rarity, any card is as likely to be found in a pack as any other (so all of the Commons are equally common, and so on). How rare is each individual card—that is, if there is a Common card called Uplift, an Uncommon called Cleaner, a Rare called Hologram, and a Very Rare called High Flux Nuke, how many of each of those four cards is in circulation relative to the others?

In a single pack, we generate 11 Commons; thus, there are 11 chances for an Uplift card to be in a booster pack. Since there are 37 common cards, however, there are 37 cards vying for those 11 slots. Therefore, the chance that an Uplift card is one of them is 11/37 or approximately 30% in any given pack (since each card is determined independently). The pack contains 3 Uncommons, each of which has a 1/90 probability of being Cleaner. Therefore, a pack contains an average of 3/90 (or 1/30) Cleaners. The pack has a 75% chance of containing a Rare (and a 25% chance of no Rares), so it has a 75/100 probability of having a 1/62 probability of generating a Hologram; multiplying those together, we have an expected 3/248 Holograms in a single booster. And finally, there is a 25% chance of containing a Very Rare, so it has a 25/100 probability of having a 1/7 probability of generating a Nuke. This gives us an expected 1/28 Nukes per booster.

As these numbers are all fractional and small, and we just care about what they are relative to one another, it may make it easier to conceptualize if we multiply all of our numbers by some large number like 1000. This gives us an expected 297.29 Uplifts, 33.33 Cleaners, 12.09 Holograms, and 35.71 Nukes per 1000 booster packs.

How do we interpret this? It means that the so-called "Very Rare" designation is actually not all that rare at all—there are about three of every individual Very Rare in circulation as there are of each Rare, and there are even more of any given Very Rare than any given Uncommon. Even though there are fewer Very Rare cards in a booster pack than any other card type, there are also fewer different kinds of Very Rare; when a Very Rare is generated at all, there are relatively few possibilities.

The lesson here is to always remember that when you have multiple independent events that have to happen (in this case, the probability of a booster pack including a Very Rare and then the probability of that card being a specific Very Rare), those probabilities are multiplied together. If you're dealing with a game that has various rarities of cards, in-game events, loot drops, or something similar, and it chooses one random item from a particular rarity, double-check to make sure that the rarer things really are more rare.

Summary

- The probability of anything is defined numerically as the number of ways the thing can happen, divided by the number of ways that anything can happen. Probabilities always range from 0 (the number of ways it can happen is zero; i.e., it never happens) to 1 (the number of ways it can happen is equal to the number of ways that anything can happen; i.e., it always happens).
- The probability of rolling a specific result on 1dn is 1/n. *Example*: the probability of rolling 2 on an eight-sided die is 1/8.
- If we have two possible results, A and B, which do not overlap (you can never have both), the probability of (A or B) is equal to the probability of A plus the probability of B. *Example*: the probability of rolling 2 or 3 on an eight-sided die is $1/8 + 1/8 = 2/8$.
- If we have two results, A and B, which do overlap (you might have A but not B, or B but not A, or A and B together), the probability of (A or B) is equal to the probability of A plus the probability of B minus the probability of (A and B together). *Example*: the probability of rolling less than 4 and/or rolling an odd number on an eight-sided die is $3/8 + 4/8 - 2/8 = 5/8$.

- If we have two entirely separate events each with its own probability, the probability of both events happening is equal to the probability of the first multiplied by the probability of the second. *Example*: the probability of rolling 2 on an eight-sided die twice in a row is 1/8 * 1/8=1/64.
- The probability of an event not happening is equal to 1 minus the probability that it happens. *Example*: the probability of not rolling 2 on an eight-sided die is 1 − 1/8=7/8.
- When the results of a die roll have numeric values, calculate the expected value of the roll (i.e., the "average" roll) by multiplying each result by that result's probability, then adding those results together. *Example*: the expected value of a four-sided die with faces showing 2, 3, 5, and 7 is (2 * 1/4)+(3 * 1/4)+(5 * 1/4)+(7 * 1/4)=17/4. If instead we found the die was loaded so that the 7 side is rolled twice as often as any of the other sides, the expected value changes to (2 * 1/5)+(3 * 1/5)+ (5 * 1/5)+(7 * 2/5)=24/5.
- When rolling large numbers of dice or doing many repeated trials, you can expect to see occasional "unlikely" streaks, but in aggregate, you will probably see something very close to what would be predicted by probability. The more dice you roll, the more pronounced this effect becomes.

Additional Resource

- James Ernest, *Volatility in Game Design*, in GenCon 2012. Full text available at https://www.crabfragmentlabs.com/s/Volatility-in-Game-Design.pdf.

Discussion Questions

1. Probability can be a tricky thing to grasp. If in a classroom or reading this as a part of a game design reading group, list things which are still unclear for you and discuss them.
2. We've learned that a little luck at the beginning of a heavily luck-based game can significantly turn the tide in one placer's favor. Can you think of a game in which early luck seems to be unbalancing?
3. What is the difference between probability and odds?

4. Select any game which has millions of simultaneous players and discuss how the law of large numbers appears in the game and may affect the outcome of the game.

5. What is a Monte Carlo simulation?

6. Thinking of probability from a purely player experience point of view, discuss a game moment in which you received an incredibly great loot drop or beat the odds in some way. Talk about the effect this had on you as a player, and if applicable, as a player in part of a community of players (like a great loot drop in *World of Warcraft*). How did you know it was rare?

7. What is the difference between a deterministic and a non-deterministic event?

8. What is the difference between an independent die roll and a dependent die roll?

9. What does 10d12+7 mean? What is the lowest, highest, and average value that this can produce?

10. From a player experience point of view, discuss how rarity affects player desire to own something (such as rare mounts in *World of Warcraft*, specific hats in *Team Fortress 2* or any game in which you are a regular player).

Sidequests

Sidequest 17.1: Bad Player

Seen on Twitter: "That awkward moment when you have a 25% chance of achieving something in a game and then you fail TEN TIMES IN A ROW. That's not a very good 1/4 chance…"

What's the probability that, out of ten attempts, all ten fail? Do you suspect this player was unlucky, or do you suspect a problem with the random-number generator in the game?

Sidequest 17.2: Kill the Elf, Redux

Earlier in this chapter, in the case study section titled "Randomness vs. Certainty," we examined a game called *Kill the Elf* where one player (the warrior) does 1 damage per turn, while the other player (the wizard) does 6 damage if they roll 6 on a d6, or 0 damage on any other roll, and both players are trying to reach a predetermined damage total before the other. We stated that this game is relatively balanced if players are racing to 4 damage. What is the actual probability of a win for the wizard, a win for the warrior, and a tie in this case? (Remember, all three probabilities should add to 1 if you do this right.)

Greater challenge: also compute the probability of a win for the wizard, win for the warrior, or tie if racing to be the first to do ten damage. This is a harder computation because you must count the number of ways for the wizard to roll 6 at least twice in 9 rolls (for a win), or exactly once in 9 rolls and then again on the tenth roll (for a draw). Use a spreadsheet and make a Monte Carlo simulation with a few thousand games, and see if it is similar to your answer. If not, look in both your math and the simulation until you find an error.

Sidequest 17.3: Horse Race, Redux

Two players are rolling 50d6, but on their first roll, one player rolls 6 and the other rolls 1. Calculating the exact probability of either player winning is difficult, but making a Monte Carlo simulation is relatively straightforward. Run the simulation in a spreadsheet program of your choice, and give an approximate answer.

Sidequest 17.4: Pig AI

The dice game *Pig*, as described in the "Case Study" section of this chapter, has a relatively simple game state. For two players, the only variables are each player's total score, which player's turn it is, and that player's running total for their current turn. Any optimal strategy, then, should only need to depend on these things in order to determine whether to continue rolling or stop.

Write your own "AI" for this game—in this case, that just means a formula that looks at three numbers (your score, opponent's score, and your current running total) and returns a simple "yes, roll again" or "no, stop now" answer. You may simplify it further, if you prefer: a formula that looks at two numbers (your score and the opponent's) and returns the number that you should stop rolling on (keep rolling if the current turn total is lower than this number, stop as soon as you reach or exceed that number). This can be written by hand as a formula or implemented in a spreadsheet program.

If going through this book with several other people (as in a classroom setting), consider having a *Pig* AI tournament. Have each player turn in their own formula and play them against each other for a few thousand games. Compare formulas and have a discussion. Why did the winning formula win? Why did the underperforming formulas lose?

Sidequest 17.5: The Amazing +1 Bonus

Imagine a very simple role-playing game (RPG) where combat is determined as follows: both players roll a d6 and add their Combat Bonus (if any). The higher number wins the combat. In case of a tie, reroll, and continue to reroll until a winner is determined.

A tenth-level Fighter has a combat bonus of +4. Determine its probability of winning against the following opponents:

- Troll (combat bonus: +3)
- Giant Spider (combat bonus: +2)
- Goblin (combat bonus: +1)
- Giant Rat (combat bonus: +0)

Hint: you might wonder, how do you handle the cases of ties when you might be rerolling those indefinitely? The answer is to ignore ties entirely, since you know the die rolling continues until you get a definite win or loss result. For example, if you find that you win with probability 0.5, lose with probability 0.25, and tie with probability 0.25, you divide the probability of winning (0.5) by the probability of winning or losing (0.75), so in that case, you would have a 2/3 probability of winning.

Sidequest 17.6: Meanwhile, Back At The Inn…

After a long day of adventuring, your RPG characters walk into the local inn. In the corner, some locals are playing a dice game and motion to you to join them if you're up for some gambling. They teach you the rules:

- There is a board, divided into eight sectors, each numbered 1 through 8. You may place one gold piece on any of the numbers. Other players may do the same, independently.
- After your bet is placed, 4d8 are rolled.
- If none of the dice show the number you guessed, you lose your wager.
- If exactly one die is showing the number you bet on, you keep your bet and gain 1 gold piece as winnings in addition (a 1:1 payout).

- If two dice are showing the number you bet on, you receive a 2:1 payout (gain 2 gold pieces).
- If three dice show the number you bet on, you receive a 3:1 payout.
- If all four dice show the number you bet on, you receive a jackpot payout of 100:1.

Assume the game is fair (i.e., the dice are not rigged in any way). What is the expected value of the gain or loss from a single play of this game?

Hint: while you should seek an exact answer for this (it can be computed by several means), also use a Monte Carlo simulation to verify your solution, as it is very easy to accidentally double-count something and get the probability wrong!

Sidequest 17.7: Collecting Dragon Eggs

There are six types of dragon eggs: red, blue, white, gold, black, and green. After completing a repeatable quest, a player receives a dragon egg of a random color, with each color having an equal probability of any other. What is the probability that a player has a complete set of one of each after repeating the quest only six times?

Greater challenge: also give the mean number of times to complete the quest in order to get at least one of each. (Hint: it's much greater than six.)

Sidequest 17.8: Rare Loot Drops

In a particular Roguelike game, when a monster is killed, it drops a piece of loot. This loot is determined by consulting a common loot table with 20 equally weighted entries and choosing one at random.

One of the entries on this table isn't a piece of loot, but rather, an upgrade: roll again on a rare loot table. The rare loot table also has 20 equally weighted entries, with one chosen at random. And one of those entries is instead to roll again on an epic loot table with 20 equally-weighted entries.

What is the probability of getting any piece of epic loot from a common drop? What is the probability of getting a particular piece of epic loot from a common drop?

18

Dependent Randomness

In This Chapter

- Dependent Events
- Card Draws and Dependence
- Computing Dependent Probability
- Case Studies

Dependent Events

In 1889, Fusajiro Yamauchi founded a company to produce hanafuda, a style of playing cards popular in Japan. In the middle of the 20th century, the company made a deal with Disney to produce packs of cards with the iconic Disney characters, to great success. The company then expanded into the toy market, and in the early 1970s, the video game market (managing to secure the rights to sell one of the earliest consoles, the Magnavox Odyssey, in Japan). The company went on to later make its own video games and the line of consoles it's best known for today: the company's name is Nintendo. If you think about it, the video game industry would be very different and much smaller today if it hadn't been for the existence of cards!

In the previous chapter, we talked about **independent** events, where the outcome of each event has absolutely no influence on future events. We considered the roll of a die as a typical, well-known independent event.

In this chapter, we examine **dependent** events, where knowing the outcome of one event actually does modify the probabilities of future events.

The typical example of a dependent event is drawing a card from a shuffled deck of cards: each card drawn influences what is left in the deck. For example, if you have a standard 52-card deck and draw the 10 of Hearts, and you want to know the probability that the next card is also a Heart, the probabilities change because your first draw already removed a Heart from the deck. Each card drawn and examined changes the possibility space (and thus the probability) of other cards that have not yet been drawn.

Card Draws and Dependence

If you have a deck of six cards numbered 1–6, and you shuffle them, draw one, then put it back, and shuffle again, that is equivalent to rolling 1d6. Each trial is independent, because of the shuffling. So one requirement of dependence in a card draw is that cards must be drawn **without replacement**.

The fact that we are looking at the cards as we draw them is also important. Removing a card from the deck without looking at it gives no additional information, so the probabilities of drawing additional cards (from our own point of reference) have not changed.

This may sound counterintuitive. Merely by flipping a card over, we magically change the probabilities? The reason for this is that we can only calculate the probabilities of the unknown based on what we *do* know. For example: if a card is drawn from a shuffled *Poker* deck of 52 cards, the probability that it is the Queen of Clubs is 1/52 (it has an equal chance of being any card in the deck). If the same deck is instead shuffled and then 51 of the cards are set aside without looking, the probability that the remaining card is the Queen of Clubs is still 1/52, because there is no additional information to go on. Now, if those 51 cards are all revealed and none of them is the Queen of Clubs, *then* the probability that the one remaining card is the Queen of Clubs is 100%. Each card revealed gives more information.[1]

It should also be noted, before moving on, that while we use "drawing cards from a shuffled deck" as the typical example in this chapter, there are plenty of other forms of dependent probability in games (just as there are many things like spinners and teetotums that look nothing like dice, but still behave the same way). Pulling out tiles from a cloth bag is a mechanic used in many tabletop games. So is the initial shuffling or other randomization of

---

[1]Note that many people harbor the fallacy that reshuffling an as-yet-unseen deck changes the outcome of the game. While this is obviously true in one sense (reordering the cards does indeed change the order they are drawn in reality), it does not change any probability calculations of what is in there.

cards, tiles, or the like, and then dealing them out face-down on a gameboard or in a tableau, so that they are not in a "deck" and might be chosen and flipped over in any order. Probability textbooks have a peculiar fascination with pulling colored balls from urns and not putting them back. All of these are equivalent to drawing cards from a shuffled deck. And just as with rolling dice, in most cases we assume that the shuffle is fair and completely random, and that the deck of cards has otherwise not been tampered with or marked in any way, so that any face-down card has an equal probability of being any of the cards that we have not yet seen.

Computing Dependent Probability

Calculating probabilities for dependent events follows the same core principles as doing the same thing with independent events: count the total number of ways to succeed, and divide by the size of the possibility space. However, with dependent probabilities it gets a bit trickier, because the probabilities change whenever a card is revealed. In practice, this means multiplying a lot of different things together, rather than multiplying the same thing by itself, if repeating a challenge several times. We are putting together everything that was done in the previous chapter, just in combination.

Drawing Two Cards

Let us start with a simple example. A player shuffles a standard 52-card deck and draws two cards. What is the probability that they've drawn a pair (two cards of the same rank)? There are a few ways to compute this, but the simplest is to start by asking: what is the probability that the first card drawn makes them completely ineligible to draw a pair (probability 0)? The answer, if course, is that the first card doesn't really matter—it can be anything at all, as long as the second card matches it. No matter what the first card is, there's still a non-zero chance to draw a matching second card. In other words, the probability of failure on the first card is 0, and thus, the probability of "success" is 1 (so long as the player *also* succeeds on the second card!).

Now, what is the probability that the second card matches the first? After drawing the first card, there are 51 cards remaining in the deck (the size of the possibility space is thus 51). Normally, there are four cards of each rank, but the first card drawn is one of those four, so there are three remaining cards that match the rank of the first card (so, the number of ways to succeed is 3). The probability of the second card matching is therefore $3/51 = 1/17$.

If a player in *Texas Hold 'Em* keeps insisting that they are dealt *yet another* pair on their initial two cards, there is a high probability they are bluffing.

Drawing Two Cards with Uneven Distribution

What if we take the previous example and add two Jokers to make it a 54-card deck? When drawing a Joker, assume the other Joker must be drawn to match as a pair, so if the first card is a Joker, then there's only one matching card (not three) in the rest of the deck. We solve this by splitting up the probabilities into two scenarios, then multiplying each possibility (first card AND second card match), and then finally adding up the (non-overlapping) scenarios (pair of Jokers OR pair of other cards).

   The first card is either a Joker (there are two in the deck, so the probability of this is 2/54) or something else (probability 52/54).

   If the first card is a Joker, then the probability of a match on the second card is 1/53 (one other Joker out of the remaining 53 cards). Multiplying this by the probability of the first card being a Joker (2/54) yields 1/1431, less than a tenth of a percent.

   If the first card isn't a Joker, the probability of a match on the second card is 3/53 (three cards of the same rank in the remaining 53 cards). Multiplying this by the probability of the first card not being a Joker (52/54) gives 78/1431, a little more than 5.5%, and less than the 1/17 probability of getting a pair in a 52-card deck (since there is an additional chance of failure if drawing a Joker on the second card but not the first).

   Since these two results (1/1431 and 78/1431) do not overlap, and we want to know the probability of *either* of them happening, we can add them together. The probability of a pair in this case is 79/1431 (still about 5.5%).

   If we really want to check our work, we could calculate the probability of all other results: drawing a Joker on the first card (1/54) but not on the second (52/53), and drawing a non-Joker on the first card (52/54) but a Joker on the second (2/53), and adding these to the other two possible results. If adding these all together, everything should sum to 1, because there should always be at least *some* result (either a pair of Jokers, a pair of non-Jokers, or two cards that are not a pair) every time.

Permutation and Combination

A lot of problems in dependent probability involve all the ways to select a particular set of things from a larger set of things. For example, in *Poker*, you might want to know the probability of drawing four-of-a-kind. If the order doesn't matter (as with *Poker*), there is a special operator, the **choose** operator (also known as **combination**), which counts the number of ways to choose some number of things among a larger number of things. The operator is defined as follows, when choosing k things out of n things[2]:

$$\binom{n}{k} = \frac{n!}{k!(n-k)!}$$

For example, the number of ways of drawing five cards from a standard 52-card deck is "52 choose 5" or

$$\frac{52!}{5!(52-5)!} = \frac{52*51*50*\cdots*3*2*1}{(5*4*3*2*1)*(47*46*\cdots*2*1)} = \frac{52*51*50*49*48}{5*4*3*2*1}$$

$$= 2,598,960$$

Thus, there are slightly less than 2.6 million unique *Poker* hands.

The choose operator assumes that order doesn't matter; drawing a Royal Flush in Spades is the same result, no matter whether the Ace was drawn first or last or anywhere in between. But sometimes, ordering does matter: for example, counting the number of ways to have first, second, and third places from an eight-player car race. When choosing k things out of n where each ordering is distinct (known as **permutation**), the formula is written as

$$P(n,k) = \frac{n!}{(n-k)!}$$

Thus, the number of unique ways to choose first, second, and third from an eight-player race is

$$\frac{8!}{(8-3)!} = \frac{8*7*6*5*4*3*2*1}{5*4*3*2*1} = 8*7*6 = 336$$

Also, the number of ways to order all eight players is $8!/(8-8)! = 8! = 40,320$.

All of the above assumes that the set of things we are randomly drawing from are all unique. A player can't usually win first *and* second places in a race, nor can they have a hand with two Aces of Spades in a *Poker* hand.

---

[2] The exclamation point is the **factorial** operator, which means you multiply all of the integer numbers between 1 and the number. 2! = 2, 3! = 6, 4! = 24, 5! = 120, and so on. Factorials get very large very quickly, and are one of the fastest-increasing functions a game designer is ever likely to encounter. By convention, 0! = 1! = 1.

However, sometimes there may be duplicates in the set. For example, if we want to know the total number of ways to get a Full House (one three-of-a-kind and one pair) in *Poker*, we only care about the rank of cards and not the suit. This means our deck contains four Aces, four Kings, and so on, with each one being equivalent for our purposes. In this case, we must take the extra step of calculating how many ways to choose the two or three matching cards for the pair and three-of-a-kind out of the four matching cards of that rank in the deck. The number of ways to have a Full House is

$$13*12*\binom{4}{3}*\binom{4}{2}=13*12*4*6=3744$$

Where do these numbers come from? We have to choose one of 13 ranks to be the three-of-a-kind and one of the remaining 12 ranks to be the pair. Note this is *not* "13 choose 2" because the order here matters: three Kings and two Aces is distinct from three Aces and two Kings. For the three-of-a-kind, we must choose three cards out of the four in the deck of matching rank (4 choose 3). For the pair, we must choose two cards out of four (4 choose 2). If we wanted the probability of a Full House, we would divide 3744 by the total number of five-card hands, 2,598,960, to get 0.00144, on the order of a tenth of a percent—so this is a very unlikely hand unless a player draws more cards or has wild cards!

Counting Shuffles

In a *Magic: the Gathering* tournament game, a player draws a reasonable opening hand with three basic land and four non-land cards… and then proceeds to draw nothing but basic land for the next five turns. There are 20 basic land cards in their 60-card deck. What is the probability that this would happen?

To calculate this, we count all of the ways that we can shuffle a deck where these conditions would hold and then divide by the total number of shuffles.

Let us first quantify the conditions we are looking at here:

- The first seven cards contain three land and four non-lands, in any random order. There are (7 choose 4)=7!/(4! 3!)=35 different ways to order these.
- The next five cards are all land. There is only one way to do this.
- The remaining 48 cards contain the remaining 12 land and 36 non-land, in any order. There are (48 choose 36)=48!/(36! 12!)=69,668,534,468 ways to order these.

- Multiplying all of these together since they must all be satisfied, we get 2,438,398,706,380, or about 2.4 trillion ways to shuffle the deck in this way. That's a lot of ways to get "land flood!"

How many ways are there to shuffle the deck? Technically, there are 60! Ways to shuffle a 60-card deck, but that's when every card is distinct. In this case, as you may notice from the above calculations, a lot of these shuffles are equivalent since we treat all "land" as identical to one another (and the same for "non-land") for the purposes of this problem. The number of ways to order 20 land would be 20!, and 40 non-land 40!, so you divide the 60! figure by both 20! and 40! to eliminate duplicate shuffles (another way to look at this: we are taking 60 cards and choosing 20 of them to be land, which is 60 choose 20; we could also choose 40 of them to be non-land, which is 60 choose 40, which gives the same result). This comes out to 4,191,844,505,805,495, or about 4 quadrillion. Dividing the number of ways to get only land in the first five turns by the total number of shuffles, we get a probability of 0.0005817 or a little less than 6 out of 10,000 games. Thankfully, that means this particular situation doesn't happen very often.

Suppose that we are concerned with more than just whether a card is land or not, and we have a deck with 10 Forest, 10 Swamp, and four copies each of 10 different non-land cards, for a total of 60 cards in the deck. How many distinct shuffles are there in this deck? Again, the answer is to first take the total number of shuffles of 60 cards (that's 60!) and divide by each duplication (there are 10! ways to swap the Forests with one another while still maintaining the same shuffle, 10! ways to rearrange the Swamps, and 4! ways to order each of the non-land cards). This gives a large number. You'll notice that when dealing with deck shuffles, the numbers do tend to get large very quickly:

$$\frac{60!}{10!10!\left(4!^{10}\right)} = 9.966E54$$

Suppose you then want to know the probability of drawing at least one copy of two specific non-land cards in a player's hand within the first ten cards. In this case, it would be easier to use negation and count the number of ways to have no copies of the first card, and the number of ways to have no copies of the second card. There is a problem: these two events are not independent (it is possible to have both at the same time), so if we add both together, we'd be double-counting the cases where the player draws no copies of either card. As a solution to this, we also count the number of ways to draw no copies of either and subtract it so that we're only counting it once again.

The number of ways to have no copies of the first card within the first ten cards: (56 choose 10), since we are choosing ten cards from the 56 that are not the first card. Once we've done that, we then multiply by 10! (total number of ways to reorder the ten cards chosen at the top of the deck) and 50! (total number of ways to reorder the remaining cards), and then divide by 10! 10! ($4!^{10}$) as before to not double-count duplicate orientations. This comes out to 4.761E54—a little more than half of the 9.966E54 shuffles.

The number of ways to have no copies of the second card within the first ten cards is the same. If we add the two situations together, we actually get more than the total number of shuffles, giving us a negative probability—but remember, this is double-counting the shuffles where neither of the two cards appear in the first ten cards.

To count the number of ways to have no copies of either the first or second card in the first ten cards, that is 52 choose 10 since we are choosing ten cards from the 52 that are neither of the two cards we care about, again multiplied by 10! and 50!, and again divided by 10! 10! ($4!^{10}$), which becomes 2.091E54.

If we add the number of ways to have no copies of the first card to the number of ways to have no copies of the second card and then subtract the number of ways to have neither, we get 7.322E54. Dividing that by the total number of shuffles with no constraints (9.966E54), we get 0.735. In other words, there is a probability of 0.735 that a player gets no copies of either or both of the cards. By negation, that means that the probability of having at least one copy of both cards is $1 - 0.735 = 0.265$. A deck that relies on putting a particular combo into play in the first three turns, therefore, would require additional card-drawing or other strategies if it wants to succeed a reasonable amount of the time!

Essential Case Studies

THE MONTY HALL PROBLEM

This brings us to a famous problem in statistics that is mainly well known for its ability to confuse people. It is named after the original host of the classic television game show *Let's Make a Deal*. In the show, the host acted as a kind of adversary, out to trick contestants and make them look like fools on national television.[3]

---

[3] Strictly speaking, this may not have been part of the show's initial design goals, but what can you say when audience members are dressed in chicken or gorilla suits?

There were a wide variety of mini-games played on the show, but the one that this problem is based on involves a choice of three doors, unoriginally called Door Number 1, Door Number 2, and Door Number 3. A contestant is given a door of their choice, for free! Behind one of the three doors, they're told, is a fabulous prize, such as a brand new car! Behind the other two doors, there's no prize at all. (Since the goal was apparently to humiliate as many people as possible, the doors were not empty, but rather they would have some silly non-prize behind them, like a goat, or a giant tube of toothpaste, or something else that was clearly *not* a brand new car.)

The contestant would pick their door. Monty Hall would get ready to reveal what was behind that door. But... wait! Before doing that, let's reveal one of the two other doors that the contestant did *not* choose and show that there isn't a car there! Since Monty knows where the car is, and there is only one car, he can always find *at least* one door to reveal that has no prize. Now, the contestant is now given the option to switch doors. Suppose they choose Door Number 3, and a goat is revealed behind Door Number 1; the contestant can keep their original Door Number 3, or they can trade it for the other unknown, Door Number 2. And this is where probability comes in: does switching doors improve the contestant's chance of winning, decrease it, or does it not matter because the probability is the same either way?

The completely counterintuitive (but correct) answer is that switching doors does increase the chance of winning. Why? Merely by revealing a door, have we somehow changed the odds? Recall our earlier examples with revealing cards from a deck, and how it is the revealing of information, not the removal of cards, that changes the probabilities—so yes, revealing information does change the probability!

On the initial choice of the player, the probability of guessing right is obviously 1/3, since there are three doors and only one brand new car. When the new prize-less door is revealed, it can't change the probability of the initial guess at all—it's still 1/3—which means that the *other* door (the only other option) must have a probability of 2/3 of being correct. If you'd like to see this for yourself, try making a Monte Carlo simulation where you switch doors every time, and another one where you don't ever switch, and see how often you win in each case, over several thousand trials.

You can look at this another way. Choose a door, which gives the probability of winning of 1/3. Monty Hall offers to trade for *both* of the other doors (sure, one of them doesn't have the car, but that is true 100% of the time). Of *course* a player should switch in this case!

You can look at it yet another way: as with the previous chapter, identify all possible outcomes and their respective probabilities. For example, suppose the car is behind Door Number 3, and you choose a random door:

- The player initially chooses Door Number 1 (probability 1/3). If they keep the door, they lose. If they switch, they win.
- They initially choose Door Number 2 (probability 1/3). If they keep the door, they lose. If they switch, they win.
- They initially choose Door Number 3 (probability 1/3). If they keep the door, they win. If they switch, they lose.
- Probability of winning after a switch: 1/3 (if they chose Door Number 1) + 1/3 (if they chose Door Number 2) = **2/3**
- Probability of winning without switching: 1/3 (if they chose Door Number 3) = **1/3**

You can count the outcomes yourself in this chart of all possible scenarios.

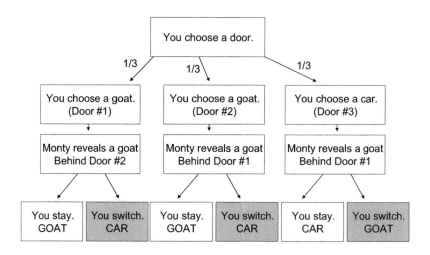

THE *REAL* MONTY HALL PROBLEM

In practice on the actual show, Monty Hall knew the solution to the so-called "Monty Hall problem" because he knew how to compute conditional probabilities even if his contestants couldn't. If he always offered the contestant the option to switch, the optimal strategy is to always switch, and if most contestants figured this out and it became common knowledge, then the game would get less interesting.

On the actual show, Monty Hall would modify the rules slightly. If the contestant chose the door with the brand new car (this does happen 1/3 of the time, so it is hardly a rare occurrence), Monty would always give the player the opportunity to switch—after all, what could be more humiliating than having a car and being tricked into trading it away for a goat? But if the contestant initially chooses a door with no prize at all, Monty would only offer to switch about half of those times; otherwise, he'd just show the contestant their brand new goat and boot them off the stage. Let us analyze this new game, where Monty Hall has the ability to choose whether or not to give the contestant the option of switching, and he always gives the option if the contestant chooses the car but only gives the option half of the time otherwise. *Now* what are the contestant's chances of winning if they keep their initial choice, compared to if they switch doors?

In this case, there are three equally likely scenarios. 1/3 of the time, the contestant correctly chooses the door with the prize; they lose if they switch, and win if they don't. Of the remaining 2/3 of the time, half of that (i.e., probability of 2/3 * 1/2 = 1/3), the contestant simply loses outright, without even having the option to trade doors. The remaining 1/3 (half of 2/3) of the time, the contestant initially chose the wrong door and is given the option to switch; they win if they switch and lose if they don't.

What is the contestant's probability of winning if they always switch doors now?

- 1/3 of the time, they lose immediately (choose wrong and have no option to switch)
- 1/3 of the time, they win (initially choose wrong, but switch)
- 1/3 of the time, they lose (initially choose right, but switch)
- The overall probability of a win by switching is **1/3**.

What about if the contestant chooses not to switch?

- 1/3 of the time, they lose immediately (choose wrong and have no option to switch)
- 1/3 of the time, they lose (initially choose wrong, and don't switch)
- 1/3 of the time, they win (initially choose right, and keep it)
- The overall probability of a win by not switching is also **1/3**.

So in this case, the contestant's overall probability of winning is 1/3, regardless of their choice. That's significantly less than the 2/3 probability of winning if they are always given the option to switch and take it (and no worse than the 1/3 probability of winning if the player never switches), so this would be a superior strategy on Monty Hall's part to reduce the number of winning contestants.

Another interesting property of this situation, if the player is given the option to switch at all, what is their probability of winning then? In this case, we have eliminated the 1/3 possibility of losing right away, so there are only two options left (analogous to having a three-card deck and revealing and discarding one of the cards). Both options are equally likely, so it turns out that if the player reaches this point, their probability of winning has improved to 1/2. Again, you can simply count up the possible outcomes manually.

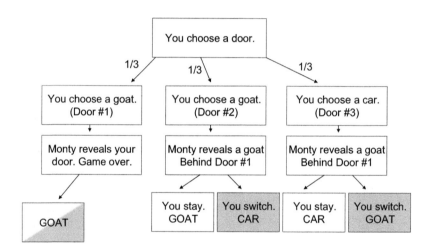

Is there any other strategy Monty could use that would reduce the contestant's probability of winning even further? What if he offers the chance to switch 1/4 of the time, or 2/5 of the time, or some other number? Let us assume that Monty offers the option of switching *if the player initially guesses right* with probability R and that he offers the option of switching *if the player initially guesses wrong* with probability W.

- 1/3 of the time, the player guesses right. Their probability of winning is $1/3 * R$ if they don't switch, and their probability of losing is $1/3 * R$ if they do switch, in this case. Additionally, their probability of winning outright is $1/3 * (1 - R)$, if their initial guess is right and they aren't given the option to switch at all.
- 2/3 of the time, the player guesses wrong. Their probability of winning is $2/3 * W$ if they switch, and their probability of losing is $2/3 * W$ if

they don't switch. Additionally, their probability of losing outright is $2/3 * (1-W)$, if their initial guess is wrong and they aren't given the option to switch.

- The overall probability of winning by not switching is $1/3 * R + 1/3 * (1-R) = 1/3$, which makes sense because the only way to win by not switching is to guess right initially, which has a probability of $1/3$.
- The overall probability of winning by switching (if given the option) is $2/3 * W + 1/3 * (1-R)$. Depending on the probabilities W and R, this could be anywhere from 0 (if $W=0$ and $R=1$, meaning that Monty *only* offers the possibility of switching if the contestant initially guessed right) to 1 (if $W=1$ and $R=0$).
- If either of these options (switching or not) is higher than the other, there is an optimal strategy for the player. Since *not* switching, by default, has a win probability of $1/3$, if Monty wants to maximize the chance of a loss, then $2/3 * W + 1/3 * (1-R)$ cannot be any greater than $1/3$. Because the contestant does get an initial choice and can always choose to stand by their first pick, there is no way to get a win probability lower than $1/3$.

The game becomes the most interesting when the probability of win by switching is the same as the probability of a win by not switching ($1/3$), because then there is no optimal strategy for the contestant. (There are many values of R and W that would lead to a win probability of $1/3$ by switching, including our initial scenario of $R=1$, $W=1/2$.) With a win probability of exactly $1/3$ for switching and $1/3$ for not switching, this is no longer a game of math, but rather a game of psychology. Did Monty offer the choice to switch because he thinks the contestant is a sucker who doesn't know that switching should mathematically be the "right" choice, and they'll stubbornly hold onto their first pick because it feels worse to have a car then trade it for a goat, than to have a goat and keep it? Or does Monty think that the contestant is smart and they'll switch, and he's only offering the chance to switch because he knows that the contestant guessed right, and he's hoping that the contestant takes the bait and falls into his trap? Or is Monty being nice, goading the contestant into doing something in their own best interest, because he hasn't given away a car in a few episodes and wants to get that excitement so that no one complains that the game is rigged? And it's up to the contestant to try to "read" Monty's expression and decide whether he's offering the option to switch because he's being nice or being mean. In spite of this game being simple, there is a lot of *psychological* depth to the play, both from Monty's side and from the contestant's.

Incidentally, the same is true for *Poker*, which helps to explain its popularity, at least in part. Most of the formats for this game involve slowly revealing cards in between rounds of betting. As with Monty Hall giving the contestant an initial choice and then a new choice, in *Poker* players all start with a certain probability of winning, and that probability then changes in between each betting round as more cards are revealed (and also, from each player's perspective with the privileged information known only to them, the players may disagree with one another over who has the mathematical advantage).

THE FALSE-POSITIVE PARADOX

The Monty Hall problem is best known from its use on a game show (and for being one of those "trick questions" that shows how unintuitive probability can be, and how easy it can be to get a simple problem wrong). Another famous problem, the False-Positive Paradox, is actually seen in many real-world situations.

It is so named because of one of its applications, medical tests. If a patient is tested by their doctor from a disease, the test either says they have the disease, or they don't; and in reality, they either have the disease being tested for, or they don't. Ideally, one would hope these two pieces of data agree; if someone has a disease and the test correctly flags them as being positive for the disease, that is a **true positive**, and if they don't have the disease and the test comes back negative, then that is a **true negative**. However, no test is absolutely perfect, and it is possible that for some people, the test result can be inaccurate. If the test says that a patient has a disease, but they actually do not, that is a **false positive**; if the test says they do not have the disease but in reality they do, that is a **false negative**. These are the four possible results, then, that someone can have from a medical test: true or false positive, and true or false negative.

Consider this problem:

- Among a certain population, 2% of people have a terrible disease, so the disease is relatively rare (but still high enough to warrant testing). On the bright side, a pretty accurate medical test is available.
- The test is 100% **sensitive**: if someone has the disease, the test detects it correctly 100% of the time. In other words, the probability of a false negative is zero.
- The test is 95% **specific**: if someone does *not* have the disease, there is a 95% probability it correctly shows as being negative, but there is the remaining 5% probability of a false positive.

- Suppose your best friend gets tested, and the test comes back positive. What is the probability that they have the disease (or, what is the probability that it's just a false positive)?

In situations like this, one way to approach the problem is to attach a number to it: assume there is a population of any number (let's say 1000) that falls exactly on this distribution, with 2% of them having the disease, and 5% of the remaining 98% getting a false positive.[4] Out of 1000 people, the expected value would be 20 people (2%) that have the disease—the true positives. Of the remaining 980 people who do not have the disease, 95% of them (931 people) have a true negative, and 5% of them (49 people) have a false positive.

Adding the false positives and true positives together, we have a total of 69 people who get a positive test result. Of these, only 20 actually have the disease. Your friend's chance of having the disease if they get a positive test, then, is 20/69, or about 29%. The probability of actually having the disease would be even lower if the disease had a lower incidence rate in the population or a higher false-positive rate; even if those are the same, a larger population would make the problem worse in the sense that more total people would be affected by an incorrect test result. This is why the problem is a "paradox": even with a positive result from the test, the probability that someone has the disease is still quite low, simply because the disease has such a low prevalence.

There are many real-world problems even outside of medicine that are affected by the False-Positive Paradox. If it could be definitively shown that there are a greater number of people of a certain race, class, or neighborhood that commit crimes, would police profiling of that population be appropriate, if the rate of criminal activity is relatively low (i.e., most citizens are law-abiding) and it's possible for "cop instincts" to be wrong and incorrectly flag a person as "probably a criminal" even when they aren't? What if we developed a pretty good (but not perfect) algorithm to detect people who are terrorists in the general population, and assuming that the total number of terrorists is a tiny fraction of the population (even less than other criminals), could this be used to justify the government covertly spying on people? What about quality control and consumer safety applications: suppose in a car assembly line, a test for defective safety mechanisms is pretty good but not perfect,

---

[4]Note that if we were going to randomly select 1000 people from a large population, the probability of them falling *exactly* on the overall probability distribution is actually quite low, just like the probability of rolling 1, 2, 3, 4, 5, and 6 once each on a roll of 6d6 is very low (as shown in the previous chapter). But in this case, we are really just using this as a method for counting, so that we can divide the total number of people in a "sample" population that fit a certain criteria by the size of that possibility space, in order to compute exact probabilities. This works no matter what number we use for the total population: 100, or 1,000, or 1,000,000, or anything else.

should all cars that fail be thrown onto the scrap heap even though most of them are perfectly fine in reality? What about mandatory drug testing of state welfare recipients (or employees of a company), where the rate of drug use is relatively low among the population and the false-positive rate for a drug test is non-zero? All of these are situations with far-reaching public policy and ethical implications, yet they can be more informed choices by a basic understanding of probability.

You may wonder what any of these situations have to do with game design. Game design is the study of systems. Law enforcement, medicine, consumer product testing, and public policy all involve systems. If you can't see the connection, consider taking any of these systems and making it into a game… and then see if the game is balanced! Or, consider running for public office yourself, some day; government could greatly benefit from more skilled game designers who know how to properly craft and balance systems.

Discussion Questions

1. As with the previous chapter, probability can be tricky—and several things in this chapter were extremely unintuitive. If in a group, discuss things that are unclear.

2. What is the difference between a dependent and independent probability event?

3. Consider two loot drop systems. In the first system, each drop is independent of the others and has a 1% chance of giving the player an epic item. In the second system, it starts at a 1% chance of an epic item but then increases by 1% every time the player doesn't get an epic item (cumulative) and resets back to 1% when they get an epic item. What's the difference in how these systems feel to a player?

4. What is the difference between the situations where you'd use permutation vs. combination?

5. Think of any card game such as a trading card game (TCG). How would the play be different if cards were replaced into the deck so that a player always had the same chance of drawing each card, rather than the probabilities changing after every card draw?

6. Give examples of how you might implement the False-Positive Paradox in a game—a situation where rare events might be signaled to players with some amount of error.

7. Take any game with die rolls. Imagine if you replaced the die rolls with a deck of cards. For example, for a 2d6 roll, use a deck of 36 cards with each possible roll represented on one of the cards, and only reshuffle the deck after it runs out. What effect would this have on play?

8. *Poker* has a luck component (the card draw) and a skill component (psychological reading of your opponents, as well as knowing the odds of having a winning hand with incomplete information). Which of the two do you think is stronger in determining the outcome of a game?

9. Why does removing cards from a deck change the probability of future draws only if you know what cards are removed, but not if they're removed without revealing them?

10. What kinds of dependent-probability calculations are easier to figure out, and which are harder? If studying this book in a group, can you come up with a probability question that no one else in the group can figure out how to solve?

Sidequests

Sidequest 18.1: Really Big Flush

In *Texas Hold 'Em Poker*, each player has two cards of their own hand plus five shared cards in the center of the table, for a seven-card "hand." These are all drawn from a standard 52-card deck (4 suits of 13 cards each, no Jokers). Players then take the best five of their seven cards to form their final hand.

A "flush" is a hand where all five cards belong to the same suit. It doesn't matter what the rank of the cards are—they can be anything—but they must all be of the same suit.

What is the probability of having a flush—that is, out of the seven cards randomly drawn from the deck, what is the probability that *at least* five of those cards belong to the same suit?

Sidequest 18.2: Multiple Turns in a Row

In the board game *The Pillars of the Earth*, players each have three actions per round, represented by pawns of their color. At the start of the round, all pawns are put in a cloth bag, and then one designated player draws one pawn out at a time, and the player whose pawn it is takes one action. In this way, turn order is randomized every round, and some players may have several "turns" in a row, which may come early or late in the round (the game balances the advantage of going early by imposing additional costs).

Assume a four player game. What is the probability that some player has all three of their tokens drawn in a row at the very start of the round?

Sidequest 18.3: *Three and Three vs. Four and Two*

Suppose you are designing a *Poker* variant that uses a six-card hand instead of the more typical five-card hands, for some reason. This suggests two new hands that do not exist in standard *Poker*. One new hand is a "Three and Three": two three-of-a-kinds (for example, three 8s and three Kings). The other is a "Four and Two": one pair and a different four-of-a-kind (for example, four Aces and two 2s).

In standard *Poker*, the various hands are ranked by rarity, so that a hand that is more rare ranks higher than one that is more common. In six-card *Poker*, which of these two new hands should be ranked higher? How much more rare is one than the other?

Sidequest 18.4: War *Lite*

The children's card game *War* is notorious for its lack of any player choices combined with its frustratingly long play time. Here is a redesigned variant that is much, much shorter:

- **Players**: 2
- **Objective**: score at least three points out of five.
- **Setup**: players take ten cards, numbered 1 through 10, and shuffle them, dealing five to each player. These remain face-down, so that neither player knows any card.
- **Play**: One at a time, each player selects one of their cards (without knowing what it is) and turns it face-up. Of the two cards chosen in this way, the higher number wins a point. Both cards are then set aside and cannot be chosen again.
- **Resolution**: After both players have played all five of their cards, the game is over, and the player with the highest number of points wins.

Now, count: how many distinct setups are there in this game? For example: one player might have all of the low cards (1–2–3–4–5) and the other all the high cards (6–7–8–9–10). Or, one player might have the odd cards

(1–3–5–7–9) and the other the evens (2–4–6–8–10). How many different initial deals are there? Be careful not to double-count!

Greater challenge: create a spreadsheet that, given an initial setup (two sets of five cards—or really, just one set of five cards, since it should be able to figure out the missing five of the other player by process of elimination), exhaustively calculate all possible plays and game outcomes. Since each outcome is equally likely, then use this to calculate the probability of each player winning, which tells you who has the advantage. Since each player can choose among five cards in any order, the total number of different orderings for each player is 5 * 4 * 3 * 2 * 1 = 120. There are two players, so there are a total of 120 * 120 = 14,400 different games that can be played off of a single distribution of cards. This number includes some duplicates, such as choosing the same set of numbers at the same time but in a different order, so if you ignore orderings and are just concerned with pairings, there are only 120 possible game outcomes.

Ultimate challenge: after doing the above, first restructure the data so that everything is in a single row. Fill Down for a number of rows equal to the total number of initial deals that you've calculated. Either by hand or by formula, exhaustively list all distinct initial deals, each in its own row. Then, sort all rows by the column that calculates the probability of winning, and find the row(s) that are as close to possible as 0.5 (that is, an even chance of either player winning). This way, if you wanted this game to only have luck during the play of the game and not on the initial distribution of cards, you could use one of those rows and distribute the cards manually instead of randomly!

Sidequest 18.5: Magic *Redux*

Consider a 60-card deck with 10 Forests and 4 Llanowar Elves (and 46 other cards). What is the probability of drawing at least one Forest *and* at least one Llanowar Elves card in an opening hand of seven cards?

Greater challenge: If a player doesn't like the cards in their opening hand of seven cards, they can choose to "mulligan" by reshuffling and then drawing a new opening hand of six cards. If they don't like that hand, they can mulligan again to reshuffle and draw five cards. If they don't like that, they can mulligan again and draw 4, and so on.

If a player feels they absolutely *must* have a Forest and Llanowar Elves in their opening hand and is willing to mulligan repeatedly if they don't get it, what is the probability that they fail to get their desired opening even if they mulligan all the way down to a two-card hand?

Sidequest 18.6: Hearthstone *Opening*

In the online TCG *Hearthstone*, the player that goes first draws three cards from their 30-card deck. They can then choose to "mulligan" any or all of the cards drawn; those are then reshuffled back into the remaining deck and an equal number of replacements are drawn (it is possible to draw the card that was just thrown away again).

Suppose that in a particular deck, 15 out of the 30 cards are cards that the player would pitch from their opening hand in order to redraw. Also suppose there is one card in particular in the deck that is highly advantageous if starting the game with it, and the deck contains two copies of that card.

Assuming a draw of three cards, throwing away any that are in the 15 that would not be kept, and then redrawing, what is the probability of starting the game with at least one copy of that one key card?

Greater challenge: In *Hearthstone*, players also draw a card on their first turn. What does the probability increase to if you include an extra random card draw from the remaining 27-card deck in your calculations, after the initial mulligan?

Sidequest 18.7: Battleship *AI*

Battleship is a two-player game played on a square grid where each player secretly places a fleet of ships of varying sizes in either horizontal or vertical alignment, anywhere on their grid (various versions differ as to whether ships are allowed to overlap). Players then take turns, each guessing one coordinate of the grid; the opponent tells them whether they hit a ship ("hit") or not ("miss"), and in some versions, must also say whether a hit sunk a ship (that is, all of the squares occupied by that ship have now been hit), and if so, which ship. The objective is to sink all of the opponent's ships first.

Let us assume a small game: a 6×6 grid with three ships, one of which has a length of 2, one with a length of 3, and one with a length of 4. Let us also assume for simplicity that players are allowed to have ships overlap one another, either partially or entirely (in the case of a single shot hitting multiple ships, the player would still only say "hit" and not say how many hits). Let's also assume that the opponent does not have to say when a ship is sunk; the only time a player is informed of anything other than "hit" or "miss" is when they achieve the final victory condition.

Calculate the total number of legal ship configurations on this grid.

Greater challenge (requires some proficiency in computer programming; the computations involved are too extensive to do by hand, and the possibility space is too large to fit in a spreadsheet): At first glance, *Battleship* appears to be a guessing game of pure chance. How would a player know where an enemy ship is likely to be if they can be anywhere? And this is how most people who learn the game play it: they start with initially guessing more or less at random, and once they get a hit, they start guessing up, down, left, or right, until they find the ends of that ship; they then return to random guesses.

We can do better. Let's assume that every possible configuration of enemy ships is equally likely. We can then simply count up how many of those configurations has part of a ship in each square, divide by the total number of possible configurations, and calculate a probability that this particular square is occupied by an enemy ship. We then simply find the square with the highest probability and fire there (choosing arbitrarily if several squares are tied for highest). Initially on an open board, this tends to give higher probabilities in the center of the board, since there are more ways to fit a ship in the center than on the edges or corners. Probability also decreases in squares that are orthogonally close to misses from previous turns and rises greatly in squares orthogonally close to hits.

Implement a computer AI that plays *Battleship* as well as possible. Test it out using a Monte Carlo simulation of randomly chosen configurations; what is the mean and median number of turns it takes to win? How does that compare to a "dumb" AI that guesses completely randomly, or a "human-like" AI that guesses randomly until it hits a ship and then follows in each direction until it finds the ends of the ship?

If you are going through this book with other people (such as in a classroom environment), you could have a tournament, pitting each person's AI against the others in a series of matches against random ship configurations to see whose AI can sink them all in the least total number of turns.

Ultimate challenge: Suppose you know that you are playing against your own AI. What is the optimal configuration of ships you can choose that takes your AI the longest to sink? In other words, what's the worst-case scenario for your AI, and how would you choose your ships to exploit that?

If doing a tournament, also create your own ship configuration. When playing your AI against another, also use each other's ship configurations.

19

Managing Luck and Skill

In This Chapter

- Beyond Randomness
- A Series of Paradoxes
- Opportunities for Skillful Play
- Frames of Reference
- The Double Axis
- Modifying Skill and Luck

Beyond Randomness

> Pinball is a good example of what makes a great game—a mixture of luck and skill. That's a very critical aspect. In the long run a more-skilled player will do better, but in the short run anyone should be able to win. There should be some randomness, which offer challenges over the game. When you get to games like Pac-Man or Mortal Kombat where there's a documentable sequence that you can execute to succeed, to me that's totally antithetical to what a game should be.
>
> *Howard Scott Warshaw, from a Digital Press interview (http://www.digitpress.com/library/interviews/interview_howard_scott_warshaw.html).*

In our brief foray into probability, there is one thing that we have so far ignored, and it is time to bring it out into the open and challenge it. By looking at random systems and how to create them, there has been an implicit, unstated assumption that this is a good thing: that randomness in games is worthwhile and makes a game better (else, we wouldn't bother learning it).

But we also know that too much randomness can also be a bad thing. Maybe children can put up with a game like *Candyland* or *Chutes & Ladders* or *War* in spite of the lack of decisions and complete dominance of luck, because they are just learning core game skills like taking turns and counting numbers… but for most adults, these aren't exactly their idea of a great time.

Perhaps, like many people, you have a general sense that there is a continuum between "completely luck-based" and "completely skill-based," and every game lies somewhere on the line, with games like *Chess* at one extreme and games like *Candyland* at the other.

You may have even encountered the terms "casual" and "core" in reference to games or gamers, and you might have a general sense that casual games tend to have more luck and hardcore games more skill.

These assumptions would seem very reasonable. However, they are not always correct.

A Series of Paradoxes

Tic-Tac-Toe has no randomness at all. It is purely a game of skill. And yet, we don't see many people attempting to make it an Olympic sport or organize televised world championships for the game. Meanwhile, a single hand of *Poker* has a very strong luck component—either players are dealt a good hand or they aren't—and yet, we still think of *Poker* as a game where skill dominates over luck.

Meanwhile, the gambling card game *Blackjack* is also highly random from hand to hand, but aside from banned strategies like counting cards, this is thought of as more of a game of chance.

Furthermore, there are physical sports like *Football* or *Baseball*, which we would naturally think of as games of skill. And yet, sports enthusiasts track all kinds of statistics on players and teams and games, treating each situation as if it were a random event: betting on games with point spreads, looking at a single play and calculating the probability of a particular team gaining or losing on that play based on past performance, and the like. If these aren't games of luck, sports fans would certainly would seem to treat them as if they were.

What's going on here? That is what this chapter is about: understanding the relationship between luck and skill.

Opportunities for Skillful Play

In cases where there is randomness but also choice in a game, a large part of whether luck or skill dominates is whether a player is rewarded for predicting and responding to the randomness. This is why there's a difference between *Poker* and *Blackjack*. In *Poker*, a skilled player can compute probabilities at the table and come up with a calculation of how likely it is they have the winning hand, and then factor that into their bet along with their perceived reactions of the opponents. The player's understanding of probability and their ability to react to those calculations has a direct relation to their performance in the game. Also, while the luck factor is high in a single hand of *Poker*, over many hands that luck tends to balance out (see about the "Law of Large Numbers" section in Chapter 17). In a long series of hands, if everyone is dealt about as many winning hands as everyone else, victory goes to the player who manages to extract the greatest amount of money from their opponents on the hands where they're winning, and loses the smallest amount on hands when they aren't, while occasionally managing to bluff their way to winning a round where they didn't even have the best hand.

In *Blackjack*, by contrast, players place their bets at the beginning of the hand before knowing what cards are dealt, and don't even have the option to "raise" or "fold" as they see additional cards come out (or if they do, it's only in very specialized situations). They make choices about whether to hit, stand, or split, but these are easily calculable probability calculations that any serious *Blackjack* player knows by heart already. We also know that this game has odds slightly in favor of the dealer, so even with optimal play, players still lose in the long run.[1] Either way, the skill of playing *Blackjack* is analogous to the skill of playing *Pac-Man*: the player follows a deterministic pattern (in the case of *Blackjack*, the "pattern" is to bet higher when the odds favor them, bet lower when they aren't, and choose actions in the game based on the player's current total and dealer's card, and so on). Optimal play in this case isn't about making interesting decisions, but rather, following an algorithm. There is skill, but it's skill at executing a well-practiced strategy—not the skill of making clever, unexpected decisions that can turn a loss into a win. Similarly, we don't think of the casino as having "skill" at *Roulette* or *Craps*, even though it certainly wins more than it loses.

---

[1] If the player counts cards successfully, or otherwise finds a way to cheat at the game, that *does* require a greater degree of skill and can also change the probabilities to favor the player rather than the casino. Casinos are very good at detecting when a player is doing this and are quick to step in and forcibly remove the player from the premises for life.

Frames of Reference

What about sports, where a clearly skill-based game is analyzed as if it were a random process? This is explained by looking at different perspectives. From the point of view of a player on a sports team, the game is won or lost on their skillful play; it's not a gamble for them (and they get paid accordingly!). But a spectator in the audience of a game has no control over the outcome, so as far as *they* are concerned, each contest behaves as if it were a random event. This is why sports betting can happen and is considered gambling: from the bettor's perspective, they are guessing about the outcome of a future event that they do not control, so for them, it really is a gamble (and if it isn't—if they have inside information or if they influence the outcome somehow—that is considered cheating).

You can see a similar effect in action games as well. In a typical first-person shooter (FPS), players are using their skill in their movement and aiming in order to shoot their opponents while avoiding getting shot themselves. This is thought of as a skill-based game, and in fact, these games are quite incompatible with randomness. For example, consider this thought experiment: suppose the designer of an FPS added a small perturbation on bullet fire from a cheap pistol, to make the weapon less accurate. And suppose a player lined someone up in their sights, pulled the trigger... and missed, because the game randomly made the bullet fly too far to the left. How would most people react to that?

They might not notice, in some cases. Action happens fast in the game. Everyone's running around, shots are fired, they miss, and players might just figure that they weren't as accurate as they thought (or their opponent was good at dodging). Or, in the case where a player is able to sneak up behind an opponent who is standing still, take a shot point-blank, and *still* miss, they'd probably feel like the game just robbed them of a skillful kill. This isn't fun and doesn't make the game any more interesting; it just makes players feel like they're being arbitrarily punished for being a good shot. Indeed, with all the factors that go into shooting at a moving target in a typical FPS, there is quite enough chaos in the system, and whether a shot hits or not is based on a number of factors that are difficult to have complete control over. Random die rolls are hardly necessary in this case.

At the same time, however, you can think of each shot fired as an independent event that could be modeled by a die roll if you are looking from an outside frame of reference, based on the relative aiming skill of the attacker and dodging skill of the target. Is there a way to increase the "luck factor" here—that is, to put players of uneven skill levels on more even ground, so that skill plays slightly less of a role in the outcome of the game? You can, but it must be done carefully.

Here is a common example from many FPS games: head shots. The typical way this works is that if a player specifically hits an opponent in the head (a much smaller target than their entire body), they do much more damage or even just get an outright kill. At first glance, this may seem like a mechanic that rewards *skill*, not luck: there's a greater degree of accuracy required in hitting such a small target. In some games, that is true; but in others, that kind of accuracy just isn't realistically possible in most situations: the action is moving too fast, the hit box around the head is too small, and most guns don't let a player zoom the camera enough at a distance to be sure of whether they're off by a pixel or two in the wrong direction. From a distance, at least, a head shot isn't something that most players can consistently rely on. But sometimes, it happens anyway, just by happy accident if the player is shooting in the correct general direction. Sometimes, through no fault of the player, they score a head shot. And this does even the playing field, slightly; without head shots, if it takes many shots to score a kill, the more skilled player almost always wins because they are better at aiming and dodging which allows them to outmaneuver and outplay a weaker player. With head shots, the weaker player occasionally gets in an outright kill (even if only by accident), making it more likely that a weaker player sees at least the occasional success. Outside of top-level tournament play, this is generally what a game designer would want for a game.

The Double Axis

How to explain the differences between the role of luck vs. skill in *Pac-Man*, *Chess* and *Candyland*, *Tic-Tac-Toe*, and *Poker*? Sure, *Chess* and *Pac-Man* and *Tic-Tac-Toe* are all games of pure skill—all elements of the three games are entirely deterministic—but the similarities end there. *Chess* is incredibly deep. *Pac-Man* isn't particularly deep, but does require a high level of precision and mastery to play well. *Tic-Tac-Toe* is simple and shallow.

Kinds of Skill

One reason these things seem to not go together is that there are many different *kinds* of skill, so it's not easy to make comparisons between games that require different kinds. *Chess* involves strategic and tactical thinking. *Pac-Man* and *Rock Band* are about fast reaction times and the ability to execute patterns flawlessly. The skill in *Poker* is partly the ability to do odds calculations in one's head and partly the ability to read the opponents' social cues while concealing their own. Even within a category, different games have a different intensity of required skill level. *Tic-Tac-Toe* and *Chess* both feature tactical and strategic skill, but *Tic-Tac-Toe*'s skill cap is very low—it's easy to master—while *Chess* requires a greater amount of skill because of its complexity and depth. *Connect Four* and *Othello* are somewhere between the two, while the number of permutations in *Go* or *Arimaa* are greater even than *Chess*.

Kinds of Luck

Just as there are different kinds of skill, there are also different kinds of luck. We can broadly classify these into two categories: those that happen *before* the player chooses an action, and those that happen *after* the player chooses an action, referred to by game designers as **Input Randomness** and **Output Randomness**, respectively.

Input randomness involves randomizing the initial setup of the game, putting the player in a different situation each time. Examples include the initial randomization of the board hexes and numbers in *Catan*, or the random map generation in *Sid Meier's Civilization* or *Minecraft*, or drawing a tile before deciding where to place it in *Carcassonne*, or the initial deal of the cards in *Freecell* solitaire. Input randomness benefits a game mainly by increasing replayability: each play involves a different setup and emergent new challenges, but without making the game feel "too random." Players can still plan in advance and rely on their actions, so there is the possibility of deep strategy even with input randomness. On the down side, if the game's *only* random elements are of this type, optimal strategies and lines of play may be evident. If the game lacks sufficient depth, it could be solvable at the table or at the very least could lend itself to "analysis paralysis" (players that deeply analyze the game state to try to find the optimal move for themselves, thus slowing down the game for everyone else).

Output randomness, by contrast, involves some kind of random element being triggered in response to a player action. Examples include to-hit and damage rolls in most RPGs, or die-rolls in many tabletop wargames: a player first declares their intention to attack an enemy, and then, they roll dice to see the outcome of the attack. Most gambling games also feature output randomness prominently: place a wager and *then* the random element determines a win or loss. The benefit of output randomness is that it adds excitement: will a player score a critical hit, or will they hit the jackpot? It allows for faster play, as players can't see too far in the future, so there's no point in getting bogged down in deep strategic decision-making. In games with some level of strategy or tactics, it allows for a different kind of skill, that of the risk/reward calculation, weighing the various outcomes and choosing whether to play more aggressively or more conservatively. On the down side, output randomness allows situations where luck dominates play; "unlucky" outcomes can lead to "cheap" losses, and the player may feel like they lost (or won) because of the dice and not because of their choices within the game.

Kinds of Uncertainty

We can also discuss different forms of randomness in terms of how the player encounters them and how they are able to deal with the uncertainty.

You can design a situation of **complete randomness** where the outcome is completely random, in such a way that the player's decision is being made blind. They come to a fork in the road and can go left or right, but receive no clues as to how the paths differ. They choose Rock, Paper, or Scissors against a new opponent that they don't know, with no information to go on in terms of their likelihood of choosing any given throw. They spin the spinner in *Candyland* and do what it says without having the ability to make a decision at all.

More insidious is that of **hidden randomness**, where the random elements are concealed from the player to the point that they may not even realize there is a random element at all (this is more common in video games than tabletop games, for obvious reasons). For example, most people who have played *Wii Sports* are unaware that there is a small random element added to the player action, weighted to favor whomever is behind. In *Wii Tennis*, for example, the ball bounces a little bit randomly from where it was hit; that random perturbation is more likely to be favorable to a player who's behind (or unfavorable if they're ahead). In *Wii Bowling*, the ball and pins are more likely to get a tiny nudge in one direction or the other based on how well or poorly a player is doing. But this random element isn't communicated to the player at all, and most players wouldn't even realize it's happening, so it isn't something players can base their decisions on.

For more strategic games where player decision-making is important, we can talk of **measured randomness**, where the exact outcome may not be known to players ahead of time, but the possibility space of what *might* happen and relative probabilities of each outcome are known to all players. *Catan* is a great example; no one knows what the dice will roll, but everyone should know that 6s and 8s are expected to happen more frequently than 2s and 12s, so the choice of where to build is an informed decision.

Kinds of Information

Yet another distinction that can be drawn is luck that comes not from a die roll, but from knowledge about the game state that is concealed from a player. In *Poker*, players don't know what's in their opponents' hands, and the "luck" in the game comes mainly from that lack of information; if the game were played with entirely open hands, then betting would be much easier, bluffing would be impossible, and the game would lose much of its interest. This can be referred to as **incomplete information**, meaning that some elements of the game state are unknown to a player, but players know exactly which elements of the game state are unknown (and generally, what the possibility space is for what those unknowns *might* be).

This is distinct from a game with **imperfect information**, where players have some information about the game state that may be incorrect, so that players aren't even sure of what they do or don't know. For example, consider the party game *Werewolf*, where one player, the Seer, gets some privileged information on one other player per round: he points at the other player and is told which of the two sides they are on. But suppose the moderator secretly rolled a d4 and gave the opposite result on a 1, as part of the Seer's ability; then the Seer still has some information, but it is unreliable.

Skill vs. Luck

And so we come back to skill and luck. Rather than being two diametrically opposed extremes on a single axis, instead they could be thought of as two separate axes. A game may require a great deal of skill, or very little, or none. A game may have a lot of elements of luck, or few, or none. The two are often inversely correlated, but not always.

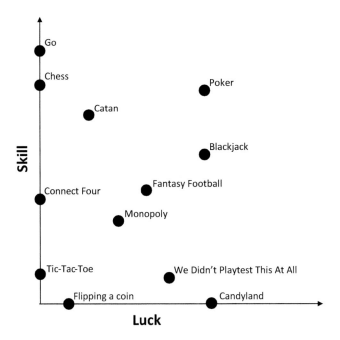

While this diagram (the dots are approximate and not places with any kind of scientific measurements) examines board and card games, the same is true in video games as well. The *Mario Kart* series, for example, is a racing game that has a relatively high luck factor, due to the random power-up blocks that are found on the track; other racing games like the *Gran Turismo* series have about the same level of driving and racing skill, but no random elements so a much lower presence of luck. First-person shooters tend to have high levels of skill and relatively little luck; *Wii Sports* has a relatively high level of luck and not as much skill.

Do These Distinctions Matter?

Is it meaningful to look at the difference between all of these different types of luck, or is it just the same rose by different names? Consider the genre of video games known as Roguelikes. In this genre, a complete playthrough of the game might take well over 50 hours of play. Yet, one common trait in these games is the presence of **permadeath**: if a player loses, not only is it game over, but their character is permanently erased. They can save a game in progress, sure (no game requires playing 50+ hours in one single session), but if the character dies, then the save file is erased. If a player is 45 hours into a 50-hour game and then they have to start from scratch, that is a lot of lost progress. One might expect such a game to be skill-based, at least: it would be terrible to lose the game just because of one unavoidable random die-roll. And yet, most of these games have die rolls for just about everything combat-related. When attacking an enemy, there might be one random roll to determine whether the character hits when attacking, then another roll to determine the amount of damage. Use of spells or skills may carry a chance of failure, where the action is wasted to no effect. Against enemy area-of-effect attacks, there might be a saving throw to reduce damage. When leveling up, improvements to stats might be randomly determined. The dungeon layout and monster and treasure placement are randomly generated. Yet, these are still games of skill, because of the nature of the randomness.

Probabilities of everything are exposed to the player, so they can calculate their chances of success in doing just about anything. Roguelikes are designed to give the player multiple ways out of a bad situation (the player might be able to heal themselves, teleport themselves or dangerous enemies away, or any number of other things, in addition to things like making sure they are protected from certain deadly status ailments and that they regularly search for traps and enemies, to avoid getting in a deadly situation to begin with). The player is never put in an unfair situation where they are sure to die, when they had no way to avoid it and have no way to respond. If the player dies—and in a typical Roguelike, players *will* die many times as they learn the game's systems—it is because they made a mistake or took an unnecessary risk. Players tend to walk into death with their eyes wide open: "sure, I'm low on health, but so is this enemy… and if I beat it I'll get a ton of treasure and experience, and if I run away then it'll heal while I'm gone and I'll have to start all over again… okay, I'll attack one more round" (and *then* they roll poorly and die). With over 50 hours' worth of die rolls, a player who takes these kinds of risks often *will* eventually roll badly and die, if they dice with death enough times. Roguelikes, above any other game genre, can only be won by understanding and mitigating risk.

Modifying Skill and Luck

A common question asked in online game design groups: what's the right level of skill or luck for a game? If the relative and absolute amounts of skill and luck in a game are under the control of the game designer, when and how should we modify these?

The answer, as with most things in game design, is "it depends." In this case, it depends mostly on the audience. For a game dominated by high levels of skill, it's important for there to be opponents in the same general skill level to play against; a *Chess* game between a novice and a grandmaster is not going to be very interesting for anyone involved. If your game already has a wide audience such that matchmaking with similar skill levels is easy (like *Chess*), this is not a problem. If you're making a brand new game and starting with a small player base, a hyper-competitive skill-based game is likely to leave some portion of your player base without any viable opponents.

The more that luck plays a role in the outcome of a game, the broader the potential audience… to a point. Games that are *too* luck-heavy become less interesting to players who really want to feel like they have some influence over winning, so it is a balancing act. Some game designers do what they can to conceal the luck elements of the game, so that their game is actually more random than it appears. This allows weaker players to win some games (more than they would if the game were entirely based on skill), while still letting strong players feel like their skill matters and is important.

Here are some ways to reduce the overall role of luck in your game:

- Reduce the possibility space of the random element. Instead of rolling d20 and choosing from twenty different possibilities, roll d10 to reduce the variance.
- Reduce the number of faces on the dice. For example, d6+4 and 5d2 both have a range of 5–10, but 5d2 is more predictable (it's far more likely to roll 7 or 8 than 5 or 10).
- Increase the total number of dice rolled. This sounds counterintuitive: why would adding *more* random elements make the game *less* random? The answer is the Law of Large Numbers: the more a random process repeats, the more that, overall, it tends toward the expected value in aggregate. This is why a single hand of *Poker* is more luck than skill (it's dominated by who got the best hand), but a series of a hundred hands of *Poker* is more skill than luck (everyone gets about the same number of winning hands, so the outcome is more influenced by who exploited their wins and cut their losses better).
- Change random events into player decisions. One possible example: instead of rolling d6 to determine some outcome, give each player six cards numbered 1 through 6, and let them choose which card to play, but they can only play each card once (and pick up all six cards to start again once they've played through them all). Or just let the player choose any number, period, and make the choices balanced so that there is no single obvious "best" choice.

- Reduce the impact of random events on the game state, so that they only provide a small modification of play position rather than a major game-changing thing.
- To increase the overall role of luck in the game, do any of the above in reverse.

There are ways to quantify "how random" something is—some way of saying, for example, that d6+4 is "more random" than 5d2 in that it is harder to predict the outcome, and we cover this later in Chapter 24.

Additional Tradeoffs

Skill and luck are not the only two elements that determine a game's feel and outcome. There are two others that can come into play in some game designs.

The first of these is time. Time is often a factor in games that feature core gameplay that involves progression, such as RPGs. As the player grinds for extra experience levels or loot, they become more powerful in the game (we examined this "virtual skill" in more detail in Chapter 11). To an extent, a player can substitute time for either luck or skill in this kind of game; their chance of surviving a difficult encounter depends partly on their character's power level in the game (a function of the amount of time they've spent grinding to level up), partly on the player's skill at the game, and partly how lucky they are with any random rolls in combat. If the combination of these factors exceeds the game's challenge level at that point in time, the player succeeds.

The second type of tradeoff, particularly popular in F2P games, is money (as in, real-world money, not in-game currency or resources). Many F2P games monetize by setting up situations where the player hits a difficulty ramp that is designed to exceed their ability, and the only way to proceed is either to spend time grinding, or pay some small amount of money to skip the grind and get to the next part of the game more efficiently. Within the game, this is often presented to the player as a money-for-time trade (you can spend several hours grinding *or* get to the same place by paying a few bucks), but since time can be substituted for skill or luck, that means money can essentially be used as a proxy for those as well.

In this chapter, we mostly focused on skill and luck since modifying the luck factor of a game comes up so often in game design (and admittedly, plotting a bunch of games on a four-dimensional chart is much harder than the 2D plot in the "Double Axis" section earlier). Still, keep in mind that relating time and money to luck and skill is exceedingly important in many games as well.

Discussion Questions

1. What role does luck play in shaping the experience of a game?

2. Choose any children's game that is all luck and no choices, such as *Chutes&Ladders*, *War*, or *Old Maid*. Propose a rules modification for children who are slightly older, have mastered the core gameplay, and would appreciate a small amount of agency (but not so much as to be overwhelming).

3. What is the difference between input randomness and output randomness?

4. If you were going to add a random element to a physical sport, would it be more appropriate to add input or output randomness, and why?

5. Think about a game you enjoy playing that you feel is primarily based on skill rather than luck. Now, suppose you found out that the game actually had a luck element to it and that it was specifically fudging the results in the background to give you an experience that made you feel more skillful than you actually are. How would this knowledge affect how you felt about the game?

6. Consider any game that gives the player information about the game state—for example, an RPG that tells the player about their character's stats and abilities, and the effects of wearing various equipment. Suppose such a game gave imperfect information, where the numbers and effects shown to the player were unreliable and may be inaccurate. How would this change the play experience?

7. Name the first ten games you can think of (any kinds of games at all). Rate each one from 1 to 10 on the separate axes of skill, luck, time, and money, in terms of how much each of those elements plays a role in the outcome.

8. Can you think of any games that either had too much or too little of an emphasis on luck? Explain the game and why you felt this way, and what you might do if you were redesigning the game to address the issue.

9. Why can adding more random rolls to a game decrease the role of luck?

10. Think of a game where the amount of luck involved is partly under player control—for example, some TCGs allow players to either choose a deck that is more consistent in its performance, or conversely that is more "swingy" (prone to doing noticeably better or worse based on a lucky draw). In such a game, suppose you have one player that favors more luck-based play while another player favors more skill-based play, and they play against each other. Which of these two players is likely to be more disappointed at the experience?

Sidequests

Sidequest 19.1: Experiments with Input and Output Randomness

Add a rule to *Go* that makes use of input randomness (in other words, randomize the start position somehow).

Add a different rule that makes use of output randomness (some kind of random element that comes into play in response to a player making a move).

Pair up with another designer, and play a seven-game series with them on a 9×9 board: one game with no rules modifications, then one game with your input randomness rule only, one game with your output randomness rule only, one game with both of your rules… and then three more games with your partner's input randomness, output randomness, and both of their rules. Which of the games was the most interesting? Which was the most skill-based? The most luck-based? Why?

Sidequest 19.2: Depth of Strategy in the Land of Candy

Consider the children's board game *Candyland*. This game is entirely luck-based and offers no player decisions at all. You can find sample rules, boards, and card lists (or photos of spinners) online, if you've never played the game.

Add, remove, or change up to three rules. In your changes, try to remove as much luck from the game as possible, substituting it with as much depth of skill as you can manage.

20

Probability and Human Intuition

In This Chapter

- Probability Isn't Always Intuitive
- Expected Value and Utility
- Cognitive Biases and Fallacies
- Design Solutions to Deal With Human Idiocy

Probability Isn't Always Intuitive

> Think of how stupid the average person is, and realize half of them are stupider than that.
>
> *George Carlin*

Now that we've learned the basics of probability, it's time to blow it all up by showing one of the two places where true odds can go horribly wrong: human psychology. (The next chapter deals with the other place, computers.) Why psychology? Because most people are terrible at having an intuition for true probabilities. So even if we make the random elements of our games perfectly fair (which, as we've seen, isn't always trivial), a lot of players end up *perceiving* the game as being unfair. Since game balance is all about players perceiving the game as fair, this is a major problem faced by game designers as they craft random systems.

We have already seen some ways where the true probabilities are not what you might intuitively guess. Many of the challenges and case studies in

Chapters 17 and 18 had unintuitive answers. We also mentioned in passing the erroneous belief that previous independent events like die-rolls influence future ones. In this chapter, we'll dig deeper into some of these errors and examine the implications as game designers.

Expected Value and Utility

By now, you should be confident in your ability to calculate the expected value of a die-roll. Calculations are important, but they aren't the whole story.

Here is an example game. Would you play?

- Money-Making Game
- Pay $1 to play
- Roll 1d20. On a roll of 19 or 20, you get $15.

It's simple to do the expected value calculation. If played 20 times, that would cost $20, but the expected return from wins is $30, for a total profit of $10 (or $0.50 per game)—a 50% advantage to the player! Yes, you should play. That's easy. Now, how about this one:

- Money-Making Game v2
- Pay $1499 to play
- Roll 1d20. On a roll of 19 or 20, you get $15,000.

Playing 20 times costs $29,980 and is expected to net the player $30,000 for a total profit of $20 (or $1 per game), twice as profitable as the original version! So you should play, right? Most people would not, because the stakes are too high relative to the expected value. This is only a 0.067% player advantage, which is tiny compared to the amount of money being wagered or won. Even if the odds favor the player, it's clearly the player advantage that dominates and not the total dollar amount being won. Let's try again:

- Money Making Mega Game
- Pay $100 to play
- Roll 1d1000000. On a roll of 1, you get $1 billion.

Playing a million times costs $100 million and the expected gain is $1 billion for a total expected profit of $900 million. This comes out to an expected gain of $900 per game—a 900% player advantage, clearly superior to both of the previous games. And yet, most people *still* wouldn't play, because the chance of winning is too low. Playing so many times would not be worth the time. What if we sweeten the pot, then?

- Money-Making Giga Game
- Pay $100 to play
- Roll 1d1000000. On a roll of 1, you get $1 trillion.

Playing a million times costs the same $100 million, but the expected gain is now $1 trillion for a total expected profit of $999.9 billion or an expected gain of $999,900 per game (a 9,999% player advantage)! Even with these ridiculously good odds, most people *still* wouldn't play. The probability of winning is still too low, and further, winning $1 trillion isn't a thousand times as life-changing as winning $1 billion, so in practical terms, the two situations are roughly equivalent for most people. Furthermore, once you get past the millions, the granularity is a bit too large for most people's minds to really conceptualize—it's hard to intuitively see a difference between a billion and a trillion beyond "they are both unimaginably large" (and therefore equivalent to most people).

So, we've learned that expected value isn't everything, and neither is player advantage; it's also about the frequency of winning. Let's try one last game:

- Money-Making Micro Game
- Pay $0.01 to play
- Roll 1d20. On a roll of 19 or 20, you get $0.20.

Playing 20 times costs $0.20 and has an expected gain of $0.40, for an expected profit of $0.20 (or one penny per game, a 100% player advantage). Yet, a lot of people would still not want to play this game, because the stakes are just too low to matter. There is a minimum threshold, mainly because time itself has value, and if someone isn't making enough money for their time, then they'll spend their time doing something else.

The lesson here is that you should still do your expected value calculations to make sure your probabilities are balanced properly… but not to rely on them exclusively, because player experience may tell a different story. In particular, most forms of math used in game balance tend to break down at the extremes (as we've mentioned before), so experimenting with edge cases is fine in playtesting but should be done with caution in a live game.

Cognitive Biases and Fallacies

Now, let's transition to a discussion of how people intuitively envision probabilities when doing off-the-cuff estimates. Under some conditions, people are actually pretty accurate at certain kinds of calculations. But in many cases, our internal calculators are following flawed algorithms.

Selection Bias

One tendency people have with estimation of probabilities is to see how easily we can recall various events and assume that ease of memory recall is proportional to the true probability. This heuristic is known as **selection bias**. If someone was rolling an unfair (weighted) die a few hundred times and the number 4 came up twice as often as random chance would dictate, they might not only notice, but even have a good sense of about how often it actually came up, if asked.

If asked which is more common, burglary (someone steals a victim's stuff when they aren't present, e.g., a home break-in while they're out) or robbery (someone steals a victim's stuff when they *are* present, e.g., a mugging at gunpoint), the first thing most people do is think about how many times they or anyone they know has been burgled or robbed, and take a guess based on that. In this case, most people would guess the correct answer (burglary is more common, and most people have first- or second-hand experience with more burglaries than robberies). So, this is a reasonable and fairly accurate method of probability estimation—except in the special cases where it fails.

Specifically, intuition fails in cases where it's easier to recall a rare event than a common one. For example, if asked which is more common, dying in a plane crash or dying in an auto accident, there is no contest: no matter how you slice the data, cars are *much* more dangerous. But a lot of people fear plane crashes more. There are several reasons for this, but one is that every time a plane crashes, it's national news, and fatal car crashes are so much more common that they are typically not mentioned on the news at all... but car crashes don't happen *that* often, so few people know all that many people who have died in cars. Thus, our intuition can lead us to believe that plane fatalities are more common than car fatalities, simply because we can remember hearing about a lot more plane crashes than fatal car crashes.

Another example is the lottery. It seems like every week or two, we might hear of someone who won some big jackpot. Since we see so many winners, it's easy to assume that winning is a lot more probable than it actually is.

If equal attention were paid to the winner as all of the people who played and lost… there wouldn't be any time left for actual news, but we would have a better intuition for just how ridiculously unlikely it is to win!

How does this affect players of games? Some events in games stick in our heads easier than others. For example, we remember our epic wins much more easily than we remember our humiliating losses (it's one of those tricks our brains play on us to make us feel good about ourselves). Absent of hard statistics, players therefore tend to overestimate their own win percentage and thus their own skill at the game. In games where players can choose their own skill level or play with or against human opponents of their choice, players have a natural tendency to choose a difficulty that's a bit harder than a 50% win probability, so they are likely to struggle a bit more and then give up in frustration… if the designers do not include mechanisms that force players into a good match for their *actual* skills (such as automated matchmaking, dynamic difficulty adjustment, or other tricks).

Self-Serving Bias

There is a certain point where an event is unlikely but still possible, where players erroneously assume it is *much* more likely than it actually is. In his keynote address at GDC in 2010, Sid Meier placed this at somewhere around odds of 3:1 or 4:1. That is, if the player had a 75%–80% probability of winning or greater, and they actually did win exactly that percentage of the time, it would feel intuitively wrong, like they are losing more than they should. His playtesters expected intuitively to win nearly all of the time (perhaps around 95% of the time) if the screen displayed a 75%–80% chance.

However, this only works with winning, not losing, so it is a **self-serving bias**. While players are *not* okay with losing a quarter of the time when they have a true 75% probability of winning, they are perfectly okay *winning* a quarter of the time when they have a 75% probability of losing!

Dunning–Kruger Effect

Related to self-serving bias is the tendency of people to estimate their own skill… *especially* if their own skill is low. For example, a clear majority of people think that they are above-average drivers, that they have a lower-than-average probability of getting into an accident, and that it's just *other* people who are idiots and menaces on the road… even though, of course, only half of the population can truly be above average at anything (by definition).

People who aren't particularly great at math or tech skills may overestimate their ability relative to their peers. And as game designers often see, *everyone* thinks they can be a better game designer than you.

Why do people who are terrible at something think they're so great at it? It turns out that the ability to judge competence at an activity comes from being competent. If a person isn't good at something, they would not be able to accurately judge which other people are experts (or if they are an expert, themselves).[1] This trait of humanity is known as the **Dunning–Kruger effect** (named after the researchers who first described it).

Think about this in the context of games. Players who are not that skilled at your game think they're better at it than they actually are. When such people enter tournaments, they lose (badly) but get frustrated because they think they should be good enough at the game to win consistently—even though they aren't. They then search for explanations to reconcile these two "facts" (that they are good at the game, but they lost): bad luck, opponents cheating, computer glitches… or even, if you can imagine, poor game balance (because clearly, if a superior player can't win the game consistently, that means the game itself is unfair).

Attribution Bias

In general, players are much more likely to accept a random reward than a random setback or punishment. And interestingly, these events are interpreted very differently, through a phenomenon known in psychology as **attribution bias**.

With a random reward, players have a tendency to internalize the event, believing that they earned the reward through superior decision-making in their play. Sure, maybe they got a bonus from a lucky die roll, but they were the ones who made the choices that led to that die roll, and their calculated risk paid off, so clearly this random benefit came about because of good decisions made on their part.

With a random setback, players tend to externalize the event, blaming the dice, the cards, or their own bad luck, but not themselves. If they see too many random setbacks, they might go so far as to say that they don't like the game because it's unfair. If emotionally invested enough in a game (such as a high-stakes gambling game), they might even accuse other players of cheating! With some video games, the logic and random-number generation is

---

[1] Tragically, this effect also works in reverse. If someone *is* extraordinarily skilled at something, they tend to assume that if it's easy for them, then it's easy for other people too, and they tend to *underestimate* their superior skills.

hidden, so we see even stranger player behavior: some players actually believe that the AI is peeking at game data or altering the numbers and cheating on purpose, because after all, it's the computer so it *could* theoretically do that. In short, people handle losing very differently from winning—in games, as in life.

Anchoring

Another way people can get probability wrong is through a phenomenon called **anchoring**. Here's how it works: the first number that a player encounters is used as an "anchor" to which all future numbers are compared. The importance of that first number is thus overstated.

This is exploited in the real world in all kinds of ways. If you go to a casino and look at any slot machine, probably the biggest, most attention-grabbing thing on there is the number of coins the jackpot is worth. This isn't an accident; people look at that number first, anchor to it, and get the idea that their chance of winning is much greater than it actually is. Casinos also sometimes use anchoring with payouts: instead of saying a payout for a standard win in *Blackjack* is 1 to 1 (meaning that you keep your wager and then get an equal amount besides), they may say that the win is 2 for 1 (meaning that you lose your initial wager in order to play the game, but if you win, then you get twice your wager)—the use of the word "for" instead of "to" implies that the player pays to play, rather than merely putting an initial wager at stake. Mathematically, 1 to 1 and 2 for 1 are identical, as in both cases, the player loses their initial wager if they lose, and keep their wager plus an equal amount as winnings if they win. However, the number 2 looks larger and thus more enticing to players.

You can also see this in some retail establishments: if, for example, a customer sees two similar cars on a used car lot and the first one that they see has a sticker price of $20,000, and the second one has a price of $18,000, the first car sets their expectations, and then the second one looks like a great deal in comparison. In department stores, sale prices often display the "original" non-sale price in big numbers, and then, the sale price under it, again to get shoppers to anchor to higher prices and then think that the sale price is a great deal because it's so much lower. In reality, it might be a terrible deal for the consumer, but absent any outside frame of reference that gives them an intuition for what a particular item normally sells for, they anchor to the first number they see.

In Sid Meier's GDC 2010 keynote, he mentioned a curious application of anchoring in his games. His playtesters—the same ones who felt it was perfectly fair to lose a third of the time when they have a 2:1 advantage (just like they were supposed to)—would feel the game was unfair if they lost a third of the time when they had a 20:10 advantage. 2:1 and 20:10 odds are identical, so what's going on here? The answer is that if the first number players see is 20, that's a big number (especially if they are used to seeing numbers that are somewhere in the 1–10 range for the first part of the game), so they feel like they have a lot of power… and it feels a lot bigger than 10 in comparison, so this feels like it should be an overwhelming advantage. (Naturally, because of self-serving bias, players are perfectly happy to accept one win out of three if they're at a 10:20 disadvantage.)

As another example, anchoring means that an RPG player who has, say, a small amount of base damage and then a bunch of bonuses added in later may underestimate how much damage they do.

The Gambler's Fallacy

People generally expect a series of random numbers to *look* random. Long streaks make a lot of people nervous and questioning whether the numbers are actually random. For example, try this: ask anyone nearby (a classmate, friend, family member, or whoever) to generate a "random" list of ten coin flips from their head—not actually flipping any coins, but just saying "Heads" or "Tails" as randomly as they can. It turns out that for most people, their list is not very random. Specifically, if a person's previous item was Heads, they have about a 60% probability of picking Tails for their next pick and vice versa. In a string of only ten coin flips, most people don't say four Heads or Tails in a row at any point… even though the probability of four-in-a-row is only 1/8, so it is actually common to see a streak of four somewhere in ten coin flips.

This is something that you can exploit as a player of games. Next time someone challenges you to *Rock-Paper-Scissors* or *Evens-and-Odds* as a way of avoiding some unpleasant task like who has to clean the bathroom, insist on playing best 3 out of 5, or best 4 out of 7, rather than a single trial. Knowing that the other person is going to switch their throw more often than not (because they don't want to appear to be "too predictable" or non-random), assume that on any given throw, they'll avoid what they threw last time, and choose your own throw accordingly. Against most people, you'll win the first throw about half of the time (as expected), and all subsequent throws you should win more often than that, giving you a definite advantage.

There are other ways that expecting things to "look" random—that long streaks *look wrong*—can lead players astray. Remember how players feel like a 3:1 advantage means they should win almost all the time, but losing a third of the time with a 2:1 advantage is okay? It turns out that if a player loses two 2:1 contests in a row, they call foul; they don't expect unlikely events to happen multiple times in a row, even though by the principles of probability, they should. When players expect a streak to be broken because they assume the probabilities have changed (even though it is a series of independent trials), that is known as the **gambler's fallacy**.

Here is another example of how the gambler's fallacy can be a pain for game designers. Suppose you make a game that involves a series of coin flips as part of its mechanics. Probability dictates that about 1/32 of the time, the first six coin flips will be exactly the same result (all Heads or all Tails). This means that if your game is played by 3.2 million players, one hundred thousand players are going to experience a six-in-a-row streak of coin flips as their very first experience on their first game. That is a lot of players, and you can bet that many of them are going to think the game is unfair!

Of those hundred thousand players, about half get six favorable coin flips in a row. Those players won't quit the game, but because of anchoring, this first experience sticks in their head and they'll have an unrealistically high expectation of winning future coin flips. When the Law of Large Numbers kicks in and they start losing about half of the time like they're supposed to, they start to feel like the game is cheating.

The other half of those hundred thousand players get six unfavorable coin flips in a row, as their first introduction to your game. These players may feel the game is unfair, or it's cheating, or the random-number generator is broken, or any other number of explanations, because they don't feel like this should happen to them. They may leave the game out of frustration, and not quietly.

The reason why the gambler's fallacy is so pervasive is that the human brain is actually shockingly good at finding and recognizing patterns. This is a great thing; it's one of the things that makes games so compelling to us (game designer Raph Koster goes into great detail on the subject in his book *A Theory of Fun for Game Design*). The side effect of this trait is that sometimes, we'll notice patterns that aren't actually there and then give artificial meaning to them that they don't really deserve.

Hot-Hand Fallacy

Related to (actually, opposite to) the gambler's fallacy is the **hot-hand fallacy**. The name comes from the sport of *Basketball*, because at some point, people started getting the idea that if a player scored two or three times in a row, that made them more likely to score additional times to keep their streak going longer (because their hand is "hot"). This was famously encoded in the sports video game *NBA Jam*, where scoring three times in a row made the player "on fire" as a mechanic that gave the player a speed and accuracy advantage, along with additional visual effects like occasionally making the basket explode in a nuclear fireball.

At first glance, the principles of probability would lead us to say that this is ridiculous. If each basket is an independent event, like rolling a die, there's no reason why previous baskets made should influence future ones. However, in reality, maybe these aren't completely independent. What if a player who scored several times now has more confidence so they can do better? What if the fans are cheering them on more, giving them a little bit of extra energy? What if the previous baskets made are a sign that the player is solidly focused on the game and in a flow state ("in the zone"), making it more likely they'll continue to perform well? Because of the psychological element, the question can't be answered purely by probability; one would also need to look at the statistics across many games to see the actual trends.

What happens if you look at the numbers? It turns out that there *is* a minor psychological effect in play, but it's the reverse of what sports fans expected: the more baskets a single player scores, the more likely that they do *not* score again in sequence.

This is a principle that works against us in games when players can build up some kind of momentum via win streaks or kill streaks, particularly if we track these streaks or tie them to in-game rewards. Why? At best, even if each game truly is independent of the others, we know that win streaks are to be expected but also anomalous. If a player's performance in a match or a play session overall falls along some kind of probability distribution (usually a bell curve, but really just about *any* distribution), they eventually get some games (or streaks, or play sessions, etc.) that fall at the upper end of their probability curve—they are doing better than they characteristically should most of the time. Because of self-serving bias, the player is attributing this not to random distribution but to their skills improving noticeably (even though in reality, they are just having uncharacteristically good performance, temporarily). What happens after that? Chances are, the next time they play, they're a bit lower on their curve. When they start losing again, they feel frustrated because they feel like they should be able to do better. This isn't exactly a great way to end a streak of wins; it taints the whole feeling. No matter how good a player does, the thrill and reward of being on a win streak is always going to be followed by what the player perceives as a setback or punishment.

Design Solutions to Deal with Human Idiocy

As you can see, game designers have some problems to deal with involving player perception. Improbable but memorable events are seen as more likely than they actually are (selection bias). Unlikely setbacks are assumed to be virtually impossible when the odds favor the player (self-serving bias).

Random events that are in a player's favor are assumed to be a result of that player's skill, while those that work against a player are interpreted as bad luck, poor game design, or cheating (attribution bias). Players grossly misestimate their own skill at the game, with weak players thinking they are experts and experts thinking they are merely average (Dunning–Kruger effect). Players overvalue the first number that they see, putting all other numbers in terms of the first (anchoring). And given a string of identical results, people may either assume that the string is more likely to be broken (gambler's fallacy) or more likely to continue (hot-hand fallacy) than probability would dictate.

The common thread through all of these errors in judgment is that even if you expose the actual probabilities of the game to your players, and if your game produces fair random numbers, players *will* complain about it because according to their flawed understanding of probability, *the game feels wrong*.

As designers, we can sit around complaining to each other about how our players are stupid and bad at math, or we can design around the problem.

Exploitation

For game designers who have no moral qualms about using their knowledge to extract large sums of money from people, going to the Dark Side is technically an option.

Lotteries, casinos, and other gambling establishments regularly take advantage of selection bias and anchoring by publicizing their big winners and the size of their biggest jackpots, making it seem like winning is more likely than it actually is. Another trick used by some casino games (particularly slot machines, video poker, and the like) is to rig the machines to give a "close but not quite" result more often than random chance would predict, such as a three-reel slot machine coming up with two Bars and then in the third reel having a Bar that is just one position off, or having four out of five cards for a royal flush come up in a video poker game. These give players the false impression that they're closer to winning than they actually are, increasing their excitement and anticipation of hitting a big jackpot and making it more likely that they'll continue to play.

Politicians often campaign on a strategy of playing off of the public's fears of vastly unlikely but well-publicized events like terrorism or natural disasters, and make promises that they will introduce legislation that keeps the public safe from these terrible threats. Interestingly, this is a campaign promise that is very likely to be held true: the events in question aren't likely to happen again, regardless!

Marketers and advertisers use the principle of anchoring to change consumer expectations of price. For example, big box stores often put large signs up throughout the store advertising special low prices on select items, and customers' brains assume that other items around those are also less expensive by comparison, even if they actually aren't. Car dealerships are notorious for this sort of tactic, such as putting two similar cars next to each other, putting a higher price on the first one that a customer is likely to see, and a lower price on the second one. The customer anchors to the first price, buys the second car, and drives away thinking they got a great deal... even though they just got ripped off.

If you *really* want to be evil, you could even become a scam artist, doing things that are illegal but highly effective. One example of a well-known scam involves writing a large number of people offering "investment advice," telling them to watch a certain penny stock between one day and the next. Half of the messages predict the stock will go up; the other half predict it will go down. Whatever actually happens, the half of the people who got the "correct" message the previous day are then given another prediction, again split into two groups, half of whom are told that a different stock will go up and the other half told it will go down. After repeating the process four or five times, the pool of people for whom you've been right every time is fairly small... but they also figure that you've been right far more often than would be predicted by random chance, so you must have a working system. Then, they give you a ton of money and you skip town with it.

This is what game designers do when they sell out: they go into marketing, advertising, political strategy, gambling, or illegal scams.

Dealing with Biases

For readers who actually want to make games, the option of changing careers to exploit brainhacks may not be so appealing. Thankfully, there are some methods game designers can use to minimize the down side from some of these effects.

One method is to actually skew the probabilities in your game to conform to the cognitive biases. Tell the player one thing and then do something else. If you know that players who are told they have a 75% probability of winning expect to actually it to act as if it were 95%, then any time you display a 75% probability on the screen, have your video game actually roll dice at a 95% win rate.[2] If the player gets one random failure, make each successive failure

---

[2] This may seem analogous to the Game Master in a tabletop role-playing game fudging a die roll behind their screen, rolling a die and then lying about the results. However, these are often different situations. In an RPG, the GM is not altering probabilities to conform to the hot-hand or gambler's fallacy; rather, they alter probabilities in the service of making for a more interesting or dramatic story.

10% less likely than pure probabilities would dictate, making long streaks less likely and super-long streaks impossible.

Be extremely careful when putting random events in your game, *especially* those with major game-altering implications. If random events work in the player's favor, that's fine; but if a player gets randomly destroyed, they don't have a good reaction. They may think they did something wrong and then try (futilely) to figure out what; they may feel annoyed that their grand strategy was torn down by a bad die-roll and there's no point to playing if the game is just going to declare a victory or loss by fiat; or they may assume the AI got jealous of their superior play and resorted to cheating (particularly in video games where the player may assume some kind of intelligence on the part of the game).

Players like seeing small gains a little and big gains a lot. They can tolerate small losses, but they *hate* big losses. In video games, that means that players typically reload from save after experiencing a sufficiently large setback, but not after a small one. In the real world, it's why gambling games like slot machines are so popular: players don't mind losing a quarter or a dollar at a time, they have occasional big wins, but never a big unexpected loss.

To deal with the hot-hand fallacy, you can simply design your game to not reward streaks of wins, downplaying their importance in the game so that a player doesn't necessarily even realize when they are on a hot streak. If streaks *are* included, they can be embedded in a positive feedback loop (giving players bonuses for streaks that increase the chance of their streak continuing) to counteract the greater chance of a miss after a string of hits.

In short, knowing that players have certain cognitive biases, one response is to change the design of your game to conform to those biases.

A Question of Ethics

The solution of changing our games to conform to player's flawed understanding of the world does not sit well with everyone. Let's be clear: this *is* dishonest. As game designers, we teach our players. If we bend the rules of probability in our games to reinforce player's incorrect ideas of how probability works, are we not doing a great disservice to our players by, essentially, teaching them something that we know is wrong? Players won't even *necessarily* walk away from our games if they are honest; *Poker*, for example, is incredibly popular and profitable… even though the game mercilessly punishes any player who harbors any flaws in how they think about probability.

It may be strange to see a question of professional ethics in a book about mathematics. This is not the last time we broach such a question. Since this *is* a book on game balance and not ethics, we don't attempt to give any definitive answers here. Rather, we simply state the questions so that each reader can come to their own conclusions.

- Is handling probability in our games a matter of professional ethics?
- Where do we draw the line between giving players what they want and showing them the enjoyment that they're paying us for vs. giving them an accurate simulated representation of reality?
- What's more important: how the game actually works or how players *perceive* it as working?

An Honest Solution

There is one other design solution that can help in some specific situations: expose the results of random processes in the game to the players, not just the stated probabilities.

As an example, if you ask players to estimate their win percentage at a game when the game doesn't track such a statistic, they probably estimate higher than the actual value. If wins, losses, and percentage are displayed every time the player goes to start a game, they gain a more accurate view of their actual performance.

If your game has a random number generator, you can track the stats of random rolls over time. For example, anyone who has played *Tetris* knows that the long straight piece never appears until just after it's no longer needed. Is the game designed to intentionally troll players? The arcade version had a neat solution: in a single-player game, the player played on one half of the screen, and the other half was used to keep track of how many of each brick type fell down. If the player felt like they were getting screwed, they could look over and see if the game really was screwing them. They could keep an eye on the stats over time, obviously seeing some variance over the course of a single level, but over time it would tend to balance out. Most of the time, players would get approximately equal numbers of each type of brick. The game was fair and could prove it with cold, hard facts displayed to the player in real time.

We can also design the user interface of our games to make probabilities easy for players to read and understand. In some versions of the board game *Catan*, each number has dots on them: a 2 or 12 has one dot, while a 6 or 8 has five dots. These make a very easy way to calculate probabilities:

the number of dots is the expected number of times that the given number is rolled on 2d6 out of every 36 rolls. All players have to do is add the dots on adjacent hexes to see how many total resources they can expect to receive from building at that location, relative to other building sites on the board.

In a *Poker* game against AI opponents, the game could let the player know after each hand who held the winning hand, and keep ongoing track of the percentage of winning hands, so the player knows that the deck shuffles and distribution of winning hands is fair. (This would be harder to do with human opponents, as it would give privileged knowledge of opponents' bluffing patterns.)

In a digital version of a board game with lots of die-rolling such as *Risk*, the game could keep track of how frequently each number of combination is rolled and allow the player to access those statistics at any time. This kind of feature is surprisingly reassuring to a player who can otherwise never know *for sure* if the randomness inside the computer is fair or not.

It's worth noting that transparency is a design choice, and not always appropriate for every game. It can also be a valid choice to deliberately conceal the nature of random systems in your game, in essence providing a puzzle for the player community to solve through their own data collection, particularly in this age of player-run Wikis and particularly for games that are community-focused such as MMOs.

Another trick that video games can use is to make the randomness more visceral and visually clear. In board games, this happens naturally: rolling dice, drawing cards, and pulling tokens from a cloth bag are all done with a player's hands, and there is something satisfying about grasping a set of dice in one's hands and throwing it at a table. Video games lack that tactile sensation and that may be part of the reason that players don't trust computerized random-number generators as much. To counteract this effect, consider adding that sensation back into the visual elements of the game. If you're generating a random number, draw a graphic of actual dice rolling on the screen. If you're drawing virtual cards from a shuffled deck, display the deck and animate the shuffling and drawing of cards to the player's hand. Even though this is just a fancy front-end to the game, psychologically it makes the game appear more legitimate to players because it actually *looks like* it's shuffling and drawing cards, or rolling dice, or what have you. (Never mind that physical cards and dice aren't entirely random either—more on that in the next chapter!)

Additional Resource

- Sid Meier, *The Psychology of Game Design (Everything You Know Is Wrong)*, at GDC 2010, viewable at https://gdcvault.com/play/1012186/ The-Psychology-of-Game-Design

Discussion Questions

1. Looking back at the five different games in the "Expected Value and Utility" section at the start of this chapter, can you derive any general rules for how to tell if a particular action with a positive expected value will be seen as a good or bad deal by players?
2. At what point does designing a game to exploit players' cognitive biases cross the line from acceptable to unacceptable?
3. Try to recall a time when you were convinced that the random-number generator of a video game was broken, because of an unlikely occurrence (either a very rare event happened several times in succession, or a very common event failed to happen for a while). Knowing what you know now, how likely is it that the game was actually in error?
4. For the same situation as in the previous question, how would you go about telling the difference between an actual bug in the game vs. you just happening to experience a statistical outlier? What tools would you need (or changes to the game interface) to verify this one way or another?
5. The list of fallacies and cognitive biases in this chapter is not a complete list; there are many others out there. Search for a list of logical fallacies or a list of cognitive biases online, pick one at random, and read it. Then, brainstorm ways that such a fallacy might either occur or be designed for in a game.
6. Of the cognitive biases and fallacies listed in this chapter, think of a time when you fell prey to one of these yourself (whether in a game or in real life). What happened?
7. Since the expected value is, by definition, the average result, why don't players always use that as their primary guideline when choosing a strategy in a game?
8. Under what conditions *do* players correctly and intuitively understand probability? Give some examples.
9. Give an example of gameplay or a particular game mechanic that you find problematic in terms of how players are likely to perceive or misunderstand it. What would you do to change it?

10. The Dunning–Kruger effect has a flip side to it that people who are actually skilled at something tend to underestimate how good they are. This manifests as something called **impostor syndrome**: the feeling that you're not that good at what you do, even if other people seem to think you are, and that you're actually just a fraud, and some day everyone around you will realize it. If you're going through this book in a group (such as a class or a book club), ask for a show of hands of who has felt this way before about game design. Did literally every hand in the room go up? It probably did. How many people were surprised at how widespread this is among game designers?

Sidequests

Sidequest 20.1: A Monopoly on Fairness

Suppose you are creating a digital version of the board game *Monopoly*. List as many methods as you can think of to prevent players incorrectly perceiving the random elements (die rolls and two shuffled decks of cards) as unfair.

Sidequest 20.2: Exploitification

Write up a one-page concept doc for a game that is specifically designed to exploit at least one of the cognitive biases or fallacies mentioned in this chapter… and then to make people aware of their internal bias, so that they are less likely in the future to fall prey to it. The game should still be fun, of course.

Sidequest 20.3: Evil Gambling Game

Design a game to be played at a casino table, with the following design goals:

- The odds should *appear* to favor the player, at first glance. (Make use of any and all cognitive biases and fallacies that you can toward this end.)
- The odds should *actually* favor the House.
- Use only the following components: one or more standard decks of cards, and/or any standard gaming dice (d4, d6, d8, d10, d12, d20), with no other specialized equipment (no wheels, ball cages, computerized machines, or similar).
- The player can only lose what they choose to wager (players will not tolerate a "reverse jackpot" where a bad result means they lose more

than what they bet, and this is difficult to enforce when a player might be betting their last remaining chips).

- The casino operator should never have to make any choices. Any choices for the "House" should be made by following strict guidelines (such as the rule in *Blackjack* that the dealer always hits on 16 or under and always stays on 17 or above).

Playtest your game with other players to see if their intuition actually leads them astray, as you intended. Modify your game accordingly based on the results of the playtest.

Additional Challenge: do the math and calculate the **house edge** of your game. Express this as a percentage of a player's bet that they can expect to lose, on average. For example, if the expected value of the result of playing the game once with a $100 bet is that the player will lose $2 per play of the game that would be a 2% house edge. If the player has choices to make or the game changes its nature over time (such as a progressive jackpot that gains more money until someone wins it), make any simplifying assumptions that you need to in order to perform your calculations, but generally assume an average (expected value) case for changing conditions, and optimal choices made on the part of the player.

Ultimate Challenge: modify your rules to optimize the house edge for your game, and adjust your math accordingly. Use the following guidelines:

- The house edge should be somewhere in the range of 0.25% (any less and the game won't be profitable enough) to 30% (any more and players won't tolerate it).
- Tend toward the lower end of the range if your game is simple and each play of the game is short. In this way, casinos may not make very much money per play of the game, but they can make it up in volume when a player plays many times.
- Tend toward the higher end of the range if your game has a large "jackpot" or other means for players to win far more than they bet. The larger the potential big win, the higher the house edge players will tolerate.
- Take a look at existing casino games with about the same profile as yours (in terms of complexity, play time, and maximum win potential) and research or calculate their house edge, and make sure yours is similar.

21

Pseudorandom Numbers

In This Chapter

- Analog Randomness
- Pseudorandomness

Analog Randomness

> At the source of every error which is blamed on the computer you will find at least two human errors, including the error of blaming it on the computer.
>
> *Gilb's First Law of Unreliability*

In the previous chapter, we learned how an otherwise fair system with randomness can be ruined by human nature. As if that weren't enough, there is even more bad news: your fair random numbers may not even be random!

A "fair d6" is to games what an ideal gas is in chemistry, or what a frictionless, massless pulley is in physics: an ideal state that is never actually seen in our imperfect reality. Go and find the nearest d6, and take a careful look at it. In many dice, the pips (dark spots) are indented, so that it is ever-so-barely weighted toward one side or another (the 1 only has one pip cut out, so that side is heavier than the 6 which has six pips removed; thus, one might expect the heavier 1 side to end on the bottom, leading to slightly more 6s rolled than pure probability for a fair d6 would dictate).

Many dice also have rounded corners; if those curves are even slightly different (and due to imperfect manufacturing processes, they probably are), the die may be slightly more likely to keep rolling when it hits certain faces. For this reason, the dice used in casinos are very different (and more expensive) than those seen in most casual games: the dice are perfectly cubic, machined within a tolerance of around ten micrometers or so, with a uniform finish (dots are painted on, with paint of a different color applied around the dots so that each side has an equal amount of paint), with weight distribution being perfectly even within a ridiculously low tolerance. Even then, one would expect some tiny imperfections—they are just small enough that the deviations from true randomness happen infrequently enough that they wouldn't interfere with the game.

Other types of dice have similar problems. If you have played tabletop RPGs for any length of time, you have probably run into at least one player who has a "lucky d20" that they bring out for critical rolls, because they *swear* to you that it rolls natural 20s more often (perhaps that player is you). And the thing is, that may not be just superstition: it is probably correct! Because of how most d20s are manufactured, they aren't perfectly round, but are slightly oblong, making it slightly less likely that they roll the numbers on the more rounded part, and more likely to roll on the flatter part. All of this, of course, is without considering the possibility of dice that are deliberately loaded, or a player that has practiced throwing dice to roll what they want, or any other form of flat-out cheating.

Coins are no better. While we would like to think that a coin flip is random with a 50% probability of either Heads or Tails, it is actually slightly more likely to flip to whichever side was face-up at the beginning of the toss (and spinning a coin can be even worse, since most coins are slightly heavier on one side than the other, leading to the heavier side being weighted down and thus being *much* more likely to have the lighter of the sides show face-up).

Shuffling a deck of cards is likewise not random. The way that a typical person shuffles (a "riffle" shuffle) is not particularly good at randomizing. For example, if you split the deck into two even parts and then merge them together with a shuffle, the cards that were previously on the top and bottom of the deck are on the top and bottom of the two different stacks; after shuffling the stacks together, the top card on one stack is probably be at or near the top of the deck, while the bottom card on the other stack remains at or near the bottom. In fact, it takes quite a few shuffles to get the deck to a state that's reasonably random... and certain types of shuffles can even, when done enough times, return the deck to its original state (often used deliberately by card-trick magicians who wish to appear to shuffle a deck while actually stacking it). Even without stacking the deck, however, you can see that all outcomes of a shuffle are not equally likely, and in fact, some outcomes are physically impossible from a single shuffle (for example, because of how a riffle shuffle works, the relative position of each card in each of the two piles remains intact; you cannot reverse the order of cards in the deck with a single riffle shuffle).

Other random devices have their own problems. For example, *Bingo* balls and lottery vacuum-based ball selection can be slightly non-random if the paint on some balls is heavier than others. Spinners in most children's board games are cheaply made, and imperfect alignment may cause greater friction in some places than others, leading to a greater chance of certain spin results. And so on.

This is a problem that casinos take great lengths to correct, as with the aforementioned expensive dice. Any perception of rigged equipment could potentially cost a casino its gambling license, and they make far too much money from an honest, long-term house advantage to want to jeopardize that. If unintentionally unfair equipment is used, savvy players could exploit the difference in true odds and payout odds to make money from the casino. Thus, it is worth a gambling establishment's while to make sure that all of their dice are as close to perfectly random as possible.

Shuffling cards is another thing casinos must be careful of, and manual shuffles have largely been replaced by automated card shufflers. These shufflers have problems of their own. Mechanical shufflers are potentially less random than human shuffles, so a careful gambler could analyze the machine to figure out which cards are more likely to clump together after a fresh deck is shuffled, gaining an advantage. Many card shufflers today are electronic, and they don't "shuffle" exactly, but rather they stack the deck card-by-card according to a randomized computer algorithm. As we'll see shortly, even these algorithms have problems.

The takeaway is that even events in physical games that we normally think of as "random" aren't always as random as we give them credit for—even without cheating. There isn't necessarily a lot we can do about this as game designers, at least not without going to great expense to include super-high-quality game components. This is a bit much for those of us who just want a casual game of *Catan*, so as players we must accept that our games aren't completely random and fair… but they are probably "close enough," and the imperfections affect all players equally, so we disregard the lack of perfect randomness (most of the time).

Pseudorandomness

Computers are entirely deterministic. If you open a computer case, you see no d6s, nor cards, nor any other random elements inside there. Unless you're willing to get some kind of special hardware that measures chaotic physical phenomena (such as the directional velocity of a particle during radioactive decay), which is greatly outside the norm for typical computer use, you are stuck with the problem that you have to use a deterministic machine to play non-deterministic games of chance.[1] Until now, we have used the word "random" to refer to computer die rolls, but the more proper term is **pseudorandom** since the numbers are not actually random. A computer uses a **pseudorandom number generator** (commonly abbreviated RNG and not PNG, because whoever coined the acronym was being a little too nontechnical) to provide pseudorandom numbers on demand.

How do computers generate pseudorandom numbers? The short version is that there are some math functions that behave very erratically, without an apparent pattern. When the function gives you one number, you simply feed that number back in to get *another* number and then feed that number in to get yet another, and so on; this produces a series of numbers that aren't random, but they do *feel* random for most purposes.

How do we decide which number to start on? We'd like to determine that randomly, but of course we can't. The starting number is called the **pseudorandom number seed** (or just "seed" for short), and once you've given the computer one seed, it then can generate new pseudorandom numbers in sequence from there. Because of this, you only have to seed the pseudorandom number generator once (this is typically done when the game first starts up). However—and this is important—if you give it the same seed, you get exactly the same results. Remember, it's deterministic! This can be very useful in testing (as you can replicate the results of a test exactly) but is not something that you'd want to do by accident in the final release.

Choosing a suitable random number seed is a subject that could take a book of its own, but generally we choose a seed that's hard for a player to intentionally replicate, such as the number of milliseconds that have elapsed since midnight. You do have to choose carefully, though; if, for example, you choose a random number seed that's merely the fractional milliseconds of the system clock (range: 0–999), then your game really just has 1000 ways of

---

[1] There are websites such as random.org that will use such equipment to generate a list of truly random numbers for you on demand. In practice, relying on third-party random data like this tends to be impractical for standard use in the game industry (or in casual game playing).

"shuffling." This is enough to appear random to casual observation, but small enough that a player might see several games that are suspiciously identical over repeated play. If your game is meant to be played competitively (PvP), a sufficiently determined player could study the game and reach a point where they could predict, from the first few pseudorandom results, which of the thousand seeds was used (and then use that to predict all future results with perfect accuracy to gain an unfair advantage). With a game meant to be played by millions of people every day, even "milliseconds since midnight" only gives 86.4 million possible seeds, and if a player starts playing the game around the same time each day, they may very well find the same seed twice.

Game developers must be even more careful when using pseudorandom numbers in games played online, particularly if the numbers are generated on the players' machines rather than on the server.[2] An example: either one player or the server generates the initial seed and that seed is then used for both players. Then, whenever either player needs a pseudorandom number, *both machines* would have to generate that number so that their respective seeds are kept in synch. Occasionally, due to a bug, one player might generate a pseudorandom number but not inform the opponent, which then puts the two players' pseudorandom number generators out of sync. The game then continues for a few turns until suddenly, one player takes an action that requires a virtual die roll, their machine rolls a success, and their opponent's machine (with a different pseudorandom number) rolls a failure. The two clients then compare their game states at some point and realize that they are different, and both players assume the other machine is cheating (oops!). These kinds of bugs can be difficult to strictly identify, because the game may continue for several turns without an error... all the way until a pseudorandom event happens differently for both players.

Saving and Loading

Even if you are just dealing with a non-networked single-player game, you still have to be careful of pseudorandom numbers because of the potential for exploits. Unfortunately, there is no way to entirely prevent saving/loading exploits, but you can at least pick your poison.

Here are some common methods to handle saving and loading:

---

[2] For the reasons explained in this paragraph, it's better to put the game logic on the server for networked multiplayer games, rather than on the client machines, so that there is only a single game state and no possibility of players getting out of synch with one another. For games where players connect to each other directly (e.g., smartphone games that connect to each other over Bluetooth), there is no server, so designate one player's device to handle all of these things and then broadcast the correct game state to other players for display on their respective devices.

Save Anywhere   Some games let a player save anywhere, at any time, under all circumstances. In these games, nothing stops the player from saving just before they have to make a big pseudorandom roll, such as a situation where they're highly unlikely to succeed but there's a big payoff if they do, and then just keep reloading from save until they succeed (imagine if your game has an in-game casino where the player can get money from hitting a jackpot: they'll just walk up to the gambling table, bet all their money, see if they win, save again if they do, and reload from save if they don't).

If you re-generate your seed each time the player reloads from save, they just keep repeating the process until they win. At this point, the player is not really playing your game the way you designed it at that point... but on the other hand, they *are* using the systems you designed, so the player isn't cheating either, strictly speaking. Your carefully balanced probabilities are thrown out the window when a player can just keep rerolling until they win.

Save Anywhere, Saved Seed   The obvious fix to the above problem is to save the random number seed as part of the game state. Then, if the player reloads after a failed random roll, they'll get the same result every time.

First, this doesn't eliminate the problem; it just adds a small barrier. The player only has to find one other random thing to do—drinking a potion that restores a random amount of health, or playing one of the gambling games but wagering a very small stake, or just choose to do the same actions in a different order—and keep trying until they find some combination of actions that works.

Second, this creates a new problem. After the player saves, they now know *exactly* what the game does at every turn, because once they start with the same random number seed the game becomes fully deterministic. This fore-knowledge can be even more powerful of an exploit. For example, if a player knows exactly how an enemy boss will act in advance, that can be even more powerful than being able to indefinitely reroll because the player can optimize ever choice they make.

Save Points   This method of having specific locations where the player can save was popular in early-generation games where memory and storage were at a premium, and only having a handful of save points in the world meant it took less space to store the player's location in a save file. However, this method also means players have to go through some nontrivial amount of gameplay between saves, which reduces reload-from-save exploits. A player might *theoretically* be able to exploit the pseudorandom numbers through the save system in this way, but in reality, they have to redo too much work to fully optimize every last action.

This causes problems for the opposite type of player. It adds a cost to "cheating," but honest players then rightfully complain that your save system won't let them walk away when they want: the game effectively holds them hostage between save points.

You'll always have one problem or the other depending on where you place your save points. For example, if you place a save point in the room just outside a very difficult boss fight, that boss might be exploitable if you are saving the current seed. If the nearest save point to that boss is 15 minutes away, then dying in that fight and having to repeat all that play just for one more chance can be intensely frustrating to *all* players.

Protected Save   You might try a save system where the player can save anytime, anywhere, but it erases their save when they reload (so the player can't just do the repeated save/reload trick). *The Nightmare of Druaga* did something like this, going so far as to detect if the player reset the game to avoid losing progress, and forced them to watch a long and boring lecture about cheating if they tried (in addition to penalizing them as if they had died). Of course, if the power went out during play, it would be treated as a loss even if the player was playing honestly. So much for being clever.

Limited Saves   You can give the player the ability to save anywhere, but limit the total number of saves (the original *Tomb Raider* did this, for example).

In that case, did you give the player a map and tell them exactly how far apart they can save, on average, so they can gauge their progress? Did you draw some big arrows on the map pointing to places where they face their greatest dangers, so that a player doesn't have to replay large sections of the map just because they didn't know the best locations to save ahead of time? If not, players can feel frustrated that the game acts as if it wants them to be psychic, knowing in advance where the optimal save spots are. And if there are optimal places for those save spots, the developer could have just done away with this "save anywhere" business and just placed save points in the proper locations to begin with.

Or, if you *did* give the player these clues, they then complain the game is too easy because it gives them complete information about where the challenges are, so they always feel prepared and never have that thrill of going into the unknown and being surprised.

You Can't Win   Finding the perfect save system is one of those unsolved problems in game design. Even with a fully deterministic game, just choosing a method of saving and loading that's fun and enjoyable and not exploitable by the player is a challenge. When pseudorandom numbers are added to the mix, you have seen how much thornier the problem gets. Either the player can manipulate the past (using save/reload to "reroll" at will) or manipulate the future (trying something out and then reloading to gain perfect foreknowledge).

If it's an intractable problem, why even mention it? Because it's still a system that must be designed, and as a game designer, it is your responsibility to think about the tradeoffs of various systems and choose the one that is most appropriate (or least damaging) to the play experience of your game. If you don't, then it's left to some gameplay programmer to figure out, heaven help you, and the system will probably be based on whatever's easiest to code and not what's best for the game or the player.

The best the designer can do in this case is to be aware of what exploits are possible and design the rest of the game to minimize the impact. For example, if you allow a save-anywhere system and it's important to not have any simple exploits to break the economy, either don't implement a casino level in the game where a player can multiply their wealth in a short period of time, or implement strict controls on how much the player can win at the casino, or implement a wide radius around the casino that prevents saving.

Interestingly, this is a problem specific to video games. Board games don't have this problem, because there is no "saving" and "reloading"!

Pseudorandom Shuffling Algorithms

Even if a suitable number seed is found, and even if the save system isn't a major issue for your particular game, there are still ways that pseudorandomness can go awry. Like bugs in the implementation code.

An example is the simple act of shuffling a deck of cards. How do you do that?

A naïve algorithm that many beginning programmers have tried is this: start with an unshuffled deck; generate two pseudorandom numbers corresponding to cards in the deck (e.g., if the deck is 52 cards, two numbers between 1 and 52… or 0 and 51, depending on what language you're using). Swap the cards in those two positions. Repeat these random swaps a few thousand times.

Aside from being horribly inefficient, does this even work as a randomizer? No, it doesn't. No matter how many times cards are swapped, there is always a *slightly* greater chance that each card appears in its original position than in any other position. This is because once it is swapped once it is equally likely to be anywhere else… but there is a non-zero chance that any given card isn't chosen to be swapped *at all*, which gives it a slightly greater likelihood of being found where it originally started. The greater the number of swaps that are performed, the lower this chance, but no matter how many swaps you do, that probability never actually becomes zero.

A better shuffling algorithm is this: start with an unshuffled deck; choose a random card in the deck; swap that card with the card in the first (or last) position of the deck. Next, choose a random card from the remaining cards (i.e., *not* the one you chose the first time) and swap it into the second (or next-to-last) position of the deck. Continue choosing cards among those you have not yet chosen already and putting them sequentially in the deck. In C++, the code might look like this (other languages may vary):

```
for (int i=DECK_SIZE-1; i>0; i--)
{
    int r = rand()%(i+1);
    tmp = Deck[i];
    Deck[i] = Deck[r];
    Deck[r] = tmp;
}
```

This algorithm is only a single loop that executes one time per card in the deck (so, 60 pseudorandom numbers and swaps for a 60-card deck). It's fast and efficient and gets you as random a shuffle as your pseudorandom number generator allows.

Except that even this algorithm isn't perfect, because of technical limitations.

At the time of this writing, most computers are 64-bit, meaning that a single computer instruction is 64 bits long and that the largest an integer number can be is 64 bits in length (so there are 2^{64}, or a little more than 18 quintillion or $1.8 * 10^{19}$) distinct integers, which means that many possible random number seeds. That is a lot of random number seeds! But how many possible shuffles are there in a 52-card deck? The first card has 52 possible spaces, the next has 51, the next has 50, and so on down to the final card that only has 1 possible remaining space it can go in when all others have been chosen. To find the total possibility space, we multiply all of these together, to get 52 * 51 * 50 * ... * 3 * 2 * 1. In mathematics, multiplying an integer number by all of the other integers smaller than it is called **factorial** (denoted with an exclamation point), so the total number of shuffles for a standard deck is 52!, which comes out to about $8 * 10^{67}$, quite a lot larger than the possibility space of our random number seed. In reality, then, the vast majority of theoretically possible shuffles of a 52-card deck can never happen under any circumstance using the latest in desktop computing. In fact, you'd need a 256-bit computer just to handle all possible 52-card deck shuffles... and even *that* isn't quite enough to handle all possible 60-card shuffles, as you might find in an online implementation of *Magic: the Gathering*.

And even then, you're dealing with an ideal case, assuming that all 2^{64} random number seeds are equally likely. If the random number seed was generated by, say, looking at the number of milliseconds elapsed since midnight, that would drop the possibility space of seeds down to the number of milliseconds in a day: about 86 million. That's a pretty tiny number of possibilities, compared to the true possibility space of a 52-card deck, or compared to the computational power of a computer. If you are reading this book on a computer, the computer that you're on could probably search for a unique sequence that matches one of 86 million possibilities, in real time, in just a few seconds. If a player correctly guessed the method of seed generation and the exact algorithm for pseudorandom number generation (such as *rand()* in the standard C++ library), it would not take very many pseudorandom results for that player to be able to determine *exactly* where they are in the sequence, and be able to predict future pseudorandom results with perfect accuracy from there, allowing them to cheat.[3]

In short, getting truly random numbers is hard. For competitive games where there's big money involved—gambling games or high-level tournaments

---

[3] Lest the reader get any ideas about using this to make easy money from an electronic game at a casino, know that casinos have excellent real-time statistics tracking to quickly tell the difference between a lucky player and a cheat. If you cheat, best case, you'll simply be ejected from the casino and banned from all other casinos for life, probably before you've won enough to make the trip worthwhile. If you're unlucky, depending on your method used, you may be prosecuted and face prison time for illegally acquiring proprietary pseudorandom number generation techniques, or sued in civil court for all your winnings, if the casino even lets you walk away with winnings in the first place. Whether you win or lose, being on the receiving end of a civil or criminal lawsuit is not a typical game designer's idea of a fun time.

of competitive skill-based games, for example—the game designers and programmers must take extra steps to ensure that their pseudorandom numbers
can't be cracked.

Discussion Questions

1. Something about any board games you own and if you know that you
   have a slightly higher chance of rolling high numbers, how would that
   alter your strategy?
2. Choose any "random" implement you'd find in a casino—dice, cards,
   and a wheel that spins. In what ways might such a device be not entirely
   random?
3. Slot machines are made to look like their reels spin randomly and
   stop in entirely random places, but in fact, they are programmed to
   intentionally produce a greater number of "near misses" (for example,
   all winning symbols except the final reel that's one position off) than
   would be predicted by random chance, because those spins generate
   excitement in the player and almost always convince them to do a few
   more spins since they appeared to be so close. If you were designing a
   slot machine's "AI," what other elements might you consider programming in to keep a player interested and prevent them from leaving?
4. What are the general tradeoffs a designer must make when designing a
   save system for their game?
5. What kinds of video games might require extra care to be taken when
   handling pseudorandom numbers?
6. What are the benefits and drawbacks of using a truly random physical
   phenomenon to generate random numbers (rather than relying on the
   computer's pseudorandom numbers) for a game?
7. Take a look at a physical board game that has any kind of random element, such as dice or cards (if you don't have a physical copy available,
   look for pictures of the components online). What kinds of less-than-
   perfect random behavior might you expect from this game's "random"
   components?
8. For the same game as the previous question, if you confirmed that the
   components weren't fully random in exactly the way you expected,
   how could a player exploit that to gain an advantage over their
   opponents?
9. Some games, such as *Slay the Spire* and *Minecraft*, actually display
   the pseudorandom number seed to the player and let the player enter

their own seed if they wish. How might this functionality be useful to players?

10. How might the functionality in the previous question be useful to the game's developers, particularly in QA?

Sidequests

Understanding the difference between "random" and "pseudorandom" has many implications for video game designers (and even board game designers, since many popular board and card games eventually have digital versions, and since board game designers may use computer simulations to assist with their game balance). Pseudorandom numbers can be a wonderful tool, and when designing a video game, they are usually the only option, but they have natural limitations in how much randomness they can actually allow... and that's without considering all-too-common software bugs and botched implementations that make a card shuffle or die roll less random than it should be.

As game designers, we must come to terms with the fact that a "random number" that is entirely random is an ideal case. In the real world, we must settle for "close enough"—and the bar for what constitutes "close enough" may change depending on whether you are talking about casual play, high-stakes competitive play, or the highly regulated gambling industry.

Sidequest 21.1: Test Your RNG

In your spreadsheet program, do this quick test: enter the formula =RAND() into cell A1, and then, Fill Down for a thousand rows. With all of those cells still highlighted, Fill Right one column, so you should have a 2×1000 block of independent pseudorandom numbers.

Now, graph these as a Scatter Plot, as if they were a thousand pairs of (x, y) coordinates.

What do you see? You can expect to see *some* areas of clustering of dots, and some areas that are sparse, but otherwise it should look fairly random with no discernible patterns, and if you re-generate all of the pseudorandom numbers, any clustering should affect entirely different areas.

This is a quick-and-dirty test for any pseudorandom number generator. There are more mathematical ways to calculate the exact level of randomness from your RNG, but this provides a simple "good enough" test for most casual game design purposes.

Sidequest 21.2: Another Card Shuffling Algorithm

Here is a slight modification of the shuffling algorithm discussed in this chapter: start with an unshuffled deck as before. Next, choose a random card, and swap with the first (or last) card in the deck. Then, choose another random card (any card, including the one that was just picked) and swap with the second (or next-to-last) card in the deck. Continue swapping any random card in the deck with each position. The C++ code for this might look like the following:

```
for (int i=DECK_SIZE-1; i>0; i--)
{
    int r = rand()%DECK_SIZE;
    tmp = Deck[i];
    Deck[i] = Deck[r];
    Deck[r] = tmp;
}
```

Does this produce shuffles as good as the original algorithm?

Hint: run all possibilities for both algorithms, assuming a "good enough" RNG, using a three-card deck. How many shuffles are in the possibility space of an actual three-card deck? Does that match the possibility space of both of these pseudorandom algorithms? Note that despite appearances, this is not a programming question; it is a probability question, asking you to count the number of ways to do something.

Sidequest 21.3: Large Deck Shuffling

In this chapter, we found that to get a fair shuffle of a 52-card deck, you'd need at least a 256-bit machine (technically a 226-bit machine would suffice, but machines are created with a number of bits that is a power of 2). How many bits would you need your computer to have to shuffle a 60-card *Magic: the Gathering* deck? What about a 100-card deck?

Sidequest 21.4: Cracking Your Own RNG

This challenge requires a bit of additional technical research and implementation skills, so should not be attempted by someone with little or no programming experience.

First, write a program to flip a coin 200 times (first generate a suitable random number seed, then use a function like *rand()* to generate a pseudorandom number between 0 and 1, round to the nearest integer such that a number below 0.5 becomes 0 and a number 0.5 or above becomes 1, and print Heads for a result of 0 and Tails for a result of 1). Or, in a spreadsheet program, flip a coin using =IF(RAND()<0.5," Heads"," Tails") and Fill Down for 200 rows.

Next, research the pseudorandom number algorithm for the RNG that you are using, and how the random number seed is generated. See if you can find the actual mathematical functions somewhere. On a 64-bit machine, this formula likely produces a repeating sequence of 2^{64} numbers, which would not be able to fit in memory of a typical desktop computer all at once... but if you can narrow down the possibility space of the initial random number seeds to a few million or less, you can keep track of *that* many possibilities, at least.

Now, use your computer to make a list of the 200 coin flips that would be generated with each seed in your possibility space, and store these lists somewhere. Write a script or program that can search through these to find the ones that match a given sequence, and to display all 200 flips from a single sequence if the search returns a unique result.

Finally, run your program or load your spreadsheet. Type the first few coin flips into your search script, and keep adding additional flips until it returns a unique result. Check the remainder of that list with the actual generated flips from your coin-flipping program or spreadsheet, to confirm that the two are the same.

How many coin flips did it take to be able to uniquely identify what the random number seed was?

Sidequest 21.5: Exploiting the Save System

Choose any video game you have available that has random elements *and* the ability to save and reload.

First, describe how it functions:

- Under what conditions can the player save (or not)?
- Does the pseudorandom number seed appear to be saved? (That is, if you reload a game in progress, do a few things that involve the game generating pseudorandom numbers, then shut down the game, and reload from the same save file again, does the same exact thing happen every single time?)

- How easily can a save file be duplicated, so that the player could reload from the same position multiple times if their first attempt doesn't work out?

After providing a description of the system, identify all potential player exploits of the system that you can think of. For each exploit, note how practical it is (for example, if a player can *theoretically* perform an exploit to gain infinite gold by abusing the save system, but in reality it happens so slowly that the player would be better served to just play the game normally, that would not be very practical).

22

Infinite Probability

In This Chapter

- An Infinite Problem
- Matrices
- State Machines
- Converting State Machines to Matrices
- Case Studies

An Infinite Problem

> This is one of the two chapters in this book – Chapter 25 being the other one – where we indulge in some pretty heavy math and technical skills to solve obscure game design problems that can't be solved any other way. The content of these chapters is not critical knowledge for game designers, does not find common use in the field, and can be safely skipped if you don't enjoy matrix operations. If you aren't afraid of a little linear algebra, however, these chapters provide an opportunity to geek out on some of the mathiest math in this book in order to do solve some really interesting problems in game design.

Until this point, we have examined probability problems that can be solved exactly by direct calculation, finding ways to count the number of results and the size of the possibility space, and then dividing the former by the latter. This is a wonderful tool that can answer a great many questions about probability in games, but there is one particular class of problems where this can't be done: those where counts can go infinite.

Here is a simple example of such a problem:

Mordenkainen's Magical Rubber Band
First-Level Spell
Choose a target. The target takes 1 damage. Then, roll 1d10. On
a 1 or 2, the spell ends. Otherwise, the target takes an additional
1 damage, and you roll again. Continue rolling in this way until
you roll a 1 or 2.

What is the expected value of the damage this spell does when cast?

- There is a 20% probability that the spell stops immediately and do just
  the 1 damage.
- There is a 16% probability (80% * 20%) that the spell does +1 damage
  once, then stops, for a total of 2 damage.
- There is a 12.8% probability (80% * 80% * 20%) that the spell does +1
  damage twice and then stops, for a total of 3 damage.

And so on… such that it has a good chance of doing a small amount of damage and a progressively smaller chance of doing a large amount of damage. But
it could potentially do an infinite amount of damage, so there is no way to just
define all the possibilities, compute the probability of each, multiply each result
by its probability, and add them all up. There are an infinite number of possibilities. You could use a Monte Carlo simulation or compute the first few hundred
possibilities and get an approximate answer that's "close enough" to take a pretty
good guess, but there are also ways to get exact solutions to problems like this.

Matrices

Before getting to the special techniques used to compute infinite probabilities,
we need to learn a mathematical tool: the **matrix** (plural: **matrices**). A matrix
is just a table of numbers, same as you might see in a spreadsheet, enclosed in
square brackets. Most of the matrices we encounter in this book (primarily in
this chapter, and in Chapter 25 when dealing with intransitive mechanics) are
square, although they don't have to be. Here, for example, is a matrix:

$$\begin{bmatrix} 4 & 5 & 2 \\ 3 & 1 & 3 \\ 0 & -1 & 1 \end{bmatrix}$$

There is also the concept of a **column vector**, which is just a matrix that is one element wide and several elements tall. (You can also have row vectors which are one element tall, though for our purposes, we only use column vectors.) Vectors and matrices don't just have to contain numbers; like spreadsheets, each item can be a variable or even an entire mathematical expression. Here is that matrix, shown next to a column vector of three variables:

$$\begin{bmatrix} 4 & 5 & 2 \\ 3 & 1 & 3 \\ 0 & -1 & 1 \end{bmatrix} \begin{bmatrix} x \\ y \\ z \end{bmatrix}$$

If you multiply a matrix by a column vector, you get another column vector. To get each position in the resulting column vector, you take the corresponding row in the matrix and multiply each element in left-to-right order with each element of the column vector in top-to-bottom order. In this case, the top element in the product would take the top row (4 5 2), each element multiplied by the corresponding element in the column vector $(x\ y\ z)$ and then added together to get $4x + 5y + 2z$. The other elements of the resulting column vector are computed the same, but using the other rows of the matrix:

$$\begin{bmatrix} 4 & 5 & 2 \\ 3 & 1 & 3 \\ 0 & -1 & 1 \end{bmatrix} \begin{bmatrix} x \\ y \\ z \end{bmatrix} = \begin{bmatrix} 4x + 5y + 2z \\ 3x + y + 3z \\ -y + z \end{bmatrix}$$

Matrices can also be used, incidentally, as shorthand for a system of equations. For example, consider the following:

$$\begin{bmatrix} 4 & 5 & 2 \\ 3 & 1 & 3 \\ 0 & -1 & 1 \end{bmatrix} \begin{bmatrix} x \\ y \\ z \end{bmatrix} = \begin{bmatrix} 5 \\ 2 \\ -5 \end{bmatrix}$$

This is shorthand for the system of equations:

$$4x + 5y + 2z = 5$$

$$3x + y + 3z = 2$$

$$-y + z = -5$$

We don't solve systems of equations in this chapter, but we do later on in Chapter 25 when we examine intransitive mechanics, so keep in the back of your mind that matrices have many applications beyond what we see in this chapter.

State Machines

Another concept we must introduce now, taken from the field of Computer Science, is the concept of a **state machine**. If you've ever taken a course in Artificial Intelligence, you have likely encountered these. They are often called **finite state machines** because state machines in actual use have only a finite number of states, but there is nothing stopping you from having, at least in the hypothetical, an infinite number of potential states.

A state machine is represented by a diagram with circles. Each circle represents a single **state** that you're in ("state" in the same sense as "state of mind" or "state of confusion," not as in Texas or New York). The diagram also contains arrows that show how you can move or **transition** from one state to another, labeled with the condition that allows the state change (this condition might be a random die roll or a fixed requirement). A state machine also has an **initial state** (denoted here by an asterisk and bolding it), and some state machines may also have one or more **final states** (states from which there are no further transitions, though not all state machines have these).

Here is the infinite state machine diagram for Mordenkainen's Magical Rubber Band.

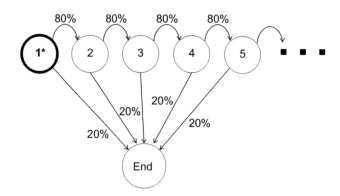

The states are labeled with the amount of damage the spell does if it reaches that point. Upon reaching the end state, the target of the spell would take damage equal to the state you were in before transitioning. It starts at 1 damage, and there's an 80% chance of transitioning to the next higher state and a 20% chance of ending, from each state. This continues indefinitely (although the probabilities get fairly negligible after a few hundred states, for practical purposes).

State machines don't have to change states by probability. Consider a stealth-action video game. In such a game, the player must sneak around, avoiding the notice of guards that typically patrol along a set path. If a guard notices something suspicious (hearing a noise, for example), they may enter a heightened state of alertness where they investigate, searching for the source of the noise or other disturbance. If at any point—either while patrolling or searching—the guard makes direct line-of-sight contact with the player, they enter a combat mode where they open fire. If the player disappears from view and stays hidden for long enough, the guard reverts to searching. If they don't find anything when searching, they return to their normal patrol. Here is this guard's finite state machine (notice there are no end states).

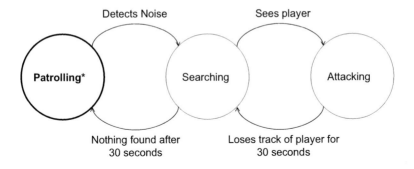

For our purposes, we'll be looking primarily at state machines that use probabilities to transition from one state to the other, but if you encounter other FSMs like this in the wild, you at least know how to read them.

Converting State Machines to Matrices

It turns out that when you have a state machine where all transitions are probabilities, this can be modeled as a matrix. As an example, let's consider the following simple FSM.

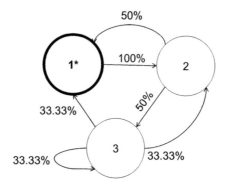

In this state machine, we start in State 1, the initial state. Every turn that it's in State 1, it transitions to State 2. Once in State 2, it has a 50% probability of going to either of the other states (1 or 3). If it makes it to State 3, it has a 1/3 probability of going to any of the three states, including remaining in State 3. So, it continues to bounce around between these three states indefinitely.

We can model this as a matrix of possibilities, where each column is the state that it's currently in, and each row is the state it might transition to at the next state change. Each item in the matrix is the probability of transitioning from the current state (column) to the new state (row):

$$\begin{bmatrix} 0 & 1/2 & 1/3 \\ 1 & 0 & 1/3 \\ 0 & 1/2 & 1/3 \end{bmatrix}$$

In the leftmost column (current State 1), there is a probability of zero of transitioning to States 1 or 3 and a probability of 1 of transitioning to State 2 (because when in State 1, it *always* goes to State 2 next). In the center column (currently in State 2), there is a 1/2 (50%) probability of going to State 1 or 3, and a probability of 0 of remaining in State 2. In the third column (current State 3), there is a 1/3 probability of going to any of the three states.

Notice that if you add up each column, all of the numbers sum to 1. This makes sense: in a state machine, you are always in exactly one state at a time, so there should always be a 100% probability of being in exactly one state after any transition.

In this example state machine and matrix, you might wonder: where do we most likely end up? Yes, the nature of this particular state machine is that we continue bouncing around between states, but suppose we let this thing go for a really long time such that our position is relatively randomized, and then at some random point, we peeked at the current state. What is the probability that it's in each of the three states? How much of its total time does it spend in each state, proportionally?

To compute this, we start with a column vector that shows our initial state. In this case, State 1 is the initial state, so we have a 100% (or 1) probability of being in State 1, and a 0% probability of starting in States 2 or 3. (If we wanted to start in a random state, we could just use probabilities of [1/3 1/3 1/3] as our initial column vector instead.)

$$\begin{bmatrix} 0 & 1/2 & 1/3 \\ 1 & 0 & 1/3 \\ 0 & 1/2 & 1/3 \end{bmatrix} \begin{bmatrix} 1 \\ 0 \\ 0 \end{bmatrix}$$

What do we get if we multiply these together? The matrix tells us the probabilities of state transitions from each state to each other state. The column vector tells us the probability of what state we're in now. Multiplying these together, then, gives us a column vector of probabilities of where we'll end up next!

$$\begin{bmatrix} 0 & 1/2 & 1/3 \\ 1 & 0 & 1/3 \\ 0 & 1/2 & 1/3 \end{bmatrix} \begin{bmatrix} 1 \\ 0 \\ 0 \end{bmatrix} = \begin{bmatrix} 0 \\ 1 \\ 0 \end{bmatrix}$$

If we start in State 1, then after the first transition, we know with certainty we end in State 2. This shouldn't be surprising; it's how the state machine is designed. And that is exactly the result we get when we multiply it out.

What do we do to figure out what happens after the *second* transition? We multiply the column vector [0 1 0] (from the first transition) by the transition matrix:

$$\begin{bmatrix} 0 & 1/2 & 1/3 \\ 1 & 0 & 1/3 \\ 0 & 1/2 & 1/3 \end{bmatrix} \begin{bmatrix} 0 \\ 1 \\ 0 \end{bmatrix} = \begin{bmatrix} 1/2 \\ 0 \\ 1/2 \end{bmatrix}$$

Again, this is not a surprise. If we know we are in State 2, there should be an equally split probability between going to States 1 or 3 after that transition. But now after two transitions, we are in an uncertain state; we no longer know for sure what state we will be in. What happens after the third transition?

$$\begin{bmatrix} 0 & 1/2 & 1/3 \\ 1 & 0 & 1/3 \\ 0 & 1/2 & 1/3 \end{bmatrix} \begin{bmatrix} 1/2 \\ 0 \\ 1/2 \end{bmatrix} = \begin{bmatrix} 1/6 \\ 4/6 \\ 1/6 \end{bmatrix}$$

Essentially, we are weighting it by taking the probability of transitions from State 1 multiplied by 1/2 (the probability that we are in that state) and the probability of transitions from State 3 also multiplied by 1/2, and add those non-overlapping probabilities together. So there is half of a 1/3 probability (which is 1/6) that we can end up anywhere if we started in State 3, or half of a 100% probability of ending in State 2, if we started in State 1.

We can continue doing this indefinitely, multiplying one transition's state probability column vector by the transition matrix to get the next state, then multiply *that* by the transition matrix to get the state after that, and so on for as long as we care to. Multiplying current probabilities by the same thing to get future probabilities is known as a **Markov chain**, named after the mathematician who invented the technique.

It turns out that if you keep doing this enough times, after about 13 iterations you get the column vector [0.3 0.4 0.3], and if you multiply *that* by the transition matrix, you get the exact same column vector as the result:

$$\begin{bmatrix} 0 & 1/2 & 1/3 \\ 1 & 0 & 1/3 \\ 0 & 1/2 & 1/3 \end{bmatrix} \begin{bmatrix} 3/10 \\ 4/10 \\ 3/10 \end{bmatrix} = \begin{bmatrix} 3/10 \\ 4/10 \\ 3/10 \end{bmatrix}$$

Since we can now multiply this column vector by the transition matrix and end up with no further changes to the probabilities ever again, this ends up being what we call a **steady state**: long term, we spend 30% of our time in States 1 and 3, and 40% of our time in State 2. Interesting, and probably not any numbers that you could guess intuitively without doing the math. And if these were the states of a guard in a stealth game, and the transitions were our estimated probabilities of state changes per unit time, we would know about how often the guard would spend in each state... and could then adjust things from there to reach the desired mix of states.

Essential Case Studies: *Chutes & Ladders*

That last state machine served as a manageable introduction to this kind of problem, but it was small and contrived. Let's look at a real game: *Chutes & Ladders*. This game is played on a board with spaces numbered 1–100. Players start off the board and each turn roll 1d6 and move that many spaces forward. If they end at the bottom of a ladder, they climb to the destination square. If they end at the top of a chute, they slide down to the square at the bottom of it. Ending a turn at the top of a ladder or bottom of a chute does nothing. Play then passes to the next player. The winner is the player who lands on the space numbered 100. They must land there by exact count; if, for example, a player is on the 97 space and rolls 4, they stay where they are and their turn is wasted.

On the traditional board, there are nine ladders, from numbered spaces 1 to 38, 4 to 14, 9 to 31, 21 to 42, 28 to 84, 36 to 44, 51 to 67, 71 to 91, and 80 to 100. There are also ten chutes: 16 to 6, 47 to 26, 49 to 11, 56 to 53, 62 to 19, 64 to 60, 87 to 24, 93 to 73, 95 to 75, and 98 to 78.[1]

If you've been suckered into playing this game with a young child, you might wonder: how long, on average, must I play this game before someone wins? How many turns does the game last? Because any player can land on a series of chutes to send them back indefinitely, the game could *theoretically* last for an infinite number of turns. However, after a certain number of turns, the probability that the game has not yet ended is so low that it can be ignored for practical purposes.[2] To analyze this game, we can view it as a finite state machine with one state per square, plus one off-the-board state ("square 0") to denote the starting position.

---

[1] Incidentally, these numbers are not accidental or random. There are very few spaces on the board that are not within reach of at least one chute or ladder (and quite a few spaces in reach of two), so that on just about every roll, there is at least a chance of something happening. The largest chute and the largest ladder each deposit the player before the other one, allowing for big gains and losses to potentially be erased in another turn or two. The final stretch (from 90 to 100) has three chutes, making it the most dangerous area in the entire game (particularly the chute at square 98, which is likely to be a threat to the player for some time since a player must land on 100 by exact count to win, and they simply lose their turn if they roll too high, which gives them more opportunities to land on 98). While the game is not particularly interesting to adults due to its complete lack of agency, the board does appear intentionally designed to maximize dramatic reversals during play. The design of the *Chutes & Ladders* board is worth studying to see how the placement of each individual element affects the play experience to create dynamic, exciting situations multiple times on most plays of the game.

[2] Because it *is* theoretically possible, however, if you did a Monte Carlo simulation, you would want to add in a failsafe. For example, after (say) 500 moves, if the game hadn't ended, you could just call it 500 and go to the next trial, preventing what might become an infinite loop where the simulated game never ends and the program hangs forever. Yes, this probably won't happen, but it is good practice, in simulations and in final game implementations too. If you design a game with a very unlikely but possible infinite loop in it, then you tweak the probabilities a bit and make that infinite process far more likely, by accident, your players are going to be very unhappy about that!

How many states would we have in our transition matrix, total? There are 100 squares on the board, plus 1 starting square off the board. However, the squares at the bottom of a ladder or top of a chute aren't *really* states, because there is no way a player can come to rest there (they always follow the chute or ladder to its other side). Eliminating those ten chute tops and nine ladder bottoms from the board, we get $100 + 1 - 10 - 9 = 82$ states total.

What does our transition matrix look like? It's big: an 82×82 matrix. It's also going to be very sparse: at any given state, there are a *maximum* of only six other states a player could transition to (since they're rolling 1d6), with a 1/6 probability of each. In some cases, there might have fewer possibilities; for example, on the square numbered 99 (this would likely be State 81 in the matrix), there is a 5/6 probability of staying in that state and a 1/6 probability of progressing to the final state (State 82 or Square 100). Once a player reaches the final state, they stay there with 100% probability. All other entries in each column are zero.

The initial column vector would have a probability 1 of starting in the initial state (State 1 in the matrix or Square "0") and probability 0 of starting in all other locations. We can then multiply this initial vector by the transition matrix to get the probability of being in each state after the first turn... then multiply that by the transition matrix to get the probability of being in each state after the second turn... and so on for a large number of turns. And then, we can analyze these column vectors collectively.

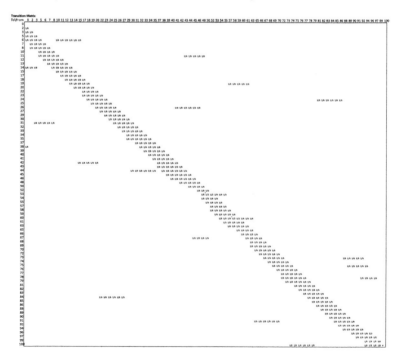

Yes, this is hard to read when shrunk this much, but it's not terribly difficult to reconstruct by looking at a copy of the board.

The first thing to look at is: where does the probability of the final state go above zero—in other words, what is the shortest possible game? It turns out that this first happens at turn 7, and it's exceedingly unlikely.

The next meaningful data point is where the probability of being in the final state first goes above 0.5, so that half of the games are longer than that and half of the games are shorter. This is the **median** length of the game. In this game, the median is 32 turns.

What if we wanted the **mean** length of the game? This is the probability of ending on any particular turn, multiplied by turn number, added up for all turns. Any individual column vector for a given turn doesn't tell us the probability of reaching any state *on that turn*—the probabilities are cumulative (the player might have reached the final state just this turn, or last turn, or ten turns ago). But you *can* get the probability of transitioning to a given state on a particular turn by subtracting the value in the previous turn's column vector from this turn's. If the probability of being in the final state this turn is 0.47634 and the probability of being in the final state last turn was 0.46301, then you know there is a 0.01333 probability that the player transitioned to the final state on the current turn only. We then multiply each individual turn number by its probability and add up. Since the game can theoretically go on infinitely, for practical purposes we can just calculate the first few hundred turns and stop adding terms when the final result doesn't change other than with rounding error, and we get a mean of about 35 turns.

We can then graph these turn-by-turn probabilities to look at the overall probability curve that the game ends on any given turn.

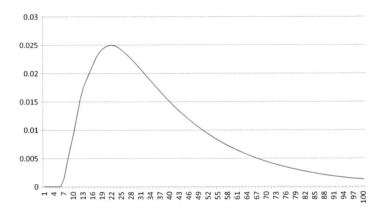

We can also look at the **mode** length of the game, the turn which has the highest probability of the game ending, relative to the other turns. This is just the peak of the above curve (22 turns in this case).

What do these numbers mean? The mean is considerably more than both the mode and the median, which means that there are some games that take a really, *really* long time to finish, and those increase the mean; but there are so few of them that they don't affect the median or mode.

You can then use this analysis to examine potential changes to the game. What if you remove the "must land on square 100 by exact count" rule and instead count it as an immediate win if you overshoot? Just modify the probabilities of the last few rows so that they're more likely to land on the final space than on themselves and recalculate. You'll find, not surprisingly, that the average length of games goes down slightly.

Want to know what happens if you add, modify, or remove extra chutes or ladders? Just modify the transition matrix accordingly. In general, you'll find that extra chutes lengthen the game and extra ladders shorten it, but not always—for example, if you have a chute that places you just before a big ladder, the addition of that chute can actually shorten the average length of the game.

You can also keep a separate count in each vector of the probability of hitting any given chute or ladder on that turn, to find the most commonly used chutes and ladders, and how often and with what probability they'll be used in any given game. (Such analysis is, perhaps, more practical in a game like *Monopoly* where players are making choices based on the probabilities of opponents landing on certain squares.)

Now, one important thing you may notice is that this method gives the mean, median, and mode for a single player. If you were playing a four-player game, and the game ends as soon as the first player reaches square 100, it's likely that the game ends on a turn significantly less than the median of 32 (because half of single-player games are below the median, and half above, so in a four-player game, you would expect two of those players to be below). On the other hand, the game itself would likely take *longer* since there are four players rolling and moving per turn, rather than one.

If you wanted to know the mean, median, and mode of total turns in a multiplayer game, how would you calculate that? Here are two approaches.

The first approach is to greatly expand the transition matrix to represent all possible game states. While each individual player can be in any of 82 separate spaces, there are four players, for a total of 82^4 states. At any given time, it is one player's turn and that is part of the state as well, so the actual size of the possibility space of the board is $4 * 82^4$, or about 180 million. You could reduce the size of this slightly by removing a few game states that would be impossible—two players on the 100 square, any player on a sufficiently high-numbered square when anyone else is on square 0, and so on—but it would still be pretty large. The transition matrix would then be $(4 * 82^4)^2$ since the transition matrix is square, with one row and one column per state, so you would need to store about 32 quadrillion numbers in the matrix alone, without even counting the column vectors. This is beyond the memory capabilities of typical computers as of this writing, so we must search for another way.

The second is to simply use your probability curve for the one-player case and generate a weighted random number that chooses a turn (simulating the length of a single game, according to the probabilities of ending on each turn). This would be like rolling a weighted die, where each face represents a specific turn, and the probability of rolling that face is the probability of the game ending on that turn only. For a four-player game, you would roll four of these numbers and then take the minimum of those four. Repeat many times in Monte Carlo fashion, and you could get a pretty good idea of when most games would end.

You could use similar tactics if, instead of ending with a single winner as soon as one player reaches square 100, you continued playing to determine second, third, and fourth place. In that case, you'd roll the same four weighted numbers, but take the *second highest* of the four (once three players have finished and determined first, second, and third place, the remaining player is in fourth place no matter how quickly or slowly they finish from there).

Yahtzee

Unlike *Chutes & Ladders*, the game of *Yahtzee* has the opportunity for players to make decisions. In this game, players roll 5d6, then can set aside any, all, or none and reroll the rest, and then repeat the reroll process a second time if desired, but after that, they have to stick with what they have. There are many different categories for scoring, and each player can only use each category once. The highest-scoring (and most difficult to achieve) category is the titular Yahtzee, or five-of-a-kind. Optimal strategy for this game is beyond the scope of this chapter, but let's take one small probability problem that's a subset of the greater one.

Assume that a player is rolling in an attempt to get a Yahtzee. That is, they ignore all other categories and just do their best to get all five dice showing the same value after the initial roll and two rerolls. This means they should always keep whatever dice belong to the most-of-a-kind they currently have and reroll the rest, so their choices are always made for them by the game state.

What is the probability they make their goal and get a Yahtzee? Here are the different states the dice can be in after each roll:

Roll	Probability of Getting This on the Initial Roll
A A A A A (Yahtzee)	6/7776
A A A A B (Four-of-a-kind)	150/7776
A A A B B (Full House)	300/7776
A A A B C (Three-of-a-kind)	1200/7776
A A B B C (Two Pair)	1800/7776
A A B C D (Pair)	3600/7776
A B C D E (Nothing)	720/7776

How were these numbers calculated? By counting the total number of ways to create each scenario and dividing by the total number of possible rolls.

- The total number of rolls is 6^5, since we are rolling five dice, six sides each, independently. Each die has six results, so there are $6 * 6 * 6 * 6 * 6 = 7776$ possible rolls. This is why every number has this in the denominator.
- There are only six ways to get Yahtzee: all 1s, all 2s, all 3s, all 4s, all 5s, or all 6s.
- To get four-of-a-kind, there are six different numbers for the four-of-a-kind itself and then five remaining possible numbers for the lone fifth die that is different from the other four ($6 * 5 = 30$). In addition, there are five ways to choose one of the five dice to be the odd one out, meaning a total of $30 * 5 = 150$ ways to get this roll.
- Full House is similar to four-of-a-kind (there are 30 different ways to choose the "A" and "B" die numbers), but there are now ten ways to choose two of the five dice to be the pair (5 choose 2 = $5!/(2!3!) = 10$), and $30 * 10 = 300$ ways to roll this.
- For the three-of-a-kind, there are now six ways to choose the triple, five ways to choose one of the remaining two dice, and four ways to choose that last die that matches neither the triple nor the other lone die; $6 * 5 * 4 = 120$. To calculate the different positions, there are five different ways to choose the "B" die and then once that is chosen, four remaining ways to choose the "C" die (the other three dice positions must be "A") so there are $5 * 4 = 20$ different ways to choose which dice have which faces. However, we must be careful not to double-count: for example, 3-4-5-3-3 (with 4 as the "B" die and 5 as the "C" die) and 3-4-5-3-3 (with 4 as the "C" die and 5 as the "B" die) are actually the same roll, and the same is true with each potential choice. There are therefore only half

as many actual rolls as first appears. We calculate 120 * 20/2 = 1200 different ways to roll three-of-a-kind. (Another way to calculate this: assume the "B" die is always higher than "C" which will then always produce a unique configuration. In that case there are (5 choose 2) = 10 different ways to choose two different die roll numbers that are not the triple, and we assign the higher of the two to the "B" die.)

- Two pair is likewise tricky, and we must be careful to avoid double-counting. Let us say the "A" pair is higher than the "B" pair. We select two different die faces from 1 to 6 to represent the "A" and "B" dice (6 choose 2 = 6!/(2! * 4!) = 15), and then, there are four remaining possibilities for the lone "C" die; 15 * 4 = 60. For choosing which dice are "A" or "B" or "C," we choose any one to be the "C" die (5 possibilities), and then of the remaining four, two are "A" (4 choose 2 = 4!/(2! * 2!) = 6), and the other two must be "B"; 5 * 6 = 30. Multiplying those together, 60 * 30 = 1800 different ways to roll two pair.

- For a single pair, let us again treat the "B," "C," and "D" dice as going from the highest to the lowest, to avoid double-counting. There are (6 choose 3) different ways to choose three different die faces for "B" and "C" and "D" (we then assign the highest of these to "B" and the lowest to "D"; 6 choose 3 = 6!/(3! * 3!) = 20), and then, there are three remaining possibilities for the "A" pair; 20 * 3 = 60 different ways to choose which faces are showing. To choose which dice are which, there are five different dice that could be "B," four remaining dice that could be "C," three remaining dice that could be "B," and then, the other two *must* be "A"; 5 * 4 * 3 = 60. Multiplying those results together, 60 * 60 = 3600 different ways to roll one pair.

- For a "nothing" roll, we choose five different numbers out of the six to be represented by "A," "B," "C," "D," and "E," assigning the highest to "A" and so on; 6 choose 5 = 6!/(5!1!) = 6. As for which die is which, there are five possible dice that could be "A," then four remaining dice to be "B," three other dice to be "C," two of the other dice to be "D," and then the last one must be "E"; 5 * 4 * 3 * 2 = 120. Multiplying those together, 6 * 120 = 720 ways to roll none of the above.

- We can check ourselves on this by adding all of these rolls up: 6 (Yahtzee) + 150 (four-of-a-kind) + 300 (Full House) + 1200 (three-of-a-kind) + 1800 (two pair) + 3600 (pair) + 720 (nothing) = 7776, which is indeed the total number of rolls. Had our sum been more than 7776, that would indicate we are double-counting in one or more of these situations. If our sum was less than 7776, we would instead look for some other possible rolls that are not accounted for.

All five dice can match (the goal state), or four dice can match (if any rerolls are left, roll the one non-matching die), three dice with a separate pair *or* two other non-matching dice (reroll both others, whether they're a pair or not), two matching dice with or without a second pair (reroll three others), or five non-matching dice (reroll all of them… or the player could keep their favorite one if they wish, as the probabilities are the same either way).

This tells us that the probability of getting Yahtzee on the initial roll is very low, less than one in a thousand. But, the player gets two rerolls. We could add up all of the many possibilities manually, but there's an easier way to do this: a finite state machine!

Rather than drawing out a state machine diagram, in this case it's simple enough to just fill in the transition matrix directly. Here's the form it takes:

$$\begin{bmatrix} 720/7776 & 0 & 0 & 0 & 0 \\ 5400/7776 & ? & 0 & 0 & 0 \\ 1500/7776 & ? & ? & 0 & 0 \\ 150/7776 & ? & ? & ? & 0 \\ 6/7776 & ? & ? & ? & ? \end{bmatrix}$$

The first column just shows the probabilities of transitioning from the first state (no matching dice) to each of the other states (pair, three of a kind, four of a kind, Yahtzee). The entries above the diagonal are all zero, because we can never transition to a previous state: if the player has three-of-a-kind and rerolls the remaining two dice, *at worst* they still have a three-of-a-kind after the roll. The probability of transitioning to a lower state is zero.

We can fill in some other numbers here easily. The probability of going from the fifth state (Yahtzee) to itself is 1. For one thing, remember that each column in a state machine must sum to 1 (there is a 100% probability of transitioning to one, and exactly one, new state on each transition—that's how state machines work), so a column with all zeros and one unknown requires that unknown to be 1. For another, it makes logical sense: if a player already has a Yahtzee, they have no need to reroll anything, so they'll stay with what they have.

The fourth column (four-of-a-kind) is also easy. The player rerolls one die, so there is a 1/6 probability of getting a match and transitioning to the fifth (Yahtzee) state, and a 5/6 probability of failing the roll and staying at four-of-a-kind.

The third column (three-of-a-kind) isn't all that terrible a calculation, either. The player rolls 2d6, which means there are 36 possible results. Of these, there is only one result (probability 1/36) of matching with both dice and going directly to the fifth state. There are ten ways (probability 10/36) of matching with one die and not the other (for example, if the player is trying to roll the number 1, the ten ways are to roll 1-2, 1-3, 1-4, 1-5, 1-6, 2-1, 3-1, 4-1, 5-1, and 6-1). The remaining 25/36 must therefore be the probability of remaining in the third state. The transition matrix now looks like this:

$$\begin{bmatrix} 720/7776 & 0 & 0 & 0 & 0 \\ 5400/7776 & ? & 0 & 0 & 0 \\ 1500/7776 & ? & 25/36 & 0 & 0 \\ 150/7776 & ? & 10/36 & 5/6 & 0 \\ 6/7776 & ? & 1/36 & 1/6 & 1 \end{bmatrix}$$

With just a pair, we're rerolling 3d6, which is the same process but just takes a little more work.

Making the roll on all three dice is easy: each die is a 1/6 probability of matching, so it is $(1/6)^3 = 1/216$.

Going from state 2 to state 4 can only happen if exactly two of the three rerolled dice match the first two, and the third one does not: 1/6 * 1/6 * 5/6 for each combination of dice that match or don't, and there are three different combinations (three ways to choose one die that does not match, out of three dice), so the probability is 3 * 1/6 * 1/6 * 5/6 = 15/216.

Going from state 2 to state 3 can happen two different ways. The first is if exactly one of the three rerolled dice matches the first two: 1/6 * 5/6 * 5/6, and again multiplied by 3 since there are three ways to choose the die that matches (or the two dice that don't), for a probability of 75/216. There is also the possibility that all three rerolled dice match each other, but do *not* match the first two. Since there are five numbers that don't match the first two, the probability here is 5/216. Adding those up, we get a probability of 80/216 that we transition from state 2 to 3.

To find the probability that we remain in state 2, we could compute it directly (calculating the ways to roll three new numbers that don't match each other or the original two, and the ways to roll three new numbers where two of them form a new pair but none of them match the original pair), but it's easier to just subtract all of the other transitions from 1: we get a probability of 1 − 1/216 − 15/216 − 80/216 = 120/216. Our final transition matrix filled in

$$\begin{bmatrix} 720/7776 & 0 & 0 & 0 & 0 \\ 5400/7776 & 120/216 & 0 & 0 & 0 \\ 1500/7776 & 80/216 & 25/36 & 0 & 0 \\ 150/7776 & 15/216 & 10/36 & 5/6 & 0 \\ 6/7776 & 1/216 & 1/36 & 1/6 & 1 \end{bmatrix}$$

What is our initial column vector? We could either have a probability 1 of starting in state 1 and probability 0 of starting anywhere else (and count that as "before the first roll"), or have a probability of 720/7776 of starting in state 1, 5400/7776 of starting in state 2, 1500/7776 of starting in state 3, 150/7776 of starting in state 4, and 6/7776 of starting in state 5 (and count that as "after the first roll").

Either way, multiplying the transition matrix by the column vector several times gives us the probabilities we are looking for. Putting the numbers in a spreadsheet and multiplying, we get the following.

Transition Matrix

To \ From	1	2	3	4	5
1	0.0926				
2	0.6944	0.5556			
3	0.1929	0.3704	0.6944		
4	0.0193	0.0694	0.2778	0.8333	
5	0.0008	0.0046	0.0278	0.1667	1.0000

Number of Rolls

0 (initial state)	1	2	3
1.0000	0.0926	0.0086	0.0008
0.0000	0.6944	0.4501	0.2560
0.0000	0.1929	0.4090	0.4524
0.0000	0.0193	0.1197	0.2448
0.0000	0.0008	0.0126	0.0460

It turns out that the result is a probability of about 4.6%, so even if a player deliberately tries for a Yahtzee to the exclusion of all else, it's a pretty rare roll[3]. On the other hand, getting four-of-a-kind actually happens fairly often (about a fourth of the time if trying for Yahtzee), and three-of-a-kind is achieved almost half of the time.

You could extend this analysis for other hands, like the probability of getting a Full House or Straight. You could also multiply the column vector by the transition matrix additional times to see the effect of allowing additional rerolls. With just one extra reroll (four rolls total), the probability of

---

[3]In a complete game, there are 13 categories and thus 13 opportunities to score. If following the strategy of going for Yahtzee exclusively over the course of an entire game, we can calculate the probability of not getting any Yahtzees by saying that the probability of failing once is 1-0.460 = 0.954, so the probability of failing 13 times is (0.954^{13}) = about 0.542, so there is slightly higher than a 50% probability. The probability of succeeding *at least* once is 1 minus 0.542 = 0.458.

a Yahtzee more than doubles, going above 10%. At ten rolls total, the probability of a Yahtzee first goes above 50%, so ten is the median number of rolls it takes to get five-of-a-kind on 5d6.

Risk

In the classic game of world domination, players place armies on a not-entirely-geographically-accurate board divided into territories. On their turn, each player receives new armies to deposit on the board in any territories they control, and then, they can attack from any of their territories to an adjacent one. At least one army must be left behind when wining an attack (to maintain control of the territory the player is attacking from), and all armies involved in an attack must be moved, which means a player cannot attack from a territory with only one army in it; they can only attack with one army from a territory that contains two; and so on. Essentially, one army in each territory doesn't count for the purposes of attacking and needs to be ignored. So for the purpose of calculating probabilities when attacking, we only consider armies beyond the first.

Other than that, the attacker can roll 1d6 per attacking army, up to a maximum of 3d6 at a time. The defender can roll 1d6 per defending army, up to a maximum of 2d6. After rolling, the highest individual die of each side is compared, and the player who rolled lowest loses one army (attacker loses the army if it's a tie). If both sides roll at least two dice, the second-highest die is also compared in the same way.

Since attacks are unlimited, either player can choose to roll less than the maximum number of dice, extending the length of combat. How many dice should each player roll? What are the probabilities of winning? There aren't all that many possibilities here. For something with this small a possibility space (maximum of 5d6 or 7776 possibilities, for three attacking and two defending dice), you can ignore math formulas and do an exact solution through naïve brute-force: use copy/paste in a spreadsheet program to give every possibility of dice rolled. With keyboard shortcuts, this could be done through brute force in just a few minutes (as mentioned in Chapter 31).[4]

If you do this, you should get the following results:

---

[4]Some programmers and mathematicians may look down on brute-force approaches as inelegant, but for small problems like this where it's not very computationally expensive anyway, sometimes it's the most efficient way. You get an exact solution (not a rough approximation as with Monte Carlo techniques), it's very easy to set up in either a spreadsheet or a few lines of code in any programming or scripting language, and because of its simplicity, it's less likely to have bugs or errors than using mathematical principles.

	2d6 (Defender)	1d6 (Defender)
3d6 (attacker)	Defender loses both: 2890/7776	Defender loses: 855/1296
	Each player loses one: 2611/7776	Attacker loses: 441/1296
	Attacker loses both: 2275/7776	
2d6 (attacker)	Defender loses both: 295/1296	Defender loses: 125/216
	Each player loses one: 420/1296	Attacker loses: 91/216
	Attacker loses both: 581/1296	
1d6 (attacker)	Defender loses: 55/216	Defender loses: 15/36
	Attacker loses: 161/216	Attacker loses: 21/36

It's easy to see from this that for each player, in any situation, the probabilities improve for them if they roll more dice. It is therefore optimal to roll as many dice as one can.

Note that this chart gives the probabilities of a single dice challenge, but assuming players continue to roll until they cannot continue further, it does *not* give a complete set of probabilities for who would win the combat. For example, if the attacker is rolling 3 dice and the defender is rolling 2, and each player loses one die, they must roll again because each player still has at least one army remaining. How do we calculate the *overall* probability of winning for each player?

Recall that to calculate the probability of two independent things happening together, multiply the two probabilities together; to calculate the probability of *either* of two independent, non-overlapping things happening, add the two probabilities together. For example, the probability of the attacker winning with two attackers vs. one defender is the probability of an outright win (125/216), *plus* the probability of an initial loss of one army (91/216) multiplied by probability of a win when it's down to one-on-one (15/36), for a combined probability of 125/216 + (91/216) * (15/36) = about 0.754.

What about the probability of the attacker winning if they start with three armies instead of two (against a lone defender)? The attacker wins outright with probability 855/1296; otherwise, they have a probability of winning equal to two-on-one (and we just calculated *that* probability already). A four-on-one contest has an 855/1296 probability if an immediate win, and a 441/1296 probability of being reduced to three-on-one (which we would need to calculate first).

What about a two-against-two battle? There is a 295/1296 probability that the attacker wins immediately, a 581/1296 probability that the defender wins immediately, and a 420/1296 probability that it is reduced to one-on-one (which we already know the probability for and can multiply by 420/1296 to get the probability of a win or loss in that case). Multiply the separate chains of events together, add them all up, and that is the probability: 295/1296 + (420/1296 * 15/36) = about a 0.36 probability of an attacker win.

For larger probabilities, at every step, we are looking at the probabilities at that step and then reducing to simpler cases, and continuing all the way down until we get to a known case (such as 2 vs. 1, or 1 vs. 1). If you have had any computer science classes, you may recognize this as **recursion** (repeating a process multiple times, with the output of one iteration feeding into the next).

For example, what is the probability of an attacker win if they start with seven attacking armies against five defenders? There is a 2890/7776 probability of the defender losing two armies (and reducing this to seven attackers and three defenders), a 2611/7776 probability of each player losing one army (reducing it to six against four), and a 2275/7776 probability of the attacker losing two armies (reducing this to five against five). Each of those probabilities is then calculated in terms of lower probabilities, until we reach a base case whose probability we already know. (Note that, because two armies are lost on each roll, there are some situations we'll never reach: seven against four, for example.)

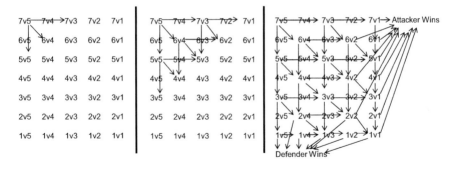

The easiest way to calculate this is in a spreadsheet. We know the probability of winning in the simplest case (one-on-one) is 15/36. To find any other probability, you'd give it the probability of each die roll result, multiplied by the cell containing that result. If you put the original one-on-one in cell A1, and B1 represented one attacker against two defenders, the probability of winning there would be 55/216 * A1. If the cell A2 represented two attackers and one defender, the probability of winning would be 125/216 + (91/216 * A1). If the cell B2 is two attackers against two defenders, the probability of winning would be 295/1296 + (420/1296 * A1). If cell E7 represents seven attackers against five defenders, the probability of winning would be (2890/7776 * C7) + (2611/7776 * D6) + (2275/7776 * E5). And so on. After you filled in the first couple of rows and columns, you could just take the same general formula for cell B3 (three attackers against two defenders) and Fill Down and Fill Right to populate the rest of the table as far as you like.

Probability of attacker winning the battle									
Att \ Def	1	2	3	4	5	6	7	8	9	10
1	0.41667	0.1061	0.02702	0.00688	0.00175	0.00045	0.00011	2.9E-05	7.4E-06	1.9E-06
2	0.75424	0.36265	0.20607	0.0913	0.04913	0.02135	0.01133	0.0049	0.00259	0.00112
3	0.91637	0.65595	0.47025	0.31499	0.20594	0.1337	0.08374	0.0535	0.03277	0.02075
4	0.97154	0.78545	0.64162	0.47653	0.35861	0.2525	0.18149	0.1234	0.08617	0.05719
5	0.99032	0.88979	0.76937	0.63829	0.5062	0.39675	0.29742	0.22405	0.16156	0.11828
6	0.99671	0.93398	0.85692	0.74487	0.63772	0.52068	0.42333	0.32948	0.25777	0.19343
7	0.99888	0.96665	0.90994	0.83374	0.7364	0.64007	0.53553	0.44558	0.35693	0.28676
8	0.99962	0.98031	0.9468	0.8878	0.81841	0.72956	0.64294	0.54736	0.46399	0.37987
9	0.99987	0.99011	0.96699	0.92982	0.87294	0.80764	0.72608	0.64641	0.55807	0.47994
10	0.99996	0.9942	0.9811	0.95393	0.91628	0.86109	0.79983	0.72397	0.65006	0.56759

This is a table that shows the probability of winning up to ten-against-ten, with conditional formatting to highlight all cells where the probability of an attacker win is at least 50%. There are some interesting findings here. When attacking and defending armies are equal, the defender has the advantage up to four-against-four (because of the benefit of winning ties), but the attacker has the advantage when it's five-against-five or more (because of the attacker's slight advantage in odds when rolling three dice against two that dominates if they roll enough times). In fact, if you extend this out to 20 against 20, eventually you'll see a point where the attacker even has the advantage even if slightly outnumbered (e.g., 17 attackers against 19 defenders)! In general, the more armies on the table, the more the probabilities favor the attacker.

A player could use this chart to determine optimal strategies. If they can guess about how many armies they're likely to get attacked with, they can figure the difference in probabilities between reinforcing various territories and choose their reinforcement strategy accordingly. For example, if they have two likely territories they'll need to defend, one with two defenders anticipating four attackers, and the other currently with four defenders and anticipating seven attackers, they can calculate which of those two places gives the best bang for the buck if they have one additional army to reinforce. Raising a four-attacking-two battle to four-attacking-three reduces the attacker's win probability by a little more than 14%; raising a six-attacking-four battle to six-attacking-five reduces the attacker's win probability by a little less than 11%. So they'd get better results, other things being equal, by adding an army to the smaller territory in this case.

A player can use similar considerations to decide where to place reinforcements to keep at least a 50% advantage as defender, if it's important to hold their borders (for example, if attempting to hold an entire continent for a turn, which grants an army bonus at the start of the next turn). If tasked with creating a digital version of this game, these are the kinds of calculations you would likely design for the AI.

As game designers, we can also notice how the combat mechanics in *Risk* affect gameplay. Probabilities tend to favor the defender in small combats, and the attacker when large numbers of armies are involved. This means that early in the game when everyone has relatively few armies on the board, defending is the dominant strategy, giving players an incentive to carve out a small area for themselves (often players try to take over South America or Australia since those have relatively few borders to defend) and just try to hold out and let the long-term bonus armies from their continent give them an advantage later on in the game. However, later in the game when players start getting massive army bonuses for continents and cards, the probabilities start to favor attacking: a positive feedback loop that helps draw the game to a close, even if everyone is playing optimally.

Discussion Questions

1. Create a custom five-state FSM, labeling all states and transitions, marking the initial state and (if any) final states, and the probabilities for each transition. This can be anything you want, for a real or imagined game system. Separately, describe in plain language what's going on.

2. For the FSM you created in the previous question, convert it to a transition matrix. (If you are going through this book in a group or a class, trade your FSM with a partner and create the transition matrix for someone else's FSM.)

3. For the transition matrix created in the previous question, use a Markov chain to determine how likely a player will be in any given state over time. Note particular points of interest, such as if/when it reaches a steady state, or when you pass a 50% chance of reaching a final state.

4. Consider this game: you can bet $1 and then flip a fair coin. If the coin lands on heads, you lose your bet. If the coin lands on tails, your bet is tripled and you can either walk away (keeping your bet) or flip again. You can only play once, ever. Model this as an infinite state machine.

5. For the game in the previous question, use a Markov chain to track the expected winnings. What do you find as the coin is flipped more?

6. For the game in the previous two questions, the expected value for flipping again is always positive, suggesting that it's always in the player's favor to flip again and never stop. But of course, if a player continues flipping the coin, they will eventually flip heads and lose everything. If you were playing this game, how would you resolve this paradox? That is, when would you stop flipping, and why?

7. Think of any game you've played that has at least one system or mechanic that could be analyzed using the techniques in this chapter. What's the game?

8. For the game you mentioned in the previous question, come up with a specific problem you could solve. For example, you might ask about the average number of turns to complete a task, or the average payoff to a particular action in the game.

9. For the problem you identified in the previous question, set up a model of the problem, such as a state machine and transition matrix.

10. Using the tools from the previous question, solve the problem and find your answer.

Sidequests

In this chapter, we learned the technique of using Markov chains to work our way forward for a repeated probability within a state machine, to analyze the effects of repeated state transitions. We also learned how to do the same thing in reverse using recursion, in order to calculate probabilities of complex events by reducing them to simpler ones. We can use this in games of pure chance to predict and optimize game length, for example. This isn't only useful in games of pure chance, however; it can also be used in games of strategy where the possibility space is known, but the exact future game state is unknown, in order to construct an optimal AI. The following challenges allow you to practice these techniques on your own.

Sidequest 22.1: Thunderstorm

Thunderstorm is a traditional children's dice game that originated in Germany. The original game is played as follows:

- **Number of players**: 2 or more, no upper limit.
- **Objective**: be the last player to be eliminated (last one standing).
- **Setup**: determine a player to go first. That player takes 6d6.
- On the first player's turn, that player rolls all 6d6 (on subsequent turns, players may roll fewer dice). After rolling,
  - If at least one of the dice rolled shows a 1, set aside all dice showing 1s, and pass the remaining dice to the next player in turn order.

- If *all* of the dice rolled are 1s, pass those dice *and all dice formerly set aside* to the next player in turn order. That player rolls all six dice on their turn.
- If *none* of the dice rolled are 1s, the player who rolled gets one strike against them. All dice that were rolled (but none that were formerly set aside) are passed to the next player. When a player gets six strikes against them, they are eliminated from the game and no longer roll dice or take turns.

Go ahead and play this game if you've never played before, in a small group. You will see that the game plays fairly quickly. Starting out, it is fairly easy to roll at least one 1 on 6d6, so the first player to roll is usually safe. But as players succeed in rolling 1s, the dice pool gets smaller and players start failing their rolls regularly. Once there is only one single die remaining, there are about four failures on average before someone finally rolls 1 and brings all of the dice back into play. At that point, the next players to roll feel some relief, as they're rolling many dice and be safe again, for the time being. *Thunderstorm* provides a surprising amount of rising and falling tension, and good pacing (which we examine in Chapter 12), considering the simplicity of its rules and the lack of any player choices.

You might wonder: how long does a single game take?

Assume a single-player version of this game. Keep playing until receiving six strikes. A player's "score" is the total number of die rolls made before being eliminated. Use a Markov chain to find the mean, median, and mode score for a single player. This can be modeled as a state machine, where each state is a unique combination of how many strikes the player has received (0 to 5), and how many dice are being rolled (1 to 6), plus one final state (six strikes received, and the number of dice are irrelevant because the game is over).

Alternate challenge: instead of a single player, model the game as a state machine that only examines the number of dice being rolled on each turn. Find the steady state, and how many turns it takes to get there. Also calculate the probability of failing a roll for each of the six states. Multiply the failure probability by the probability of being in that state. Add those together to get the probability of a failure ("strike") on any given turn.

Now, let's make the simplifying assumption that in a multiplayer game, each player has an equal probability of getting a strike (this is not strictly accurate, since the first player is rolling 6d6 on the first turn and thus would be expected to have a slightly different probability than the other players in sequence). Players continue to accumulate strikes until they are eliminated, so the total number of strikes in an *N*-player game is going to be somewhere between 6 * (N – 1) and 6 * (N – 1) + 5, because all but one player has six strikes at the end (elimination) and the winning (non-eliminated) player has somewhere between zero and five strikes. Using this range, come up with a range of average die rolls.

Greater challenge: extend the alternate challenge above: using any technique you can, find the expected value of the number of strikes in an N-player game. Multiply *that* by the probability of a strike in steady state to get expected number of turns in a game, in terms of N.

Ultimate challenge: examine the first-player advantage (or disadvantage) in a two-player game. Here, you need to consider not only the steady state in the long term, but also the initial rolls before steady state has been established. In the Markov chain, calculate the probabilities of a strike for all odd turns and all even turns, and keep track of the cumulative number of expected strikes for each player. Which player's probability of losing crosses 50% first?

Do the same for a three-player game, and a four-player game, and five-player, and so on. Do you see any patterns emerging, in terms of which position in turn order is the most (or least) favorable?

Sidequest 22.2: Hi Ho! Chery-O

This children's game with a theme of picking cherries from trees can be described, abstractly, as follows:

- **Players**: 2 or more
- **Objective**: be the first player to reach at least 10 points
- **Setup**: all players begin the game with 0 points. Choose a player to go first.
- **Play**: on a player's turn, they spin a spinner that produces one of seven equally likely results (equivalent to rolling 1d7). The results are: gain 1 point; gain 2 points; gain 3 points; gain 4 points; lose 1 point; lose 2 points; or reset their score to 0.

Let us first consider the single-player case. For one player, this can be modeled as a state machine with 11 states (scores of 0–9, and then a final state that contains all scores of 10 or above). Using Markov chains, calculate the mean, median, and mode turns it takes a single player to complete the game. Graph the probability curve of the probability of ending the game on the y-axis, and the turn number on the x-axis, up to 100 turns.

Greater challenge: use a Monte Carlo simulation to find the average game length for a four-player game.

Ultimate challenge: suppose you want to change the game to a median game length of ten turns for the single-player case. Without changing the mechanics of the seven spinner results, modify the probabilities of each spinner space (so that players are rolling a *weighted* d7, essentially) to get the median game length as close to exactly ten turns as you can. You need to restructure your spreadsheet so that you can enter weights in a series of cells, and the Markov chain calculations must take these weights into account. Then, play around with the weights by hand, or use a Solver to optimize.

Repeat this challenge, but you must keep the weights as even (you are now rolling a fair 1d7) but modify the mechanics, instead. Each of the seven spaces must determine the state transition, through any means that occurs to you (it might add or subtract points, set a player's score to any constant value, or even transition to the same state as a "null" move—anything that can be modeled in a state diagram). Modify the values of these spaces and, again, try to get the median game length down to 10 as above.

Which of these two methods was easier? Did you find it more challenging to tweak the probabilities, or change the core mechanics?

Sidequest 22.3: *Mordenkainen's Magical Rubber Band*

Consider that magic spell at the start of this chapter: it does 1 damage, with an 80% probability of doing +1 damage (repeating until the player fails the die roll). Calculate the expected value of damage from this spell using a Markov chain. Since this is an infinite state machine, just consider the first couple hundred states (anything after that amounts to a rounding error).

Repeat the calculation as a Monte Carlo simulation to verify your answer.

Alternate challenge: You can also solve this algebraically. This can be modeled as a sequence of probabilities, where damage $D_n = 1 + 0.8 * D_{n+1}$. In this particular case, since this holds true for every state (each state is the same as every other), $D_n = D_{n+1}$, which means you can reduce the equation to $D = 1 + 0.8 * D$. Solve this simple equation for the damage, and confirm that it gives the same answer as the other two methods above.

Sidequest 22.4: Kill the Elf *as a State Machine*

In Chapter 17, we examined a game called *Kill the Elf*. It is a two-player game. One player (the warrior) does 1 damage per turn; the other player (the wizard) rolls 1d6 and has a 1/6 probability of doing 6 damage per turn, and a 5/6 probability of doing no damage per turn. The expected values of these are the same in the long term, but in the short term, we found that a race to 6 damage greatly favors the wizard. Challenge 17.2 asked to compute the probability of a win if racing to 4 damage or 10. But what if we wanted to find the amount of damage that gave the closest to 1:1 odds of the warrior and wizard winning, for any values between 1 and 1000? That could potentially get quite unwieldy if we just used our standard probability tools.

But we can model this as a state machine, where the state is the number of times the wizard hits:

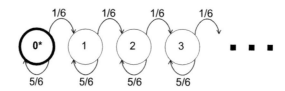

This becomes a fairly simple transition matrix. Construct that matrix, and use an initial column vector that shows a probability 1 of starting in state 0. Using a Markov chain, you can then determine, for any number of turns, the probability breakdown of what state the player is in (multiply by 6 to get the amount of damage done so far). For any given turn, you can see the probability of doing any amount of damage (keeping in mind that on turn n, the warrior has done exactly n damage).

What trends do you see as the amount of required damage increases? Between 1 and 1000, what value gives the odds that are closest to 1:1 (even chance of the warrior or wizard winning, i.e., the smallest absolute difference between the expected win rate of the wizard and 50%)?

Sidequest 22.5: Horse Race, *Exact Solution*

Chapter 17 also introduced a dice contest between two players, where each player rolls 50d6 and we must calculate the probability of either player winning if one player rolls a 1 and the other player rolls a 6 on the first turn. In Challenge 17.3, we performed a Monte Carlo simulation to get an estimate of this probability and noted that an exact solution would be challenging.

We can model the horse race as a finite state machine, where the state is the difference between the two players' scores (some states may be negative numbers!). The initial state is 5 (because one player has 6 points and the other player has 1 point, after the first roll). Each subsequent roll may change the state anywhere from +5 to −5, depending on the rolls (there are only 36 different results for each turn, and you should be able to calculate the probability of each state transition easily enough at this point). At any point, being in a positive state means the player who rolled the initial 6 is winning; being in a negative state means the player who rolled the initial 1 is winning; and being in state 0 means the players are currently tied.

Since there are 50 turns (and the first turn, by the problem statement, puts us in state 5), the states after all 50 turns ranges from −240 to 250, for a total of 491 states. That is very possible to do in a spreadsheet, but tedious. Instead, let's take a simpler case: a ten-turn game (which has states ranging from −40 to 50, for 91 states total). Using a Markov chain, determine the probability of the player who initially rolled 6 winning the game (i.e., the probability of ending in *any* positive-numbered state) after each turn. Graph the win probability on the *y*-axis and the turn number on the *x*-axis, from turns 1 through 10 (turn 1, since it is fixed in state 5, should be a probability 1 of winning).

What pattern do you see emerging, from the graph? How would you expect the probability to change for a 50-turn game, or a 100-turn game, or a 500-turn game?

Sidequest 22.6: Two in a Row

A deck containing three black cards and three red cards is shuffled randomly, and the cards are dealt out in order. What is the probability of flipping at least two black cards in a row?

This can be done by brute force, but if it were much larger (say, if looking at an entire deck with 26 black and 26 red, and looking for a string of at least 5 in a row), it would become quite unwieldy, and trying to compute it by conventional methods seems like it should be easy until you try, at which point it starts to feel impossible. However, this can be modeled as a state machine!

Each state consists of *three* numbers rather than just one. The first number is the number of black cards remaining in the deck. The second number is the number of red cards remaining in the deck. The third number is the number of black cards in a row, currently. The initial state is (3, 3, 0).

With the first card drawn, we can draw either a black card (probability 3/6) transitioning to state (2, 3, 1) or a red card (probability 3/6) transitioning to state (3, 2, 0). State (2, 3, 1) has a probability 2/5 of drawing a second black card, transitioning to (1, 3, 2) which is a final state, because no matter what is drawn after that, we know that we have encountered a run of two black cards in a row; there is also a probability 3/5 of drawing a red card after the initial black card instead, transitioning to state (2, 2, 0). The partial state diagram looks like the following.

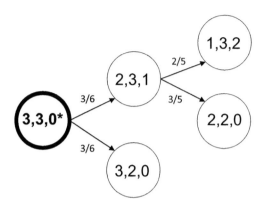

You could extend this state diagram to include all possibilities. Then, for each final state that includes a run of at least two black cards, multiply all of the probabilities to get there (in this case, the probability of reaching state (1, 3, 2) is 3/6 * 2/5 = 1/5). Add the probabilities of all such final states and that is the probability of encountering a run of at least two cards.

How would you model this in a spreadsheet? The first number is between 0 and 3. The second number is between 0 and 3. The third number is between 0 and 2. This gives a maximum of 4 * 4 * 3 = 192 states. You could simply number the states as a single three-digit number (the initial state would be 330). For greater efficiency, if the three numbers are (a, b, c), you could have that correspond to the state number 12a + 3b + c, which would be unique for any valid combination of the numbers. (We could get even more efficient, since some states like (3, 3, 3) are impossible, but the number is small enough that we can ignore that detail for now.) As with the *Risk* case study in this chapter, each state (a, b, 2) for all numbers a and b is considered a positive final state, and we can compute the probability of reaching that state by going back to the previous (a + 1, b, 1). Any state (m, n, 1) can be reached from (m + 1, n, 0). Any state (x, y, 0) can be reached from either (x, y + 1, 0) or (x, y + 1, 1). Going recursively, you get back to (3, 3, 0) eventually through all paths. By multiplying each state's probability by the probability of transitioning there from a previous state—the probability of drawing a black card from state (*black, red, streak*) is black/(black+red), and the probability of drawing a red card is red/(black+red)—you should be able to get the probability of transitioning at some point to any given state. Add up all the probability of reaching all final states with *streak* = 2 and that gives you the probability you're looking for.

Ultimate challenge (requires programming): A gambler sits down at a *Blackjack* table, which is dealing cards from an eight-deck shoe; this means the cards are being dealt from a collection of 32 Aces, 128 "tens" (10, Jack, Queen or King), and 256 "spots" (number cards 2 through 9). Assume a fair, random shuffle, and assume that the entire shoe is dealt through. What is the probability that at some point, the player sees at least one run of at least 10 "tens" dealt in a row?

(An equivalent problem, since each card is either a "ten" or it isn't: imagine a string of 416 computer **bits**—ones or zeros[5]; 128 of these bits are ones. The remaining 288 bits are zeroes. Aside from that constraint, they are ordered randomly. What is the probability that the entire string contains at least one section of 10 or more ones in a row?)

This is equivalent to the earlier problem, but instead of an initial state of (3, 3, 0), you have an initial state of (128, 256, 0) and final states have a run of 10 instead of 2. There are about 400,000 potential states here, too many to enumerate with a hand-drawn state diagram. Even populating a spreadsheet can be unwieldy for this, unless you can develop some kind of trick to populate cells in an automated fashion. However, it can be quite feasible to solve this problem in a programming language, using a recursive function call.

---

[5] The word "bit" is short for "binary digit" because the binary number system uses just zeros and ones.

23

Situational Balance

In This Chapter

What Is Situational Balance?

In Chapter 8, we studied the balance of transitive mechanics. In Chapters 17 and 18, we looked at probability theory. In this chapter, we combine these topics to balance mechanics that are transitive, sort of, but where their value changes depending on the game state. There isn't a well-accepted term for these kinds of mechanics, so in this book, we call it situational balance.

Consider damage that affects all targets in an area (**AoE** or Area of Effect), as opposed to an attack that only hits a single enemy. You would expect something that does 500 damage to all enemies in an area to be more valuable than something that does 500 damage to a single target, other things being equal. But how much more valuable? It depends. If fighting a single enemy one-on-one, it isn't any more valuable; it does 500 damage whether it targets just that enemy or all other (non-existent) enemies in the vicinity. On the other hand, if fighting 50 enemies all clustered together in a swarming mass, the AoE attack is 50 times as valuable as a single-target spell. Maybe at some point in the game, there are giant enemy swarms, and other times, the player fights a single lone boss. How do you balance the value of AoE compared to an equivalent single-target attack?

Or consider an effect that depends on what the opponent does in a PvP game. As an example, in the first edition of *Magic: the Gathering*, there was a spell called Karma that did damage to the opponent equal to the number of their Swamps in play, every turn. Against a player who has 24 Swamps in their deck, this single card could kill them very dead, very fast. Against a player with no Swamps at all, the card is absolutely worthless under normal circumstances. But if the player who plays Karma also has *other* cards in their deck that can turn the opponent's land into Swamps, then the value of Karma depends on the player's ability to combine it with other card effects (that may or may not be drawn from a shuffled deck). But Karma still has to have a fixed cost; how does a game designer choose something appropriate?

Another common type of balance is a healing effect. In most games, characters have a maximum health value (usually wherever they start at), and if they are already at maximum health, then healing is completely worthless. On the other hand, healing can make the difference between winning and losing if they're almost dead, and fighting against something else that's almost dead, and they just need to live long enough to take one or two more actions. How do you balance a healing effect where its value ranges from near-zero to near-infinite depending on the situation?

In all of these cases, finding the right cost for an effect on your cost curve depends on the situation in the game, so in this book, we refer to these types of effects as **situational effects**, and the process of balancing these is referred to as **situational balance**. How do we balance something that must have a fixed cost, even though its benefit changes? The short answer is that we use probability to figure out an *expected value* of the benefit. Depending on the nature of the effect, we may also look at the maximum or minimum possible value of the benefit. The final balanced cost of the thing is generally somewhere in that range.

For situational effects, often the *best* way to find the true value of its benefit is through playtesting and analytics (see Chapters 13 and 15). However, that requires us to have already built the game and had players playing it in order to get real data on how it is used in actual play. But we do not always have sufficient budgets to playtest a game thoroughly before release in the real world; we don't always want to wait until after release to use large-scale analytics to balance the game; and even if we do, we still have to start *somewhere*, so we need to make our best initial, educated guess. This chapter provides some techniques to assist in making that first guess.

A Simple Example

Let us start with a simple example: an extremely oversimplified version of the *d20* combat system, used in *Dungeons & Dragons* third edition. Here is how this system works: each character has two stats, their Base Attack Bonus (BAB) and Armor Class (AC). Each round, every character gets to make one attack against one opponent. To attack, they roll 1d20 and add their BAB, and compare the total to the target's AC. If the attacker's total is greater or equal, they hit; otherwise, they miss. A default "plain vanilla" character starts with a BAB of 0 and an AC of 10. Thus, with no further bonuses, a vanilla character should be able to hit another vanilla character 55% of the time.

Here's an important question for this system: are AC and BAB balanced? That is, if a character gets an extra +1 to their BAB (making it more likely for them to hit), is that equivalent to +1 AC (making it less likely for them to get hit by an enemy)? Or is one of the two stats more powerful than the other?

First, realize that we cannot fully answer this question because we don't know how much damage gets dealt on a hit or how much health a character has (i.e., how many times a character can survive being hit or how many times a character has to successfully hit an enemy to defeat it). But assuming these are equal (or equivalent), it doesn't actually matter. Whether an enemy gets killed after being hit once or 5 times or 100 times, as long as it's equally vulnerable to the character, the character's hit percentage (compared to the opponent's) is the main determiner of success. They hit the opponent a certain percentage of the time, the opponent hits them a certain percentage of the time, and the player wants their character's hit percentage to be higher than the opponent's. If it takes the same number of hits to kill the character as it does to kill the opponent, a higher number of required hits means less variance in the rolls (the Law of Large Numbers kicks in and makes a victory virtually certain for someone with a higher hit percentage, with a sufficiently high number of die rolls), while a smaller number of required hits means the player with the lower hit percentage has a better chance of getting lucky enough to overcome the odds against them.

So, in this system, it's not the absolute hit percentage that matters, but the hit percentage *compared to the opponent*. If both the character and an enemy have a 5% chance of hitting each other (both have low BAB and high AC), then both hit each other very infrequently. If they both have a 95% chance of hitting each other (high BAB, low AC), they hit each other just about every time. Either way, they exchange blows as often as one another. This means that gaining a +5% probability of hitting the opponent (+1 BAB) is just as good as reducing the opponent's probability of hitting the character by −5% (+1 AC). Assuming the character needs to hit as often as they get hit, the two stats are indeed equivalent against a single opponent in one-on-one combat.[1]

What if we aren't limited to a one-on-one fight? What if the character is alone, surrounded by four enemies? Now, they attack once for every four attacks made against them. In this case, +1 AC is four times as powerful as +1 BAB, because a die roll that involves the character's AC is made four times as often as a die roll that involves their BAB.

What if it's the other way around: a party of four adventurers are working together to take on a lone powerful monster, like a giant. Assuming the giant can only attack one adventurer at a time, +1 BAB is now more powerful. But if the giant spreads out its attacks evenly, it only attacks each individual adventure every four rounds, so each adventurer is attacking once per round but only getting attacked 0.25 times per round, on average. In this case, +1 BAB is four times as powerful as +1 AC.

Even in a one-on-one setting, there may be a difference if fighting against an opponent with different damage and different health. If the opponent does twice as much damage as the character when hitting, and both have the same health, then avoiding the opponent's damage is twice as important as hitting the opponent, so AC is twice as powerful as BAB in that battle. If character and opponent do the same amount of damage but the character has twice as much health, they only have to hit half as often as the opponent to win. In this case, BAB is twice as useful as AC, since every time the character hits that is equivalent to their getting hit twice; it's more important to emphasize connecting with vital hits than avoiding one of the opponent's weak hits.

In practice, in most *D&D* campaigns, GMs are fond of putting their adventuring party in situations where they're outnumbered and outpowered; the setting of the game is ideal for characters that become heroes, overcoming impossible odds to triumph over evil, and it feels more epic to throw characters into challenging situations. That means that in everyday use, AC is likely to be more powerful than BAB. The two stats are *not* equivalent on the cost curve, even though the game behaves as if they should be, and any GM who wants the game to feel balanced should design their adventures accordingly.

---

[1]One exception to this: if a character's AC or BAB is so much higher than the opponent's corresponding stat, that they have already increased their hit percentage to 100% or above, or reduced the opponent's hit percentage to 0% or below, then (as stated in our simplified system) additional bonuses to that stat provide no additional benefit.

Implications for Game Designers

Granted, this *is* an oversimplification. But we can see something interesting emerge from this simple system: the value of attacking is higher if more powerful than the opponent, and the value of defending is higher when less powerful.

If you're creating a game where you know what the player encounters ahead of time—say, a first-person shooter or role-playing game with levels that are designed by hand—you can use your knowledge of upcoming challenges to balance the game. For example, if you have a game using our simplified *d20* combat system and you know that the player is mostly fighting in situations where they're outnumbered, you can change AC on the cost curve to be more valuable and thus more costly. Or, if you desire BAB and AC to be equivalent and balanced with each other, you could change the mix of encounters in the game so that the player is outnumbered about as often as they outnumber the enemy. Aside from making BAB and AC balanced with each other, this also adds replay value to the game: going through such a game with a high BAB is going to be a very different experience than going through the game with high AC; in each case, a different set of encounters are hard or easy, giving the player a different perspective and different level of challenge in each encounter.

Versatility

What if our simplified *d20* combat system worked in such a way that the player could freely convert AC to BAB at a one-for-one rate, at the start of any combat? Now, all of a sudden, the two stats are equivalent to each other, and a +1 bonus to either is more powerful and versatile relative to any other bonuses in the rest of the game.

Okay, so a complete re-spec of the player's character isn't something that happens in unlimited fashion on demand in most RPGs, but there *are* plenty of games where the player can swap out one situational thing for another. First-person shooters (FPSs) are a common example. The player might be carrying several weapons at a time, each of which is specialized: maybe a rocket launcher against big slow targets or clusters of enemies, a sniper rifle to use at a distance against single targets, or a knife or chainsaw for close-quarters attacks. Each weapon is better in some situations than others, but as long as it's possible to switch from one to another with minimal delay, it's the *sum* of weapon situations that matters rather than *individual* weapon limitations.

A large pile of situational weapons for every occasion is much better than a single jack-of-all-trades, master-of-none weapon, in this case.

But suppose we made the cost of switching weapons higher: perhaps a five-second delay to put one weapon back in the character's pack and take out another. Now all of a sudden, the limitations of individual weapons play a greater role, and a single general-purpose weapon may end up becoming more powerful than an entire suite of situational weapons.

We can modify the situational balance simply by modifying the cost of switching between different tools, weapons, stat distributions, or overall strategies.

Complete Inability to Change

Let us take one extreme case: the player can't switch strategies at all. An example might be a simple role-playing game (RPG) where players can only carry and equip one armor and one weapon at a time, and whenever they acquire a new one, it automatically gets rid of the old. Here, the calculation is fairly straightforward: what they have is their only option, so we have to look at it across all situations. This looks like an expected value calculation. So you can ask: in what situations does this object have a greater or lesser value, how often does the player encounter those situations (the probability), and how much greater or lesser is its value in those situations (the result)? Multiply each probability by its result, and add all of the separate scenarios together.

Here is a simple example: suppose you design a sword that does double damage against dragons. Suppose that 10% of the meaningful combats in your game are against dragons. Let's also assume that in this game, damage has a linear relationship to the cost curve, so that doubling the damage of a weapon makes it exactly twice as good.

In this case, 90% of the time the sword acts normally, and 10% of the time it's twice as good:

$$90\% * 1.0 + 10\% * 2.0 = 1.1$$

In this case, "double damage against dragons" is worth 1.1 times as much as a sword that just does standard damage all of the time: a +10% modifier to the base cost.

Here's another example: you design a sword that is 1.5 times as powerful as other swords in its class, but it only does half damage against trolls. Let's further assume that "half damage" is a huge liability: it takes away the player's primary way to do damage, so they must rely on other sources that are less efficient. This would greatly increase the chance that they end up dead if they run into a troll at a bad time. So in this case let's say that "half damage" doesn't just mean 50% value, but rather that it actually makes the sword a net negative, a liability. Specifically, if a standard sword has a value of 100 (and this sword has a value of 150 because of its 1.5× damage), at half damage it has a value of −250 against trolls. But let's also say that trolls are pretty rare, only 5% of the encounters in the game. We can calculate the value of this risky sword:

$$150 * 0.95 + (-250) * 0.05 = 130$$

Thus, this sword would be worth 30% more than a plain 100-value sword. More to the point, you can see how there are a lot of design knobs you could turn to modify the balance here. You can obviously change the raw cost or benefit of an object, perhaps adjusting the damage in special situations, or adjusting the base values that affect every *other* situation. But you can also change the frequency of situations (the places where trolls or dragons are encountered) in the entire game, or even just in the immediate area surrounding where the player finds the sword. After all, if the player finds the sword that is useless against trolls in a region of the game that has no trolls, it's not much of a drawback, even if the rest of the game is *covered* in trolls.

Unrestricted Ability to Change

Let's examine the other extreme, where the player can carry around as many situational objects as they like and can switch between them freely and instantly. In this case, the limitations of each object don't matter nearly as much as the strengths, because there is no opportunity cost to gaining a new capability. In this case, if we want to compute the value of a new object, we look at the benefits of what the player has collected thus far and figure out what the new object adds that can't be done better by something else. Multiply this added benefit (relative to what they could do without the new object) by the percentage of the time that benefit is useful. This is the value of the new object.

It's not usually that simple, however. The player may pick up objects in a different order on each playthrough, if the game isn't entirely linear. The player may be using suboptimal strategies, using objects that aren't *perfect* for the situation but which can still be useful. In short, you don't actually know how often something will be used in such a game, because the frequency of use depends on what other tools the player has already acquired, and the player's preferred play style.

Let us take another example: perhaps you create a variety of swords in a game, and the player can switch between the swords they've acquired at any time with no penalty. Each sword does double damage against one class of monster, half extra damage against a different class of monster, and *no* damage against a third class of monster, and standard damage against all other monster types. Assume the swords are all otherwise equal, and each class of monster is encountered as frequently (and is as dangerous) as the others:

Sword	2 × Damage Against…	1.5 × Damage Against…	Ineffective Against…
Slayer	Dragons	Trolls	Slimes
Legend	Beasts	Goblins	Trolls
Vermillion	Slimes	Demons	Bunnies
Master	Undead	Dragons	Goblins
Heavenly	Demons	Bunnies	Humans
Magic	Goblins	Undead	Golems
Broken	Bunnies	Slimes	Dragons
Ginormo	Humans	Golems	Beasts
Samurai	Golems	Humans	Undead
Lost	Trolls	Beasts	Demons

These swords should obviously cost the same. However, they do not actually give equal value to the player at any given point in time; it depends on how many swords they have collected already.

For example, suppose the player buys the Slayer sword, which does extra damage against dragons and trolls. After that, the Lost sword isn't quite as powerful an increase anymore; it does double damage against trolls, but the player could already do extra damage against trolls. Going from a 1.5× to 2× multiplier is not as much of an increase as going from 1× to 2×.

If the player fully optimizes, they can buy just five swords (say, Slayer, Vermillion, Magic, Samurai, and Lost) and have at least *some* bonus against all ten monster types. From that point on, extra swords have severely diminishing returns, and thus, their cost should go down.

How might you handle such a thing in practice? Here are a few ideas (you can probably think of others):

- Change costs during play. If the player buys all ten swords from the same merchant (or sword manufacturing company), reduce the cost of future swords. You could even work this into the narrative, framing it as the character getting a discount for being such a good customer. You could even go so far as to give the player a "customer loyalty card" in the game and have the merchant stamp the card.

- Keep the costs the same. This does mean the player would have diminishing returns if they buy more swords, and it would be a meaningful choice for the player to decide how many is enough.
- If the player is getting more money over time as they progress through the game, even if the costs are kept constant, it's still effectively a diminishing cost because the amount of time spent exploring or fighting that is required to buy another sword is decreasing.
- You could spread out the locations where the player can get each sword, so that you know ahead of time which ones the player probably has early or late in the game. You can cost each sword differently because you know which ones the player encounters after they already have a sizeable sword collection.

If you add a cost to switching swords, the effect of diminishing returns would decrease proportionally, but you could still use any or all of these methods to balance the costs—just with less intensity.

Versatile Objects

So far, we have only considered situations where the game objects are fixed and specialized, and the character's versatility depends on their ability to change between them. But what if an object *itself* is versatile and can be used in several situations? This happens a lot in turn-based and real-time strategy (RTS) games, for example, when individual units may have several functions.

For example, a typical relationship in an RTS game is that there are three classes of units: archers, footmen, and fliers. Archers are strong against fliers; fliers are strong against footmen; and footmen are strong against archers (this is called an intransitive relationship, and we examine this more fully in Chapter 25). Now, suppose you designed a new unit, the wizard, which is strong against *both* footmen and fliers, but not quite *as* strong against fliers as archers are, and not as strong against footmen as fliers are. So, if an archer can take down a flier while losing only 20% of its health, maybe a wizard loses 50% of its health. Wizards may not be as good against fliers as archers are, but wizards are good for other things too, so they are more versatile.

Another example might be a typical first-person shooter, where knives and swords are easily the best weapons if standing next to an opponent, while sniper rifles are great at a long distance. Meanwhile, a machine gun might be moderately useful at most ranges, but not *quite* as good as anything else. If a player has a machine gun, they'll never be caught with a completely ineffective weapon, but they'll also never have the perfect weapon for the job.

How much is this kind of versatility in an object worth? Its value is in direct proportion to uncertainty. If a player knows ahead of time that they're playing on a small map with tight corridors and lots of twists and turns, knives are more useful than sniper rifles. On a large map consisting primarily of wide open space, it's the other way around. If a single map has a combination of open and close areas, a weapon that can be useful in both types of spaces is more valuable.

What if map selection is random, and players must select their weapons before learning what level they'll be playing on? Maybe, there's a 50% chance of getting a map that favors knives, and a 50% chance of getting a map that favors sniper rifles. What's the best strategy now? Taking the versatile weapon is mildly useful in each case, but not as powerful as a player who picked the specialized weapon and guessed right. That kind of choice is not very interesting: players must choose blindly ahead of time, and then most of the game comes down to who was a lucky guesser… unless the players are given a mechanism to change weapons during play to adjust to the map, or they can take multiple weapons with them. Which brings us back to the fact that versatility comes in two flavors: the ability of an individual game object to be useful in multiple situations and the ability of the player to swap out one specialized game object for another. The more easily a player can switch between game objects or strategies, the less useful versatility within a single object becomes.

Shadow Costs

Back in Chapter 8 when looking at cost curves, we noted that "costs" do not just mean the raw resource cost of an object, but also other drawbacks or limitations. These other non-resource costs tend to come up a lot in situational balancing. In the field of economics, these are called **shadow costs** because they are a cost that's hidden behind the resource cost.

Here's an example of a shadow cost from the real world. Suppose you buy a cheap alarm clock for $5, which seems like a great deal at the time. But there is an additional cost in time (and transportation) to go out and buy it, so if it's sold far away from where you live, that reduces the value of the deal to you. If the clock is cheaply made (or poorly designed so that you accidentally set it for PM instead of AM) and fails to wake you up one morning which causes you to miss a critical appointment, this may cost you additional time and money to reschedule. If it breaks in a few months because of its cheap components, the time it takes you to return or replace it is an extra cost on top of that.

While the sale price of the alarm clock is only $5, the *actual* cost when factoring in all of these shadow costs is much higher, perhaps even making it more expensive in total than a better-made alarm clock with a higher price tag.

In games, there are two kinds of shadow costs that seem to come up a lot in situational balance: sunk costs and opportunity costs. We explain these in the following sections.

Sunk Costs

A **sunk cost** is a setup cost that must be paid first, before gaining access to the thing that was originally desired. A common example of this is a tech tree (common in RTS, RPG, and MMO games). As one example, in the original *StarCraft*, to build most kinds of units a player must first build a structure that can manufacture them. The structure may not do anything practical or useful, *other* than allowing its owner to build a special unit. So, if a player has to build a Gateway (costing 150 minerals) to be able to build a Cybernetics Core, and then a Cybernetics Core (costing 200 minerals) to be able to build Dragoon units, and a Dragoon unit costs 125 minerals and 50 gas, and these things are used for nothing else, then one Dragoon unit actually ends up costing a total of 475 minerals and 50 gas, which includes 350 minerals' worth of sunk costs. This is a very large cost compared to the base cost of the unit itself!

Of course, if that player builds ten Dragoons, then the sunk cost is said to be **amortized** across all ten of them. The total cost of one Gateway, one Cybernetics Core, and ten Dragoons is 1600 minerals and 500 gas, which comes out to 160 minerals and 50 gas per Dragoon—a unit price much closer to the listed cost of a Dragoon.

If the Gateway or Cybernetics Core provides additional benefits, such as unlocking other types of buildings or units or offering specialized unit upgrades, then we could also consider part of the cost of those buildings going to those other things, rather than being part of the Dragoon cost.

Still, you can see that if a player must pay some up-front cost merely for the privilege of being able to pay an additional cost for something, you must be careful to include the sunk cost in your analysis. If the sunk cost can be amortized over multiple future purchases, the amount of the sunk cost should be based on an expected value: *how many* Dragoons are built in a typical game where the player builds both a Gateway and Cybernetics Core? When costing Dragoons, the designer had to factor in the up-front costs as well.

You can also do this the other way around: rather than choosing the cost of the final purchase while factoring in the shadow costs, instead cost the prerequisite purchases based on not only its immediate benefits, but also the potential future benefits it enables or unlocks. Tech trees are a prime example of this method; some RPGs feature special abilities or feats that can be chosen on level-up that are only marginally useful on their own, but that have prerequisites for some very powerful abilities much later. This can lead to interesting short-term/long-term decisions, where a player can take a good ability now *or* a less powerful ability now to get a *really* powerful ability later.

Sunk costs can be seen in other kinds of games, too. In many RPGs, the player may have a choice between paying for consumable items (which are cheap, but can only be used once), or reusable versions of those same items (which are more expensive, but unlimited use). Maybe, the player can buy a Potion for 50 gold, or a Machine of Unlimited Potion Making for 500 gold (the machine is a better value if they expect to create more than ten Potions). Or a player might have a choice of paying for a one-way ticket on a shuttle for 10 gold or a Lifetime Pass for 1,000 gold (the pass is worthwhile only if they take the shuttle 100 times). Or a player purchases a Shop Discount Card which gives 10% off all future purposes, but costs 5,000 gold for the card (a worthwhile purchase if they expect to spend at least 50,000 gold on future purchases). These kinds of choices aren't always as interesting to the player, because the game expects them to estimate how many times they'll use something… but without telling them how much longer the game is or how many times they can expect to use the reusable thing, so it is a blind decision. Still, as game designers who can make reasonable estimates of the expected value of these kinds of items, we can do our own calculations and balance the items accordingly. If we do it right, our players should at least trust that the cost is relative to the value by the time they have to make a buy-or-don't-buy decision in our games.

Opportunity Costs

The second type of shadow cost, which we refer to as an **opportunity cost**, is the "cost" of giving up something else, reducing versatility. One example from games with tech trees is a situation where the player must choose between different branches of a tech tree, where each one locks the other. For example, if a player learns Fire magic in some games, it immediately locks them out of learning any Ice spells and vice versa. Another example happens in quest systems, where a player may get two competing quests, and they must decide which of the two to complete (each one automatically causes the other to fail). In many trading card games (TCGs), merely including certain cards in a deck either prevents a player from including other cards (if they are of competing factions and deckbuilding rules only allow one faction or the other in a deck) or limits a player in other ways (if each faction has its own unique resource type, like the five mana colors in *Magic: the Gathering*, each additional faction in a deck makes it harder to get all of the resources needed). In all of these situations, taking an action in the game *now* prevents taking some other action *later* (or adds an additional cost to doing so).

In this case, these initial actions have a hidden cost: in addition to the explicit resource cost of taking the action right now, players also pay a cost later in decreased versatility. The action adds a constraint on future actions. How much is that constraint worth as a cost? That depends entirely on your particular game and how its mechanics fit together. But remember that the cost is not zero, and be sure to factor this into your cost curve analysis.

Essential Case Studies

How do all of these concepts work in practice? Let us take a look at some more simple examples to get the general idea.

A SCROLL OF FIRE AND ICE

How do the numbers for balancing versatility work in practice? That depends on the nature of the versatility and the cost and difficulty of switching.

Imagine a game with an arena where individuals face off against each other in one-on-one combat. Inside the arena, all players have either an Ice attack or a Fire attack (never both and never neither) and both are equally popular among the player community. Before entering the arena, a player can buy a Protection from Ice enchantment that cuts Ice damage by half, or a Protection from Fire enchantment that reduces Fire damage by half, and each of these costs 10 gold. There's also a third option, Protection from Fire and Ice, which acts as both, as a package deal. How much should this third option cost to make it balanced?

This depends on how much is known about the next opponent. If a player knows ahead of time that they're about to face a Fire opponent, then it should cost the same as Protection from Fire: 10 gold. The versatility offers no added value, because they already know the optimal choice.

If they have no way of knowing the next opponent's attack type until it's too late to do anything about it, then it should cost 20 gold, the same as buying the Fire and Ice protections separately. Here, versatility offers exactly the same added value as buying both; there is no effective difference between buying the two of them separately or together.

What if you design the option to buy one of the two scrolls (Fire or Ice) before the combat starts, and then if the player guessed wrong, at the start of the fight they can immediately call a time-out and buy the other one? In this case, players would normally spend 10 gold to buy one of the two right away, and there's a 50% probability of guessing right (so they only spend 10 gold), and a 50% probability of guessing wrong (they'd have to then spend an extra 10 gold, for a total of 20, to gain this protection). The expected value here is (50% * 10) + (50% * 20) = 15 gold, so that is what the combined package should cost if purchased up front, in this case.

What if the game is partly predictable, where a player has some general idea of whether the opponent uses Fire or Ice attacks, but can't be completely sure (say they can view the next opponent's avatar, and many player avatars look fire-ish or ice-ish, but a few players intentionally make their avatar look like the opposite of what they use to throw off the opposition)? The proper cost for the protection-from-both package is somewhere between the extremes of 10 and 20 gold, depending on just how certain a player can be.

SPLASH DAMAGE

Returning to one of the initial questions in this chapter: for things that do damage to multiple targets instead of just one at a time, *other things being equal*, how much of a benefit is that AoE damage?

Generally, you'd take the expected value of the number of targets hit and multiply. If enemies come in clusters from 1 to 3 in the game (evenly distributed), then the expected number of targets would be 2 per attack. In that case, an AoE attack would be considered twice the benefit of an equivalent single-target attack.

Now, "other things being equal" is very tricky here, because in most games, other things *aren't* equal. For example, in most games, enemies don't lose any offensive capability until they're completely defeated; with just 1% of health remaining, an enemy can still do just as much damage with their greatest attack as they could with full health. In such a game, doing *partial* damage to an enemy isn't nearly as important as doing *lethal* damage. Spreading out the damage slowly and evenly among several enemies would be less efficient than using single-target high-power shots to selectively take out one enemy at a time, since each enemy killed reduces the offensive power of the enemy forces, while an AoE attack that does damage evenly won't do that for a while.

If the enemy force has varying amounts of health among its constituents, such that an AoE attack would actually knock out individual enemies at a reasonable rate, we encounter another problem: a dwindling enemy force reduces the total damage being dealt by the AoE attack over time! If the player is doing 100 damage to five enemies at the start of combat, that's 500 damage per attack, total. Once the weakest enemy falls, they only do 400 damage. By the time the enemies are down to a lone survivor, it's only 100 damage per attack. So, you have to consider this as well: in a typical encounter, how often are enemies clustered together... *and* how long do they stay that way throughout the encounter?

ELEMENTAL STRENGTHS AND WEAKNESSES

Many games have attacks that are strong or weak against certain enemy types. The simplest way to calculate this is to multiply the extra benefit (or liability) if it were always present, by the expected percentage of the time that the player encounters the relevant enemy type.

However, as noted earlier in this chapter, you must be very careful of what the extra benefit or liability is really worth. "Double damage" is rarely worth exactly double the base benefit. For example, if a character's base attack does enough damage to take down an enemy in one attack already, doubling that damage does nothing for them. Double damage against the weakest enemies in the game isn't particularly useful, because the player can probably kill the weak ones easily without the bonus. Double damage against the final boss of the game is much more valuable, because it is (literally) the last thing the player needs!

Meanwhile, "half damage" isn't necessarily half of the base benefit. If enemies have armor that reduces damage by a certain flat amount, half damage against a high-armor enemy might mean that it takes *zero* damage from attacks! If a player's primary attack is rendered less effective, they may have to rely on other means of doing damage: spells, techniques, or consumables that are more expensive or limited use, and may run out before they finish the level they're on.

ALTS AND SIDEBOARDS

Some games support the use of situational objects that can be brought into play when needed, but can be safely ignored in cases where they're suboptimal. Examples are situational weapons in an FPS that can be carried as an "alternate" sidearm, specialized units in an RTS that can be built when needed and ignored otherwise, or situational cards in a TCG that can be "sideboarded" and only put in a deck against specific opponents. In all of these cases, the utility of the objects depends on things outside of player control: what map the game is played on, what units the opponent is building, or what cards are in the opponent's deck.

In these cases, the most obvious thing to do would be to cost them according to the likelihood they'll be useful. For example, suppose there's a card that does 10 damage against a player who is playing Red spells in *Magic: the Gathering* and that most decks use two of the five colors, so that (if the colors are balanced in the metagame) 40% of players are using Red in open play. Intuitively, you might cost this the same as a card that did $40\% * 10 = 4$ damage to any player, unrestricted. If the player had to choose whether to use this in their deck with no advance knowledge of the opponent's deck, this would be a reasonable method.

But, in many cases, a player *does* know what their opponent is playing. In many tournament formats, players play three games against each opponent, and they are allowed to modify their play deck with cards from a 15-card "sideboard" in between games. A player could put this 10-damage-against-Red card in their sideboard for the first game, and swap it in for subsequent games against Red opponents only. Played this way, a player is virtually assured that the card works 100% of the time. The only cost is the opportunity cost of using a discretionary card slot in the sideboard and that is a *metagame* cost. As we noted back in Chapter 8, costing game objects based on the metagame is tricky and prone to error. At best, we can say that this fictitious situational 10-damage spell should cost a *little* less than an unrestricted 10 damage to compensate for the metagame cost, but it shouldn't be 60% off unless we *really* wanted to encourage its use as a sideboard card by intentionally undercosting it.

The same is true with a specialized unit in an RTS game, assuming it has no sunk cost to earn the capability of building it. If a particular unit is useless most of the time, then a player loses nothing by simply not exercising the option to build it. But when it *is* useful, players build it, and they'll know it's useful in that case. Again, a specialized unit should be costed with the assumption that whatever situation it's designed for actually happens near 100% of the time. (If players must pay extra for the versatility of being able to build the situational unit in the first place, *that* cost is what you'd want to adjust, based on a realistic percentage of the time that such a situation is encountered in typical play.)

With an alternate weapon in an FPS, a lot depends on exactly how the game is structured. If the weapons are all free (no resource cost to purchase), but players can only select one main weapon and one alternate, you need to make sure that the alternates are balanced against each other; i.e., each one is useful in equally likely situations—or rather, that if you multiply the benefit by the expected probability of receiving that benefit, *that* should be the same across all alternate weapons. In other words, some alternate weapons might be extremely powerful in a narrow set of circumstances, while others are mediocre but can be used just about anywhere, and those two types might be balanced if the numbers all agree.

PLAYING THE METAGAME

In the collectible card game *Hearthstone*, about 10% of the minions in the game are Mech ("Mech" is a keyword that has no direct in-game consequences, but is referenced on a number of cards). Which of the following effects would be more powerful: "Destroy all Mechs in play" or "Destroy all minions in play except for Mechs"? Keep in mind that both of these would affect not just the opponent, but the one who played the effect as well.

If assuming that both players stick to the percentages, both of these effects on the surface seem the same, since they affect players equally; one of them will destroy 10% of the minions in play, and the other will destroy 90%, so they are different but equal. However, this is actually not the case, because players choose what cards to put into their decks. A card that affects both players will primarily be included in decks that are specifically constructed to favor the player who is playing the card. A "destroy all Mechs" card might be included in a deck with no Mechs of its own; a "destroy all non-Mechs" card would surely be included in a deck that contains Mechs exclusively. A player has no control over what their opponent puts in their own deck, but they have complete control over the contents of their own.

In this context, the "destroy all non-Mechs" effect can be expected to wipe out most or all of the opponent's forces while leaving the player's Mech army unscathed. This makes it quite powerful, and such an effect, if it existed, would likely have a profound effect on *Hearthstone*'s metagame. By contrast, "destroy all Mechs" would often do nothing against an opponent, unless the current metagame or other conditions strongly favored Mech-heavy decks for other reasons.

METAGAME COMBOS

We've examined many cases where the player has no control over how often they'll encounter a specialized situation. But what if the player does have control? What if some game object isn't particularly useful on its own, but creates a powerful combined effect with something else? Examples would be dual-wielding weapons in an FPS, "support" character classes in an MMO, card combos in a TCG, or support towers that improve adjacent towers in a Tower Defense game. These are all situational in a different way: they reward the player for playing a certain type of *meta*game.

To understand how to balance these, we return to the concept of opportunity costs. Specifically, these objects all have a metagame opportunity cost: players have to take some other action in the game *completely apart from the thing we're trying to balance* in order to make that thing useful. There are a few ways to go about balancing combos like this.

One option is to take the power of the combo in aggregate, find a suitable cost for that, and then divide the cost up among the individual components based on their utility outside the combo. Here is an example from an early edition of *Magic: the Gathering*: a pair of cards, Lich and Mirror Universe.

Lich instantly reduced the player who played it to zero life points, but added extra rules to effectively turn the player's cards in play into their life. It's an extremely risky card, because if it ever leaves play, then the player is left with zero life and thus loses the game immediately! Even without that risk, it had questionable value: it helps when losing by giving some extra time, but a card that's primarily useful when losing means the player must be playing to lose… which isn't generally a winning strategy.

Mirror Universe is a card that allows the player to swap life totals with the opponent. This isn't as risky as Lich (the player is in control of when they use it), but still only useful when the player is losing, and not very easy to use effectively. But combine the two cards, and it's an instant game win: the player's life total becomes zero (but without dying), then they swap life totals with the opponent!

This is an extreme example, where two cards individually are fairly weak, don't work all that well in any other context, but become all-powerful when used together. The best answer for a situation like this might be to err on the side of making their *combined* cost equal to a similarly powerful game-winning effect (perhaps marked down slightly since it requires a two-card combination, which is harder to achieve than just playing a single card).The next question: how do you split the cost between the two cards—should one be very cheap and the other expensive, or should they both cost about the same (somewhere in the middle)? Their respective costs could be weighted according to their relative usefulness. Lich does provide some side benefits (like drawing extra cards in place of gaining life, since drawing an extra card in this game is usually more powerful than gaining a single life point), but it has a seriously nasty drawback in that the player loses immediately if the Lich card ever leaves play. Mirror Universe, meanwhile, has no drawback. If anything, Mirror Universe has the psychological benefit that the opponent might hold off on attacking because they wouldn't want to *almost* kill the player, only to have them swap life totals and then plink them to death with a small-damage effect. And that is, more or less, how the two were actually costed in the game: combined they had a cost of ten mana (higher than just about any other effect in the game at the time, and certainly in the realm of a reasonable cost for a game-winning threat), with Lich costing four mana and Mirror Universe costing 6.

What about a less extreme example? A support character in an MMO might offer a lot of healing and attribute bonuses that help the rest of their team. On their own, they may have *some* non-zero value (they can always attack enemies directly if they have to, and if they can heal and buff themselves they might even be reasonably good at it; in any case, they're still a warm body that can distract enemies by giving them something else to shoot at). But their true value shows up in a group, where they can take the best members of the group and make them better.

As a simple example, suppose you're designing a special ability for a support character that increases a single ally's attack value by 10%, and they can only have one copy of this buff active at a time. To calculate the value of this ability, assume a group of adventurers of similar level, and find the character class among those with the highest attack value. In a group, this ability would have an expected value of 10% of that highest attack value. Obviously, the ability would be less useful if the player is solo, or if they're in a group that doesn't have any good attackers, so you'd have to figure the percentage of time that the support character could expect to be traveling with a group where this buff was useful, and factor that into the numbers. In this case, the opportunity cost for including a strong attacker in the party is usually pretty low (most groups would have at least one of those anyway), so this support ability would almost always operate at its highest level of effectiveness, and it could be balanced accordingly.

In general, when dealing with situational effects that players have some control over, a rule of thumb is to decide on the *opportunity costs* for setting up the situation and then factoring that in as a "cost" to counteract the added situational benefit.

MULTI-CLASSING

On the subject of character classes, consider so-called "multi-class" characters, commonly found in tabletop RPGs. Generally, such a character gains versatility, in that they have access to the unique specialties of several character types... but in exchange for that, they tend to be lower level and less powerful in all of those types than if they were dedicated to a single class. How much less powerful would a multi-class character have to be so that multi-classing feels like a viable choice, but not one that's overpowered?

This is a versatility problem. The player typically doesn't know what kinds of situations their character will face in the future, so they're trying to prepare for everything. After all, if they knew exactly what to expect, they would pick and choose the most effective single character class and ignore the other one. However, they probably do have some *basic* idea of what they're going to encounter, or at least, what capabilities the rest of their party is currently lacking.

One extreme would be to make a dual-class character exactly half as powerful in each class, so that it adds up (i.e., a Level 5 Fighter/Thief would be considered the same as a Level 10 Fighter or a Level 10 Thief), which would make sense if the characters had absolutely no idea of what they were facing and needed some coverage from both classes. At the other extreme, a dual-class character could be just as powerful as single-class (a Level 10 Fighter/Thief would be equivalent to a Level 10 Fighter or Thief), which would be appropriate if the players have complete foreknowledge of the adventure and would only need one or the other. In most cases, the reality is somewhere between the two extremes, so a starting guess of making a single class 1.5 times as powerful as a dual class would be reasonable, and the designer could then adjust from there as needed based on playtesting.

"Either/or" choices in games like TCGs follow a similar pattern, where you design a single object that can do one thing *or* another, and the player chooses among the possible effects when they put the object into play. Maybe you create a card in a TCG that can bring a creature into play *or* make an existing creature bigger. Or in an RPG, you might make a lump of rare metal that can be fashioned into either a great suit of armor *or* a powerful weapon. In these cases, assuming the player knows the value of each choice (but they can choose only one), the actual cost is probably going to be more than either option individually, but less than both combined. If two choices are radically different in value (one is powerful, the other is worthless), then it's closer to just the value of the better one. If all available choices have similar value to one another, then a rule of thumb is to start the cost at 1.5 times the value of either choice and adjust from there.

PvE AND PvP

Designing PvE games (where one or more players are cooperating in a team and working against the computer, the system, the AI, etc.) is different from designing PvP games (where players are in conflict with each other) when it comes to situational balance.

PvE games are easier. You're designing the environment. You're designing the levels. You're designing the AI. You already know what is "typical" or "expected" in terms of player encounters. Even in games with procedurally generated content where you don't know *exactly* what the player will encounter, you know the algorithms that generate the encounters—or you should, anyway, since you're the one who designed them—so you can figure out the expected probability that the content generator produces certain kinds of encounters and within what range.

Because of this, you can do expected-value calculations fairly easily and come up with a reasonable initial guess for your costs and benefits, when dealing with the situational parts of the game.

PvP is a bit trickier, because players can vary their strategies. "Expected value" doesn't exist, as such, when players don't know what to expect from their opponents, or where it depends on a constantly shifting metagame. In these cases, playtesting and analytics are the best methods we have for determining typical use, which we discuss in more detail in Chapters 13 and 15.

Discussion Questions

1. What are situational effects, as described in this chapter?
2. Which is more powerful generally, offense or defense, if you're outnumbered? Try and think of a general mechanic or system that would change this around so that the opposite were true.
3. If your character can change weapons and equipment at any time, what does that do to the value of a single piece of equipment that itself is versatile?
4. If your character can't easily change weapons or equipment, what does that do to the value of a single piece of equipment that itself is versatile?
5. What is a sunk cost?
6. There is a logical fallacy called the "sunk cost fallacy" that causes people to consider their sunk costs when assessing value, even though those costs can't be recovered. For example, some gamers may choose to continue playing a game they paid $60 for even though they are not having any fun, and would have more fun playing a free game on their phone, because they feel like they should get that $60 of value out of the game that they already paid for. Think of a way to apply the sunk cost fallacy to the design of a game, either by manipulating players into doing

something they might not otherwise do or by working against this to get players to overcome it.

7. Choose a game where you play a single customizable character, such as an RPG. What are the opportunity costs when optimizing your character in this game?

8. What design purpose do elemental strengths and weaknesses serve in a game? How do they offer the player interesting choices, if done well?

9. Think of any game that has both single-target and AoE attacks, and look up their respective costs and damage. Based on what you see, how much do you think the designers of that game felt AoE was "worth"—that is, what was their expected value of AoE targets, in order to balance that with an otherwise similar attack that only affects one enemy?

10. Repeat the previous question's exercise for another type of situational effect, such as elemental attacks where some enemies are weak against that element.

Sidequests

In this chapter, we examined how to cost objects in a transitive game where their benefit varies depending on the game state. Mostly, the idea is to figure out the *expected value* of the benefit (using probability) and then use that as if it were the actual value. Depending on the game, however, you also might consider the best-case or worst-case value, taking into account the opportunity costs to get the average or best case.

We also found that as designers, we have many more options when balancing conditional elements in our games. We can modify costs and benefits as usual, but we can also change the other systems or the design of levels or encounters in order to keep the object the same but change its expected-value benefit.

Additionally, we noted that versatility *itself* can be considered a benefit, and that *how much* of a benefit it is depends on the player's ability to plan ahead (foreknowledge) as well as the player's ability to change their mind in the middle of the game (cost of switching). The value of foreknowledge is inversely proportional to the cost of switching, as well.

Lastly, we showed two special kinds of shadow costs to watch out for when balancing, because if you forget about them and don't take them into account when balancing your game, the costs feel wrong and you won't know why.

Sidequest 23.1: Desktop Tower Defense

Tower defense games are wonderful exercises for looking at situational balance. The way the genre works is that enemies ("creeps") are wandering across the map toward their goal. Along the way, the player can place towers that automatically attack any creep in range. Towers cost resources to build. Creeps that are killed give additional resources to build more towers. Over time, towers get more powerful, but the creeps get stronger. When too many creeps have reached their goal without getting eliminated by the towers, the game ends in a loss. The player's goal is to maximize the efficiency of their towers' total damage output per the resources spent, so these games present the player an efficiency problem.

By the nature of the game, just about everything in it is situational. Merely calculating how much damage a tower does depends on many things. The key stat is DPS (damage per second), which is affected by how much damage it does per attack multiplied by the rate of attacks per second. But both of these numbers depend on other things.

For example, some towers do AoE damage, so their damage is multiplied when clusters of creeps travel together. Other towers do heavy damage to one creep at a time, so swarms are dangerous to them: they take out a few creeps in the swarm, but the rest get through unscathed. Some towers do a small amount of damage per shot but take a lot of shots, so their DPS can be high against unarmored creeps or zero against creeps with high armor that can ignore low-damage shots. Some towers do big damage but only in a small radius, so their total damage output depends on the map and how many creeps walk through their area and how long they can stay there. Some towers may do little or no damage, but slow creeps down for a time, increasing the amount of time they stay in range of other nearby towers (and possibly causing them to cluster together, increasing the value of nearby AoE). Some towers boost the damage, range, or other abilities of nearby towers, but don't do anything themselves. Some towers do extra damage (or no damage) against certain types of creeps (such as ground attacks being ineffective against flying creeps). In some games, players can place the towers anywhere on the map so that they aren't just attacks, but also the walls in a maze that they construct; the benefit of a tower isn't just its damage output, but also the nature of the maze that they've constructed and where that tower is placed within. In many games, they can purchase additional towers or spend money to upgrade additional towers, so there is a tradeoff between concentrated damage coming from a single tower vs. spreading out the damage but also requiring more physical space to put more towers (in addition to the relative resource costs). As a case study for situational balance, few genres are better.

One of the games that popularized the genre is *Desktop Tower Defense 1.5*.[2] In this game, there are nine towers, but for this challenge, we only consider two of them: the Swarm tower (which only works against flying enemies but does massive damage to them) and the Boost tower (which increases the damage of all orthogonally and diagonally adjacent towers). If a player were to build a block of Swarm and Boost towers to wreck all fliers, the prime spot to put those would be the center of the map (flying creeps in this game start at the top of the screen traveling down, and the left of the screen traveling right, so placing these towers in the center is a great way to maximize the number of creeps crossing their path).

Suppose a Swarm tower costs \$640 and does 480 DPS. A Boost tower costs \$500, does 0 damage on its own (so two adjacent Boost towers do nothing for one another), and gives a 50% damage bonus to all orthogonally and diagonally adjacent Swarm towers. For example, a single Swarm tower surrounded by eight Boost towers would cost \$4640 and have a total damage of 2400 (for a DPS/\$ efficiency of 0.517).

Specifically, let's assume a 4×3 block of squares, right in the center of the board, and the player has decided to put either a Swarm or Boost tower at each of the 12 locations. Assuming that they wish to minimize cost and maximize damage, what is the optimal placement of these towers? Find the tower configuration that has the highest total DPS. Also find the tower configuration that gives the highest efficiency (DPS/\$). Is this the same configuration, or are they different?

From there, you can also figure out if the two tower types (Swarm and Boost) are balanced with each other. Calculate the contribution to DPS from Swarm towers alone, and divide by the cost of all of the Swarm towers. Then, calculate the boosted contribution to DPS from the Boost towers in your optimal configuration, and divide by the cost of those Boost towers. Which tower type has greater efficiency, or are they both the same?

Greater challenge: You can take this to any further level of analysis. Flying enemies only come every seventh round, and Swarm towers do zero damage to non-flying enemies, so the *actual* damage efficiency of a block of Swarm and Boost towers would be your calculated amount divided by 7. You can then try to calculate the optimal DPS of additional tower types (which affect six of the seven levels with non-flying creeps) to decide which is more

---

[2]It is recommended that anyone taking on this challenge play the game a few times. It can be played in a web browser and is available for free at http://jayisgames.com/games/desktop-tower-defense-15/.

efficient: a combination of ground-only and flying-only towers, or using only towers that can attack *both* ground and air. You can try to figure out the optimal damage efficiency of all nine tower types versus the seven types of creeps that appear with equal frequency.

And then, of course, you can test your theories on the game itself to see if you can get a high score. If performing this challenge in a group, you could even hold a tournament to see who can get the highest score, after everyone analyzes the game to the extent of their ability.

Sidequest 23.2: DOOM

The classic game that popularized the first-person shooter genre, *DOOM*, has long since been available for free as open-source software[3], making it useful for study. The original game features the following weapons:

- **Fists**: This does 2–20 damage per hit and can be used 123.5 times per minute, for an expected DPS of 22.64. It can only hit in close range. It does 10× damage if the player is under a Berserk powerup. It can be used infinitely (it has no ammo that can run out).
- **Chainsaw**: This also does 2–20 damage per hit but attacks 525 times per minute, for an expected DPS of 96.25. Like the fists, it can only hit at close range and has no ammo, although it does not benefit from the Berserk powerup.
- **Pistol**: This does 5–15 damage per hit and can fire 150 shots per minute, for an expected DPS of 25. It uses bullet ammo (a player can hold up to 200 bullets). It is highly accurate, but low power.
- **Chaingun**: This does 5–15 damage per hit and fires 525 shots per minute, for an expected DPS of 87.5. It uses the same bullet ammo as the Pistol. While its damage output is high, it does burn through ammo at a very fast rate (holding the fire button down burns through the entire bullet store in less than 23 seconds).
- **Shotgun**: This sends out seven pellets in a highly random direction, each of which does 5–15 damage (so firing at an enemy up close and hitting with all seven deals 35–105 damage per blast—but the damage is significantly less if firing at an enemy further away, due to the spread causing many pellets to miss). It can fire 56.8 times per minute, for an

---

[3]Anyone taking on this challenge should play through the game or at least look up some online FAQs, strategy guides, or videos to (re)familiarize themselves. The game is available for download at https://github.com/id-Software.

expected DPS of 66.27 if all pellets hit. It uses shotgun shell ammo (players can hold up to 50 shells).

- **Rocket launcher**: This fires a rocket that travels in the direction fired until it hits something, and is the only weapon with AoE damage extending from the blast. It does 20–160 damage on a direct hit to an enemy and then does 0–128 additional damage to all enemies in proximity based on distance from ground zero of the blast (meaning that an enemy being hit actually takes a total of 20–288 damage). It uses rocket ammo (players can hold up to 50 rockets). It can fire up to 105 shots per minute, for an expected DPS of 287 if firing a continuous stream of rockets into an enemy and keep scoring direct hits. However, it is dangerous to use at close range, because the player can take damage from their own rocket's blast damage.

- **Plasma gun**: This fires rapid-fire projectiles that are more powerful than the Chaingun, doing 5–40 damage per projectile and firing at a rate of 700 projectiles per minute, for an expected DPS of 262.5. It uses energy cells as ammo, and players can carry 300 cells at a time.

- **BFG 9000**: This gun fires off a projectile after a short delay, making it harder to aim. Its damage is 100–800 damage on a direct hit, and then after another delay, it sends out additional rays in a scatter pattern (similar to a shotgun spread but with much longer range). There are 40 of these extra rays, and they do 49–87 damage each. The gun can fire 52.5 shots per minute. Thus, if fired point-blank so that an enemy is hit with the main projectile and every additional ray, this would do a whopping 2,773.75 expected DPS. It uses energy cells as ammo, same as the plasma gun (spending 40 cells per shot).

Analyze the balance of these weapons. Do any of them become useless in certain regions of the game? Are any weapons strictly better than others, or does each one serve a useful role? Choose one of the weapons and presume that it was removed from the game; what effect do you think that would have on gameplay, and how would the player need to compensate?

24

Statistics

In This Chapter

- What Is Statistics?
- Fundamental Statistical Calculations
- Outliers
- Statistical Significance
- The Z Test
- Correlation
- Common Mistakes

What Is Statistics?

One of the fascinating things about game balance is that different aspects of balance touch other fields, both inside and outside of game development. In our discussion of pseudorandom numbers in Chapter 21, we came dangerously close to programming and computer science. When examining psychology in Chapter 20, we examined a question of professional ethics. In Chapter 11, we noted that the visual design of a level can be used as a reward by signifying progression to the player: game design as influenced and expressed by visual art. In this chapter, we examine (among other things) where game design intersects business, by looking at ways to measure player purchasing behavior and relating it to game balance.

In Chapter 13, we look specifically at analytics, taking measurements or tracking some data in a game and then analyzing it to draw conclusions about the game's balance. This chapter provides a set of tools that allow us to extract useful information from those measurements.

In common use, the words "probability" and "statistics" are often used interchangeably, but in fact they are two distinct but related branches of mathematics. In probability, you are given a random process that is described (such as a die roll with a certain probability distribution of outcomes), and the goal is to predict what the outcome looks like when the random mechanics are set in motion. Statistics works like probability in reverse: you're given a set of data up front, which represents the outcome of some random process. Your goal with statistics is to reverse-engineer the data to figure out the nature of the randomness that caused it to happen.

To a layperson, "statistics" has a connotation of an exact science (you may occasionally hear someone make an argument by saying "these are cold, hard statistics" or "the numbers don't lie"). In reality, however, statistics is messy, and you shall see that game designers (and even professional statisticians) disagree about the core principles of statistics, even more than they disagree about the core principles of systems design. This is one thing that probability and statistics *do* have in common: neither one is guaranteed. Probability can tell you that there's a one in six chance of rolling a 4 on 1d6, but it doesn't tell you what number a player actually sees when they roll the die. Likewise, statistics can tell you from a series of die roll results that you're 95% sure that these results are consistent with rolling a fair 1d6, but that means there's a 5% probability that you're wrong. You can increase your certainty by collecting more data, but the probability of being wrong never quite reaches zero.

Fundamental Statistical Calculations

When someone asks for the "average" of something, they are usually talking about the **mean** average. To get the mean of a set of values, first add them all up and then divide by the number of values:

$$m = \frac{v_1 + v_2 + v_3 + \cdots + v_n}{n}$$

(where m is the mean, each v is a value in the data set, and n is the number of values). This is similar to the expected value of a probability, except that the expected value is a theoretically balanced set of die rolls, and the mean is the actual average of a set of real-world die rolls. Calculating the mean is easy and useful, because it is usually pretty close to the expected value.

There are other kinds of averages other than the mean, but the only other one we'll examine here is the **median**. To calculate the median, take all of your values and sort them from the smallest to the largest, then pick the one in the center.[1] For example, if you have five values and they are 1, 2, 5, 8, and 24, the median is 5 (the value in the middle). By definition, half of the values are below the median, and half are above (not counting the median itself). When someone says that "half of the population is always below average," they are talking about the median, not the mean.

On their own, the mean and median are both useful, but you learn much more when comparing the two with each other. With both the mean and median, you learn whether the values tend to be weighted to one side or are symmetric about the mean.

Here's an example: in the United States, the median household income in 2014 was $51,939, but the mean was $72,641. What does it tell us when the mean is much higher than the median? In this case, it means that there are a few ridiculously large numbers on the high end that don't affect the median but that do pull up the mean. This makes sense: it's hard for household income to go far below zero, so there is a limit to how low the most dirt-poor people can earn; but at the high end, the United States has quite a few billionaires who are making very large amounts of money each year.

Now let's consider the other way around, with a median that is noticeably higher than the mean. One such situation might be a class average grade, where most students are clustered around 75%–85%, but one lazy student is currently getting a zero in the class. This pulls down the mean average a bit, but has virtually no effect on the median. This also tends to happen with any game that has an online scoreboard of some kind: a small minority of players are incredibly good at the game and posting massive scores, while everyone else who is just a mere mortal has a score that's much closer to the median.

In some situations, the mean and median may be very close together, meaning that the extreme ends aren't skewing your data. This might mean that you don't have any extremes, or it might mean that the extremes are equally spaced from the mean and happen about as often on the high end as they do on the low end. How do you tell the difference between a situation where every value is very close to the mean, and one where the values are spread out a lot but still have the same mean? Here, we introduce another statistical tool that shows just such a distinction: the **standard deviation**.

---

[1] If you're curious what to do if you have an even number of values so that there are *two* values in the middle rather than one, you calculate the mean of those two central values and *that* is the median.

To calculate the standard deviation, first calculate the mean of the data set. Then, for each individual data point in the set, first subtract it from the mean and then square the result (that is, multiply the result by itself). Add all of these squares together, then divide by the total number of data points, and finally take the square root of that whole thing:

$$SD = \sqrt{\frac{(v_1 - m)^2 + (v_2 - m)^2 + \cdots + (v_n - m)^2}{n}}$$

Simply, the standard deviation represents how "spread out" your data is. About two-thirds of the data set is within one standard deviation from the mean, and well over 90% of the data is within two standard deviations. That means the size of your standard deviation is relative to how big the mean is. A mean of 50 with SD of 25 looks a lot more spread out than a mean of 5000 with SD of 25. A relatively large standard deviation means your data is all over the place; a very small standard deviation means your data is clustered tightly together in a narrow range.

To give an example, let us compare two random die rolls: 1d11+1 and 2d6. Both of these give a number in the range of 2–12. Both have an expected value of 7. If we rolled a large number of dice for both of these and rolled exactly according to the expected probabilities, both the mean and median would be 7 for both. But they have very different probability distributions: with 2d6 a player is much more likely to roll seven than they are to roll 2 or 12, but with 1d11+1, they're just as likely to roll any result as any other. However, in this case, the standard deviation for 1d11+1 would be about 3.3, while the standard deviation for 2d6 is only about 2.4. Thus, for 1d11+1, the range of 4–10 fits within one standard deviation of the mean; for 2d6, the range of 5–9 fits within one standard deviation. This may not seem like much of a difference... until the dice start rolling.

Case Study: A Tutorial Level

Suppose you're making a game and looking at the time it takes playtesters to get through the first tutorial level. What you *want* is for it to take about 5 minutes. Here is what you actually get when you measure the time through the level:

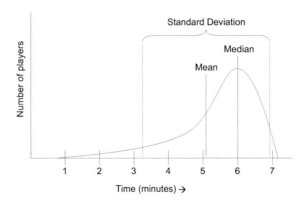

The mean is 5 minutes (exactly what you want), but the median is 6 minutes, with a standard deviation of 2 minutes. Is that good or not? What does this tell us?

Most people take between 3 and 7 minutes. This might be good or bad depending on just how much of the level is under player control. In many games, the tutorial is fairly standardized and linear, which would make this feel like a pretty large range. The other cause for concern is the median being higher than the mean, suggesting that most players take longer than 5 minutes (so the tutorial is probably running longer than intended). To bring down the mean, a few people got through the level *really* fast, suggesting that some players may have found an unintentional shortcut or exploit, or else skipping through all of the intro dialogue, which might get them stuck or frustrated if they continue without learning the core mechanics of the game. On the bright side, no one took hours to complete the tutorial (else the mean would be much higher than the median instead).

Just by looking at three numbers (mean, median, and standard deviation), we have identified potential issues in a level. However, while we know that *something* is happening, we don't know *why* exactly; there are multiple possible explanations, including some that may not even be listed above. This is typical for the use of statistics. A designer must therefore be careful not to misuse these numbers. Even if you find one logical explanation for why the numbers are as they are, remember there could be other valid explanations as well. In the above example, we don't know what is causing the median to be shorter than the mean or its implications for the design of the game. We could spend time thinking of all possible explanations, and then collect and examine more data that would help us differentiate between the various potential root causes. For example, if one fear is that players are skipping through all of the intro dialogue, we could measure time spent reading dialogues in addition to just the total level time and run another playtest. We return to this concept in the following chapter on analytics.

There's another lesson here: in this example, we didn't say *how many* play-testers there were, to get this data! The greater the number of tests in your sample, the more accurate the final analysis (for the same reason that the more times a die is rolled, the closer it probably is to the expected values). If we only had three testers in this analysis, the mean, median, and standard deviation are nearly meaningless if we're trying to predict general trends. If this data came from a few thousand playtests, it is probably much more accurate.

Outliers

When you have a set of data and some points are *way* above or below the mean, statisticians call those points **outliers** (pronounced "out-liars"). Since these tend to change the mean much more than the median, if you encounter a situation where the mean and median are noticeably separated, it's probably because of outlier data.

When doing statistical analysis, you might wonder what to do with the outliers. How do you even decide what counts as "outlier" as opposed to just a point toward the high end of the normal range? Once outliers are identified, do you include them, ignore them, or keep them in their own special group? As with most things in game design and in life, it depends.

If you're just looking for normal, usual play patterns, it's better to discard the outliers from the data set and pretend they don't exist. By definition, out-liers do not arise from typical play. If instead you're looking for edge cases, you not only want to include your outliers, but also pay close attention to them. For example, if you're trying to analyze the scores that players achieve so you know how many digits have to fit on a leaderboard, realize that the high-score list is going to be dominated by outliers at the top of the range. In any case, if you have any outliers at all, it's usually worth investigating further to figure out what caused them in the first place. Going back to the earlier example of time to complete a tutorial level, if most players take 5–7 minutes but a small minority of players get through in 1 or 2 minutes, that suggests those players found some kind of shortcut or exploit, and you'll want to review the level and any other records of play to figure out how they did that. If most players take 5–7 minutes, but instead you have one sole outlier where a player took an hour, *that* is probably because the player put the game on pause or had to walk away for a while and just left the game idle. If several people took that long, it might be the same… or it might be that some players are having so much fun playing around and using the level as a sandbox that they didn't care about advancing to the next area, or it might be that some fundamental aspect of the game was completely unclear to them, and they were too polite to just rage-quit in 5 minutes like a normal player who gets frustrated. In that case, you should investigate further, because if some players are running into problems, you want to eliminate that possibility if you can. If there are players that find some aspect of the tutorial really fun, that's also good to know while designing the other levels of the game.

Statistical Significance

Here's a situation that comes up frequently in statistics: you have two sets of data and want to know if they are both driven by the same process, or if they were different. This can happen when you are collecting play data from a game, then make a change to the game, and then collect that same data and want to know what effect (if any) your change had. It can also happen in the case of an **A/B test** where two versions of the game are created simultaneously, each with one key difference, and then, the same playtest data is collected from each version after playtesters are randomly assigned to one version or the other.

Being able to tell if two groups are distinct is important and not trivial. After all, if 100d6 are rolled and then the results are split randomly into two sets of 50d6, you'll probably see slightly different means and standard deviations among the two groups, even though they are both driven by exactly the same random process. They'll probably be close, and the larger the number of dice rolled, the closer they're likely to be, but it probably won't be an *exact* match. How close is "close enough" that we can say they are from the same data set with no differences between the process that created both sets? Looking at it the other way, how different is "different enough" that we can say there is an actual difference between the two sets?

Here's the bad news: we can never know for sure. If I roll 50d6 and 50d20 and compare the two data sets, it is theoretically possible (though highly unlikely) that the d20 set rolls low enough that the two sets end up looking similar. Even if we roll 5000d6 and 5000d20 and compare, or even more dice, we can never get the possibility down to exactly zero; there's always a minuscule chance that through random chance, the two highly distinct data sets appear similar. Thus, when comparing two sets and deciding whether there are statistical differences, we must accept that there is always a possibility that our analysis is wrong.

We can calculate the probability that we are wrong and that we are seeing what *looks* like a statistical difference but really is only due to random variation, and then we can set a bar for **statistical significance**, that is, the minimum probability of being right (what statisticians call **confidence**, expressed as a percentage or probability) before we say that the data does indeed show enough of a difference to count as being distinct. If the minimum acceptable confidence is too low, then we may see what we *think* are a lot of statistical trends and differences that are false; if the required confidence is too high, we discard and ignore genuine trends.

For whatever reason, in most fields (not all), the standard for statistical significance is a 95% confidence level: that is, there is *at most* a 5% chance of being wrong. It may be a bit scary to realize that when reading any given published and peer-reviewed scientific study, there may be as high as a 1 in 20 chance that the conclusions are incorrect (even if the study itself was conducted flawlessly, with a solid design). That said, the bar must be set *somewhere*, and this is as good a balance as any between finding correct results most of the time without requiring such strict standards that experiments become impractical. After all, if game developers required 10,000 playtesters just to get any reasonable numbers, most of them would be unable to draw any conclusions! So, keep in mind that even under ideal conditions, the statistics *may* lie to you, and be aware of what your confidence is when drawing conclusions about the balance of your game.

The Z Test

While it may seem like bad news that statistical analysis is always uncertain, there is a silver lining: we can calculate whether there are statistically significant differences between two data sets, we can calculate the confidence level, and the calculations are relatively simple to do. One common technique is the **Z test**, which follows a three-step process:

1. Compute the **standard error** (SE), which is calculated as the standard deviation divided by the square root of the number of data points:

$$SE = \frac{SD}{\sqrt{n}}$$

2. Next, calculate the **z-score**, which is the difference between the sample's mean and the established prior mean, divided by the standard error: $z = \dfrac{m_{\text{sample}} - m_{\text{population}}}{\text{SE}}$

3. Lastly, look up the z-score in a table or use the formula NORMSDIST(z) in a spreadsheet program to get the probability that a set of random data in the general population would be below the sample mean.

There are limitations to the Z test. In order to use it, there must already be an established mean from prior data to compare your new data set with (if comparing two data sets with each other, you would have to choose one of them to treat as the "established" data and the other as a new sample). Also, the Z test assumes that your data is generated by a normal (bell-curve-shaped) probability distribution. Luckily, most real-world behaviors *do* fall along a normal distribution or something closely resembling it, but keep in mind that if you are comparing (say) two sets of 1d12, the z-score may not be the best statistical tool.

Let us take an example. Suppose we are making a game and run a large initial playtest with 1000 testers, and it takes them a mean of 5 minutes with standard deviation of 2 minutes to finish the tutorial level. Now, you make some changes to the level in the hopes of reducing the time. You then run a second, small playtest with only 16 playtesters, and it takes them a mean of 4:40 with a standard deviation of 2 minutes. It seems like your changes are a success: you knocked 20 seconds off the mean! But is this change statistically significant, or did you just see random variation?

Computing time units to seconds for ease of calculation, the established mean is 300 seconds and the new mean is 280 seconds, with a standard deviation of 120 seconds in both cases. The number of data points in the new playtest is $n=16$.

$$\text{The standard error is : SE} = \frac{120}{\sqrt{16}} = 30$$

The z-score is $z = \dfrac{280 - 300}{30} = -\dfrac{2}{3}$. In other words, the new mean is two-thirds of a standard error unit below the established mean.

Looking up the z-score in a spreadsheet, we get NORMSDIST($-2/3$) = 0.252493. In other words, there's about a 25% chance that the sample is a result of random variation, and about a 75% chance that the change actually is responsible for the reduction in playtest time. So, your changes are *probably* doing what they were supposed to, but the data don't show statistical significance. Note that you could improve the significance by adding more people to the playtest.

Correlation

Another common situation is to look for the relationship between two things to see if they are related. For example, if you are creating an online TCG and the players are complaining that a certain card is overpowered, you might want to know if there's a relationship between using that card in a deck and winning. If you're making a fighting or brawling game and want to make sure matches are short, you might look for the relationship between each character and match length for games featuring that character. If you're designing a tabletop RPG, you might be interested in how often certain character classes are used together in the same party, when players are given free control over what class their character is. In short, you might want to know if two sets of data are entirely independent, or if they are **correlated**.

There are two types of correlations. A **direct correlation** means that two sets of numbers follow the same trajectory. If one goes up, the other goes up. If one goes down, the other goes down. The opposite is an **inverse correlation**, where the two sets of numbers go in opposite directions. If one is going up, the other is going down. Here, we are talking about general trends and not absolutes. Yes, if two things are **perfectly correlated**, then the correlation is absolute and exact, and you can be certain of exactly what happens to one of the things if you know the other. But most relationships are a bit more chaotic, so occasionally two directly correlated items go in opposite directions because of random variance, but more often than not they'll track together. A measure of how often two correlated things behave in this manner—how strong the correlation is—is the **correlation coefficient**.

We usually do not compute the correlation coefficient by hand, but instead have a computer do it for us. In a spreadsheet program, the function CORREL(array1,array2) takes in two sets of data, which can be given by cells or cell ranges, and it computes the correlation coefficient between the two sets. Since a correlation is looking at pairs of data (what happens to one thing when the other goes up), the two sets must be of the same size, and they must be given so that each data point in one set corresponds to the proper data point in the other set.

The correlation coefficient is a number between −1 and 1. If the coefficient is −1, that means the two are perfectly inversely correlated: when one goes up, the other goes down by the exact same proportion, 100% of the time. A coefficient of 1 means the two are perfectly directly correlated: both go up or down in perfect synchronicity. A coefficient of 0 means the two are uncorrelated: they behave independently, with absolutely no trends or tendencies that could be predicted at all.

Most strong correlations are not going to be exactly 1 or −1, because there is some small amount of noise (random variance) in the system that makes things behave imperfectly. Most things that are uncorrelated don't have a correlation coefficient of exactly 0 for the same reason: there is usually at least *some* slight correlation, if minor, just from random chance. But the further from 0 and the closer to 1 or −1, the stronger the correlation appears to be.

Common Mistakes

Mark Twain is credited as saying that there are three kinds of lies: lies, damn lies, and statistics. His intent was probably not to say that statistics is useless, but rather that it can appear to lie to you if you're not careful. What follows are some cautionary tales about how statistics can go horribly wrong, and what to do to avoid the wrong conclusions.

Anscombe's Quartet

Take a look at these four sets of 11 data points each.

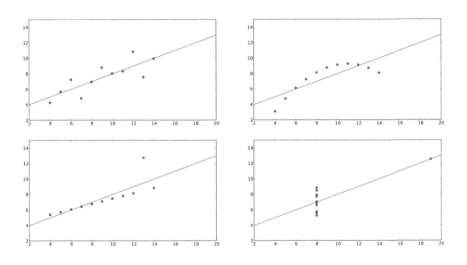

These are known as **Anscombe's Quartet**, a famous representation of data in the field of statistics. These all obviously represent *very* different sets of data with different natures. At the top left is a fairly linear relationship with a little bit of error. The top right data is a parabolic (not linear) curve. Bottom left is an extremely strong linear correlation with one outlier. Bottom right is also a linear correlation with one outlier, except this time the line is vertical. What's the relationship between these four data sets? It turns out that each one has a mean of 9 for x, a mean of 7.5 for y, and the standard deviations of x and y are nearly identical across the four sets. The correlation between x and y is the same in all four cases, as well. The lesson here is that you shouldn't just look at statistical numbers without also graphing or otherwise visualizing the raw data; looking only at mean, median, and standard deviation can be misleading. Statistical tools can be useful to clarify what you're seeing in the raw data, but don't neglect the data and look only at statistical calculations derived from it.

Sample Size

Statistical analysis of data is only as good as the sample. One common problem is that if you don't have a large enough sample, it's difficult to achieve statistical significance. The more data points you have, the better. Here's one example: suppose a player is building a deck for a *Magic: the Gathering* tournament. One of the most important things in a *Magic* deck is to have the proper ratio of land (the primary way to gain resources) and spells (which require those resources to put into play). If they have too much land, they can cast all the spells they need, but they just don't have that many spells so they fall behind to an opponent who can cast a lot more spells. If they don't have enough land, then they won't be able to cast their spells because they'll be starved for the necessary resources.

Now, let's say that a player has their deck and wants to know if it has the right amount of land, so they shuffle the deck as well as possible, then deal an opening hand, and play a few mock turns to see if it feels like they're getting enough. Then, they put those cards aside and do this again with the remaining deck, and continue drawing sample hands throughout the entire deck. Then, if it seems like they have too much land more hands than not, they take some land out; if they consistently have too little land, they put some more in. Then, they reshuffle and try again until they get through the entire deck with it feeling just right. On the surface, this seems like a pretty good quick-and-dirty way to get the right amount of land in there, without having to count everything and do a ton of statistical analysis. But, let's say that it just so happens that on one shuffle of the deck, the land is very evenly distributed and not clustered so that most of the time it seems like the player is doing okay after a turn or two… so they call it good, and enter the tournament. Then, in the tournament they find that they're consistently not drawing enough land and lose game after game. After the tournament is over, they count and see that there are only 16 land in the 60-card deck (where 20 land is far more typical for most decks).

What happened here, and how did these calculations go so far off? The problem was the attempt to analyze the deck through statistical methods, but with a sample size that was too small to draw meaningful conclusions.

Sample Bias

Small sample size isn't the only way to screw up your data. Here's another example: suppose you're making a game aimed at the casual market. To gauge difficulty, you have everyone on the development team play through the game to get some baseline data on how long it takes to play through each level and how challenging each level is.

On most development teams, the developers are *not* casual gamers, so a playtest like this is not representative of the target market. Your development team is probably far more skilled at the game than the average player (due partly to their experience playing games for many years, and partly their inside knowledge of the inner workings of the game), so they are likely to get through the game far more quickly and with less resistance than most casual players who would be playing the game for the first time.

Another example: a publisher runs a focus test of a game in development with a female protagonist, and the focus group nearly unanimously said that they would have preferred a male lead. The publisher then demands that the developer change the main character's gender. This might be a reasonable demand, if the focus group is representative of the target audience. But what if you found out that the game is intended for the mass market, but the focus group was all male? That would be a different story.

In short, when collecting playtest data, do your best to recruit playtesters that are as similar as possible to the target market, in addition to finding as many testers as possible so that the random variation gets filtered out. Your analysis is only as good as your data!

Programming

Even if you use statistics honestly, there are still things that can go wrong. For video games, the quality of playtest data is often at the mercy of the programming team, because the programmers are the ones who must spend time writing code to collect any data that the designer is asking for. Programming time during game development is always limited, so at some point, someone (either the designer or the producer) must make a tradeoff between having the programming team implement data collection or having them implement the actual game. This is easier to get through the pipeline in some companies than others, but at many development studios, "analytics" falls into the same category as audio, localization, and playtesting: tasks that are ignored during most of development, pushed off to the end of the development cycle, and then rushed through after it's too late to make useful changes. If the game design relies on being informed by statistical analysis, make sure to impress upon others the importance of this from early on in development.

Even if you get plenty of programming resources to implement data collection, software has bugs, and it is always possible that some of the data collected is flat out incorrect. Always look at the raw data and see if it makes sense, or if it's possible that there are any bugs that are skewing the data. It helps if you can collect some data independently by hand and then spot-check to make sure it's being collected properly in code (for example, if you're measuring the number of player deaths on each level, observe a playtester play through a particular level and manually count every time they die, and then compare to what the software tells you).

Miscalculation

To be fair to programmers, even doing statistical analysis by hand is error-prone. Even if the programming code is (miraculously) bug-free, it is still very possible for you as the designer to accidentally mess up your calculations and get the wrong answer, just like it is with probability calculations. However, probability at least has some sanity checks built in to make the wrong answers *look* wrong; for example, if you ever find a probability that is less than 0 or greater than 1, you know that something is incorrect and can go back to check your figures. With statistics, you don't generally know what you're looking for or what you expect the answer to be. As such, you should proceed with caution, and use every method you can think of to independently verify your numbers and calculations.

Correlation and Causality

One of the most common errors in statistics is when a correlation is found between two things: when one goes up, the other always seems to go up (a direct correlation) or down (an inverse correlation). Correlations are useful, but often people assume the most obvious causal relationship when a correlation is found. However, this is something that *can't* be detected from statistics alone.

Let's take an example. In the original board game *Puerto Rico* (with no expansions or modifications), there's a strong correlation in tournament play between winning and buying the Factory building. Let's suppose, for example, that out of every 100 tournament games, the winner owned a Factory in 95 of them. The natural assumption here is that Factory must clearly be overpowered and that it is causing players to win. But this perfectly reasonable conclusion can't be assumed without additional information, because some other equally valid conclusions are possible.

For example, what if it's the other way around, where winning causes the player to buy a Factory? This sounds strange, but one potential scenario would be that Factory helps the player who is already winning, so it's not that Factory is *causing* the win, but rather that a player in the lead is strongly incentivized to buy a Factory for some reason.

Another possibility is that something else not even mentioned here is unbalanced and that thing causes the player to *both* buy a Factory *and* win the game. Maybe an early-game purchase sets the player up for buying the Factory easily and that early-game purchase is also the thing that most contributes to a player's winning. In this case, the Factory is a symptom and a by-product of some other overpowered game object, and not the root cause.

Lastly, it's possible that buying a Factory and winning the game are actually uncorrelated, and the correlation seen in the data is just a statistical anomaly, and the sample size isn't large enough for the Law of Large Numbers to kick in. This is seen in popular culture in many places, where things that obviously have no relation to one another happen to have strong correlations anyway (there's even a website dedicated to finding these: http://www.tylervigen. com/spurious-correlations). As we learned in probability, if you take a lot of random things you'll be able to see patterns. With enough data sets, some of them are probably correlated, if only by random chance.

Frequentism and Bayesianism

One final point to make is that there are actually two ways of looking at both probability and statistics. Even the basic question of what we're measuring, at a fundamental level, is something that reasonable people can disagree on. There are two general approaches, referred to as **frequentism** and **Bayesianism**.

In short, frequentism is the math that we have studied in this (and most other) texts, regarding expected values, statistical significance, and so on. Bayesianism is how most humans actually reason intuitively. For example, suppose you're in your apartment and can't find your portable phone, but it has one of those charging stations where you can press a button and it causes the phone to make a sound. A frequentist approach would be to listen for the sound and head in that direction. A Bayesian approach would be to also take into account the places in the apartment where you typically talk on the phone, where you know the phone is likely to be based on past experience, and go to whichever of those seems most in the direction of the sound you're hearing, and search there first.

To illustrate, consider this problem: you have a coin that may or may not be fair. You flip the coin 100 times and get 71 heads, 29 tails. You flip the coin again. What is the probability that the next flip is tails?

A frequentist solution to the problem is straightforward. We observed 29 tails out of 100 flips, so with this data, our best guess is that it's an unfair coin with a 29% probability of flipping tails, with the limited information that we have.

A Bayesian solution is more complicated and goes into much more heavy math than this book covers. In short, this approach is that the probability isn't a constant 29%. Rather, the probability is *itself* a random variable, with a distribution of possible values. To solve this requires something called the Beta function, some light calculus, and Google searching if you are interested. Suffice to say that this approach gives a slightly different answer than the frequentist solution and that the Bayesian solution is probably a little more realistic if used in the real world.

Discussion Questions

1. Suppose you find two things in a game that are strongly correlated. What are the four different possible explanations for this observance that you should examine?
2. What is the difference between probability and statistics?
3. What does it tell you if the mean is far below the median?
4. What does it tell you if the mean and median are almost exactly the same? (There are several possibilities for this.)
5. What does the standard deviation tell you about the nature of a data set?
6. What can you do to improve the statistical significance of a data analysis?

7. What is an outlier?
8. What are the conditions required to use a Z test? What kinds of situations does it NOT help with?
9. Why is it important to look at your raw data and not just the mean, median, standard deviation, and other derived calculations?
10. How can you avoid sample bias in playtesting? Why would you want to?

Sidequests

Sidequest 24.1: Gender in Games

It's well recognized that the video game industry has a lack of diversity, i.e., an underrepresentation of women and minorities, compared to the general human population. Let us just consider women for the time being.

There are many possible explanations for why this is. Identifying the root cause is important if the industry wants to improve its diversity, because each explanation suggests an entirely different solution. For example, you might see the following theories proposed:

- Overall, women are less interested than men in technical fields. This could be biological, but more likely is cultural. Thus, the number of qualified women entering the field is low. (Solution: more outreach at the primary school and college level to get younger women interested in game development as a future career choice.)
- Women might be interested in careers in games under normal conditions, but too many studios send signals in their job postings that discourage women from applying. (Solution: make the job application process more inclusive.)
- Women might be applying to game studio job postings in equal numbers, but there's an unconscious gender bias at male-dominated studios which favors male over female applicants. (Solution: hiring managers and interviewers at game studios should identify their internal biases, and eliminate or correct for them when evaluating candidates.)
- Women might be getting job offers, then turning them down to seek some other career opportunity outside of games. (Solution: make offers that are more competitive, or at least do a better job of marketing the position to female applicants when sending formal job offers.)

- Or, it might just be a coincidence. This year the industry is mostly male, and five years from now it might be mostly female. The industry's hiring practices are a meritocracy, and any skewing of diversity in one direction or the other is just acceptable statistical variation. If it's an unexpectedly heavy swing in one direction, that's just an outlier that corrects itself over time. (Solution: do nothing because there isn't a real problem.)

If you're working at a game studio that seeks greater diversity in its future hires, obviously the desire would be to identify the actual problems without spending effort "fixing" things that aren't problems at all. This can be aided with statistics.

The Applicant Pool

Let us suppose that, overall, among all game-related job postings across the entire game industry, applicants are 15% female. Now, suppose at *your* particular studio, you've made one hire per year over the last five years. For each open position, you've received 100 applications. The applications had a mean of 90 men and 10 women (10% female) with a standard deviation of 5. Your company is obviously below the industry average, but is the difference statistically significant? What is the confidence level—the probability that the difference in gender disparity at your studio (compared to the industry at large) is *not* just due to random variation? (*Hint:* use the Z test.)

Selection Bias

Let us further suppose that this year for your studio's most recent job posting, there were exactly 20 women within the 100 total applicants and that the studio narrowed down the applications to a smaller pool of ten promising candidates to interview. Of those ten, only one was a woman. This puts the percentage of women interviewed at half of the percentage who applied, suggesting a possible bias in the first round of candidate selection. Is *this* difference statistically significant? (*Hint:* to use the Z test here, you must find the standard deviation of a sample, but "male" and "female" are not numbers where a standard deviation could be calculated. To work around this, treat gender as numeric—for example, treat females as 1 and males as 0—and then compute the mean and standard deviation for the sample.)

Sidequest 24.2: The Average Dalmuti

The card game *The Great Dalmuti* features a custom 91-card deck. Each card has a number on it from 1 to 13, and the number is both the card's value in the game *and* the number of that card in the deck (there's only a single 1 card, two 2s, nine 9s, thirteen 13s, and so on).

If you draw a single card at random from a randomly shuffled complete deck, what is the mean, median, and standard deviation of the number you expect to draw? (You may find it helpful to do this in a spreadsheet rather than by hand.)

Alternate Challenge

If you're looking for a simpler challenge to do by hand, calculate the mean, median, and standard deviation of a modified d10 roll, where the die has the following ten faces: 1, 1, 1, 1, 2, 2, 2, 3, 3, 4.

25

Intransitive Mechanics and Payoff Matrices

In This Chapter

- Intransitive Mechanics
- Solving Intransitive Mechanics

Intransitive Mechanics

> Good ol' rock… nothin' beats that!
>
> *Bart Simpson in The Simpsons, Season 4, Episode 19,*
> *just before losing to Lisa's throw of Paper.*

Way back in Chapter 8, we encountered transitive mechanics: those where game objects are balanced along a curve that relates their total costs to their total benefits. In other words, better things cost more. The implicit assumption for that kind of balance is that "better" has some kind of meaning: that it is possible to compare two game objects and see one as strictly better than the other.

Not all game mechanics work that way. In some cases, one object may be strong against something and weak against something else, so that "better" is not an absolute, but a relative term to relate two objects to each other (and each relationship is different). These kinds of mechanics are geekily called **intransitive**. The simplest and most familiar example is *Rock-Paper-Scissors*.

Talking about the absolute benefit or value of Rock is meaningless, because it depends entirely on what the opponent throws.

It's worth asking: if intransitive mechanics are just glorified *Rock-Paper-Scissors*, what's the appeal? Few people would consider it a fun night of gaming to get some friends together for a few hours of *Rock-Paper-Scissors*, so why should we enjoy a game that uses the same core mechanics and just themes them differently?

For one thing, intransitive mechanics are at least more interesting than having one single dominant strategy (perhaps you could call that *Rock-Rock-Rock*) because there is three times the variety in play. For another, an intransitive *mechanic* can be embedded in a larger game that still allows players to change or modify their strategies in mid-game. Players may make certain choices in light of what they observe other players doing—sometimes in real time—and playing a series of *Rock-Paper-Scissors* matches in an action-based game where a player has but a few milliseconds to react can be dynamic and exciting.

Intransitive mechanics appear in many types of games, in some form or other. For example,

- In fighting games (such as the *Street Fighter* or *Mortal Kombat* games), a typical pattern is that normal attacks are stopped by blocking, blocking can be punished by throwing, and attempting to throw the opponent can be countered by a normal attack.
- In many real-time strategy (RTS) games (such as the *Warcraft* series), flying units absolutely destroy infantry, infantry units work well against ranged units, and ranged units are great at taking down flying units.
- Turn-based strategy games (such as the *Advance wars* series) may have several layers of intransitive relationships between their pieces. For example, heavy tanks might lose to anti-tank infantry, which in turn are less cost-efficient and thus ineffective against normal infantry, but normal infantry is slaughtered by tanks.
- First-person shooters with vehicles (such as the *Halo* series) may have intransitive relationships between vehicles and weapons. For example, heavy weapons like rocket launchers might be great against large tanks (since the tanks are big, slow, and easy to hit from a distance). Tanks are great against light vehicles, since they don't have the firepower or range to take the tank down and they are absolutely destroyed by the tank's close-range weaponry once they approach. Light vehicles are, in turn, great against heavy weapons, because they can dodge and weave around slow incoming rockets.

- MMORPGs and tabletop role-playing games (RPGs) often have some character classes that are particularly good at fighting against other classes (and weak against still others) in one-on-one combat.
- The metagame in TCGs is often intransitive. A dominant deck emerges which beats most other decks. A counter-deck is developed that is designed specifically to win matches against the dominant deck. Other decks that might lose to the dominant deck become strong against the counter-deck, since the counter-deck is tuned to beat the dominant deck but is inefficient against everything else.
- Some relationships are not so obvious. For example, consider a game where one kind of unit has long-range attacks (such as a sniper), which is defeated by a short-range attacker who can turn invisible (an assassin), which then in turn is defeated by a medium-range attacker that can see invisible units (a heavy soldier), which in turn can be taken down by the sniper's long-range attacks.
- Some relationships are purely mathematical. In *Magic: the Gathering*, creatures have power (the amount of damage they do) and toughness (the amount of damage that it takes to kill them). In combat, if two creatures fight each other, they each do their power in damage against the other's toughness simultaneously, *unless* one of the creatures has the First Strike ability, in which case that creature attacks first, and only receives damage in return if the other creature it's fighting is still alive. In this way, a 1/3 creature (that is, power of 1 and toughness of 3) kills a 2/1 First Strike creature while surviving. A 2/1 First Strike creature kills a 3/2 creature, and a 3/2 creature kills a 1/3 creature. These three creatures might not even necessarily be designed with the intention of being intransitive, but that's what ends up happening.
- In games with bluffing mechanics (like *Poker*), players make choices based on what they've observed other players doing in the past and use that to predict the opponents' future moves. This can be particularly interesting in games with partial but incomplete information.

Hopefully, you can see the breadth and variety that intransitive mechanics can take. Just because a game has intransitive elements, doesn't mean it's as dull as *Rock-Paper-Scissors*.

There is one additional reason why game designers should become familiar with intransitive mechanics: they serve as a kind of "emergency brake" on runaway dominant strategies. Even if you don't know if your game is balanced, and even if you don't know what strategies will emerge in the player community, intransitive relationships between game objects or strategies can at least prevent a single dominant strategy that invalidates everything else, because it's destined to be weak to at least one counter-strategy. Even if the game itself is unbalanced, intransitive elements allow for a metagame correction to keep overpowered elements in check. This is obviously not an ideal thing to rely on exclusively (*that* would be lazy design, indeed), but better to have at least *some* safety net than not, especially in games where major game balance changes can't be easily made after the fact.

Solving Intransitive Mechanics

What does a "solution" even look like with intransitive mechanics? It can't be a cost curve, because no choice is strictly better or worse than the others. Instead, it's a *ratio* of how often a player should choose each available option and (in an asymmetric game) how often they expect their opponent to choose each of *their* options. For example, with an intransitive relationship between archers, infantry, and fliers, a solution might be something like "build an army of 30% archers, 50% infantry, 20% fliers (or a ratio of 3:5:2)."

As a game designer, you might prefer that certain game objects be used more or less frequently than others or you might prefer each object to be used exactly as often as any other. In any case, by changing the relative costs and availability of each object, you can change the optimal mix of objects that players use in actual play. By designing the game specifically to have one or more optimal ratios of your choosing, you know ahead of time how the game is likely to develop. For example, you might design a particular Dreadnaught unit that is expensive, powerful, and impressive-looking, but you want it to also only happen rarely during normal play so that it creates a truly spectacular moment when it's used. If you understand how your costs of each unit affect their relative frequencies of use, you can design a game like this intentionally, or at least take a pretty good initial guess. (Or, if it seems like your players are using one strategy more than the others during playtesting, this kind of analysis can help shed light on why that might be.)

What would we expect the solution of *Rock-Paper-Scissors* to look like? Since each throw is (theoretically) as good as any other, the expectation would be that the optimal ratio is 1:1:1, meaning that you should choose each throw about as often as the others. If you chose any other strategy (say, 1:2:1, favoring Paper), then your opponent could choose a dominant counter-strategy of 0:0:1 (all Scissors) which would win more than it would lose. But with 1:1:1, there is no other strategy that can dominate it. That is what we'd expect intuitively, and it turns out this *is* what we'll find, but it's important to understand how to get there mathematically so that we can solve more challenging and complex problems that aren't so obvious.[1]

Solving Basic Rock-Paper-Scissors

First, let's examine all possible outcomes of the game. Let us call our own throws *R*, *P*, and *S* (with capital letters), and our opponent's throws *r*, *p*, and *s* (with lower-case letters). Since winning and losing are normally considered equal and opposite (that is, winning once and losing once balance each other out) and draws are right in the middle between the two, let's call a win +1 point, a loss −1 point, and a draw 0 points.[2] We now construct a table of results:

	r	*p*	*s*
R	0	−1	+1
P	+1	0	−1
S	−1	+1	0

This table is just from our own perspective. For example, if we through (R)ock and the opponent throws (s)cissors, we win, for a net +1 to our score. Our opponent's table would have inverted values.

What do *r*, *p*, and *s* actually represent? Since our opponent's move is unknown ahead of time and outside of our direct control, these can be thought of as the probabilities that the opponent will choose each respective throw. We can model the opponent as a weighted random variable!

We can also think of *R*, *P*, and *S* (our own choices) as representing the expected value of the results from our choosing any given throw: in the field of game theory, this would be called the **payoff**.

We can then perform a set of expected value calculations, multiplying each outcome by its probability, to get the payoffs for each throw:

$$R = 0r - 1p + 1s = s - p \qquad P = 1r + 0p - 1s = r - s \qquad S = -1r + 1p + 0s = p - r$$

[1] "Game Architecture and Design" (Rollings & Morris), Chapters 3 and 5, was the first game-design-related book to document the solving of intransitive games as shown in this chapter. This book takes things a bit farther, but those authors deserve credit for the original idea.

[2] The process used here would actually work for *any* point values, but the numbers of +1 for win/0 for draw /−1 for loss are the easiest to work with.

Let us suppose that we knew our opponent was using an unwise strategy of $r = 0.5$, $p = s = 0.25$. What is our best counter-strategy? Plugging those values into the above equations, we get the payoffs $R = 0$, $P = 0.25$, $S = -0.25$. Since P has the best payoff of all three throws, assuming the opponent doesn't vary their strategy at all, our best counter-strategy is to throw Paper every single time. If we do this, we expect to gain 0.25 points per throw (that is, out of every four throws, we expect to win one more game than we would lose). In fact, we can find that if our opponent merely throws rock the *tiniest, slightest bit* more often than the others, like a strategy of $r = 0.3334$, $p = s = 0.3333$, our net payoff for Paper is positive (and better than the other two throws), and our best strategy is still Paper every time. This is actually a significant finding; it tells us that intransitive mechanics can be fragile, where even a slightly suboptimal play strategy can lead to a completely dominant counter-strategy on the part of the opponent.

Toward a Steady State

Of course, if we notice the opponent playing too much rock and we counter with an all-Paper strategy, if the opponent notices they would be wise to respond with an all-Scissors strategy, which would then push us to respond with all-Rock, and so on. If we are both adjusting our strategies to counter each other, do we ever reach any point where both of us are in some kind of stable steady state?

To answer this question, we first must lay out a few rules.

Theorem 1

If the game mechanics are symmetric, the solution is the same for both players.

In other words, if both players have exactly the same set of options and they work the same way, then the opponent's probability of choosing Rock should be the same as our own. This should be self-evident.

Theorem 2

Among the set of all strategies worth choosing *at all*, each strategy has the same payoff.

If any payoff were less than the others, it would no longer be worth choosing; a player is better off taking an option with a higher expected payoff instead. If any payoff were higher than the others, players would choose that one exclusively as the optimal play and ignore the others. Thus, all potential moves that are worth taking must have the same payoff as one another.

Theorem 3

In symmetric zero-sum games, the payoff for all viable strategies is zero.

This is specific to games that are both zero sum and symmetric. If they are symmetric, from Theorem 1, it means that the solution must be the same for both players, which means the payoffs must also be the same. Since the game is zero sum, by definition, the payoffs must sum to zero. The only way for two equal numbers to sum to zero is if both numbers are themselves zero.

We can use these theorems, since *Rock-Paper-Scissors* is indeed a symmetric, zero-sum game. Specifically, we know that the payoffs R, P, and S must be equal to each other, and they must be equal to zero. This lets us rewrite our equations from above, replacing the payoffs with zero:

$$0 = s - p$$

$$0 = r - s$$

$$0 = p - r$$

We can also add one more equation, since we know the opponent must select exactly one of the three throws, and their probabilities must add up to 1:

$$r + p + s = 1$$

We can solve this system of four equations with three unknowns using simple algebra. Rewriting the first three equations, we find that $s = p$, $r = s$, and $p = r$ (in other words, all three variables are equal to each other). Substituting p and s for r in the final equation gives

$$r + r + r = 1; \quad r = \frac{1}{3}$$

Since s and p are the same as r, that means our solution is that $r = p = s = 1/3$. This is a ratio of 1/3:1/3:1/3 (or 1:1:1 if you prefer), which is what we expected to find.

Does this mean that the optimal strategy in *Rock-Paper-Scissors* is to throw randomly each time (say, by rolling a die secretly before each throw and doing what the die says)? No. There is a difference between choosing each throw about as often as any other and playing randomly with no regard to what the opponent has done. In an actual *Rock-Paper-Scissors* tournament, a truly random strategy would win a third of its matches, lose a third, and draw a third, for a net score of 0. Winning a tournament would require a better record than that!

As we noted back in Chapter 20, humans are terrible at trying to appear random on purpose. In actual play against a human opponent in the real world, the best strategy is to detect and exploit patterns in the opponent's play, while at the same time masking any apparent patterns in one's own play. The ratio of 1:1:1 does not specify which throw a player must choose at any given time—that is where the skill of anticipating the opponent's future moves comes in—but just that over time, we would expect the best strategies to show close to a 1:1:1 ratio of the throws, because any deviation from that hands the opponent a clear counter-strategy that wins more often than not... at least, until the player readjusts their strategy back to 1:1:1.

Solving Rock-Paper-Scissors *with Costs*

We have now written a definitive mathematical proof of the optimal strategy for *Rock-Paper-Scissors*. That may be gratifying, but it wasn't particularly surprising. Let us apply the same method to solve a slightly harder game, one that adds costs. (As an example of an intransitive mechanic with costs: in a fighting game, attacks may beat throws while throws beat blocks and blocks beat attacks, but each of these does a different amount of damage, so they each have different "costs" in the sense that each choice puts a different amount at risk.)

Let us make a simple change to *Rock-Paper-Scissors*: every win using Rock counts double. (This might seem like more of a benefit than a cost, but for a symmetric zero-sum game, a cost to a player is an equal benefit to their opponent, so the two terms are essentially interchangeable.) How does this rule change affect the optimal strategy? Think about what you might guess, intuitively, and write that down before reading on.

As before, we start with a payoff table:

	r	p	s
R	0	−1	+2
P	+1	0	−1
S	−2	+1	0

We then use this to construct our three payoff equations:

$$R = 0r - 1p + 2s = 2s - p$$

$$P = 1r + 0p - 1s = r - s$$

$$S = -2r + 1p + 0s = p - 2r$$

This new game is still symmetric and zero sum, and both players must choose exactly one throw, so we still have the additional conditions that $r + p + s = 1$ and $R = P = S = 0$. Our equations then become

$$2s = pr = sp = 2r$$

$$r + p + s = 1$$

Again, we solve by hand using algebra, putting the first three equations in terms of r and then substituting in the final equation:

$$r + p + s = r + (2r) + (r) = 4r = 1; r = \frac{1}{4}$$

Substituting $r = 1/4$ into the earlier equations, we get $s = 1/4$ and $p = 1/2$. Our optimal ratio of r:p:s is actually 1/4:1/2:1/4 (or 1:2:1). Is that what you guessed? Probably not, as it is entirely unintuitive! If we double the wins for Rock, the end result is that *Paper* gets chosen more often. In retrospect it makes sense: since Scissors is such a risky play, players are less likely to choose it; if a player knows their opponent is unlikely to choose Scissors, their throw of Paper is unlikely to lose (it either wins or draws), so it is actually Paper—not Rock—that gets played more often.

Thus, if you had a fighting game where a successful throw does twice as much damage as a successful attack or block,[3] you'd expect to see twice as many attack attempts as throws or blocks!

---

[3] If it seems strange to think of blocking as doing damage equal to an attack, suppose that blocking enables the player to launch an unblockable counterattack.

Solving Rock-Paper-Scissors *with Incomplete Wins and Losses*

In most RTS games, players pay resource costs to produce units. While some units are strong or weak against others, it's not complete dominance; a weak unit may still do some small amount of damage to a stronger one, and a sufficiently large swarm of units can still take down a unit that they are "weak" against. How do we model something like that?

Let's take a simple example where Knights that are strong against Archers, Archers that beat Dragons, and Dragons that beat Knights. Specifically, assume that if a player sends one unit against another of the same type, there's no net gain or loss on either side (they kill each other, so both players lose the same amount). But with unequal units, it's a different story. When a Knight attacks an Archer, the Archer is killed, but the Knight still loses 20% of its health to the initial arrow volley before it closes the ranks. Against Dragons, Archers lose 40% of their health due to counterattacks, but they do take down the Dragon. But let's say that Dragons can take out a Knight while taking no damage in return at all—there's not much a swordsman can do when being roasted with fire from 50 feet above.

Finally, let's say that Knights cost 50 gold to produce, Archers cost 75, and Dragons cost 100. What's the solution now?

As before, we start with the payoff table, using K, A, and D to represent the payoffs for choosing a Knight, Archer, or Dragon, and k, a, and d being the probabilities of the opponent choosing each:

	k	a	d
K	0	+65	−50
A	−65	0	+70
D	+50	−70	0

These numbers deserve some explanation. In the case of both players choosing the same thing (say, both choose Knights), each player is paying the same amount (50 gold) and losing that unit. Since we are still representing this as a zero-sum game, a loss of 50 gold for one player is equivalent to a gain of 50 gold for their opponent, so the two cancel each other out to 0.

When a Knight meets an Archer, the Archer dies (a 75 gold advantage), but the Knight loses 20% of its health (the Knight costs 50 gold, so losing 20% of the Knight "costs" 10 gold), so the actual outcome is that the Archer player is up a net 65 gold. Likewise, when an Archer meets a Dragon, the Dragon dies (+100 gold), but the Archer loses 40% of its health (loss of 40% of 75 gold, or

−30 gold) for a net gain of 70 gold. When a Dragon kills an enemy Knight, the Knight dies (+50 gold) and the Dragon doesn't get hurt at all, for a net gain of 50 fold; the Dragon's cost of 100 gold doesn't come into play in this scenario, because the Dragon's owner may have spent some fold to purchase it, but they haven't lost anything… at least, not yet! The numbers are all inverted when the player *loses* a unit to the opponent, since the game is symmetric.

So, in the case of differing unit costs and incomplete victories, the hard part is just altering the payoff table. From there, the process is the same. As before, since we have a symmetric and zero sum game, we know that $K = A = D = 0$, and $k + a + d = 1$. This gives us these equations:

$$K = 0k + 65a - 50d = 0; \quad 65a = 50d$$

$$A = -65k + 0a + 70d = 0; \quad 65k = 70d$$

$$D = 50k - 70a + 0d = 0; \quad 50k = 70a$$

$$k + a + f = 1$$

Solving the second and third equations to put a and d in terms of k and then substituting in to the final equation, we get

$$d = \frac{13}{14}k$$

$$a = \frac{10}{14}k$$

$$k + \left(\frac{10}{14}k\right) + \left(\frac{13}{14}k\right) = 1; \quad k = \frac{14}{37}$$

$$a = \left(\frac{10}{14} * \frac{14}{37}\right) = \frac{10}{37}; \quad d = \left(\frac{13}{14} * \frac{14}{37}\right) = \frac{13}{37}$$

So, in this case the solution is $k{:}a{:}d = 14{:}10{:}13$, a fairly even mix of units, with Knights being a little more common and Archers a little less. If you instead wanted Dragons to be relatively rare, you might change their costs, or the relative costs or damages of other units. As we've seen, simple changes to one game object may have unpredictable effects on the others, so the easiest way to get the numbers right would be to put them in a spreadsheet and fiddle either with the numbers manually or with an automated Solver.

Solving Asymmetric Rock-Paper-Scissors

So far, all of our examples have assumed symmetry: both players have the exact same set of throws, and both players win or lose the same amount on any particular combination of throws. But not all intransitive games are perfectly symmetric; of the examples mentioned at the start of this chapter, in fact, most of them are not.

Let's take *Rock-Paper-Scissors* and make it asymmetric. Suppose that we designed a variant where there was a deck of cards, and each card alters the game in some way for the next throw. This round, you flip a card that looks like the following.

Rock On!

For the next round, starting player gets 2 points for a win with Rock.

This card only affects one of the two players; let's say that this particular card happens to affect a player, giving *them* two points for a win with Rock, but giving no such bonus to their opponent. How does this change our analysis?

It actually complicates the situation a great deal. With a symmetric game, we know that each player's probabilities and payoffs are identical to each other. With asymmetry, those may not be the same anymore, so we have doubled the number of variables we need to solve for, making this double the work, although the general process is still similar otherwise. Let us suppose for this example that there are two players, A and B, and Player A has the double-Rock-win bonus. What is the optimal strategy for A? What about B? And how much of an advantage does this card give to Player A, if any?

Instead of just a single payoff table, we now have two of them:

Player A	r_b	p_b	s_b
R_A	0	−1	+2
P_A	+1	0	−1
S_A	−1	+1	0

Player B	r_a	p_a	s_a
R_B	0	−1	+1
P_B	+1	0	−1
S_B	−2	+1	0

We cannot rely on our old trick of setting all payoffs equal to zero, because we don't know if the payoffs for Players A and B are equal (in fact, intuition tells us they probably aren't, since one player has an asymmetric advantage). However, we do at least know that the payoffs for Player A are all equal to one another, the same is true for Player B's payoffs, and since the game is still zero sum, we know that the payoff for Player A is equal to the opposite of that of Player B. Also, since each player still must choose exactly one throw, the probabilities for each player still add to 1. We now have this intimidating set of equations:

$$R_A = P_A = S_A = X \qquad\qquad R_B = P_B = S_B = -X$$

$$r_B + p_B + s_B = 1 \qquad\qquad r_A + p_A + s_A = 1$$

$$R_A = 2s_B - p_B = X \qquad\qquad R_B = s_A - p_A = -X$$

$$P_A = r_B - s_B = X \qquad\qquad P_B = r_A - s_A = -X$$

$$S_A = p_B - r_B = X \qquad\qquad S_B = p_A - 2r_A = -X$$

We *could* do this the hard way through substitution, but an easier way to handle this by rewriting the payoff tables as matrices. Here is the **payoff matrix** for Player A:

$$\begin{bmatrix} 0 & -1 & 2 & X \\ 1 & 0 & -1 & X \\ -1 & 1 & 0 & X \end{bmatrix}$$

This represents the bottom three equations above, in shorthand. The right-most column represents the right side of the equation. The leftmost column represents r_B, the next column is p_B, and the third column is s_B. Thus, the top row of the matrix is equivalent to saying $0r_B - 1p_B + 2s_B = X$, without the variables and equal sign. We could keep this in its raw equation form, but you may find it easier to manipulate the numbers if you only have to worry about numbers and can forget the letters for the time being.

We know that in algebra, we can multiply both sides of an equation by the same number and it is still true (if $a = b$, then $na = nb$ for any number n). Also, if we add the left side of two equations together and the right side of two equations together, the resultant sum is still true (if $a = b$ and $c = d$, then $a + c = b + d$). Lastly, since each row in the matrix represents a separate, independent equation, we can reorder the rows as we see fit; their order does not matter. Our goal is to manipulate this matrix so that it is in **triangular form**:

$$\begin{bmatrix} * & ? & ? & ? \\ 0 & * & ? & ? \\ 0 & 0 & * & ? \end{bmatrix}$$

In a matrix in triangular form, every value under the diagonal (the entries marked with an asterisk) is zero. All entries on the diagonal itself must be non-zero. All other entries above the diagonal (marked with a question mark here) can be any value, zero or non-zero.

Right now, Player A's payoff matrix is not in triangular form, but we can manipulate it using our three tricks (rearranging the rows, multiplying all entries in a single row by a constant, and adding two rows together) in various combinations in order to get it there. It's usually easiest to start at the top left, go down the left column changing the values one at a time, and then start with the diagonal entry in the second column and go down from there, and so on one column at a time. If we do that, the first problem is that the top left entry (which is on the diagonal) is zero, and we need it to be non-zero. The simplest way to fix that is to swap the top and middle rows:

$$\begin{bmatrix} 1 & 0 & -1 & X \\ 0 & -1 & 2 & X \\ -1 & 1 & 0 & X \end{bmatrix}$$

Notice that this also happens to place a zero immediately underneath the first diagonal, which is what we need. To eliminate the −1 on the left in the bottom row, we can add the top and bottom rows together to get [0 +1 −1 2X] and replace the bottom row with that:

$$\begin{bmatrix} 1 & 0 & -1 & X \\ 0 & -1 & 2 & X \\ 0 & 1 & -1 & 2X \end{bmatrix}$$

We only have one more entry to eliminate, the +1 on the bottom row. To eliminate that, we can add the bottom two rows together to get [0 0 +1 3X] and replace the bottom row with that:

$$\begin{bmatrix} 1 & 0 & -1 & X \\ 0 & -1 & 2 & X \\ 0 & 0 & 1 & 3X \end{bmatrix}$$

This matrix is now in triangular form. To see why triangular form is useful, we can now rewrite these as normal equations again:

$$1r_B + 0p_B - 1s_B = X$$

$$0r_B - 1p_B + 2s_B = X$$

$$0r_B + 0p_B + 1s_B = 3X$$

We can then solve these equations from the bottom up, using substitution: $s_B = 3X$

$$s_B = 3X$$

$$-1p_B + 2(3X) = X; \quad p_B = 5X$$

$$r_B - (3X) = X; \quad r_B = 4X$$

At this point, we may not know what Player A's payoffs are, but we *do* know that the solution for Player B is $r_B:p_B:s_B = 4:5:3$. Since $r_B + p_B + s_B = 1$, we can even give exact amounts: $r_B = 4/12$, $p_B = 5/12$, $s_B = 3/12$. Incidentally, this also lets us solve for X: if $r_B = 4X = 4/12$, then $X = 1/12$ (confirmed by finding the same value for p_B and s_B).

We can use the same technique with Player B's payoff equations to figure out the optimal strategy for Player A. Again, the payoff tables were as follows:

Player A	r_b	p_b	s_b
R_A	0	-1	+2
P_A	+1	0	-1
S_A	-1	+1	0

Player B	r_a	p_a	s_a
R_B	0	−1	+1
P_B	+1	0	−1
S_B	−2	+1	0

This makes the payoff matrix for Player B:

$$\begin{bmatrix} 0 & -1 & 1 & -X \\ 1 & 0 & -1 & -X \\ -2 & 1 & 0 & -X \end{bmatrix}$$

Again, we must get this into triangular form. This time, let's try swapping the top and bottom rows, to get

$$\begin{bmatrix} -2 & 1 & 0 & -X \\ 1 & 0 & -1 & -X \\ 0 & -1 & 1 & -X \end{bmatrix}$$

To eliminate the +1 in the center row, we can't simply add two rows together…, but we can multiply the center row by 2 first, before adding it to the top row (or multiply the top row by 1/2, but most people find it easier to multiply whole numbers rather than fractions). Multiplying the center row by 2 gives [+2 0 −2 −2X], and adding that to the top row gives [0 +1 −2 −3X], which we then replace in the center row:

$$\begin{bmatrix} -2 & 1 & 0 & -X \\ 0 & 1 & -2 & -3X \\ 0 & -1 & 1 & -X \end{bmatrix}$$

All that's left now is to eliminate the −1 in the bottom row, which can be done by adding the bottom two rows together to get [0 0 −1 −4X], providing the following matrix in triangular form:

$$\begin{bmatrix} -2 & 1 & 0 & -X \\ 0 & 1 & -2 & -3X \\ 0 & 0 & -1 & -4X \end{bmatrix}$$

Again, writing in standard equation form, then solving the bottom row and working our way back up with substitution, we get

$$-2r_A + 1p_A + 0s_A = -X$$

$$0r_A + 1p_A - 2s_A = -3X$$

$$0r_A + 0p_A - 1s_A = -4X$$

$$s_A = 4X$$

$$p_A - 2(4X) = -3X; \quad p_A = 5X$$

$$-2r_A + (5X) = -X; \quad r_A = 3X$$

Our solution, then, is $r_A{:}p_A{:}s_A = 3{:}5{:}4$, or $3/12{:}5/12{:}4/12$ after substituting into $r_A + p_A + s_A = 1$. This is slightly different from Player B's optimal strategy of $4/12{:}5/12{:}3/12$ (the probabilities of Rock and Scissors are swapped between the two players).

How much of an advantage does Player A have over Player B, if any? It turns out, we already found that out earlier, because the advantage is equal to the payoff. We set these equations up assuming that the payoff for Player A is X, and the payoff for Player B is $-X$. Earlier, we established that $X = 1/12$. This means that if both players play optimally, the advantage from this situation is surprisingly small: out of 12 games, Player A only wins one extra game over Player B.

Solving Rock-Paper-Scissors-Lizard-Spock

So far, all of the intransitive mechanics we've analyzed have only three choices. Can we use the same technique if there are more than three? Yes, and we do exactly the same thing, just more of it.

In the game *Rock-Paper-Scissors-Lizard-Spock*, two new throws are added to the original game. Rock smashes Scissors and squashes Lizard; Paper covers Rock and disproves Spock; Scissors cuts Paper and Lizard; Lizard poisons Spock and eats Paper; and Spock vaporizes Scissors and Rock. The payoff table looks like this (using "z" for Lizard to avoid the lower-case "l" that looks like the number one, and "k" for Spock so as to not get confused with Scissors):

	r	p	s	Z	k
R	0	−1	+1	+1	−1
P	+1	0	−1	−1	+1
S	−1	+1	0	+1	−1
Z	−1	+1	−1	0	+1
K	+1	−1	+1	−1	0

Since this game is symmetric and zero sum, we know that $r + p + s + z + k = 1$ and $R = P = S = Z = K = 0$. Solving by hand as before, we end up with the unsurprising solution of 1:1:1:1:1 (or a probability of 1/5 for each of r, p, s, z, and k).

Solving Rock-Paper-Scissors-Dynamite

Not all intransitive mechanics are equally balanced. In some cases, even without weighted costs, some throws are just better in every way than other throws. Recall that we've said the payoffs for all throws that are worth doing at all are equal to each other; here, we encounter a throw that is *not* worth doing at all, so we can see how to treat it.

Suppose we added a fourth throw to *Rock-Paper-Scissors*, "Dynamite" (shown by a closed fist with thumb up). Dynamite beats Rock (by explosion), and Scissors beats Dynamite (by cutting the wick). Arguments could be made about whether Dynamite beats Paper or vice versa, but let us say for now that Dynamite beats Paper. In theory, this makes Dynamite and Scissors both seem like great choices, because both of them beat two out of three of the other throws. It also makes Rock and Paper seem like weak choices, because they each lose to two of the other three throws. But what do we find when we do a mathematical analysis?

Here is the payoff table:

	r	p	s	d
R	0	−1	+1	−1
P	+1	0	−1	−1
S	−1	+1	0	+1
D	+1	+1	−1	0

Before going further, we see an immediate problem: looking closely at both the *P* and *D* row, we see that Dynamite is better than or equal to Paper *in every situation*. Both lose to Scissors, both beat Rock, but against each other Dynamite wins. In other words, there is no reason to *ever* choose Paper, because whenever a player might be tempted to use Paper, it's better to take

Dynamite instead. Using terminology from the field of game theory, we can say that Paper **is dominated by** Dynamite.

If we merely converted the above payoff table into a 4×5 payoff matrix and tried to solve as we did earlier, we would find some very strange behavior and before too long realize that it isn't solvable (or at least, that the only "solutions" make no sense, like having probabilities r, p, s, or d that are less than 0 or greater than 1). This is because we would be operating under the assumption that all payoffs are equal ($R = P = S = D$), but in this case that is not true. Paper is not worth taking, ever, and should have an expected payoff that is strictly less than that of Dynamite.

How do we deal with this? By systematically eliminating all choices that are dominated. In this case, that simply means removing the P row and p column from the payoff matrix:

	r	s	d
R	0	+1	−1
S	−1	0	+1
D	+1	−1	0

We now check again to see if, after the first elimination, any other strategies are now dominated. In this case, they aren't, so we're back to the same exact payoff table as the original *Rock-Paper-Scissors*, but with Paper being renamed to Dynamite.

Solving Rock-Paper-Scissors-Jackhammer

What if we create a new throw to add to *Rock-Paper-Scissors* that isn't dominated by anything, but works a little bit differently from the other throws? Consider the throw "Jackhammer" (signed by holding the hand in a fist, but held sideways as if grasping the handle). Jackhammer smashes through Rock, is given a citation for excessive noise by Paper, and draws with Scissors because the two can't interact much. In other words, Jackhammer works like the reverse of Scissors, beating what loses to Scissors and losing to the throw that beats Scissors. Now, we have the following payoff table:

	r	p	s	j
R	0	−1	+1	−1
P	+1	0	−1	+1
S	−1	+1	0	0
J	+1	−1	0	0

Here, no throw is strictly better than any other—there are no dominated strategies. Since the game is zero sum and symmetric, and both players must choose exactly one throw, we know that $r + p + s + j = 1$, and $R = P = S = J = 0$. Our payoff matrix becomes

$$\begin{bmatrix} 0 & -1 & 1 & -1 & 0 \\ 1 & 0 & -1 & 1 & 0 \\ -1 & 1 & 0 & 0 & 0 \\ 1 & -1 & 0 & 0 & 0 \end{bmatrix}$$

Note that the rightmost column is 0 and not X because the payoff is known to be zero for each throw. Now we work to put this in triangular form. First, we rearrange the rows to get non-zeros along the diagonals:

$$\begin{bmatrix} 1 & -1 & 0 & 0 & 0 \\ -1 & 1 & 0 & 0 & 0 \\ 1 & 0 & -1 & 1 & 0 \\ 0 & -1 & 1 & -1 & 0 \end{bmatrix}$$

Now that the leftmost diagonal is non-zero, we can go down. If we eliminate the -1 in the second row by adding it to the first row, we get [0 0 0 0 0]. We can also eliminate the leftmost +1 in the third row by subtracting it from the first row to get [0 −1 +1 −1 0]. Replacing the second and third rows, respectively, we get

$$\begin{bmatrix} 1 & -1 & 0 & 0 & 0 \\ 0 & 0 & 0 & 0 & 0 \\ 0 & -1 & 1 & -1 & 0 \\ 0 & -1 & 1 & -1 & 0 \end{bmatrix}$$

Curious! We get a row that's all zeros. This gives us absolutely no useful information (it represents the equation $0 = 0$, in case you ever had any doubt that zero equals itself). As if that weren't enough, the bottom two rows are exactly the same as each other, so the last row is redundant and again tells us nothing we didn't already know. Since the second row is all zero and the diagonal must be non-zero, there is no way to put this in triangular form; it does not have a unique solution. Putting back into equation form, we only have two useful rows of information, and thus two equations:

$$+1r - 1p + 0s + 0j = 0; \quad r = p 0r - 1p + 1s - 1j = 0; \quad j = s - p$$

Substituting these into $r + p + s + j = 1$, we can put all other variables in terms of s:

$$1 = r + p + s + j = \left(p\right) + p + s + \left(s - p\right) = 2s + p$$

$$p = 1 - 2s$$

$$\left(\text{substituting into } r = p\right): \quad r = 1 - 2s$$

$$\left(\text{substituting into } j = s - p\right): \quad j = 3s - 1$$

We can therefore set one variable, s, to any number and use it to calculate the others. Can we set s to anything at all? No—remember that these are all probabilities, so they must all stay within the range of 0 (if the throw would never be chosen) to 1 (if players would always choose it). This lets us limit the range of s.

From the equation $j = 3s - 1$, we know that s must be at least 1/3 (otherwise j would be negative), and at most 2/3 (otherwise j would be greater than 100%). From the other two equations, $p = r = 1 - 2s$, we can see that s must be within the range of 0–1/2. Combining those two ranges, s must be between 1/3 and 1/2. This is a significant result for this problem: it tells us that no matter what, Scissors is an indispensable part of all ideal strategies!

At the lower boundary condition ($s = 1/3$), we find that $p = 1/3$, $r = 1/3$, $j = 0$, which is one valid strategy—the same strategy as plain *Rock-Paper-Scissors*. At the upper boundary ($s = 1/2$), we find $p = 0$, $r = 0$, $c = 1/2$. We could also opt for any strategy in between: for example, $s = 2/5$, $p = 1/5$, $r = 1/5$, $c = 1/5$. There are an infinite number of valid strategies, since there are an infinite number of values between 1/3 and 1/2.

You might wonder: are any of these infinite strategies "better" than the others, such that a single one would win more often than the others? A definitive answer for such a question requires far more game theory than we can go into in this chapter, but the short version is "it depends" based on what assumptions a player makes about how rational their opponents are, whether players are capable of making occasional mistakes when implementing their strategy, and how much the players know about how their opponents play, among other things. For our purposes here, assuming that all players follow their chosen strategy perfectly, we can say that any of these strategies is as good as any other.[4]

---

[4]Also, for our purposes, we could say that Jackhammer is probably not a good addition to the core game of *Rock-Paper-Scissors*, as it allows one winning strategy where Jackhammer can be completely ignored, and another optimal strategy where both Paper and Rock are ignored, making us wonder why we're wasting time making content that may never even see play by sufficiently skilled players!

Solving Game of Malkav

We have considered many variations of *Rock-Paper-Scissors*, but one thing we haven't yet considered is a situation where players have a different selection of choices—not just an asymmetric payoff, but an asymmetric *game*. What if one player has, say, six possible throws and their opponent only has five? You might think that such a problem would be unsolvable for a unique solution (there are six unknowns and only five equations, after all), but it turns out we can use some advanced techniques to solve such a game uniquely, under the right conditions.

The collectible card game *Jyhad* (later renamed *Vampire: the Eternal Struggle*) had a card in an early set called Game of Malkav. When the card was played, all players secretly choose a number from 1 to 5… except the player who played the card, who can choose a number from 1 to 6. All choices are revealed simultaneously, and everyone gains health equal to the number they selected… *unless* another player happened to choose a number that is *exactly one less* than what the player chose, in which case they *lose* that much health instead. For example, if one player chooses the number 4 and any other player chooses the number 3, the first player would lose 4 health and the other player would gain 3; if no one else chose 3, then the player who chose 4 would instead gain 4 health. The dynamics of this game can get complicated with multiple players, but let's consider the case of just two players. Let's also make the simplifying assumption that the game is zero sum: that gaining 1 health is equivalent in value to the opponent losing 1 health.[5]

We might wonder: what is the expected payoff of playing this card? Does the additional option of choosing 6 when the opponent can only choose up to 5 make a difference? What's the best strategy and expected payoff (for both players)? In short, is this card worth playing in a deck… and if so, when played, how should players decide what to choose?

As usual, we start with the payoff table, calling the player choices P_1 through P_6, and the opponent choices o_1 through o_5:

	o_1	o_2	o_3	o_4	o_5
P_1	0	+3	−2	−3	−4
P_2	−3	0	+5	−2	−3
P_3	+2	−5	0	+7	−2
P_4	+3	+2	−7	0	+9
P_5	+4	+3	+2	−9	0
P_6	+5	+4	+3	+2	−11

---

[5] Strictly speaking, this is usually *not* a correct assumption, and the value of healing vs. damage varies based on relative health totals, but we treat it this way for now as a starting point for understanding what this card is actually worth, and what advantage (if any) it grants to the one who plays it.

For example, if we choose 3 (P_3) and the opponent chooses 5 (o_5), we gain 3 health, opponent gains 5 health, so we lose 2 health relative to the opponent (shown in the chart as -2).

We might start by looking for any dominated rows or columns, but there do not appear to be any. If we try to solve this through our previous methods (go ahead and attempt it!), the numbers get complicated quickly, and it ends up being unsolvable once you progress. The reason is that there are six equations and five unknowns, which means there should be some redundancy... except in this case, none of the rows end up canceling to 0 or becoming equivalent to each other, which means we end up with at least two equations that contradict each other. So there must actually be some dominated strategies here, but they aren't immediately obvious. But we *can* find them.

The method we follow is to find the best move for each player, *if* they had perfect foreknowledge of what the opponent was doing ahead of time. For example, if the opponent knows we will throw P_1, their best move in that row is o_5 (giving us a net health gain of -4). Now we continue by reacting to their reaction: if we know the opponent will choose o_5, our best move in that column is P_4. Against P_4, the best result for the opponent in that row is o_3. Against o_3, our best result in that column is P_2. If we were to draw this as a series of arrows pointing to the optimal responses, it would look like the following.

	O_1	O_2	O_3	O_4	O_5
P_1:	0	+3	-2	-3	-4
P_2:	-3	0	+5	-2	-3
P_3:	+2	-5	0	+7	-2
P_4:	+3	+2	-7	0	+9
P_5:	+4	+3	+2	-9	0
P_6:	+5	+4	+3	+2	-11

Against P_2, the opponent has two equally good moves in that row: o_1 and o_5. We consider both options.

If the opponent chooses o_5, the best response in that column is P_4, and then, we continue around in the intransitive sequence $o_5 \rightarrow P_4 \rightarrow o_3 \rightarrow P_2 \rightarrow o_5 \rightarrow \dots$ indefinitely. If instead the opponent chooses o_1, the best response in that column is P_6. The opponent's best move against P_6 is o_5, and the best response to o_5 is P_4 again, which leads to the intransitive sequence $o_5 \rightarrow P_4 \rightarrow o_3 \rightarrow P_2 \rightarrow o_1 \rightarrow P_6 \rightarrow o_5 \rightarrow \dots$ which continues to loop forever. Graphically, these loops look like the following.

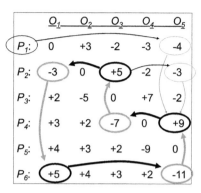

All of that covers the chain that starts at P_1. What if we start at a different place, such as initially throwing P_3? The opponent's best counter-move is o_2, our best answer to that is P_6... and that leads us back to the $o_5 \rightarrow P_4 \rightarrow o_3 \rightarrow P_2 \rightarrow o_1 \rightarrow P_6 \rightarrow o_5$ loop.

What if we start with P_5? The opponent's best response is o_4, which begs the response P_3, and we just covered the case of starting at P_3. We have already covered the cases of starting at P_2, P_4, and P_6 already from the earlier cases.

What if we start with o_1 through o_5? These are all covered in earlier sequences. There is nothing more to analyze. Our final diagram looks like the following.

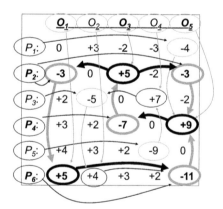

We can see that no matter what we start with, eventually after repeated moves and counter-moves, only a small subset of moves actually end up being part of the intransitive nature of this game (the repeated path is bolded above). The only moves that matter are o_1, o_3, o_5, P_2, P_4, and P_6. Any other choice ends up being strictly inferior: for example, at any point where it might be advantageous to play P_6 (that is, the player expects a positive payoff), there is no reason they'd want to play P_5 instead.

By using this technique to find the intransitive loops hidden in a large set of choices, you can sometimes reduce the possibility space to a smaller set of viable choices[6]... or at worst, you can prove that all of the larger set are, in fact, viable. In the Game of Malkav problem, we can reduce the payoff table to the subset of meaningful values:

	o_1	o_3	o_5
P_2	−3	+5	−3
P_4	+3	−7	+9
P_6	+5	+3	−11

From there, we put into a payoff matrix. We realize this is *not* symmetric, so the payoff is an unknown (again we'll call it X here):

$$\begin{bmatrix} -3 & 5 & -3 & X \\ 3 & -7 & 9 & X \\ 5 & 3 & -11 & X \end{bmatrix}$$

As before, we start by going down the first column in order, to put the matrix in triangular form. Adding the first two rows gives [0 −2 +6 2X]. To get rid of the +5 in the third row, we can multiply the third row by 3 and multiply the first row by 5, and then add them together to get [0 +34 −48 8X]:

$$\begin{bmatrix} -3 & 5 & -3 & X \\ 0 & -2 & 6 & 2X \\ 0 & 34 & -48 & 8X \end{bmatrix}$$

To zero out the +34 in the third row, we multiply the second row by 17 and then add to the third row, to get [0 0 54 42X]. Since we can multiply any row by a constant, we can reduce this to a smaller number by multiplying by 1/6, which changes this row to [0 0 9 7X]. Replacing the third row with this result, we get our matrix in triangular form:

---

[6]Occasionally, you'll find a game where there are one or more locations in the payoff table that are equally advantageous for *both* players, so that we expect all players to be drawn to those locations and stay there after repeated play. The Prisoner's Dilemma is one well-known example. In game theory, these points are called **Nash equilibriums**, named after the mathematician who first wrote about them.

$$\begin{bmatrix} -3 & 5 & -3 & X \\ 0 & -2 & 6 & 2X \\ 0 & 0 & 9 & 7X \end{bmatrix}$$

By substituting from the bottom up, we get $o_5 = 7X/9$, $o_3 = 4X/3$, and $o_1 = 0X/9$. Since $o_1 + o_3 + o_5 = 1$, this gives us the values $X = 9/29$, $o_1 = 10/29$, $o_3 = 12/29$, $o_5 = 7/29$. Since X is the payoff for the player who played the card, this tells us that the card is worth less than a third of a point of health, on average—not particularly powerful, although the possibility of sudden large swings may (or may not) make it more worthwhile in real-world play. We also know the optimal strategy for the opponent, if facing this card.

This doesn't tell us the best strategy for the player who played the card, however. To do this, we must flip the matrix so that we are looking at the opponent's payoffs (O_1, O_3, O_5) and the current player's probabilities (p_2, p_4, p_6). Since the opponent has the opposite payoff, we treat their payoff as $-X$, and all other results in the matrix are likewise inverted (a net gain of $+3$ for the player is -3 to the opponent). This **transposed** payoff matrix is

$$\begin{bmatrix} 3 & -3 & -5 & -X \\ -5 & 7 & -3 & -X \\ 3 & -9 & 11 & -X \end{bmatrix}$$

We then put that matrix in triangular form:

$$\begin{bmatrix} 3 & -3 & -5 & -X \\ 0 & 3 & -17 & -4X \\ 0 & 0 & -9 & -4X \end{bmatrix}$$

Solving, we get $p_6 = 4X/9$, $p_4 = 32X/27$, $p_2 = 43X/27$. Substituting the known value $X = 9/29$ from before, we get $p_6 = 12/87$, $p_4 = 32/87$, $p_2 = 43/87$ (and we can confirm that $p_2 + p_4 + p_6 = 1$).

Solving Three-Player Rock-Paper-Scissors

The Game of Malkav gets far more complicated in multiplayer situations. While we won't attempt to solve it for a large group, it's worth showing the much simpler case of three-player *Rock-Paper-Scissors* to see how this analysis extends to multiple players. After all, many games with intransitive mechanics involve more than just a single head-to-head two player situation. Some games involve teams or free-for-all environments.

Teams are actually straightforward. If there are exactly two teams, treat each team as a single "player" for analysis purposes. Free-for-all situations are much harder because each player must take into account all possible combinations of moves among all opponents. As we'll see, complexity increases dramatically with each successive player. Three-player games are obnoxious but still very possible to solve by hand. Four-player games are the upper limit of what most people would reasonably attempt. If you want to solve a six-player free-for-all intransitive game where each of the six players has a different set of options and an asymmetric payoff matrix that covers every combination of throws among all players… well, technically it can be done, but it would take far too long to do by hand, and you would likely want to enlist the aid of a computer and a professional game theorist to do it for you.[7]

How does three-player *Rock-Paper-Scissors* even work, mechanically? Let's invent the rules. If all players make the same throw, *or* all players choose different throws (one Rock, one Paper, and one Scissors, in any combination), call that a draw, because there is no obvious way to choose a winner. If two players make the same throw and the third player chooses a different throw (so that there are only two distinct throws being used among the three players), one of those throws beats the other. In that case, each player gains a point for each other player whose throw they beat, and each player loses a point for each player they lost to. For example, if Albert and Betty each throw Paper and Charles throws Scissors, then Charles gets +2 points and Albert and Betty each get −1. If instead Charles had thrown Rock, then Albert and Betty would get +1 point each, and Charles would get −2. (The reason we choose these numbers is to keep the game zero sum so that the math is easier. You could choose any other scoring method, however.)

Of course, we know because of symmetry that the solution to three-player *Rock-Paper-Scissors* is identical to the two-player game, $r{:}p{:}s$ = 1:1:1. So, let's throw in the same wrinkle as before: any player winning with Rock counts it as a double win (since this is zero sum, that also means that losses with Scissors count as a double loss). In the two-player case, we found the solution

[7]Actually, at the point where you're dealing with that kind of complexity, a more practical approach is to just use playtesting and analytics to find how players are actually making their choices. One thing that the field of game theory has learned is that the more complex the game, the longer it takes human players to converge on the optimal strategies. For a highly complex game, therefore, playtest data gives you a better idea of how the game actually plays "in the field" than doing the math to prove optimal solutions, because the players won't find the optimal solutions anyway. (Another design solution is to simplify the mechanics, if they're really that complex.)

of $r{:}p{:}s = 1/4{:}1/2{:}1/4$. Let's find out if this changes in the three-player case, since there are now *two* opponents which make it even more dangerous to throw Scissors—and even more profitable to throw Rock.

The trick to solving the three-player game is to look at the problem from only one player's perspective at a time and treat that player's opponents collectively as if they were just one single opponent. In this case, we might construct a payoff table that looks like this:

	rr	rp	rs	pp	ps	ss
R	0	−1	+2	−2	0	+4
P	+2	+1	0	0	−1	−2
S	−4	0	−2	+2	+1	0

Since there are three equations here and six unknowns, that would suggest this is not uniquely solvable. But the good news is that the game is symmetric, which means we *can* solve it, because we know that the probabilities of the opponents are the same. While there are six outcomes, each is just the multiple of two individual probabilities, and the probability of *r*, *p*, and *s* is the same for both opponents.

There is one thing to be careful of: there are actually *nine* combinations of throws for the opponents, not six, because three of them are duplicated above (for example, with *rp*, that could mean your left-hand opponent throws Rock and the right-hand opponent throws Paper, or vice versa). A more accurate payoff table would look like this:

	Rr	rp	pr	rs	sr	pp	ps	sp	ss
R	0	−1	−1	+2	+2	−2	0	0	4
P	+2	+1	+1	0	0	0	−1	−1	−2
S	−4	0	0	−2	−2	+2	+1	+1	0

We can use the simplified payoff table above that only has six columns. It just means that when doing so, we must remember to multiply *rp*, *rs*, and *ps* each by 2, since there are two ways to get each of them. Note that we haven't made a distinction between which opponent is which; for this game, it doesn't matter because it is symmetric, so the probability of *any* other player throwing Rock is the same as the other players.

Since we're dealing with two variables per entry rather than one, this doesn't present so well in matrix form. In theory, we could split this into three smaller matrices, each of which represents the first opponent's choice, and then having each matrix give the three choices for the second player; then we could solve each matrix individually and combine the solutions into one at the end. That's a lot of work, though, so instead let's write this longhand as a system of equations and solve algebraically instead:

$$R = 2(-rp) + 2(2rs) - 2pp + 4ss = 0$$

$$P = 2rr + 2(rp) + 2(-2ps) - 2ss = 0$$

$$S = -4rr + 2(-2rs) + 2pp + 2(ps) = 0$$

$$r + s + p = 1$$

The 0 at the end is because we know this game is symmetric and zero sum.

Where do you start when solving something like this? A useful starting place is to use $r + s + p = 1$ to eliminate one of the variables by putting it in terms of the other, then substituting that into the three payoff equations above. If we eliminate Rock ($r = 1 - s - p$) and substitute, after multiplying everything out and combining like terms we get

$$R = -4pp + 2ps - 2p + 4s = 0$$

$$P = -2p - 4s + 2 = 0$$

$$S = 2pp - 6ps + 8p + 4s - 4 = 0$$

Now we are down to three equations and two unknowns—progress! We could isolate either p or s in either the top or bottom equation by using the quadratic formula, which would yield two possible results (we might be able to eliminate one if it strays outside the probability bounds of 0–1). However, the middle equation is much easier, so let's solve that one instead: $p = 1 - 2s$. Substituting that into the top and bottom equation gives the same result, so at least we know that there is no contradiction in the system. After multiplying everything out and combining like terms, we get $20ss - 26s + 6 = 0$.

Now, we do have to use the dreaded quadratic formula. If it's been too long since you've used it for anything practical, the formula can be used for any equation of the form $ax^2 + bx + c = 0$, where x is the variable and a, b, and c are numbers:

$$x = \frac{-b \pm \sqrt{b^2 - 4ac}}{2a}$$

In our case, $a = 20$, $b = -26$, and $c = 6$. This yields two solutions, one using the "+" and one using the "−" in the top row. Calculating in our case, we find $s = (26 + 14)/40$ and $s = (26 - 14)/40$… that is, s can either be 100% or 30%. Are both of these valid solutions? To find out, we substitute back to find the other two variables. Remember that $p = 1 - 2s$ which lets us find p; and then $r = 1 - s - p$ which gives us r. This gives us two solutions: $r = 100\%$, $p = -100\%$, $s = 100\%$; and $r = 30\%$, $p = 40\%$, $s = 30\%$. That first solution is obviously invalid (p is shown as negative, but probabilities cannot be below zero), leaving us with only a single valid solution: $r{:}p{:}s = 3{:}4{:}3$.

Answering our original question, it turns out that multiple players *do* have an effect on the "rock wins count double" problem, but it might not be the result we expected. With three players, it's actually *closer* to 1:1:1 than it was with two players! Perhaps the likelihood of a draw when one player chooses Rock, another chooses Paper, and another chooses Scissors makes Scissors a less risky play than it would be in a two player game; even if one opponent does choose Rock, the other might choose Paper instead, making the difference between a quadruple-loss and a draw.

Summary

In this chapter, we learned a powerful trick for being able to evaluate intransitive mechanics using linear algebra. This is about as complicated as it gets, bringing together elements of cost curves, probability, and statistics, which is why this chapter appears at the end of this book and not at the beginning. The process is the same:

- First, make a payoff table.
- Then, eliminate all dominated choices from both players. Compare all pairs of rows to see if any pair contains one row where each entry is strictly better to or equal than the other. Do the same for the columns. Continue doing this until all remaining choices are viable.
- Find all intransitive "loops" by finding the best opposing response to each player's initial choice. Eliminate rows or columns that do not contain any elements of any loop.
- After the elimination steps, all remaining rows and columns are viable choices. Using only those, construct a payoff matrix for each player:
  - All of the payoffs for a single player are equal to one another.
  - In a zero sum game, payoffs for all players sum to zero (one player's payoff is X, then the opponent's payoff is $-X$ in a two player game, for example).
  - In a symmetric zero-sum game, all payoffs are equal to zero.

- Add one additional equation: if each player must choose exactly one action, then the probabilities of all choices sum to 1. In an asymmetric game, the probabilities of each individual player's choices sum to 1, so this may be *several* similar equations in that case.

- Using algebraic substitution, triangular-form matrices, spreadsheets, or any other means you have at your disposal, solve for as many unknowns as you can. If you manage to learn the value of X (the payoff for one player), it tells you the expected gain or loss for that player. Summing all players' X values tells you if the game is zero sum (if they all add to zero), positive sum (if they add to a number greater than zero), or negative sum (if they add to a number less than zero), and by how much overall... if you didn't know that information from the start.

- If you can find a unique value for each probability that is between 0 and 1, those are the optimal probabilities with which you should choose each throw. For asymmetric games, the optimal solution may be different for each individual player. This is your solution.

- For games with more than two players, choose one player's payoffs as the point of reference and treat all other players as a single combined "opponent." The math gets much harder for each player you add over two: a three-player game gives you a system of quadratic equations, a four-player game provides a set of cubic equations, a five-player game gives quartic equations, and so on.

The field of game theory is vast and covers a wide variety of other games not covered in this chapter. In particular, it is also possible to analyze games where players choose sequentially instead of simultaneously and also games where players can negotiate ahead of time, make pleas or threats to each other, coordinate their movements, and so on—as might be found in positive sum games where two players can cooperate with each other to get ahead of their opponents.[8]

Discussion Questions

1. When playing plain *Rock-Paper-Scissors* against a new opponent, which throw do you tend to open with and why?
2. How much of plain *Rock-Paper-Scissors* is luck versus skill? Did you change your mind on this after reading this chapter?

---

[8] If you are interested in learning more about game theory, the author of this book recommends *Game Theory: a Critical Text* (Heap & Varoufakis) as a useful and fairly accessible introduction to the field.

3. What's the difference between transitive and intransitive mechanics?

4. Give an example of a game that has *both* transitive and intransitive elements. How do these interact with each other in that game?

5. Propose one or two new throws to add to *Rock-Paper-Scissors* other than the ones listed in this chapter. How would your new throw(s) work (what do they beat and what beats them)?

6. Do the mathematical analysis for the new throw you proposed in the previous question. With that throw in the game, what is the optimal strategy? Do you think this throw is a good addition to the core game, and why or why not?

7. Suggest a new scoring system for plain *Rock-Paper-Scissors* (wins with Rock count for x points, wins with Paper are worth y points, and wins with Scissors give z points, for some values of x, y, and z). Intuitively guess, for this new scoring system, what the optimal strategy will be. Then, do the analysis to find the actual answer. How close was your guess?

8. For two players trying to use a fast way to determine something like who goes first in a game, *Odds and Evens* is more efficient than *Rock-Paper-Scissors* since there are never any ties (in *Odds and Evens*, one player chooses odds, one chooses evens, then both players choose either the number 1 or 2 and add both numbers together; if the result is odd, the Odds player wins, and if the result is even then the Evens player wins). What is the most efficient way you can think of to determine who goes first in a three-player game? Can you extend your solution up to an arbitrary number of players?

9. Consider this scoring system for *Rock-Paper-Scissors*: one of the players has wins counted double if they win with Rock, the other player has their wins counted double if they win with Scissors. Take a guess: do you think either player has an advantage in this matchup, and if so, by how much? Now do the analysis to see how close your guess was.

10. In addition to *Rock-Paper-Scissors-Lizard-Spock*, there are other variants that include yet more throws, including RPS 25 and RPS 101 (that have 25 and 101 different throws, respectively—you can find charts for these by searching online). Are these variants with a greater variety of throws an improvement on the original, or are they worse? Why?

Sidequest 25.1: Three-Player Rock-Paper-Scissors *with Fewer Draws*

While reading through the three-player *Rock-Paper-Scissors* example in this chapter, you may have noticed that our rules could have been simplified further. Imagine if we simply said that players get +1 point for each opponent that they would win against, and −1 point for each opponent that they would lose against.

Simple, right? And identical to our more complicated rules in the plain three-player case.

However, this provides a different result when playing with the "Rock wins count double" rule. Specifically, in that case, if one player throws Rock, one throws Paper, and one throws Scissors, it is no longer a draw. The Rock player would gain *two* points from the presence of Scissors and only lose *one* point to Paper, for a net gain of 1. The Scissors player would likewise have a net loss of 1, and the Paper player would have a net score of 0 for the round. The rules simplification would appear to make Scissors more risky and Rock less so.

Solve the game again with this new rule. What is the optimal strategy now?

Sidequest 25.2: A Fighting Game

In this chapter, we tried two methods to add a fourth throw to *Rock-Paper-Scissors*, but never with compelling results that led to an optimal strategy that always required all four throws. This might make you wonder if such a game is possible or if we are always destined to be limited to three. Here is a simple game that represents a street fight[9]:

- **Players**: 2
- **Objective**: be the first to reduce the opponent's health to 0.
- **Setup**: both players start at 10 health.
- **Play**: the game is played in a series of rounds. Each round, both players choose one of four moves: Fast Attack, Fierce Attack, Special Attack, and Throw. The round is resolved as follows:
    - Fast Attack does 1 damage, and counters Special Attack and Throw (so an opponent playing Fierce Attack against Fast Attack would take 1 damage and do nothing in return).
    - Fierce Attack does 2 damage and counters Fast Attack.
    - Special Attack does 3 damage and counters Throw.
    - Throw does 4 damage.
- **Resolution**: when either player loses their last point of health (dropping to 0 or negative), the game ends. If *both* players lose their last health on the same round, the game is a draw. Otherwise, the player with any health remaining is the winner.

---

[9]This game was inspired by an as yet unpublished project by game designer Nathan Davis.

Try playing this game. Simply write the four moves on index cards or small slips of paper, have your opponent do the same, and then select one card each round. You can keep track of health remaining in your head or on a piece of paper.

You probably noticed that the strategy for the game starts to change once player health totals are uneven, and especially when either player's health gets very low (if a player has only two health remaining, a Throw is no more useful than a Fierce Attack, for example, since both end the game).

Let us only take the simplest case: the start of the game where both players have 10 health. On that initial throw, what is the optimal strategy?

Greater challenge: Solve the game for both players, in the case where one player has 3 health and the other player has 10 health. In other words, for the player that has 10 health, the payoff for a successful Throw is now the same as the payoff for a successful Special Attack. You may either treat that payoff as 3 (the amount of damage done) or infinite (because connecting with either of those immediately ends the game in a win). Note that this game now has asymmetric payoffs, because the player with 3 health may still have reason to choose any of the four throws. What is the optimal strategy for each player?

Ultimate challenge: Solve the game for *all* cases, where the optimal strategy is a function of both players' remaining health. Write an "AI" in a spreadsheet program that chooses a throw randomly based on your strategy and the current score. If going through this book with several other people (as in a classroom setting), have a Fighter AI tournament! Have each player turn in their own formula, and play them against each other for a few thousand games. Compare formulas and have a discussion. Why did the winning strategy win? Why did the underperforming strategies lose?

Sidequest 25.3: Five Cards Battle

Here is another game[10]:

- **Players**: 2
- **Objective**: be the first player to earn the most points after five rounds.
- **Setup**: each player takes a set of five cards, numbered 1 through 5. A third deck of point cards, also numbered 1 through 5, is shuffled and placed face down.

---

[10] This game is based on one of the mini-games from *Suikoden II*. In that mini-game, players used sets of cards numbered 1 through 13 instead, and tying for a point card leaves that card on the table so that the following round's winner gets several point cards at once. These rules have been removed for this challenge, as they complicate the analysis considerably.

- **Play**: the game is played in a series of up to five rounds. At the start of each round, a card from the shuffled deck of point cards is flipped face up. The current round is worth a number of points equal to the face value of that card. Each player chooses one card from their set of five cards, and both players reveal simultaneously. The higher number claims the point card and scores that many points. In case of a draw, no one gets the points, and the point card is just put aside. Both players also set aside the cards they chose for that round; those cards may not be played again.
- **Resolution**: after all five rounds have been played, the player with the most points wins. If both players are tied in points, the game is a draw. If one player reaches 8 points or more before all five rounds are finished, that player wins immediately (because they already have a majority of the points).

It's easy to see that there is no single dominant strategy. If the opponent plays completely randomly (20% probability of playing each card on the first round), a player can come out far ahead by playing the number in their hand that matches the points that each round is worth (play the 3 on the 3-point card, the 5 on the 5-point card, etc.)—against a random strategy, this "matching" strategy wins *far* more often than it loses.

But "matching" is not a dominant strategy either; it can be easily beaten by playing cards that are one higher than the point card (and playing 1 on the 5-point card). Against a matching strategy, this "+1" strategy loses the 5-point card but wins all four of the others, for a guaranteed win of 10 points against 5 points.

Does the "+1" strategy dominate? No, it can be beaten with a "+2" strategy, which in turn loses to a "+3" strategy, which then is beaten by "+4" which in turn is beaten by "matching" again, so these strategies are all intransitive. Essentially, the goal of this game is to guess what the opponent is about to play and choose a card that is exactly one higher than that (or play 1 on the opponent's 5).

Since each strategy is as good as any other if choosing between matching, +1, +2, +3, and +4, you might wonder if it's a matter of just choosing one of those strategies at random… but as we already discovered, the matching strategy beats random play! That means the optimal strategy is probably *not* 1:1:1:1:1, but some other ratio. Find the optimal strategy for the first card play of the game.

Hint: think of the problem like this. For any given play, there are only five strategies: matching, +1, +2, +3, or +4. A player may end up shifting strategies from round to round (as with *Rock-Paper-Scissors*), but with no other information on the first round there are only these five strategies to choose from, and each of these choices may help or hurt depending on what the opponent does. The payoff table looks like this, assuming you'd be initially intending for both players to follow the strategy for all five plays, so you could solve this as a payoff matrix:

	Matching	+1	+2	+3	+4
Matching	0	−5	+3	9	+13
+1	+5	0	−7	−1	+3
+2	−3	+7	0	−9	−10
+3	−9	+1	+9	0	−11
+4	−13	−3	+10	+11	0

Greater challenge: Create an algorithm in a spreadsheet program that plays the full game in a series of rounds, where the "AI" only knows the current point card, past point cards, current scores of both players, and past cards played by both players, and with only that information must choose one of its remaining cards. Your AI's strategy should be able to beat the constant matching, +1, +2, +3, and +4 strategies 100% of the time, *and* should be able to beat a random strategy more than half the time. It does not have to work well against any other strategies except those six. There are many possible solutions to this.

Ultimate challenge: As with the previous exercise, write an "AI" strategy for playing the full game in a series of rounds, where it can look at the current point card, past point cards, current scores of both players, and past cards played by both players, and choose one of its remaining cards, in a spreadsheet program. This time, your goal is to create the strongest strategy you can, against *any* opposing strategies… then play your AI against your friends' AIs. Discuss who played what strategies, which strategies won or lost, and why.

Part III

Spreadsheets

No book on game balance would be complete without a comprehensive section on the tool used the most by game designers when balancing games: spreadsheets. Most game designers love spreadsheets, and even those that don't love them still use them heavily out of necessity. If you are already a spreadsheet expert, that's great! But if you aren't, this section of this book is meant to get you from "never heard of it" to "competent and comfortable" so that you can use spreadsheets to assist in doing the kind of balance work used throughout this book. And even if you are, you may benefit from scanning this section for lesser-known tricks; spreadsheet programs have hundreds of obscure features, and chances are pretty good there are at least a few things in here you haven't heard of.

This means you need to get access to a spreadsheet program of some kind. Microsoft Excel (for Windows) and Numbers (for Mac/iOS) are two popular programs. If you're on a budget, the Calc program in OpenOffice is free, multi-platform, and open source (you can find it at https://www.openoffice. org/download). Another popular and free alternative is Google Spreadsheets, which can be operated in a browser and is stored online (accessible at https:// docs.google.com/spreadsheets). Screenshots in this book are mostly from Google Spreadsheets, as it is popular in the game industry as of the time of printing of this book, due to its ease of sharing among distributed teams.

26

Making Lists

When you open a spreadsheet program, you mostly see a grid, separated into individual rectangles called **cells**. Each cell exists in a column (given by the letter at the top of the column) and a row (given by a number at the left side of the row). Normally, in a new spreadsheet you see cell A1 at the top left highlighted; that is where your cursor is, and if you type something, that is where your typing goes. You can use the arrow keys to move around to different cells, or you can click on a cell directly using the mouse to teleport the cursor there.

To enter information into the current cell, simply start typing. When you are finished, hit Enter to place what you just typed into the spreadsheet in that cell. Different spreadsheets have varying behavior for what happens here; in some, Enter also moves the cursor to the next cell down, while in others, it keeps the cursor over the current cell. You can also hit the Tab key to move the cursor to the right (Shift+Tab to move to the left), and if you are in the middle of typing in a cell, it places that information into the cell before moving.

You may notice while you are typing that the text appears in two places: in the cell itself and also in the formula bar at the top of the spreadsheet.[1] The formula bar is circled in the following figure.

---

[1] In Excel and Numbers, notice that somewhere on the formula bar, there are three small buttons: an X, a check mark and a button labeled f_x. Of these, the X button is the most meaningful to you right now. If you ever start editing a cell and then realize you made a mistake—maybe you clicked on another cell by accident, and now it's putting that new cell into your formula and you didn't want it to—you can always hit the X, and it cancels any changes you made, reverting the cell to its previous state. The check mark button does the opposite, taking what you've written in the formula bar and putting it in the cell, overwriting any information that may have been there before (same as hitting Enter, but without moving the cursor anywhere). We deal with the f_x button at a later time; it deals with functions, which can help you do many useful calculations. The X and check mark do not appear on Google Spreadsheets, however.

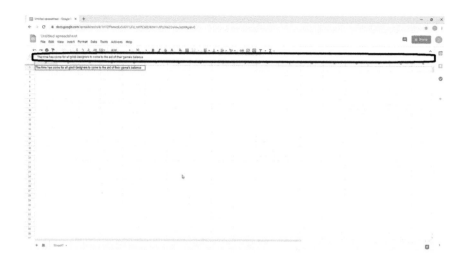

Notice also that whatever cell your cursor is in, the row and column are both highlighted.[2] If you're working on a large spreadsheet, this is a useful way to find and reorient yourself at a glance. Here, cell L23 is highlighted, and you can also see that the headings for column L and row 23 are also a different color.

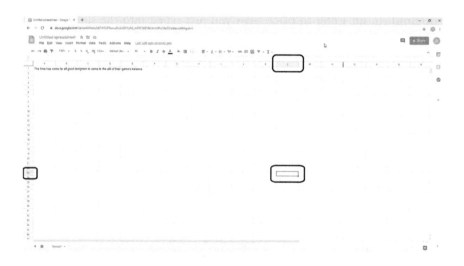

---

[2]In Excel, the current cell coordinates also appear to the left of the formula bar buttons. (More on this in Chapter 33.)

Sidequests

Sidequest 26.1

If you've never used a spreadsheet before, or you haven't used one in a while, take a few minutes to (re)familiarize yourself with the interface. Load up the program of your choice. Use the arrow keys and mouse to move around to different cells. And then enter some text in order to make some kind of list— a to-do list for next week, a grocery shopping list, a list of all of the t-shirts that you own, or anything really. This gets you used to the basic interface and navigation and gets you ready for the more complex skills that follow in future chapters.

27

Basic Formatting

Suppose you were making a list of milestones for your current project and forgot to add one in the middle.

Typing all of that over again is a hassle, but there are other options. The simplest, perhaps, is to insert a new row. Just move your mouse cursor over the row heading, right-click, and insert a row either above or below where you clicked[1]:

---

[1] There is some variation among spreadsheet programs (some simply have "Insert Row" or "Insert Column" and always insert the new one where you have selected, pushing everything else down or to the right).

You can also do the same for columns, and you can also do the same thing from the Insert menu.

What if you want to insert several rows? Right-clicking to insert one at a time is tedious if you have to insert a hundred extra rows. In that case, simply select the number of rows you want to insert, and then right-click, and you can insert a number of rows equal to how many you have selected. Again, you can do this with columns as well.

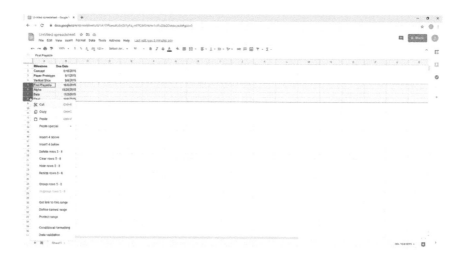

What if you have several columns and only want to insert a row into some of them, but not all? Insert Row inserts an entire row, not part of one.

In this case, your best bet is to select everything you want moved down, and copy and paste. There are quite a few ways to select more than one cell at a time:

- Hold the Shift key down while moving around with the arrow keys. This selects a rectangular block of cells.
- Click on one cell with the mouse and then drag to another cell. This also selects a rectangle.
- Click on individual cells (or click-and-drag) with the mouse while holding the Shift key down. This selects multiple cells that do not necessarily have to be adjacent or in any shape. If you make a mistake and select something that you weren't supposed to, Shift+Click it a second time to deselect.
- Click on a row or column heading to select all cells in that row or column. You can Shift+Click to select multiple rows and/or columns, and you can click and drag to select multiple adjacent ones at a time.
- Click the top left corner of the spreadsheet (where the row and column headings meet, shown below) to select all cells in the current worksheet. The shortcut Ctrl+A also does this.

	A	B	C	D	E	F	G	H
1	Milestone	Due Date		Week	Team Size			
2	Concept	8/18/2015		1	2			
3	Paper Prototype	9/1/2015		2	2			
4	Vertical Slice	9/8/2015		3	3			
5	First Playable	10/6/2015		4	6			
6	Alpha	10/20/2015		5	6			
7	Beta	11/3/2015		6	7			
8	Final	12/8/2015		7	10			
9				8				
10				9				
11				10				
12				11				
13				12				
14				13				
15				14				
16				15				

Once you have your cells selected, you can copy them (Ctrl+C) or cut them (Ctrl+X), and then paste elsewhere (Ctrl+V). These commands are also in the Edit menu and are available when right-clicking a cell with the mouse.

Another thing you can do when selecting multiple cells is to clear them (press the Delete key). This doesn't shift any other cell positions around; it just removes the contents of the affected cells, leaving them blank. (If you make a mistake and do this by accident, you can Undo with Ctrl+Z; if you accidentally Undo, you can Redo with Ctrl+Y.)

If you want to remove a row and have everything beneath it conveniently shift upwards so that you don't have to manually cut and paste it, you can delete a row by selecting that row and then right-clicking on the row header (the option appears just below the ability to insert a new row). You can also do this with columns; everything to the right of the deleted column(s) shifts leftward. You can also delete the current row or column that the cursor is on from the Edit menu. This is the primary difference between "Clear" and "Delete": clearing cells just makes their contents blank, but deleting them actually changes the position of other cells below or to the right.

One very convenient property of row and column insertion and deletion, as well as cut/paste functionality: the spreadsheet automatically updates any values that pointed to it previously. For example, suppose you have a formula in cell B1 that references A1, and then, you insert a new row at the top of the spreadsheet so that these two cells are now A2 and B2. The formula in B2 now references A2, without you having to go in there and update it manually.

If you later cut A2 and pasted into A5, the formula in B2 then references A5. We will go into more detail on references in the next two sections.

One last thing: you might have noticed in the previous examples that the headers in row 1 are bolded. An individual cell can have its text formatted as **Bold** (Ctrl+B), *Italic* (Ctrl+I), <u>Underlined</u> (Ctrl+U), or ~~Strikethrough~~ (Alt+Shift+5). This affects all cells that are currently selected and the entire contents of the cells. If you want a single cell to have mixed formatting (such as a cell that contains a text paragraph with one or two bolded words), edit the text in the cell by double-clicking it, and then, select the relevant text and format it.

Sidequests

Sidequest 27.1

Take the list you made from Sidequest 26.1 in the previous chapter. Insert a new row at the top of your list. In this new row, put a heading or title, and bold it.

Also, practice inserting new rows, adding bogus values, and then removing them through various means.

28

Formulas, References, and Graphs

Game designers find many uses for spreadsheets when balancing their games. As an example, let's consider a game where the player is a merchant moving trade goods from one city to the next, buying where prices are low and selling when they're high. Let's start by entering some trade goods and their respective buy prices manually in their own columns, as we did in the previous chapter.

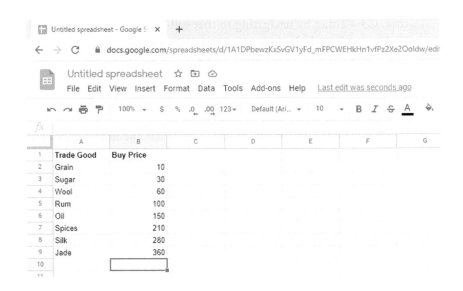

Spreadsheets are also useful for calculating formulas for us so we don't have to do calculations manually.

To enter a formula:

- Click in a cell.
- Enter=followed by the calculation you want. Example: =5+2.
  - You can use numbers, the arithmetic operators (+, −, * and /), and importantly, you can use other cells by their name (the letter and number) which uses whatever value is currently in that other cell. Example: =A5+2. This is called a **reference** to the other cell.

To put this in practice, create a third column heading for the Return On Investment in cell C1. We want this to start off at 50% (or 0.5) in the first row and then increase by an additional 50% in each successive row. Enter 0.5 in the first row (in the above case, this would be cell C2). Then, in the cell below that, type =C2+0.5. You'll see that the new cell correctly calculates to 1 (or 100%).

We then want the cell below that one (C4) to be equal to C3+0.5, and then, C5 should be C4+0.5, and so on. We could enter these manually, but there is an easier way: Fill Down.

To Fill Down:

- Highlight the cell that has the formula you want to repeat—in this case, C3—either by navigating to that cell with the arrow keys or else clicking on it with the mouse cursor.
- Select that cell, and all the other cells below it that you want to copy the formula to, down to C9. You can do this by clicking and dragging with the mouse, or highlighting C3 with the keyboard and holding Shift while using the arrow keys to select them all.
- Select Fill Down as a menu option, or else use the keyboard shortcut Ctrl-D.

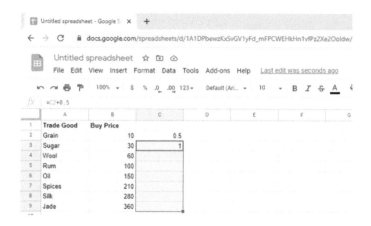

You'll notice that the formula propagates down, and the return column is filled with each cell taking the cell above it and adding 0.5 (you can confirm this by selecting any cell and looking at the formula that appears).

Likewise, you can Fill Right by selecting a horizontal group of cells, then select Fill Right as a menu option or use the keyboard shortcut Ctrl-R. If you want to fill a single cell both right *and* down into a rectangular area, simply select the area and then Fill Right and Fill Down separately.

You might wonder if it's possible to Fill Up or Fill Left. While there are menu options for these, there are no keyboard shortcuts. However, there is another way to fill in any arbitrary direction, using the mouse. You might notice in the figure above, a small blue filled square in the bottom right of the selected area. If you start with a single cell selected and click and drag that square in any direction, it will fill all the cells you cover as you drag the mouse. (You can also click and drag that square with multiple cells selected, but it has a slightly different behavior then.)

From here, we can calculate the sell price and profit: the profit is the buy price multiplied by the return, and the sell price is the profit added to the buy price. Let's add those: label column D "Sell Price" and column E "Profit" in the first row. In E2, the formula would be =B2*C2 (again, the profit is the buy price in B2 multiplied by the return in C2). In D2, the formula is =B2+E2 (the sell price is the buy price plus profit). You can then Fill Down in those columns to calculate the sell price and profit of the remaining trade goods. (Note: you can also Copy the cells and then Paste them for the same result: for example, Copy D2, then highlight D3 through D9 and Paste, and it will paste the formula from D2 into all of the other highlighted cells, but updating the actual cells in the formula so that E3=B3*C3, E4=B4*C4, and so on down the line.)

Untitled spreadsheet

File Edit View Insert Format Data Tools Add-ons Help   Last edit was seconds ago

100% $ % .0 .00 123▾   Default (Ari...▾   10   ▾   B I S̶ A ✧. ⊞

fx   =D9-B9

	A	B	C	D	E	F	G
1	Trade Good	Buy Price	Return	Sell Price	Profit		
2	Grain	10	0.5	15	5		
3	Sugar	30	1	60	30		
4	Wool	60	1.5	150	90		
5	Rum	100	2	300	200		
6	Oil	150	2.5	525	375		
7	Spices	210	3	840	630		
8	Silk	280	3.5	1260	980		
9	Jade	360	4	1800	1440		

Graphing

To visualize the relationships between these numbers, we can graph them, either individually or on the same graph. Let's start by creating a single line graph. To create a line graph:

- Select the entire set of data (including the labels on the left and right). In this case, this would be the entire block of cells from A1 down to E9.
- In the Insert menu, one of the options is Chart. Select the line graph, and you'll see something like this (you can then click and drag to move it around on the sheet so it's not visually obstructing your data cells).

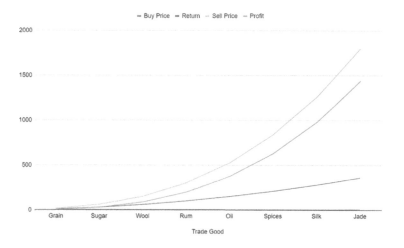

Return shows up as a flat line on the bottom simply because its number is so small compared to the others.

You might wonder how the shapes of these graphs compare, if they were not all on the same scale. For this, you can make a graph for each individual column (just highlight the one column and Insert another line graph). Note that in this case, the axis on the bottom is unlabeled instead of showing the trade good names, since we left out Column A when constructing these charts.

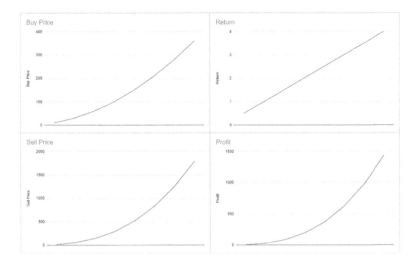

Here, we can see that Return is clearly linear; Buy Price is what a triangular curve looks like (increasing faster as you get higher, but in a relatively gentle way compared to exponential increases); and Sell Price and Profit both have a much more sharply increasing curve. Thus, we can see how a linear relationship and triangular relationship can combine to form something that increases at a much faster rate than either one alone.

Sometimes, curves don't perfectly fit a known formula, but you would like to find one. A useful feature in spreadsheet graphs and charts is that of a **trendline**, which is a best-fit approximation to your data points, drawn on the graph as a separate line or curve. To add a trendline:

- Go to the Customize tab when creating the chart (or if the chart already exists, click on the chart to select it, and then from the top-right menu, select Customize).

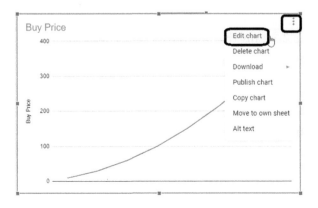

- Select Series, scroll down, and you'll see a Trendline checkbox.

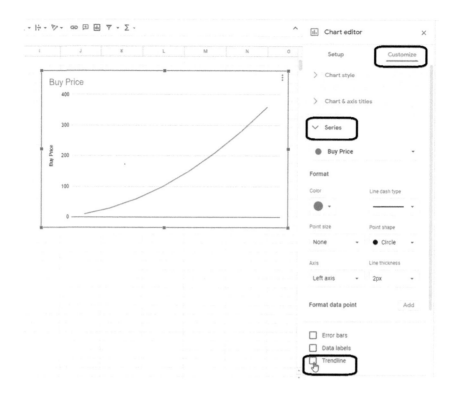

- You have several choices for a trendline: Linear, Polynomial, Exponential, Logarithmic, Power Series, or Moving Average (some spreadsheet programs offer different options). Linear means it finds the straight line where the distance between the line and each point is minimized. Exponential finds a curve of the form $y=a^x$ for some constant a that again attempts to minimize the distance between the curve and each point. Polynomial does the same, but for a curve of the form $y = a + bx + cx^2 + dx^3 + \dots$ up to the specified **degree** of the polynomial. Degree 2 means that the highest-order term is x^2, degree 3 means it goes to x^3, degree 4 means it goes up to x^4, and so on.

When displaying the trendline, there are two additional options of note. One is the Label, which defaults to "None" (it does not display at all on the chart's legend, if there is one) Custom (it does appear on the legend) or to Use Equation (where it shows the actual equation used for the trendline). The latter is useful if you later want to use the trendline as a mathematical model to extrapolate the curve.

The other option is a nondescript checkbox, Show R^2. This gives the R-squared value of the curve. R-squared is a useful way to tell, generally, how good a fit your trendline is. R-squared ranges from 0 (worst fit) to 1 (exact fit that passes precisely through every single data point). There is no set cutoff for which we can say R-squared is "good" or "bad" but, for example, if your trendline has an R-squared of 0.988, then you can call it a strong approximation, and if it is 0.42, then you might try some other trendline option to see if a different equation form provides a better fit.

Sidequests

Sidequest 28.1: Graphing Common Curves

To practice graphing, start with a blank spreadsheet. In column A, create the numbers 1 through 100. (Hint: put the number 1 in A1 and then in A2 put =A1+1 and then Fill Down to A100, so you don't have to type it all manually). Now, in column B, use the formula for triangular numbers $(n^2 - n)/2$ to calculate each of the first hundred triangular numbers in sequence. Graph this second column to see what a triangular curve looks like in the long term.

Greater challenge: create a third column that shows a 10-to-1 linear relationship (just ten times the corresponding number in column A), and a fourth column that shows an exponential relationship where the first number is 1 and each successive number is 1.1 multiplied by the previous one. Graph these other two rows individually, and then graph all four curves (identity, triangular, linear, and exponential) on the same graph.

29

Absolute References

Suppose you want to create a level/XP curve, where you relate the number of experience points the player must get in order to reach the next level. Suppose you want this to be triangular, but you also want it to be multiplied by a constant: say, to reach level N, you need $N * (N - 1) * K$ experience points, where K is some constant. You're not sure what you want K to be yet, so you'd like to make it something you can fiddle around with easily in a spreadsheet until the numbers look right.

You'd like to have something that looks like the following.

As a general principle, when you have a task that needs to be repeated, it's better to get the computer to do it than to repeat it yourself. If you type the same formula many times, it's easy to accidentally mistype once, which could throw all of your numbers off (and that's not even mentioning how tedious it is to spend your time typing and retyping the same thing). With that said, how can we build this Level/XP curve with the least amount of effort and repetition?

In the Level column, we want the numbers 1 through 20. There are a few ways to get that result without having to type each number individually:

- Type the number 1 into a cell (cell B5, in the above case). In the cell below, type the formula =B5+1 (which equals 2, of course). Then, Fill Down from there. You'll notice that the formula is updated, so that each cell is looking at the one above it. More on this in a moment.

- As above, start with typing the number 1 into a cell, and then below that, type a formula to add 1 to the original cell. Copy (Ctrl+C) the second cell. Then, select the remaining 18 blank cells below it and Paste (Ctrl+V). It will paste the one individual copied cell into all the other selected cells, and it updates the formula for each cell the same way that Fill Down does.

- You might notice, if you look closely, a small square in the bottom right corner of the cell cursor. After highlighting one or more cells, clicking and dragging from that corner causes the spreadsheet to attempt to continue the pattern. For example, if you type 1 into cell B5 and 2 into B6, then highlight both of them and then drag the square down, and it creates the rest. (This trick tends to only work with simple sequences like 1, 2, 3... and gets confused if you give it anything much more complicated. It can still be a time-saver when you just want a quick list of numbers.)

Now, for the XP column, in cell C5 we would like to use the formula =B5*(B5-1)*C2. This correctly gives the number 0. However, what happens if we Fill Down from there? Cell C6 immediately below shows the formula =B6*(B6-1)*C3. That C3 is a problem; that cell is blank! We would like it to increment B5 to B6 (and B7, B8, and further as we Fill Down) while leaving C2 alone from the original formula.

In spreadsheet lingo, there are two ways to reference a cell by its name: **absolute** and **relative**. So far, we have used relative references, meaning if cell C5 references C2 in its formula, it is not actually looking in C2; it is looking three cells above its current position. If you copy C5 and paste into, say, H9, the new formula pasted in H9 isn't looking at C2, but rather three cells above itself (in H6). Likewise, if you Fill Down or Fill Right or Copy/Paste, any relative references to cells updates so that they are now relative to the new cells being filled into.

It is possible to give an absolute reference to a cell, meaning that you are referring to a specific named cell in the spreadsheet and that reference doesn't update even if the original cell moves, is copied and then pasted, or is filled into new cells. To do this, put a dollar sign before the row and column: $C$2 instead of C2.

In the case of our spreadsheet here, use the following formula in C5, and then Fill Down to C24, and it works properly: =B5*(B5-1)*$C$2. You can now change the value in cell C2 and all of the XP values update accordingly.

Another thing you may have wondered about with that screenshot was why cell C2 was a different color than the rest. You can change the background color of any cell or cells: just highlight them, then click the paint bucket tool, and select a color. This has no effect on functionality; it is purely cosmetic. Just as programmers may talk about "coding style," individual game designers may have their own "spreadsheet style": use of certain colors in order to denote various types of data. For example, you might choose to color all computed cells a certain color in order to let the viewer know that these should not be changed, while using a different color for cells that contain values that *are* meant to be fiddled around with. You might also color entire rows or columns a certain color to differentiate them into general categories (maybe you color costs and limitations in one color, and benefits and strengths in a separate color). There is no industry standard in the use of colors; it is up to you to choose coloration that is representative and, more to the point, consistent throughout your spreadsheets. We go into more detail about this in Chapter 33.

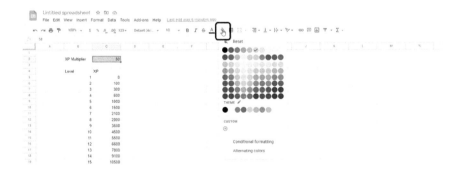

Color is not the only way to give information. In computer programming, the code is often hard to decipher just by looking at it; the same can be true for complicated formulas or nonstandard layouts of data in a spreadsheet. Programmers add comments to their code in order to provide additional information to make it easier to understand what's going on. Spreadsheets offer two primary ways to do this.

The first, and simplest, is to type text into a cell. If you include a column of data for "design notes," you can add these wherever they are needed. However, sometimes it is not practical to use cells for this purpose, or it would be is ambiguous what the comment is referring to. In this case, you can also leave a comment attached to a specific cell: just right-click the cell and select Insert Note.

You can then proceed to type your notes on the cell, and it shows up as a black triangle in the corner of the cell from that point on. If you want to edit or modify the note, you can select Insert Note again. To remove a note, select Clear Notes. To view an existing note, move the mouse to hover over that cell and the comment pops up.

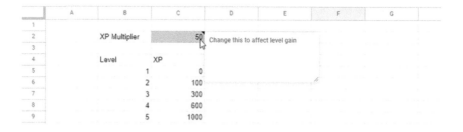

In most other spreadsheet programs, this functionality is called a Comment instead of a Note. Confusingly, Google Sheets also has an Insert Comment option, which works similarly to a note. The difference is that, because Google Sheets is meant to be online and collaborative, Comments have your name attached to them and they have a "Resolve" button that removes it. You can also have multiple Comments on a single cell that are displayed as a threaded conversation. Comments in Google Sheets, then, are meant as a way for one person on a design team to raise questions or issues to others who are working on the same spreadsheet. This functionality is obviously not standard in most other standalone spreadsheets that are run locally on a single machine.

One last helpful thing is being able to navigate through a spreadsheet quickly. If you have more cells that fit on the screen—perhaps thousands of cells if you Fill Down, for example—you might want to go from the top to the bottom without having to scroll manually one cell at a time. By holding the Ctrl button down and using arrow keys to navigate, you can move much faster. If the current highlighted cell is blank and you're holding Ctrl down while moving, the cursor jumps to the next non-blank cell (or to the extreme edge of the sheet if all the data is blank). If the current cell is non-blank, Ctrl jumps to the last non-blank cell in sequence so that you can find the edge of the current block of data. For this reason, you generally want to organize your spreadsheets to have all of your related data in adjacent cells, and not leave a blank row or column in between every piece of data just to add some visual spacing (the way you'd leave a blank row to add whitespace in a text document)—doing so only serves to make navigation less efficient.

Likewise, it can be useful to select multiple cells, mostly for copying/pasting purposes or else to delete them *en masse*. While you can do this by clicking and dragging with the mouse, you can also hold the Shift key down while moving the cursor with the arrows. And as you might imagine, holding Shift *and* Ctrl down while using the arrows can be used to select a large area very quickly—to select a contiguous rectangular block of cells, just put the cursor in one corner (or click anywhere in the general area and use Ctrl and arrows to get to one corner), and then Shift+Ctrl with arrows to get to the opposite corner.

Sidequests

Sidequest 29.1: Graphing Supply and Demand

MMOs that allow trading of items for game currency within some kind of in-game market or auction house provide a remarkably pure representation of economic principles in action. Suppose that at a certain point in time in *EVE Online*, the demand curve for one unit of Megacyte was $y = 500,000 - 50x$, and the supply curve was $y = 45x$ (in both cases, x is the price, and y is the number of units that a buyer is willing to buy or a seller is willing to sell at that number—see Chapter 6 for more on economics).

In a spreadsheet, create some cells to represent these equations. Create one column where x varies from 0 to 10,000 in increments of 100, another column representing the demand curve at each point, and a third column representing the supply curve at each point. You should be able to use formulas for everything (even the numbers for x can just add 100 to the previous x) and then Fill Down for a hundred rows.

Next, create a chart (either a scatter plot or line graph) that shows both supply and demand curves on the same chart, as shown in the previous chapter. Finally, play around with labeling: label the x axis as "Price" and the y axis as "Quantity"; add "Megacyte" as a header or title above the chart; and either remove the legend that appears by default or label the legend with "Supply" and "Demand" for the two curves.

30

Advanced Formatting

In game design, spreadsheets are most commonly used to keep track of game elements, but they have other uses as well. One of these is to use the grid-like nature of a worksheet to serve a similar purpose to graph paper.

One useful feature of spreadsheets is the ability to resize rows and columns. By placing the mouse cursor between two row or column headings, you can click and drag to resize an individual row or column. You can also select one or more row or column headings and then right-click on any of them to select Resize if you want to specify an exact column width or row height.

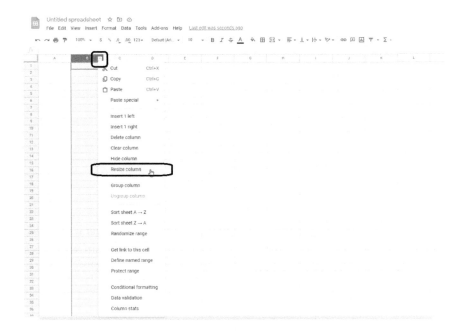

Sometimes, you might wish to combine several cells into a single rectangular block, mostly for appearance purposes (you could resize the row or column, but that affects every cell in there, rather than just one single cell). For example, if you have a lot of column headings in the top row, you might wish to group those headings by category. While you can color-code each category, it is nice to add an additional heading with the category name, like Core Stats, Damage Range, and Spells here:

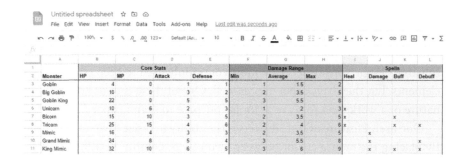

As you can see above, this is entirely possible! This functionality is called Merge Cells. First, select all cells that you'd like to merge into one, then click the Merge button in the toolbar, and select Merge All.

The cells have now merged into one. If you need to un-merge them, just select the merged cell, click the same button, and Unmerge. You can also access merge functionality from the Format menu.

You might wonder, if you need to refer to the value inside a merged cell, what cell do you reference? The value is stored in the cell in the top left. For example, if you have merged cells E2:H5 as above and put a number in that merged cell, you could get the value of that number by referencing cell E2 (but not the others).

In some cases, you may want to logically group a set of cells together, without merging them. For example, you might have several charts in a single worksheet and want to make them distinct. Again, you could color-code the background of various regions to set them apart; but another thing you can do is to draw a border around them.

To draw a border around one or more cells, first select the cells and then use the Border tool. You can create a border around the entire selected area:

You might have noticed some thick vertical and horizontal lines in the very first example in this section (the one with monster stats and category headings). Those were made by selecting an entire row or column and then adding a Border along one of the sides.

Lastly, just as it is sometimes useful to use background color to draw attention to cells, logically group them together, or differentiate them by using several colors, it is also possible to change the color of the text in a cell, using the Text Color tool.

As you can see here, a common layout for a spreadsheet is to have each row as one game object (enemies, weapons, cards, character classes, etc.) and each column as an attribute or property of each object, with columns grouped together by category. Each cell represents whether the object in that row has that attribute (and if so, how much of it).

At the far right, you can place a column with a formula that weights the various traits for each row, adding the benefits and subtracting the limitations and costs. This produces a final value where the particular game object falls along its cost/power curve (see Chapter 8 for more detail on this type of analysis). If the costs are subtracted from the benefits and everything is scaled to an identity curve, a value of 0 means the object is balanced, a positive value means it's above the curve (too powerful), and a negative value means it's below the curve (too weak). This method is highly intuitive: higher numbers are more powerful, and the further away from zero the object's value is, the more out of balance.

As a general principle, it is desirable to separate parts of a single complex formula into several simpler formulas. This makes the formula easier to understand and conceptualize, and makes it easier to check for and detect errors. In the case of a cost/power curve spreadsheet, at the very least, having a separate column to perform a subtotal of costs and another for the subtotal of benefits would be warranted. If there are a lot of mechanics, grouping them into logical categories and subtotaling each of those in a separate column also helps. You may also find it helpful to format these computed columns, for example by giving them a differently colored background, to make it clear these are not cells that should be filled in manually. In the example below, "Mana Subtotal" is a formula that computes the total cost from the mana cost components.

Card	Color Mana Cost	Colorless Mana Cost	Mana Subtotal	Power	Toughness	Flying	Lifelink	Trample	First Strike	Reach	Haste	Swampwalk	Dea
G for 0/3 Defender, Reach	1	0	3	0	3					1			
W1 for 2/1 Flying	1	1	4	2	1	1							
B1 for 2/1 Lifelink	1	1	4	2	1		1						
GG for 3/2 Trample	2	0	6	3	2			1					
WW for 2/2 First Strike, Pr	2	0	6	2	2				1				
BB for 2/2 First Strike, Pro	2	0	6	2	2				1				
W2 for 2/2 Flying	1	2	5	2	2	1							
B2 for 2/2 Swampwalk	1	2	5	2	2							1	
G3 for 2/4 Reach	1	3	6	2	4					1			
R3 for 3/2 Haste	1	3	6	3	2						1		
U3 for 2/4 Flying	1	3	6	2	4	1							
W3 for 3/2 Flying	1	3	6	3	2	1							
WW2 for 2/3 Flying, First S	2	2	8	2	3	1			1				
GG3 for 3/5 Deathtouch	2	3	10	3	5								
WW3 for 4/4 Flying, Vigilar	2	3	10	4	4	1							
WW3 for 5/5 Flying, First S	2	3	10	5	5	1	1			1			
GG4 for 6/4 Trample	2	4	12	6	4			1					
GG5 for 7/7 Trample	2	5	15	7	7			1					

If you have more rows or more columns than can fit on a single screen, you'll quickly find it frustrating to read. For example, suppose you are examining a game object in row 70; you might see many numbers in the various columns, but then you must scroll back up to see the column headings in the top row, and then back down again to find the row, and by the time you locate your row, you might have forgotten which column is which again.

There is a better way: **Freeze.**[1] You can direct a spreadsheet to "freeze" the topmost row or rows, and/or the leftmost column or columns, in place. When you do this, those headings are always displayed, no matter where you are in the spreadsheet. In Google Sheets, the option is under the View menu; you can freeze rows or columns independently. This makes it much easier to read. If you want to stop this behavior, the option to unfreeze is in the same menu.

You can tell if rows or columns are frozen by a thick bar that shows the boundary. You also notice quite obviously if you scroll, and some of the spreadsheet stays in one place, as you can see here when the user has scrolled a few columns to the right.

---

[1]In Excel, this option is called **Freeze Panes**. Why "panes"? Excel was originally made for the Windows operating system, and in the early days of programming for Windows, a single window (an application currently running) might be divided into several different areas that each behaved like a mini-window, and these were called panes (because Window Panes, get it?). The term isn't as widely used today, but it still sticks around in spreadsheets.

	Card	G Flying	H Lifelink	I Trample	J First Strike	K Reach	L Haste	M Swampwalk	N Deathtouch
5	GG for 3/2 Trample			1					
6	WW for 2/2 First Strike, Pr				1				
7	BB for 2/2 First Strike, Pro				1				
8	W2 for 2/2 Flying	1							
9	B2 for 2/2 Swampwalk							1	
10	G3 for 2/4 Reach					1			
11	R3 for 3/2 Haste						1		
12	U3 for 2/4 Flying	1							
13	W3 for 3/2 Flying	1							
14	WW2 for 2/3 Flying, First S	1			1				
15	GG3 for 3/5 Deathtouch								1

On the subject of formatting, there are two things we can do with that "Benefits Minus Costs" column that can make it easier to immediately identify cards that are the most in need of attention. First is Conditional Formatting. This is a way to add formatting (usually background fill color or text color, though you can do other formatting such as italic or bold) to a cell only if the contents of the cell meet certain conditions that you specify. You can have multiple conditions active and choose the order that they execute.

To show how this works, let's first add a format rule to turn the cells in Benefits Minus Costs red if they're below zero (that is, below the curve) and another rule to turn the cells green if they're above zero (above the curve). First, select the cells that you want conditionally formatted (in this case, we click the header of column S to select the entire Benefits Minus Costs column), and then choose Conditional Formatting from the Format menu.

Doing this opens a sidebar on the right side of the screen that looks like this.

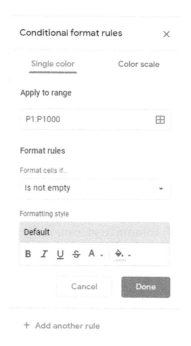

Here, you can adjust the range of cells that are affected by the formatting rule if you wish and choose the condition (in this case "Less than" and then 0), and adjust the style by choosing a background color or other formatting options. After doing this, we click "Add another rule" at the bottom and format cells to have a green background if greater than 0. Then, we click Done. From that point on, if we move the cursor over one of the affected cells, we see the conditional formatting rules in effect on that cell.

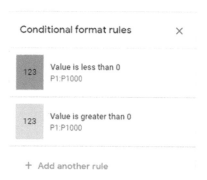

By hovering the mouse over a rule (here, the red rule is highlighted), you see a trash can icon that lets you delete that rule, and four dots on the left that you can click and drag to reorder the rules so they execute in a different order. Order is important because in Google Sheets, once one of the rules is found to apply, all of the formatting in that rule is applied and any rules further down are ignored.[2]

Our spreadsheet column now looks like the following.

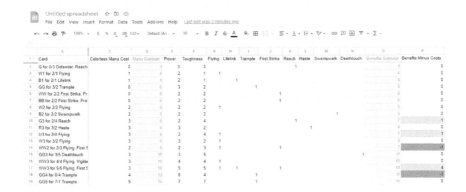

That's better, in that we can instantly see at a glance which cards are off the curve. But what if we want instead to see deeper colors depending on how far off the curve it is, so that color information is more granular? To do this, we remove the existing formatting rules and add a new rule on our balance column.

---

[2]In some spreadsheet programs, you can choose whether each Conditional Formatting rule stops execution of later rules, or whether you can have multiple rules in effect that are layered on top of one another. For example, if you want numbers that are greater than 10 to be italicized and numbers between 5 and 15 to be bolded (with numbers between 11 and 15 being both italicized and bolded), you could do that in just two rules if you can specify to not stop after the first rule. In Google Sheets, this would take three formatting rules: one to bold the numbers between 5 and 10, bold and italicize between 11 and 15, and italicize 16 and above.

At the top of the Conditional Formatting sidebar when adding a rule, you can choose a color scale instead of a single color, which lets you color cells along a gradient, either from one color to a second color (black to white), or with three colors (high end, midpoint, and low end). You can specify the colors of the midpoint and the two extremes, and also how to compute the minimum, maximum, and midpoint values: as specified numbers, minimum/maximum values along the range of cells being formatted, or as a percentile. In the above example, we determine the minimum and maximum values as the lowest and the highest in the column, formatting them as a red and green background, respectively, and formatting the value of 0 as white and using that as the midpoint (even though 0 isn't the mean or median of the column). Now our column looks like this, where the +1 and +4 values are shaded differently.

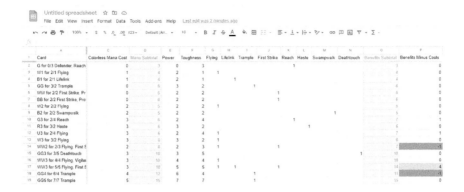

Now, the game objects that are above or below the curve should be visually distinct in that column. Another natural thing we might want is to order each game object from most above the curve to most below, in order to cause all objects of similar power level to cluster together. To do this, spreadsheets offer the ability to Sort.

In general, the way this works is that you first select a range of rows that you want sorted. Then, from the Data menu, select Sort Range.

This brings up a dialog where you can specify which column to sort by, and whether it is sorted in ascending (A to Z) or descending (Z to A) order. Note that while it shows this as if it were alphabetical, it also sorts numerically ascending or descending if the data is numeric, or in date order for date/time cells.

In this case, we sort by the Benefits Minus Costs column, descending so it goes from most overpowered at the top to most useless at the bottom. Had we selected all rows including the header row at the top, we would check the "Data has header row" so that the header did not accidentally get sorted as well, but it is usually easier to just leave that unchecked and not bother selecting the header row.

However, we have many cards in this list that have the same value of 0, so we might want to specify a second column to use as a "tiebreaker" to sort by. To do this, click "Add another sort column" and specify a second column (in this case, we might choose to reorder by card name secondarily, or else perhaps the Cost Subtotal column to order things from smallest to largest). You can continue to do this as many times as you wish, adding additional tiebreakers to sort things that have the same values in all previous sorting criteria. When you're ready, click the Sort button, and all of the rows are reordered based on the sort you chose. In this case, we chose to sort by column P (descending) and then secondarily by column O (ascending).

If you sort and get a result that you weren't expecting, such that it feels like you just screwed up your entire spreadsheet, don't panic—you can Undo (Ctrl-Z, also available in the second button from the left on the toolbar, or at the top of the Edit menu).

Lastly, there are some useful ways to format your cells to make them easier to read, all of which are accessible in the toolbar.

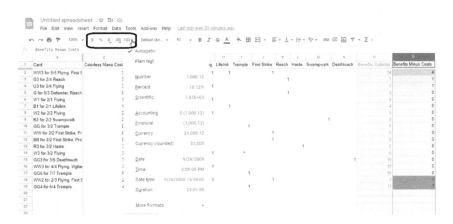

If you select one or more cells, rows, or columns, you can click one of the buttons shown above to change the appearance of the numbers: showing as currency (dollar sign and two decimals), a decimal with a specified number of decimal places (if it extends to more decimal places, the appearance in the main sheet is shortened and rounded accordingly, although this doesn't change the actual value for computation purposes—if you format it to only show whole numbers and type 1.4 into a cell, it appears as 1 in the main sheet, but if you then have another cell that multiplies that value by 10, the result is 14 and not 10). Also, the true value of a cell is shown in the formula bar if you select the cell.

There are four other formatting buttons on the toolbar worth knowing for now.

Of these, the leftmost lets you choose horizontal text alignment within a cell (by default, text is left-justified and numbers are right-justified, but you can change that around—it sometimes makes it easier to read if you center text in column headings, for example). The next button over lets you choose vertical alignment (starting at the top, bottom, or vertically centered within a cell). By default, this makes no obvious difference because cells are a single line high, but if you resize the height of cells, it helps to make the text easier to read.

The third button in the circled area above lets you choose how word wrap works within a cell. By default, if there is too much text to display inside a single cell, it just appears to bleed into adjacent cells to the right, or be cut off if there is any data in those cells. But you can change it to Wrap, which causes the vertical height of the cell to resize itself automatically to the length of the text, and have the text wrap within a cell. Here is what happens to our sheet when we turn on Wrap for the card names in column A.

The fourth button lets you rotate text within a cell so that it's vertical or at an angle. This can sometimes be helpful, for example, with column headings if there are a lot of them and you want to make the whole sheet more compact, but still want to be able to read the headings.

You can also access these formatting options in the Format menu.

Sidequests

Sidequest 30.1: Build a Level

Try resizing all columns so that the column width is the same as the row height in order to make virtual graph paper. Draw a border around a 20×20 grid. Then, fill some of the cells in with a black background to make a crossword puzzle, or a maze, or a dungeon layout. That's right—you can use a spreadsheet as a simple level design tool!

Sidequest 30.2: UI Design

Mock up a screen layout for a video game. Assume screen resolution of 1280×960 pixels, with each cell representing a 32×32 block of pixels (this means your screen is 40 cells wide and 30 cells high). Some examples might be

- Design the inventory management screen for an action-RPG.
- Design the main screen for an FPS, showing where various gameplay elements (health, ammo, status effects, etc.) are displayed.
- Design the main menu for a game, showing options to start a new game, load from save, view the credits, and exit the game, and any other appropriate options you might think of. Show where each button goes.
- Find a screenshot for any of the above kinds of screen layouts for an existing game, use a painting program to identify the pixel coordinate ranges of each element on the screen, and recreate that layout in a spreadsheet.

Use color and text to identify where the various screen elements are displayed on the screen, and use borders to separate the screen elements from one another as well.

Sidequest 30.3: Cost Curve Formatting

To practice formatting a cost/power curve spreadsheet, first do one of the Main Quests in Chapter 8, or Sidequest 8.2 (in the latter case, add a column on the right that subtracts the gold costs from the DPS benefits such that it is equal to zero if the weapon is on the curve, and also add a few more weapons of your own design that are above and below the curve to varying degrees).

If you'd like to refresh your memory from previous chapters, insert a new row at the top, and use Merge Cells within that new top row to group the categories into logical groups (such as "benefits" and "costs"—or even more granular if that makes sense for you). Color-code each group, except for the "Benefits Minus Costs" row in the far right—leave that one alone for now.

The item on the far left column (A) should contain the name of each game object, and the top two rows (1 and 2) should be headers. Freeze the first column and the first two rows in order to lock those in place. Try scrolling to the right and down to confirm that they stay put, then use the Ctrl and arrow keys to quickly get back to the top left.

For each column that is represented by a number, Format the cells in some reasonable way. They may be integers, fractions, decimals, or percentages.

For the Benefits Minus Costs column, which should be 0 if the game object is balanced, negative if it's below the curve and positive if it's above: use Conditional Formatting to highlight anything too far away from the curve. You could do this by using three tiers, too weak (less than zero, or else less than some threshold you choose if you want to count a very slightly negative value as "close enough"), too strong (greater than zero by a sufficient amount), and balanced (neither of the other two categories). Or you could take a reasonable maximum and minimum for how far something can be above or below the curve, then format the column as a gradient between the two.

Lastly, Sort your spreadsheet by the Benefits Minus Costs column (ascending or descending, your choice) so that all of the things that are too far from the curve are all clustered at the top and bottom. Make sure not to sort the two header rows at the top by mistake!

31

Math Functions

So far, all of our formulas have just involved numbers, references to other cells, and simple arithmetic operators. You will run into situations where you'll need more advanced functionality, and for that, spreadsheets include what are called **functions**. There are many functions to explore, but the syntax for each one is the same: each function is invoked by writing its name, then an open parenthesis, then any **parameters** that the function requires (if any), and then a closing parenthesis.

Functions can be used within any formula in a spreadsheet. A function can be used on its own, or it can be added to or multiplied by some other number, cell, or another function. For functions that take parameters, one of those parameters might even be another function, which itself could contain yet another function. When computing the value of a cell, the spreadsheet takes any functions and first computes the value of their parameters, and then uses those values to compute the final value of the function itself. (Do remember, however, that you must start every function with an equal sign.)

Pseudorandom Functions

Let's dive in with an exploration of pseudorandom numbers. These can be useful for modeling random systems, and spreadsheets have lots of probability-based functions to support this.

The bread and butter of pseudorandomness in spreadsheets is the RAND() function. This function takes no parameters at all and gives a floating point (decimal) number between 0 and 1. It can theoretically be 0, but never 1. This is important to know when rounding; for example, if rounding down to the nearest integer, this function always returns 0, but if rounding up to the next highest integer, it is usually 1 but can theoretically be 0. If rounding (up or down) to the nearest integer, it would return 0 half the time and 1 the other half.

What if you want to generate a number within a range that isn't 0 to 1? RAND() can be multiplied and/or added to in order to get any range. For example, if you want a number between 150 and 250, that would be =RAND()*100+150. Multiplying 100 by a number between 0 and 1 gives a number between 0*100 and 1*100, so the range is now 0 to 100. Adding 150 to that number increases the range from 0+150 to 100+150, or between 150 and 250.

What if you want an integer number, such as rolling 1d6? =RAND()*6+1 gives a number between 1 and 6.99999999. To get just the whole number portion—that is, rounding down to the lower integer number—use the function FLOOR(). This function takes two parameters. The first is the number to be rounded. The second is the number to round to; for nearest integer, use 1, but you can also use 100 to round down to the lower hundred, or 0.1 to round down to the lower tenth, or 33.52 to round down to the next lower multiple of 33.52. For 1d6, the, you would use =FLOOR(RAND()*6+1,1). Likewise, there is a function CEILING() that rounds up to the next higher number, and MROUND() that rounds up or down, whichever is closest.[1]

That's a bit unwieldy for just rolling a simple six-sided die, but there is a simpler function for integers. RANDBETWEEN() is a function that takes two parameters, a lower bound and an upper bound, and returns a pseudo-random integer within that range, inclusive. =RANDBETWEEN(1,6) is 1d6, and =RANDBETWEEN(0,1) is a "coin flip" that gives either 0 or 1.

What if you want to roll 2d6? You might be tempted to do =RANDBETWEEN(1,6)*2, but that would not roll 2d6, it would roll 1d6 and multiply the result by 2 (you cannot get a result of 7 this way, for example). Instead, you call the function twice: =RANDBETWEEN(1,6)+RANDBETWEEN(1,6). Alternatively, put =RANDBETWEEN(1,6) in two separate cells and then add them together in a third cell. (The latter might be easier if you're rolling a lot of dice: for 100d6, use =RANDBETWEEN(1,6) in one cell, Fill Down for a total of 100 rows, and then SUM() them in one final

---

[1] There's also another set of functions that round up and down: ROUNDDOWN(), ROUNDUP(), and ROUND(), which work similarly to FLOOR(), CEILING(), and MROUND(), respectively, except their second parameter is the number of digits to round to: 0 means round to the nearest integer, 1 is to the nearest tenth, 2 to the nearest hundredth, and so on... and if negative, the second parameter being −1 means round to the nearest ten, −2 to the nearest hundred, etc.). These are less versatile and intuitive, which is why this book uses FLOOR(), CEILING(), and MROUND(), but you may encounter these other functions in the wild so be aware that they exist and are slightly different.

cell. The SUM() function takes any number of parameters, each of which is a cell or range of cells, and it gives the result of adding all of them up. For example, if your 100d6 are in cells A1:A100, then =SUM(A1:A100) would give the total of those cells (you can also use =SUM(A1:A50,A51:A100) or =SUM(A1:A10,A25:A50,A77:A100,A51:A76,A11:A24) although you probably wouldn't want to).

If you're wondering about those colons in the previous example, that is how to specify a **range** of cells in a spreadsheet. By giving two single cells separated by a colon, that tells the spreadsheet to use all of the cells inside the rectangle with those two cells at opposite corners. Thus, A1:A5 has five cells (A1, A2, A3, A4, and A5), C3:D4 has four cells (C3, C4, D3, and D4), and E24:D22 contains six cells (D22, D23, D24, E22, E23, and E24, though conventionally we usually specify a range giving the top-left cell first and the bottom-right cell last, and the spreadsheet program may even helpfully reorder this for you once you type it in). Additionally, you can specify an entire row or column by omitting the other: =SUM(A:B) adds together everything in column A and column B, and =SUM(3:3) adds everything in row 3.

You might notice that when there is a RAND() or RANDBETWEEN() somewhere in your spreadsheet and you edit or modify a different cell, the number changes. That's because every time you make any change to the sheet, it recalculates everything (this is why any cells with other functions like SUM() update immediately if you change the cells they're referencing, too). To force a recalculation—that is, to roll the dice again without having to modify cells—simply hit Ctrl+R in Google Spreadsheets.[2] This can be useful when you just want to use a Monte Carlo simulation and repeat it several times to make sure that your results are falling in a sufficiently narrow range.

Statistical Functions

On the subject of Monte Carlo simulations, there are some other functions that are often useful. If you need to take the average (mean) of a large set of numbers, one thing you can do is SUM() them all and then divide by the

---

[2]Other spreadsheet programs may have a different control for this. For example, in Microsoft Excel, you would hit F9. In Numbers for iOS, a hotkey doesn't exist, so you might just enter bogus data in a blank cell or make a checkbox in a cell and just toggle it by clicking on it. If you're in an unfamiliar spreadsheet program and want to figure out how to do this, "Recalculate Cells" is the search term you want to use to find it online.

number of things you're adding. That is the mathematical definition of the mean, after all. However, this can be prone to error if you ever add more cells, which throws off your count, and then you have to remember to go back and adjust the calculation. An easier way is to use the AVERAGE() function. Like SUM(), it takes any number of parameters which are all cells or cell ranges, and it averages all cells that contain numbers (and, conveniently, ignores cells that are blank or contain text or other non-numeric data—so if you have all of your data in a single column like column C, and the only thing in that column is your data and a header row, you can take the mean with =AVERAGE(C:C) instead of having to give an exact cell range, and you won't have to update anything if you add more rows of data).

What if you have a lot of data rows and you're not sure how many there are? Perhaps you have some exported playtest data from your game that you've loaded into a spreadsheet, and some rows are blank because they represent incomplete games or accidental crashes, but you'd like to get a sense of how many there are. The COUNT() function takes any number of cells or cell ranges as parameters, just like SUM() and AVERAGE(), except that COUNT() gives you the total number of cells with numeric data.[3]

While AVERAGE() gives the mean, there is also the MEDIAN() function which gives the median average (that is, the value within a group of values that would be in the center, if you sorted them from lowest to highest). And yes, there is also a MODE() function that gives the mode average (the value that appears the greatest number of times in the data set). Other useful functions include MAX() and MIN() which give the largest and smallest value in the set of values you give them, respectively, and STDEV() which calculates the standard deviation (which is harder and error-prone to calculate manually). All of these functions are like SUM() and AVERAGE() in that you can provide any number of parameters, with each parameter being a number, cell, or cell range.

One other function that can be useful when doing statistics and analytics is the CORREL() function. This takes exactly two parameters, each of which is a range of cells (and both ranges must have the same dimensions). It compares these two sets of cells, element-to-element, and gives the correlation coefficient: -1 if the two are perfectly inversely correlated, 0 if uncorrelated, and 1 if perfectly directly correlated.

---

[3] Weirdly, spreadsheets treat calendar dates and times of day as numeric data, so if you have a column with some dates and some numbers and you try to SUM() or AVERAGE() them, you get some very strange results! These cells are also tallied in the COUNT() function.

Conditional Functions

Often, you want to test if the value of a cell meets a certain condition (for example, rolling a percentage chance of success using RAND() and then having a separate cell that determines whether the roll succeeded). For this kind of situation, the IF() function is both useful and versatile. IF() takes three parameters. The first is a **Boolean** (true or false) expression, usually a comparison of one thing to another; the second is a value to return if the expression is true; and the third is a value to return if the expression is false. Some examples are given as follows:

- =IF(A2>4,1,0) checks to see if cell A2 is greater than 4; if it is, this formula is 1, otherwise, it's 0. This form of comparison is common in situations where, for example, you want to see how many items meet certain criteria.
- =IF(B5="Fire",C5," ") sees if the value in B5 is the text "Fire" (note the quotation marks, which differentiate text from numbers). If it is, then this formula is equal to whatever is in cell C5. Otherwise, the cell shows up as blank (a pair of quotation marks with nothing between them denotes an empty cell). Note that if we changed "Fire" to "" in this expression, it would check to see if B5 was blank. You might use this to set certain stats for all enemies that have a certain elemental affiliation, for example.
- =IF(C1>=3,IF(C1<=6,15,0),0) returns 15 if the value in C1 is between 3 and 6 inclusive, and 0 otherwise. Notice how we can have an IF() inside another IF(), which programmers refer to as **nested** ifs. While this looks fancy and complicated, really all that is happening is that all three parameters of IF() can be expressions or formulas, not just numbers.
- Another way to do that last one is using the logical function AND(), which takes any number of parameters and returns *true* only if they are all true, and *false* otherwise. The expression in the previous example could be rewritten as =IF(AND(C1>=3,C1<=6), 15,0). Other useful logical functions are OR() (returns *false* only if all of its parameters are false and *true* if even a single one is true) and NOT() (takes a single argument evaluates it to *true* or *false* and then returns the opposite).

In a Monte Carlo simulation, you'll often be repeating some IF() trial many times (usually one per row), and what you'd like to do is add up the results.

For example, if you have a random die roll that results in either success or failure, you might want to know the average success rate. One way to do this would be to have a column that uses IF() with the success criteria as the first parameter, 1 for success and 0 for failure, and then in another cell, you would take the AVERAGE() of that column to calculate the rate of success. However, there is a more compact way to calculate something like that: the COUNTIF() function. This function takes two parameters: the first is a range of cells, and the second is some Boolean criteria that's used to test each cell in the range. COUNTIF() then gives a count of all cells in the range that meet the given criteria.

The syntax for the criteria is tricky. If you are just checking if it's equal to a value, simply provide that value (if it's text and not numeric, enclose the text in quotation marks). If instead you are comparing the cell to a value or an expression, enclose the entire expression in quotes. Some examples are given as follows:

- =COUNTIF(A:A,5) looks at the entire column A and counts the number of cells with the exact numeric value of 5.
- =COUNTIF(A:A,B2) looks at column A and counts the number of cells that match the value of B2.
- =COUNTIF(B3:D5,"x") examines the nine cells B3, B4, B5, C3, C4, C5, D3, D4, and D5 and counts the number of them that have exactly "x" as text.
- =COUNTIF(C:C,">=14") counts the number of cells in column C that have a value greater than or equal to 14.

What if you wanted to count all cells that did not meet your criteria? Subtract the COUNTIF() from COUNT() of the same range. For the first example above, =COUNT(A:A)-COUNTIF(A:A,5) would give the number of cells in the column A with any numeric value that was not 5.

While COUNTIF() returns the number of cells that meet a criteria, occasionally you may want to sum the contents of the cells that meet your criteria. To do this, use the SUMIF() function, which has the same parameters as COUNTIF(). For example, suppose you're simulating a combat against an armored enemy, where all damage of 3 or below is ignored (but higher damage goes through normally). If the combat round damage results are in E2:E6, then the total damage would be =SUMIF(E2:E6,">3").

Monte Carlo vs. Brute Force

When trying to do probability computations for your game (see Chapters 17–18), there are three ways to figure out the chance of a player finding the Extremely Rare Item on your loot drop table, or what have you. You can use probability theory to add up all the possible ways to do the thing, all the ways to do *anything*, and divide the former by the latter. You can use a Monte Carlo simulation, where you just make a few thousand random die-roll attempts and see what they average out to. Or you can brute-force the problem, laying out every possible result and counting them.

Of these three, novice designers tend to overuse the Monte Carlo method. While it's a powerful tool, it's also the only one of these three that does not give an exact answer, but an approximation (that will change every time you Recalculate Cells). Using probability theory is ideal, if you have the knowledge to do so. If you don't, as inelegant as it seems, an exhaustive brute-force analysis is often the easiest way.

As a simple example, if you're rolling 2d6, there are only 36 possibilities, so it's not terribly hard to write each possibility out manually and add them all together. In many ways, it's less trouble than doing a Monte Carlo simulation of 2d6 for several thousand rolls, and it even gives you an exact solution instead of Monte Carlo's approximation. Enumerating every single possibility seems like an admission of naivete, and most programmers would flinch at the idea of it, but it can be practical and is a useful tool in the game designer's toolkit.

Things get a little harder if you have a greater number of possibilities, but it is often still very possible for most real-world problems that a designer encounters. To get a sense of the scope of the problem, just calculate the total size of the possibility space. For example, if you're rolling 7d4, the total number of possibilities is 4*4*4*4*4*4*4 (you can use a calculator, or just type =4*4*4*4*4*4*4 or =POWER(4,7) or =4^7 into a blank cell in a spreadsheet). This gives 16,384 possibilities, which seems like a lot to write out one at a time by hand… but a spreadsheet can easily hold that many rows, and there are a few tricks we can use to cut down the time considerably.

One way to do this is through the selective use of copy and paste, and the arrow, Ctrl, and Shift keys. Let us do this in columns A through G, starting in row 1 for simplicity (we should expect to end on row 16,384 if we do everything properly). We start by writing the numbers 1 through 4 in cells A1:A4. These numbers are repeated throughout the series. When you're done, the cursor should be in cell A4. Now move to the right (B4) using the right arrow key or Tab key after you type 4 in cell A4, and put a 1 in B4. Next, hold Ctrl down and press the up arrow, which jumps to the next value above… except the row is blank and there isn't one, so it just jumps to the top cell at B1. Put a 1 here as well. Now, hold Shift and Ctrl down, and press the down arrow. This selects everything down to the next value in B4.

Now, press Ctrl+D to fill down, and the intermediate cells B2 and B3 now hold the value 1 as well.

Notice how the cursor is still at the top of the range, in B1. Press the left arrow to move back to A1 (this deselects the range of B1:B4), and hold Ctrl+Shift+down arrow to highlight A1:A4. Next, press Ctrl+C to copy that range. Hold Ctrl (without Shift) and press down arrow to jump to the bottom of that range (the cursor moves to A4), and then press down arrow without holding anything else in order to go down one cell to A5. Now, Ctrl+V pastes a copy of the values from A1:A4 just below.

Now, to fill the column to the right with the value 2, first move to the bottom (Ctrl+down arrow) and then press right arrow to go to column B. Enter 2 here. Next, Ctrl+up arrow moves to the previous block of 1s, and then, down arrow moves to the first empty cell. Enter 2 here as well. Now, select every cell in between the bottom and top (Ctrl+Shift+down arrow) and then fill down (Ctrl+D) to fill the 2s. The cursor should now be in cell B5, at the top of that range. Left arrow moves it to A5, then Ctrl+Shift+down arrow selects A5:A8. Copy (Ctrl+C), then Ctrl+down arrow, and another plain down arrow to move to cell A9. Paste (Ctrl+V) to put the numbers in cells A9:A12. Repeat the process to add 3s to B9:B12 and then to paste 1-2-3-4 from A13:A16 and add 4s to B13:B16.

Now, all of that may have been a lot of work just to add values to 16 cells in two columns; you probably could have done that faster by hand, and in fact, you might have started out that way. Keep in mind, though, that this method scales to any size. Now, you can add 1s to cells C1:C16, then copy A1:B16 down to A17:B32, then add 2s to cells C17:C32, and so on until all cells down to row 64 are complete. The rows now contain every possible result of rolling 3d4. Adding a third die took just as much time as adding a second die, even though you added a total of 12 new rows for your second die but 48 rows for your third die.

Repeat the process with column D, filling data down to row 256, and you have 4d4. Keep going with columns E:G, and you'll have 7d4, all 16,384 possibilities, in just a few minutes.

If that seems like a method that's too "brute force" and not mathematical enough for you, an alternative would be to use a formula. In column A, create the numbers 0 through 16,383, through any method you like. Then, use the following formulas in the first row and then fill down to the bottom:

- Cell B1: `=MOD(A1,4)+1`
- Cell C1: `=MOD(FLOOR(A1/4),4)+1`
- Cell D1: `=MOD(FLOOR(A1/(4^2)),4)+1`
- Cell E1: `=MOD(FLOOR(A1/(4^3)),4)+1`
- Cell F1: `=MOD(FLOOR(A1/(4^4)),4)+1`
- Cell G1: `=MOD(FLOOR(A1/(4^5)),4)+1`
- Cell H1: `=MOD(FLOOR(A1/(4^6)),4)+1`

What's going on here? The MOD() function takes two parameters, divides the first by the second, and gives the remainder.[4] The B column simply takes the remainder of each number in A after dividing by 4—which gives the sequence 0, 1, 2, 3, 0, 1, 2, 3, 0, 1, 2, 3, and so on. Since d4s range from 1–4 and not 0–3, we add 1 at the end, which makes the sequence 1, 2, 3, 4, 1, 2, 3, 4, repeating for all rows. This also makes it clear why we start counting at 0 and not 1 in column A: if we start at 1, the expression becomes 2, 3, 4, 1, 2, 3, 4, 1, … which would still ultimately contain everything we want, but would be out of sequence. It's easier to read if we start counting at 0.

---

[4] The name "MOD" is short for the word modulo which is the mathematical term for the remainder of integer division.

We want column C to also cycle between 1 and 4, but four times slower than column B. To do this, we first divide column A by 4, taking no remainder (hence the FLOOR() function). Alternatively, we could use the QUOTIENT() function, which works just like MOD() but returns the result of the integer division rather than the remainder: =MOD(QUOTIENT(A1,4), 4)+1. Column D has to do the same thing, but cycling four times slower than column C (and thus sixteen times slower than column B). Each successive column repeats the same pattern, but even slower. This method is even faster than brute force, but is more complicated and may require troubleshooting to make sure all the formulas work properly.

Sidequests

When dealing with either Monte Carlo simulations or brute-force calculations, things can be either fast or tedious, depending on how well the designer has honed their skills in this area. To practice your skills, it's time for a race! If you have one or more friends or classmates who are going through this book with you, gather everyone together, each person at their own computer.

Sidequest 31.1: 4d6 Brute Force Speedrun

First, do a Monte Carlo simulation of the probability that a 4d6 roll totals somewhere between 13 and 15, inclusive. This involves writing some formulas to calculate a single 4d6 roll and then either using IF() in each row to determine if it has the correct total and then AVERAGE() to find the mean of all rows, or else using COUNTIF() on all rows to calculate the frequency of this event in one shot. "Re-roll" a few times and take a guess as to what the true probability is. If doing this with friends, see if you all agree.

Then, figure it out using a brute-force approach. There are 1296 different ways to roll 4d6. Using Fill, copy and paste, or any formulas that occur to you, create 1296 rows, one for each unique 4d6 roll, and then perform the same calculation on these to get an exact solution. Typing 1296 separate rows in manually is error prone and slow, so find ways to do this that are as fast and error-free as you can think of. A spreadsheet expert would be able to do this in under 5 minutes; how fast can you go? (And, how close was your Monte Carlo guess, above?)

Sidequest 31.2: Correlation of Chance

Once you're done with that, let's take a closer look at the CORREL() function. You might have heard (from this book or elsewhere) that "correlation does not mean causation," but let's take a moment to examine what correlation *does* mean and how it appears in real-world data, to see why correlations can be useful but also misleading.

Start with a fresh spreadsheet and in cell A1, put =RAND() to choose a random number from 0 to 1. Fill Right to cell B1, and then in both columns, Fill Down to row 1000. We now have two sets of 1000 pseudorandom numbers, one set per column.

In some free cells, type: =CORREL(A1:A10,B1:B10) and =CORREL(A1:A50,B1:B50) and =CORREL(A1:A100,B1:B100) and finally =CORREL(A1:A1000,B1:B1000). In reality, of course, we know there is no true correlation; each number is an independent pseudorandom number, so there is no reason why a higher number in one list would cause the corresponding number in the other list to be higher or lower. You would expect a correlation of zero between the two lists. But you'll notice it is not exactly zero, because random variation causes some small correlation, if only by random chance. Press Ctrl+R a few times and see what the general range of each correlation is. For the 1000-sized list, the correlation tends to be very small, usually less than 0.05. The correlation between the first hundred elements may be as high as 0.1 or 0.2. With fifty elements, the correlation varies more widely, sometimes being close to zero and occasionally giving something very high (considering the source being a list of pseudorandom numbers)—maybe you'll even see a correlation above 0.5 (or below −0.5). With only ten elements, you might even see a correlation of 0.8 or higher (or below −0.8), making the two lists appear very strongly correlated one way or the other.

Now, what would you expect to see if you take STDEV() of a list of pseudorandom numbers that range from 0 to 1? Through some math that we need not go into at this point, the standard deviation of a uniform distribution from 0 to 1 (this is what RAND() is) is or $\dfrac{1}{2\sqrt{3}}$ about 0.2887. Is that what you get when you take STDEV(A1:A1000)? What about STDEV(A1:A10)? Repeat the same exercise with AVERAGE() and MEDIAN(), both of which you'd expect to be 0.5 but you'll see it varies slightly one way or the other.

To visualize what's going on here and what a correlation looks like, highlight all the cells in A1:B1000 (remember, you can hold Shift+Ctrl down while moving your cursor to select an entire block of cells) and create a

Scatter Plot, which will create a graph with 1000 points displayed (treating the pair in each row as a set of x, y coordinates). Now add a linear trendline and display the R-squared value. If you've forgotten how to do this, review the graphing part of Chapter 28. In this plot, you'll probably see a horizontal line with an R-squared very close to zero. Next, create similar plots but with only 10 or 50 pairs of points, see how those vary, and compare the R-squared values of your trendlines to the values you get from CORREL(). Try other trendlines, like polynomial or exponential, to see what those look like for completely random data.

The lesson you'll learn here is that you should be very careful to understand the nature of your data when correlations are found, and to not rely *too* much on curve fitting (especially if extrapolating beyond your current data set). Note, for example, that an exponential curve and a sigmoid (S-shaped) curve both look very similar when you're hitting that first initial hockey-stick-shaped upswing... but common sense tells you that, for example, the number of active players in your game can't be exponential (even if it's a good curve fit so far) because there are only so many people on the planet who can play your game, so it has to level off eventually!

32

Deck Shuffling

The choose operator is known in spreadsheets as the COMBIN() function. =COMBIN(60,7) gives the total number of 7-card starting hands drawn from a 60-card *Magic: the Gathering* deck, assuming all cards are distinct (you would have to take additional steps if some cards are duplicated in the deck, as is typical). The reason for the strange name is that drawing a number of cards from a deck without replacement where order does not matter is sometimes called a **combination** by mathematicians.

When order does matter, that is called a **permutation**, and the corresponding spreadsheet function is called PERMUT(). If you want the number of ways to select the top ten players out of a thousand (where the ordering within the top ten matters), you would use =PERMUT(1000,10). These are handy functions when you don't want to take the time to remember the mathematical formulas.

Aside from that, there are a few functions which are useful in simulating a random shuffle. We've already encountered RAND() which produces a pseudorandom number from 0 to 1. Additionally, there is a function called RANK() which takes two parameters: first, a value; and second, a range of cells. RANK() looks up the value within the range and tells you what position it is in, numerically: 1 if it is the highest number in the list, 2 if it's the second highest, 3 if it's the third highest, and so on.

Try this: in cells C1:C52, simply put =RAND() so that each contains a pseudorandom number. Then in D1, write =RANK(C1,$C$1:$C$52) and then fill down to D52. The D column now has the numbers 1 through 52 in a random order[1]!

---

[1]It is technically possible for RAND() to produce two of the exact same number, in which case you wouldn't get the numbers 1 through 52. However, this is exceedingly unlikely, so for quick-and-dirty simulation purposes, it is good enough.

That's fine if you have a deck of cards numbered 1 through 52, but what if you have a standard deck of cards instead? It would be nice to create some kind of lookup table that converts the numbers 1 through 52 into a set of actual cards. There is a function that does this, called VLOOKUP(). This function is a bit finicky; what it's meant to do is take a table (for spreadsheet purposes, a rectangular block of rows and columns), find a value in the leftmost column, and return the corresponding value in one of the other columns. It takes three parameters: first, a value ("key") to look up; second, the range of cells that comprises the table; and third, which column to return a value from once it finds the key in the first column. This third parameter is a number, where 1 means the leftmost column, 2 means the column just to the right of the leftmost, 3 is two columns to the right of the leftmost, and so on. But it always looks up the key in the leftmost column, so you cannot use VLOOKUP() with data sorted any which way; the data being matched must be on the left.

To illustrate, let's extend our card shuffler above that currently just randomizes the numbers 1 through 52. In cells A1:A52, write the numbers 1 through 52 in order. In cells B1:B52, write the names of the 52 cards in a standard deck (you may wish to abbreviate a single number or letter for the rank and suit, e.g., "AS" for Ace of Spades, "TC" for Ten of Clubs, and "5D" for Five of Diamonds).[2] This gives you an unshuffled "deck" of cards in column B.

If typing 52 cards manually seems tedious to you, there is an easier way. Off to the side in cells J1:J13, write the ranks of the cards: A, 2, 3, 4, 5, 6, 7, 8, 9, T, J, Q, K (or however you prefer). Copy and paste that a few times so that you have four sets of ranks from J1:J52. Then, put a suit (C, D, H, or S) in K1 and Fill Down to K13, and repeat the process with the other three suits down to K52. Now, reading columns J and K together, you have a suit and rank. Next, in cell B1, instead of writing the name of the card, combine J1 and K1 as follows: =CONCAT(J1,K1) and then Fill Down. This function takes any number of parameters that are cells, ranges of cells, or data, treats each one as a string (that is, a series of characters) and sticks them together in order as its own string. If you wanted to get fancy, you could write the ranks and suits out as complete words (Queen and Hearts, for example) and then use =CONCAT(J1," of ", K1) to have the card show as "Queen of Hearts."

---

[2] If you want to get fancy, in Microsoft Excel, you can even use Insert Symbol... from the Insert menu, to use characters corresponding to the four card suits. Google Spreadsheets does not have this functionality; however, if you create that symbol in another program, you can Copy and Paste into the spreadsheet.

Now, in cell E1, write the following: =VLOOKUP(D1,$A$1:$B$52,2) and then fill down to E52. This takes the value in D1 (one of the randomized numbers from 1 to 52), finds the corresponding sorted number in column A, and then finds the card name right next to that number in column B (the third parameter is 2, meaning look at the second column in the data range, which in this case is column B). Column E now has a shuffled deck of cards!

If it bugs you that VLOOKUP() requires your keys to all be on the left, there is an alternative, using a pair of other functions. MATCH() is a function that looks up the position of a key within a range of cells that is either a single column or row. Its first parameter is the key that you want to look up, and the second parameter is the cell range. If it finds the key in the topmost or leftmost position, it gives a value of 1; if it's the one just below or to the right of that, it gives a value of 2; and so on. There is an optional third parameter, which determines what to do if the key is not found. The third parameter can be 1 (the default if it's omitted), which assumes the list is sorted in ascending order and returns the closest position without going over if the key is not found; or it can be −1 if the list is in descending order and you want the opposite; or it can be 0 if the list is unsorted and you're looking for an exact match only. Usually, you'll want to use 0. MATCH() is helpful in looking up a key in an arbitrary position (as opposed to the leftmost position).

The other function that goes with MATCH() is the INDEX() function, which takes three parameters. First is a range of cells. The second parameter is 1 for the topmost row, 2 for the next to top row, and so on. The third parameter is 1 for the leftmost column, 2 for the column just to the right of that one, and so on. For example, INDEX(A1:D4,2,3) gives the contents in cell C2, because that is the second row from the top and third column from the left in that cell range. INDEX(E3:G5,3,1) gives the contents in cell E5, because that is the third row from the top and the column on the left within the block of E3:G5.

We could, therefore, simplify our earlier spreadsheet. Starting over, put the 52 card names in cells A1:A52. In cells B1:B52, use =RAND(). In cell C1, write =INDEX($A$1:$A$52,RANK(B1,$B$1:$B$52), 1) and then fill down to C52. We don't even need MATCH() in this case, although it can come in handy if, for example, you're looking up some item in a loot drop table.

If you just want to show a shuffled deck of cards, it may bother you that you have four other columns' worth of data that could confuse someone else. By selecting one or more rows or columns (by clicking on the headings) and right-clicking, one of the options is to Hide Rows or Hide Columns. Try selecting columns A through D, and Hiding them—they look like they're gone now, and all that's left is your glorious shuffled deck. You can see a small right-arrow symbol in the header of column E, to indicate that one or more columns are hidden just to its left. If you had only hidden columns B through D, you would also see a left arrow in the header of column A, showing that one or more columns to its right are hidden.

In practice, avoid hiding if you can. It is very easy to not notice hidden columns or rows (your only indications are one or two tiny triangles, plus a gap in the lettering of columns or numbering of rows). Copying and pasting across a hidden range of cells is error-prone and may not give you the results you expected, and if you are writing a formula that references a range of cells that crosses a hidden range that you didn't notice was there, you may have errors and not understand why until you realize there's something hidden there. If you absolutely must hide your data to show a cleaner spreadsheet, you may find it easier to put the intermediate data on a separate worksheet, and have your formulas reference the cells on that worksheet (we cover how to do that in Chapter 33).

Why bother mentioning Hide functionality if you're being cautioned not to use it? Because at some point, you may be looking at someone else's spreadsheet that has hidden rows or columns, or you might accidentally hide some of your own data when you meant to select something else from the right-click menu, and it's useful to be able to identify and correct. If you want to access those hidden cells, just click on that tiny arrow in the row or column header and they all reappear.

Loot Drops

In many games, the player runs around beating up monsters for gold, experience, and loot; if the stuff that comes out of a defeated enemy is randomized, that is referred to as a **loot drop**. Game designers construct loot drop tables to determine which loot will drop from which enemies and at what frequencies. This can be simulated in a spreadsheet.

A loot drop table functions similarly to a deck of cards, except that in most cases, each individual drop is independent of the others, so the "deck" would be shuffled every single time. Building a large deck shuffler (as above) just to get a single drop from the first entry is overkill, and also impractical if you wanted to simulate multiple drops at once since you'd have to do multiple shuffles in order to keep the drops independent of each other.

There is another, easier way to do this, using a powerful function called INDIRECT(). This function takes a single parameter, a string, and it takes that string and interprets it as if it were a cell reference instead. For example, =INDIRECT("B3") is the same as simply writing =B3. In this case, however, we can build our own custom string in order to select one of a random range of cells.

Try this: create a table of six different pieces of loot, in cells A1:A6. These can be anything you want: 1000 Gold, the Artifact of Untold Awesomeness, a coupon for 10% off at the general store, whatever. Now, in cell B1, we're going to select one of these items at random. Enter this formula: =INDIREC T("A"&RANDBETWEEN(1,6)).

The ampersand (&) in this formula takes two strings and sticks them together (this is called **concatenation**; different spreadsheet programs have different names for functions that concatenate strings, but all of them allow & to build a string out of several smaller strings without a function). So, what this is doing is generating an integer between 1 and 6, attaching an "A" in front of it so that we get something between A1 and A6, and then using INDIRECT() to take the value of that particular cell. If you wanted to do multiple drops, you could simply take this formula in B1 and Fill Down.

You can likewise use concatenation to build strings from component parts. For example, consider this table.

	A	B	C
1	Flame	Sword	of Haste
2	Ice	Dagger	of Stunning
3	Lightning	Mace	of Health
4	Sharp	Staff	of Strength
5	Dull	Flail	of Agility
6		Hammer	

We can create a random weapon as follows:

```
=INDIRECT("A"&RANDBETWEEN(1,6))&INDIRECT("B"&RANDBETW
EEN(1,6)) &INDIRECT("C"&RANDBETWEEN(1,6))
```

This formula takes one element from each of the first three columns and sticks them together. Put an extra space at the end of each word in column A and at the beginning of each entry in column C so that you don't end up with "IceDaggerofStunning." Note also the blank cells in A6 and C6, so that you might just get a "normal" weapon.

Up to this point, we've assumed each entry in a loot table has an equal probability of being chosen, like individual cards in a deck, but what if you want some items to be more common or rare than others? There are a few ways to do this.

The simplest is to include multiple entries for the more common drops. If you have one common drop that you want to fall 60% of the time, a rare drop that should fall 30% of the time, and an epic drop that the player gets 10% of the time, you could make a list of ten items with six of them being the common drop, three being the rare, and one being epic.

What if you have probabilities that don't have nice round numbers? Maybe your analytics team has determined that your common drops should happen 55.79744% of the time for optimal monetization, and your tech team has told you that a loot table with 10,000,000 different entries would take up too much memory so it would be impractical in the extreme. What then?

In this case, we can use VLOOKUP() in a different way. Consider the following loot table.

	A	B
1	0	Common
2	0.65	Uncommon
3	0.95	Rare
4	0.99	Legendary
5	0.999	Epic

The numbers in column A are cumulative percentages, so that if we generate a random number between 0 and 1, anything between 0 and just under 0.65 is Common (so 65% of the loot will be common), anything from 0.65 to 0.95 is Uncommon (30%), anything between 0.95 and 0.99 is Rare (4%), anything from 0.99 to 0.999 is Legendary (0.9%), and anything higher than 0.999 is Epic (0. 1%).

In order to choose a rarity from this weighted table, use the following formula:

```
=VLOOKUP(RAND(), A1:B5,2)
```

This generates a number between 0 and 1 and looks it up in the A column, by default choosing the highest number without going over. It then returns the corresponding item in column B.

Sidequests

Sidequest 32.1: Shuffling a Deck

Let's practice shuffling some cards. In *Magic: the Gathering*, a typical deck has 60 cards, some of which are spells (which help win the game but must be paid for in mana) and lands (which typically provide one mana each per turn to power spells). Only one land card can be played each turn, and mana does not carry over from one turn to the next, so the amount of mana a player has available on any given turn is either the current turn number or the number of lands they have drawn so far, whichever is less.

Assume that a player is using a deck with 20 land and 40 spells, and that they draw seven cards as their opening hand at the start of the game and then one card on each turn. Simulate a single shuffle of this deck and then calculate the turn number when the player first reaches 6 mana. Recalculate the cells (Ctrl+R) a bunch of times; what seems to be the average turn? (You may wish to simply copy and paste your data a few hundred times and take the average of those results.)

Sidequest 32.2: Poker Probabilities

Time for some practice with COMBIN() and PERMUT(). Calculate the probabilities of some or all five-card *Poker* hands drawn from a standard 52-card deck:

- Pair (two of the five cards are the same rank)
- Two Pair (four of the five cards form two pairs of different ranks)
- Three of a Kind (three of the five cards are the same rank)
- Straight (all five cards have consecutive ranks, such as 2-3-4-5-6; Aces are high, so A-2-3-4-5 does not count)
- Flush (all five cards are of the same suit)
- Full House (three of the five cards are the same rank, and the other two cards are a pair)
- Four of a Kind (four of the five cards are the same rank)
- Straight Flush (all five cards have consecutive ranks, and are of the same suit)
- Royal Flush (T-J-Q-K-A of the same suit)

Be careful not to double-count: for example, A-A-A-A-K should not count as Two Pair, even though it is technically two separate pairs of Aces. Also note that there are some *Poker* hands that contain none of the above, so if you add up all of these hands, you get less than the total number of all possible five-card hands.

Sidequest 32.3: Automated Game Design

Using concatenation and INDIRECT(), try making a random game idea generator! Create several columns in different categories (perhaps one for genre, one for setting or theme, one for platform, etc.—use your imagination), and populate each column with several options. Then choose one item from each column to build a single string that describes a random game idea. Next time you feel like doing a game jam, bring out your random game idea generator and use it to give yourself a random constraint!

33

Organizational Formatting

Until this point, we have focused mostly on the functional aspects of spreadsheets. In those situations where we've focused on the aesthetic elements, we have done so mostly for the purpose of making the spreadsheet easy to maintain. In short, we have approached spreadsheets as if they were a programming language: we treat each cell as a variable and each formula as code.

But code itself is rarely the front end of a program. Spreadsheets, on the other hand, are often not only the code but also the user interface. When designers complete their spreadsheets, they do not compile it to an executable; rather, they share the spreadsheet with other people, who then look at the sheet directly. For this reason, proper formatting of spreadsheets may serve a similar purpose to using a consistent coding style, but the author of a spreadsheet is given many more tools for this purpose.

In this way, proper and consistent formatting is more than just making your spreadsheet look nice. It serves the practical purpose of making it much easier to navigate your spreadsheet, find the data you're looking for, and make changes or additions without making as many mistakes. Spreadsheets aren't just about storing data and calculating formulas; they're about communicating the results of those calculations back to you (or others on your team), so learning how to get your spreadsheets to communicate clearly can be critical and save you a lot of time and headache.

Working with Worksheets

Sometimes, you have multiple elements of a spreadsheet that are related but separate, and it's nice to put them in different areas. For more complex sheets, putting everything in a single spreadsheet in different areas can get a bit unwieldy and difficult to navigate. If, for example, you have character stats in A1:E10, a weapon list in J1:L30, armors in N1:P30, accessories in R1:T30, the XP/level curve in A15:B55, and secondary stat lookup tables in F40:M80, all that information is important but hard to look through or organize in a cohesive way on a single sheet. You could simplify things by hiding columns and rows, but as pointed out in the previous chapter, it's not always obvious what is hidden (or even that anything is hidden). A better way is to use multiple worksheets in the same document.

If you look at the lower left corner of the below figure, you see three things: a plus sign, an icon with a bunch of lines, and a tab named "Sheet1" by default.

If you double-click on the name Sheet1, it highlights and you can give it a more meaningful name (you can also find the Rename option on the sheet's menu, if you click the downward-pointing triangle on the sheet tab).

To add a new sheet, click the + icon. You can add as many sheets as you need, generally one per purpose. To navigate to a different worksheet, you can click on its tab at the bottom, or you can click on the icon with all the horizontal lines and select the worksheet from the list there. Or, to go to the next or previous worksheet in sequence, hold Ctrl+Shift and press PgUp or PgDn.[1] If you want to reorder the worksheets to make it easier to navigate in this way, simply click and drag one sheet left or right to the desired new position.

You may wonder, why bother creating multiple **worksheets** (those are the tabs) in a single **spreadsheet** (that's the entire document containing one or more worksheets) instead of just creating multiple spreadsheets? If the various worksheets are completely separate, that may be the best thing to do, but if

---

[1] Every spreadsheet program has hotkeys to navigate to the next or previous worksheet, though they vary from one program to the next, so if you aren't using Google Spreadsheets, you should look that up to see how to do this in your own program. When going back and forth between tabs a lot, it's much faster to use a keyboard shortcut than to go back and forth with the mouse.

you want the cells on one worksheet to reference the cells on another, that is much easier to do in a single spreadsheet than to try to get one spreadsheet file to reference an entirely separate document.

To reference a cell in a different worksheet within the same spreadsheet, use the worksheet name followed by an exclamation point and then the cell name. For example, if you are in the Character tab above and want to look up the value in cell B5 in the Weapons tab, you would write =Weapons!B5. If you forget the syntax, you can also just type the equal sign, then click on the Weapons tab and click on cell B5 to select it, and then hit Enter, and it fills in the target cell or range of cells for you.

Note that cells in other worksheets can also be named by either absolute or relative references. If you write =Weapons!B5 and fill down a few rows, you see =Weapons!B6, =Weapons!B7, and so on in the next cells down. If instead you write =Weapons!$B$5 and fill down a few rows, you'll see =Weapons!$B$5 in all of the other cells.

If the worksheet name has any spaces in it, you must enclose the name in single quotes. In the above sheet, if you wanted to access cell A3 of the Leveling Curve tab, you'd have to type ='Leveling Curve'!A3 and if you forget the quotes it will give you an error.

Cell Formatting

In the toolbar, there are a variety of buttons, most of which involve changing the appearance of any cells that are currently selected:

- The buttons near the left that format cells, change how data is presented: as currency with a dollar amount, as a percentage with a percent sign, as a decimal shown to a chosen number of places, or others such as a formatted date or time (selectable through the drop-down "123" button).
- To the right of the format buttons, you can choose the font and font size. These are not used often because you can zoom in or out to change

the size of everything.[2] However, it can sometimes be useful to make the font in some cells larger for emphasis, especially if you increase the width of the column or height of the row as well.

- Past the font formatting, the text in cells can be **bolded**, *italicized*, or ~~struck through~~ (it can also be <u>underlined</u> by pressing Ctrl+U). Other options such as alignment and word wrapping are available in the Format menu.
- You can also change both the color of the text and the color of the background. Note that changing these to the same color makes the text invisible.
- Finally, you can add a border around either a single cell or a rectangular block of cells. The border may go all the way around or only affect one side, and it can be thick or thin. You may, for example, select a column and then add borders on the right side only in order to draw a solid line between that column and the one to its right. Or you might draw a thick border around a block of cells to outline it, visually isolating it from the rest of the sheet.

In addition to making the worksheet look pretty, formatting can be used to make the sheet much easier for another person to understand and use. As one example, consider the different types of cells you may have in a spreadsheet (the following is not an exhaustive list):

- **Data**: constant words or numbers that are hardcoded. Examples might be the names of each weapon in the game or the numeric stats of all the enemies.
- **Inputs**: fields that are meant to be modified by hand in order to get additional results. For example, perhaps you haven't yet settled on the costs or stats of some military units in a strategy game, but you have a formula that tells you if a given unit is above or below the curve. In that case, the costs and stats are fields that the designer is meant to modify and play around with until they get things balanced.
- **Calculations**: intermediate formulas that depend on other fields, such as data or inputs. It's often useful to break up one complex formula into several simpler steps—it makes the formula easier to troubleshoot if there are problems and makes it easier for another person to understand what is going on.

---

[2]In Google Spreadsheets, there is no "zoom" command; instead, just use the zoom in/out functionality of whatever Web browser you are using. In other spreadsheet programs, there is typically a zoom feature in the View menu, or through one or more keyboard or mouse shortcuts.

- **Controls**: a special kind of input field that is used to control which of several other things happen. For example, in a card game, you might have different cost curves for different card types. The card type could therefore be a control field, where the balance formulas use an IF() function to determine which formula to use based on card type.
- **Outputs**: the final calculations that you may care about.

However, all of the above are still just cells, and by default, they look the same. Here is where formatting can be used to make functionality obvious. By using different background colors for each type of field consistently throughout your sheet (and perhaps throughout all spreadsheets that you do, ever—the spreadsheet designer's equivalent of "coding style" for programmers), you can denote which fields the viewer is expected to mess around with, which fields they should ignore, and which fields they should look to for answers. For example, calculation fields can use a light gray background with dark gray text (similar to how unselectable menu options in many programs are grayed out), in order to signal the viewer that these fields should not be changed and can generally be ignored. By making input cells bright yellow or a similar color that stands out, or adding a thick border around them, you imply that the viewer can and should modify these values. Making output cells bolded can draw attention to their importance; you might color them their own special color as well or even use conditional formatting to modify their colors based on the final values (e.g., changing the background to red for an item that is far off of the cost/power curve).

Using borders and background color shading can also be used to divide and organize a worksheet into functional sections. For example, if making a sheet to compare the costs and benefits of cards in a trading card game (TCG), you might make the cost columns one background color and the benefits another color. If there are several types of benefits (perhaps core stats, passive special abilities, and activated special abilities, or some other logical grouping), you might color them all different shades of the same color, in order to visually show that they are distinct but related.

You can also use comments to describe functionality (much like adding comments to code in a programming language). You can either do this by commenting individual cells (in which case it is up to the viewer to move the mouse over the cell to read the comment) or by typing text into some cells directly (as with a header row or column, or else a "notes" field for each game object). A little text to explain what is going on can go a long way to making a spreadsheet easy to use and understand.

Data Validation

For input cells in particular, it can sometimes be useful to limit the values to something reasonable. One way to do this is through data validation. Select a cell or block of cells, then click the Data menu, and select Data Validation. You can also right-click a cell and select Data Validation from that menu. This opens a popup menu where you can tell it which cells are being validated, what the criteria are (is the input a number within a range of values, or a value from a list that is contained elsewhere in the spreadsheet, for example), and then what to do if the data ever becomes invalid (showing a warning or rejecting the change entirely). You can also use validation for calculated fields, when troubleshooting, if you know that a certain calculation is supposed to be within a given range (such as a probability always being between 0 and 1).

Data validation can also be used to create a dropdown list of values within a cell, useful for input cells where you only have a few options and want to make sure the user doesn't type the wrong thing. To do this, use "List of Items" as the criteria.

Simply enter the different values the field can be separated by commas. Or, if the different values already exist in the spreadsheet elsewhere, you can use "List from a Range" and give it the cells. Make sure the "Display in-cell button to show list" is checked. Click Save, and the affected cell or cells now contain a clickable arrow, which then opens up the list of options to select from:

Long Text

Sometimes, you'll want to store large amounts of text in a single cell: card or rules text, character dialogue, quest descriptions that players can see, or designer notes or other text that's internal to the development team. For text-heavy cells, there are several ways to format text fields that may be useful. Text fields like this tend to take more room than the small size of a cell would allow. If you have a cell with longer text than the cell accommodates, it displays normally, appearing to stretch across further cells in that row, so long as they are blank.

The text in the above example is still all in cell A1; cells B1:E1 are blank. Now, if one of them had data added to them, the text in A1 would be truncated on its display.

As you can see, even though the rest of the text in A1 is no longer displayed, it is still considered part of the contents of the cell.

Suppose instead you want to force all the text to display. You can change the width of the column (click the division between two adjacent columns and drag it to resize) to allow for more horizontal space, and you can also Merge Cells (described in Chapter 30) to allow a single piece of text to display in a larger cell.

Additionally, you can turn on Word Wrap, which forces the column height to be tall enough to support all of the text. To do this, select the relevant cell or cells and then click on the Format menu, and then choose Text Wrapping > Wrap (you can also use the text wrap button on the menu bar).

Note that if you have a very long text string, this may make the column even taller than the screen! In that case, you may want to widen the column as well.

This can be useful if, for example, you want a large cell that contains documentation, rules text, or similar. If putting something like that in your spreadsheet, it won't be long before you wonder if you can add a carriage return to break up the text in a single cell into several paragraphs. And you can: just hold Alt and press Enter.

Named Formulas

Another thing you can do to make your formulas more meaningful is to give them a name. After all, which of these is easier to understand at first glance, for a formula that's calculating damage: =BaseDamage*Multiplier-TargetArmor or =$D$7*$C$1-$F$7? Well, actually, that depends. The former is certainly more meaningful, but the latter tells you where the data being referenced actually resides, so it is a matter of taste. But you *can* give names to individual cells, or even entire ranges of cells, and use those names in your formulas.

To do this, click the Data menu and select Named Ranges:

This brings up a tab on the right that lets you define a range of cells (this can also be a single cell) along with a name for it. Note that since the cell or cell range is named, this is treated as an absolute (not relative) reference; copying and pasting or filling down/right doesn't change the named reference.

Sidequests

Sidequest 33.1: Human or Robot?

This chapter covered a lot, so let's start by reviewing some techniques we've learned in previous chapters and then extend it with multiple worksheets.

Suppose we flip ten fair coins in a row, so that each flip is either Heads or Tails. Start by doing a brute-force enumeration of all 1024 possible results of ten flips, one per row, using the first ten columns (one per flip); review

Chapter 31 if you've forgotten how to do this. In the next column(s) over, calculate the size of the longest run of Heads or Tails. For example, the sequence
HTTHHHTTHH would be 3 (the run of three Heads in a row in the middle of the sequence), while TTTTHHTTTH would be 4 (the four Tails at
the start), HTHTHTHTHT would be 1 (there are no runs of two or more in
a row), and HHHHHHHHHH would be 10 (ten Heads in a row).[3]

You can then use COUNTIF() on the column that tracks the maximum
streak in order to get the probability of a maximum run of 1, 2, 3, and so on
up to 10. Do so, confirm that the sum of all ten probabilities is 1, and then
plot them on a graph to see what the probability distribution is like and how
often you'll see a maximum streak of each length.

Now, create a second worksheet. On this sheet, use RANDBETWEEN()
to choose a pseudorandom number between 1 and 1024, and create ten cells
and use INDEX() or INDIRECT() to pull up the ten coin flips in the row on
the first worksheet that correspond to the RANDBETWEEN() result—for
example, if the number is 412, find the coin flips in the 412th row. Finally,
display the maximum number of heads or tails in that row, which you've
already calculated in that row.

Format the coin flips on this second worksheet to make it clear that these
are output fields that shouldn't be modified.

Elsewhere on the same worksheet, include ten coin flip input fields that
should be entered, and format them appropriately to make that functionality
clear. For each, use data validation to make sure each one is Heads or Tails
(or "H" or "T," or however you formatted it originally). You can either reject
all bad inputs or create a dropdown list for each field.

Now, calculate the maximum run of Heads or Tails for the ten input coin
flips, in the same way that it was computed on the first worksheet for all 1024
rows there. Use whatever formatting you see fit (colors, borders, or what have
you) to make it clear that the maximum run is a computed output field that
should not be modified, but that is important for viewing.

Finally, using either an extra text field with an IF() function or conditional
formatting, highlight whichever of these two rows—the one from the pseudorandom coin flips or the one from the human-entered input fields—has
the higher max streak (choose arbitrarily if there's a tie).

Now, find a friend. Instruct them to think of ten "random" coin flips in
their head, without flipping any actual coins. Enter those into the input field

---

[3]There are many ways to do this. One way is, if the data is in A1:J1024, let columns K through T
keep track of the cumulative number of Heads or Tails in a row. Column K can always be 1. Column L:
IF(B1=A1,K+1,1), and then fill right and down from there. Then in cell U1, use MAX(K1:T1) to get the
highest run in that row, and fill down.

for the human-generated coin flips. The machine-generated coin flips will, of course, appear in the other output field. As discussed in Chapter 20, most humans are terrible at acting randomly, and the row with the highest max streak is probably the computer's best guess for which of the two rows was truly random and which was made by a human trying to be random. Was this "AI" correct in its guess? Try it with several friends and see how often it's correct!

Sidequest 33.2: Word Cloud

To practice text formatting, try using Merge Cells, Word Wrap, carriage returns after each letter to make some words appear vertical,[4] and a variety of fonts, font sizes, and formats to make a word cloud that looks cool. Fill every cell with a background color such that you don't see the gridlines any more. Here's a small example of a set of words related to game design.

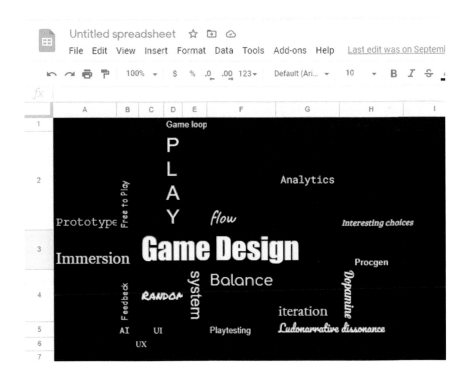

---

[4] Most spreadsheet programs will let you change the orientation of text so that it displays sideways or at an angle, but it's done differently in each. In Google Sheets, you can do this in the Format menu under Text Rotation; in Excel, you can right-click on a cell and Format Cells and then select the Alignment tab and look for Orientation.

34

Times and Dates

One thing we have not addressed so far is date formatting. Days and dates aren't particularly useful for most game balance tasks (unless you're dealing with timestamped analytics data from your game server), but it can be very useful for organizing your work, time, and schedule. While it is usually producers/project managers and not game designers tasked with scheduling and budgeting in larger game companies, for smaller projects (or even just to keep oneself organized, personally), the designer may come up with their own schedule. Spreadsheets offer a number of useful features to assist.

TODAY() is a useful function that requires no parameters and gives the current date, normally displayed in a date format such as mm/dd/yyyy (you can change the appearance with cell formatting, the same way that you would change the display of a number).

On its own, TODAY() doesn't do much—you can probably look at a corner of your computer screen to see the current date (and time, for that matter)—but it becomes far more useful when you realize that addition and subtraction work exactly as you'd expect for dates (subtraction, in particular, gives the difference between two dates, as the number of days between them). As such, if you have a future date as the deadline for a task, subtracting TODAY() from that date gives the number of days remaining before the deadline, and adding a number to a date gives that many days after the date (for example, =TODAY()+7 gives the date for a week from today). You can also use these in comparisons: =IF(G7<TODAY(),"OVERDUE","") is blank, unless the date in G7 happened in the past, in which case it says "OVERDUE."

If you organize tasks by week, the WEEKNUM() function takes a single parameter of a date and gives the number of the current week within the year (from 1 to 53—the year is just a day or two longer than 52 weeks, so the final days are in week 53). If the WEEKNUM() of two dates is the same, that means they take place in the same week—at least, assuming they are also in the same year. If you want to check the year, there is a YEAR() function that takes a date as a parameter and gives the year as an integer.

If you organize tasks by month, the MONTH() function works the same as WEEKNUM(), except it returns a number from 1 (representing January) to 12 (representing December). If you want to count how many tasks are due in the current month, make a column that gives the MONTH() of each row's due date and then use COUNTIF() to count how many items in that column have the same value as MONTH(TODAY()).

A date in Google Sheets can contain the day/month/year, but it can also contain the time of day—there is no individual "time" format; it is just considered part of a date. To get the date *and* time, use the function NOW(), which works just like TODAY() except it contains the current hour, minute, and second in addition to the date. To separate out the individual time elements, you can use the functions HOUR(), MINUTE(), and SECOND() which each take a date/time as a single parameter and give back the number of the hour (from 0 to 23), minute (from 0 to 59), and second (from 0 to 59), respectively. Note that just like RAND() and RANDBETWEEN(), the functions TODAY() and NOW() only update when data is changed in the sheet or when you force a recalculation with Ctrl+R. In the File menu under Spreadsheet Settings, you can change a particular spreadsheet to recalculate automatically every minute or every hour (but not every second, nor "never, not even when a cell changes" so you'll have to find workarounds for those).

You can also use the TIMEVALUE() function, which takes the parameter of a date/time and gives the fraction of the current day that has elapsed (where 0 is midnight and 1 is 11:59 pm). To get the number of seconds elapsed, multiply this fraction by 86,400 (that's 24 * 60 * 60, the number of seconds in a day). If you want to do arithmetic with times of day, taking the difference between one time and another, or adding a number of seconds from one time to another, use TIMEVALUE()—if you try to do this with a date/time such as NOW(), it treats integers as days and not time of day. You can do this by adding fractions of a day, however; for example, =NOW()+0.25 gives the current date and time plus 6 hours.

Also on the subject of schedules and task lists is the desire to mark tasks as complete, so that they can be tracked over time or flagged when behind. Some spreadsheets support putting a checkbox in a cell, although Google Sheets does not (at least directly). A simpler alternative is to just have the user put something in the cell, such as an "x" or "*" to mark it as complete. Then, you might, for example, count the number of tasks that are or aren't done. We've already talked about the COUNTIF() function, which can tell you how many cells in a range match a specific value, but in this case, it's prob-ably easier to use to simply check how many cells are blank or non-blank, so that you can put any symbol you want (and not have to worry about, for example, the difference between "x" and "X"). To accomplish this, there are two functions, each of which takes a cell or range of cells as a parameter: COUNTBLANK() and COUNTA(). The former gives the number of cells in the range that are empty, and the latter gives the number of cells in the range that are not. There is also a function ISBLANK(), which takes a single cell as a parameter and gives TRUE if it is blank and FALSE if it contains anything—useful as the condition in an IF() function.

Sidequests

Sidequest 34.1

To practice the scheduling functions, create a spreadsheet with a task list of things you are currently working on, along with a deadline for each task that you can enter manually. Also have a column you can "check off" in some way to denote that the task is complete. Have the sheet calculate the number of days remaining before the task is due: have it be blank if the task is already complete, display the word "OVERDUE" if the task is incomplete and the due date is in the past, or display a number if the task is incomplete and the due date is today or in the future. Additionally, at the top of the sheet above the task list, create a cell to show the total number of incomplete tasks remaining and the number of tasks that are overdue.

Sidequest 34.2

To practice everything else covered in this section, create a spreadsheet imple-mentation of a simple idle game where the player starts at 0 XP and Level 1, and gains +1 XP per second. Create one cell that contains the current time/date via NOW() and another that contains the time/date when the character was first created (make this one an input field where you can just copy the NOW() cell and Paste Values to start it off). Create a triangular leveling curve where it takes some number of XP to reach Level 2, then progressively more XP to reach each successive level. In four other cells, compute the following:

- Current Level
- Current total XP

- XP to next Level
- A bar graph showing where the player is between the start of the current Level and the start of the next (where the graph would be empty when you just leveled up and full when you are just about to level up)

Use formatting to make the spreadsheet easy to understand.

Greater challenge: create clickable buttons in the spreadsheet that add 1 XP per click (your total XP would then be the sum of the XP added via clicking, and the XP added via time). Most spreadsheets support different ways of adding buttons and giving them functionality via a scripting language, but like graphs inside of cells, each does it differently. For Google Sheets, you start by clicking the Insert menu and selecting Drawing, designing the visual look of a button, and then clicking and dragging it inside the spreadsheet to put it where you want it, and then choosing Script Editor from the Tools menu to create a script that increments the value in a particular cell. This is highly advanced and technical functionality that is beyond the scope of this book, but can be found through reading the spreadsheet's own documentation if you want to take that extra step.

Ultimate challenge: implement a full idle game where the player can spend their XP to purchase powerups that increase the rate of XP gain from that point forward. Do not allow the player to spend enough to decrease their Level, but do give some kind of bonus per Level (perhaps a bonus to how many XP are gained per click). This may require several buttons, each with its own script.

35

Iterative Calculations

The user interface for all spreadsheets was clearly designed with the assumption that the users would be entering data or formulas into blank cells far more often than editing existing cells, because the default behavior if you start typing in a cell is to overwrite what's already there. All spreadsheet programs do have the means to edit an existing cell, however, so it's useful to learn how to do so in the program(s) that you use. You can always double-click on a single cell to edit, or move the cursor to a cell and then click in the formula bar above the top of the worksheet, but being able to navigate with keyboard only feels a lot faster and more efficient to most people than going back and forth between keyboard and mouse.

While this book has concentrated mostly on Google Sheets for its examples, there is one feature that appears in Microsoft Excel and OpenOffice Calc but not elsewhere, which can be useful for simulating incremental differences over time or over each turn: iteration. Before explaining this, we need to examine **circular references**.

A circular reference is where the formula in a cell references itself, or one cell references a second cell which then references the first cell, or any number of cells that reference one another in a circular loop. For example, if cell A1 has the formula =A2+1 and cell A2 has the formula =A1+1, that is a circular reference. Under normal conditions, this causes an error. After all, the cells are all supposed to recalculate at the same time, so two cells that depend on each other leave the question of which one updates first (or if they both keep going infinitely, how would the spreadsheet not get stuck)? Most of the time, if you create a circular reference it's by accident, so it is useful to receive a dire warning from the spreadsheet program letting you know that you screwed up.[1]

In Excel, however, if you go to the File menu, select Options, and then go to the Formulas tab, you can turn on Enable Iterative Calculation. This sets the maximum number of iterations Excel will attempt in order to resolve a circular reference.

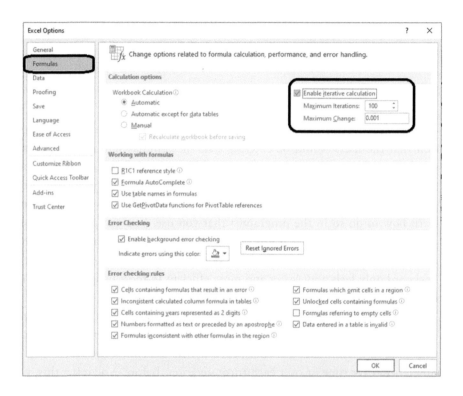

If you set maximum iterations at 100 and have cell A1 showing =A1+1, then every time you recalculate cells (by modifying a cell or pressing F9 in Excel, the equivalent of Ctrl+R in Google Sheets), the value in that cell increments by 100. If you set maximum iterations at 1, it only increments by 1, which is generally what you'll want if you enable this option.

This functionality can be useful for simulating turn-based or time-based effects in a single playthrough. For example, you can have the "turn" or

---

[1] In Microsoft Excel, a useful tool for tracking down circular-reference errors is to go to the Formulas menu, then select **Trace Precedents** or **Trace Dependents**. For the selected cell or cells, these options will show arrows pointing to which cells reference which other cells. There is similar functionality in OpenOffice Calc, but not in Numbers (iOS) or Google Spreadsheets at the time of this writing. If it is added later, the bolded terms in this note are what you would search for online.

"time" increment itself by 1 on each iteration and have other variables increment based on the game state (in other cells), also on each iteration. Imagine, for example, making an idle game where each iteration represents 1 second of game time, and the player's currency increments by their currency-per-second.

This could also be used to model player vs. player (PvP) games, such as fighting games, brawling games, MMOs, or MOBAs, to track things like character health and/or growth over time, especially when dealing with attacks that are timed or that have cooldowns. Consider having a global "timer" cell that tracks time elapsed and increments itself by one unit of time (in however much granularity is meaningful in the game). For example, an attack with a cooldown might be implemented as follows:

- Cell A1 represents a powerful attack that should always be spammed as soon as it's out of cooldown, marked with "X" if it is the next action and blank otherwise: =IF(B1>0," ","X").
- Cell B1 represents the amount of time left on cooldown, set to 10 when the attack is performed and decremented by 1 for every second elapsed: =IF(B1>0,B1-1,IF(ISBLANK(A1),0,10)).

If you had multiple attacks with cooldowns, you could have Cell A1 compute some kind of priority for this attack based on its utility, but only if it's not under cooldown (and a priority of zero if it is under cooldown, meaning it can't be selected in that case). Then, in a separate column, each cell would check to see if its own priority was equal to the MAX() of all priorities, and if so, it would trigger (and enter cooldown). You could also keep a global timer that just increments itself by 1 each iteration and then a move history where it would keep track of whichever move was chosen on the current time:

- Cell J1 as the global timer: =J1+1
- Cell K1 is a formula that contains whatever move is being performed this turn
- Cells L1:L20 contain the numbers 1 through 20
- Cell M1: =IF($J$1=L1,$K$1,M1) and then fill down to M20.

What if you are using Google Sheets, or another spreadsheet program that doesn't support iteration? Then, this kind of iteration is still possible, but requires a bit more room on the sheet, and a bit more copying and pasting. In this case, attempt to put everything necessary to track the game state in a single unit of time on one row. Then, have each row refer to the previous row. To extend the above example, let's assume the same situation, but starting with the initial game state on row 1 (this would be hardcoded and not contain formulas, since it is the fixed initial setup). On row 2,

- **A2**: `=IF(B1>0," ","X")`
- **B2**: `=IF(B1>0,B1-1,IF(ISBLANK(A2),0,10))`
- **J2**: `=J1+1`
- **K2**: a formula that contains the move being performed this turn
- **L2 and M2**: no longer necessary, as the record of moves being performed is now recorded in column K, one move per row (rather than being in a single cell that continually overwrites itself).

If the data for the game is too complex to fit on a single row in a way that's remotely readable, then you can spread it out on multiple rows and just copy and paste down. If it takes four rows to display the game state at a single point in time, for example, then the initial state is in rows 1:4, first turn after that is in rows 5:8, the next turn is in rows 9:12, and so on, with each cell referencing the relevant cells from the four-row block above where it resides. In this case, it may be worth adding a horizontal border at the top or bottom of each block, to make each game state visually distinct from the adjacent ones. Another alternative in this case would be to create four worksheets and spread the calculations throughout row 1 of each.

Sidequests

Sidequest 35.1: Rock-Paper-Scissors *AI Pair*

Implement a pair of randomized *Rock-Paper-Scissors* AIs playing against one another.

If you use a spreadsheet program that supports iteration: have cells A1 and A2 that use RANDBETWEEN(1,3), and cells B1 and B2 that convert the number to Rock ("R"), Paper ("P"), or Scissors ("S"), using a pair of nested IF() functions. In cell B3, choose the winner, again using a series of nested Ifs: display 1 for player 1 (row 1), 2 for player 2 (row 2), or 0 for a draw game. Then, in cell C1, have a timer that increments by 1 each iteration. In column D, list the numbers 1 through 30, sequentially. In column E, track the winners of the first 30 games, based on the "time" in C1 and the result in B3.

Greater challenge: also add a master reset button in cell C2: change all other formulas in C1 and column E to be blank if C2 is *not* blank, or have them proceed normally if C2 is blank. The user would manually set or clear C2 in order to reset the board and start again.

You may also wish to do the following in order to compare and contrast methods.

If you use a spreadsheet program that does *not* support iteration: columns A and B use RANDBETWEEN(1,3) as above, and columns C and D convert A and B into "R" or "P" or "S," respectively. Column E shows the winner of the game in the current row, and column F can be numbered 1 through 30 as the sequential number of the game on the current row. Fill down the first row for 30 rows.

36

Fancier Graphing

Copying and pasting is surprisingly versatile within a spreadsheet. For example, if you copy a single cell, then select several cells and then paste, it pastes the single cell's contents into all of the selected cells—an alternative to Fill Down/Fill Right that can work even on oddly shaped areas.

When copying and pasting a block of cells, there are two options that are sometimes useful for designers that are accessed by right-clicking and selecting Paste Special from the menu. The first of these is **Paste Special/Values**, which does not copy the formulas, but rather the values in the cells. For example, try this: put the number 1 in cell A1, then in A2 put =A1+1 and fill down for a few dozen cells. Now, copy all of those cells, then right-click on cell B1, and Paste Special/Paste Values Only. Column B now appears to be the same as column A… but if you look at the formula in A2, it still says =A1+1, but in cell B2, it simply says 2. If you then copied and pasted, say, B10 to D10 on its own, it would still show the value of 10, rather than B9+1.

One use for this is to "lock down" values that are constantly recalculated, such as those that use RAND() or RANDBETWEEN(). Normally, you want these to keep re-rolling every time a cell is updated, but if you want to preserve a particular roll (perhaps you're using a sheet to roll the stats for a character for a tabletop RPG and want to just roll once and then keep the results permanently), simply copy and then Paste Special/Values.

Another useful feature is **Paste Special/Transposed**. Imagine if you're working on a chart, and after getting a lot of data in there, it occurs to you that you should have organized it so that what you have in rows are in columns (and vice versa). This comes up often when creating charts and graphs, for example, if you realize that everything is sideways. Luckily, this can be easily fixed. You can swap rows and columns while preserving all of the data and formulas by copying a rectangular block of cells and then doing Paste

Special/Paste Transpose. If, for example, you copy a 3×4 block of cells and paste the transpose, it shows a 4×3 block.

You can also paste just the formatting of a cell in the same way, if you want to, for example, create a new block of cells that you want to be formatted the same as a different block, and don't want to spend the time selecting borders, background colors, text colors, and so on individually by hand again. Another handy tool is the **format painter** in the toolbar.

To use this tool, first have a single cell highlighted by your cursor that you want to copy the formatting from. Then, click the button. Once you've done that, click another cell, a row or column heading, or click and drag to select a range of cells, and everything you selected will have the formatting copied from your original cell. You can also "paint" the formatting this way by selecting a group of cells, and the spreadsheet will treat it as if you're copying and pasting the formatting of the cells together as a group. This is also sometimes the easiest way to *remove* formatting; for example, to remove all special formatting from an entire worksheet, simply select an empty unformatted cell, click the format painter button, and then click the top left corner of the spreadsheet in order to select the entire spreadsheet. In just three clicks, all the formatting is removed.

Graphing Options

Another feature that has more options than when it first appears is graphing data on charts. We have made some simple charts before (as a reminder, highlight some data and then select Chart from the Insert menu), but you can do a lot to improve the appearance and visualization of a chart.

By right-clicking anywhere on the chart area, you have access to many options.

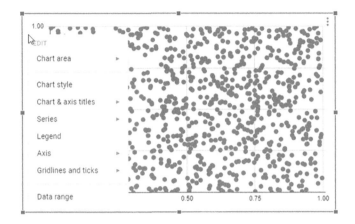

From the main right-click menu, you can add a title to the top of the chart. It's useful to get in the habit of doing this. In spreadsheets with several graphs, the title alone can make it clear which is which; additionally, if the graph is ever taken out of the context of the sheet itself, having a clear label can help to explain what it is. Likewise, the Axis submenu allows you to add labels on the horizontal and vertical axes of the graph, and again it's good to always label these for clarity. The Axis submenu also lets you change the range of numbers on the horizontal and vertical axes; the spreadsheet's default values aren't always what you want (for example, if you have values ranging from 0 to 1, it might decide for some reason to have the axis go from 0 to 1.2).

The Series submenu lets you change the appearance of a **data series** (that is, a single set of data on the chart—each chart can have many separate series, each with its own color and appearance). For points on a scatter plot or line graph, you can change the color, size, and shape of the points for a series, for example. If the data series being used isn't what you intended, or if you want to add another data series on the same graph, you can do this through right-clicking Edit (on the chart) and then selecting Series in order to bring up the Chart Editor sidebar with the selected series selected. If the Chart Editor is already visible on the screen, you can edit an existing series by selecting the Customize menu, then Series; or you can add a new series by selecting the Setup menu and clicking Add Series.

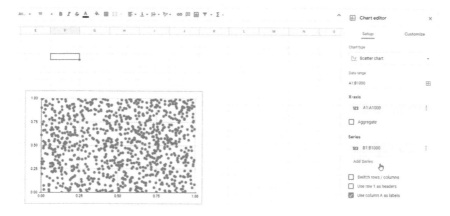

From there, you can edit the range of cells that the data series is drawing from, or you can add one or more new series by giving it a cell range.

Kinds of Charts

There are a number of visualization tools worth exploring within spreadsheets. We have already encountered the scatter plot, which lets us draw pairs of (x, y) points on a coordinate grid. Another visualization tool is the line graph. While a scatter plot just shows pairs of points where the ordering doesn't matter, a line graph shows a series of points in succession, allowing you to track one value going up or down as another value changes (for example, looking at how DAU changes over time, or how the average length of a game session changes compared to character level). To create a simple line graph, highlight data within a single row or column. Then, select Chart from the Insert menu, and choose the line graph.

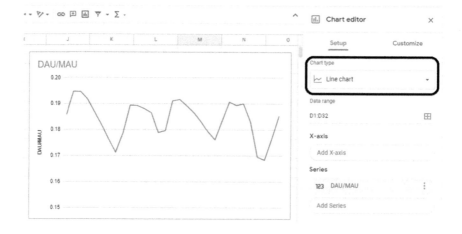

This might be fine in some cases, but more often you'd like the x-axis to be labeled with corresponding data (dates if you're graphing DAU over time, for example). In this case, you'll need *two* rows or columns, making sure that the one on the top (or left) is the x-axis headings. Then, check the "Use row (number) as headers" box if your data is in rows, or the "Use column (letter) as labels" box if your data is organized in columns.

If your data is unsorted, your graph will look like the tangled mess above, where it attempts to connect the dots in order. The simplest way to fix this is to just sort everything by your header row or column first, but you can also force the x-axis labels to be put in order by checking the "Aggregate" checkbox.

If you have several sets of data that you'd like to display on the same chart, follow the same steps as before, but put each data set in its own row or column, and select all of them.

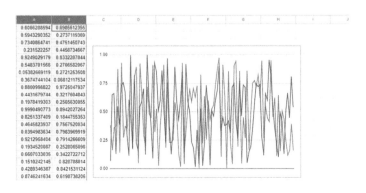

Also of use is a **bar graph** (Google Sheets refers to this as a **column chart**), which is created the same way as a line graph, except you select Bar Graph from the menu. Bar graphs and line graphs show essentially the same data—one or more series of points graphed on the *y*-axis for each spot on the *x*-axis—but a line graph makes it easier to track changes to *y* as the *x* variable changes (such as changes over time or changes with respect to player level), while a bar graph puts more visual weight on the relative height of each column, so it is more useful for side-by-side comparisons of several data sets on a point-by-point basis.

In some cases when graphing data, you may want to show not just the data but also the standard error, as a way of visualizing how reliable the data is. Generally, if you have two data points whose error bars overlap, that means they are not statistically significantly different; also, in general, small error bars are an easy way to see that the data is highly reliable, while large ranges of error indicate that reality may be significantly off from what the data show and you should therefore not put too much confidence in this data set. To show error bars, after selecting the chart type, click on the Customize tab, then Series, and you'll see the option to add error bars (you can do this with both line and column charts). You can set error bars to be a percent of the value, a constant amount from all values, or several other things. If you know your standard error, for example, you might calculate that and then use it as a constant error bar.

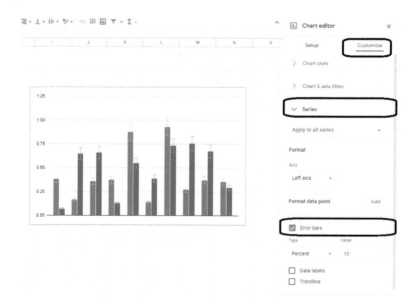

Lastly, you might notice that when you insert a chart that it tends to take up a lot of space and obstructs the view of part of your spreadsheet. What if you wanted instead to have a lot of graphs, perhaps one line graph per row of data when you have 50 rows? You might want to do this when your data isn't very granular, you're looking for general trends, and there are a *lot* of graphs that you'd like to compare side by side. For example, if each row represents the player population within a different zone in an MMO over time, and there are several dozen zones, it may be easier to put a single population-versus-time graph in a single cell at the end of each row so that you can see all of the zones in a single column on a single screen, as a bird's eye view of where the heaviest populations are. Or, if you're balancing a list of game objects along a cost curve, you could show each object's power level relative to the others.

To add a chart within a single cell, you don't go to the Insert menu. Instead, in the target cell, use the SPARKLINE() function. This function is somewhat complicated because of its versatility. You can specify all kinds of options, including range, color, axis information, and what type of chart it is. SPARKLINE() takes two arguments. The first is simply the data range. The second is a set of options, enclosed in {curly braces} with each option expressed as the option name, then a comma, and then the value for that option. If you include multiple options, they are separated from each other with a semicolon.

There are many options, so if you want something specific, it may be easiest to simply look up the online help for the function. But the one you'll need to know for most of your charts is "charttype" which is the option that specifies what kind of chart you're embedding in the cell. Values are "line" for a line graph or "column" for a column chart, among others. For example, here is what a line graph looks like for a series of random data.

Sidequests

Sidequest 36.1: Tiny Graphs

In one column, write multiples of 5 (a linear function). In the second column, write out the first ten triangular numbers, starting at 1 and ending at 55 (a polynomial function). In the third column, write 1.5 raised to the power of 1 through 10 (an exponential function). In the fourth column, use the formula =RANDBETWEEN(1,50) ten times (a uniform pseudorandom function). Graph all four on the same line chart.

Then, for each column, create a SPARKLINE() that shows a line chart for that column only.

Note how whenever you recalculate the cells, that random column keeps changing, as does its graph. Select those ten RANDBETWEEN() cells, then Paste Special/Values in the same place, replacing the formulas with fixed values. Note how when you press Ctrl+R to recalculate cells, the "random" column no longer changes after that.

37

Matrix Functions

In this book, we cover a few situations that involve matrix multiplication, particularly in Chapters 22 and 25. While there are other software packages that specialize in matrix operations, it is possible to do these in a spreadsheet. This is not the simplest thing to do in spreadsheets (at times, it can be downright unwieldy, and this is definitely a more advanced-level task), but it can be more convenient if the rest of your work is in a spreadsheet so that you don't have to deal with exporting data back and forth between different programs. With that said, let's get started.

Let's start by taking a matrix and multiplying it by a column vector. The result of this multiplication is another column vector, where each entry is equal to its row in the matrix multiplied by the column vector; to multiply a row by a column, multiply the first item (leftmost or topmost) of the row by the column, then the next item, then the next, and add all of these products together. For a 3×3 matrix and a 1×3 vector, the formula for the multiplication looks like this:

$$\begin{bmatrix} a & b & c \\ d & e & f \\ g & h & i \end{bmatrix} \begin{bmatrix} x \\ y \\ z \end{bmatrix} = \begin{bmatrix} ax + by + cz \\ dx + ey + fz \\ gx + hy + iz \end{bmatrix}$$

Matrices are, conveniently, blocks of numbers and formulas laid out in a square grid, so we can treat each element of each matrix above as a cell in a spreadsheet, using the matrix and vector on the left as input fields that the user can mess around with, and the resulting column vector on the right as an output field that is calculated by formula.

Implementing a Markov Chain

As an example, let's compute a Markov chain in a spreadsheet (see Chapter 22 for more details). This is where we start with a transition matrix that gives us the probability of switching between several states, where the state we're transitioning *from* is in each column, and the state we transition *to* is in each row. We can also SUM() each column to make sure it adds to 1, since we are always exactly in one state at a time. Then, in another column over, enter the initial state as a column vector (which should also sum to 1). If, for example, we take the simple state machine example from Chapter 22 where State 1 always moves to State 2, State 2 has a 50/50 chance of moving to States 1 or 3, and State 3 has an equal chance of changing to any state (including itself), this would look like.

To get the entries for one half (in column C), you could enter 0.5 or =1/2. For the entries of a third (column D), enter =1/3 rather than typing the decimal, to avoid rounding errors.

Now, to keep track of the number of transitions elapsed, we put 0 in G1 (because that is our initial state) and then want to put 1 in H1, 2 in I1, and so on; one way to do this is to put =G1+1 in cell H1 and then highlight a bunch of cells to the right (start at H1 then hold Shift+right arrow about twenty times or so), and then fill right (Ctrl+R—that's right, the same hotkey that recalculates cells with RAND() in them).

What about calculating the new column vectors? Remember, here we want to multiply the first row (B2:D2) of the transition matrix, piecewise, by the column vector (G2:G4) to get the first entry in the next column vector (H2). We might be tempted do this manually here, entering =B2*G2+C2*G3+D2*G4 into cell H2, and following suit for every other row and column. Actually, since we would *like* to fill down in the current column and fill right across all other columns, we would want to use absolute and relative references selectively: for each row in the matrix, the columns B, C, and D are fixed (we do *not* want to be multiplying by any other columns, although the row varies from 2 to 4), and the reverse is true for the column vectors (in H2:H4, the formula contains G2:G4, so the columns 2, 3, and 4 are fixed), so we would actually need =$B2*G$2+$C2*G$3+$D2*G$4. And it works if you put that in H2, then fill down (Ctrl+D) to H4, and then fill right (Ctrl+R) for 20 rows or so. You can also fill right on row 5 to confirm that the total of each subsequent column vector remains 1.

However, this method can get a bit unwieldy for larger transition matrices, such as the one in *Chutes & Ladders* that we also examined in Chapter 22. Would you really want to manually type in 82 multiplications? Could you do it without making a single error (or could you easily track down errors if you made them)? There is another way; it is a little more complicated, but well worth it to save time.

What we would like to do is take the sum of the piecewise products of $B2:$D2 and G$2:G$4, but ($B2:$D2) * (G$2:G$4) doesn't work, for starters because those two ranges are different shapes (one has dimensions of 1×3, the other 3×1). Luckily, spreadsheets have a function TRANSPOSE() which flips horizontal to vertical orientation and vice versa, similar to Paste Special/Transpose (covered in the previous chapter), so we can do TRANSPOSE($B2:$D2) * (G$2:G$4), except that doesn't work either—it gives a series of three cells, each of which is the product of one of the cells in that result. We would like to sum them together: =SUM(TRANSPOSE($B2:$D2)*(G$2:G$4)) which is the correct formula, but *still* won't work, because by default a spreadsheet doesn't know how to multiply a cell range by another—that operation isn't defined. There is, however, a way to get around this: treat each cell range as an **array** instead of a cell range. Multiplying one array by another works exactly the way we want it to here. In order to do this, enter that formula, but instead of hitting Enter, hit Ctrl+Shift+Enter. In Google Sheets, this then appears as =ArrayFormula(SUM(TRANSPOSE($B2:$D2)*(G$2:G$4))). You can also use the ArrayFormula() function[1] manually instead of using the keyboard shortcut. And finally, this works, and you can fill it down and to the right to see each transition.

---

[1] Be aware that ArrayFormula() is specific to Google Sheets; other spreadsheet programs use a similar (or same) hotkey but represent this differently in the actual formula (Excel, for example, puts {curly braces} around the formula instead). This can cause problems if exporting from Google Sheets and importing into another spreadsheet program, so be prepared to fix this manually if you do so.

In this particular case, there is no final state; it just keeps bouncing around indefinitely. However, in other situations (such as our example from Chapter 22 of calculating the average number of turns to reach the final square in *Chutes & Ladders*), there is a final state, and we might be trying to compute how long it takes to reach the final state, on average.

The median number of transitions is simply the first transition where the probability goes above 0.5. You can simply label the final state's row in the column vectors "Median" since this is essentially the cumulative probability that the final state is reached, so once it reaches 0.5, that means half of the games take longer and half take less time, so that one value is the median number of turns before reaching the final state.

To get the probability that you transitioned into the final state in each transition and not a prior transition, subtract the probability of being in the final state in the current column vector from that of the previous column vector. To find the mode (that is, the transition with the greatest probability of reaching final state at that specific time), first find the maximum value among these probabilities, using the MAX() function. This tells you what the highest value is, but not which transition; to find the location of the column, use the MATCH() function, as described in Chapter 32.

To find the mean (expected value) number of transitions to reach the final state, you also use the probability of transitioning to the final state on each individual transition (this is the probability) but multiply it by the number of the transition (this is the outcome). Then, as with all expected-value calculations, sum all of the (probability * outcome) products together. If the probabilities are in cells H6:ZZ6, for example, and the transition count is H1:ZZ1, then again you could do =ArrayFormula(SUM((H1:ZZ1)*(H6:ZZ6)).

Calculating a Payoff Matrix

To solve intransitive relationships (as described in Chapter 25), we first describe a payoff matrix that details how much a player is ahead or behind if they and their opponent each choose some combination of moves in a head-to-head game such as *Rock-Paper-Scissors*. We then multiply that matrix by a column vector that gives the probability of each move the opponent can do. The result gives the expected value of each move that the player might choose.

Here's what is actually going on mathematically: you have a payoff matrix (M) which is multiplied by a column vector of probabilities (c) and gives a column vector of payoffs (p). This can be written as

$$Mc = p$$

As detailed in that chapter, we know that the payoffs are all equal to one another so that p is just the same number repeated in every position. What number is that? Well, it can really be any number at all; by changing the number, we just multiply the final probabilities vector c by some constant. If we want the probabilities in c to sum to 1, we can scale p accordingly or just adjust our answer after the fact by dividing each element of c by the sum of all elements of c. One caution in this case is that we should not make p equal to all zeros, even in a zero sum game where the payoffs actually are zero. In this case, the only solution is typically for c to also be all zeros, which is technically accurate but not useful for our purposes here.

So, we know p, and we also know the payoff matrix M, but what we don't know are the probabilities of a player choosing each throw; we want to solve the above equation for c. If this were just basic algebra, we would divide both sides by M, which is really multiplying both sides by the multiplicative inverse of M. And that is, more or less, what we do here: multiply both sides by the inverse of M (mathematicians would write this as M^{-1}).

With matrices, the inverse is a little different than with basic multiplication: when a matrix is multiplied by its inverse, the result is the identity matrix I (1s along the diagonal and 0s everywhere else). This is the "identity" because it can be multiplied by any other column vector or matrix and the result is the thing you multiplied it by, unchanged (the same way that the number 1 is the multiplicative identity, as multiplying anything by 1 gives you the same thing you started with).

Thus, if we multiply both sides of the above equation $Mc = p$ by M^{-1}, we get

$$M^{-1}Mc = M^{-1}p$$

$$c = M^{-1}p$$

In other words, if we multiply the inverse of M by our payoff column vector, the result is our relative probabilities for each throw. How do we find the inverse of a matrix, though? Finding it by hand is a pain, and at that point, you may as well just solve the system of equations by hand and forget matrices entirely. But there are two helpful functions in spreadsheets that do the work for us. The first is MINVERSE() which takes a single argument, a cell range that is treated as a matrix, and returns the inverse. Of course, this on its own won't work, because a single cell can't hold an entire matrix. Additionally, we'll want to multiply that matrix by our column vector, which can be done with the MMULT() function, which takes two arguments, both cell ranges that represent matrices that can be multiplied together (in our case, the square inverse payoff matrix and the payoff column vector).

And then, as before, we hold Ctrl and Shift down and press Enter (or use the ArrayFormula() function in Google Sheets) to tell the spreadsheet to treat this as a single element of the output array and fill that formula down to cover an entire column vector.

For example, suppose our payoff matrix is in cells B2:D4, and our column vector with 1s in it is in E2:E4. Then in F2, use the formula: =MMULT(MINVERSE(B2:D4), E2:E4) and press Ctrl-Shift-Enter. The cells F2:F4 now contain your probability column vector:

This would be the solution for a *Rock-Paper-Scissors* game where wins with Rock count double. You may notice that the "probabilities" are massive, and certainly not between 0 and 1. We can fix this, again, by simply dividing each one by the sum of them all.

The other thing that might bug you is the slight rounding error that comes from cell C4. Why not just put the number 1 in there like it obviously should be? The answer is that some matrices don't have an inverse, so MINVERSE() returns a *#NUM!* error. If you get this error, then you can try changing one of the values ever so slightly, to see if it clears up the problem. If it does, then an exact solution can't be found through matrix inversion, but you can use other methods, or just use a tiny perturbation in any one cell to get something close enough that you can probably figure out the "real" solution (in the above case, 0.25/0.5/0.25).

Solvers

There is one other feature that isn't native to most spreadsheet programs, but can be used through some kind of add-on. The feature in question is a **solver**:

you give it one or more cells that it is allowed to modify, and another cell and a value you'd like that cell to become. It then tries to find some combination of values for the input cells in order to get the output cell to the desired value, or as close as possible. Different solvers work differently in terms of how they find the values, how much tolerance they have if an exact solution can't be found, and what parameters they offer, but it is generally worth your time to search the Web for this add-on.[2] You may not use it often, but there are times when you'll find the functionality to be a great time-saving measure, compared to having to solve a multi-dimensional system of equations by hand.

Sidequests

Sidequest 37.1: Trust but Verify

Take any of the examples in Chapter 22 that involve Markov chains, and replicate the findings in this book by doing the work yourself inside a spreadsheet.

Alternate challenge: Do the same for any payoff matrix solutions in Chapter 25.

Sidequest 37.2: Build a Matrix Auto-Solver

Create a general auto-solver for a 3×3 payoff matrix, but also implement a backup solution that converts the matrix to triangular form (see Chapter 25 for more on this). This may involve replicating the matrix several times, doing things one step at a time:

1. If the diagonals are all zero, find a row with a non-zero first element and swap its position with the top row.
2. If the cell immediately under the top diagonal is non-zero. If the top diagonal has a value of a and the cell under it is b, multiply the entire second row by $-a/b$ and then add each element to that of the first row.
3. Repeat this step for the bottom left cell in order to make that zero as well.
4. If the middle cell in the second row is zero, and the middle cell in the bottom row is not, switch the positions of those rows.

---

[2] For Google Sheets, click the Add-ons menu, select Get add-ons, and then search for the Linear Optimization add-on made by Google. There are other third-party solvers available which you can also explore. For other spreadsheet programs like Excel, you'll have to search for a solver on your own, but many exist, and any popular spreadsheet program has at least one available for free.

5. Using a similar method to above but with the middle and bottom rows, make the center cell in the bottom row zero by multiplying and adding to the middle row.

If a non-zero element cannot be found in step 1 or 4, or if the entire bottom row is all zeros after step 5, then the payoff matrix does not have a single solution, but rather an infinite number of potential solutions (as with the *Rock-Paper-Scissors-Jackhammer* example from Chapter 25). In any of these cases, it's sufficient to display an error to this effect. Otherwise, you now have a matrix in triangular form; now use formulas to solve it using substitution and proudly display the column vector of probabilities as your solution. Check this against the MMULT(MINVERSE()) solution to ensure they give similar values.

Greater challenge: Extend your auto-solver to handle 4×4 payoff matrices.

Ultimate challenge: Do some research on third-party Solver add-ons, and use one of them to guarantee a certain ratio of Rock to Paper to Scissors in the basic game, with the only modification being weights on the values of winning (but not introducing additional throws). For example, if you wanted players to throw 1 Rock for every 2 Paper and every 4 Scissors, what would each win have to be worth for every combination in order to produce that as the optimal strategy?

Appendix

Game Genres

We refer to many game genres throughout the course of this book. For those unfamiliar with these genres, here is a brief introduction to them, as well as a description of some of the games referenced. Genres are listed in alphabetical order.

Genre: 4X

This strangely named genre is a shortening of a description of the core game loop: eXplore, eXpand, eXploit, and eXterminate. Most games in this genre are turn-based strategy games played on a grand scale, where the player begins by simply exploring their surroundings and finding ways to produce basic resources, which they can then use to expand their empire (by building cities and upgrading them, and building units to further explore the unknown). These games often feature multiple interlocking systems: a light combat system where military units battle on the map (usually a simple die roll to determine wins and losses when they attack), an economic system, a tech tree to give the player access to more powerful units and city upgrades, and often other systems specific to the game. The game that popularized the genre is the *Sid Meier's Civilization* series.

Related to 4X games are **turn-based tactics** games, such as the *Advance Wars* series and *Wargroove*. These games lack the complexities of multiple systems and a tech tree, but they do have the four "X" elements: players begin with a series of military forces and use them to explore a map, take over strategic locations that give them resources, and use those resources to build additional military units.

Genre: Adventure

While many games are officially classified as "adventure games" in their own marketing or in genre descriptions, this category is overly broad and thus challenging to describe. In this book, we use the term to mean games that feature exploration as their core mechanic, though it is often mixed with something else such as a combat system. Examples include the *Legend of Zelda* series, *Tomb Raider* series, *Assassin's Creed* series, *Dishonored* series, and *God of War* series. Some of these are more action-oriented and have only light exploration (and might be properly called "Action-Adventure"), while others have more of a balance between the two. Games with only exploration and no combat at all would generally be classified as another genre, the walking simulator (discussed later in this Appendix). Meanwhile, the related genre known as **survival-horror** has similar core mechanics to other adventure games, but casts the player as relatively weak compared to the enemies that surround them, and focuses more on the player surviving through stealth, ingenuity, running away, and only occasional fighting; the *Resident Evil* franchise is one of many examples of the survival-horror genre.

Genre: Arcade

While these might more properly be called "action games" since the core experience involves fast action and reaction to avoid losing, all of the examples of pure action games used in this book originated in video arcade form. Arcade games mentioned in this book include *Crazy Climber*, *Gauntlet*, *Gravitar*, *Ms. Pac-Man*, *Pac-Man*, *Pong*, *Robotron 2084*, *Spacewar!*, *Space Invaders*, *Tempest*, and *Tetris*. Arcade games tend to be quite challenging and were designed that way intentionally because the arcade business model expected players to finish their game in an average of 3 minutes or less. As such, these games share much in common with "masocore" games (discussed later in this Appendix), but in that case, the games are designed to be difficult in order to provide an extreme challenge, as opposed to being difficult to force the player to lose and stop playing.

One subgenre of action-arcade games is the **shmup** (short for **shoot-em-up**) that involves the player moving their avatar and shooting all around them, generally while moving or scrolling in one direction or another. *Asteroids* and *Defender* are examples of early shmups, though the *Gradius* and *R-Type* series are better examples of the form. Shmups themselves have a further subgenre, the **bullet hell** game, so called because the main feature is a large number of enemies shooting an even larger number of bullets at the player, where the focus is on maneuvering their avatar rapidly to avoid getting hit; *Ikaruga* and *Raiden* were early games to popularize this form, and some role-playing games such as *Undertale* and *Nier: Automata* use bullet-hell mechanics as part of some of their combats.

Genre: Battle Royale

Battle Royale isn't technically a genre so much as a format or structure of play. Battle Royale games throw a large number of players (usually about a hundred) into a single chaotic free-for-all experience. Players that lose are eliminated and can restart a new match immediately (with a new set of opponents). While there can only be one winner, players tend to spend more actual time winning than losing: elimination happens quickly (and the player can immediately return to play again), while winning can take a bit longer since it involves besting 99 other players. While most games of this type are first-person shooters (FPSs) (*PlayerUnknown's Battlegrounds (PUBG)*, *Fortnite*), it is possible to use this format with something else, such as *Tetris 99* which pits a hundred players against each other playing competitive *Tetris*.

Genre: Free to Play (F2P)

This is also technically not a genre, but a business model. F2P games are, as the name suggests, free: players do not have to pay any money to download them and start playing. However, these games offer purchases inside of the game, and players are encouraged to spend money once they are actively playing. Some of these purchases are cosmetic in nature (buying fancy clothes to decorate your avatar), while others have gameplay effects (powerful weapons or items to improve a player's chances in combat against other players, or consumable limited-use items that give a player a temporary boost to help them get past difficult points in the game). The F2P model became quite popular on social media platforms like Facebook for a time (peaking around 2009–2010) and became the standard model for mobile/tablet games as well as many MMOs.

Some of the F2P games discussed in this book focus on competitive play between players (the browser game *Archmage*, the Facebook games *Mafia*

Wars, *Warbook*, and *Bejeweled Blitz*, and the mobile game *Clash of Clans*). Others were more social in nature and involved players building their own custom space and then visiting their friends (the Facebook games *FarmVille* and *Ravenwood Fair*). Still others are primarily single-player experiences, such as the action games *Diner Dash* and the similar *Gordon Ramsay Dash*; the **match-3** puzzle games *Candy Crush Saga*, *Puzzle & Dragons*, and *Merge Dragons*; and idle games *AdVenture Capitalist* and *Clicker Heroes*.

Genre: Fighting/Brawling

Fighting games, so called because of the *Street Fighter* series that popularized the genre (though there are many others in this genre, such as the *Mortal Kombat* series), involve two or more players each controlling a character and attempting to punch, kick, or otherwise land hits on their opponent while dodging or blocking to avoid getting hit themselves. Most games in this genre provide each player a life meter that goes down when they are hit, and reducing the opponent's life meter to empty is the goal. The games involve fast-paced action with lots of counterplay, as players are continually launching attacks and reacting to their opponents' moves.

An offshoot of this genre, sometimes just called fighting games but sometimes called **brawling** games to distinguish them (the series that popularized this sub-genre was *Super Smash Bros.*, and one of its more popular games was *Super Smash Bros. Brawl*), is a bit more chaotic, often allowing more players at once. The win condition is usually not to reduce the opponent's life to zero, but rather to knock them off of a floating platform, though connecting with more moves does make the opponent more susceptible to getting knocked out of the area.

Genre: First-Person Shooter (FPS)

The FPS genre perhaps takes the award for the clearest description in a genre name: the games in this genre all use a first-person camera view (the player sees things through their character's eyes directly), and they all involve running around, aiming, and especially shooting. Popular FPSs include the *DOOM*, *Gears of War*, *Halo*, *Half-Life*, and *Quake* series.

As the requirements for inclusion in this genre are relatively broad, there's a lot of design space to work in, and there have been many variants and hybrids that bring other gameplay elements into the FPS. Some games opt to be much more realistic military simulations (where just one or two bullets can end your life), such as the *Call of Duty* and *Modern Warfare* series. Some games add a stronger emphasis on story as well as character growth akin to RPGs, such as *Destiny* and the *BioShock* and *Borderlands* series. Other games focus on online team play, either cooperative (*Left 4 Dead* series) or competitive play against other teams (*Team Fortress 2*, *Overwatch*). Still others focus more on stealth than gunplay (*Thief: The Dark Project*, *Hitman* series).

Genre: Game Shows

Televised game shows involve contestants competing in a variety of tasks (sometimes cerebral, sometimes physical) for cash or other prizes. Since there are potentially millions of people watching at home (and hundreds more in a live studio audience), these games tend to be designed with an emphasis on being fun to watch; being fun to *play* is secondary (though many game shows do have home versions for people to play with their family). This book mentions two game shows, *Jeopardy!* (which focuses on trivia knowledge) and *Let's Make a Deal* (which includes some tasks that require knowledge of retail item prices, and others that are mostly psychologically trying to "read" the host's intentions).

Genre: Idle Games

Sometimes called "incremental games" (but referred to as "idle games" in this book), this is the genre that was never meant to be. The original idle game, *Cookie Clicker*, was initially designed as parody, mocking the progression mechanics of early-generation F2P games like *FarmVille* but eliminating virtually all of the gameplay, other than clicking on screen elements to produce resources (or, more importantly, to purchase automated resource generators). The game ended up being popular in its own right for its core advancement mechanic being compelling, and it spawned an entire genre of games with numeric progression at their core, such as *AdVenture Capitalist* and *Clicker Heroes*.

Genre: Masocore

Masocore is more of a description of the play experience, than an actual genre; masocore games can be any genre, so long as they are obnoxiously, ridiculously difficult. The core experience of masocore games is to throw up impossible-seeming barriers, so that the player can feel skilled and powerful when they overcome the challenge. Masocore games usually (but not always) feature very short play times before the player dies, but also don't set the player back very much so that they are free to try again. Masocore games exist in many genres: platformer (*Super Meat Boy, Celeste*), action/arcade (*Super Hexagon, Getting Over It With Bennett Foddy*), and Action-RPG (*Dark Souls, Bloodborne*) are mentioned in this book. While the genre is of course niche and limited to an audience that enjoys the extreme challenge, it is mentioned a lot in this book because it exists at an extreme end when dealing with balancing game difficulty.

Genre: Massively Multiplayer Online Game (MMO)

MMOs (sometimes MMORPGs since most of them are role-playing games, but in this book, we shorten the genre to "MMO" for brevity) involve a theoretically unlimited number of players all inhabiting the same world. Most games of this type are Action-RPGs, but designed for a large audience, and thus involve many kinds of systems: combat (solo, team co-op, and competitive), leveling, exploration, economic, and social, among others. As of this writing, the most well-known MMO is *World of Warcraft*, though in this book we also mention the much earlier *Ultima Online*, and the outer-space sci-fi world of *EVE Online*.

Related to MMOs are **Virtual Worlds** (sometimes abbreviated VWs) such as *Second Life* which feature an emphasis on social elements but do not inherently involve combat or leveling. as well as MUDs (short for "Multi-User Dungeon") which can be thought of as early-generation text-based precursors to MMOs.

Genre: Multiplayer Online Battle Arena (MOBA)

MOBAs are an extension of real-time strategy (RTS) and tower defense games that have two teams of players facing each other. Each player controls a single character, who they move around the world to attack AI monsters and opposing players. Eliminating targets gives them gold and experience, which they can use to upgrade their character. The ultimate goal of the game is to destroy the opposing team's base, located on the opposite side of the map, while protecting their own team's base. MOBAs mentioned in this book include *League of Legends*, *Heroes of the Storm*, *Defense of the Ancients 2 (DotA 2)*, and *Monday Night Combat*.

Genre: Party Game

Party games are meant to be played in a mid- to large-sized group, usually in person, and thus feature an emphasis on inter-player interactions. Because this genre is described by the audience and the situation they're playing in, the kinds of mechanics seen in this genre are broad. The hybrid digital board game/minigame collection *Mario Party* is one example of a party game; the cooperative music game series *Rock Band* is another.

One popular subgenre of party games, sometimes referred to as **hidden role** or **social deduction**, involves players each secretly assigned to one of several teams. Depending on the game and the role, players may or may not know who else is on their team, but through discussion and occasional outright accusation, players try to discover the teams of other players. The original game of this genre is *Mafia* or *Werewolf* (same game rules, just with different themes), where a small number of mafiosos (or werewolves) terrorize a village, eliminating one of the other players at a time; in between these murders, the rest of the players make accusations trying to find out who the killers are and, through majority vote, choose one player to eliminate (who may or may not be one of the killers). Many other games exist in this subgenre, including the popular online game *Among Us*.

Genre: Platformer

Platformers involve jumping, movement, and traversing a space as their core mechanic, as the player avoids both enemies and environmental hazards such as deadly falls or traps. The game that popularized the genre was *Super Mario Bros*.

This genre is highly diverse and has many subgenres. One of these is the **puzzle platformer** which focuses less on action skills and more on puzzle solving, through a combination of exploration and figuring out how to manipulate the environment. Two examples of these are *Braid* (which features a unique unlimited time-rewind mechanic) and *Inside* (where the focus is more on manipulating objects in the environment to progress).

Another popular variant of the platformer is the **Metroidvania** (named after two popular series of this type, *Metroid* and *Castlevania*, though ironically the *Castlevania* series had a number of games in it that were pure action platformers before it released an actual Metroidvania game). Other examples of this form are *Cave Story* and *Ori and the Blind Forest*, both of which featured combat and movement upgrades as well as more of an emphasis on emotional storytelling.

Genre: Roguelike

The Roguelike genre is named after the game *Rogue*, and as such designers and scholars will disagree on what *exactly* constitutes a Roguelike, but generally they involve turn-based movement (though there are real-time games that would call themselves Action-Roguelikes if not Action-RPGs) in a procedurally generated dungeon (thus, the player is always exploring a new space and can never simply memorize a game's map layout). The games generally are RPG-like, with combat and exploration as the core mechanics, as well as leveling and equipment systems. Enemies often drop random loot, adding to the player's anticipation as even a relatively minor enemy might occasionally drop a powerful item.

The first Roguelikes (*Rogue, Angband, Nethack*) were text-based and played on PC, though more recent games feature actual graphics and sometimes appear on console (*The Nightmare of Druaga*). While early Roguelikes (and "pure" Roguelikes) tend to be very long, with it taking dozens or even hundreds of hours to play through, they can be short, such as *Desktop Dungeons* where a single play can be completed in about 10–15 minutes. Early games in this genre were extremely punishing, with permadeath (permanently deleting the player's saved game if the player dies, forcing the player to restart from scratch if they make a mistake); more recent games tend to either unlock new functionality on death to make it feel like less of a penalty than a progression, or feature shorter play times so that the player dying doesn't set them back multiple hours to get back to where they were.

There are also many games that have Roguelike elements but that combine the feel of procedural generation and deadly combat with another genre. The first hybrid Roguelike was *Spelunky*, which was part Roguelike and part platformer, and was popular enough to encourage experimentation with other genres: *Rogue Legacy* (Roguelike/Metroidvania), *FTL* (Roguelike/Tactical Combat), *Dungeon of the Endless* (Roguelike/Tower Defense), and *Slay the Spire* (Roguelike/Deck-builder), to name a few.

Genre: Roleplaying Game (RPG)

RPGs are difficult to clearly define as a genre, but they tend to feature combat, an in-depth character progression system, and an emphasis on exploration and story. **Tabletop RPGs** (usually played in person) usually involve most players controlling a single character, while one player known as the **GM** (Game Master, essentially the lead storyteller, referee, and arbiter) controlling everything else. While tabletop RPGs often have many intricate systems for combat or other conflict resolution, they tend to be quite open-ended, where a player can describe in detail what their character is doing, and then the GM can make a judgment call about what happens. *Dungeons & Dragons* is perhaps the best-known tabletop RPG.

By contrast, computer/console RPGs (sometimes abbreviated **CRPG**) are much more rules-based, as the computer is acting as GM, often with just a single player controlling a character or a small group ("party") of characters. Among "pure" CRPGs, one could subdivide into two general styles. One of these, the Japanese RPG (**JRPG**) named after the country that popularized them, focuses much more on numeric systems, character leveling, and "grinding" (repeated combats to get more levels and in-game currency to buy better equipment) while keeping the overall progression between areas mostly linear so as to provide a well-crafted story; examples include the *Final Fantasy* and *Dragon Quest* (*Dragon Warrior* in the US) series. The other, the **Open-World RPG**, gives the player much less direction but much more agency to go wherever they will, and thus places more emphasis on exploration and an overall feeling of being one small part of a vast and epic world, where the player can choose their own objectives rather than following a script; examples include the *Wizardry*, *Fallout*, and *Elder Scrolls* series, and *Shroud of the Avatar* (a spiritual successor to the *Ultima* series).

Some games play like one continual RPG combat, played in real time, where exploration and combat are mixed; these are sometimes called **Action-RPGs** (**ARPGs** for short), as they focus more on action than a traditional RPG. Examples of ARPGs include the *Diablo* series (which popularized the form), *Dungeon Siege 2*, *Baldur's Gate*: *Dark Alliance*, *Bloodborne*, and most of the games from the studio Supergiant (*Bastion, Transistor, Pyre*). As many of these games involve procedurally generated dungeons, their core gameplay is closer to Roguelikes than RPGs, and you may occasionally find these called Action-Roguelikes, but the term **Action-RPG** is in more common use as of this writing.

Lastly, there are some games that focus much more on turn-based tactical combat and less on exploration. These are sometimes referred to as **Tactics**

RPGs, **Tactical RPGs**, or **Strategy/Tactics** games, depending on who is writing about them. Examples include *Final Fantasy Tactics*, the *Fire Emblem* series, *Mutant Year Zero*, and the *X-COM* series. Other games have Tactics RPG elements with some modifications: *Empire of Sin* combines this form of tactical combat with an empire-building sim, while *Into the Breach* mostly dispenses with the concept of leveling up and character progression in order to focus more on customizable character builds.

Genre: Real-Time Strategy (RTS)

Real-time strategy games (popularized by the *Warcraft* and *StarCraft* series) behave similarly to 4X games, but played on a much shorter time scale and, as the name would suggest, in real time. Players start on a map with a small handful of units that they can order to explore the nearby area. Some units can build structures that will let them build yet more units, upgrade units, or provide localized defense. Some units can mine the map for resources used in building. Other units are more military in nature and are used to attack the opponents' units and their base of operations. The goal is generally to wipe the opponent from the map.

Games in the RTS genre have often included mod tools that allow players to create rules modifications to the game and share those with the game community. As a result, several other genres have been created from what were originally community-built RTS mods, notably tower defense games and MOBAs (mentioned elsewhere in this Appendix).

Genre: Sandbox

Sandbox games, as the name implies, are characterized by giving the players a fun space to play in but not giving them much in the way of goals. The player can move around the world, interacting with things. While there may in fact be some goals or a storyline, the main focus is just on the joy of interacting with things: creating grand constructions and crafts in *Minecraft*, or creating total chaos in *Grand Theft Auto* or *Red Dead Redemption*.

Related to these are **Sim** games (short for simulation), which includes several subgenres including **city-builder sims** (*Sim City*) and **social sims** (*The Sims*).

Genre: Sports

Sports inherently involve competition (though many games do as well). Most sports are physical in nature (*Tennis, Baseball, Basketball, Soccer,* or *Football*—this last one is its own sport in the United States, and what Americans call *Soccer* is referred to as *Football* elsewhere; therefore, in this book we usually specify *American Football* to differentiate it). That said, some sports do not necessarily use a player's physical prowess directly, but rather through the use of tools or equipment (motor sports such as auto racing, or table games like *Pool* or *Pocket Billiards*), but are still generally referred to as sports.

Video game simulations of (real or imagined) sports are also referred to as being in the "sports" genre, although this is of course distinct from *actual* physical sports. Examples include simulated auto racing (the realistic *Gran Turismo* series that closely simulates the real-world physics of auto racing, and the more whimsical *Mario Kart* series that has players driving while also launching various traps, projectiles, and other hazards to slow their opponents), simulated two-on-two *Basketball* (the arcade game *NBA Jam*), and the various simplified versions of sports found in *Wii Sports*. *Rocket League* is an interesting case here: a video game that plays very similarly to *Soccer* except played with cars, in a way that would be impossible (or at least highly dangerous and impractical) if done in real life, yet still feels sports-like.

Other physical games, such as the playground game *Tag*, might not be considered a sport, mainly because they lack an ultimate goal (kids can play *Tag* until they're tired, but there isn't an actual win condition—they just run around chasing or being chased until they decide to call the game over or until an adult makes that decision for them).

Genre: Tabletop Games

The field of games that aren't video games is vast, and it's difficult to even find an appropriate term to refer to all of them; sometimes, they are called **non-digital** games (but this implies digital is somehow the default, even though these games have been around for thousands of years), **analog** games (as opposed to "digital"), **board games** (though many feature cards, dice, or other components with no board at all), or **tabletop** games (though they can be played in other locations such as the floor). In this book, when referring to these, we use the term **tabletop** as the lesser evil.

Tabletop games aren't a genre *per se*, and in fact, they can be subdivided into as many genres as video games are, although the genres are different:

- **Abstract strategy** games focus on strategic decision-making ("abstract" is added when there is no clear theme; examples include *Chess*, *Checkers*, *Go*, *Tic-Tac-Toe*, *Connect Four*, *Risk*, *Othello*, *Arimaa*, and *Backgammon*.
- **Auction** games center around bidding and auction mechanics. Perhaps the best example is *Modern Art* which features five different kinds of auctions, and players can act as both bidders and auctioneers; other auction games include *Medici* and *Ra* (both focused on bidding on a set of goods where some are more useful to some players than others), *Queen's Necklace* (where the prices of unpurchased goods get reduced every turn), and *Fist of Dragonstones* (a series of blind simultaneous bids where players are trying to both assess the value of what's up for auction, and how badly their opponents want it).
- **Card** games primarily involve a deck of cards, and thus, mechanics like shuffling, being dealt a hand of cards, and selecting and playing cards from one's hand are common mechanics. Some card games use a standard poker deck (*Blackjack*, *Bridge*, *Freecell*, *Poker*, *Slap Jack*, *War*), while others use a custom deck deliberately designed for that game: the trading and collection games *PIT* and *Bohnanza*, the **deck-builder** *Dominion* (similar to a TCG except players acquire cards during play and don't own a collection outside of the game), the **take that/screw-your-neighbor** games *Family Business*, *Nuclear War*, and *Plague and Pestilence* (where players generally play cards to attack or hurt other players in a vicious cycle), the unfair strategy game *The Great Dalmuti* (which gives players unequal starting positions), and the aptly named *We Didn't Playtest This At All*.
- **Cooperative** games (sometimes abbreviated **co-op** or **coop**) involve players working together towards a common goal, and either winning or losing as a team; the opposition comes from the game systems themselves, rather than from an opposing player or team. Examples include *Pandemic*, *Flash Point: Fire Rescue*, *Wok Star*, *Hanabi*, *Lord of the Rings* (the board game, specifically), *Magic Maze*, *Pandemic*, *Sentinels of the Multiverse*, and *Space Alert*. These have a wide variety of mechanics and are classified primarily by the relationship between players as unconditional allies.
  - Some games might be thought of as **semi-cooperative**: *most* of the players work together as a team, but there are one (or a small

number) of players who provide the opposition. Sometimes, this is done in the open (in *Descent: Journeys in the Dark*, one player controls all of the monsters in a dungeon crawl, while the other players work together as an adventuring party; in *Scotland Yard*, one player is a criminal on the run from the others who play detectives). Sometimes, the player's role is secret (in *Shadows Over Camelot Dead of Winter*, and *Battlestar Galactica*, one or more players may or may not secretly be traitors who win if the rest of the team fails). In *Betrayal at House on the Hill*, all players initially work together, and part way through the game one of them (determined randomly) turns traitor and from that point on works against the others.

- **Dice** games primarily use dice as their only or main material component, so these games involve rolling dice and then reacting to the rolls. Examples include the casino game *Craps* (players simply bet on the outcome of a series of die rolls with no further decision-making), the **push-your-luck** game *Farkle* (players can choose to stop on their turn to take what they've earned, or they can continue rolling to get more points… but risking everything they've won so far), and the games *Roll Through the Ages* and *Yahtzee* (both involve rolling a set of dice and then optionally choosing to reroll some or all of them once or twice, and then deciding how to score what was rolled).

- **Roll-and-move** games (the preferred term in game design; also called **track games** by game historians since they generally involve moving along a linear track) have players using some random element such as dice, cards, or a spinner to move their piece forward along a path, the objective being to reach the end first. Due to the lack of player agency in the core mechanic, these games tend to be the most popular with young children who are still developing their proto-game-playing skills like taking turns, counting spaces, and being a good sport. Examples in this book include *Candyland* and *Chutes & Ladders* (also sometimes *Snakes & Ladders*). Other notable examples that go beyond the simplest form include *Clue* (a game where three decks of cards are dealt out evenly to the players except for one missing card each, and the players have to take guesses to try to deduce which cards are missing; the rolling and moving restricts where they are on the board, and which cards they're allowed to guess); *Hare & Tortoise* (rather than moving randomly, players can gain resources by moving backward or pay resources to move forward); and *Monopoly* (players roll to move around a board and purchase property, but landing on opponents' property forces them to pay money to the opponent, the goal being to bankrupt all opponents).

- **Territory-based** games involve a map that, like real-world geography, is not divided into a neat grid but rather a series of contiguous territories, sometimes forming natural choke points or areas that can be easily surrounded and assessing the map and where to move is key to the strategy. Perhaps the best-known game of this type is *Risk*, but this book also discusses the similar games *Vinci* and *Small World*, as well as the games *Diplomacy* and *Advanced Civilization* that focus less on combat and more on negotiation and unstable alliances.

  - Other games may not take place on a territory-based map but something more regular, yet still have strong elements of territorial control. Mentioned in this book: the **tile-laying** game *Carcassonne* (in this case, the board is built of tiles drawn from a bag over the course of play, and players attempt to control areas on the tile map that is built), the trading and negotiation game *Catan* (players build on a hex grid map that is constructed randomly at the start of the game and then generate resources based on where they have built), the card game *Hacker* (players build an interconnected computer network out of cards and then attempt to hack into various areas in the network to control as many nodes as possible), the city-building *Lords of Vegas* and *Manhattan* (players compete to take over and control the most profitable blocks of land), and the route-building *Ticket to Ride* (players compete to be the first to build routes between various cities, attempting to connect specific distant cities within their own rail network).

Genre: Tower Defense

Tower defense games involve the player building and upgrading a series of defensive, usually immobile structures along a path. Automated enemies ("creeps") attempt to cross the area from their starting points to the location the player is trying to defend. The defensive towers automatically attack any creep in range, and there are generally a wide variety of tower types that have different amounts of damage, rates of fire, ranges of effect, and other special abilities such as area-of-effect attacks, debuffs like slowing creeps or making them more vulnerable, or buffing other nearby towers. Examples include *Desktop Tower Defense* (an early Flash game that popularized the genre) and *Kingdom Rush* (a mobile F2P tower defense game).

Genre: Trading Card Game (TCG)

Also sometimes referred to as **collectible card games** (**CCG**s), though TCG is more commonly used as of this writing (ironic, in that many online TCGs don't actually feature trading, though many digital TCGs do allow trading—and of course, all physical TCGs do). TCGs focus on a player collecting cards and then using some subset of cards from their collection to build one or more decks of cards. When playing the game against another player, each player brings their own custom-made deck (generally according to certain rules restricting things like how many cards can be in the deck or how many copies of the same card can be included). From there, it proceeds as a card game, usually with players taking turns, drawing and playing cards from their own deck. Most TCGs (unlike other card games) include a play field where players can put cards into play that stay there permanently until removed by the opponent's actions. TCGs generally have some kind of resource used to pay to bring cards into play, so cards have costs to use, and managing resources (and choosing a deck that follows a smooth resource ramp) is part of the strategy of play. The first and best-known TCG is *Magic: the Gathering*; other games discussed in this book include the physical card games *Yu-Gi-Oh*, *Netrunner*, *Vampire: the Eternal Struggle*, and the digital *Hearthstone*.

Genre: Walking Simulator

This genre is almost entirely exploration and narrative. The name was originally a pejorative, making fun of the idea that all the player is doing is walking around and not fighting or solving difficult puzzles or anything, the name stuck, and now it's seen more neutrally as there have been many popular and successful games of the genre. In most walking simulators, the player can't lose and there is only light puzzle solving; the joy is in exploring the space and learning about the environment, as well as the things that may have happened there. Because the player is learning the history of a space by exploring it, these games tend to have heavier themes involving death, psychological horror, or a general sense of foreboding to act as a counterweight to the player's natural curiosity. Examples in this book include *Life is Strange*, *To the Moon*, *Night in the Woods*, and *What Remains of Edith Finch*.

Index

Note: *Italic* page numbers refer to *figures* and page numbers followed by "n" refer to notes

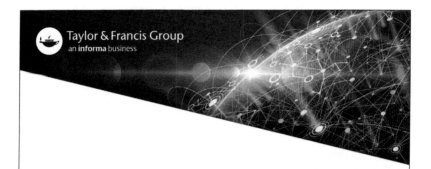